EDITOR: Dominic Bates
MANAGING EDITOR: Dan French
INFORMATION EDITORS: Chris Wingrove, Des de Moor

DESIGN AND PRODUCTION BY THINK PUBLISHING
Project Editor: Emma Jones
Sub Editors: Rica Dearman, Richard Rees
Art Director: Lou Millward
Designer: James Collins
www.thinkpublishing.co.uk

Cover photograph: Dawn view from Glastonbury Tor,
Somerset by Guy Edwardes/Getty
Back cover photographs (from top): Catherine Leckenby,
Chris Ord, Philip Roxby, Dan French

PRINTED AND BOUND BY BGP, COLCHESTER, ESSEX
walk BRITAIN 2007 is printed on UPM Cote
which is manufactured using wood products certified
by the Forestry Stewardship Council

TRADE DISTRIBUTION BY CORDEE LTD
3a de Montfort Street, Leicester LE1 7HD
☎ 0116 254 3579 Email: sales@cordee.co.uk

ACCOMMODATION ADVERTISING
☎ 020 7339 8527 Email: yearbook@ramblers.org.uk

COMMERCIAL ADVERTISING
Think Publishing
The Pall Mall Deposit, 124-128 Barlby Road,
London W10 6BL
☎ 020 8962 3020
Email: advertising@thinkpublishing.co.uk

PUBLISHED BY
The Ramblers' Association
2nd Floor, Camelford House
87-90 Albert Embankment, London SE1 7TW
☎ 020 7339 8500 Fax: 020 7339 8501
Email: ramblers@ramblers.org.uk
www.ramblers.org.uk
Registered charity no. 1093577 and a company limited by
guarantee in England and Wales (no. 4458492)

Ramblers' Association Scotland
Kingfisher House, Auld Mart Business Park
Milnathort, Kinross KY13 9DA
☎ 01577 861222 Fax: 01577 861333
Email: enquiries@scotland.ramblers.org.uk
www.ramblers.org.uk/scotland

Ramblers' Association Wales
3 Coopers Yard, Curran Road, Cardiff CF10 5NB
☎ 029 2064 4308 Fax: 029 2064 5187
Email: cerddwyr@ramblers.org.uk
www.ramblers.org.uk/wales
www.ramblers.org.uk/cymru

Ramblers Holidays
Box 43, Welwyn Garden City AL8 6PQ
☎ 01707 331133 Fax: 01707 333276
Email: info@ramblersholidays.co.uk
www.ramblersholidays.co.uk

WE

CPRE

**Welcome to the 2007 edition of walk BRITAIN, the
official handbook and accommodation guide of the
Ramblers' Association.**

This book is divided into three distinct parts:

THE RAMBLERS' WORK where you'll find news of all our
campaigns, recent successes and forthcoming initiatives, plus details
about how you can volunteer, join and other ways to support us.

WALKER'S TOOLKIT which contains information that's essential
for every walker – from 'how to' guides for reading maps and
reporting a footpath problem, to FAQs about rights of way and
countryside access. You'll also find clothing and equipment advice,
details of long distance paths, local Ramblers Groups listings and lots
of useful contacts.

ACCOMMODATION listing over 2,000 walker-friendly B&Bs,
self-catering cottages, hostels, bunkhouses, campsites and group
accommodation. There are full-colour maps to help you plan your
trips showing the location of B&Bs, long distance paths and national
parks. And regional introductions offering lots of ideas for walks and
places to visit that will inspire you to explore the British countryside.

For all the latest information about walking in Britain, visit our website
www.ramblers.org.uk which also features all the accommodation
in this book searchable by postcode, county, long distance path or
national park and is linked to our nationwide Group Walks Finder.

We hope you enjoy reading **walk BRITAIN** and find it useful.
Please let us know what you think with the feedback form on p123
and don't forget to use your Ramblers Discount Vouchers (see p121)
at any B&B listed with a 🍽 symbol.

CONTENTS

ACCOMMODATION

The Ramblers' Work

THE RAMBLERS' ASSOCIATION

The Ramblers' Association is Britain's biggest walking charity, the only one dedicated to:

- **Promoting** walking for everyone as a healthy, fun, inexpensive activity
- **Safeguarding** Britain's unique network of public paths
- **Increasing** opportunities for responsible access for everyone to our beautiful open countryside
- **Protecting** the countryside and green spaces from harmful and polluting developments
- **Educating** the public about their rights and responsibilities, and the health and environmental benefits of walking so that everyone can enjoy our wonderful heritage

We receive no direct funding from central government and are entirely dependent on the generosity of our members and supporters. If you would like to help, the simplest way is to join (see p21).

ABOUT US

PRESIDENT'S FOREWORD

've been a walker and rambler all my life. I've walked from youth hostel to youth hostel in the Lake District, Snowdonia and Yorkshire; I've traversed the backbone of England along the Pennine Way; I've tramped the glens and mountains of Scotland. And I've loved every moment of it. There have been long, lingering sunlit days with the birds in song, the trees rustling and the meadows green in the rolling countryside. There have been struggles through the pouring rain, arriving damp and drenched and triumphant at the other end. There have been glimpses of heaven in this beautiful but fragile earth. And none of it would have been possible if I hadn't been able to get out into the countryside and savour the fresh air, the fine views and the landscape bequeathed to us over the generations.

And it wouldn't have been possible, either, if the Ramblers' Association hadn't been there over the decades, to fight for the rights of walkers, campaign for access, bring walkers together, and ensure that the footpaths are free for all to use. None of this has been easy. It's been down to thousands of people, in local groups up and down the land, over many years, using the paths, removing obstacles, insisting that local councils do their duty, negotiating with landowners, providing guidance and advice, and generally promoting the benefits of walking.

And it's been down to the patient campaigning and lobbying work of the Ramblers' Association nationally, too. For over 100 years, people were arguing and campaigning to legislate for a 'right to roam' in open countryside, mountain and moorland. Thanks to the Ramblers, it's now on the statute book, and it means that there is a genuine right of responsible access for everyone – no matter who or what they are – to areas of open landscape that before were forbidden territory.

> '**I've traversed the backbone of England and tramped the glens and mountains of Scotland. And I've loved every moment of it**'

There's still a lot to be done, of course. Access to coastal and woodland areas, local battles over paths and places, and the need to spread the word about the enjoyment and benefit that walking can bring to young and old alike. The work of the Ramblers' Association will be needed for years to come. We can all be proud to be part of an organisation that means and does so much.

Chris Smith

Rt Hon Lord Smith of Finsbury
President of the Ramblers' Association

RICHARD ELSE

CATHERINE LECKENBY

PROMOTING WALKING

COUNTRYSIDE AGENCY/ANDY TRYNER

Walking hit the headlines last year when new transport figures showed that trips on foot in Britain had declined by 16% over 10 years. It doesn't take much imagination to spot the connection with other headline-grabbing figures: 22% of men, 23% of women and over 16% of children are obese; only 37% of men and 24% of women exercise at least 30 minutes a day, five days a week – the recommended minimum for good health; and low levels of physical activity cost the NHS over £8billion a year.

Getting Britain back on its feet

The decline of walking is undoubtedly a major contributor to today's unhealthy, inactive lifestyles, with their high and rising levels of heart disease, diabetes and depression. This sorry situation is the result of decades of treating the car as king, and allowing our streets and public spaces to become through-routes for drivers at the expense of everyday walking. Other countries have done things differently and it shows. In places like France, Austria and Sweden, 25-30% of urban trips are on foot, more than twice the level in Britain.

We want to see the decline in walking slowed, halted and ultimately reversed over the next couple of decades. To help achieve this, we've been looking at ways to encourage people to take more regular, local walking trips, including in urban areas where most of us live. We want to reach everyone who will benefit, including black and minority ethnic groups, young people and people in deprived inner-city areas who are often not attracted to traditional walking initiatives.

Ambassadors for everyday walks

Our Get Walking Keep Walking programme aims to get people walking independently. It includes an informal Welcome to Walking session, several short, led walks exploring the local area, follow-up sessions and motivational items like pedometers, log books and maps. A key feature is the involvement of walking ambassadors – trained volunteers who can give individual advice and support.

Last year we trialled the programme in south London with parents of young children, people from the Bengali and Somali communities (see below right), and mental health patients. We want to roll it out more widely and in other English cities, so we're bidding for National Lottery funding as part of the Active Travel Consortium, in partnership with other organisations like Living Streets and Sustrans.

Also in south London, Little Legs Big Strides (pictured) uses a similar approach to promote everyday walking to pre-school children, their older siblings and their parents. We're working in partnership with local children's centres and Sure Start schemes in a one-year project funded by a charitable trust that launched in September last year.

Leading walks for all

A recent survey found that more Ramblers Groups are welcoming new walkers with shorter, easier and family-friendly walks. At least a quarter now offer alternatives to the traditional day-long country walk (four Groups are entirely dedicated to family walking), and for the first time this year, we've highlighted Groups offering easier walks in the Ramblers Areas and Groups listings (p68).

Other successes include the Walking Out project in Sheffield, now in its fourth year; the three lively Friends

'We want to see the decline in walking slowed, halted and ultimately reversed over the next couple of decades'

LOUISE HILLYER

RICHARD MANN/GUZELIAN

OUR CAMPAIGNS

'We're working with Olympic organisations to ensure walking plays its part in making this the most sustainable Games ever'

Groups offering shorter walks in Essex; and Northumbria Short Circuits, a new Group running easy walks all over north-east England.

In Scotland we've increased our support for shorter walks with a new Easy Walks brand and a helpful factsheet (contact Ramblers Scotland to order). And the Cerrig Camu/Stepping Stones scheme aimed at people 'graduating' from health walks should soon be operating in every local authority area in Wales.

Ramblers volunteers are also helping people with disabilities to enjoy the outdoors. London Blind Ramblers works with around 30 Ramblers Groups to provide a full programme of walks with sighted guides all over south-east England, and similar projects exist in Brighton, Cardiff and Sheffield.

A national and Olympic profile

Welcome to Walking Week in September – already the Ramblers' flagship countrywide walking event – this year includes National Day of Walking on 16 September. We'll be working to promote the day as a major national event and a great opportunity to publicise the benefits of walking, (keep an eye on our website for further details).

The 2012 Olympic and Paralympic Games may be a few years off, but preparations are already well underway, and we're working with Olympic organisations to ensure walking plays its part in making this the most sustainable Games ever. In Scotland, we're also involved in Glasgow's bid to host the Commonwealth Games in 2014.

Another vital task is to win the hearts and minds of decision-makers. Politicians, civil servants and health professionals are now much more positive about walking, but enthusiasm is rarely matched by cash, and we're still waiting on the government's promise of more NHS funding for prevention rather than cure. So there's still plenty of work to do, but we remain optimistic about the prospects of creating a healthier, more sustainable and civilised Britain where more people choose to walk.

For the latest on our campaigns to promote walking, visit www.ramblers.org.uk/walking

IN FOCUS: RAMBLING IN HEADSCARVES

Women from a Bengali community project based at Elephant and Castle, south London, enthusiastically embraced the benefits of walking – once they'd mastered the art of clipping a pedometer onto a salwar kameez (tunic and trousers).

CAROLINE WATSON

The women were participating in a pilot of the Ramblers' new Get Walking Keep Walking programme to support regular everyday local walking for health, run in partnership with Charterhouse in Southwark.

Participants found walking a much more comfortable and welcoming alternative to gym or exercise classes, and relished the opportunity to explore their local streets and green spaces on foot. Some were surprised to discover that the river Thames was within easy walking distance of their homes.

"Walking has been really stereotyped as something all-very English that you do in the countryside," walker Navy Choudhury told the BBC, who reported on the initiative. "But it's good for your mind as well as your body. It's de-stressing, you meet new people – there are so many benefits."

FOOTPATHS IN ENGLAND AND WALES

COUNTRYSIDE AGENCY/NICK SMITH

'Across the country, we're involved in campaigns and legal cases to protect, extend and improve the path network'

For walkers, the public rights of way network is the single most important way of gaining access to the countryside. It is a precious resource and is, in theory, protected by an array of laws. But despite this, the latest Audit Commission figures show only 67% paths in England are classified as easy to use – down 3% on the previous year.

So the efforts of Ramblers volunteers to improve this situation remain vital through practical work, campaigning, path surveys and reporting of problems.

Successful legal challenges

Across the country, we are involved in extensive casework to protect, extend and improve the path network: appearing at public inquiries, defending against diversions and closures, and serving legal notice on highway authorities to ensure paths are kept open and maintained.

Last year there were many successful cases for the Ramblers, including the restoration of the Chimney Steps path on the Isle of Wight (see right), and the saving of a bridleway at South Tawton on Dartmoor after the landowner's last-ditch attempt to remove it from the definitive map was defeated in the High Court.

We also secured the reopening of the popular and useful seafront path that runs under Southend-on-Sea's famous pier, which had been blocked for more than two years. After constant letter-writing and lobbying failed to prompt the council into action, the Ramblers issued a summons against them for the offence of obstructing the highway, resulting in a speedy resolution.

And there was more good news with the enactment of the Natural Environment and Rural Communities Act. This goes some way towards tackling the problem of off-road vehicles using public rights of way, by closing the legal loophole (in respect of recent and future claims) that allowed modern motor vehicles to drive on routes historically recognised for use by horse-drawn vehicles.

First case to House of Lords

In an exciting year ahead, we'll be taking our first ever case to the House of Lords to challenge a legal ruling.

'The most basic thing people can do about footpaths is walk them. Use Your Paths aims to walk all rights of way in England and Wales by September'

The law assumes that if the public use a path for 20 years, it is automatically deemed a public right of way unless there is sufficient evidence that the landowner had no intention to dedicate it. Until recently, it was generally accepted that landowners had to direct their objections at path users by putting up 'No right of way' signs, locking gates or ordering walkers off the route during those 20 years to ensure it remained private. But in 1999, the High Court ruled that a landowner could defeat such a right of way claim by producing evidence of virtually any sort of which the public were unaware, such as private letters to solicitors.

The Ramblers, and many leading experts on rights of way, believe this interpretation of the law is wrong and contrary to previously upheld principles. It makes it far more difficult to claim a right of way based on presumed dedication, and means Ramblers volunteers can waste months of time making claims for paths, only to be defeated by evidence they knew nothing about. The aim of our appeal to the House of Lords is to try to get the law put back as it was.

Campaigns involving more walkers

Campaigning is a key part of the Ramblers' work on footpaths, and last year saw the launch of many successful new campaigns with a greater emphasis on steps every walker can take to help us in our work.

The most basic thing we could ask people to do about footpaths is to walk them. So in March 2006, the Use Your Paths Challenge was born aiming to get all recorded rights of way in England and Wales walked by September this year. The Challenge got off to a fantastic start, and within a few months walkers across the country had logged on to www.useyourpaths.info and recorded walking over 15,000 grid squares. To find out how to take part, visit the website, ☎ 020 7339 8554, or see the advert overleaf.

We've always encouraged walkers to report footpath problems to their local authority. So when it came to discussing projects that would recruit more active volunteers, we immediately thought about how we could build on this vital work. The result is the Footpath Guardian project – a flexible scheme in which anyone can take part (see p19 for full details).

Ongoing fight for better paths

But our 'bread and butter' work remains targeted campaigns to improve the condition of rights of way. Across England and Wales, local volunteers are working hard to make the case for investment in rights of way, and for stronger policies to protect and secure an open and usable path network. With diminishing budgets to spend on footpaths, we continue to press councils to meet their legal obligations, while illustrating the wider value of our rights of way.

For all the latest footpath campaign news, visit www.ramblers.org.uk/footpaths

IN FOCUS: RESTORATION VICTORY FOR THE CHIMNEY STEPS
These ancient steps are a public right of way linking the sea to the downs on the south coast of the Isle of Wight, offering spectacular views as you climb. They needed massive repairs and were closed to the public, with the Isle of Wight Council unable to foresee carrying out the necessary work for many years. This prompted a four-year battle with the council, with the Ramblers' Isle of Wight Area seeking a legal order against them, compelling the council to repair the footpath. Eventually, with the support of the Ramblers' Legal Panel and our honorary solicitor, Jerry Pearlman, the necessary magistrates' court order was obtained, obliging the council to carry out the repairs. The result is that this stunning path is now open for everyone to use.

TAKE UP THE CHALLENGE

at www.useyourpaths.info

WANT TO BE PART OF THE BIGGEST-EVER WALKING PROJECT IN THE UK?

The Ramblers' Association is challenging all walkers to help us walk the entire length of the rights of way network in England and Wales before September 2007. It's never been done before. There are 140,000 miles (225,000 km) of paths and to help make this enormous task more manageable, we've broken the challenge up into 1 km grid squares – just right for a quick trip out on our marvellous path network!

TO TAKE PART:

1. **Choose** a grid square (or squares) to walk. You'll find the national grid on most maps.
2. **Walk** all the public rights of way (see the map key for information) in your chosen square(s).
3. **Report** any problems you come across (obstructions, missing signposts etc) to the relevant council (see the website for details).
4. **Log on** to www.useyourpaths.info to let us know you've completed your square(s).

And that's it – simple and fun!

For more information, and to keep a check on everyone's progress:
Visit: **www.useyourpaths.info**
Email: **challenge@useyourpaths.info**
Call our **Challenge Hotline: 020 7339 8554**

THE USE YOUR PATHS CHALLENGE   MAKE A DIFFERENCE

FREEDOM TO ROAM IN ENGLAND AND WALES

MRS GILLIAN LAUDER

OUR CAMPAIGNS

This year sees the 75th anniversary of the Kinder Scout Mass Trespass when six walkers were imprisoned following scuffles with gamekeepers, prompting the Ramblers' Association's formation three years later. We've been campaigning hard for a public right of access to the countryside ever since, which culminated in the statutory right to roam contained in the Countryside and Rights of Way (CRoW) Act 2000 that was fully rolled out at the end of 2005. So we're pleased to report that, after some initial apprehension from landowners and others, there have been very few conflicts or problems (unlike in 1932!), and walkers have been enjoying their new right of access to open countryside across England and Wales.

Protecting and promoting our new right

Ramblers volunteers and staff are still working hard though to ensure that the new access arrangements work well in practice and can be enjoyed by the public. We have been monitoring restrictions on access land to prevent unjustifiable closures to walkers, and are working with the Countryside Agency, the Countryside Council for Wales and local authorities to make sure appropriate infrastructure, including signage, is in place. Ramblers volunteers

'75 years after the Kinder Scout Mass Trespass, walkers are enjoying their new right to roam in England and Wales with few problems'

continue to ably represent walkers' interests on Local Access Forums, established to advise local authorities on how to improve access within their areas.

We are also doing what we can to help promote the new right of access to the public. So last year saw the creation of a new breed of Ramblers volunteer – the Access Promoter (see overleaf). Recruits came from around Derbyshire and Wales to help us spread the word about the benefits and opportunities provided by the new right to roam in their locality, and their excellent work includes distributing literature and giving presentations to local community groups. The Access Promoters project is only a pilot project at this stage, but we hope to roll it out nationally across England and Wales in 2008.

Targeting coastal access

As well as consolidating what we've already won, we're also looking to the future. Having secured the long sought-after right of access to open countryside, we're considering what our future priorities should be. Following a consultation with volunteers and experts, a revised access campaign strategy will be produced later this year.

Meanwhile, the issue of coastal access continues and promises to make this forthcoming year an exciting one. There is no doubt that the British public

'A general right of public access to the coast already exists in Scotland, Scandinavia and Portugal – we want one in England and Wales, too'

KEVIN MATTHEWS

a stretch of coast by Osborne House forms the only break in the Isle of Wight Coastal Path that circumnavigates the island. A general right of public access to the coast already exists in Scotland, Scandinavia and Portugal – we want one in England and Wales, too.

Green light for Wales coastal path

In Wales, there has been a warm welcome to new access land. In May, Environment Minister Carwyn Jones cut the cake celebrating right to roam's first birthday at a special event in Caerau joined by local people, councillors and Local Access Forum members. A total of 21% of Wales is now mapped as access land including forestry land dedicated by the Welsh Assembly.

We have now achieved a commitment from the Assembly to a coastal path around Wales, with further consideration being given to a statutory right of access to coastal areas. Local path networks will be developed around coastal communities and particular attention will be given to the needs of those with disabilities. We plan to use local partnerships to deliver Wales's coastal access programme, but are still looking for the money to fund it. There's a great deal of work for Ramblers Wales to do!

For all the latest news from the Ramblers' access campaign, visit www.ramblers.org.uk/freedom

feel a strong affinity with the coast and wish to visit it. A recent poll commissioned by the Ramblers in May last year found that 94% of those surveyed believe the public should have a legal right to walk in England and Wales's coastal areas – including beaches, foreshore (the beach between high and low water), cliffs, estuaries and sea banks. Contrary to popular belief, no such right currently exists.

The government is concluding a year-long study into extending the CRoW Act to cover coastal areas, and will issue a document for public consultation early this year detailing the options for improving coastal access. The Ramblers will be campaigning vigorously for the CRoW Act's extension to secure a legal right to walk along the coast – subject to safeguards protecting wildlife, habitats and property.

Such a measure could eradicate several high-profile gaps for walkers along England's coast. A four-mile long 'missing link' still blights the South West Coast Path between Clevedon and Weston-super-Mare, and

OUR CAMPAIGNS

ROGER MITCHELL

IN FOCUS: ACCESS PROMOTERS TAKE ON THE CHALLENGE

One of our new Access Promoters is Peter Moody, 63, from Sheffield. He is enthused by the task facing him. "I've discovered that many groups I am contacting know very little about the realities of the right to roam," he says. "They've heard about it through the media but don't always know exactly what it means. I think it's vital that the Ramblers ensure our new right is explained accurately to the wider public, and I'm very happy to be involved in this kind of work. Once people are confident in their rights as walkers, they can go on to make the most of what the great British countryside has to offer."

SAIRA MALIK-ADAMS

Peter added that recent research has shown 41% of walkers are women, so he's been especially pleased that some of the first presentations he'll be delivering will be to local Women's Institute groups!

If you would like to know more about Access Promoters, call the Freedom to Roam team on ☎ 020 7339 8570.

COUNTRYSIDE PROTECTION

MAGGIE DONNELLY

A beautiful countryside benefits everyone, which is why countryside protection has always been a key charitable aim of the Ramblers' Association. Visitors benefit from clean air, inspiring views and the chance to learn more about nature. Even people who never leave town benefit – from the land used to grow our food, the mountains that filter our water, or the trees and moors that sustain the air we breathe.

Threats to the countryside come in many forms. Inappropriate development or land management and, increasingly, climate change all have the potential to damage our unique landscape beyond repair. The Ramblers' Association monitors these developments, and takes action to protect and enhance our countryside.

Pipelines and phoneboxes

Over the past year, we have had numerous successes exerting our influence. Developers of a gas pipeline

through Wales committed to minimising disruption to footpaths and rights of way. Phoneboxes in rural Teesdale were saved from demolition. And government recognised the importance of conservation and environmental protection in its official policy statements. From individual members writing letters to their local council, to being part of large national coalitions in meetings with senior civil servants, action can be taken at many levels to ensure the benefits of our landscape are felt both now and in the future.

Parks and projects

We are continuing to campaign for the best possible South Downs National Park. This was first promised as a 'gift to the nation' in 1999, and now a legal judgement has become the latest obstacle to maximising the protection of this area of outstanding natural beauty. National park status will prevent the Downs (pictured below) being over-run by the massive development planned for the South East of England, and preserve the unique landscape for future generations. We will work with others to ensure the government makes this designation as soon as possible over the coming year.

'Our influence has saved footpaths and rural phoneboxes from developers, and swayed Government policy to recognise environmentalism's importance'

Other important concerns include the proposed relief road through the South Dorset Area of Outstanding Natural Beauty, the construction of a 10-mile barrage across the Severn Estuary, and the giant power line between Beauly and Denny in the Scottish Highlands. Each of these has the potential to cause damage which will be felt not only in the local area, but have important repercussions throughout the country.

We need you
The strength and influence of the Ramblers campaigning relies on the fact that we have a dedicated and active membership. Whatever you can do to help us protect and enhance the beauty of the countryside will make a difference. Campaigning doesn't have to be on national or regional issues – local developments can also have a big impact on the places where we enjoy walking.

Easy actions and information are sent regularly by email to people who subscribe to our Take Action e-newsletter (see p19). You could choose to receive our regular Countryside Update bulletin, which contains all the latest countryside campaign news. Ramblers in Scotland and Wales can also receive information and action on developments in the Welsh Assembly and Scottish Parliament. Many local Groups also have a dedicated countryside volunteer – get in touch to find out how you can support them, or even consider taking up the post yourself (see Ramblers Areas and Groups, p68).

All the latest countryside news and campaign updates can be found at www.ramblers.org.uk/countryside

SCOTSVOICE

OUR CAMPAIGNS

IN FOCUS: TACKLING CLIMATE CHANGE
The Ramblers' Association recognises the need to tackle climate change, and the responsibility we all have to reduce our carbon footprint. We have campaigned against the expansion of airports, for the provision of better trains and buses, and to promote walking as a means of carbon-free transport. We also recognise the need for increased use of renewable energy.

Current government policy has led to large subsidy payments for the construction of giant, industrial-scale on-shore wind turbines – often in the most remote and unique landscapes. We are concerned about the impact of these turbines on the countryside, especially when a range of alternatives exist.

We are still pushing for a change in the 'Renewables Obligation' funding system to encourage technology that is more sensitive to the surrounding landscape, such as off-shore wind turbines. The government recognised the need for this in its 2005 Energy Review and we are pressing for speedy reform. We also want to encourage 'micro-

'Scotland alone has over 400 applications for wind farms and we're campaigning to prevent their irreparable damage to our landscape'

generation' of electricity, close to where it is used, for example through roof-top solar panels.

We have also campaigned against the most damaging proposals in sensitive areas, and claimed a big victory in March 2005 when planning permission was rejected for England's largest wind farm at Whinash Ridge, between the Yorkshire Dales and Lake District National Parks. There are currently over 400 applications for wind turbine stations in Scotland alone, and we will continue our campaign to end the unfair economic advantage given to these developers over developers of other alternative energy, and to prevent irreparable damage to our landscape.

THE RAMBLERS' ASSOCIATION IN SCOTLAND

JANCY DAVIES

Scotland's access legislation – which came into effect in 2005 – is now bedding in and enables all walkers, cyclists, horse-riders and canoeists to enjoy the wonderful variety of Scotland's outdoor opportunities with greater confidence.

Path disputes and creation

However, last year we faced a number of challenges to its implementation, ranging from the Scottish Golf Union trying to restrict access on golf courses, to rich landowners and developers. Some of these disputes have led to court cases to defend these attacks on our access rights.

Local Access Forums now operate in all areas of the country and new path networks continue to appear on the ground. These are making it easier for visitors and residents of Scotland alike to find walks for all abilities, in both rural and urban areas.

New Groups, shorter walks

Last June marked the completion of our Promoting Walking project, funded by the Scottish Executive through the Paths for All Partnership. The 15-month scheme set up five new Ramblers Groups and encouraged a fifth of all Scotland's Groups to organise regular programmes of short walks, often linked to public transport. Some Groups have begun working with their local health walk schemes to provide a 'next step' for walkers, and our North Berwick Group now organises regular family walks.

'We want a new national park on the Isle of Harris and are working on proposals for a coastal and marine national park in 2008'

Wild hopes

Wild land is an important part of the Scottish countryside experience, and we are campaigning to maintain the wild qualities of our uplands. Whether it's telecommunication masts, wind turbines or power lines in insensitive locations, or the impact of grazing by sheep and deer, we have continued to lobby government for policies that protect the wildness of the Scottish hills for the enjoyment of future generations of walkers.

Winds of change

The Scottish Parliamentary and local elections will take place in May this year. This gives us an excellent opportunity to get our own objectives for the outdoors included in the political commitments of the next government.

We want to see walking and physical activity integrated into all relevant policy areas, and new criteria to be developed to guide wind farm development. Wind turbines have an important role to play in meeting renewable energy and climate change objectives, but

RICHARD MANN

we believe that land-based turbines should in future be no more than 50 metres in height and be located on land of minimal heritage value.

We'll also be working with Scottish Natural Heritage on proposals for a coastal and marine national park in Scotland, to be announced in 2008, as well as our campaign to establish Scotland's third land-based national park on Harris in the Western Isles.

Getting fit for the Olympics

Building on the success of our promoting walking work, this year we'll be focusing on our Get Fit For Tomorrow project. The aim is to encourage people to raise their fitness levels through walking, in association with major sporting events. We want to use the Olympic Games in

2012 and the prospective Glasgow Commonwealth Games in 2014 to inspire everyone to walk a minimum of 30 minutes each day.

We are also working to develop new walking groups across Scotland, particularly in deprived areas such as Glasgow, and continue to encourage our Groups to include walks with wide public appeal.

For all the latest information about Ramblers Scotland, visit www.ramblers.org.uk/scotland

DATES FOR THE DIARY

JANUARY	26 Dec–2	Festival of Winter Walks, www.ramblers.org.uk/winterwalks
MARCH	10–11	Ramblers Scotland Annual Conference, Dunblane Hydro Hotel
	16–18	The Ordnance Survey Outdoors Show, Birmingham NEC
	24–25	Ramblers Wales Council, Mount Sorrel Hotel, Barry
	30–1 April	Ramblers' Association General Council, Reading University
APRIL	24	75th Anniversary of the Kinder Scout Trespass
	28–7 May	Scottish Outdoor Access Festival, www.outdooraccess-scotland.com
MAY	21–25	Walk to School Week
JUNE	16–24	Green Transport Week, www.eta.co.uk
	23–1 July	Use Your Paths Week
SEPTEMBER	15–23	Welcome to Walking Week (TBC), www.ramblers.org.uk/walks
	16	National Day of Walking
	22	In Town Without My Car Day
	22	Final day of Use Your Paths Challenge, www.useyourpaths.info
DECEMBER	26–1 Jan	Festival of Winter Walks, www.ramblers.org.uk/winterwalks

OUR CAMPAIGNS

This is called a TV.

The people inside it move. The people watching it don't.

Weird.

Blacks
THE OUTDOOR EXPERTS

Get 10% off with your Ramblers' Association members card at all Blacks stores.*

BECOME A MEMBER

Join us at a specially discounted rate using the form overleaf. Benefits of membership include:

- **walk BRITAIN**, our annual handbook and accommodation guide

- **walk**, our quarterly colour magazine

- Discretionary discounts at outdoor stores, including 10% off at Millets and Blacks

- Newsletters covering local and regional issues affecting your Area (where published)

- Membership of a local Group with a programme of walks and social events. Members may also participate in events and walks run by any other Ramblers' Association Group

- Access to the Ramblers Map Library. The Library stocks all OS Landranger and Explorer maps, and members can borrow up to ten maps at a time for a small fee plus p&p. Contact the Map Library Service at our central office for details or see p54

GET INVOLVED

If you want to turn your love of walking into action, the Ramblers can offer some great opportunities to get stuck in. Whether you have ten minutes spare here or there, or want to commit more regular chunks of time, there's always a way to make a difference.

If you're always very busy…

…Sign up to our Take Action e-newsletter

Every month you can receive our lively e-newsletter which will keep you informed about our campaigns and suggest some short, sharp actions that you can take. Visit www.ramblers.org.uk/volunteer, click on 'Sign up for our newsletter' and enter your email address to subscribe!

…Keep your eyes open for footpath problems*

Something you can do when you're out and about walking! If you come across a blocked or overgrown path, a stile or bridge that is dilapidated, or any other footpath problem, let us and the local authority know about it. Either fill in the footpath report form on p49 following the instructions on the neighbouring page. Or become a Footpath Guardian and get a colourful pack telling you what to look out for and what to do. Contact our Footpath Campaign team for your free pack on ☎ 020 7339 8582 or register online at www.ramblers.org.uk/volunteer.

…Take part in the Use Your Paths challenge*

Pick up a map, choose a grid square and walk the paths within it! Until September 2007 we are aiming to get every path in England and Wales

walked. Once you have walked the paths, mark it off on our interactive map at www.useyourpaths.info, then pick another square! See p10 for full details.

If you've got a bit more time…

…Forgotten Paths Project*

If you have an interest in archives and research, the Forgotten Paths Project could be for you. At least 20,000 paths are at risk of being lost for ever. Volunteers with time and enthusiasm for research can help us keep these paths by identifying them. Find out more and get the Forgotten Paths pack from our Footpath Policy team on ☎ 020 7339 8530 or rightsofway@ramblers.org.uk

…Get involved with your local Group and Area

Every local Group is different, but they are all run entirely by volunteers and organise a range of activities. Leading walks is the most visible of Group activities and new leaders are always welcome. As important as leading walks is publicising them. Groups put together walk programmes, list walks on the Group Walks Finder, and publicise their activities in local information centres and through local media. Groups are active in footpath, access and countryside work. They monitor the condition of local footpaths, lobby over developments that affect walkers, or run local campaigns to raise

SUPPORTING US

awareness. Many Groups also carry out practical work to improve footpaths, clearing paths or repairing stiles.

Areas work to support and coordinate the efforts of their various Groups and to ensure that the voice of the Ramblers is heard loud and clear across their patch.

Getting involved with your Group or Area is a great way to keep informed about the issues facing walkers locally and to do something about them. Opportunities include traditional committee roles to shorter-term or

more infrequent commitments. Whatever you would like to offer, your Area or Group will be delighted to hear from you. Contact details for all Areas and Groups are listed on p68.

(* = In England and Wales only)

For more details of opportunities to volunteer or get involved with the Ramblers, visit www.ramblers.org.uk/volunteer

OTHER WAYS YOU CAN HELP

Following in your footsteps – Last year saw the creation of a long distance path showcasing some of the finest scenery in the country thanks to a generous legacy left by John Musgrave of Devon (see p127). Once you have provided for your loved ones, why not help leave the world a better place like John did and include the Ramblers in your will? For a copy of our free guide to making and updating your will, ☎ 020 7339 8511, or see the advert on p12.

THE RAMBLERS SHOP
In 2006, we launched our Ramblers Shop, which features many items at a significant discount! We also receive a donation for every purchase you make, helping raise money for our vital charitable work. Visit our shop – www.ramblers.org.uk/shop – and follow the links or call the numbers below.

Breakdown car cover and cycle insurance – The ethical Environmental Transport Association offers car breakdown cover and cycle insurance with up to 50% off, while also making a donation to the Ramblers for the life of each policy. ☎ 0800 212 810 and quote Ramblers' Association 1269-4001.

Ordnance Survey maps – Aqua3 offers a 10% discount on both standard paper and waterproof maps, with a 10% donation to the Ramblers for each map sold. Apply online and get free p&p, or ☎ 0870 777 0791, quoting the Ramblers.

Digital mapping – Get the latest software from Anquet at a 15% discount and a donation will also go to us. ☎ 0845 330 9570 and quote RA150.

Cottage holidays – Cottages4you has over 15,000 holiday homes across the UK and Europe and will donate 10% of the booking to the Ramblers. Browse online at the Ramblers Shop or ☎ 0870 197 1654 quoting the Ramblers' Association.

Ramblers Credit Card – Change your credit card and help change the world! Run by the ethically guided Co-operative Bank, we receive £15 for every new cardholder, £2.50 on first use, and donations for every transaction thereafter. ☎ 0800 002 006 to apply.

Ramblers Insurance – UIA is an ethical insurer offering low-cost, high quality insurance and will give between £5 and £15 to the Ramblers for every home, travel or motor policy taken out. You can get a no obligation quote from ☎ 0800 013 0064, quoting reference RAMG, or buy online and save even more money. See the advert on p125.

Gift Aid – If you say yes to Gift Aid, we can claim an extra 28p per pound donated, even on membership fees. This doesn't cost you a penny, but can raise hundreds of thousands of pounds for us! So, even if you are already a member, you can sign the form opposite, go to our website, or ☎ 020 7339 8595.

Direct Debit – Over 50% of members pay their subscriptions by direct debit, which saves them trouble and greatly reduces our administration costs and bank charges. To sign up, please complete the bottom half of the form opposite.

Ramblers Holidays was set up in 1946 to support the work of the Ramblers' Association, and still makes a kind and considerable donation to the Ramblers' Association every year for our core charitable work. For a brochure call ☎ 01707 331133, or see the adverts on the inside of the front and back covers.

Our thanks go to **Millets** for its continuing support and sponsorship of this book and we would like to draw your attention to its pages (pp18, 23 and 64-67).

SPECIAL DISCOUNT MEMBERSHIP OFFER

If you are not yet a Ramblers member, use this form to get 20% off your first year's subscription, plus one month extra free for joining by Direct Debit.

If you are already a member, why not introduce a friend to this special offer and give them this form, or use it to sign up to Gift Aid or Direct Debit if you haven't already?

The Ramblers

IT IS A CONDITION OF THIS OFFER THAT YOU PAY BY DIRECT DEBIT

Yes, I/we would like to join the Ramblers

Title_____ Name(s)_____

Address_____

_____ Postcode_____

Phone number_____ Email_____

(I am happy for the Ramblers to contact me by email)

Date(s) of Birth _____ _____ RA Group (if you have a preference)_____

If you have no preference you will be placed in a group according to your postcode

BO

Tick the box that suits you best: ☐ **Individual £19.20** (normally £24) ☐ **Joint* £25.60** (normally £32)

☐ **Reduced Individual+ £14** ☐ **Reduced Joint*+ £18**

*Joint membership is available for two adults living at the same address.

+Reduced rates are available and are intended for people who, through whatever circumstances, cannot afford the standard rates.

The offer is valid until December 2007. The offer is not open to existing members.

We occasionally exchange members' names and addresses with other like-minded organisations, which may be of interest to you. These are for use once only, and will not lead to further mailings. However, if you would prefer to be excluded from any such exchanges, please tick this box. ☐

giftaid it If you are a UK tax-payer, please complete this simple section to increase the value of any donation or membership subscription you may make by 28% at no extra cost to you.

I want the Ramblers' Association to treat all donations I have made for the six years prior to this year (but no earlier than 6/4/2000), and any I make until further notice, as Gift Aid donations.

Title_____ Full name_____ Date_____

Ramblers Membership Number (if currently a member)_____

You must pay an amount of Income Tax (or Capital Gains Tax) at least equal to the tax that the Ramblers' Association will reclaim on your donation (currently 28p for each £1 you pay). You can cancel this declaration at any time.

Instruction to your Bank or Building Society to pay by Direct Debit

DIRECT Debit

Please fill in the whole form and send it to: The Ramblers' Association, FREEPOST SW15, London SE1 7BR

Ramblers Membership Number (if currently a member)

Details of the Bank/Building Society

Originator's Identification Number 9 2 2 6 7 0

To: The Manager	Bank/Building Society

Branch Sort Code

Address

Reference Number (for office use)

Postcode

Instruction to your Bank/Building Society – Please pay The Ramblers' Association Direct Debits from the account detailed in this Instruction subject to the safeguards assured by the Direct Debit Guarantee.

Name(s) of Account Holder(s)

Signature(s)

Bank/Building Society account number

Date

Banks/Building Societies may not accept Direct Debit Instructions for some types of account.

SUPPORTING US

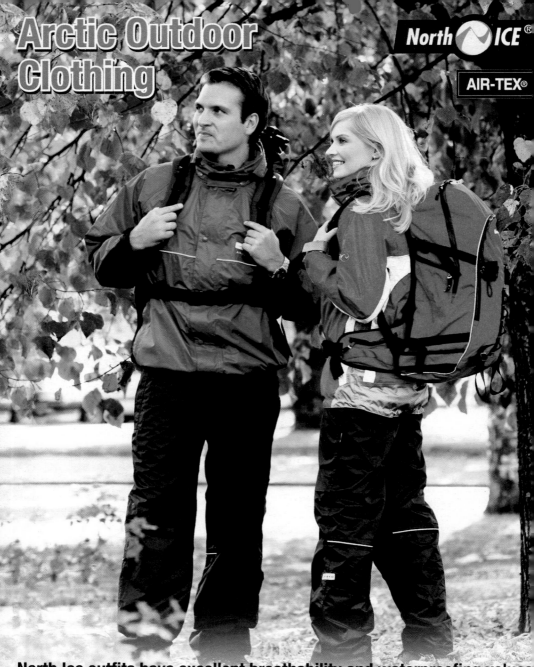

Arctic Outdoor Clothing

North ICE

AIR-TEX®

North Ice outfits have excellent breathability and waterproofing values
Every Outdoor suit comes with an amazing bonus pack of clothing.

Visit our website for further details and
latest offers or call us at 0845 389 0370

www.northice.co.uk

Walker's Toolkit

LONG DISTANCE PATHS

These pages give information on a selection of long distance paths and routes in Britain, offering thousands of miles of excellent walking through a huge variety of dramatic landscapes. Nearly all of them can be used as the basis for shorter walks, or walked in sections as well as a longer, single trek.

Walking advice

If you are planning your first extended walking trip, we recommend you practise on day walks before setting out to ensure you can comfortably walk the distance you intend to cover each day. Don't forget that, unless you have arranged luggage transfer, you will probably be carrying a heavier pack than you would on a day walk.

EASY routes offer generally level walking through areas where transport and assistance are usually close at hand and, while attractive to all, are especially recommended for the less experienced or energetic.

CHALLENGING routes have sections across difficult or remote terrain, which should only be attempted by those who have a little experience and navigational skill and are properly equipped, especially in bad weather. The majority fall somewhere in between.

All routes are signed unless otherwise stated, though standards vary. We recommend you always take a path guide and map even when following a well-signed trail. There are now many hundreds of walking routes in Britain and only space for a selection in this guide. The Ramblers website lists many more routes, in much more detail – see www.ramblers.org.uk/info/paths.

Accommodation

All routes listed are cross-referenced in the B&B section and appear on the maps for each region. Accommodation within 3.2km/2 miles of paths listed here is indicated by a note under its location. You can also use the path listings on the Ramblers website to search for nearby accommodation.

Comprehensive accommodation lists are available for some paths via their own website or printed publication and these are indicated with the abbreviation (AC) in the listings.

Luggage carriers are listed on p57. Many accommodation providers are also willing to transfer your luggage. Look for the ! symbol in the accommodation section.

Maps

Sheet numbers refer to Ordnance Survey Explorer 1:25 000 maps. The latest editions show the exact line of route for almost all the trails below. You can buy the full range of OS Explorer maps in both weatherproof and paper versions from Aqua3 through the Ramblers website at a special discount, and we'll also receive a donation for every map sold – see p20.

Strip maps and digital maps are available for some routes. These cover the route itself and some of the countryside on either side. For more on maps see p51.

Publications

Where indicated, these can be obtained from the Ramblers Bookshop (see p95) or directly from local Ramblers Areas and Groups.

Publications with ISBN numbers can be ordered from bookshops and internet retailers, or direct from the publisher (see p95). Some publications are less widely available, in which case we've given ordering details in the listing itself. Guides include at least sketch maps and those marked (OS) have extracts from Ordnance Survey mapping.

SYMBOLS AND ABBREVIATIONS

✸ new listing
🗿 National trail (England and Wales)
🖐 Long distance route (Scotland)

(AC) includes accommodation listings
(OS) includes Ordnance Survey map extracts
TIC Tourist/Visitor Information Centre

Cambrian Way

Cardiff to Conwy 440km/274 miles
CHALLENGING
A spectacular but very mountainous unsigned coast to coast route across Wales from north to south via the Brecon Beacons, Cader Idris and Snowdonia, devised by Ramblers volunteers. Through the Beacons a new partly signed route, the Beacons Way, covers some of the same route, but offers some easier alternatives.
MAPS OL12, OL13, OL17, OL18, OL23, 151, 152, 187, 213, 215
PUBLICATIONS CAMBRIAN WAY GUIDEBOOK (AC), ISBN 0 950958 03 4, £5.50 FROM AJ DRAKE. BEACONS WAY GUIDEBOOK (OS), ISBN 1 902302 35 4, £12 FROM BRECON BEACONS NATIONAL PARK (P99) OR VISIT WWW.BRECONBEACONSPARKSOCIETY.ORG
CONTACT CAMBRIAN WAY, 2 BEECH LODGE, 67 THE PARK, CHELTENHAM GL50 2RX, WWW.CAMBRIANWAY.ORG.UK

Cateran Trail

Blairgowrie, Bridge of Cally and Spittal of Glenshee 101km/63 miles
A lengthy heart-shaped trail with a spur from Blairgowrie, over varied terrain from rolling pastures to the foothills of the Cairngorms with excellent views and stunning scenery throughout. Mostly moderate walking with a more challenging section from Enochdu to Spittal of Glenshee.
MAPS 381, 387
PUBLICATIONS THE CATERAN TRAIL ISBN 1 898481 21 0, RUCKSACK READERS £10.99
CONTACT PERTH AND KINROSS COUNTRYSIDE TRUST ☎ 01738 475340 WWW.PKCT.ORG/CATERANTRAIL

🗿 Cleveland Way

Helmsley to Filey Brigg 177km/110 miles
Horseshoe-shaped route that first follows the western and northern edges of the North York Moors National Park to Saltburn, then the beautiful coastline via Whitby and Scarborough: this last section is now part of the international North Sea Trail project. The whole route is accessible by public transport, and some sections are accessible for people with disabilities: contact the national trail officer for more information. The Link through the Tabular Hills connects Helmsley with the coast near Scalby via a more direct route (77km/48 miles), creating a complete circuit of the national park.
MAPS OL26, OL27, 301
PUBLICATIONS OFFICIAL GUIDEBOOK (OS), ISBN 1 854108 54 9, AURUM PRESS, £12.99. ALTERNATIVE GUIDEBOOK: THE CLEVELAND WAY: WITH THE YORKSHIRE WOLDS WAY AND LINK (OS), ISBN 1 852844 47 7, CICERONE, £12
LUGGAGE CARRIERS BRIGANTES, COAST TO COAST HOLIDAYS, SHERPA VAN
CONTACT NATIONAL TRAIL OFFICER ☎ 01439 770657 WWW.NATIONALTRAIL.CO.UK/CLEVELANDWAY (AC)

Clwydian Way

Prestatyn, Llangollen, Corwen and Denby 243km/152 miles total
A roughly bottle-shaped route through splendid but little-known walking country and historic towns in the Clwydian Range and the Vale of Clwyd. The main 195km/122-mile circuit is complemented by an alternative 48km/30-mile moorland section linking Mynydd Hiraethog and Denbigh.
MAPS 255, 256, 264, 265
PUBLICATIONS GUIDEBOOK (OS), ISBN 1 901184 36 6, NORTH WALES AREA (SEE P94), £5.95
WWW.CLWYDIANWAY.CO.UK (AC)

Coast to Coast Walk

St Bees to Robin Hood's Bay 304km/190 miles
CHALLENGING
Unsigned route devised by Alfred Wainwright to link the Irish Sea and the North Sea via three national parks: the Lake District, Yorkshire Dales and the North York Moors. Popular and scenic, but notably demanding, it was named the second best walk in the world in a recent experts' poll.
MAPS OL4, OL5, OL19, OL26, OL27, OL30, 302, 303, 304
WEATHERPROOF STRIP MAP (WEST), ISBN 1 85137 410 8, AND WEATHERPROOF STRIP MAP (EAST), ISBN 1 851374 40 X, HARVEY MAPS, BOTH £8.95. DIGITAL EXPLORER STRIP MAP £99.95 FROM MEMORY-MAP (SEE P95)

PUBLICATIONS A COAST TO COAST WALK BY A WAINWRIGHT, ISBN 0 711222 36 3, FRANCES LINCOLN £11.99. ACCOMM GUIDE, £3 FROM DOREEN WHITEHEAD, BUTT HOUSE, KELD, RICHMOND DL11 6LJ, BUTTHOUSE@SUPANET.COM. CAMPING GUIDE £2.99 FROM ROCKUMENTARY PRESS, 11 CLIFF TOP, FILEY YO14 9HG, ROCKUMENTARYPRESS@YAHOO.CO.UK
LUGGAGE CARRIERS BRIGANTES, COAST TO COAST HOLIDAYS, COAST TO COAST PACKHORSE, SHERPA VAN
HOSTEL BOOKING YHA

COLERIDGE WAY

Coleridge Way

Nether Stowey to Porlock 58km/36 miles
A walk linking the Quantock and Brendon hills, Exmoor National Park and the Somerset coast through a landscape that inspired the Romantic poet Samuel Taylor Coleridge, including numerous delightful villages. Launched in 2005, the route is now fully signed.
MAPS OL9, 140
PUBLICATIONS FREE OVERVIEW LEAFLET FROM PORLOCK TIC ☎ 01643 863150. DETAILED DESCRIPTION AND MAPS ON WEBSITE WWW.EXMOOR-NATIONALPARK.GOV.UK/ COLERIDGEWAY (AC)

✸ Copper Trail

Minions, Bodmin, Camelford, Five Lanes 100km/60 miles
A circuit around bleak and beautiful Bodmin Moor, including prehistoric remains, mining heritage and open access land. Launched by a local businesses partnership in 2005.
MAP 109
PUBLICATIONS GUIDEBOOK £4.95 + £1 P&P FROM BEST OF BODMIN MOOR (SEE BELOW)

COPPER TRAIL

CONTACT BEST OF BODMIN MOOR, LOWER TRENGALE FARM, LISKEARD PL14 6HF WWW.BOBM.INFO (AC)

Cotswold Way
Bath to Chipping Campden
163km/101 miles
Scenic, popular and undulating route through classic English countryside first proposed by Gloucestershire Ramblers in the 1950s and due to relaunch as a national trail this year: for news about route improvements see website. Part of the Cotswold Round, a lengthy circular walk (see Macmillan Way).
MAPS OL45, 155, 167, 179
WEATHERPROOF STRIP MAP, ISBN 1 85137 342 X, HARVEY MAPS, £9.95
PUBLICATIONS GUIDE, ISBN 1 873877 10 2, REARDON PUBLISHING, £5.95. HANDBOOK (AC, FACILITIES, TRANSPORT), ISBN 1 873877 79 X, GLOUCESTERSHIRE AREA RA (SEE P86), £2.95. ALTERNATIVE GUIDE: THE COTSWOLD WAY (OS), ISBN 1 85284 449 3, CICERONE £12, INCLUDES MANY RECENT ROUTE IMPROVEMENTS. AN OFFICIAL TRAIL GUIDE (OS) IS DUE IN 2007.
LUGGAGE CARRIERS COMPASS, SHERPA VAN
CONTACT NATIONAL TRAIL OFFICE
☎ 01453 827004
WWW.NATIONALTRAIL.CO.UK/COTSWOLD

Cowal Way
Portavadie to Ardgartan near Arrochar 75km/47 miles
Across the Cowal peninsula from Loch Fyne to Loch Long, with grassy hills, heather moorland, forest plantations, prehistoric heritage and rich wildlife all within easy reach of Glasgow. Includes some more remote and strenuous sections.
MAPS 362, 363, 364
PUBLICATIONS GUIDE £4.99 + P&P FROM DUNOON VISITOR INFORMATION CENTRE
☎ 08707 200629 OR WWW.COLGLEN.CO.UK (AC)

Cumbria Way
Ulverston to Carlisle 112km/70 miles
Through the heart of the Lake District National Park via Langdale and Borrowdale, Coniston, Derwent Water and Caldbeck. A good

introduction to the area keeping mainly to the valleys, with some higher exposed ground.
MAPS OL4, OL5, OL6, OL7, 315
WEATHERPROOF STRIP MAP, ISBN 1 841373 34 9, HARVEY MAPS, £8.95.
PUBLICATIONS GUIDE, ISBN 1 855681 97 8, DALESMAN PUBLISHING, £2.99
LUGGAGE CARRIERS BRIGANTES, SHERPA VAN
HOSTEL BOOKING YHA

CUMBRIA WAY

Dales Way
Leeds, Shipley or Harrogate to Bowness-on-Windermere 205km/128 miles total **EASY**

the dales way

Originally inspired by local Ramblers, this fairly easy-going, mainly waterside trail links the Yorkshire Dales and the Lake District. The original route runs from Ilkley to Bowness, and three links connect with big towns in the lower Dales.
MAPS OL2, OL7, OL10, OL30, 297 (MAIN ROUTE), 288 (SHIPLEY), 289 (LEEDS)
WEATHERPROOF STRIP MAP, ISBN 1 851373 69 1, HARVEY MAPS, £9.95
PUBLICATIONS. GUIDEBOOK, ISBN 0 906886 72 4, AVAILABLE FROM ADDRESS BELOW, £5.99. HANDBOOK (AC, FACILITIES, TRANSPORT), £1.50 + P&P FROM WEST RIDING AREA (P92)
LUGGAGE CARRIERS BRIGANTES, SHERPA VAN
USER GROUP DALES WAY ASSOCIATION, 3 MOORFIELD ROAD, ILKLEY LS29 8BL
WWW.DALESWAY.ORG.UK (AC)

Derwent Valley Heritage Way
Ladybower Reservoir, Bamford to Derwent Mouth, Shardlow 88km/55 miles **EASY**
Along the river Derwent from Ladybower Reservoir in the Peak District via the Derwent Valley Mills World Heritage Site and the city of Derby to its confluence with the river Trent near Shardlow. A fascinating combination of rich natural landscapes, industrial heritage and famous estates.
MAPS OL1, OL24, 259, 260
PUBLICATIONS THE DERWENT VALLEY

HERITAGE WAY, ISBN 0 711729 58 1, JARROLD £11.99 (OS). BASIC ROUTE DESCRIPTION AND OVERVIEW MAP ON WEBSITE WWW.NATIONALHERITAGECORRIDOR.ORG.UK

Essex Way
Epping to Harwich 130km/81 miles **EASY**
Pioneered by Ramblers and CPRE members, this walk heads across quiet countryside via Dedham Vale and Constable country to finish at the Stour estuary. The unsigned 24km/15-mile Epping Forest Centenary Walk, created to celebrate the centenary of the saving of the Forest for public enjoyment, connects Manor Park in east London with Epping.
MAPS 174, 175, 183, 184
PUBLICATIONS GUIDE BOOKLET, ISBN 1 852812 48 6, ESSEX COUNTY COUNCIL (SEE P109), £3.50. CENTENARY WALK GUIDE £1 + 30P P&P FROM EPPING FOREST INFORMATION CENTRE
☎ 020 8508 0028
WWW.CITYOFLONDON.GOV.UK/OPENSPACES

FIFE COASTAL PATH

Fife Coastal Path
North Queensferry to Newport on Tay 107km/67 miles
Around the firths of Forth and Tay, through historic towns and villages, excellent countryside and attractive beaches, combining surfaced seaside promenades and rougher coastal tracks. The route is now part of the international North Sea Trail.
MAPS 367, 370, 371
PUBLICATIONS GUIDE, ISBN 1 841830 57 7, MERCAT PRESS, £12.99. PATH MAPS AND OTHER USEFUL INFORMATION ON WEBSITE BELOW.
CONTACT FIFE COAST AND COUNTRYSIDE TRUST
☎ 01333 592591 WWW.FIFECOASTALPATH.COM (AC)

Glyndŵr's Way
Knighton to Welshpool 206km/128 miles
A beautiful route through mid-Wales visiting many sites associated with the fifteenth century hero Owain Glyndŵr. Forms a rough triangle with Offa's Dyke Path as the third side and Machynlleth as its westernmost point.

MAPS 201, 214, 215, 216, 239
DIGITAL EXPLORER STRIP MAP £49.95 FROM
MEMORY-MAP
PUBLICATIONS GUIDE, ISBN 1 854109 68 5,
AURUM PRESS, £12.99. FOR ACCOM GUIDE SEE
OFFA'S DYKE PATH
CONTACT NATIONAL TRAIL OFFICER
☎ 01654 703376
WWW.NATIONALTRAIL.CO.UK/GLYNDWRSWAY (AC)

🌢 Great Glen Way

Fort William to Inverness 117km/
73 miles
From the West Highland Way along
the fault line of Glen Mor and the
northwest shores of Loch Lochy and
Loch Ness, following the course of
the Caledonian Canal. Lower level
and less demanding than some other
Scottish routes.
MAPS 392, 400, 416
WEATHERPROOF STRIP MAP, ISBN 1 851373 84 5,
HARVEY MAPS, £9.95
PUBLICATIONS GUIDEBOOK, ISBN
1 898481 24 5, RUCKSACK READERS, £9.95.
ACCOM & SERVICES GUIDE (AC) FREE + P&P
FROM OUR CENTRAL OFFICE
LUGGAGE CARRIERS ABERCHALDER, GREAT
GLEN BAGGAGE, GREAT GLEN TRAVEL, LOCH NESS
INDEPENDENT HOSTELS IBHS
CONTACT GREAT GLEN WAY RANGER SERVICE
☎ 01320 366633
WWW.GREATGLENWAY.COM (AC)

🌢 Hadrian's Wall Path

Newcastle to Bowness on Solway
130km/81 miles
From the bustling Newcastle
quaysides to the remote North
Pennines alongside the line of
the wall built in the year 122 to
mark the northern limit of the Roman
empire. Please help to look after the
monument by following the
conservation advice issued by the
National Trail Office.
MAPS OL43, 314, 315, 316
WEATHERPROOF STRIP MAP, ISBN 1 851374 05 1,
HARVEY MAPS, £9.95.
DIGITAL EXPLORER STRIP MAP £49.95 FROM
MEMORY-MAP
PUBLICATIONS GUIDEBOOK (OS), ISBN
1 854108 93 X, AURUM PRESS, £12.99. ESSENTIAL
GUIDE (FACILITIES, TRANSPORT, SUGGESTED
ITINERARIES ETC), ISBN 0 954734 20 3,
HADRIAN'S WALL PATH TRUST, £3.95. ACCOM
GUIDE (AC) FREE + P&P FROM OUR CENTRAL
OFFICE. NUMEROUS SHORTER AND CIRCULAR
WALKS GUIDES FROM NATIONAL TRAIL OFFICE
(SEE BELOW)
LUGGAGE CARRIERS BRIGANTES,
SHERPA VAN, WALKERS BAGGAGE TRANSFER,
WALKING SUPPORT
HOSTEL BOOKING YHA

CONTACTS
NATIONAL TRAIL OFFICER
☎ 0191 269 1600
WWW.NATIONALTRAIL.CO.UK/HADRIANSWALL
(AC)
HADRIAN'S WALL INFORMATION LINE
☎ 01434 322002
WWW.HADRIANS WALL.ORG (AC)
USER GROUP HADRIAN'S WALL PATH TRUST
C/O NATIONAL TRAIL OFFICER

Heart Of England Way

Milford near Stafford to Bourton on
the Water 161km/100 miles
A green route across the West
Midlands linking Cannock Chase with
 the Cotswolds, through
mainly gentle low-lying
country with woodlands,
canals and agricultural land.
MAPS OL45, 204, 205, 219, 220, 232, 244
PUBLICATIONS GUIDEBOOK, ISBN
0 947708 40 5, WALKWAYS, £7.50. ACCOM LIST
(AC) FREE + P&P FROM OUR CENTRAL OFFICE
USER GROUP HEART OF ENGLAND WAY
ASSOCIATION, 50 GEORGE ROAD, WATER ORTON,
BIRMINGHAM B46 1PE
WWW.HEARTOFENGLANDWAY.ORG

Herefordshire Trail

Ledbury, Ross-on-Wye, Kington,
Leominster and Bromyard
246.5km/154 miles
A circuit around the county visiting all
the market towns, with numerous
 pretty villages and attractive
countryside including
commons, woodlands, hills,
farmlands, waterside and
characteristic black and white
architecture. Created by local
Ramblers in partnership with
Herefordshire council.
MAPS OL13, OL14, 189, 190, 201, 202, 203
PUBLICATIONS THE HEREFORDSHIRE TRAIL,
BY THE HEREFORD GROUP (SEE P87).
WEBSITE WWW.HEREFORDSHIRETRAIL.COM
(AC)

Icknield Way Path

Bledlow to Knettishall Heath near
Thetford 206km/128 miles
Follows prehistoric trackways from
the Chilterns into East Anglia,
passing many sites of
archaeological interest and
connecting the Ridgeway and
Peddars Way as part of a lengthy
off-road route along ancient ways
between the Dorset coast and
the Wash (see Ridgeway). The
original walking route runs from
Ivinghoe Beacon; there are now
alternative multi-user sections from

Bledlow to Ivinghoe, running
parallel to the Ridgeway, and
from Aldbury to Pegsdon (Icknield
Way Trail).
MAPS 181, 193, 208, 209, 210, 226, 229
PUBLICATIONS GUIDEBOOK (FROM
IVINGHOE) £4.50 + P&P. ACCOM LIST (AC) £1
+ P&P AVAILABLE FROM DAVID NORTHRUP, 5
PERNE AVENUE, CAMBRIDGE, CB1 3RY. GREATER
RIDGEWAY GUIDE: SEE RIDGEWAY. BLEDLOW –
IVINGHOE LEAFLET FROM BUCKINGHAMSHIRE
COUNCIL, DOWNLOADABLE FROM THEIR WEBSITE
UNDER WALKS AND RIDES (P109). ICKNIELD WAY
TRAIL LEAFLET FROM NORTH CHILTERNS TRUST
☎ 01582 412225
WWW.NORTHCHILTERNSTRUST.CO.UK
USER GROUP ICKNIELD WAY ASSOCIATION,
1 EDGEBOROUGH CLOSE, KENTFORD,
NEWMARKET CB8 8QY,
WWW.ICKNIELDWAYPATH.CO.UK

Isle Of Anglesey Coastal Path

Llanfaethlu, Amlwch,
Beaumaris, Holyhead
200km/125 miles
Fairly easy walking around the edge
of Anglesey, through diverse coastal
scenery mainly within an area of
outstanding natural beauty, with
many attractive villages. Easily
accessed by bus (details in
publications, below).
MAPS 262, 263
PUBLICATIONS GUIDEBOOK (NEW 2006)
ISBN 1 902512 13 8, FROM HOLYHEAD
VISITOR CENTRE, ☎ 01407 762622, OR
DOWNLOAD ROUTE INFORMATION FROM
WEBSITE, WWW.ANGLESEYCOASTALPATH.COM
(AC)

Isle Of Wight Coastal Path

Circular from Ryde 105km/65 miles
Popular coastal circuit round an
island well-loved by walkers,
via chines, saltmarshes, cliffs and
holiday resorts, with plenty of
accommodation and good public
transport links. Connects with a
number of other routes heading
inland including the 22km/
14-mile Tennyson Trail from
Carisbrooke to Alum Bay and the
18km/11-mile Bembridge Trail from
Shide to Bembridge.
PUBLICATIONS COASTAL PATH AND INLAND
TRAILS GUIDE £3 + P&P FROM ISLE OF WIGHT
TOURISM OR DOWNLOAD ROUTE GUIDES FROM
ISLAND BREAKS WEBSITE (SEE BELOW).
LUGGAGE CARRIER BAG TAG
CONTACT ISLE OF WIGHT TOURISM
☎ 01983 813800
WWW.ISLANDBREAKS.CO.UK (AC)

London Loop

Erith to Rainham via Kingston, near circular around Greater London 241km/150 miles **EASY**

A fascinating mix of waterside, parkland, nature reserves and countryside on the urban fringe, within easy reach of central London by public transport. The Loop and sister inner orbital path the Capital Ring (115km/72 miles via Woolwich, Crystal Palace, Richmond and Finsbury Park, fully opened in 2005) were pioneered by Ramblers volunteers and the London Walking Forum, and both are now Transport for London strategic walking routes.

MAPS 160, 161, 162, 172, 173, 174
PUBLICATIONS LOOP AND RING GUIDEBOOKS (OS) £12.99 + P&P EACH FROM RAMBLERS CENTRAL OFFICE. FREE LEAFLETS FOR MOST OF THE LOOP AND ALL OF THE RING ALSO AVAILABLE, ☎ 0870 240 6094, WWW.TFL.GOV.UK/WALKING

Macmillan Ways

Macmillan Way: Boston to Abbotsbury 464km/290 miles
Macmillan Way West: Castle Cary to Barnstaple 163km/102 miles
Abbotsbury-Langport Link: 38.5km/24 miles
Cross-Cotswold Pathway: Banbury to Bath 138km/86 miles
Cotswold Link: Chipping Campden to Banbury 33.5km/21 miles

A network of attractive routes linking the south coast, Bristol channel and North Sea coast of England, taking in the Cotswolds, the Quantocks and the Fens. The main route runs diagonally across England from south to east, while the western route links the north Devon coast to the east coast, or to the south coast via the Langport link.

The Cross-Cotswold option uses one of the most popular sections of the main route with additional town links providing public transport connections, while the Cotswold Link connects with the Cotswold Way to create the Cotswold Round, a 331km/207-mile circuit via Chipping Campden, Banbury, Cirencester and Bath.

MAPS MAIN ROUTE/ABBOTSBURY LINK: OL15, OL45, 117, 129, 142, 156, 168, 191, 206, 207, 223, 233, 234, 248, 249, 261
WEST: OL9, 129, 140, 141, 142
CROSS-COTSWOLD PATHWAY/LINK: OL45, 155, 156, 168, 179, 191, 206
PUBLICATIONS MACMILLAN WAY GUIDEBOOK £9 + P&P, MACMILLAN WAY WEST GUIDEBOOK £6.25 + P&P FROM MACMILLAN WAY

ASSOCIATION (SEE BELOW). NORTH-SOUTH SUPPLEMENT FOR THE MAIN ROUTE, GUIDES TO OTHER LINKS AND SPURS, PLANNERS, UPDATE SHEETS, ACCOMMODATION LISTS AND NUMEROUS OTHER PUBLICATIONS AND MERCHANDISE FROM USER GROUP BELOW.
USER GROUP MACMILLAN WAY ASSOCIATION ☎ 01789 740852
WWW.MACMILLANWAY.ORG

MIDSHIRES WAY

Midshires Way

Princes Risborough to Stockport 363km/230 miles

A walking link between southern and northern England, from the Ridgeway in the Chilterns to the Pennine Bridleway and Trans Pennine Trail via historic estates, farmland and the Peak District National Park. Generally gentle walking incorporating sections of numerous other trails including the North Bucks Way, Brampton Valley Way and High Peak Trail. In the north, the 25km/15.5-mile Etherow-Goyt Valley Way connects Stockport with Longdendale in the Peak District via two country parks.

MAPS OL1, OL24, 181, 192, 207, 223, 233, 244, 246, 259, 260, 269
PUBLICATIONS MIDSHIRES WAY GUIDE ISBN 1 850058 778 7, SIGMA LEISURE £7.95. ETHEROW-GOYT VALLEY WAY GUIDE £2.25 FROM TAMESIDE COUNCIL (P113)

Monarch's Way

Worcester to Shoreham 982km/610 miles

Britain's second longest signed route follows in the footsteps of Charles II on his flight from the Battle of Worcester, a meandering course from the West Midlands to the south coast taking in many historic sights.

MAPS OL45, 116, 117, 119, 120, 121, 122, 129, 130, 131, 132, 141, 142, 143, 155, 167, 168. 204, 205, 218, 219, 220, 221, 242
PUBLICATIONS GUIDEBOOK IN THREE VOLS:

1. THE MIDLANDS, ISBN 1 869922 52 2; 2. THE COTSWOLDS, THE MENDIPS AND THE SEA, ISBN 1 869922 28 X; 3. THE SOUTH COAST, THE DOWNS AND ESCAPE, ISBN 1 869922 29 8, ALL FROM MERIDIAN, ALL £6.95. ACCOM LIST (AC) 75P FROM MONARCH'S WAY ASSOCIATION (SEE BELOW).
USER GROUP MONARCH'S WAY ASSOCIATION ☎ 0121 429 4397
WWW.MONARCHSWAY.50MEGS.COM

Nene Way

Badby to Sutton Bridge 177km/110 miles **EASY**

Along the valley of the river Nene as it first meanders through quiet Northamptonshire countryside then straightens out onto a canalised section towards Lincolnshire and the Wash.

MAPS 207, 223, 224, 227, 234, 235, 249
PUBLICATIONS LEAFLET PACK BADBY TO WANSFORD £3 + P&P FROM NORTHAMPTONSHIRE COUNTY COUNCIL (SEE P112). LEAFLET WANSFORD TO WHITTLESEA FREE FROM PETERBOROUGH COUNCIL PUBLIC RIGHTS OF WAY OFFICE (P112). LEAFLET WHITTLESEA TO SUTTON BRIDGE FREE FROM CAMBRIDGESHIRE COUNCIL PUBLIC RIGHTS OF WAY OFFICE (P109)

Nidderdale Way

Circular from Pateley Bridge 85 km/53 miles

Around the valley of the river Nidd, an area of outstanding natural beauty on the edge of the Yorkshire Dales, including gritstone outcrops and rough, open moorland. Much of the route has good public transport connections: information from Nidderdale AONB (p100).

MAP 298
WEATHERPROOF STRIP MAP, ISBN 1 851373 92 6, HARVEY MAPS, £6.95
PUBLICATIONS WALK CARD PACK £2.95 + P&P FROM YORKSHIRE FOOTPATH TRUST, 37 HAZEL GARTH, YORK YO30 1HR
CONTACT NIDDERDALE AONB (P100)

NORTH DOWNS WAY

North Downs Way

Farnham to Dover 245km/153 miles

Along the chalk ridges and wooded downland of Surrey into Kent, with an optional loop via Canterbury, often running parallel to the ancient trackway of the Pilgrim's Way. The 55km/ 24-mile St Swithun's Way continues along the line of the trackway from Farnham to Winchester.

MAPS 137, 138, 145, 146, 147, 148, 150 (AND 132, 144 FOR ST SWITHUN'S WAY) **WEATHERPROOF STRIP MAPS,** WEST (FARNHAM TO THE MEDWAY) ISBN 1 851373 67 5 & EAST (MEDWAY TO DOVER) ISBN 1 851373 79 9, HARVEY MAPS, BOTH £9.95

PUBLICATIONS GUIDEBOOK (OS), ISBN 1 845109 65 0, AURUM PRESS, £12.99. ST SWITHUN'S WAY ROUTE CARD PACK AVAILABLE FROM HAMPSHIRE COUNTY COUNCIL (SEE P111). ACCOMMODATION AND TRANSPORT DETAILS ON WEBSITE BELOW

CONTACT NATIONAL TRAIL OFFICE ☎ 01622 221525 WWW.NATIONALTRAIL.CO.UK/NORTHDOWNS (AC) ST SWITHUN'S WAY WEBSITE WWW.HANTS.GOV.UK/WALKING/SWITHUNS/

Offa's Dyke Path
Chepstow to Prestatyn 283km/ 177 miles **CHALLENGING**
A varied walk from the Severn estuary to the Irish Sea through the border country of England and Wales via Knighton, Welshpool and Llangollen, with around 100km/60 miles alongside the eighth century earthwork of Offa's Dyke itself. Although not as challenging as more mountainous routes, there are some remote sections with rough paths and numerous ups and downs.

MAPS OL13, OL14, 201, 216, 240, 256, 265 **WEATHERPROOF STRIP MAPS,** SOUTH (CHEPSTOW TO KNIGHTON) ISBN 1 851374 56 6, NORTH (KNIGHTON TO PRESTATYN) ISBN 1 851374 51 5, HARVEY MAPS, BOTH £9.95

PUBLICATIONS OFFA'S DYKE PATH SOUTH (CHEPSTOW TO KNIGHTON) (OS), ISBN 1 854109 87 1; OFFA'S DYKE NORTH (KNIGHTON TO PRESTATYN) (OS), ISBN 1 854109 76 6, AURUM PRESS, BOTH £12.99. OFFA'S DYKE & GLYNDŴR'S WAY ACCOM GUIDE (AC), £4, ROUTE DESCRIPTIONS SOUTH TO NORTH AND NORTH TO SOUTH, A CAMPING AND BACKPACKING GUIDE, CIRCULAR WALKS BOOKS AND NUMEROUS OTHER ITEMS ALL FROM OFFA'S DYKE ASSOCIATION (SEE BELOW)

LUGGAGE CARRIERS SHERPA VAN **USER GROUP/CONTACT** OFFA'S DYKE ASSOCIATION ☎ 01547 528 753 WWW.OFFASDYKE.DEMON.CO.UK NATIONAL TRAIL OFFICE ☎ 01547 528192 WWW.NATIONALTRAIL.CO.UK/OFFASDYKE (AC)

Peddars Way and Norfolk Coast Path
Knettishall Heath near Thetford to Cromer 146km/91 miles **EASY**
Effectively two routes: the Peddars

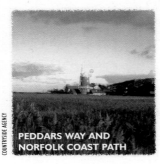

PEDDARS WAY AND NORFOLK COAST PATH

COUNTRYSIDE AGENCY

Way runs northwards through the Norfolk countryside to near Hunstanton, connecting with the Icknield Way Path to form the last link in a continuous chain of ancient trackways from the south coast. The coast path then runs eastwards via Sheringham. Many sections are suitable for people with special access needs: more information from the National Trail Office (below). Two other easy routes connect to provide a lengthy circuit of Norfolk, the 90km/56-mile Weavers Way from Cromer to Great Yarmouth via the Broads, and the 123km/77-mile Angles Way eastwards along the Waveney and Little Ouse rivers back to Knettishall Heath.

MAPS 229, 236, 250, 252, 252 (AND OL40, 238 FOR WEAVERS WAY; OL40, 230, 231 FOR ANGLES WAY)

PUBLICATIONS PEDDARS WAY/COAST PATH/WEAVERS WAY GUIDE BOOKLET (AC) AND ANGLES WAY GUIDE BOOKLET (AC) £2.70 + P&P EACH FROM NORFOLK AREA (SEE P90). PEDDARS WAY AND NORFOLK COAST PATH OFFICIAL GUIDEBOOK (OS) ISBN 1 854085 2 2, AURUM £12.99. GREATER RIDGEWAY GUIDE: SEE RIDGEWAY

CONTACT NATIONAL TRAIL OFFICE ☎ 01328 850530 WWW.NATIONALTRAIL.CO.UK/PEDDARSWAY (AC)

Pembrokeshire Coast Path
Amroth to Cardigan 299km/186 miles
Some of the most spectacular coastal walking in Britain, mainly along clifftops and almost all within the Pembrokeshire Coast National Park, including Wales' only marine nature reserve and 17 Sites of Special Scientific Interest (SSSIs). Some steep climbs but also sections suitable for people with special access needs. At Cardigan the Path links with the 101km/63-mile Ceredigion Coastal Path, which is still under development

but already walkable; both paths will eventually form part of a continuous walking route around the Welsh coast.

LUGGAGE CARRIERS PEMBROKESHIRE DISCOVERY, TONY'S TAXIS **MAPS** OL35, OL36 (CEREDIGION COAST OL23, 198, 213)

PUBLICATIONS GUIDEBOOK (OS), ISBN 1 854109 75 8, AURUM PRESS, £12.99. EASY ACCESS GUIDE £2.95 + P&P, WALK LEAFLETS FOR INDIVIDUAL SECTIONS AND CIRCULAR WALKS, VARIOUS OTHER PUBLICATIONS FROM PEMBROKESHIRE COAST NATIONAL PARK (P99). WALKING THE CEREDIGION COAST FREE + P&P FROM OUR CENTRAL OFFICE OR DOWNLOADABLE FROM WWW.WALKCARDIGANBAY.COM (AC). WALKING THE CARDIGAN BAY COAST FROM CARDIGAN TO BORTH, ISBN 1 902302 09 5, KITTIWAKE £3.95

CONTACT PEMBROKESHIRE COAST NATIONAL PARK TEL 01437 720392 WWW.PEMBROKESHIRECOAST.ORG.UK (AC)

Pennine Bridleway
Hartington or Middleton Top to Byrness 560km/350 miles
A route for walkers as well as horse riders and cyclists, running roughly parallel to the Pennine Way but along easier paths to the west of the hilltops. The southern section, 188km/117 miles from the Peak District to the South Pennines, is already open, including the Mary Towneley Loop, a 68km/42-mile circuit around Todmorden and Bacup. A further 142km/89 miles from the Loop to the Fat Lamb Inn, Cumbria, opens this year. The rest is mainly walkable already, though as yet unsigned: see website for the latest situation.

MAPS SOUTHERN SECTION OL1, OL21, OL24; NORTHERN SECTION OL2, OL19, OL41 **WEATHERPROOF STRIP MAP,** ISBN 1 851374 06 X, HARVEY MAPS, £9.95

PUBLICATIONS GUIDEBOOK TO DERBYSHIRE/SOUTH PENNINES SECTION (OS), ISBN 1 854109 57 X, AURUM PRESS, £12.99. ACCOM AND SERVICES GUIDE (AC), FREE + P&P, FROM OUR CENTRAL OFFICE.

CONTACT PENNINE BRIDLEWAY TEAM ☎ 0161 237 1061 WWW.NATIONALTRAIL.CO.UK/PENNINE BRIDLEWAY (AC)

Pennine Way
Edale to Kirk Yetholm 429km/ 268 miles **CHALLENGING**
A high and wild trail along the backbone of England from the Peak District to the Scottish Borders. Pioneered by Ramblers activist Tom Stephenson, it is the oldest as well as one of the toughest of Britain's signed walking trails.

PATHS & ACCESS

MAPS OL1, OL2, OL16, OL19, OL21, OL30, OL31, OL42, OL43
HARVEY WEATHERPROOF STRIP MAPS: SOUTH (EDALE TO HORTON), ISBN 1 851374 31 0; CENTRAL (HORTON TO GREENHEAD), ISBN 1 851374 26 4; NORTH (GREENHEAD TO KIRK YETHOLM) ISBN 1 851374 21 3, £9.95 EACH FROM HARVEY MAPS. DIGITAL EXPLORER STRIP MAP £99.95 FROM MEMORY-MAP.
PUBLICATIONS GUIDEBOOKS SOUTH (EDALE TO BOWES) (OS), ISBN 1 854108 51 4; NORTH (BOWES TO KIRK YETHOLM) (OS), ISBN 1 854109 62 6, AURUM PRESS, BOTH £12.99; TRANSPORT AND ACCOM LIST (AC) FREE + P&P FROM OUR CENTRAL OFFICE
LUGGAGE CARRIERS BRIGANTES, SHERPA VAN
HOSTEL BOOKING YHA (ASK ABOUT PENNINE HIGHLIGHTS AS A SHORTER ALTERNATIVE TO THE WHOLE WALK)
CONTACT NATIONAL TRAIL OFFICE
☎ 0113 246 9222
WWW.NATIONALTRAIL.CO.UK/PENNINEWAY (AC)
USER GROUP PENNINE WAY ASSOCIATION
☎ 01434 607088
WWW.PENNINEWAYASSOCIATION.CO.UK

✳ Ribble Way
Longton to the source of the Ribble near Ribblehead 114km/71 miles

A riverside walk originally championed by local Ramblers from the wide-open Ribble estuary through rolling pastoral countryside via Preston and Clitheroe, then cutting through rough Pennine moorlands to reach remote Cam Fell.
MAPS OL2, OL41
PUBLICATIONS GUIDEBOOK (NEW 2006) ISBN 1 85284 456 6, CICERONE £10. ROUTE MAPS ARE AVAILABLE ON LANCASHIRE COUNCIL'S WEBSITE (P111)

🌢 Ridgeway
Overton Hill near Avebury to Ivinghoe Beacon 137km/85 miles
A route along 'Britain's oldest road' past the ancient hillforts of the North

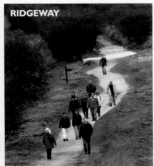
RIDGEWAY

Wessex Downs, across the Thames and through the wooded countryside of the Chilterns. With the Wessex Ridgeway, Icknield Way Path and Peddars Way it forms a continuous 583km/363-mile walking route following ancient ways from the south coast to the Wash, the complete route of which is described in the *Greater Ridgeway Guide* below.
MAPS 157, 170, 171, 181
WEATHERPROOF STRIP MAP, ISBN 1 8541373 14 4, HARVEY MAPS, £8.95.
DIGITAL EXPLORER STRIP MAP £49.95 FROM MEMORY-MAP
PUBLICATIONS GUIDEBOOK (OS), ISBN 1 845130 63 4, AURUM PRESS, £12.99; RIDGEWAY COMPANION (AC), ISBN 0 953520 77 3, NATIONAL TRAIL OFFICE (SEE BELOW), £3.95; GREATER RIDGEWAY GUIDE (OS), ISBN 1 852843 46 2, CICERONE, £12.95
CONTACT NATIONAL TRAIL OFFICE
☎ 01865 810224
WWW.NATIONALTRAIL.CO.UK/RIDGEWAY (AC)
USER GROUP FRIENDS OF THE RIDGEWAY, 18 HAMPTON PARK, BRISTOL BS6 6LH
WWW.RIDGEWAYFRIENDS.ORG.UK

Rob Roy Way
Drymen to Pitlochry 126km/79 miles
Connecting the West Highland Way with the Tay valley, this unsigned route includes rich woodlands, remote moors and heaths, dramatic mountain views, impressive built heritage and sites connected with Scotland's most famous outlaw, Rob Roy MacGregor (1671-1734).
LUGGAGE CARRIER BIKE AND HIKE, TROSSACHS TRANSFERS
MAPS 347, 365, 378, 386
PUBLICATIONS GUIDEBOOK, ISBN 1 898481 26 1, RUCKSACK READERS, £10.99
WEBSITE WWW.ROBROYWAY.COM (AC)

Saints' Way
Padstow to Fowey 42km/26 miles
Attractive coast to coast trail across Cornwall, following a route possibly taken by the Celtic saints.
MAPS 106, 107
PUBLICATIONS GUIDE, £3.99 + P&P FROM CORNWALL COUNTY COUNCIL (SEE P109)

Sandstone Trail
Frodsham to Whitchurch 51km/32 miles
An airy walk following the sandstone ridge that rises dramatically from the central Cheshire plain, including rock outcrops, woodlands, castles and historic churches. Can be walked easily in three sections of

SANDSTONE TRAIL
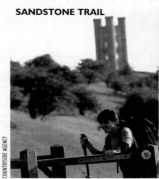

around 17km/10.5 miles each, with a seasonal weekend bus service.
LUGGAGE CARRIER BYWAYS BREAKS
MAPS 257, 267
PUBLICATIONS FREE LEAFLET + P&P FROM OUR CENTRAL OFFICE, INFORMATION PACK (AC) FROM CHESHIRE COUNCIL COUNTRYSIDE SERVICES (P109) OR SEE WWW.CHESHIRE.GOV.UK/WALKING

Severn Way
Plylimon to Bristol 360km/225 miles
Britain's longest riverside walk follows the Severn from its source in the wild mid-Wales moorlands to its wide estuary on the Bristol channel via Welshpool, Shrewsbury, the World Heritage Site at Ironbridge, Worcester and Gloucester. The Way ends officially at Severn Beach (337km/210.5 miles) where a link path continues into central Bristol.
MAPS OL14, 167, 179, 190, 204, 214, 215, 216, 218, 241, 242
PUBLICATIONS GUIDEBOOK £6.95 FROM RECREATION DEPARTMENT, ENVIRONMENT AGENCY, HAFREN HOUSE, WELSHPOOL ROAD, SHELTON, SHREWSBURY SY3 8BB
WEBSITE WWW.SEVERNWAY.COM (AC)

Shropshire Way
Shrewsbury, Wem, Grindley Brook, Long Mynd, Ludlow 264km/165 miles total
A tour devised by local Ramblers, combining bracing hill sections and

SHROPSHIRE WAY

PATHS & ACCESS

Enjoy a FREE magazine on us

Choose from one of our leading countryside and regional titles:

Dalesman

At the very heart of Yorkshire Life, Dalesman features a detailed Accommodation and What's On Guide along with monthly featured walk.

Plus there's stunning photography alongside articles on the county's history, wildlife, people and places.

Countryman

We'll bring you closer to the British Countryside with detailed features on our all-important rural heritage. Each issue covers:

• Birds and wildlife
• Country People
• Traditions
• Crafts and
• Rural issues

Cumbria

Enjoy an intimate view of the Lake District and an appreciation of the pressures and delicate balance that exists between sustainable tourism and rural economy. Cumbria Magazine reveals Lakeland' hidden Gems, provides a full What's On Guide and detailed accommodation listing.

Claim your FREE magazine. Complete and return the form below or call: **0845 053 9066** and quote "WALK Britain 07" when ordering.

✂

FREE ISSUE REQUEST

Please send me the following magazine: ☐ Dalesman ☐ Countryman ☐ Cumbria

Title _____ Forename _____ Surname _____

Address _____

_____

Postcode _____ Telephone _____

Return to: Country Publications Ltd, The Water Mill, Broughton Hall, Skipton, North Yorkshire BD23 3AG

We may contact you (by post, telephone or email) with details of other special reader offers. ☐ Please tick here if you do not wish this to happen.
We do occasionally share information with other carefully selected organisations who may send you information about their product and services by post. ☐ If you do not wish this to happen then please tick here .

celebrated sights like Wenlock Edge, the Long Mynd and the Wrekin with gentler, more pastoral walking in the valleys. A narrow, wiggling circuit from Shrewsbury with two alternative routes is combined with a spur to Grindley Brook and the Llangollen Canal. A good network of leisure buses operates in the area: see www.shropshirehillsshuttles.co.uk.
MAPS 203, 216, 217, 241, 242
PUBLICATIONS GUIDEBOOK, £6.99 + P&P FROM SHROPSHIRE AREA (SEE P90)

Solent Way
Christchurch to Emsworth
112km/70 miles

Across the south of Hampshire via beaches, clifftops, marshes, heaths, ancient woodlands, riverside villages and the historic waterfronts of Southampton and Portsmouth. The Way is signed from Milford but *Pub Walks* (below) describes a route from Christchurch. The Bournemouth Coast Path, signed as European path E9, links Sandbanks (Poole) and the South West Coast Path to Milford: the guide below includes sections with alternative clifftop and prom routes.
MAPS OL22, 119, 120 (AND OL15 FOR POOLE)
PUBLICATIONS PUB WALKS ALONG THE SOLENT WAY, ISBN 1 853067 38 5, COUNTRYSIDE BOOKS, £7.95. LEAFLET WITH ROUTE OVERVIEW, FREE + P&P FROM RAMBLERS CENTRAL OFFICE. DETAILS ALSO AVAILABLE AT WWW.HANTS.GOV.UK/WALKING. EXPLORING THE BOURNEMOUTH COAST PATH, ISBN 1 8530690 8 6, COUNTRYSIDE BOOKS £7.99

South Downs Way
Eastbourne to Winchester 161km/ 101 miles
Exhilirating route along the rolling chalk downs of Sussex and Hampshire, through the heart of the future national park.
MAPS 119 (VERY SMALL PART), 120, 121, 122, 123, 132
HARVEY WEATHERPROOF STRIP MAP £9.95 + P&P FROM OUR CENTRAL OFFICE

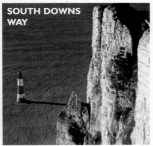

SOUTH DOWNS WAY

COUNTRYSIDE AGENCY

PUBLICATIONS GUIDE (OS), ISBN 1 85410 966 9, AURUM £12.99. ALONG THE SOUTH DOWNS WAY GUIDE IN BOTH DIRECTIONS (AC), £6 + P&P. AVAILABLE FROM SOUTH DOWNS SOCIETY (SEE P99)
CONTACT NATIONAL TRAIL OFFICER
☎ 023 9259 7618
WWW.NATIONALTRAIL.CO.UK/SOUTHDOWNS

South Tyne Trail
Source of the South Tyne near Garrigill to Halwhistle
36.5km/23 miles **EASY**

A route created with the help of local Ramblers following the South Tyne and Tyne rivers through the remote and lesser-visited countryside of East Cumbria and the North Pennines to end near Hadrian's Wall. From Alston to Haltwhistle it follows an old railway line with easy access. More ambitious walkers can follow the full length of both the Tyne (Garrigill to Tynemouth 133km/83 miles) and North Tyne (Hexham to Alston and Deadwater 76km/47.5 miles) as both linear and linked circular walks using the additional publications below: note these longer routes include more challenging sections.
MAPS OL31, OL42, OL43, 316
PUBLICATIONS SOUTH TYNE TRAIL LEAFLET £2 FROM EAST CUMBRIA COUNTRYSIDE PROJECT (BELOW). WALKING THE TYNE AND WALKING THE NORTH TYNE GUIDEBOOKS FROM NORTHUMBRIA RAMBLERS (SEE P90)
CONTACT EAST CUMBRIA COUNTRYSIDE PROJECT
☎ 01228 561601, WWW.ECCP.ORG.UK

South West Coast Path
Minehead to Poole 1014km/630 miles
Britain's longest national walking route, a spectacular and massively popular continuous path around almost the entire southwest peninsula. Although never too remote, there are some arduous cliff-top sections with steep climbs and descents. The national trail website below includes plentiful suggestions for short and easy walks as well as information about the whole trail.
MAPS OL9, OL15, OL20, 102, 103, 104, 105, 106, 107, 108, 110, 111, 115, 116, 126, 139
HARVEY WEATHERPROOF STRIP MAPS: A SERIES OF SIX MAPS COVERING THE TRAIL IS IN THE PROCESS OF BEING PUBLISHED. CONTACT HARVEY FOR MORE DETAILS (P95).
DIGITAL EXPLORER STRIP MAPS, MINEHEAD TO FALMOUTH AND FALMOUTH TO POOLE, £99.95 EACH FROM MEMORY-MAP (P95)
PUBLICATIONS SOUTH WEST COAST PATH OFFICIAL GUIDES IN FOUR VOLUMES, AURUM £12.99 EACH (OS): MINEHEAD TO PADSTOW ISBN

SOUTH WEST COAST PATH

CHRIS ORD

1 85410 97 7 4, PADSTOW TO FALMOUTH ISBN 1 85410 85 0 6, FALMOUTH TO EXMOUTH ISBN 1 85410 76 8 2, EXMOUTH TO POOLE ISBN 1 854109 88 X. SOUTH WEST COAST PATH GUIDE (ROUTE DESCRIPTION ONLY, NO MAPS, UPDATED ANNUALLY, AC) & SOUTH WEST COAST PATH THE OTHER WAY ROUND, ROUTE DESCRIPTION FROM POOLE TO MINEHEAD TO BE USED IN CONJUNCTION WITH OTHER GUIDES, £3.50 BOTH FROM SOUTH WEST COAST PATH ASSOCIATION (SEE BELOW) WHO CAN ALSO SUPPLY OTHER LITERATURE AND MERCHANDISE
CONTACT NATIONAL TRAIL OFFICER
☎ 01392 383560
WWW.SOUTHWESTCOASTPATH.COM (AC)
USER GROUP SOUTH WEST COAST PATH ASSOCIATION ☎ 01752 896237
WWW.SWCP.ORG.UK

♿ Southern Upland Way
Portpatrick to Cockburnspath
341km/212 miles **CHALLENGING**
Scenic coast to coast trail through southern Scotland via Sanquar, Moffatt and Melrose, combining some remote and demanding stretches with sections suitable for families.
MAPS OL32, OL44, 309, 310, 320, 321, 322, 328, 329, 330, 345, 346
PUBLICATIONS GUIDE(OS), ISBN 1 841830 77 1, MERCAT PRESS, £16.99; ACCOM LEAFLET (AC) FREE + P&P FROM OUR CENTRAL OFFICE. SHORTER WALKS LEAFLETS FROM RANGER SERVICES OR DOWNLOADABLE FROM WEBSITE (SEE BELOW)
LUGGAGE CARRIERS SOUTHERNUPLANDWAY.COM, WAY FORWARD
CONTACT RANGER SERVICE ☎ 01387 260184 (WEST) OR ☎ 01835 830281 (EAST)
WWW.DUMGAL.GOV.UK/SOUTHERN UPLANDWAY (AC)

♿ Speyside Way
Buckie to Craigelachie, Tomintoul or Aviemore 135km/84 miles total
Following the fast-flowing river Spey south from the Grampian coast through classic malt whisky country, along forest trails and an old railway track to the famous Highland resort of Aviemore.
MAPS 403, 419, 424
WEATHERPROOF STRIP MAP, ISBN 1 851373 37 3, HARVEY MAPS, £9.95
PUBLICATIONS GUIDE (INCLUDES FULL ROUTE MAP), ISBN 1 841830 46 1, MERCAT PRESS, £14.99. ACCOM GUIDE (AC) FREE + P&P FROM OUR CENTRAL OFFICE

PATHS & ACCESS

CONTACT SPEYSIDE WAY RANGER'S OFFICE
☎ 01340 881266
WWW.SPEYSIDEWAY.ORG.UK (AC)

St Cuthbert's Way

Melrose to Lindisfarne
100km/62 miles
Pilgrimage path on the
border between England and
Scotland, following in the footsteps of
a seventh-century saint and linking the
Pennine and Southern Upland Ways.
Easy except for a remote upland
stretch between Kirk Yetholm and
Wooler.
LUGGAGE CARRIERS CARRYLITE,
SHERPA VAN
MAPS OL16, OL44, 339, 340
**HARVEY ROUTE MAP £7.95 (INCLUDED WITH
GUIDE BELOW)**
PUBLICATIONS GUIDE, ISBN 0 114957 62 2,
THE STATIONERY OFFICE, £9.99
CONTACT JEDBURGH TIC TEL 01835 863435
WEBSITE WWW.STCUTHBERTSWAY.NET (AC)

Staffordshire Way

Mow Cop Castle to Kinver
Edge 147km/92 miles
A north-south route across
the county, from gritstone hills on the
edge of the Peak District via the steep
wooded slopes of the Churnet Valley
('Staffordshire's Rhineland'), Cannock
Chase and more gentle pastoral
scenery and parkland to the sandstone
ridge of Kinver Edge. Sister path The
Way for the Millennium, designed for
easier walking, crosses at Shugborough
on its way from Newport to Burton
upon Trent (65km/41 miles).
MAPS OL24, 219, 242, 244, 259, 268
PUBLICATIONS GUIDEBOOK, £5 AND WAY FOR
THE MILLENNIUM, £3.50 AVAILABLE FROM
STAFFORDSHIRE COUNTY COUNCIL (P113). ACCOM
LEAFLET (AC) FOR BOTH PATHS FREE
+ P&P FROM OUR CENTRAL OFFICE

Suffolk Coast And Heaths Path

Manningtree to Lowestoft
106km/92 miles **EASY**
Through the tranquil
landscapes of an area of outstanding
natural beauty in a less-visited part
of England: beaches, estuaries and
wild heaths. The original route starts
at Felixstowe, while an extension,
the Stour and Orwell Walk,
negotiates the river estuaries via
Ipswich to Manningtree. The
96km/60-mile Sandlings Walk
provides an inland alternative

through the heathland between
Ipswich and Southwold.
MAPS OL40, 197, 212, 231
PUBLICATIONS SUFFOLK COAST AND STOUR
AND ORWELL PACKS INCLUDING PUBLIC
TRANSPORT (AC), £4 EACH AND SANDLINGS WALK
PACK, £4.75 FROM SUFFOLK COASTS AND HEATHS
PROJECT (SEE BELOW)
CONTACT SUFFOLK COAST AND HEATHS PROJECT
(P101)

Teesdale Way

Dufton to Warrenby,
Redcar 161km/100 miles
Along the Tees from its source in
the Cumbrian Pennines through
wild and remote moorland and
gentler countryside to the industrial
cityscapes of Teesside and on to
the North Sea, including ten circular
walks. A shorter path, the Tees
Link, connects Middlesbrough
Dock to High Cliff Nab,
Guisborough (17km/10.5 miles)
via Guisborough Forest.
MAPS OL26, OL31, 304, 306
PUBLICATIONS THE TEESDALE WAY ISBN
1 852844 61 2, CICERONE £10 (OS). TEES LINK
LEAFLET FROM TEES FOREST (P101)

Thames Path

Source of the Thames near Kemble
to London and Crayford Ness
311 km/194 miles **EASY**
A splendid and very popular riverside
walk pioneered by Ramblers
members from the remote
Cotswolds to Britain's biggest city,
passing world-famous sites such as
Oxford, Windsor, the central London
riverfront and Greenwich. The
national trail ends officially at the
Thames Barrier where a well-
signed16km/10-mile extension
continues eastwards towards Erith
and the marshes. The whole route
through London is now one of
Transport for London's six strategic
walking routes.
MAPS 160, 161, 168, 169, 170, 171, 172, 173, 180
DIGITAL EXPLORER STRIP MAP £99.95 FROM
MEMORY-MAP (P95)
PUBLICATIONS GUIDEBOOK (OS) £12.99 +
P&P, COMPANION (AC ETC) £4.75 + P&P FROM
OUR CENTRAL OFFICE; THE THAMES PATH GUIDE
FROM BARRIER TO SOURCE, ISBN 1 852844 36 1,
CICERONE £12. FREE LEAFLETS COVERING LONDON
SECTION INCLUDING EXTENSION,
☎ 0870 240 6094, WWW.TFL.GOV.UK/WALKING.
CONTACT NATIONAL TRAIL OFFICE
☎ 01865 810224
WWW.NATIONALTRAIL.GOV.UK/THAMESPATH (AC)

Trans Pennine Trail

Southport to Chesterfield, Leeds, York
or Hornsea 560km/350 miles total
Multi-user route from
Merseyside to
Humberside via Stockport
(Manchester) and Doncaster, with
connecting spurs to Chesterfield via
Sheffield, Leeds via Wakefield, York
and Beverley linking all the major cities
of northern England, interestingly
mixing rural and urban walking. Much
of the route, which was created with
the help of local Ramblers, is
wheelchair and pushchair accessible
and easily reached by public transport,
and the section from Liverpool to Hull
is part of European path E8. Walkers
following the linear coast to coast
route from Southport to Hornsea
need only route maps 1 and 3 below,
while map 2 covers the central north-
south spurs.
MAPS OL1, 268, 275, 276, 277, 278, 279, 285,
288, 289, 290, 291, 292, 293, 295
ROUTE MAPS:1 IRISH SEA—YORKSHIRE; 2
DERBYSHIRE & YORKSHIRE; 3 YORKSHIRE—NORTH
SEA; £4.95 FROM TRANS PENNINE TRAIL OFFICE
(SEE BELOW)
PUBLICATIONS VISITOR GUIDE (AC) £4.95
FROM TRANS PENNINE TRAIL OFFICE (SEE BELOW)
CONTACT TRANS PENNINE TRAIL OFFICE
☎ 01226 772574
WWW.TRANSPENNINETRAIL.ORG.UK
USER GROUP FRIENDS OF THE TRANS
PENNINE TRAIL, 164 HIGH STREET, HOOK, GOOLE
DN14 5PL. SEE ALSO WEBSITE ABOVE

Two Moors Way

Ivybridge to Lynmouth
166km/103 miles
An outstanding route pioneered by
local Ramblers linking wild and remote
Dartmoor to the spectacular North
Devon coast via the Dart Valley and
Exmoor, mainly easy going with some
challenging stretches and unsigned
sections across the moors. The
southern end links with the well-signed
Erme-Plym Trail from Ivybridge to
Plymouth (21km/13 miles) to provide
a coast to coast route across Devon.

TWO MOORS WAY

PATHS & ACCESS

MAPS OL9, OL20, OL28, 113, 114, 127
ILLUSTRATED ROUTE MAP £1.50 + 50P P&P FROM
TWO MOORS WAY ASSOCIATION (SEE BELOW)
PUBLICATIONS TWO MOORS WAY
GUIDEBOOK, £4.95 AND ACCOM LIST (AC), 50P,
BOTH FROM TWO MOORS WAY ASSOCIATION (SEE
BELOW). ERME-PLYM TRAIL SHOWN ON OS MAPS:
SEE ALSO WWW.DISCOVERDEVON.COM/WALKING
LUGGAGE CARRIERS CAN BE ARRANGED BY
ACCOMMODATION PROVIDERS LISTED IN GUIDE
USER GROUP TWO MOORS WAY ASSOCIATION,
COPPINS, THE POPLARS, PINHOE, EXETER EX4 9HH

Valeways Millennium Heritage Trail

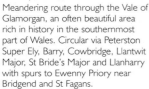

Circular from St Fagans
111km/69 miles
Meandering route through the Vale of
Glamorgan, an often beautiful area
rich in history in the southernmost
part of Wales. Circular via Peterston
Super Ely, Barry, Cowbridge, Llantwit
Major, St Bride's Major and Llanharry
with spurs to Ewenny Priory near
Bridgend and St Fagans.
MAP 151
PUBLICATIONS ROUTE CARD AND BOOKLET
PACK £6.99 + £1.50 P&P FROM VALEWAYS
(SEE BELOW).
CONTACT VALEWAYS ☎ 01446 749000
WWW.VALEWAYS.ORG.UK

Viking Way

Barton upon Humber to
Oakham 225km/140 miles
EASY
A trail pioneered by Ramblers
volunteers from the Humber Bridge
south along the Lincolnshire Wolds
through territory once occupied by
Vikings to Horncastle and Lincoln,
finishing near Rutland Water.
MAPS 234, 247, 272, 273, 281, 282, 284
PUBLICATIONS GUIDEBOOK £3.95, FACTSHEET
(AC) FREE FROM LINCOLNSHIRE COUNTY COUNCIL
(SEE P111)

Wealdway

Gravesend to Eastbourne
129km/80 miles
Attractive and quiet walk devised by
local Ramblers from the Thames
estuary to the south coast via the Kent
and Sussex Weald and Ashdown
Forest. The southern section runs
parallel and sometimes together with
the Vanguard Way, an 107km/66-mile
route from Croydon to Newhaven.
At Croydon you can continue along
the Wandle Trail for 19km/12 miles to
join the Thames Path at Wandsworth.
MAPS 123, 135, 147, 148, 163 (AND 146, 161 FOR
VANGUARD WAY/WANDLE TRAIL)

PUBLICATIONS GUIDEBOOK IS OUT OF PRINT.
VANGUARD WAY GUIDEBOOK £2.95 FROM
CROYDON GROUP (SEE P79). WANDLE TRAIL MAP
FREE FROM SUTTON LIBRARY
☎ 020 8770 4700, WWW.WANDLETRAIL.ORG

Wessex Ridgeway

Marlborough to Lyme Regis
219km/136 miles
From deepest Wiltshire along
ancient paths via the edge of Salisbury
Plain and Cranbourne Chase to the
Dorset Coast. Connects with the
Ridgeway as part of a series of trails
linking Wessex and East Anglia.
MAPS 116, 117, 118, 130, 143, 157
PUBLICATIONS GUIDE (OS), ISBN
1 854106 1 3 9, AURUM, £12.99. GREATER
RIDGEWAY GUIDE: SEE RIDGEWAY

West Highland Way

Milngavie, Glasgow to Fort William
153km/95 miles **CHALLENGING**
A popular trail following old drove,
military and coach roads from the edge
of Scotland's biggest city via its largest
freshwater loch, Loch Lomond, and first
national park to the foot of its tallest
mountain, Ben Nevis, connecting with
the Great Glen Way. Two riverside
walkways effectively extend the walk in
the south through Glasgow city centre
and beyond: the Kelvin-Allander
Walkway from Milngavie to the Clyde
near the Tall Ship (14.5km/
9 miles), and the Clyde Walkway from
Partick station to the Falls of Clyde at
New Lanark (64km/40 miles).
MAPS 347, 348, 364, 377, 384, 392 (AND 335, 342
AND 343 FOR THE WALKWAYS)
HARVEY ROUTE MAP £9.95 (INCLUDED WITH GUIDE
BELOW)
DIGITAL EXPLORER STRIP MAP £49.95 FROM
MEMORY-MAP (P95)
PUBLICATIONS GUIDEBOOK, ISBN
1 841831 02 6, MERCAT PRESS, £16.99; ACCOM
LEAFLET (AC) FREE + P&P FROM OUR CENTRAL

WEST HIGHLAND WAY

OFFICE. FIT FOR LIFE! MAP INCLUDING ALL
GLASGOW WALKWAYS AND THE CLYDE WALKWAY
LEAFLET PACK, BOTH FREE FROM GLASGOW TIC,
☎ 0141 204 4400
LUGGAGE CARRIERS AMS, SHERPA VAN,
TRAVEL-LITE, TROSSACH TRANSFERS
INDEPENDENT HOSTELS IBHS
CONTACT WEST HIGHLAND WAY RANGER
☎ 01389 722199
WWW.WEST-HIGHLAND-WAY.CO.UK (AC)

❋ Wherryman's Way

Norwich to Great Yarmouth
56km/35 miles **EASY**
Links Norwich to the coast and
Angles Way through the heart of
the unique landscapes of the Broads
along the river Yare, once plied by
boats known as wherries. This new
route, launched in 2005, also boasts
public art and good public transport
connections including a riverbus.
MAPS OL40
WEBSITE WWW.WHERRYMANSWAY.NET

Wye Valley Walk

Chepstow to Plylimon,
Hafren Forest 218km/
136 miles
Along the the river Wye via
Monmouth, Hereford, Builth Wells
and Rhayader to the source deep in
rugged and remote Hafren Forest,
crisscrossing the border of England
and Wales along dramatic limestone
gorges and through rolling countryside
and uplands.
MAPS OL13, OL14, 188, 189, 200, 214
PUBLICATIONS GUIDEBOOK £9 + FREE
ACCOM LIST (AC) FROM WYE VALLEY AONB
(SEE P101)
WEBSITE WWW.WYEVALLEYWALK.ORG

Yorkshire Wolds Way

Hessle, Kingston upon Hull to Filey
127 km/79 miles
One of the least known national trails,
but well worth getting to know, this
route through rolling chalk hills
between the North Sea coast and the
Humber estuary celebrates its 25th
anniversary this year. Some easy
access sections are described on the
website below.
MAPS 293, 294, 300, 301
PUBLICATIONS GUIDEBOOK (OS), ISBN
1 854109 86 3, AURUM, £12.99. CIRCULAR
WALKS GUIDES AVAILABLE FROM NATIONAL TRAIL
OFFICE (SEE BELOW)
CONTACT NATIONAL TRAIL OFFICER
☎ 01439 770657, WWW.NATIONALTRAIL.CO.UK/
YORKSHIREWOLDSWAY (AC)

EUROPEAN LONG DISTANCE PATHS

E-paths are designated by the European Ramblers' Association (ERA). They largely follow sections of existing trails and are not usually signed in their own right except at major junctions. Route names shown in red below indicate that the route has a full entry in the LDPs section; otherwise brief details of further information sources are given. For an overview of the E-paths, visit www.era-ewv-ferp.org or see our website. E-paths are also now shown on OS Explorer maps.

E2 Atlantic – Mediterranean

Stranraer – Harwich or Dover 1400km/875 miles

The main route takes in the Southern Uplands, Pennines, Yorkshire coast, Wolds and Fens to connect with the ferry for Hoek van Holland. A western branch visits the Peak District, Cotswolds, Thames Valley and North Downs on its way to Dover (this branch continues from Oostende but there is currently no direct ferry: an alternative is the ferry to Calais and the E9 coastal path). The two routes rejoin in the Belgian Kempen and continue along the celebrated GR5 via the Ardennes, Lake Geneva and the French Alps to the Mediterranean coast at Nice. An Irish section to the Galway coast is planned, making a total length of 4850km/3030 miles.

FROM STRANRAER

SOUTHERN UPLAND WAY TO MELROSE 258KM/161 MILES
ST CUTHBERT'S WAY TO KIRK YETHOLM 51KM/32 MILES
PENNINE WAY TO MIDDLETON IN TEESDALE 180KM/113 MILES

EASTERN ROUTE VIA HARWICH

TEESDALE WAY AND TEES LINK TO GUISBOROUGH 125KM/77.5 MILES
CLEVELAND WAY TO FILEY 99KM/62 MILES
YORKSHIRE WOLDS WAY TO HESSLE THEN VIA HUMBER BRIDGE TO BARTON UPON HUMBER 131KM/82 MILES
VIKING WAY TO RUTLAND WATER 233KM/146KM
HEREWARD WAY TO ELY 117KM/73 MILES
INFORMATION FROM RUTLAND, PETERBOROUGH AND CAMBRIDGESHIRE COUNCILS (P108). AN IMPROVED AND NEWLY-SIGNED ROUTE FOR THE HEREWARD WAY THROUGH PETERBOROUGH OPENED IN 2006.
FEN RIVERS WAY TO CAMBRIDGE 27KM/17 MILES: GUIDE FROM CAMBRIDGESHIRE RAMBLERS (P85)
ROMAN ROAD LINK TO LINTON 18KM/11 MILES: NOT YET SIGNED AND NO GUIDE, BUT THE ROMAN ROAD IS OBVIOUS ON OS MAPS.
ICKNIELD WAY PATH TO STETCHWORTH 15KM/9.5 MILES
STOUR VALLEY PATH TO STRATFORD ST MARY 83KM/52 MILES: GUIDE £3.50 FROM DEDHAM VALE AND STOUR VALLEY AONB (P100)
ESSEX WAY TO RAMSEY THEN LINK PATH TO HARWICH INTERNATIONAL 28KM/17.5 MILES

WESTERN ROUTE VIA DOVER

PENNINE WAY TO STANDEDGE 200KM/125 MILES OLDHAM WAY TO MOSSLEY 15KM/9.5 MILES: CONTACT OLDHAM COUNCIL (P112)
TAMESIDE TRAIL TO BROADBOTTOM 13KM/8 MILES: CONTACT TAMESIDE COUNCIL (P113)
ETHEROW GOYT VALLEY WAY TO COMPSTALL 8KM/5 MILES: SEE MIDSHIRES WAY (GOYT WAY) TO MARPLE 4KM/2.5 MILES
PEAK FOREST CANAL TO DISLEY 4KM/2.5 MILES: CONTACT BRITISH WATERWAYS (P103)
GRITSTONE TRAIL TO RUSHTON SPENCER 33KM/20.5 MILES: CONTACT CHESHIRE COUNCIL (P109)
STAFFORDSHIRE WAY TO CANNOCK CHASE 76KM/47.5 MILES
HEART OF ENGLAND WAY TO BOURTON-ON-THE-WATER 159KM/99.5 MILES
OXFORDSHIRE WAY TO KIRTLINGTON 41KM/25.5 MILES: GUIDEBOOK £5.99 FROM OXFORDSHIRE COUNCIL (P112)
OXFORD CANAL WALK TO OXFORD 16KM/10 MILES: CONTACT BRITISH WATERWAYS (P103) OR SEE WWW.WATERSCAPE.COM/OXFORD_CANAL
THAMES PATH TO WEYBRIDGE 146KM/91 MILES
WEY NAVIGATION TO GUILDFORD 25KM/15.5 MILES: CONTACT NATIONAL TRUST ☎ 01483 561389
NORTH DOWNS WAY TO DOVER 193KM/120.5 MILES

E8 Atlantic – Istanbul

Liverpool–Hull 300km/188 miles

In Britain this path entirely follows the Trans Pennine Trail (see above), connecting via the Dublin ferry with the Irish Waymarked Ways network. From Rotterdam it heads for the Rhine Valley, the Romantische Straße, the Northern Carpathians and the Bulgarian Rodopi mountains to Svilengrad on the Turkish border, a total of 4390km/2750 miles, though some of the Eastern section of the route is incomplete.

E9 European Coastal Path

Plymouth–Dover 711km/444 miles, plus Isle of Wight loop 68 km/43 miles

Along or parallel to the south coast of England, including some of its most famous coastal sites. The path provides an alternative to the mainland route of the E9, with which it connects by ferry at Roscoff, Calais and several points between. Additionally, it links the Saxon Shore Way and South West Coast Path to provide a continuous signed route of almost 1,000 miles around southern England from Gravesend to Minehead. The complete route will eventually stretch 5000km/3125 miles from Capo de São Vincente in the southwest corner of Portugal to Narva-Jõesuu on the Baltic coast at the Estonian-Russian border.

FROM PLYMOUTH

SOUTH WEST COAST PATH AND FERRY TO POOLE 343KM/214 MILES
BOURNEMOUTH COAST PATH (SEE SOLENT WAY) TO MILFORD ON SEA 30KM/19 MILES

SOLENT WAY TO LYMINGTON 11KM/7 MILES
ISLE OF WIGHT LOOP VIA FERRY TO YARMOUTH
ISLE OF WIGHT COASTAL PATH TO THE NEEDLES 11KM/7 MILES
TENNYSON TRAIL (SEE IOW COASTAL PATH) TO CARISBROOK 21KM/13 MILES
LINK TO NEWPORT 5KM/3.5 MILES
BEMBRIDGE TRAIL (SEE IOW COASTAL PATH) TO BEMBRIDGE 18KM/11 MILES
ISLE OF WIGHT COASTAL PATH TO RYDE 13KM/8 MILES THEN FERRY TO PORTSMOUTH

MAIN ROUTE

SOLENT WAY TO PORTSMOUTH, REJOINING ISLE OF WIGHT ALTERNATIVE 60KM/37.5 MILES.
SOLENT WAY TO LANGSTONE HARBOUR, HAVANT 16KM/10 MILES
STAUNTON WAY TO QUEEN ELIZABETH COUNTRY PARK 19KM/12 MILES: CONTACT HAMPSHIRE COUNCIL (P111)
SOUTH DOWNS WAY TO JEVINGTON 111KM/69.5 MILES
1066 COUNTRY WALK TO RYE 56KM/35 MILES: CONTACT BATTLE TIC
☎ 01424 773721
SAXON SHORE WAY TO DOVER 65KM/39 MILES: NEW GUIDEBOOK (2006) FROM KENT COUNCIL (P111).

RIGHT TO ROAM FAQs

Where does the new legislation apply?

The Countryside and Rights of Way (CRoW) Act provides a legal right of access to approximately one million hectares of open, uncultivated countryside in England and Wales, which is defined in the legislation as mountain, moor, heath and down, as well as registered common land.

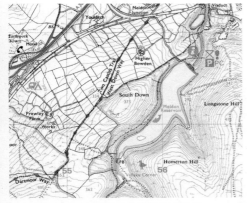

ORDNANCE SURVEY MAPPING © CROWN COPYRIGHT

How can I find out where I can walk?

Ordnance Survey has re-issued all of its Explorer maps to show access land, which is indicated by a light yellow area surrounded by a narrow pale orange border. Orange 'i' symbols pinpoint access information points. To avoid confusion, a border of light magenta dashes now represents the boundaries of national parks.

In addition, Natural England provides an open access website where walkers can find details of access land throughout the country. While in Wales the Countryside Council for Wales hosts a similar resource. See p47 for details.

What am I allowed to do on access land?

The new law provides a right of access for walkers only, and does not confer any additional rights for cyclists or horse-riders (though where additional rights are currently allowed or tolerated, they are likely to continue). Dogs are permitted on some areas of open country, but must be kept on a lead on access land between 1 March and 31 July and at any time in the vicinity of livestock. Furthermore, dogs may be banned temporarily or permanently from some areas of land. Access at night is permitted but may be subject to local restrictions. Walkers are responsible for their own safety at all times.

How is access managed locally?

Access is managed by local authorities or, in national parks, by the national park authority. They have the power to enact and enforce by-laws that will apply to open access land in their jurisdiction, subject to consultation with the relevant local access forum and countryside body. They also have powers to set up the necessary infrastructure to make the new access land easily available to walkers including the power to appoint wardens, erect and maintain notices and improve means of access.

What is a local access forum?

Local access forums, made up of landowners, users and others with an interest in the land, have been established to advise access authorities on the local application of the new law. This may mean commenting on access management or the need for signage or the necessity or otherwise of a proposed long-term local access restriction.

Are landowners able to close their land for any reason?

The Act allows landowners to close their land for up to 28 days a year (including some Saturdays and Sundays) for any reason. Natural England and the Countryside Council for Wales should be informed of these closures and can make the information publicly available. Landowners may apply for further closures or restrictions, on a temporary or permanent basis, for public safety, land management or fire risk. There may also be restrictions to protect wildlife or areas of historic interest or on the grounds of national security.

What should I do if I see a misleading notice?

Please contact your local authority (see p108) using the problem report form on p49, and then inform the Ramblers' Association in England or Wales.

What if there is no way onto the access land?

Access authorities must provide ways of getting to access land, ideally in consultation with the landowner but by order if necessary. If you find there is no way of getting to the access land then please contact your local authority (see p108) using the problem report form on p49, and then inform the Ramblers' Association.

**For more information, see
www.ramblers.org.uk/freedom**

What if you knew you could always find your way to the next camp?
What if you had an eXplorist GPS?

The Magellan® eXplorist™ family offers real value in a lightweight, rugged, water-resistant handheld GPS. Easy to operate with just one hand, it features TrueFix GPS technology, an advanced, intuitive file management system and plenty of memory for all your tracks and route history.
The eXplorist 210 has 22 MB of memory whereas the eXplorist 400, 500 & 600 use Secure SD cards for memory storage, which one is the right one for you?

For more information, please go to www.magellanGPS.com

RIGHTS OF WAY FAQs

What is a right of way?

A right of way is a path that anyone has the legal right to use on foot, and sometimes using other modes of transport.

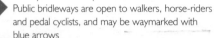 Public footpaths are open only to walkers, and may be waymarked with yellow arrows

 Public bridleways are open to walkers, horse-riders and pedal cyclists, and may be waymarked with blue arrows

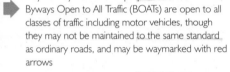 Restricted byways are open to walkers, horse-riders, pedal cyclists and horse-drawn carriages and may be waymarked with purple arrows

Byways Open to All Traffic (BOATs) are open to all classes of traffic including motor vehicles, though they may not be maintained to the same standard as ordinary roads, and may be waymarked with red arrows

Legally, a public right of way is part of the Queen's highway and subject to the same protection in law as all other highways, including trunk roads.

What are my rights on a public right of way?

Your legal right is to 'pass and repass along the way'. You may stop to rest or admire the view, or to consume refreshments, providing you stay on the path and do not cause an obstruction. You can also take with you a 'natural accompaniment', which includes a pram, pushchair or wheelchair (though you may find the surface of the path is not always suitable), or a dog. However, you should ensure that dogs are under close control. Note that there is no requirement for stiles to be suitable for use by dogs.

How do I know whether a path is a public right of way or not?

The safest evidence is the official 'definitive map' of public rights of way. These maps are available for public inspection at the offices of local surveying authorities (see Local Authorities, p108). In addition, public rights of way information derived from them is shown by the Ordnance Survey on its Explorer and Landranger maps.

Some rights of way are not yet shown on definitive maps. These can quite properly be used, and application may be made to surveying authorities for them to be added to the map. The inner London boroughs are not required to produce definitive maps, though this does not mean there are no rights of way in inner London.

How does a path become public?

In legal theory most paths become rights of way because the owner 'dedicates' them to public use. In fact very few paths have been formally dedicated, but the law assumes that if the public uses a path without interference for some period of time – set by statute at 20 years – then the owner had intended to dedicate it as a right of way.

A public path that has been unused for 20 years does not cease to be public (except in Scotland). The legal maxim is 'once a highway, always a highway'.

Paths can also be created by agreement between local authorities and owners or by compulsory order, subject, in the case of objection, to confirmation by the Secretary of State for the Environment, Food and Rural Affairs, or the National Assembly for Wales.

Can a landowner put up new gates and stiles where none exist presently?

No. Not without seeking and getting permission from the local authority and then complying with any conditions to that permission. Maintaining stiles and gates is primarily the owner's responsibility, but the local authority must contribute 25% of the cost if asked and may contribute more if it wishes. If stiles and gates are not kept in proper repair the authority can, after 14 days' notice, do the job itself and send the bill to the owner.

How wide should a path be?

The path should be whatever width was dedicated for public use. This width may have arisen through usage, or by formal agreement, or by order, for example if the path has been diverted. The width may be recorded in a statement accompanying the definitive map but in many cases the proper width will be a matter of past practice on that particular path.

Is it illegal to plough up or disturb the surface of a path so as to make it inconvenient to use?

Yes, except where the path is a footpath or bridleway that runs across a field (as opposed to alongside a field edge). In this case the landowner can plough or otherwise disturb the path surface provided it is not reasonably convenient to avoid doing so. The path must be restored

reasonably necessary. Unless injury to the property can be proven, a landowner could probably only recover nominal damages by suing for trespass. But of course you might have to meet the landowner's legal costs. Thus a notice saying 'Trespassers will be Prosecuted', aimed for instance at keeping you off a private drive, is usually meaningless. Criminal prosecution could only arise if you trespass and damage property. However, under public order law, trespassing with an intention to reside may be a criminal offence under some circumstances. It is also a criminal offence to trespass on railway land, sometimes on military training land, and land which has been specifically designated under the Serious Organised Crime and Police Act 2005.

A fuller version of this text is available as a factsheet (FS7) and on our website. *Rights of Way* is the definitive guide to rights of way law and practice published by the Ramblers and Opens Spaces Society (see p40). Order either from the Ramblers Bookshop, p95

OUTDOOR ACCESS IN SCOTLAND FAQs

BRITAIN ON VIEW/ROD EDWARDS

What is the Land Reform (Scotland) Act?
The Land Reform (Scotland) Act 2003 establishes a statutory right of responsible access and is accompanied by the Scottish Outdoor Access Code (see p47). For a full explanation visit www.ramblers.org.uk/scotland.

How will the Act affect my access to the Scottish countryside?
There has long been a general presumption of access to all land unless there is a very good reason for the public to be excluded. The access legislation confirms this presumption, and walkers in Scotland now have a statutory right of access to all land, except for areas such as railway lands, quarries, harbours, airfields and defence land where other laws apply. Walkers should act responsibly when exercising their right of access, and follow the Scottish Outdoor Access Code (see p47).

Are there rights of way in Scotland?
Yes, but they are less extensive than in England and Wales because there is a tradition of access to most land. Rights of way do exist, but there is no legal obligation on local authorities to record them, so they don't appear on Ordnance Survey maps, though paths and tracks are shown on these maps as geographical features and you have a right to walk on most of these. ScotWays (see p104) keeps a catalogue of rights of way, signs many of them and maps and describes the major rural routes in its publication Scottish Hill Tracks. It is expected that Core Paths will largely supersede the existing arrangements for rights of way.

What is a Core Path?
Local authorities have new duties and powers to develop Core Path Networks by adopting and improving existing paths and creating new ones. Councils have until February 2008 to produce plans for these networks. Core paths will eventually appear on OS Explorer maps. Scottish Natural Heritage and local authorities have developed The Scottish Paths Record database as a tool to help develop path networks.

THE COUNTRYSIDE CODE

RESPECT – PROTECT – ENJOY

If you follow the Countryside Code wherever you go, you'll get the best enjoyment possible and you'll help to protect the countryside now and for future generations.

Be safe – plan ahead and follow any signs

Even when going out locally, it's best to get the latest information about where and when you can go; for example, your rights to go on to some areas of open land may be restricted while work is carried out, for safety reasons, or during breeding season. Follow advice and local signs, and be prepared for the unexpected.

Leave gates and property as you find them

Please respect the working life of the countryside, as our actions can affect people's livelihoods, our heritage, and the safety and welfare of animals and ourselves.

Protect plants and animals, and take your litter home

We have a responsibility to protect our countryside now and for future generations, so make sure you don't harm animals, birds, plants or trees.

Keep dogs under close control

The countryside is a great place to exercise dogs, but it's every owner's duty to make sure their dog is not a danger or nuisance to farm animals, wildlife or other people.

Consider other people

Showing consideration and respect for other people makes the countryside a pleasant environment for everyone – at home, at work and at leisure.

For the full Code, including advice for land managers, contact Natural England or Countryside Council for Wales (see pp107–108)

SCOTTISH OUTDOOR ACCESS CODE

Everyone has the right to be on most land and water for recreation, education and for going from place to place, providing they act responsibly. These access rights and responsibilities are explained in the Scottish Outdoor Access Code.

The key points are:

When you're in the outdoors

- take personal responsibility for your own actions and act safely
- respect people's privacy and peace of mind

- help land managers and others to work safely and effectively
- care for your environment and take your litter home
- keep your dog under proper control
- take extra care if you're organising an event or running a business

If you're managing the outdoors

- respect access rights
- act reasonably when asking people to avoid land management operations
- work with your local authority and other bodies to help integrate access and land management
- respect rights of way and customary access

For more detailed advice, contact Scottish Natural Heritage (see p108)

HOW TO REPORT A PATH PROBLEM

What is a path problem?

There are many types of footpath problem – too many to list here – but the selection below give a good idea of the type of problem that should be reported. If you have any doubts, please contact our central office.

- **Natural vegetation** – undergrowth, overgrowth, hedgerow encroachment, overhanging branches, fallen trees, etc.
- **Path 'furniture'** – missing or broken stiles, bridges, gates, signposts, waymarks, etc.
- **Agriculture-related** – ploughing, cropping, manure, slurry, etc.
- **Man-made problems** – barbed wire, buildings, fences, walls, rubbish, rubble, etc.
- **Miscellaneous** – misleading notices, dangerous animals, surface problems, etc.

Reporting the problem

When you come across a path problem on a walk in England and Wales simply follow these steps:

1. Note down the location and details of the problem. Grid references are very useful (help with these can be found on p53). Photos are useful too, so if you've got your camera take a few shots of the problem.

2. Write to the Public Rights of Way Officer at the relevant highway authority. (Highway authorities are the county, unitary, metropolitan, or London borough council for the area in question – i.e. not district, town, parish, or community councils. See p108 for full listings.) Use the form opposite, or a letter or email is just as good. Outline the details of the problem you encountered, giving as much information as possible. Remember to include your contact details.

3. Make a copy of your form or letter to the highway authority and send this to our central office. This will be forwarded to our local footpath secretary for information. You can also do this online at www.useyourpaths.info/report.php.

4. If possible, we would encourage you to go out and check on any promised action and satisfy yourself that the problem has been resolved.

5. If the problem has not been resolved within a reasonable timescale (say, three months), write again to the highway authority requesting action.

And in Scotland?

In Scotland, access authorities now have a duty to uphold access rights to land generally as well as paths. Contact the access officer in the relevant local authority area or national park (see the access section of www.ramblers.org.uk/scotland). Copy any correspondence to the Ramblers Scotland office and to your Group's access and footpath officer. For further advice ☎ 01577 861222 or email enquiries@scotland.ramblers.org.uk

Enjoy protecting your local footpaths? Then see p19 for details of how to become a Footpath Guardian

PATH OR ACCESS PROBLEM REPORT FORM

Please complete this form to report a footpath or access problem following the instructions opposite.

WHERE WAS THE PROBLEM? Please give as much information as you can

Path report ☐

District_____

Parish/Community_____

From (place) _____

Grid ref._____

To (place)_____

Grid ref._____

Path N° if known_____

Access report ☐

Nearest Town/Village_____

_____

At Grid ref. _____

(and if applicable)
Grid ref._____

Date problem encountered _____

County/unitary authority_____

WHAT WAS THE PROBLEM? Be precise: quote grid references for any specific point or draw a sketch map if you think it will help. If anyone spoke to you, please give details, including their name and address if known.

PLEASE GIVE YOUR DETAILS

Name_____

Address_____

_____

Email_____

Telephone_____   **Tick box for more Report Forms** ☐

Send this form to
Your relevant local highway authority **and** the Ramblers' Association,
2nd Floor, 87-90 Albert Embankment, London SE1 7TW
☎ 020 7339 8500 • Fax 020 7339 8501

THE CHARITY
WORKING FOR
WALKERS
www.ramblers.org.uk

MAPS FOR WALKERS

Ordnance Survey maps

The best and most comprehensive walkers' maps of Britain are the 1:25 000 scale Ordnance Survey (OS) Explorer series in orange covers. They include a range of geographical features and landmarks at a high level of detail, including field boundaries, heights shown as contours and 'spot heights', railway stations and tram stops. They also show rights of way (except in Scotland), permissive paths, many long-distance paths, off-road cycle paths, open access land (including new access land in England and Wales), locations of shorter circular walks and nature trails, information centres and visitor attractions.

Another OS series, 1:50 000 Landranger maps in pink and silver covers, also include footpaths and selected tourist attractions, but show less detail; OS are now marketing them as maps for planning days out rather than navigating on the ground.

Bookshops, information centres, larger newsagents and even some garages stock their local OS sheets. Maps can also be bought from specialist retailers, over the internet or direct from the OS, who can also supply a free Mapping Index showing all the sheet numbers.
Ordnance Survey ☎ 0845 605 0504
www.ordnancesurvey.co.uk

Or buy OS maps online from **Aqua3** through the Ramblers website and earn a **10% discount** with free postage. The Ramblers receive a 10% donation for every map sold this way.

Other paper maps

While no other publisher covers all of Britain at detailed scales, a number of other specialist publishers do offer maps of use to walkers. The most important is Harvey who produce very clear specialist walkers' maps of certain popular upland areas and long-distance paths at 1:25 000 and 1:40 000 scales. The maps also usually include useful information and addresses, and most are printed on weatherproof paper.
Harvey Maps ☎ 01786 841202 (credit card hotline) www.harveymaps.co.uk

In urban areas street atlases can be more useful than OS maps. The **Philips** series is probably the best for walkers since most rights of way and other off-road paths, parks and open spaces – and even some promoted routes – are clearly shown.
Philips ☎ 020 7644 6940 (general enquiries), ☎ 01903 828503 (mail order) www.philips-maps.co.uk

Electronic maps

Electronic mapping systems for home PCs enable you to print OS maps at a variety of scales, to plan and annotate routes, and link up to a GPS or pocket PC to take out on your walk – but make sure your hardware is compatible with the system you want to buy. The main suppliers are:
Anquet Maps ☎ 0845 270 9020 www.anquet.co.uk
Hillwalker (ISYS) ☎ 0845 166 5701
www.hillwalker.org.uk
memory-map ☎ 0870 740 9040
www.memory-map.co.uk
TrackLogs ☎ 01298 872537 www.tracklogs.co.uk

Mapping websites allowing you to view extracts from Landranger and street maps by grid reference, postcode or place name include www.streetmap.co.uk, www.multimap.com, www.map24.co.uk and the OS site.

Learning more about maps

In addition to the map and compass tutorial on the next page of this book, the free *Map Reading Made Easy* from OS is an excellent brief introduction and is downloadable from their website.

Two particularly useful books are available from the Ramblers Bookshop (see p95 to order). *Navigation and Leadership: a manual for walkers* is the Ramblers' official bible on the use of map and compass and leading group walks. Julian Tippett's *Navigation for Walkers* is a great beginners' guide which includes OS map extracts, (the author also helped produce the tutorial overleaf).

See the Maps section on our website which lists navigation course providers and suggestions for further reading. This information is also available as a printed factsheet – FS2 (see p96).

MAPS & TRANSPORT

HOW TO USE A MAP AND COMPASS

For effective navigation, in addition to the appropriate maps, you should also carry:

- a **compass** – in lowland areas you could rely purely on map-reading skills, but using map and compass together, provided you have the basic skills, will help you follow your route with much more accuracy, particularly in woods. In the hills a compass is essential, especially when visibility is poor. Choose an **orienteering** or **protractor** compass with a rectangular baseplate of reasonable size so it can be turned while wearing gloves, and clearly marked km/m scales that can be read in poor light
- a reliable **watch**, to help judge speed, monitor progress and plan for future journeys
- a **torch**, especially on short winter days
- something to **protect** non-waterproof maps, such as a polythene bag or map case.

A **GPS** will provide an accurate check of position at any time, and can be programmed to provide directions for a complete route. It is, though, essential to be well practised in its use.

Map interpretation

Maps are simply an accurate picture of the ground as seen from above, scaled down from life size and with symbols to show particular features and landmarks. On a 1:25 000 map such as an OS Explorer, one unit of length on the map represents 25,000 units on the ground, so 1cm on the map represents 25,000cm, that is 250m or 0.25km on the ground. On a 1:50 000 map, 1cm on the map represents 500m on the ground.

To find out what features the different **symbols** represent (buildings, different kinds of church, electricity pylons, roads and railways, woods, orchards, scrub or marsh and so on) consult the key shown on the map. The best way to learn these symbols is to relate them to the way they appear on the ground.

Some map markings do not show on the ground, such as council boundaries (unless these follow a physical feature such as a river or ditch), contours and grid lines. Rights of way marked on maps will often be visible as a distinct path or track on the ground, but in less well-walked areas the path may not be visible.

Footpaths and bridleways are marked as green dashes on Explorer maps (magenta on Landranger).

Remember: although a good map will remain useful

for at least a few years, the landscape is ever-changing and you should not be surprised if some features on the ground do not agree with your map.

To **measure the approximate distance of your route**, take a piece of thin string and lay it carefully along the exact route on the map, then lay it straight along the scale line on the map's margin. With practice, you'll soon learn to estimate the distances involved by eye, but don't forget the extra effort of climbing hills when calculating how long the route will take to walk.

Contours are lines connecting points of equal height above sea level. Together with spot heights, they are the means used by the map-maker to portray the shape of the land, its height, the form taken by hills and valleys, steepness of slopes, and so on. On Explorer maps, the interval between contours is five metres in lowland areas and 10 metres where mountainous. At random points along many of the contour lines a number is shown to indicate its height, always printed so that the top of the number points uphill. Every fifth contour line is printed more thickly than the others. The closer together contours are the steeper the ascent or descent for the walker. **Spot heights** – shown as a number beside a dot – appear at strategic points, often along roads where they level out at the top or foot of a hill. These can be a useful guide where contour height numbers are infrequent.

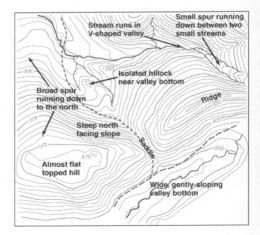

Grid references

All OS maps are criss-crossed by vertical and horizontal **grid lines** (coloured blue on Explorer maps) which are 4cm apart on 1:25,000 scale maps and 2cm apart on the 1:50,000 scale. A **grid reference** uses six figures

How to take or locate a 6-figure grid reference

What is the grid reference of the church?

1. Identify the 1km square containing the church. Do this by selecting its left and bottom sides (imagine a letter 'L' bounds the square).

2. Take the numbers on the edge of the map for these two sides (downstroke of the 'L' first, as you would write it). This gives: 31_25_ (Note: 3125 is the 4-figure grid reference of the square).

3. Now an extra figure must be added to each pair of numbers to specify to the nearest 100m where the church lies within the square. Estimate the number of tenths (100m) the church lies from the two sides, once again starting with the downstroke. It is seven-tenths from the downstroke and four tenths from the horizontal stroke, so the 6-figure grid reference is: 317254.

To find a point on a map using a 6-figure grid reference, simply do the reverse. Remember to start with the eastings (the first three figures) and then move up the northings (the last three). A helpful reminder is the

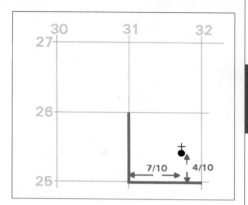

saying: "go along the corridor and then up the stairs". Many compasses also contain a **romer** – a rectangular scale on the clear-plastic baseplate – that makes estimating the tenths easier, though make sure you have the correct romer for the scale of your map.

to identify a particular spot on a map that is 100 metres square. The first three specify the vertical lines (the eastings) and the second three the horizontal (the northings). Sometimes four figure grid references are used to give a rough location (the map grid square).

Using the compass

There are three basic techniques detailed here that should be mastered with a compass:

- **Setting the map** – aligning the map in the direction you are facing so features on the map match those on the ground.
- **Travelling on a bearing** – walking over open ground on a bearing taken from the map.

- **Checking the direction of the path** – e.g. at a junction in a wood where you can see no other landmarks to help you.

Setting the map

Setting the map (or orientating the map) helps relate the map to the countryside by turning the map so that your direction of travel is at the top. When done, all features on the map and on the ground are seen to lie in the same direction from your current position, and the north edge of the map points to north on the ground. The map can be set by aligning it to prominent features in the landscape, or by compass (see below).

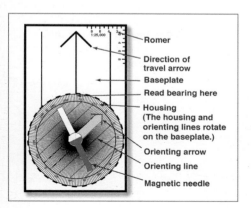

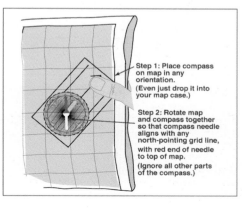

Travelling on a bearing

If you want to travel from your present position to a landmark you cannot see due to poor visibility, use the following procedure:

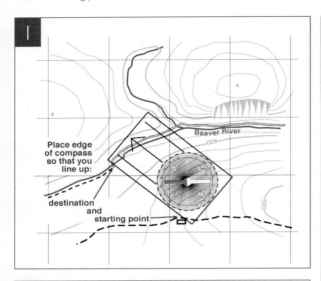

Place edge of compass so that you line up:

destination and starting point

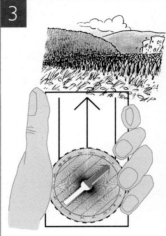

Take the compass off the map, and hold it as shown.

Turn your whole body to align the compass —red end of needle on orienting arrow ("red on red").

Now walk ahead on the line of the direction of travel arrow.

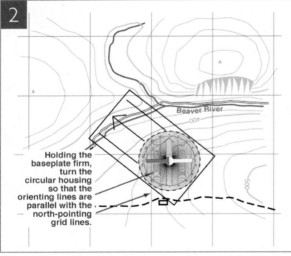

Holding the baseplate firm, turn the circular housing so that the orienting lines are parallel with the north-pointing grid lines.

NB *You can also use this procedure to check the direction of a path.*

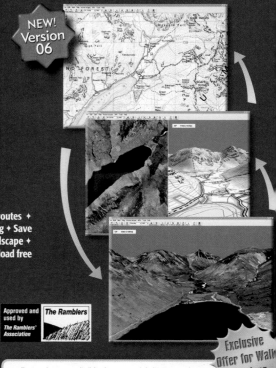

PUBLIC TRANSPORT

Help avoid pollution and congestion by combining walking and public transport. You can plan more flexible walks such as linear walks, and forget worries like parking, car crime and whether or not you should have a pint along the way.

For information about **train** services and fares, including an online journey planner, use:
National Rail ☎ 0845 748 4950, textphone 0845 605 0600 www.nationalrail.co.uk

For long distance **coaches**, use:
National Express ☎ 020 7529 2000
www.nationalexpress.com
Scottish Citylink ☎ 0141 332 9644, 0870 550 5050 (enquiries and bookings) www.citylink.co.uk

For **local transport** information, including online journey planners for local bus, metro/underground, tram/light rail and ferries, use:

Transport Direct www.transportdirect.info
Transport for London ☎ 020 7222 1234
www.tfl.gov.uk
Traveline ☎ 0870 608 2608,
textphone 0870 241 2216
www.traveline.org.uk

There is an increasing number of services for **countryside visitors**, especially in popular areas during the summer. They often run on Sundays and bank holidays and offer economical ticket deals for those planning linear walks. See the information section of our website, and:
Countrygoer ☎ 01943 607868 www.countrygoer.org

Travel information for **people with disabilities** is available from:
Tripscope ☎ 0845 758 5641 www.tripscope.org.uk

We encourage **Ramblers Areas and Groups** to organise walks by public transport wherever possible, and our annual Welcome to Walking Week, coinciding with In Town Without My Car Day (European car-free day) in September includes a wide range of car-free walks. Ramblers walk leaders in need of advice on organising walks by public transport should contact the Countryside team at our central office, who can put you in touch with our network of regional transport contacts.

MAPS & TRANSPORT

LUGGAGE CARRIERS

Aberchalder ☎ 01809 501411
AMS ☎ 01324 823144
www.ams-scotland.com
Bag Tag ☎ 01983 861559
www.bagtagiow.co.uk
Bike and Hike ☎ 01877 339788
www.bikeandhike.co.uk
Brigantes ☎ 01729 830463
www.brigantesenglishwalks.com
CarryLite ☎ 01434 634448 www.carrylite.com
Coast to Coast Holidays ☎ 01642 489173
www.coasttocoast-holidays.co.uk
Coast to Coast Packhorse ☎ 017683 71777
www.cumbria.com/packhorse
Compass (Carry a Bag) ☎ 01242 250642
www.compass-holidays.com

Great Glen Baggage Transfer ☎ 01320 351322
www.invermoriston.freeserve.co.uk/BaggageTransfer
Great Glen Travel ☎ 01809 501222
www.greatglentravel.com
Loch Ness Travel ☎ 01456 450550
www.lochnesstravel.com
Sherpa Van Project ☎ 0871 520 0124
www.sherpavan.com
southernuplandway.com ☎ 0870 835 8558
www.southernuplandway.com
Tony's Taxis (Pembrokeshire) ☎ 01437 720931
www.tonystaxis.co.uk
Travel-Lite ☎ 0141 956 7890
www.travel-lite-uk.com
Trossachs Transfers ☎ 01360 660466
www.trossachs-transfers.co.uk

Sore Feet?

You love the outdoors, but sometimes your feet cant quite go the distance. Do they burn, ache or blister after being on your feet all day?

This is because during walking and hiking, the pressure exerted on each foot can be up to four times your normal body weight. Therefore, all this rigorous exercise accelerates wear and tear on the feet.

The good news is that through identification and intervention, most foot problems can be lessened or even prevented, keeping you in the great outdoors for even longer.

Take your first step towards healthier feet today by visiting **foothealthcare.com.** Our website has a wealth of information on how to keep your feet in tip top condition, plus advice on the best foot care products for walking and hiking

Now you can enjoy your outdoor pursuits with the reassurance of putting your best foot forward every time!

Prothotics Professional
Anatomically designed insoles to enhance motion control, alignment and shock absorption

Prothotics Semi-Flex
Designed with a carbon arch support for control, stability, maximum support and optimal comfort

Airplus Gel Heel Cups
The revolutionary lightweight gel provides superior shock absorption and comfort for painful heels and calves

Gehwol Antiblister Cream
The anti-inflammatory effect prevents chafing and blisters and soothes tired feet

Spiky
Anti-slip shoe covers to prevent accidents in icy, snowy or slushy conditions

foothealthcare.com

Europe's number one consumer footcare provider

WHAT TO WEAR WALKING

GEAR

A huge range of clothing is available to make your walking easier, safer and more comfortable, and most walkers find the gear that suits them through experience. **The golden rules** are: be comfortable, dress for the sort of weather and terrain you are likely to meet, and never underestimate the changeability of British weather.

It's advisable to buy your outdoor gear from a specialist supplier who can give you expert advice (such as Millets, whose stores we list on p65). A directory of suppliers is available on the Ramblers website **www.ramblers.org.uk/info/equipmentshops**

Footwear – boots or shoes?

Feet are probably the most important part of a walker's body, so treat them with care. If you want to walk regularly in all kinds of weather, especially on longer walks out in the countryside, you should invest in specialist walking footwear.

- **Walking boots** with tough moulded soles are the best all-round solution, protecting and keeping feet warm and dry, providing grip and supporting the ankles – essential on steep slopes.
- **Walking shoes** are a lighter alternative to boots, offering tough protective soles with good grip, but no ankle support.
- **Good quality trainers** are cheap and lightweight, but usually not waterproof and give limited support and protection.
- **Walking sandals** for lowland use in summer have solid soles suitable for a variety of surfaces, but give no ankle support and less protection from undergrowth and sharp rocks, so should be used with great discretion.

Socks

Boots are more comfortably worn with good walking socks. Modern socks are often made from synthetic looped material, and have extra padding around toes and heels to cushion impact without potentially irritating raised seams. Some even 'wick' sweat outwards or are waterproof.

Some walkers wear two pairs of socks – a thin cotton or synthetic pair next to the skin, and a thicker pair on top. This helps cushion the feet and prevent blisters.

GOLD 2006 walk READER AWARDS www.ramblers.org.uk

GOLD 2006 walk READER AWARDS www.ramblers.org.uk

Meindl boots and Merrell walking shoes

Good walking socks are tough enough to last a while. Discard heavily worn or holed socks, don't attempt to repair them. On long walks bumps, holes and darning stitches can cause irritation and blistering.

Clothing – waterproof and windproof wear

In the British climate, a good quality **waterproof** (not just showerproof) and windproof jacket or anorak is essential. Look for something with at least a hood (or provision for a hood to be attached) and spacious pockets for maps and snacks. A cheap lightweight cagoule is adequate, but if you plan to do a lot of walking, consider a jacket made from 'breathable' material which allows sweat out but stops rain getting in.

To stop trousers and socks getting wet or muddy, consider waterproof **overtrousers**, or **gaiters** – knee-high waterproof leggings that attach to the boot. Both have their champions, but can be difficult to put on or remove.

Inner layers

The basic principle of outdoor clothing is the **layering** system. Several thin layers are more useful than one thick sweatshirt or large jumper since warm air is trapped between layers and provides better insulation, and you can add or remove layers according to the weather and level of activity.

The **base layer** nearest the skin is best made of thin synthetic material with the capability of 'wicking' moisture away from the skin and drying quickly. Natural fibres like cotton are not recommended since they absorb sweat and make you clammy. Wicking base layers work especially well with breathable jackets.

Between base layer and jacket you can add one or more **insulating layers**, usually made of an open-weave or knit fabric. An ordinary

Bridgedale socks

sweatshirt, jersey or high street fleece will suffice, but a good fleece specially designed for outdoor use could offer more warmth and comfort. Some are also windproof, keeping you warmer in cold winds even without a top layer, and a zipped front allows you to alter ventilation.

Trousers

Tracksuit bottoms or everyday casual trousers are fine for the average lowland walk, though can irritate and chafe on long walks.

Modern synthetic **walking trousers** are popular among regular walkers, being lightweight, loose-fitting and quick-drying with handy pockets. Some walkers wear walking shorts in fine weather, though long trousers offer better protection against brambles, nettles and ticks and should always be carried in case the weather changes.

Rohan walking trousers

Don't wear denim jeans as they restrict movement, lack pocket space, chafe when wet and take a long time to dry. They have a high wind-chill factor, meaning you can get very cold in them, especially when they get wet.

Head and hands

Up to 40% of body heat is lost through the head, so it is essential to protect your head and ears. A **warm hat** is a must in winter, especially in the hills, and can be worn under a jacket hood.

When sunny, wear a **sunhat** and use **sun cream** on your face and any bare patches of skin. You may be out in the sun for long periods without shelter, and even with a cooling wind or in cold weather you can still burn.

Gloves are important in cold weather, especially for those with circulatory problems. To walk comfortably and with good posture you should be able to swing your arms freely, so putting your hands in your pockets is not an option.

See the Ramblers Bookshop p95 to order factsheet FS3 for more details about walkers' clothing and equipment and a buyer's guide

Berghaus base layers, fleeces and waterproof jackets

GEAR

WHAT EQUIPMENT TO TAKE

Karrimor backpacks and Berghaus daysacks

Equipment checklist

On lowland walks you should also consider carrying:

- ☑ **Map**, **compass** and **navigation equipment**
  (See How to use a map and compass, p52)
- ☑ Full **water bottle** and/or thermos flask adequate
  for your walk
- ☑ **Extra clothing** including hat and gloves,
  especially in winter
- ☑ **Food**, unless you're absolutely sure you can eat on
  the way
- ☑ **Emergency rations**
- ☑ A **first aid kit** and any medicines you might need
- ☑ Optionally, a **mobile phone**

And don't forget to make room for non-essential items
that might make your walk more enjoyable, such as a
notebook, pencil, camera, guidebooks etc.

Rucksacks

Wherever you walk, rucksacks or backpacks are the
best means of carrying what you need – they leave
your hands free and are far more comfortable than a
shoulder bag over a long distance. Modern rucksacks
are made of tough, waterproof nylon or polyester
fabric and lightweight alloy frames.

The simplest rucksack is a small **daysack**, which is
usually frameless and has only shoulder straps so that
all weight is carried on the shoulders. Larger, more
sophisticated **travel packs** and **backpacks** have
frames, hip-belts and chest straps to help distribute
weight more evenly across the back. Many models
now have ventilation features to avoid a sweaty
back, and some are designed especially to fit women
or children.

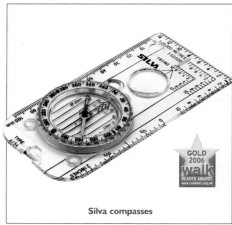

Silva compasses

Always choose the best size rucksack for the
purpose. A daysack of around 20 litres capacity is fine
for walks of a day or less, but quickly become
uncomfortable across the shoulders if too heavily
loaded. For weekends and short breaks, or
when you need to carry more equipment,
there are various medium-sized packs
of 30-55 litres. For longer holidays or
serious backpacking with camping
equipment, large packs with a
capacity of 55-75 litres are
available. You should also look for
additional features, such as ice-axe
loops, key clips and concealed
security pockets.

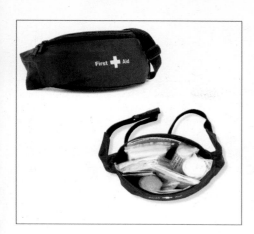

First Aid Kit

A basic first aid kit should include:

- ☑ 10 **plasters** in various sizes
- ☑ 2 **large sterile dressings** for severe bleeding
- ☑ 1 **medium sterile dressing** for larger wounds
- ☑ 4 **triangular bandages** to support suspected broken bones, dislocations and sprains
- ☑ 1 **eye pad** in case of a cut to the eye
- ☑ 4 **safety pins** to secure dressings
- ☑ **Disposable gloves** for good hygiene

Ready-made first aid kits for walkers are available from outdoor shops and St John Supplies.

See First Aid and Emergencies p105 for details of first aid and health suppliers

GEAR

For more demanding walks in hills or mountains you may need additional equipment, such as:

- ☑ A **survival bag** – a heavy-duty bag for body insulation in an emergency
- ☑ **Torch** and spare batteries
- ☑ **Whistle**
- ☑ **Water purification tablets**
- ☑ **High-energy rations** such as mint cake, chocolate and dried fruit

If you are likely to meet heavy snow or ice, wear a pair of heavy-duty winter walking boots that can be fitted with **crampons** – metal spike attachments that give a better grip in icy conditions that are not suitable for all boots – and carry an **ice axe**. Learn how to use them both properly – in the hands of a novice they can cause, rather than prevent, accidents (see appropriate courses on our website www.ramblers.org.uk).

Many hillwalkers carry a **kisu** shelter or **bothy bag**. Like a tent without poles, it is made of lightweight waterproof nylon with a draw cord round the base, is big enough to sit inside and allows two or more people to share bodyheat. Available in a range of sizes, you should carry one that is adequate for the size of your party.

LOCAL MILLETS STORES

ABERDEEN	167/168 Union Street AB11 6BB	01224 596230
ABERGAVENNY	Unit 3 Cibi Walk NP7 5AJ	01873 858944
ABERYSTWYTH	3 Great Darkgate Street SY23 1DE	01970 612119
ALDERSHOT	1/2 Wellington Centre GU11 1DB	01252 345979
ALTRINCHAM	101 George Street WA14 1RN	0161 9269794
AMBLESIDE	Unit 12 Market Cross Shopping Centre LA22 9BT	01539 433956
ANDOVER	29 High Street SP10 1LJ	01264 324877
ASHFORD	Unit 24 Park Mall TN24 8RY	01233 634192
AYLESBURY	13 Market Square HP20 2PZ	01296 397599
AYR	58 High Street KA7 1PA	01292 610516
BAKEWELL	Unit 3 Rutland Square DE45 1BZ	01629 815143
BALLYMENA	Unit 33 Fairhill BT43 6UG	02825 646098
BANBURY	9 High Street OX16 5DZ	01295 263189
BANGOR	261 High Street LL5 7IPB	01248 361263
BARNSTAPLE	91 High Street EX31 1HR	01271 342937
BASILDON	21A Town Square SS1 4IBA	01268 272771
BASINGSTOKE	11/12 Potters Walk RG21 7GQ	01256 364649
BATH	25/28 High Street BA1 5AJ	01225 471500
BEDFORD	3 West Arcade, Church Street MK40 1LQ	01234 357375
BELFAST	1 Cornmarket BT1 4DA	02890 242264
BEVERLEY	16 Butcher Row HU17 0AE	01482 868132
BEXLEYHEATH	119 The Broadway DA6 7HF	0208 3035089
BICESTER	26/27 Crown Walk OX26 6HY	01869 324854
BIGGLESWADE	2 Market Square SG18 8AP	01767 312089
BIRKENHEAD	32/34 Borough Pavement CH41 2XX	0151 6661350
BIRMINGHAM	35 Union Street B2 4SR	0121 6431496
BIRMINGHAM	62 New Street B2 4 DU	0121 6430885
BISHOP AUCKLAND	63/65 Newgate Street DL14 7EW	01388 602555
BISHOP STORTFORD	26 South Street CM23 3AT	01279 651452
BLACKPOOL	22 Church Street FY1 1EW	01253 628430
BLANCHARDSTOWN	Unit 149 Blanchardstown Centre DUBLIN 15	00353 18222160
BODMIN	27/31 Fore Street PL31 2HT	01208 79003
BOGNOR REGIS	38 London Road PO21 1PZ	01243 837340
BOLTON	53/55 Victoria Square BL1 1RY	01204 366563
BOSCOMBE	13 Sovereign Centre BH1 4SX	01202 300720
BOSTON	16 Market Street PE21 6EH	01205 361753
BOURNEMOUTH	39 Old Christchurch Road BH1 1DS	01202 295911
BRACKNELL	46 High Street RG12 1LL	01344 485 524
BRADFORD	43A Darley Street BD1 3HN	01274 725343
BRAINTREE	86/88 High Street CM7 1JP	01376 554742
BRECON	16 High Street LD3 7AL	01874 624634
BRENTWOOD	7 Chapel High CM14 4RY	01277 223669
BRIDGEND	Brackla Street Centre CF31 1EB	01656 657945
BRIDGWATER	5 Fore Street TA6 3NQ	01278 422243
BRIGHTON	Unit 3 Air Street BN1 3FB	01273 777125
BRIGHTON	153 Western Rd BN1 2DA	01273 329435
BRISTOL	10 Broadmead BS1 3HH	0117 9221167
BRISTOL	9/10 Transom House BS1 6A	0117 926 4892
BROMLEY	65 High Street BR1 1JY	0208 460 0418
BURGESS HILL	Unit 77, Church Walk, The Martlets RH15 9BQ	01444 258448
BURNLEY	64/66 St James Square BB11 1NH	01282 831803
BURTON ON TRENT	12 St Modwens Walk DE14 1HL	01283 562488
BURY ST EDMUNDS	2 Buttermarket IP33 1DB	01284 755521
BUXTON	53/55 Spring Gardens SK17 6BJ	01298 25660
CAMBERLEY	33 High Street GU15 3RB	01276 65680
CAMBRIDGE	18/19 Sidney Street CB2 3HG	01223 307046
CANTERBURY	47 Burgate CT1 4BH	01227 479698
CARDIFF	109/111 Queen Street CF1 4BH	02920 340341
CARDIFF	10 Duke Street CF10 1AY	02920 390887
CARLISLE	59 English Street CA3 8JU	01228 529206
CARMARTHEN	1 Red Street SA31 1QL	01267 235906
CHELMSFORD	34 High Chelmer CM1 1XR	01245 269989
CHELTENHAM	117 High Street GL50 1DW	01242 520692
CHELTENHAM	(Clearance) 240 High Street GL50 3HF	01242 262592
CHESHAM	35 High Street HP5 1BW	01494 791920
CHESTER	15/17 Northgate CH1 1HA	01244 329331
CHICHESTER	4 South Street PO19 1EH	01243 786627
CHIPPENHAM	17/18 High Street SN15 3ER	01249 652533
CHISWICK	167 Chiswick High Road W4 2DR	0208 9945807
CIRENCESTER	34 Cricklade Street GL7 1JH	01285 651250
COLCHESTER	17/18 High Street CO1 1DB	01206 574615
COLCHESTER	16 Short Wyre Street CO1 1LN	01206 577040
COVENTRY	41 Smithford Way CV1 1FY	02476 224841
COVENTRY	19 Smithford Way CV1 1FY	02476 837048
CRAWLEY	16 Haslett Avenue RH10 1HS	01293 541003
CREWE	7 Queensway CW1 2HH	01270 255446
CROYDON	52 High Street CR0 1YB	0208 688 6066
CROYDON	40/44 St George's Walk CR0 1YJ	0208 6881730
CWMBRAN	14 Monmouth Walk NP44 1PE	01633 871279
DARLINGTON	5/7 East Row DL1 5PZ	01325 485806
DERBY	1 East Street DE1 2AU	01332 342368
DEVIZES	29 The Brittox SN1 0IAJ	01380 730281
DONCASTER	54 High Street DN1 1BE	01302 739659
DORCHESTER	16 Cornhill DT1 1BQ	01305 251637
DORKING	5 South Street RH4 2DY	01306 887227
DUDLEY	205/206 High Street DY1 1PB	01384 252974
DUMFRIES	28 Munches street DG1 1ET	01387 739954
DUNDEE	23 Cowgate DD1 2HS	01382 223744
DUNSTABLE	14 Nicholas Way LU6 1TD	01582 663460
EAST GRINSTEAD	23 London Road RH19 1AL	01342 300977
EASTBOURNE	146/148 Terminus Road BN21 3AN	01323 728340
EDINBURGH	12 Frederick Street EH2 2HB	0131 220 1551
ELGIN	Unit 13 St Giles Centre IV30 1EA	01343 556550
ELTHAM	122 Eltham High Road SE9 1BJ	0208 8502822
ELY	26 Market Place CB7 4NT	01353 664023
ENFIELD	21 Palace Gardens EN2 6SN	0208 363 1682
ENNISKILLEN	Unit 24 Erneside Centre BT74 6JQ	02866 328580
EPSOM	17 High Street KT19 8DD	01372 721557
EVESHAM	33 Bridge Street WR11 4SQ	01386 446759
EXETER	207 High Street EX4 3EB	01392 255811
EXMOUTH	42 Chapel Street EX8 1HW	01395 267144
FALMOUTH	11 Market Strand TR11 3DB	01326 313348
FAREHAM	80/82 Osborne Mall, Hampshire PO16 0PW	01329 283088
FARNBOROUGH	Unit 5/7 The Mead GU14 7RT	01252 371663
FARNHAM	2/3 West Street, Surrey GU9 7DN	01252 711338
FELIXSTOWE	52 Hamilton Road IP11 7AJ	01394 672203
FLEET	158 Fleet Road GU51 8BE	01252 620636
GALWAY	Unit 37 Headford Road	00353 91569433
GATESHEAD	31 The Galleria NE11 9YP	0191 460 3153
GLASGOW	Unit 2B Sauchiehall Street G2 3ER	0141 332 5617
GLENROTHES	56 Unicorn Way, Kingdom Centre KY7 5NU	01592 753217
GLOUCESTER	4 Southgate Street GL1 2DH	01452 412803
GRAVESEND	Unit 4 Anglesea Centre DA11 0AU	01474 362889
GREAT YARMOUTH	20/21 Market Place NR30 1LY	01493 857040
GREENOCK	45 Hamilton Way PA15 1RQ	01475 726425
GRIMSBY	22 Baxtergate, Freshney Place DN31 1QL	01472 362449
GUERNSEY	9 The Pollett GY1 1WZ	01481 725888
GUILDFORD	21 Friary Street GU1 4GH	01483 573476
HALIFAX	11 Crown Street HX1 1TT	01422 342644
HAMILTON	17 Duke Street ML3 7DT	01698 284691
HANLEY	10/12 Upper Market Square ST1 1NS	01782 214560
HARLOW	5 Eastgate CM20 1HP	01279 438165
HARROGATE	15/15A Beulah Street HG1 1QH	01423 526677
HARROW	324A Station road HA1 2DX	0208 4273809
HASTINGS	12/13 York Building, Wellington Place TN34 1NN	01424 203589
HAVERFORDWEST	25 Bridge Street SA61 2AZ	01437 767300
HAVERHILL	17 High Street CB9 8AD	01440 713682
HAYWARDS HEATH	98 South Street RH16 4LJ	01444 457214
HEMEL HEMPSTEAD	221 The Marlowes HP1 1BH	01442 265218
HEREFORD	12/14 Eign Gate HR4 0AB	01432 264196
HERTFORD	18 Fore Street SG14 1BZ	01992 584427
HEXHAM	24 Fore Street,Hexham NE46 1LZ	01434 608324
HIGH WYCOMBE	4/5 Church Square HP11 2DE	01494 522100
HITCHIN	26 Market Place SG5 1DT	01462 432567
HORSHAM	18 West Street RH12 1TV	01403 262851
HULL	24/26 King Edward Street HU1 3SS	01482 210389
HUNTINGDON	Unit 5 St Germain Walk PE29 3FG	01480 413554
ILFORD	154 High Road IG1 1LL	0208 478 7341

GEAR

INVERNESS	24 High Street IV1 1JQ	01463 714387
IPSWICH	16 Hacket Street IP4 1AY	01473 254704
IPSWICH	14/16 Carr Street IP4 1EJ	01473 211797
ISLE OF MAN	13 The Strand Shopping Centre IM1 2ER	01624 615668
JERSEY	29/31 King Street JE2 4WS	01534 725449
KENDAL	26/28 Highgate LA9 4SX	01539 736866
KENSINGTON (London)	176 Kensington High Street W8 7RG	0207 9377141
KESWICK	85/87 Main Street, Cumbria CA12 5DT	01768 775524
KETTERING	3/5 Newland Street NN16 8JH	01536 481261
KIDDERMINSTER	21 The Bull Ring DY10 2AZ	01562 740127
KING'S LYNN	SU17A The Vancouver Centre PE30 1DE	TBC
KINGSTON	3/5 Thames Street KT1 1PH	0208 546 5042
LANCASTER	7 Cheapside LA1 1LY	01524 841043
LEEDS	117/118 Kirkgate LS1 6BY	0113 242 9892
LEEDS	Unit 24 St Johns Ctre, 110 Albion Street LS2 8LQ	0113 2342395
LEEDS - WHITEROSE	Unit 28 Whiterose Centre LS11 8LU	0113 276 1149
LEEK	34 Derby Street ST13 5AB	01538 383731
LEICESTER	121/123 Granby Street LE1 6FD	0116 254 2402
LEIGH	Unit 33 Spinning Gate Ctre,Ellesmere St WN7 4PG	01942 671944
LEIGHTON BUZZARD	47 High Street LU7 1DN	01525 371623
LETCHWORTH	5 Commerce Way, Garden Sq Ctre SG6 3DN	01462 679583
LEWISHAM	205 Lewisham High Street SE13 6LY	0208 852 1909
LICHFIELD	19 Tamworth Street WS13 6JP	01543 262003
LINCOLN	321/322 High Street LN5 7DW	01522 567317
LIVERPOOL	15 Ranelagh Street LI 1JW	0151 709 7017
LIVINGSTONE	Unit 68, Almomdvale Centre EH54 6HR	01506 437 728
LLANDUDNO	80 Moystn St LL30 2RP	01492 879 593
LLANELLI	42 Stepney Street SA15 3YA	01554 751657
LOUGHBOROUGH	4 Market Street LE11 3EP	01509 236413
LOUTH	78 East Gate LN11 9PG	01507 602711
LOWESTOFT	71 London Road North NR32 1LS	01502 572239
LUTON	Unit 125 Arndale Centre LU1 2TN	01582 724514
LYMINGTON	52 High Street SO41 9AG	01590 675144
MACCLESFIELD	45 Mill St SK11 6NE	01625 427477
MAIDSTONE	Unit 34A Fremlin Walk ME14 1QT	01622 674137
MANCHESTER	133 Deansgate M3 3WR	01618 351016
MANCHESTER	Unit 49 Arndale Centre M4 2HU	0161 832 7547
MANSFIELD	48 Westgate NG18 1RR	01623 629446
MERRY HILL	11 Merry Hill, Brierley Hill DY5 1QX	01384 261671
MIDDLESBROUGH	40 Linthorpe Road TS1 1RD	01642 240863
MILTON KEYNES	21/23 Crown Walk MK9 3AH	01908 672322
MONMOUTH	21 Monnow Street NP25 3EF	01600 719187
NEATH	12 Queen Street SA11 1DL	01639 637216
NEWARK	25 Middlegate NG24 1AL	01636 640842
NEWBURY	68/69 Northbrook Street RG13 1AE	01635 40070
NEWCASTLE U LYME	53 High Street ST5 1PN	01782 612968
NEWCASTLE U TYNE	121/125 Grainger Street NE1 5AE	0191 232 1100
NEWPORT (Gwent)	3 Llanarth Street, Gwent NP20 1HS	01633 246 309
NEWPORT (Isle of Wight)	21 St James Square PO30 1UX	01983 525995
NEWRY	Unit 30, Buttercrane Quay BT35 8HJ	02830 263565
NEWTON ABBOT	17 Queen Street TQ12 2AQ	01626 353405
NEWTOWNABBEY	Unit 70/71, Abbey Centre BT37 9AQ	02890 865520
NORTHAMPTON	24 Market Square NN1 2DX	01604 621898
NORWICH	9/11 St Stephens Street NR1 3QN	01603 622708
NORWICH	Boston House, 5 Orford Hill NR1 3QB	01603 625645
NOTTINGHAM	12 Exchange Walk NG1 2NX	0159 417456
NUNEATON	14/15 Abbey Gate Centre CV11 4HL	02476 385625
OBAN	71 George Street PA34 5NN	01631 571122
ORPINGTON	178 High Street BR6 0JW	01689 826794
OXFORD	42/43 Queen Street OX1 1ET	01865 790676
OXFORD	17 Turl Street OX1 3DH	01865 247110
PAIGNTON	37/39 Victoria Street TQ4 5DD	01803 529578
PAISLEY	29 The High Street PA1 2AF	0141 8471013
PENZANCE	105 Market Jew Street TR18 2LE	01736 363204
PERTH	182/186 High Street PH1 5PA	01738 622248
PETERBOROUGH	47 Bridge Street PE1 1HA	01733 341371
PETERBOROUGH	97 Bridge Street PE1 1HG	01733 561000
PETERSFIELD	8 Rams Walk GU32 3JA	01730 260317
PLYMOUTH	39/40 New George Street PL1 1RW	01752 665521
PONTYPRIDD	80 Taff Street CF37 4SD	01443 400086
POOLE	9 Kingland Crescent BH15 1TA	01202 661307
PORTSMOUTH	213/215 Commercial Road PO1 4BJ	02392 851653
PRESTON	28 Market Place PR1 2AR	01772 884433
PRESTON	23 Miller Arcade PR1 2QA	01772 250242
PUTNEY	98 High Street SW15 1RB	0208 788 2300
RAMSGATE	8 Queen Street CT11 9DR	01843 594220
READING	4/5 St Mary's Butts RG1 2LN	0118 959 5228
REDCAR	15/17 High Street TS10 3BZ	01642 483924
REDDITCH	12 Kingfisher Walk B97 4EY	01527 595229
REDHILL	29 High Street RH1 1RD	01737 765177
RHYL	60/62 High Street LL18 1ET	01745 353178
RINGWOOD	7 The Furlong Centre BH24 1AT	01425 480047
ROMFORD	42/44 South Street RM1 1RB	01708 743751
ROTHERHAM	18 Howard Street S60 1QU	01709 382502
RUGBY	Uuit 28 clock towers shopping centre CV21 3JT	01788 578 106
SAFFRON WALDEN	37/39 King Street CB10 1EU	1799 529343
SALISBURY	38/39 Old George Mall SP1 2AF	01722 341 583
SCARBOROUGH	6/7 Westborough YO11 1UH	01723 367869
SCUNTHORPE	116 High Street DN15 6HB	01724 849890
SHEFFIELD	71 The Moor S1 4PF	0114 2722194
SHREWSBURY	6/7 Mardol Head SY1 1HD	01743 353686
SITTINGBOURNE	119 High Street ME10 4AQ	01795 472544
SKIPTON	30 Sheep Street BD23 1HX	01756 793754
SLOUGH	186/188 High Street SL1 1JS	01753 520981
SOUTHAMPTON	104 East Street SO14 3HH	02380 228797
SOUTHEND	4/19 York Road SS1 2BH	01702 463316
SOUTHPORT	4/8 Tulketh Street, Merseyside PR8 1AQ	01704 534017
SOUTHSEA	5 Palmerston Road PO5 3QQ	02392 732461
St. ALBANS	19/21 French Row AL3 5DZ	01727 856328
St. HELENS	2/4 Cotham Street WA10 1SQ	01744 739941
STAFFORD	13 Gaolgate Street ST16 2BQ	01785 251912
STAINES	111A High Street TW18 4PQ	01784 469820
STAMFORD	63 High Street PE9 2LA	01780 481346
STIRLING	20/22 Murray Place FK8 1DQ	01786 451141
STOCKPORT	29/31 Princes Street SK1 1SU	0161 477 4160
STRATFORD UPON AVON	Unit 21A Town Square Shopping Centre CV37 6JN	01789 414857
STROUD	34 Kendrick Street GL5 1AQ	01453 764646
SUDBURY	14 North Street CO10 1RB	01787 375883
SUTTON	86 High Street SM1 1JG	0208 643 4251
SUTTON COLDFIELD	56 The Parade B72 1DS	01213 554931
SWANSEA	234 High Street SA1 1NZ	01792 655637
SWINDON	Sub Unit 4 The Parade SN1 1BA	01793 514941
TALLAGHT	Unit 315 The Square DUBLIN 24	003531 4621119
TAUNTON	20 East Street TA1 3LP	01823 332782
TELFORD	207 Dean Street TF34BT	01952 201002
TONBRIDGE	70 High Street TN9 1SD	01732 355247
TORQUAY	49 Union Street TQ1 1ET	01803 297588
TROWBRIDGE	40 The Shires BA14 8AT	01225 762871
TRURO	11 Pydar Street TR1 2AX	01872 240973
TUNBRIDGE WELLS	3/7 Camden Road TN1 2PS	01892 519891
UCKFIELD	136 High Street TN22 1QN	01825 766176
WAKEFIELD	28 Little Westgate WF1 1JY	01924 371120
WALSALL	9 The Bridge, West Midlands WS1 1LR	01922 624462
WARRINGTON	28 Golden Square Shopping Centre WA1 1QE	01925 417050
WATFORD	Unit A8 The Harlequin Centre WD7 2TB	01923 212427
WEST THURROCK	Unit 338 Lakeside Shopping Centre RM20 2ZH	01708 864366
WESTON-S-MARE	98 High Street BS23 1HS	01934 621930
WEYMOUTH	74 St Mary Street DT4 8PJ	01305 786002
WHITEHAVEN	19/20 King Street CA28 7LA	01946 694655
WIGAN	24/26 Market Street WN1 1HX	01942 245330
WIMBLEDON	34 The Broadway SW19 0BB	0208 946 6644
WINCHESTER	149 High Street SO23 9AY	01962 841970
WINDSOR	42 Peascod Street SL4 1DE	01753 620405
WITNEY	Unit 18A, Woolgate OX28 6AP	01993 778775
WOKING	31 Commercial Road GU21 6XR	01483 721551
WOKINGHAM	37 Peach Street RG4 0IXJ	01189 798097
WOLVERHAMPTON	2 Wulfrun Centre WV1 3HF	01902 423797
WORCESTER	7/8 The Shambles WR1 2RF	01905 25672
WORTHING	95 Montague Street BN11 3BN	01903 236066
WREXHAM	24 Queen Street LL11 1AL	01978 261267
YATE	5 West Walk BS37 4AX	01454 312823
YEOVIL	22 Middle Street BA20 1LY	01935 423156
YORK	4/6 Market Street YO1 8ST	01904 620618
YORK	Unit 3, Queens House, Micklegate YO1 6JH	01904 653567

GEAR

RAMBLERS AREAS AND GROUPS

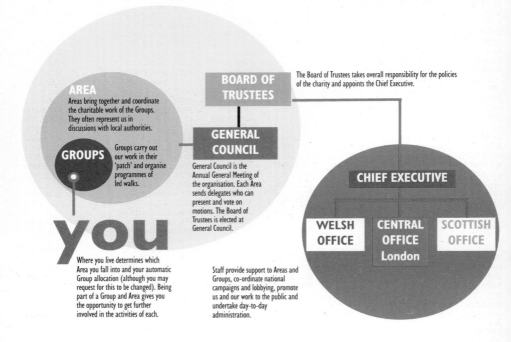

AREA
Areas bring together and coordinate the charitable work of the Groups. They often represent us in discussions with local authorities.

GROUPS
Groups carry out our work in their 'patch' and organise programmes of led walks.

BOARD OF TRUSTEES

The Board of Trustees takes overall responsibility for the policies of the charity and appoints the Chief Executive.

GENERAL COUNCIL
General Council is the Annual General Meeting of the organisation. Each Area sends delegates who can present and vote on motions. The Board of Trustees is elected at General Council.

CHIEF EXECUTIVE

WELSH OFFICE   **CENTRAL OFFICE London**   **SCOTTISH OFFICE**

you

Where you live determines which Area you fall into and your automatic Group allocation (although you may request for this to be changed). Being part of a Group and Area gives you the opportunity to get further involved in the activities of each.

Staff provide support to Areas and Groups, co-ordinate national campaigns and lobbying, promote us and our work to the public and undertake day-to-day administration.

The Ramblers' structure

The Ramblers' Association operates across the whole of Britain, although Scotland and Wales have their own devolved structure within the organisation. It is a democratic organisation where members have a say and become involved in our work. Our network of Areas and Groups gives us a fantastic combination of a strong national voice and effective local action.

There are just over 50 Areas. These largely correspond to county boundaries in England and to other regional boundaries in Scotland and Wales. Each Area, and each subsidiary Group within it, is managed and run entirely by volunteers.

Area and Group activities

Our Groups carry out conservation work in their localities, walk and socialise together. Each Group listed organises its own programme of led walks. Most walks are now on the Group Walks Finder www.ramblers.org.uk/walksfinder, otherwise you can request a programme by sending a SAE to the Group secretary.

Many work from home so if you telephone, please do so at reasonable times.

Many Groups also publish details of upcoming walks and activities on their own websites, which are all linked from www.ramblers.org.uk/info/localgroups.

A variety of walks offered

Most Groups and Areas offer a mixed programme of long and short walks, but some offer regular programmes of shorter, easier walks and/or walks aimed at families with young children, generally no more than 8km/5 miles and taken at an easy pace. We've marked these with ● in the listings. For more information about these walks contact the Area or Group directly or see www.ramblers.org.uk/walking.

There are also a number of Groups for people in their 20s and 30s known as hike 20–30s Groups. These are highlighted in blue.

All details were correct in October 2006 but changes may take place during the year.

ENGLAND

AVON
Bath & North East Somerset; Bristol and South Gloucester

AREA SECRETARY
Ms Jill Fysh, 43a Springfields, Ableton Lane, Severn Beach, Bristol BS35 4PP
☎ 01454 633001 jillfysh@aol.com
www.avon-ramblers.org.uk

GROUP SECRETARIES
Bath Mrs M Wright, 47 Dovers Park, Bathford, Bath BA1 7UD ☎ 01225 858047 wright_marilyn@hotmail.co.uk
www.tompson.demon.co.uk/
Bathramblers/Bathhome.htm

Bristol ● Mr Barry Smith, 81 Leighton Road, Upper Westow, Bath BA1 4NG
☎ 01225 423341 [mobile 07906 403992]
www.bristolramblers.org.uk

Brunel 20s–30s Walking Group
www.brunelwalking.org.uk. See
www.ramblers.org.uk/info/localgroups or contact our central office for current details

Kingswood Mrs Nicola Phelps, 10 Cloverlea Road, Warmley, Bristol BS30 8LF ☎ 0117 985 8825 ronphelps@supanet.com
www.kingswoodramblers.pwp.
blueyonder.co.uk

Norton Radstock Mrs Sally Haddon, 4 Dymboro Close, Midsomer Norton, Bath BA3 2QS

Severnside Mrs Gill King, 42 Riverside Park, Severn Beach, Bristol BS35 4PN
www.severnside-ramblers.org.uk

Southwold (Yate) Miss Sharifa Naqui, 3 Brake Close, Sherbourne Park, Bradley Stoke, Bristol BS32 8BA
☎ 01179 697246
sharifa.naqui@ukgateway.net
www.southwold-ramblers.co.uk

BEDFORDSHIRE
AREA SECRETARY
See www.ramblers.org.uk/info/
localgroups or contact our central office for current details

GROUP SECRETARIES
Ivel Valley Mrs Rachel Bryce, 7 Wood Close, Biddenham, Bedford MK40 4QG
☎ 01234 823603
www.ivelvalleywalkers.org.uk

Lea & Icknield Miss SH Lewis, 21 Simpson Close, Leagrave, Luton LU4 9TP ☎ 01582 847273

Leighton Buzzard Mr John Hartley, 57 The Paddocks, Leighton Buzzard, Beds LU7 2SX ☎ 01525 372525
leightonramblers2.mysite.wanadoo-
members.co.uk

North Bedfordshire Mrs Linda Tongue, 25 Field Cottage Road, Eaton Socon, St Neots, Cambs PE19 8HA
☎ 01480 350345
lindatongue@yahoo.co.uk

Ouse Valley Mrs B M Leaf, 117 High Street, Blunham, Bedfordshire MK44 3NW
www.ousevalleyramblers.co.uk

BERKSHIRE
AREA SECRETARY
Mr Cliff Lambert, Marandella, 1 Lawrence Mead, Kintbury, Hungerford RG17 9XT ☎ 01488 608108

GROUP SECRETARIES
Berkshire Walkers Ms Caroline McDonagh, 49 Sharnwood Drive, Calcot, Reading, Berkshire RG31 7YD
www.berkshirewalkers.org.uk

East Berkshire ● Mr Gerald Barnett, 9 Fremantle Road, High Wycombe, Bucks HP13 7PQ ☎ 01494 522404 [memberships enquiries, Mrs Welch
☎ 01753 662139]
www.eastberksramblers.org

Loddon Valley Mr David Turner, 9 Meadow Walk, Wokingham, Berkshire RG41 2TG ☎ 01189 784364
nwty.lwyrykxy@ntlworld.com
www.lvra.org.uk

Mid Berkshire Ms Elizabeth Cuff, Donkey Pound Cottage, Beech Hill, Reading, Berkshire RG7 2AX
☎ 0118 988 2674
www.mbra.org.uk

Pang Valley Dr C Howlett, 3 Western Elms Avenue, Reading RG30 2AL
☎ 0118 9590436
chris.howlett@telco4u.ne

South East Berks Mrs Rania Turner, 8 Arden Close, Bracknell RG12 2SG
☎ 01344 420015
turnerrania@hotmail.com

West Berkshire ● Mr Fred Carter, Elvira, Main Street, West Ilsley, Newbury RG20 7AW ☎ 01635 281621
fred@silkartwork.fsnet.co.uk
www.wberksramblers.org.uk

Windsor & District Miss JM Clark, 7 Dyson Close, Windsor, Berkshire SL4 3LZ ☎ 01753 866 545

BUCKINGHAMSHIRE & WEST MIDDLESEX
Buckinghamshire plus the London boroughs of Brent, Ealing, Harrow, Hillingdon and Hounslow

AREA SECRETARY
Mr D Bradnack, 47 Thame Road, Haddenham, Aylesbury, Bucks HP17 8EP
☎ 01844 291069 [before 9pm]
bradnackd@aol.com
www.bucks-wmiddx-ramblers.org.uk

GROUP SECRETARIES
Amersham & District Mrs Madeleine Moody, White Cottage, 93 St Leonard's Road, Chesham Bois, Amersham HP6 6DR ☎ 01494 727504

Aylesbury & District Mr Jim Cornwell, 41 Archer Drive, Aylesbury HP20 1ER
☎ 01296 336588

Chilterns 20s–30s Walking Group
www.chilterns2030s.co.uk or see
www.ramblers.org.uk/info/localgroups or contact our central office for current details

Chilterns Weekend Walkers See
www.ramblers.org.uk/info/localgroups or contact our central office for current details

Hillingdon ● Ms Vivien Kermath, 92 Hill Road, Pinner HA5 1LE
☎ 020 8866 1062
Vivkermath@aol.com
www.hillingdonramblers.org.uk

Hike MK Group Mr Bryan Mitcham, 20 Curlew, Watermead, Aylesbury HP19 0WG
www.mk-northbucks2030s.org.uk

Milton Keynes & District Mr John West, 45 Blackdown, Fullers Slade, Milton Keynes MK11 2AA
☎ 01908 564055
john.f.west@btinternet.com
www.mkramblers.org.uk

North West London Miss Heather Lee, 12b Wellesley Road, Harrow, Middlesex HA1 1QN ☎ 020 8863 7628
heatherlee@mynow.co.uk

West London Mr Tom Berry, 128 Park Lane, South Harrow, Middlesex HA2 8NL ☎ 020 8422 3284
www.btinternet.com/
~westlondongroupra

Wycombe District ● Mr John Esslemont, 4 Park Farm Way, Lane End, High Wycombe, Buckinghamshire HP14 3EG
☎ 01494 862699 [membership enquiries]
beebee@bbrooksbank17.fsnet.co.uk
www.geocities.com/perrir_uk/walking/
frames.html

CAMBRIDGESHIRE & PETERBOROUGH
AREA SECRETARY
Ms Jill Tuffnell, 62 Beche Road, Cambridge CB5 8HU
☎ 01223 362881
web.ukonline.co.uk/cambs.ramblers

GROUP SECRETARIES
Cambridge Ms Jill Tuffnell , 62 Beche Road, Cambridge CB5 8HU
☎ 01223 362881

DAVID SIMMS

RAMBLERS GROUPS & PUBLICATIONS

Cambridge 20s & 30s Walking Group
Mr Iain Simpson,
13 Cratheme Way, Cameron Road,
Cambridge CB4 2LX
enquiries@walkcambridge.org
www.walkcambridge.org

East Cambridgeshire Mrs Sue
Summerside, Mow Fen Hall, 4a Silt Road,
Littleport, Ely, Cambs CB6 1QD
☎ 01353 861435

Fenland Mrs SL Ledger, 18 Alexandra
Road, Wisbech, Cambs PE13 1HS
☎ 01945 587135

Huntingdonshire Mr William
Thompson, 2 Bankers Walk, Ramsey,
Huntingdon, Cambs PE26 1EG
☎ 01487 812022

Peterborough Mr P Bennett, 93
Woodhurst Road, Stanground,
Peterborough, Cambs PE2 8PQ
☎ 01733 553828

Peterborough Younger Walkers
Miss KL Hornsby, 11 Albany Walk,
Peterborough PE2 9JN
☎ 01733 557381
web.ukonline.co.uk/cambs.
ramblers/pbg_20-30_info.htm

CHESHIRE
See Merseyside & West Cheshire,
South & East Cheshire, and North
& Mid-Cheshire Areas

CORNWALL
AREA SECRETARY
Mrs Christine James, Chy-Vean,
Tresillian, Truro, Cornwall TR4 8BN
☎ 01872 520368
www.racornwall.org.uk

GROUP SECRETARIES
Bude/Stratton Mr Peter Judson,
Meadowcroft, Bagbury Road, Bude,
Cornwall EX23 8QJ ☎ 01288 356597

Camel District (Wadebridge) Mrs
Daphne Windle, 4 Sarahs Close, Padstow,
Cornwall PL28 8BJ ☎ 01841 533283
www.racamelgroup.org.uk

Caradon Ms C Craze, 3 Culverland Park,
Liskeard, Cornwall PL14 3HY
☎ 01579 348973

Carrick ● Mr JB Jennings, 7 Moresk
Close, Truro, Cornwall TR1 1DL
☎ 01872 278317

Newquay Mrs E Smith, Ferryman Rest,
Luthewllan Barn, Trevean Way, Newquay,
Cornwall TR7 1TW ☎ 01637 879965

Restormel ● Mrs Jane Sloan, Brouard
Cottage, Fore Street, Grampound, Truro
TR2 4QT ☎ 01726 883214

West Cornwall (Penwith & Kerrier)
Mrs Sylvia Ronan, Trebant, Ludgvan,
Churchtown, Penzance, Cornwall
TR20 8HH ☎ 01736 740542
sylv@west-cornwall-footpaths.com

CUMBRIA
See Lake District Area

DERBYSHIRE
West Derbyshire, Amber Valley, Derby,
South Derbyshire and Erewash
districts of Derbyshire. See also South
Yorkshire & North East Derbyshire,
and Manchester Areas

AREA SECRETARY
Mr John Hayes, The Old Rectory,
Old Brampton, Chesterfield, Derbyshire
S42 7JG ☎ 01246 569260

GROUP SECRETARIES
Amber Valley Mrs MA Siddons,
Overdene, Ridgeway Lane, Nether Heage,
Nr Belper, Derbyshire DE56 2JT
www.ambervalleyramblers.org.uk

Derby & S Derbyshire Mrs Pat
Vaughan, Greenways, 13 Evans Avenue,
Allestree, Derbys DE22 2EL
☎ 01332 558552
sec@derbyramblers.org.uk
www.derbyramblers.org.uk

Derbyshire Dales Miss Amanda Higton,
231 Chesterfield Road, Matlock,
Derbyshire DE4 5LE ☎ 01629 582661
Amandahigton@aol.com
www.derbyshiredalesramblers.org.uk

Derbyshire Family Rambling Group
● The secretary ☎ 01332 841975
or 01332 554756
www.derbyshirefamilyrambling.org.uk

Erewash Ramblers Mr Tony Beardsley,
14 York Avenue, Sandiacre, Nottingham
NG10 5HB ☎ 0115 917 0082
aebbooks@ntlworld.com
erewashramblers.org.uk

DEVON
AREA SECRETARY
Mrs EM Linfoot, 14 Blaydon Cottages,
Blackborough, Cullompton, Devon
EX15 2HJ ☎ 01884 266435
website.lineone.net/~devon.ramblers

GROUP SECRETARIES
Bovey Tracey See www.ramblers.org.uk/
info/localgroups or contact our central
office for current details

Devon Bootlegs Mr Michael Sanderson,
51 Ribston Avenue, Exeter EX1 3QE
☎ 01392 460907
www.geocities.com/devonbootlegs

East Devon Mr Andy Mack,
3 Cadbury Gardens, East Budleigh,
Budleigh Salterton EX9 7EU
☎ 01395 442748.

Exeter & District Mrs JD Fly, Volant,
53 Bilbie Close, Cullompton
EX15 1LG ☎ 01884 839080

Moorland Miss PD Dorrington,
52 Hillside Road, Saltash, Cornwall
PL12 6EY ☎ 01752 843800
pdorrington@wistmans.fsnet.co.uk
website.lineone.net/
~northdevon.ramblers

North Devon Mrs Pauline Newbound,
Mauretania, Town Bridge, Burrington,
Umberleigh EX37 9LT
☎ 01769 520421
website.lineone.net/
~northdevon.ramblers

Plymouth Ms Vereleen Finch,
39 Ponsonby Road, Plymouth PL3 4HP
☎ 01752 263670
www.plymouthramblers.org.uk

South Devon Mr Robert A Woolcott,
The Lodge, 43 Seymour Drive,
Watcombe, Torquay TQ2 8PY
☎ 01803 313430

South Hams Mr Peter Boult,
Bridge Cottage, Frogmore,
Kingsbridge TQ7 2NU
☎ 01548 531701

Tavistock See www.ramblers.org.uk/info/
localgroups or contact our central office for
current details

Teignmouth & Dawlish Mrs Anne
Mccallister, 21 Southdowns Road, Dawlish
EX7 0LB ☎ 01626 864046
anne@mccallister.fsnet.co.uk

Tiverton Mrs MA Cox, 18 Anstey
Crescent, Tiverton EX16 4JR
☎ 01884 256395

Totnes Miss EM Evans,
7 North Street, Totnes TQ9 5NZ
☎ 01803 840403

DORSET

AREA SECRETARY
Mr Jim Scott, Bankside, Holt Lane, Holt, Wimborne, Dorset BH21 7DQ
☎ 01202 885870
www.dorset-ramblers.co.uk

GROUP SECRETARIES
Dorset Young Walkers Ms Cheryl Hadnutt, Flat 4, 51 St Albans Avenue, Bournemouth BH8 9EG
☎ 01202 510592
Dorothy200705@hotmail.com
www.dorsetyoungwalkers.org.uk

East Dorset Mrs Margaret Kettlewell, 12 Limited Road, Bournemouth BH9 1SS
☎ 01202 522467 [membership enquiries, Mr Jim McDonald ☎ 01202 691709]
marg788@ntlworld.com

North Dorset Mr AT Combridge, Green Bushes, North Rd, Sherborne, Dorset DT9 3JN
☎ 01935 812809

South Dorset Mr Stan Faris, 4 Long Acre, New Street, Portland, Dorset DT5 1HH
☎ 01305 820957

West Dorset Mrs Jacqueline Stow, 21 Glebe Court, Beaminster DT8 3EZ
☎ 01308 863081

DURHAM

See Northumbria and North Yorkshire & South Durham Areas

EAST YORKSHIRE & DERWENT

East Riding of Yorkshire, York and the old rural districts of Derwent, Easingwold, Flaxton, Malton, Norton, and Filey; part of Scarborough, Ryedale and Hambleton

AREA SECRETARY
Mr Malcolm Dixon, 8 Horseman Avenue, Copmanthorpe, York YO23 3UF
☎ 01904 706850
m.s.dixon@care4free.net
www.eastyorkshireramblers.org.uk

GROUP SECRETARIES
Beverley See www.ramblers.org.uk/info/localgroups or contact our central office for current details

Driffield Mr John Jefferson, Delamere, 2 Spellowgate, Driffield YO25 5BB
☎ 01377 252412
john@spellowgate.fsnet.co.uk

Get Your Boots On Mr Paul Rhodes, 23 Ash Street, York YO26 4UR
[membership enquiries, Cath Guest
☎ 07749 840885] www.gybo.org.uk

Howden & Goole Mrs Carol Edwards, The Lawns, 72 High Street, Hook, Goole DN14 5NY ce.gv@dsl.pipex.com

Hull & Holderness Mrs Lynn Clark, 169 Hathersage Road, Hull HU8 0EX
☎ 01482 783666
www.hullramblers.org.uk

Pocklington Mr Tony Ashbridge, 4 Burnaby Close, Molescroft, Beverley, East Yorkshire HU17 7ET ☎ 01482 861215
www.pocklingtonramblers.org.uk

Ryedale c/o Mr Mike Mcgrory, 2 Acres Close, Helmsley, North Yorkshire YO62 5DS ☎ 01439 770 940 [membership enquiries, R Fielden ☎ 01482 882499]
rayfielden@rayfielden.karoo.co.uk
www.ryedaleramblers.org.uk

Scarborough & District Mr Dennis Muir, 6 West Avenue, Scalby, Scarborough, North Yorks YO13 0QB ☎ 01723 377222

York Miss Vera Silberberg, 41 North Parade, Bootham, York YO30 7AB
☎ 01904 628134
vsilberberg@fish.co.uk
www.communigate.co.uk/york/yorkramblers2

ESSEX

Essex plus London boroughs of Waltham Forest, Redbridge, Havering, Barking & Dagenham and Newham

AREA SECRETARY
Mr Len Banister, 41 Gordon Avenue, Highams Park, London E4 9QT
☎ 020 8527 8158
Talkingwalking@aol.com

GROUP SECRETARIES
Basildon Greenway Mr Reg Hartley (acting) 57 Grange Avenue, Wickford SS12 0LY [membership enquiries ☎ 01277 625493]

Brentwood Mr Mick Dodge, 27 Bruce Grove, Wickford SS11 8RB
☎ 01268 765475 [membership enquiries ☎ 01277 220781] Mickdodge@aol.com
www.brentwoodramblers.org.uk

Chelmer & Blackwater Mrs Pauline Ellis, 85 Hoynors, Danbury, Chelmsford CM3 4RL ☎ 01245 227727
www.chelmerandblackwater-ramblers.org.uk

Colchester Mr KJ Clark, Vine Cottage, 366 London Road, Stanway, Colchester CO3 8LU
www.colchester-ramblers.ccom.co.uk

East Essex Friends ● Mrs Jan Palmer, 6 Victoria Road, South Woodham Ferrers, Chelmsford CM3 5LR
☎ 01245 321050
www.eastessexfriends.plus.com

Essex Friends ● Mrs Jeanie Lamb, 96 Waverley Crescent, Wickford, Essex SS1 7LS ☎ 01268 768546
jeanie.lamb@homecall.co.uk

Essex Young Ramblers A Vincent-Jones, Flat 14, Nelmes Court, Hornchurch, Essex RM11 2QL ☎ 01708 473253
essexwalkinggroup@tesco.net

Havering & East London
Mr Ken Richards, 26 Arundel Road, Harold Wood, Romford, Essex RM3 0RT ☎ 01708 375559
www.havering-and-eastlondon-ramblers.org.uk

Lea Valley Friends ● Mrs Margaret Brown, 11 Harford Road, London E4 7NQ ☎ 020 8529 1602
www.communigate.co.uk/london/leavalleyfriendswalkinggroup

Maldon & Dengie Hundred
Ms Jill McGregor, 29 Doubleday Drive, Heybridge, Maldon CM9 4TL
☎ 01621 842595
jill.mcgregor@itsyourhome.co.uk
www.maldondengieramblers.org.uk

North West Essex Mr David Harvey, 18 Clydesdale Road, Braintree, Essex CM7 2NX ☎ 01376 342090

Redbridge Ramblers ●
www.redbridgeramblers.org.uk or see www.ramblers.org.uk/info/localgroups or contact our central office for current details

Rochford & Castle Point Mrs Janet Paton, 11 Arundel Gardens, Rayleigh, Essex SS6 9GS ☎ 01268 786620
www.btinternet.com/~bta.wga/rochford-ramblers

South East Essex Mrs Carol Clark, 146 Kenneth Road, Benfleet SS7 3AN
☎ 01268 758855 www.e-cox.fsnet.co.uk

Stort Valley Mr Chris Abbott, 68 Glebelands, Harlow, Essex CM20 2PB
☎ 01279 305 725
chris.abbott@cammarchitects.com
www.geocities.com/stortvalleywalkers

Tendring District Mrs Ann Jones, Wayside, Hall Road, Great Bromley, Colchester CO7 7TS ☎ 01206 230563
www.tendringramblers.co.uk

Thurrock Mr Stan Dyball, 29 Bishops Road, Corringham, Stanford Le Hope, Essex SS17 7HB ☎ 01375 676442

Uttlesford Mrs Ann Corke, Roston House, Dunmow Road, Thaxted, Dunmow CM6 2LU ☎ 01371 830654

West Essex Mr Mike Whitley, 62 Beresford Road, Chingford, London E4 6EF ☎ 0208 8542737
www.westessexramblers.org.uk

GLOUCESTERSHIRE

AREA SECRETARY
Mrs Mavis Rear, 106 Malleson Road, Gotherington, Cheltenham, Glos GL52 9EY ☎ 01242 674470
mavis.rear@tesco.com

GROUP SECRETARIES
Cirencester Mrs Karen Appleby, 46 Rendcomb Drive, Cirencester GL7 1YN
karen.appleby@openwork.uk.com

Cleeve Mr John Gerrard, 20 The Hyde, Winchcombe GL54 5QR
☎ 01242 602229
johngerrard@tesco.net

Forest of Dean Mrs Olive Jeanes, Beechenhurst, Church Road, Undy, Caldicot NP26 3HF ☎ 01633 889460
undyite@yahoo.co.uk
myweb.tiscali.co.uk/deanforest

Gloucester Mrs Rosemary Parker, 62 Ermin Park, Brockworth, Gloucester GL3 4DP ☎ 01452 618404

Gloucestershire Walking Group
Miss Sue Davis, 12 Kings Road,
Cheltenham GL52 6BG ☎ 01242 234996
www.gwg.org.uk

Mid-Gloucestershire Mrs Sheila
Houston, 22 Leckhampton Road,
Cheltenham GL53 0AY ☎ 01242 210398
sheila210398@aol.com

North Cotswold Group See
www.ramblers.org.uk/info/localgroups or
contact our central office for current details

South Cotswold Mr Bernard Smith,
139 Thrupp Lane, Thrupp,
Stroud GL5 2DQ ☎ 01453 884013
smith.bernard@tesco.net
www.southcotswoldramblers.org.uk

HAMPSHIRE

AREA SECRETARY
Mr D Nixon, 27 Brading Avenue,
Southsea, Hants PO4 9QJ ☎ 023 9273
2649 david@nixond2.fsnet.co.uk
www.hants.gov.uk/hampshireramblers

GROUP SECRETARIES
Alton Group See www.ramblers.org.uk/
info/localgroups or contact our central
office for current details

Andover Mr Phil Wood, 9 Kingsmead,
Anna Valley, Andover, Hampshire
SP11 7PN ☎ 01264 710844
www.hants.gov.uk/raag

Eastleigh Mrs PD Beazley, 16 Windover
Close, Bitterne, Southampton SO19 5JS
☎ 023 8043 7443
secretary@eastleighramblers.
wanadoo.co.uk
www.hants.org.uk/eastleighramblers

Hampshire 20s & 30s Walking Group
Miss Gillian Neild, 33 Queens Road, North
Warnborough, Hook RG29 1DN
Neild@verdu.com
www.hants.gov.uk/hantswalk2030

Meon Mrs C Coxwell, 19 New Road,
Fareham, Hants PO16 7SR
☎ 01329 827790

New Forest Group Mrs Audrey Wilson,
16 West Road, Dibden Purlieu,
Southampton SO45 4RJ
☎ 023 8084 6353
www.newforestramblers.org.uk

North East Hants Mrs Mary Hill,
25 Church Road West, Farnborough,
Hants GU14 6QF ☎ 01252 547429

North Hampshire Downs Mr Mike
Taylor, 19 Inkpen Gardens, Lychpit,
Basingstoke, Hants RG24 8YQ
☎ 01256 842468
taylor@mgksb.wanadoo.co.uk
www.hants.org.uk/ramblersnhd

Portsmouth Mrs MG Haly,
95 Winstanley Road, Stamshaw,
Portsmouth PO2 8JS ☎ 023 9269 3874

Romsey Mr Tom W Radford,
67 Rownhams Lane, North Baddesley,
Southampton SO52 9HR ☎ 023 8073
1279 tom.radford@virgin.net
www.romseynet.org.uk/ramblers/
ramblers.htm

South East Hants ● Mr D Nixon,
27 Brading Avenue, Southsea PO4 9QJ
☎ 023 9273 2649
david@nixond2.fsnet.co.uk
www.hants.org.uk/sehantsramblers

Southampton Mr John Catchlove,
4 Sandringham Court, 18 Winn Road,
Southampton SO17 1EN
☎ 023 8055 3883
www.hants.gov.uk/sotonram

Waltham ● Mrs WE Bassom,
3 Mayfair Court, Botley, Southampton
SO30 2GT ☎ 01489 784946

Wessex Weekend Walkers
Ms HE Stacey, 18 Langham Close, North
Baddesley, Southampton SO52 9NT
☎ 07884 486676
www.wessexweekendwalkers.org.uk

Winchester Mrs Penny Farncombe,
7 Fairfax Close, Winchester SO22 4LP
☎ 01962 620126 .
penny.farncombe@ntlworld.com
www.hants.gov.uk/wramblers

HEREFORDSHIRE

AREA SECRETARY
Mr Phil Long, 5 Gillow Cottages,
St Owens Cross, Hereford HR2 8LE
☎ 01989 730697 gillowcot@talktalk.net

GROUP SECRETARIES
Hereford Mr Arthur Lee, 61 Bredon
Grove, Malvern, Worcs WR14 3JS
☎ 01684 575044
arthur@bredon61.fsnet.co.uk

Leadon Vale Ms Isobel Gibson,
41 Jubilee Close, Ledbury HR8 2XA
☎ 01531 635139
isobel.gibson@talk21.com

Mortimer Mrs Pat Bickerton,
35 Mortimer Drive, Orleton,
Ludlow, Shropshire SY8 4JW
☎ 01568 780827
patbickerton@btinternet.com

Ross-on-Wye ● Mr Sam Phillips,
Thelsam, Chapel Road,
Ross-on-Wye HR9 5PR
☎ 01989 563874 samph13@gmail.com

HERTFORDSHIRE &
NORTH MIDDLESEX

Hertfordshire plus London boroughs of
Barnet, Enfield and Haringey

AREA SECRETARY
Mr DS Allard, 8 Chilcourt,
Royston SG8 9DD ☎ 01763 242677
www.ramblers-herts-
northmiddlesex.org.uk

GROUP SECRETARIES
Dacorum Mr Norman Jones,
47 Cedar Walk, Hemel Hempstead
HP3 9ED ☎ 01442 211794
www.dacorumramblers.com

East Hertfordshire Miss PA Hemmings,
16 Smiths Green, Debden,
Saffron Walden CB11 3LP
☎ 01799 541308
www.easthertsramblers.co.uk

Finchley & Hornsey Mrs Julia Haynes,
33 Links Road, Cricklewood, London
NW2 7LE ☎ [membership enquiries
Mrs V Mallindine ☎ 020 8883 8190]
See Area website for further details

North Hertfordshire Mrs Frances Fakes,
Vine Cottage, 31 High Street,
Offley, Hitchin SG5 3AP
☎ 01462 768495
david.v.smith@zen.co.uk
See Area website for further details

North London & South Herts
Mr M Noon, 100 Wynchgate,
London N14 6RN ☎ 020 8886 0348
[membership enquiries ☎ 020 8441 0920]
See Area website for further details

Royston Mrs Katherine Heale,
4 The Brambles, Royston SG8 9NQ
☎ 01763 246988
See Area website for further details

Watford & Three Rivers
Mrs VM Buckley, 4 Firbank Drive,
Watford WD19 4EL
☎ 01923 222591
See Area website for further details

INNER LONDON ●

AREA SECRETARY
Ms Clare Wadd, 8a Archel Road,
London W14 9QH
☎ 020 7386 1835
clare.wadd@virgin.net
www.innerlondonramblers.org.uk

GROUP SECRETARIES
Blackheath Ms D O'Toole,
67 Flintmill Crescent, London SE3 8LU
☎ 020 8319 8593
www.blackheathramblers.org.uk

Hammersmith & Wandsworth
Mrs M Jones, 27 Rannoch Road, London
W6 9SS ☎ 07796 684522 [membership
enquiries Mr Esbester ☎ 020 8646 5545]

Hampstead Mr KD Jones, Flat 4, 144
Agar Grove, Camden, London NW1 9TY
☎ 020 7485 2348 [evenings only]
kevin_jones@onetel.com

Kensington, Chelsea & Westminster
Ms June Mack, 8N Grove End House,
Grove End Road, London NW8 9HN
☎ 020 7289 0305 [membership enquiries,
Susan Gunning ☎ 020 7589 6600]
junemack@grovend.freeserve.co.uk
http://users.whsmithnet.co.uk/
kcw.ramblers

Metropolitan Walkers Mr Graham Pett,
Ground Floor Flat, 32 Leigh Road,
London N5 1AH ☎ 07986 277117
secretary@metropolitan-walkers.org.uk
www.metropolitan-walkers.org.uk

North East London Ms S Milsome,
2 Thames Village, Hartington Road,
London W4 3UE
☎ 020 8994 0171 www.nelr.co.uk

South Bank
www.southbankramblers.org.uk or
see www.ramblers.org.uk/info/
localgroups or contact our central office
for current details

ISLE OF WIGHT
AREA SECRETARY
Mrs Jenny Mitchell, Flat 6, Northcliff Heights, Northcliff Gardens, Shanklin PO37 6ES ☎ 01983 861238 jenreflex@yahoo.co.uk

GROUP SECRETARIES
Isle of Wight Mr David Skelsey, Madeira, Hunts Road, St Lawrence, Ventnor PO38 1XT ☎ 01983 854540 wdskelsey@aol.com

Wight Sole Mr Gary Clarke, 70 Newport Road, Cowes PO31 7PN ☎ 01983 299511 wightsole@yahoo.co.uk www.wightsole.org.uk

KENT
AREA SECRETARY
Mr Arthur Russ, 7 Barnfield Road, Riverhead, Sevenoaks TN13 2AY ☎ 01732 453863 arthur.russ@waitrose.com www.kentramblers.org.uk

GROUP SECRETARIES
Ashford (Kent) Mr PB Whitestone (acting), Summer Hill, Fosten Green, Biddenden Ashford TN27 8ER ☎ 01580 291596 ashford-ramblers.org.uk

Bromley Miss Barbara Phelps, 60 St Georges Road West, Bromley BR1 2NP barbara.phelps@btopenworld.com

Canterbury Mr R Cordell, 162 Broadway, Herne Bay, Kent CT6 8HY ☎ 01227 361 902 raycordell162@hotmail.com

Dartford Ms Joyce Gathercole, 10 Amberley Road, London SE2 0SF ☎ 020 8310 2453

Maidstone Mr PD Royall, 18 Firs Close, Aylesford, Maidstone ME20 7LH ☎ 01622 710782 [membership enquiries, W Williams ☎ 01634 371906] www.maidstoneramblers.org.uk

Medway Mrs DM Ashdown, 94a Hollywood Lane, Wainscott, Rochester ME3 8AR

North West Kent Mr Ken Conie, 63 Crofton Avenue, Orpington BR6 8DY ☎ 01689 851358

Sevenoaks Mrs SE Penzer, 62 Oakhill Road, Sevenoaks, Kent TN13 1NT ☎ 01732 461536

Tonbridge & Malling ● Miss B Stead, 43 Copse Hill, Leybourne, West Malling ME19 5QR

Trailfinders (East Kent) 20s–40s Mr Mike Harries, 99 Newbury Avenue, Maidstone ME16 0RE ☎ 01622 763685 [mobile 07742 444779] mike@harries1962.freeserve.co.uk

Tunbridge Wells Group See www.ramblers.org.uk/info/localgroups or contact our central office for current details

West Kent Walking Group Mr N Houghton, 29 Foley Street, Maidstone, ME14 5BD westkentwalking@yahoo.co.uk www.home.freeuk.net/wkwo

White Cliffs Mrs R Hodges, 25 William Avenue, Folkestone, Kent CT19 5TL ☎ 01303 258022 rhonahodges@hotmail.com

LAKE DISTRICT
Cumbria plus Lancaster district of Lancashire

AREA SECRETARY
Mr Peter Jones, 44 High Fellside, Kendal LA9 4JG ☎ 01539 723705 pcj@ukf.net www.ralakedistrict.ukf.net

GROUP SECRETARIES
Carlisle Mrs Mabel Little, 29 Kelvin Grove, Morton Park, Carlisle CA2 6HE ☎ 01228 529650 See Area website for further details

Furness Mrs Pam Leverton, 6 Churchill Drive, Millom, Cumbria LA18 5DD ☎ 01229 772217 See Area website for further details.

Grange over Sands Mrs Wendy Bowen, Hollyhow, Hazelrigg Lane, Newby Bridge, Ulverston, Cumbria LA12 8NY ☎ 015395 31785 See Area website for further details

Kendal ● Mr Lester Mather, 5 Airethwaite, Kendal, Cumbria LA9 4SP ☎ 01539 731788 walking@ignetics.co.uk See Area website for further details

Lancaster Ms Joy Greenwood, 59 Avondale Road, Edgeley, Stockport, Cheshire SK3 9NY joygreenwood25@yahoo.co.uk

Penrith Mr Dave Dixon, Oaklea, Beacon Edge, Penrith, Cumbria CA11 8BN ☎ 01768 863155 davedixon@talktalk.net www.penrithramblers.org.uk

Summit Good Mr Rob Milligan, 12 Brackenfield, Bowness-on-Windermere LA23 3HL ☎ 07773 896512 robmilligan@ukonline.co.uk www.lakedistrictwalkers.co.uk

West Cumbria Mr Mike Murgatroyd, Huyton Hey, Brundholme Road, Keswick, Cumbria CA12 4NL ☎ 017687 75755 mjmurgatroyd@onetel.co.uk

LANCASHIRE
See Lake District, Mid-Lancashire, and North East Lancashire Areas

LEICESTERSHIRE & RUTLAND
AREA SECRETARY
uk.geocities.com/ramblingjohn/ Leics.html or see www.ramblers.org.uk/ info/localgroups or contact our central office for current details

GROUP SECRETARIES
Coalville ● Mr KM Pare, 103 Tressall Road, Whitwick, Coalville LE67 5QE ☎ 01530 833967 webmail@coalvilleramblers.org.uk www.coalvilleramblers.org.uk

Hinckley Mrs Barbara Elliston, 20 Surrey Close, Burbage, Hinckley LE10 2NY ☎ 01455 238881 www.hinckleyramblers.cjb.net

Leicester Mr TG Bates, 9 Main Street, Scraptoft, Leicester LE7 9TD ☎ 0116 241 8887 http://leicesterramblers.co.uk

Leicestershire & Rutland Walking Group Ms Jo Pagett, 21 Riverside Walk, Asfordby, Melton Mowbray LE14 3SD ☎ 01664 812934 secretary@lrwg.org.uk www.lrwg.org.uk

Loughborough & District Mrs Joyce Noon, 8 Ribble Drive, Barrow-upon-Soar, Loughborough LE12 8LJ ☎ 01509 414519 uk.geocities.com/ramblingjohn/ Loughborough.html

Lutterworth Mrs Y Coulson, 12 Elmhirst Road, Lutterworth LE17 4QB ☎ 01455 552265

Melton Mowbray ● Mrs Gillian Lant, 94 Scalford Road, Melton Mowbray LE13 1JZ ☎ 01664 500516 jbgramblers@btinternet.com www.meltonramblers.org.uk

Rutland Mrs Margaret Wright, 7 Forsells End, Houghton-on-the-Hill LE7 9HQ ☎ 0116 243 2550

LINCOLNSHIRE
AREA SECRETARY
Mr Stuart Parker, 129 Broughton Gardens, Brant Road, Lincoln LN5 8SR ☎ 01522 534655 [includes answerphone] S.w.parker@btinternet.com www.lincscountyramblers.co.uk

GROUP SECRETARIES
Boston Mr RM Warren, 6 Gilder Way, Fishtoft, Boston PE21 0QS ☎ 01205 351854

Gainsborough Mr MA Clapham, 69 Beckett Avenue, Gainsborough DN21 1EJ ☎ 01427 615871

Grantham Mr Derek Booles, 4 Dovedale Close, Grantham NG31 8EA
☎ 01476 403533

Grimsby & Louth Mrs Joan Johnson, 50 Gayton Road, Cleethorpe DN35 0HN
☎ 01472 509396
grimsbylouth.rambers@ntlworld.com
uk.geocities.com/tjrambler

Horncastle Mr Gordon Vessey, 51 Elm Crescent, Burgh Le Marsh, Skegness PE24 5EG ☎ 01754 810049
See Area website for further details

Lincoln ● Mrs Mary Glen, 130 Fulmar Road, Harts Holme Fields, Lincoln LN6 0LA
☎ 01522 689387
See Area website for further details

Lincolnshire Walking Group
Mr Stuart Parker, 129 Broughton Gardens, Brant Road, Lincoln LN5 8SR
☎ 01522 534655 [includes answerphone]
S.w.parker@btinternet.com
www.lincswalkinggroup.org.uk

Scunthorpe Mrs Janet Atkinson, 30 Conference Court, Scunthorpe DN16 3SZ ☎ 01724 350118
See Area website for further details

Skegness Mr A Malcolm, 9 Winston Drive, Skegness PE25 2RE
☎ 01754 899878
www.skegnessramblers.gothere.uk.com

Sleaford ● Mr Dave Houghton, 19 Eastgate, Heckington, Sleaford NG34 9RB ☎ 01529 461220
See Area website for further details

Spalding Mrs WA Hicks, 2 Jubilee Close, Spalding PE11 1YD ☎ 01775 725531
www.spaldingramblers.org.uk

Stamford Mrs Fran Jacklin, 15 Perth Road, Stamford PE9 2TX
☎ 01780 752736
fran@jacklin-stamford.fsnet.co.uk
See Area website for further details

LONDON

For Inner London boroughs see Inner London Area, for Outer London boroughs see Buckinghamshire & West Middlesex, Essex, Hertfordshire & North Middlesex, Kent, and Surrey Areas

MANCHESTER & HIGH PEAK

Former Greater Manchester plus High Peak district of Derbyshire

AREA SECRETARY
See www.ramblers.org.uk/info/localgroups or contact our central office for current details

GROUP SECRETARIES
Bolton Mrs Pat Hall, 92 Bradshaw Road, Bolton BL2 3EW
homepage.ntlworld.com/boltonramblers

Bury Mrs Megan Smith, 87 Bankhouse Road, Bury, Lancashire BL8 1DY
☎ 0161 764 8598

Mad Walkers (Manchester & District) Mr John Ireland, 13 Rawson Road, Bolton BL1 4JG ☎ 01204 496310
johnaj.ireland@virgin.net
www.madwalkers.org.uk

New Mills ● Mr John Biggins, 39 Grasmere Crescent, High Lane, Stockport SK6 8AL ☎ 0161 4277303
www.nmramblers.freeserve.co.uk

Oldham Ms Janet Hewitt, 2 Hillside Avenue, Carrbrook, Stalybridge, Cheshire SK15 3NE ☎ 01457 834769
www.oldhamramblers.org.uk

Rochdale ● Mrs S Blatcher, 5 Enfield Close, Rochdale, Lancashire OL11 5RT
☎ 01706 641041

Stockport Mrs L Sangster, 98 Mile End Lane, Great Moor, Stockport SK2 6BP
☎ 0161 4838774

Wigan & District Mr K Rourke, 8 Hawthorn Avenue, Orrell, Wigan WN5 8NQ ☎ 01942 203265

MERSEYSIDE AND WEST CHESHIRE ●
Merseyside plus Chester and Ellesmere Port districts of Cheshire

AREA SECRETARY
Miss GF Thayer, 53 Bramwell Avenue, Prenton, Wirral CH43 0RQ
☎ 0151 6089472

GROUP SECRETARIES
Cestrian (Chester) Ms F Parsons, 32 Wetherby Way, Little Sutton, South Wirral CH66 4NY ☎ 0151 3391178

Liverpool Mrs M Hems, 19 Moorcroft Road, Liverpool L18 9UG ☎ 07980 856101 www.liverpoolramblers.co.uk

Merseyside 20s–30s Walkers Group
Ms B Roche, 212 Pilch Lane, Liverpool L14 0JQ ☎ 07880 535221
bernie_roche@hotmail.com
www.fillyaboots.org.uk

Southport Mr D Wall, 22 Dunbar Crescent, Southport, Merseyside PR8 3AB
☎ 01704 579924

St Helens Mrs C Walsh, 13 Owen Street, Toll Bar, St Helens WA10 3DW
☎ 01744 601608

Wirral Mr Gordon Clarke, 19 Stevenson Drive, Wirral CH63 9AH ☎ 0151 334 3435

MID LANCASHIRE
Lancashire; Blackpool, Fylde, Preston, South Ribble, Chorley, West Lancashire and Wyre boroughs

AREA SECRETARY
Mr D Kelly, 4 Buttermere Close, Bamber Bridge, Preston PR5 4RT ☎ 01772 312027
www.lancashire-ramblers.org.uk

GROUP SECRETARIES
Chorley www.chorleyramblers.com or see www.ramblers.org.uk/info/localgroups or contact our central office for current details

Fylde Group Mr David Stokes, 7 Cedar Close, Newton With Scales, Kirkham PR4 3TZ ☎ 01772 671134
www.fylderamblers.org.uk

Garstang & District Mrs C Stenning, 20 Meadowcroft Avenue, Catterall, Garstang PR3 1ZH ☎ 01995 601478

Lancashire Walking Group Mrs R Kirk, 68 Broadriding Road, Shevington, Wigan WN6 8EX ruth.kirk@blueyonder.co.uk
www.lypwc.org.uk

Preston Mr A Manzie, 3 Ruthin Court, Dunbar Road, Ingol, Preston, Lancs PR2 3YE ☎ 01772 736467
prestonra@prestonra.co.uk
www.prestonra.co.uk

South Ribble Mr BA Kershaw, 2 Moss Way, New Longton, Preston PR4 4ZQ
nursic54@tiscali.co.uk

West Lancashire Mr WG Wright, 49 River View, Tarleton, Preston PR4 6ED
☎ 01772 812034 wgwright@tesco.com
www.westlancsramblers.org.uk

NORFOLK
AREA SECRETARY
Mr Derek Goddard (acting), 49 Lindford Drive, Eaton, Norwich NR4 6LR
☎ 01603 612644
dgoddard@my-emails.com
http://homepage.ntlworld.com/bcmoore/NorfolkRA

GROUP SECRETARIES

Fakenham See www.ramblers.org.uk/info/localgroups or contact our central office for current details

Great Yarmouth Mrs Annie Sharrock, Aldebaran, The Street, West Somerton, Norfolk NR29 4EA ☎ 01493 393671 annie.pas@btopenworld.com

King's Lynn Ms Lynda Jones, 8 Lancaster Drive, Long Sutton, Spalding PE12 9BD ☎ 01406 362254

Mid-Norfolk Mrs Carol Jackson, Mandola, Mill Street, Elsing, Dereham, Norfolk NR20 3EJ ☎ 01362 637752

Norwich Group Mr Derek Goddard, 49 Lindford Drive, Eaton, Norwich NR4 6LR ☎ 01603 612644 dgoddard@my-emails.com See Area website for further details

Sheringham & District Group ● Mrs Edwina Moore, 20 Creake Road, Sculthorpe, Fakenham NR21 9NG ☎ 01328 862771

Southern Norfolk Mrs Jean Aldridge, Wacton Common, Long Stratton, Norwich NR15 2UP ☎ 01508 530289

Wensum Mr Tony Smith, 3 Priors Drive, Old Catton, Norwich NR6 7LJ ☎ 01603 423085

NORTH AND MID CHESHIRE

The district of Vale Royal and the western part of Macclesfield district

AREA SECRETARY

Mrs Daphne Armitage, Birchtree Bungalow, Red Lane, Appleton, Warrington WA4 5AB ☎ 01925 268540 nmc-ramblers.org.uk

GROUP SECRETARIES

Halton Mr Norman Lidbury, 50 Deepdale Drive, Rainhill, Prescot L35 4NW ☎ 0151 4260925 n.lidbury@blueyonder.co.uk See Area website for further details

Cheshire Walkers Mrs Sarah Talbot, 217 Edgeley Road, Stockport SK3 0TL www.cheshirewalkers.org.uk

Vale Royal and Knutsford Mrs Daphne Armitage, Birchtree Bungalow, Red Lane, Appleton, Warrington WA4 5AB

Warrington Mr M & Mrs B Elebert, Yellow Lodge, Park Lane, Higher Walton, Warrington WA4 5LW bernielebert@hotmail.com See Area website for further details

NORTH EAST LANCASHIRE

Lancashire; Ribble Valley, Pendle, Burnley, Rossendale, Blackburn and Hyndburn districts

AREA SECRETARY

Mrs Sue Baxendale, 101 Blackburn Road, Clayton-Le Moors, Accrington BB5 5JT ☎ 01254 235049

GROUP SECRETARIES

Blackburn & Darwen Miss Glenda Brindle, 103 School Lane, Guide, Blackburn BB1 2LW ☎ 01254 671269

Burnley & Pendle Mrs M Broadley, 18 Station Road, Padiham BB12 8EB ☎ 01282 778 153

Clitheroe ● Mr Ben Brown, 2 Chorlton Terrace, Barrow, Whalley, Clitheroe, Lancs BB7 9AR ☎ 01254 822851

Hyndburn Mr Trevor Whittaker, 25 Harwood New Road, Great Harwood, Nr Blackburn BB6 7TD www.hyndburnramblers.co.uk

North East Lancashire 20s–30s Group Mr John Haworth, 32 Stanhill Lane, Oswaldtwistle, Accrington BB5 4QF www.nelancs20s30s.co.uk

Rossendale Mr Peter Aizlewood, Lynwood, 265 Haslingden Old Road, Rossendale BB4 8RR ☎ 01706 215085 peter.aizlewood@ntlworld.co

NORTH YORKS & SOUTH DURHAM

Cleveland; Co Durham except Derwentside, Durham and Chester-le-Street districts; North Yorkshire; present Richmondshire district and the former urban and rural districts of Bedale, Helmsley, Kirkbymoorside, Northallerton, Pickering, Stokesley, Thirsk and Whitby now forming part of the Hambleton and Ryedale districts, see also West Riding Area; East Yorks and Derwent Area

AREA SECRETARY

Dr David Leyshon, 11 Ripley Road, Norton, Stockton On Tees TS20 1NX ☎ 01642 553796 david.leyshon@btinternet.com www.bigwig.net/nysd_ramblers

GROUP SECRETARIES

Barnard Castle Mrs E Vlaming-Helmer, Hollin Croft, Romaldkirk, Barnard Castle, Co Durham DL12 9EL ☎ 01833 650192 www.barnardcastleramblers.org.uk

Cleveland ● Mr Alan Patterson, 141 Castle Road, Redcar TS10 2NF ☎ 01642 474864

Crook & Weardale Mrs K Berry, 11 Wood Square, Bishop Auckland, Co. Durham DL14 6QQ ☎ 01388 608979 http://members.aol.com/crookramblers

Darlington Mr Bryan Spark, 3 Thirlmere Grove, West Auckland, Bishop Auckland, Co Durham DL14 9LW ☎ 01388 834213 bspark@addisonandco.co.uk

Darlington Dales & Hills Mr Simon Cummings, 20 Burnhope, Newton Aycliffe DL5 7ER ☎ 01325 320911 [evenings only] darlingtonhiking@hotmail.co.uk www.darlingtonhiking.co.uk

Northallerton Group web.onetel.net.uk/~murraykent or see www.ramblers.org.uk/info/localgroups or contact our central office for current details

Richmondshire Mrs V Darwin, 4 Sycamore Avenue, Richmond, North Yorks DL10 4BN ☎ 01748 822845

NORTHAMPTONSHIRE

AREA SECRETARY

Mrs Pamela Barrett, 132 Wellingborough Road, Earls Barton, Northampton NN6 0JS ☎ 01604 812556 barrett670@aol.com www.northants-area-ra.info

GROUP SECRETARIES

Daventry Mrs Penny Alexander, 14 Coronation Road, Newnham, Daventry NN11 3EY ☎ 01327 310945

Kettering ● Mrs Rira East, 38 Hawthorn Avenue, Mawsley NN14 1TH info@kra-g.org www.kra-g.org

Northampton Miss J Hammond, 37 Knights Court, Little Billing, Northampton NN3 9AT ☎ 01604 518517 www.northamptonra.org.uk

Northants 20s & 30s Walking Group Mr John Hadley, 19 St Peters Avenue, Rushden, Northants NN10 6XW secretary@letsgetreadytoramble.or.uk www.letsgetreadytoramble.org.uk

Wellingborough & District Mrs Pamela Barrett, 132 Wellingborough Road, Earls Barton, Northampton NN6 0JS ☎ 01604 812556 barrett670@aol.com www.wellingboroughramblers.org.uk

NORTHUMBERLAND

See Northumbria Area

NORTHUMBRIA ●

AREA SECRETARY

Mrs Judith Taylor, 2 The Poplars, Gosforth, Newcastle-upon-Tyne NE3 4AE ☎ 0191 285 3482 robt_taylor@lineone.net northern.ra-area.org.uk

GROUP SECRETARIES

Alnwick Mr Colin Mcclure, The Acorns, Acklington Road, North Broomhill, Morpeth NE65 9XD ☎ 01661 822929 colsy195@hotmail.co.uk

Berwick Mr John Bamford, 112 Main Street, Spittal, Berwick-on-Tweed TD15 1RD ☎ 01289 302559

Chester le Street Mr Brian Stout, 37 Kirkstone Drive, Carrville, Durham City DH1 1AH ☎ 0191 3864089

Derwentside Mrs Sheila Jeffreys, 7 Ferndene Court, Moor Road South, Newcastle-upon-Tyne, Tyne & Wear NE3 1NN ☎ 0191 285 8442 Sheila@jeffreyss.fsnet.co.uk

Durham City Mr Cliff Ludman, 5 Church Street, Durham DH1 3DG ☎ 0191 386 6886 cliff.ludman@ramblers.durhamcity.org.uk

RAMBLERS GROUPS & PUBLICATIONS

Gateshead Mrs Hilary Clark,
15 Shibdon Park View,
Blaydon, Tyne & Wear
NE21 5HA ☎ 0191 4143643

Hexham Mrs Rosalind Blaylock,
10 Quatre Bras, Hexham,
Northumberland NE46 3JY
☎ 01434 604639

Morpeth Mrs Margaret Siggins,
17 Kingswell, Carlisle Lea, Morpeth,
Northumberland NE61 2TY
☎ 01670 518031

Northumbria Family Walking Group
● Mrs Liz Smith, 18 Bath Terrace,
Newcastle-upon-Tyne NE3 1UH
☎ 0191 2132102

Northumbria Short Circuits ●
Mrs Mary Moore, 2 Kingsway Avenue,
Gosforth, Newcastle-upon-Tyne NE3 2HS
☎ 0191 285 6890
mtmoore@waitrose.com

Northumbria Walking Group
Ms Gill Atkinson
northumbria_walking_group@hotmail.com

Ponteland Mr Colin Braithwaite,
105 Western Way, Ponteland, Newcastle-
upon-Tyne NE20 9LY ☎ 01661 822929

Sunderland Mrs Pat Jackson,
73 Houghton Road, Hetton-le-Hole,
Houghton Le Spring DH5 9PQ
☎ 0191 526 0434

Tyneside Mrs Pennie Porter, 4 Angerton
Gardens, Fenham, Newcastle-upon-Tyne
NE5 2JB penny@angerton.fsnet.co.uk

NOTTINGHAMSHIRE
AREA SECRETARY
Mr Rod Fillingham, 1 Albany Close,
Arnold, Nottingham NG5 6JP ☎ 0115
9204066 www.nottsarearamblers.co.uk

GROUP SECRETARIES
Broxtowe Dr Alan Brittain,
23 Banks Road, Toton,
Nottingham NG9 6HE ☎ 0115 9720 258
harveybrittain@yahoo.co.uk
www.broxtoweramblers.co.uk

Collingham Ms Anne Burns, 69 Harcourt
Street, Newark NG24 1RG
anneburns39@ntlworld.com

Dukeries Mr A Gamble,
35 Greenwood Crescent,
Boughton, Newark NG22 9HX
☎ 01623 861376

Gedling ● Mrs Jenny Fillingham, 1 Albany
Close, Arnold, Nottingham NG5 6JP
☎ 0115 9204066
www.innotts.co.uk/ramblers/

Hucknall Ms Sarah Smith, 306 Belper
Road, Stanley Common, Ilkeston
DE7 6FY ☎ 07968 267846
sarahs306@aol.com

**Mansfield & Sherwood
Walking Group** Mr Malc Lawson,
2 Northfield Drive, Mansfield,
Nottingham NG18 3DD
☎ 01623 460941
secretary@mansfield-ramblers.co.uk
www.mansfield-ramblers.co.uk

Newark Mr Richard Legg, 43 Ropewalk,
Southwell, Nottingham NG25 0AL
☎ 01636 812318
www.newarkramblers.co.uk

Nottingham Mrs Margo Cameron,
46 Sandford Road, Nottingham NG3 6AJ
☎ 0115 8718927

Notts & Derby Walking Group
Ms Wendy Ferguson, 10 Bishops Gate,
Woodville, Swadlincote DE11 8DT
Wendyferguson196@hotmail.com
www.ndwg.co.uk

Notts Weekend Walkers Mr Kevin
Matthews, 44 The Downs, Silverdale,
Nottingham NG11 7DY
☎ 0115 914 5653
notts.walkers@ntlworld.com

Ravenshead Mr Allan Rogers, 63 Quarry
Road, Ravenshead, Nottingham NG15
9AP ☎ 01623 797321

Retford Mrs Judith Anson, Townrows
Farm, High Street, Elkesley DN22 8AJ
☎ 01777 838763

Rushcliffe Mr Richard Parrey,
61 West Leake Road, Kingston On Soar
NG11 0DN ☎ 0115 9830730
richard.parrey@btinternet.com
www.theburks.org/ramblers

Southwell Ms Margaret Macdonald,
4 Waterside, North Muskham, Newark,
NG23 6FD ☎ 01636 677395

Vale of Belvoir Mrs Linda Pitt,
4 Rockingham Grove, Bingham,
Nottingham NG13 8RY
☎ 01949 876146

Worksop Mrs Cherry Keates,
46 Snipe Park Road, Bircotes, Doncaster
DN11 8DG

OXFORDSHIRE
AREA SECRETARY
Mr Patrick Lonergan, 35 Cherwell Close,
Abingdon OX14 3TD ☎ 01235 202784
patlon@ntlworld.com
www.ramblers-oxon.org.uk

GROUP SECRETARIES
Bicester & Kidlington Mr Colin
Morgan, 11 Spruce Drive, Bicester
OX26 3YE ☎ 01869 369603

Cherwell Ms Hazel Lister, 3 Bowling
Green, Farthinghoe, Brackley NN13 5PQ
☎ 01295 710227
hazel@lister8280.fsbusiness.co.uk

Didcot & Wallingford Mrs V Tilling,
The Cedars, Brookfield Close, Wallingford
OX10 9EQ ☎ 01491 839221
janicetilling@aol.com

Henley & Goring See www.ramblers.
org.uk/info/localgroups or contact our
central office for current details

Oxford Mrs Moissa Perot, 35 Boulter
Street, Oxford OX4 1AX

Oxon 20s & 30s Walking Group
Miss Sam Band, 4 Chestnut Road, Oxford
OX2 9EA www.oxon2030walkers.org

Thame & Wheatley Mrs JE Noyce,
27 Worminghall Road, Ickford, Aylesbury,
Bucks HP18 9JB ☎ 01844 339969

Vale of White Horse Mr Patrick
Lonergan, 35 Cherwell Close, Abingdon,
Oxon OX14 3TD ☎ 01235 202784
patlon@ntlworld.com

West Oxfordshire Mr Clive Jones,
49 Harefields, Oxford OX2 8HG
☎ 01865 514663

SHROPSHIRE
AREA SECRETARY
Mrs Marion Law, 3 Mead Way,
Shifnal, Shropshire TF11 9QB
☎ 01952 462855
marionlaw@rapidial.co.uk
www.shropshireramblers.org.uk

GROUP SECRETARIES
Market Drayton Mrs Heather Morris,
10 Golf Links Lane, Wellington,
Telford TF1 2DS
☎ 01952 242910

Oswestry Mrs Alison Parker,
11 St Johns Hill, Ellesmere SY12 0EY
☎ 01691 623026

Shrewsbury & Mid-Shropshire Mrs
Chris Cluley, Birches Farm, Clun, Craven
Arms SY7 8NL ☎ 01588 640243

Shropshire Young Ramblers
Mr Paul Tanner, 4 Bridge Way, Shawbury,
Shrewsbury SY4 4PG
paul.tanner@rnac.com

South Shropshire ● Ms S Sharp,
Brookside, Eagle Lane, Cleobury Mortimer,
Kidderminster DY14 8RA
☎ 01299 271099
susan.sharp@eggconnect.ne

Telford & East Shropshire Mrs Anne
Sumner, 18 Shrewsbury Road, Edgmond,
Newport TF10 8HU ☎ 01952 810444

SOMERSET
AREA SECRETARY
Ms Mary Henry, 22 Linden Grove,
Taunton TA1 1EF ☎ 01823 333369
www.somersetramblers.org.uk

GROUP SECRETARIES
Clevedon Mrs Sue Shewan,
25 Honeylands, Portishead, Bristol
BS20 6RB ☎ 01275 848075

Family Countryside Walkers ●
Ms Mary Henry, 22 Linden Grove,
Taunton, TA1 1EF ☎ 01823 333369

Mendip Mrs Valerie Evans, Brook
Cottage, Cannards Grave Road, Shepton
Mallet BA4 5RE ☎ 01749 347124
www.mendipramblers.co.uk

Sedgemoor Mrs Peggy Frampton, 15
Church House Road, Berrow, Burnham-
on-Sea TA8 2NG ☎ 01278 783270

Somerset Walking & Activity Group
www.funwithswag.org.uk or see
www.ramblers.org.uk/info/localgroups or
contact our central office for current details

South Somerset ● Mr Ian Rendall,
3a Tintern, Abbey Manor Park, Yeovil
BA21 3SJ ☎ 01935 421235
www.somersetramblers.co.uk/
southsom.htm

Taunton Deane Mr Robert Camp,
7 Wilton Close Taunton, TA1 4EZ
☎ 01823 331058
www.tauntonramblers.org.uk

West Somerset Mr Geoffrey Taylor,
1 Culvercliffe Court, Minehead TA24 5UP
☎ 01643 705288
geoff@woodhouse.co.uk

Woodspring Ms D Smith, 50 Rowan
Place, Weston-super-Mare BS24 7RQ
☎ 01934 518082.

SOUTH & EAST CHESHIRE

Cheshire; Crewe & Nantwich and
Congleton districts plus eastern section
of Macclesfield district

AREA SECRETARY See www.ramblers.
org.uk/info/localgroups or contact our
central office for current details

GROUP SECRETARIES
Congleton Group See www.ramblers.
org.uk/info/localgroups or contact our
central office for current details.

East Cheshire Mr Ian Mabon,
Highwinds, 15 Churchfields, Bowdon,
Altrincham, WA14 3PL
☎ 0161 928 3437 [fax also]
ian.hilltop@zetnet.co.uk

South Cheshire Mr P Callery,
45 Broughton Lane, Wistaston,
Crewe CW2 8JR ☎ 01270 568714
www.ramblerssouthcheshire.org.uk

SOUTH YORKS & NE DERBYSHIRE

Former South Yorkshire plus North East
Derbyshire; Chesterfield, and Bolsover
districts of Derbyshire

AREA SECRETARY
www.syned-ramblers.org.uk or see
www.ramblers.org.uk/info/localgroups or
contact our central office for current details.

GROUP SECRETARIES
Barnsley & Penistone Mrs C Wood,
25 Cloverlands Drive, Mapplewell,
Barnsley S75 6EB ☎ 01226 384041

Bolsover District Ms Daeana Walker,
53 Somerset Drive, Brimington,
Chesterfield S43 1DL
☎ 078170 45266
daeanawalker@yahoo.co.uk
**Chesterfield & North East
Derbyshire**
Mrs Gill Stone, Garth Derwen,
195 Old Road, Chesterfield,
Derbyshire S40 3QH ☎ 01246 566020
family@garthderwen.freeserve.co.uk
Chesterfield 20s & 30s Miss Rachael
Burnett, 29 Cross London Street, New
Whittington, Chesterfield S43 2AG
www.chesterfieldyoungramblers.co.uk
Dearne Valley Group Ms Pauline
Gibbons (acting) ☎ 01709 571169
www.dearnevalleyramblers.org.uk
Doncaster ● Mr David Gadd,
5 Wong Lane, Tickhill,
Doncaster DN11 9NH
david.gadd5@btinternet.com
Rotherham Metro District
Mrs Ann Balding, 2 Calcot Green,
Swinton, Mexbrough,
South Yorks S64 8SY
Sheffield ● Mr Peter Wood, 17
Woodend Drive, Sheffield,
South Yorks S6 5HB
☎ 0114 234 1217
woodlandview17@hotmail.com
www.sheffield.ramblers.care4free.net
Sheffield Walking Group Ms D Terry,
38 Linaker Road, Sheffield S6 5DT
www.sheffieldwalkinggroup.org.uk

STAFFORDSHIRE

Staffordshire plus Dudley, Sandwell,
Walsall and Wolverhampton districts of
former West Midlands

AREA SECRETARY
http://homepages.tesco.net/~staffsra,
www.ramblers.org.uk/info/localgroups or
contact our central office for current details

GROUP SECRETARIES
Biddulph www.biddulphra.freeuk.com
or see www.ramblers.org.uk/
info/localgroups or contact our central
office for current details

Bilston Mrs J Tyler, 50 Wellington Place,
Wednesfield, Willenhall, West Midlands
WV13 3AB ☎ 01902 633849
www.bilstonramblers.org.uk
**Black Country 20s & 30s Walking
Group** Ms Sarah Andrews, 33 Lapwing
Close, Cheslyn Hay, Walsall WS6 7LL
www.blackcountrywalkinggroup.netfirms.com
Chase & District ● Mr Roy Roobottom,
19 Winchester Court, Wildwood, Stafford
ST17 4TB ☎ 01785 663131
royroobottom@yahoo.co.uk
East Staffordshire ● Mrs Jane King,
39 Faraday Avenue, Stretton, Burton-on-
Trent DE13 0FX ☎ 01283 543483
Leek Mrs Shirley Lunt, 17 Rennie
Crescent, Cheddleton, Leek ST13 7HD
☎ 01538 360907 www.raleek.co.uk
Lichfield Mr Malcolm Day, 2 Fontenaye
Road, Coton Green, Tamworth B79 8JZ
☎ 01827 700590
Mid Staffordshire Mrs Shirley Benn,
11 Porlock Avenue, Stafford, Staffs
ST17 0HS ☎ 01785 603646
homepage.ntlworld.com/brian.benn/ra
Sandwell Miss V Dubois, 47 Gladys
Road, Smethwick B67 5AW ☎ 0121
4296148 www.sandwellramblers.org.uk
Staffordshire Walkers Mr Steven
McLuckie, 9 Leacroft Road, Penkridge,
Stafford ST19 5BU
www.staffs-walkers.org.uk
Stoke/Newcastle Mr Graham Evans,
65 Pacific Road, Trentham, Stoke-on-Trent
ST4 8RS ☎ 01782 642872 [membership
enquiries ☎ 01782 787948]
http://hyperhelp.co.uk/ra/index.htm
Stone Mr G Greensides, Ambleside,
111 Lichfield Road, Stone ST15 8QD
☎ 01785 813067 george.greensides@
tesco.net www.stoneramblers.com
Stourbridge ● Mrs D Pearce, 17 Ibstock
Drive, Stourbridge, West Midlands
DY8 1NW ☎ 01384 359463
Walsall Mrs Alice Harrison,
30 Clarendon Place, Pelsall, Walsall, West
Midlands WS3 4NL ☎ 01922 683411
Wolverhampton Mr Geoff Lewis,
73 Albert Road, Wolverhampton
WV6 0AG ☎ 01902 422531
geoff@lewis02.co.uk
wton-ra.atspace.com

SUFFOLK

AREA SECRETARY
Mr Phil Snelling, 12 Market Place,
Lavenham CO10 9QZ ☎ 01787 248079
phil.snelling@amec.com
www.suffolkramblers.org.uk

GROUP SECRETARIES
Alde Valley Ms Anne Hubert-Chibnall,
133 High Street, Wickham Market,
Woodbridge IP13 0RD ☎ 01728 747966
tulasim@visa.com
Bury St Edmunds Mrs JM Bolwell, 42
Cloverfields, Sandpit Lane, Thurston, Bury
St. Edmunds IP31 3TJ ☎ 01359 231301
www.burystedmundsramblers.org.uk

Explore
Lee Valley Regional Park

The Park is a regional and national destination for sport and leisure stretching for 10,000 acres between Ware in Hertfordshire down to the river Thames at the East India Dock Basin, and provides activities which suit all ages, tastes and abilities.

For more information all about the Park and what you can do call 0845 677 0601* or visit

www.leevalleypark.org.uk

*local rate number

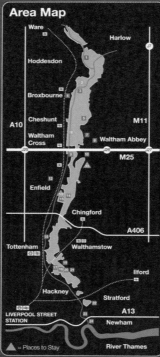

Area Map

Ware
Harlow
Hoddesdon
Broxbourne
Cheshunt
M11
Waltham Cross
A10
Waltham Abbey
M25
Enfield
Chingford
A406
Tottenham
Walthamstow
Ilford
Hackney
Stratford
A13
LIVERPOOL STREET STATION
Newham
River Thames

▲ = Places to Stay

1. Rye Meads Nature Reserve & Rye House Gate
2. Lee Valley Caravan Park, Dobbs Weir
3. Lee Valley Boat Centre & Lee Valley Leisure Po
4. The Old Mill & Meadows
5. Lee Valley Park Farms
6. YHA Lee Valley Cheshunt
7. Cornmill Meadows Dragonfly Sanctuary
8. Abbey Gardens
9. Rammey Marsh
10. Gunpowder Park
11. Lee Valley Camping & Caravan Park, Sewardst
12. Myddelton House Gardens
13. Lee Valley Camping & Caravan Park, Picketts L
14. Lee Valley Athletics Centre
15. Picketts Lock Golf Course
16. Tottenham Marshes
17. Walthamstow Marsh Nature Reserve
18. Lee Valley Ice Centre
19. Lee Valley Riding Centre
20. Middlesex Filter Beds & Nature Reserve
21. Lee Valley WaterWorks Nature Reserve & Golf
22. Three Mills
23. Bow Creek Ecology Park
24. East India Bock Basin

Lee Valley Park

Open spaces and sporting place

Ipswich & District ● Mr John Laycock, 8 Church Lane, Henley, Ipswich IP6 0RQ
☎ 01473 831236
laycock.family@btinternet.com
www.ipswichramblers.co.uk

Newmarket & District
Mrs CC Lee, Corner Cottage, Sharps Lane, Horringer, Bury St Edmunds IP29 5PW
☎ 01284 735971 cclwalk@aol.com
www.newmarketramblers.co.uk

Stour Walking Group
Miss Cheryl Nice, 16 Prior Close, Halstead CO9 1AX
☎ 01787 477706 or 07974 010889
www.stourwalkinggroup.co.uk

Stowmarket Mrs JJ Thompson, 2 Harvest Close, Haughley, Stowmarket IP14 3PZ
www.stowmarketramblers.org.uk

Sudbury Mrs I Kay, 6 Chaplin Walk, Great Cornard, Sudbury CO10 0YT
☎ 01787 370019
ingrid@ingridkay.wanadoo.co.uk
www.sudburyra.freeserve.co.uk

Waveney Group Mrs Anne Crosland, 16 Holmere Drive, Church Meadow, Halesworth IP19 8TR
☎ 01986 873662
croslandanne@btinternet.com

SURREY

Surrey plus London boroughs of Richmond, Kingston, Merton, Sutton and Croydon

AREA SECRETARY
Mr Graham Butler, 1 Leaside Court, Lower Luton Road, Harpenden AL5 5BX
☎ 01582 767062
Butlergc1@aol.com

GROUP SECRETARIES
Croydon Mr W Haug, 22 Danvers Way, Caterham CR3 5FJ ☎ 01883 344011
walter.haug@virgin.net
www.croydonramblers.org.uk

East Surrey Group Mrs Lisa Dunning, 143 Hillbury Road, Warlingham CR6 9TG
www.eastsurreyramblers.org.uk

Epsom & Ewell ● Mr David Newman, 56a Acacia Grove, New Malden KT3 3BU
☎ 020 8949 3471
david.mayumi@virgin.net
www.epsomandewellramblers.co.uk

Farnham & District Ms Gaynor Ross, 10 Ridgway Hill Road, Farnham GU9 8LS
☎ 01252 722930
gaynorross@ferdys.freeserve.co.uk
www.farnhamramblers.org.uk

Godalming & Haslemere
Mrs Cynthia Chard, 1 Hill House, Ockford Road, Godalming GU7 1QX
☎ 01483 416907
www.godalmingandhaslemereramblers.org.uk

Guildford Mr Philp Mansley, 40 Guildown Road, Guildford GU2 4EY
☎ 01483 854451
www.guildfordramblers.org.uk

Kingston ● Mr M Lake, 87 Porchester Road, Kingston-upon-Thames KT1 3PW
☎ 0208 541 3437
martin.h2o@tiscali.co.uk
www.geocities.com/kingstonramblers

Mole Valley Mrs J Kucera, 120 Carlton Road, Reigate RH2 0JF ☎ 01737 765158 [membership enquiries Mrs Marles ☎ 01372 454012]
myweb.tiscali.co.uk/molevalleyramblers

Reigate Mr Glyn Jones, 12 Briars Wood, Horley RH6 9UE ☎ 01293 773198
glynjones@siemens.com
www.reigateramblers.org.uk

Richmond Mr W Westcott, 47 Capel Gardens, Pinner HA5 5RF
☎ 020 8429 0886 [membership enquiries, Ms Jennifer Berry ☎ 020 8943 0836]
ramblers@hampton-hill.fsnet.co.uk
www.richmondramblers.co.uk

Staines Pat Pratley, 76 Hetherington Rd, Charlton Village, Shepperton TW17 0SW
☎ 01932 711355
www.stainesramblers.co.uk

Surrey Area Weekend Walkers
Mrs Sue Ward saww_enquiries@hotmail.com www.saww.org.uk or see www.ramblers.org.uk/info/localgroups or contact our central office for current details

Surrey Heath Mrs C Norris, 11 Warwick Close, Camberley GU15 1ES
☎ 01276 26821

Surrey Under 40s Miss Geraldine Thompson, 74 Tanyard Close, Brighton Road, Horsham, West Sussex RH13 5BW
☎ 01403 240168
surrey_young-ramblers@hotmail.com
www.surreyyoungwalkers.org.uk

Sutton & Wandle Valley ● Peter Rogers, 8 Claygate Court, All Saints Road, Sutton SM1 3DB ☎ 020 8641 4339 [membership enquiries ☎ 020 8643 2605] peterogs@aol.com
www.suttonandwandlevalleyramblers.org.uk

Woking & District ● web.ukonline.co.uk/wokingramblers or see www.ramblers.org.uk/info/localgroups or contact our central office for current details

SUSSEX
AREA SECRETARY
Mr Nigel Sloan, Kervesridge, Kerves Lane, Horsham RH13 6ES
☎ 01403 258055 [membership enquiries Anne Parker ☎ 01243 536080]
nigelsloan2001@yahoo.co.uk
www.sussex-ramblers.org.uk

GROUP SECRETARIES
Arun-Adur Miss GM Agate, 136 Abbey Road, Sompting, Lancing BN15 0AD
☎ 01903 761352
www.arun-adur-ramblers.org.uk

Beachy Head Miss M O'Brien, Southease, Folkington Lane, Folkington, Polegate BN26 5SA
☎ 01323 482068

Brighton & Hove ● Mrs FM Leenders, 14 Middle Road, Brighton BN1 6SR
☎ 01273 501233
www.brightonandhoveramblers.org.uk

Crawley & North Sussex
Mrs V Sherrington, 37 Cook Road, Crawley RH10 5DJ ☎ 01293 535852

Heathfield & District
Mrs R Brown, Chant House, Eridge Lane, Rotherfield TN6 3JU
☎ 01892 852153

High Weald Walkers Mr N Singer, Croft Lodge, Bayhall Road, Tunbridge Wells, Kent TN2 4TP
☎ 01892 523821
norbert@singerm.fsnet.co.uk
www.highwealdwalkers.org.uk

Horsham & Billingshurst Ms Angie Alderson, 34 Glovers Road, Reigate RH2 7LA ☎ 01737 240047
angiea1@onetel.com

Mid Sussex ● See www.ramblers.org.uk/info/localgroups or contact our central office for current details

Rother Mr LE Pringle, Merrymead, 57 Westfield Lane, St Leonards-on-Sea, TN37 7NE
☎01424 752452
admin@rotherramblers.org.uk
www.rotherramblers.org.uk

RICHARD MANIN/GUZELIAN

South West Sussex Mrs Anne Parker, 11 Palmers Field Avenue, Chichester PO19 6YE ☎ 01243 536080 anne_parker@tiscali.co.uk southwestsxramblers.mysite.wanadoo-members.co.uk

Sussex Young Walkers Group Ms B Bruzon & Mr D Hammond, 30 Northiam Road, Eastbourne BN20 8LP ☎ 01323 639172

WARWICKSHIRE

AREA SECRETARY
Mr Michael Bird, 16 Melford Hall Road, Solihull, West Midlands B91 2ES ☎ 0121 705 1118

GROUP SECRETARIES
Bear 20s–30s Walking Group Mr Steven Bick, 11 Normandy Close, Hampton Magna, Warwick, Warwickshire CV35 8UB ☎ 01926 400842 stephen@sbick.wanadoo.co.uk www.bearwalkinggroup.co.uk

Castle Bromwich Mr Andrew Moore, 108 Shopton Road, Birmingham B34 6PH ☎ 07779 205183

City of Birmingham Group ● Ms Ceri Dittrich (acting), 10 Peel Walk, Harborne, Birmingham B17 8SR ☎ 0121 429 6253 uk.geocities.com/bhamramblers @btinternet.com

Coventry ● Mr Tom O'Sullivan, 94 Dunhill Avenue, Coventry CV4 9PX ☎ 02476 471404 tom.osullivan1@btinternet.com www.coventryRA.org.uk

Mid Warwickshire Mrs Beryl Shone, 23 Stephenson Close, Old Milverton Rd, Leamington Spa, Warks CV32 6BS ☎ 01926 335999 www.midwarksramblers.org

Rugby Mr Tony Harris, 16 Fishers Close, Kilsby, Rugby, Warks CV23 8XH ☎ 01788 822996 anthony.harris2@btinternet.com uk.geocities.com/rugbyramblers

Solihull Mrs Sheila Woolley, 36 Alderwood Place, Princes Way, Solihull, West Midlands B91 3HX ☎ 0121 7055753 www.solihullramblers.co.uk

South Birmingham Ms Jackie Spearpoint, 63 Oak Farm Road, Birmingham B30 1ET ☎ 0121 459 1479 jackie.spearpoint@virgin.net www.sbramblers.pwp.blueyonder.co.uk

Southam Mr Colin Harwood, 44 Pendicke Street, Southam, Warks CV47 1PF ☎ 01926 812820 www.southamramblers.org.uk

Stratford upon Avon Mrs Judy Leavesley, 16 Icknield Row, Alcester, Warwicks B49 5EW ☎ 01789 764798 www.stratfordramblers.com

Sutton Coldfield Mr Geoff Jones, 3 Shenstone Close, Four Oaks, Sutton Coldfield, West Midlands B74 4XB ☎ 0121 353 0405 obrigado1087@tiscali.co.uk www.suttoncoldfieldramblers.co.uk

West Midlands Walking Group Mr Andy Page, 28 Seymour Close, Coventry CV3 4ER ☎ 02476 304825 andy_page@fsmail.net www.wmwg.co.uk

WEST MIDLANDS
See Warwickshire and Staffordshire Areas

WEST RIDING
AREA SECRETARY
Ms Gwendoline Goddard, Spring Bank, Hebden Bridge, West Yorks HX7 7AA ☎ 01422 842558 gwendoline.goddard@3-c.coop

GROUP SECRETARIES
Bradford Mr Malcolm Pitt, 1 Highfield Close, East Morton, Keighley BD20 5SG ☎ 01274 563426

Calderdale Mrs Diane Hall, 11 School Close, Ripponden, Halifax, Yorks HX6 4HP ☎ 01422 823440

Castleford & Pontefract Mr Chris Halton (acting), The Grange, 38 Regent Street, Castleford, West Yorks WF10 5RN ☎ 01977 515469

Craven Ms Diane Lindsay ☎ 07944 809119 or see www.ramblers.org.uk/info/localgroups or contact our central office for further details

Dewsbury Mr Michael Church, 58 Alexandra Crescent, Birkdale Road, Dewsbury, West Yorks WF13 4HL ☎ 01924 462811 church_mj@yahoo.com

Harrogate ● Mrs Clare Sandercock, 3 Burrell Close, Wetherby LS22 6YA ☎ 01937 520174 cmsandercock@djinter.net www.willouby.demon.co.uk/ ramblersassociation/harrogategroup.htm

Huddersfield Mr John Lieberg, 11 Woodroyd Avenue, Honley, Huddersfield, West Yorks HD9 6LG ☎ 01484 662866

Keighley Mr Jeff Maud, 50 Cliffe Lane South, Baildon, Bradford, West Yorkshire BD17 5LB ☎ 01274 59771

Leeds Ms JB Morton, 6 Lawns Green, New Farnley, Leeds, West Yorks LS12 5RR ☎ 0113 279 0229 jeanne.morton@ntlworld.com www.leedsramblers.co.uk

Leeds & Bradford 20s & 30s Mr Timothy Williamson, 91 Valley Road, Pudsey LS28 9EU ☎ 0113 2570260 tim@dynamicdatadesign.co.uk www.takeahike.org.uk

Lower Wharfedale Revd David Morling, Lorindell, 61 Layton Lane, Rawdon, Leeds LS19 6RA ☎ 0113 250 3488 david@morling.co.uk

Ripon Mr Ay Clothier, 49 Boroughbridge Road, Knaresborough, N Yorks HG5 0ND ☎ 01423 865412

Wakefield Ms Jeanette Douglas, 19 Clifton Avenue, Stanley, Wakefield, West Yorks WF3 4HB ☎ 01924 820732

Wetherby & District Mrs Pauline Clarke, 7 Raby Park, Wetherby, West Yorks LS22 6SA ☎ 01937 583378

WILTSHIRE & SWINDON
AREA SECRETARY
Mrs Joan Crosbee, 2 Kennet View, Fyfield, Marlborough SN8 1PU ☎ 01672 861359 joancrosbee@tesco.net www.ramblers-wilts.org.uk

GROUP SECRETARIES
Chippenham Mrs Kath Parkinson, 6 Silbury Road, Curzon Park, Calne SN11 0ES ☎ 01249 811445

Mid Wiltshire Mrs Valerie Thomas, 6 Orchard Close, Devizes, Wiltshire SN10 5JU ☎ 01380 725214 val@dhtdev.freeseve.co.uk

North East Wiltshire ● Mr Peter Gallagher, 10 Folkstone Road, Swindon SN1 3NH ☎ 01793 537472 peg.456@virgin.net

South Wiltshire See www.ramblers.org.uk/info/localgroups or contact our central office for current details

West Wiltshire Mrs Jill Elliott, 152 Bath Road, Bradford-on-Avon, Wilts BA15 1SS ☎ 01225 862566

Wiltshire Wanderers Mr Martin Lucas, 10 Foreman Street, Calne SN11 8PE ☎ 01249 816467 mart75@yahoo.com

WORCESTERSHIRE
AREA SECRETARY
Mr RA Hemmings, 25 Whinfield Road, Worcester WR3 7HF ☎ 01905 451142 richard_a_hemmings@lineone.net

GROUP SECRETARIES
Bromsgrove Group Mrs Jean Deakin, 106 Salwarpe Rd, Charford, Bromsgrove B60 3HS ☎ 01527 875385

Evesham Ms DK Harwood (acting), 12 Queen's Rd, Evesham WR11 4JN www.communigate.co.uk/worcs/ ramblersevesham

Redditch Mrs Ann Hawkins, 58 Cherington Close, Redditch B98 0BB

Worcester ● Mr Clive Burkin, 35 Impney Green, Droitwich WR9 7EL ☎ 01805 774111 ramblers@impneygreen.demon.co.uk

Worcestershire 20s & 30s Mr James Baker, 19 St Peters Crescent, Droitwich, Worcestershire WR9 8QD ☎ 01905 799036 ramblers20-30@fsmail.net worcestershire20.mysite.orange.co.uk

Wyre Forest ● Mr Hugh Buttress, 132 Elan Avenue, Stourport-on-Severn, Worcester DY13 8LR ☎ 01299 878181

WALES

CARMARTHENSHIRE
AREA SECRETARY
Mr Alwyn Williams, 77 Denham Avenue, Llanelli SA15 4DD ☎ 01554 773597

GROUP SECRETARIES

Carmarthen & District Mr David Bush, 31 Eldergrove, Llangunnor, Carmarthenshire, Dyfed SA31 2LQ ☎ 01267 230994 david.bush@ btinternet.com mysite.wanadoo-members.co.uk/carmarthen/index.html

Dinefwr ● Mr David Foot, Ty Isaf, Taliaris, Llandeilo SA19 7DE ☎ 01550 777623 mysite.freeserve.com/beauchamp/index.html

Llanelli ● Mrs Nina Clements, 53 Heol Morlais, Trimsaran, Kidwelly SA17 4DF ☎ 01554 810979 nina_clements@yahoo.co.uk www.llanelliramblers.org.uk

CEREDIGION

AREA SECRETARY
Sue Johnson, 16 Clos Ceitho, Llanbadarn Fawr, Aberystwyth SY23 3TZ ☎ 01970 612649 sue.johnson1@gmail.com

GROUP SECRETARIES
Aberystwyth ● Ms Shirley Kinghorn, 16 Bryn Glas, Llanbadarn, Aberystwyth, Dyfed SY23 3QR ☎ 01970 624965 users.aber.ac.uk/dib/AberRamblers

Cardigan & District ● Mrs Kathy Gill, Abersylltyn, Cwm Cou, Newcastle Emlyn, Dyfed SA38 9PN ☎ 01239 710858 mysite.wanadoo-members.co.uk/cardigan/index.html

Lampeter Ramblers ● Mr Phillip Lodwick (acting), Penrhyn, Cwmann, Lampeter SA48 8JU ☎ 01570 442181 philip@lodwickchemist.freeserve.co.uk

DYFED

See Carmarthenshire, Ceredigion and Pembrokeshire Areas

GLAMORGAN

Bridgend; Cardiff; Rhondda, Cynon Taff; Swansea; Vale of Glamorgan; and West Glamorgan
AREA SECRETARY
Mr John Thomas, 7 Parc Afon, Porth CF40 1JF ☎ 01443 681082 tigerbayramblers@hotmail.com

GROUP SECRETARIES

Bridgend & District ● Mr John Sanders, 3 Bryn Rhedyn, Pencoed, Bridgend CF35 6TL ☎ 01656 861835 john@pencoed9.wanadoo.co.uk alex-penyfai.homecall.co.uk

Cardiff ● Ms Diane Davies, 9 Cyncoed Rise, Cyncoed, Cardiff CF23 6SF ☎ 029 2075 2464 dianedaviesandks@btinternet.com www.btinternet.com/~cardiff.ramblers

Cynon Valley ● Mr Allan Harrison, 8 Stuart Street, Aberdare CF44 7LY ☎ 01685 881824 allan.harrison1@btopenworld.com alex-penyfai.homecall.co.uk

Maesteg Mr Steve Luke, 33 Maiden Street, Maesteg CF34 9HP ☎ 01656 733729 lukee@btinternet.com www.maestegramblers.org.uk

Merthyr Valley ● Mr Andrew Richards, 8 St Davids Close, Penpedairheol, Hengoed, Mid Glamorgan CF82 8BL ☎ 01443 833719 ajeffreyrichards@yahoo.co.uk

Neath Port Talbot Mr David Davies, 2 Cwrt Coed Parc, Maesteg CF34 9DG ☎ 01656 733021 dave@gecarpentry.co.uk alex-penyfai.homecall.co.uk

Penarth & District Ms Lorraine Davies, 3 Barrians Way, Barry, CF62 8JG ☎ 01446 407595 lorraine.davies@ntlworld.com uk.geocities.com/jungjames@ btinternet.com/penarth/penarth.html

Taff Ely (Llantisant) ● Mr Jeff Brown, 2 Shadow Wood Drive, Miskin, Pontyclun CF72 8SX ☎ 01443 239743 jeff_tjbrown@btinternet.com

Tawe Trekkers Mr Doug Morgan, 100 Bryn Road, Brynmill, Swansea SA2 0AT ☎ 07766 652837 tawe@hotmail.co.uk www.tawetrekkers.org.uk

Tiger Bay Ramblers ● Ms Nina Ley, 42 Ty Wern Avenue, Cardiff CF14 6AW ☎ 029 2062 8892 ninaley@hotmail.co.uk www.tigerbayramblers.org.uk

Vale of Glamorgan ● Mr Ian Fraser, 44 Millfield Drive, Cowbridge CF71 7BR ☎ 01446 774706 ian.fraser@elwa.org.uk alex-penyfai.homecall.co.uk

West Glamorgan www.westglamorganramblers.org.uk or see www.ramblers.org.uk/info/localgroups or contact our central office for current details

GREATER GWENT

Blaenau Gwent; Caerphilly; Monmouthshire; Newport; and Torfaen

AREA SECRETARY
Mr Mike Williams, 7 Cwm Sor Close, New Inn, Pontypool NP4 0NN ☎ 01495 753040 mike@cwmsor78.freeserve.co.uk

GROUP SECRETARIES
Gelligaer ● Mrs Dolores Price, 26 Tyn Y Coed, Ystrad Mynach, Caerphilly CF82 7DD ☎ 01443 813220 dolores.p@virgin.net www.ramblersgelligaergroup.co.uk

Islwyn Ms Maggie Thomas, 15 Carlton Terrace, Cross Keys, Newport NP11 7BU ☎ 01495 273057 maggie.thomas@virgin.net www.islwyn-ramblers.itgo.com

Lower Wye Mrs Dawn Davies, 5 Crown Meadow, Coal Way, Coleford GL16 7HF ☎ 01594 837157 dawn@davies421.wanadoo.co.uk www.lowerwyeramblers.org.uk

North Gwent ● Miss Liz Kennedy, 19 Cambridge Gardens, Beaufort, Ebbw Vale NP23 5HG ☎ 07976 913083 northgwentramblers@yahoo.co.uk www.northgwentramblers.co.uk

Pontypool Mrs Barbara Whitticase, Glantawell, Llanfihangel Talyllyn, Brecon, Powys LD3 7TH ☎ 01874 658386 www.pontypool-ramblers.org.uk

South Gwent Mr Ken Phillips, 39 Penylan Close, Bassaleg, Newport NP10 8NW ☎ 01633 894172 information@south-gwent-ramblers.co.uk south-gwent-ramblers.co.uk

RAMBLERS GROUPS & PUBLICATIONS

NORTH WALES
Isle of Anglesey; Conwy; Denbighshire; Flintshire; Gwynedd; and Wrexham

AREA SECRETARY
Mr Ron Williams, 11 Fron Las, Holywell, Clwyd CH8 7HX ☎ 01352 715723
ronanol@macunlimited.net

GROUP SECRETARIES
Bangor-Bethesda Mr Hugh Griffiths, 2 Trefonwys, Bangor, Gwynedd LL57 2HU ☎ 01248 353252

Berwyn ● Mr John Kay, Erw Fain, Llantysilio, Llangollen, Clwyd LL20 8BU ☎ 01978 861793 gmoss@ukonline.co.uk
www.berwynra.org.uk

Caernarfon/Dwyfor ● Canon Edmund Plaxton, 1 & 2 Tyn-y-Maes, Y Fron, Upper Llandwrog, Caernarfon LL54 7BW ☎ 01286 880188
Edmundrachel@aol.com

Clwydian ● Mr Eldryd Ankers, 14 Bron Yr Eglwys, Mynydd Isa, Mold, Clwyd CH7 6YQ ☎ 07799 668779
clwydianramblers@woodlawn.
wanadoo.co.uk

Conwy Valley ● Mr Frank Parry, 4 Brompton Park, Rhos On Sea, Colwyn Bay LL28 4TN ☎ 01492 547967
frankperry@tiscali.co.uk
www.conwyvalleyra.org.uk

Deeside ● Mr Jim Irvine, 30 St Davids Drive, Connahs Quay, Flintshire CH5 4SR ☎ 01244 818577
deesideramblers@btinternet.com
www.deesideramblers.org.uk

Eryri 20.30 Mrs Delyth Roberts, Tre Wen, Groeslon, Waunfawr, Caernarfon LL55 4EZ ☎ 01286 650295
walk20.30@btopenworld.com
www.eryri2030.org.uk

Meirionnydd ● Ms Val Goslin, 4 Highgate, Penrhyndeudraeth, Gwynedd LL48 6RG ☎ 01766 770770
val@valgoslin.vispa.com

Vale of Clwyd ● Mr Malcolm Wilkinson, 49 Victoria Road West, Prestatyn, Denbighshire LL19 7AA ☎ 01745 888137
malcolmray@supanet.com
www.voc-ramblers.org.uk

Walkers on Wales Dr F Lloyd-Williams, Plas Wern, Waen, St Asaph LL17 0DY ☎ 07702 955344 ffionlw@talk21.com
www.walkersonwales.fsnet.co.uk

Wrexham ● Mrs Anne Cooper, 33 Fford Llywelyn, Smithy Lane, Wrexham, Clwyd LL12 8JW ☎ 01978 312515
llywelyn.cooper@talktalk.net

Ynys Môn ● Mrs Rhiannon Pritchard, 14 Llanfaes, Llanfaes, Beaumaris LL58 8RH ☎ 01248 490534

PEMBROKESHIRE
AREA SECRETARY
Ms Christine Morris, 24 St Lawrence Close, Hakin, Milford Haven, Dyfed SA73 3NE ☎ 01646 697543
christine.morris12@tiscali.co.uk

SARAH BOVE

GROUP SECRETARIES
Pembrokeshire ● Ms Christine Morris, 24 St Lawrence Close, Hakin, Milford Haven, Dyfed SA73 3NE ☎ 01646 697 543 christine.morris12@tiscali.co.uk
www.pembrokeshireramblers.org.uk

POWYS
AREA SECRETARY
Mr KM Jones, 1 Heyope Road, Knucklas LD7 1PT ☎ 01547 520266
secretary@powysramblers.org.uk
www.powysramblers.org.uk

GROUP SECRETARIES
4 Wells Mr Derek Cosslett, 2 Gilfach Cottage, Newbridge On Wye, Llandrindod Wells LD1 6HS ☎ 01597 860519
cosslet@tiscali.co.uk
www.fourwells.powysramblers.org.uk

East Radnor Mr KM Jones, 1 Heyope Road, Knucklas LD7 1PT ☎ 01547 520266 secretary@powysramblers.org.uk

Welshpool ● Mrs Lynda Dabinett, Pentre Isaf, Llangyniew, Welshpool SY21 0JT ☎ 01938 810069

SCOTLAND

ARGYLL & BUTE
See Strathclyde, Dumfries & Galloway Area

CENTRAL FIFE & TAYSIDE
See Forth Valley, Fife & Tayside Area

DUMFRIES & GALLOWAY
See Strathclyde, Dumfries & Galloway Area

FORTH VALLEY, FIFE & TAYSIDE
Angus; City of Dundee; Clackmannanshire; Falkirk; Fife; Perth & Kinross; and Stirling

AREA SECRETARY
Mr David Galloway, 5 Doocot Road, St Andrews, Fife KY16 8QP ☎ 01334 475102

GROUP SECRETARIES
Blairgowrie & District Miss AM McRuvie, 5 Grampian Crescent, Kirriemuir, Angus DD8 4TW ☎ 01575 572415

Brechin Ms Ursula Shone, 4 Park Road, Brechin, Angus DD9 7AF ☎ 01356 626087

Broughty Ferry Miss M Cameron, 19 Gillies Place, Broughty Ferry, Dundee DD5 3LE ☎ 01382 776250

Dalgety Bay & District ● Mr David Thomson, Sand Dollar House, High Street, Aberdour, Burntisland KY3 0SW ☎ 01383 860324
davidthompson@tesco.net
www.dalgetybayramblers.org.uk

Dundee & District Mrs AC Cowie, 32 Ballindean Terrace, Dundee, Tayside DD4 8PA ☎ 01382 507682

Forfar & District Mrs Jenny Mcdade, 21 Duncan Avenue, Arbroath DD11 2DA ☎ 01241 870695

Glenrothes Mr Doug Jolly, 16 Orchard Drive, Glenrothes, Fife, Scotland KY7 5RG ☎ 01592 757039
douglas-jolly@virgin.net

Kinross & Ochil Ms Karen Bernard, 4 St Serfs Place, Crook Of Devon, Kinross KY13 0PL ☎ 01577 842246

Kirkcaldy Mr WH Gibson, Flat 5, 2 Darney Terrace, Kinghorn, Fife KY3 9RF ☎ 01592 891319

Perth & District Miss EJ Bryce, 2 Hawarden Terrace, Jeanfield, Perth PH1 1PA ☎ 01738 632645

St Andrews & North East Fife ● Ms Pat J Ritchie, 63 St Michaels Drive, Cupar, Fife KY15 5BP ☎ 01334 653667

Stirling, Falkirk & District Ms JA Cameron, 17 Buchany, Doune FK16 6HD ☎ 01786 841178

Strathtay Ms Clair Robertson, West Wing, Pitnacree, Ballinluig, Perthshire PH9 0LW ☎ 01887 840324

Tayside Trekkers Ms M Nicol, 7 Coastguard Cottages, Fife Ness, Crail, Anstruther KY10 3XN ☎ 01333 450611
shelliwelly@aol.com
www.taysidetrekkers.co.uk

West Fife Mrs ME Wrightson, 24 Orwell Place, Dunfermline KY12 7XP
☎ 01383 729994

GRAMPIAN
Aberdeenshire; City of Aberdeen; Moray

AREA SECRETARY
Ms Anne Macdonald, 64 Grant Road, Banchory, Aberdeenshire AB31 5UU
☎ 01330 823255

GROUP SECRETARIES
Aberdeen ● Miss Alison Mitchell, 32 Gordon Road, Mannofield, Aberdeen AB15 7RL ☎ 01224 322580
alisonmmitchell@talktalk.net
www.aberdeenramblers.org.uk
Inverurie Ms MT Corley, 60 Gray Street, Aberdeen AB10 6JE
☎ 01224 318672
Moray ● Mrs EM Robertson, Abbey Bank, Station Road, Urquhart, By Elgin, Moray IV30 8LQ ☎ 01343 842489
Stonehaven Mr I Forbes, 11 Burnside Gardens, Stonehaven AB39 2FA
☎ 01569 766553

HIGHLAND & ISLANDS
Highland; the Western Isles; Orkney and Shetland

AREA SECRETARY
www.highlandramblers.org.uk or see www.ramblers.org.uk/info/localgroups or contact our central office for current details

GROUP SECRETARIES
Badenoch & Strathspey See Area website or www.ramblers.org.uk/info/localgroups or contact our central office for current details
Inverness Mrs Moira Livingstone, Nooralain, 21 Green Drive, Inverness IV2 4EX ☎ 01463 231985
analbo@dsl.pipex.com
Lochaber & Lorn Ms Jean O'Brien, Flat 1, 75-83 High Street, Fort William PH33 6GD ☎ 01397 701957

LOTHIAN & BORDERS
City of Edinburgh; East Lothian; Midlothian; Scottish Borders; West Lothian

AREA SECRETARY
Mr Arthur Homan-Elsy, 55 Deanburn Road, Linlithgow, West Lothian EH49 6EY
☎ 01506 842897
areasec@lothian-borders-ramblers.org.uk
www.lothian-borders-ramblers.org.uk

GROUP SECRETARIES
Balerno Mr RJ Bayley, 65 Silverknowles Drive, Edinburgh EH4 5HX
Coldstream Mrs MA Taylor, East Cottage, Lees Farm, Kelso Road, Coldstream TD12 4LJ ☎ 01890 883137
East Berwickshire Mrs E Windram, 20 Hinkar Way, Eyemouth, Berwickshire TD14 5EQ ☎ 018907 51048

Edinburgh ● Miss D Giles, 81b Lothian Street, Bonnyrigg, Midlothian EH19 3AF
Edinburgh Young Walkers Ms Sarah Emmerson, 11/15 Wardlaw Place, Edinburgh EH11 1UA ☎ 0131 313 1879
edinburghyoungwalkers@hotmail.com
Linlithgow ● Mr John Davidson, 16 Friars Way, Linlithgow EH49 6AX
☎ 01506 842504
Livingston Group ● Mrs V McGowan, 4 Larbert Avenue, Deans, Livingston EH54 8QJ ☎ 01506 438706
Midlothian Walkers & Hillwalkers Miss LJ McKie, 48 The Square, Newtongrange, Dalkeith, Midlothian EH22 4PX
midlothianwalkers@hotmail.com
Musselburgh Mr GC Edmond, 54 Northfield Gardens, Prestonpans, East Lothian EH32 9LG ☎ 01875 810729
North Berwick ● Mrs IR Mcadam, 23 Gilbert Avenue, North Berwick, East Lothian EH39 4ED ☎ 01620 893657
Tweeddale Mrs F Hunt, 8 Craigerne Drive, Peebles EH45 9HN
☎ 07763 169896

PERTH & KINROSS
See Forth Valley, Fife and Tayside Area

SCOTTISH BORDERS
See Lothian & Borders Area

STIRLING
See Forth Valley, Fife and Tayside Area

STRATHCLYDE, DUMFRIES & GALLOWAY
Argyll & Bute; City of Glasgow; Dumfries & Galloway; East, North & South Ayrshire; East & West Dunbartonshire; East Renfrew; Inverclyde; North & South Lanarkshire; Renfrewshire

AREA SECRETARY
Ms Elizabeth Lawie, Burnside Cottage, 64 Main Street, Glenboig, Lanarkshire ML5 2RD ☎ 01236 872959

GROUP SECRETARIES
Bearsden & Milngavie Mr Andrew Summers, 47 Burnbrae Avenue, Bearsden, Glasgow G61 3ET
lilias@asummers. wanadoo.co.uk
www.bearsdenand milngavieramblers.co.uk
Biggar Mrs Sue Wigram, The Granary, Annieston Farm, Symington, Biggar ML12 6LQ ☎ 01899 308920
Clyde Valley Mr Harry Read, 6 Maybole Gardens, Hamilton, Lanarkshire ML3 9EU
☎ 01698 828207
secretary.cvr@scotsol.plus.com
www.cvramblers.supanet.com
Cumbernauld & Kilsyth ●
Mrs H Shearer, 7 Avonhead Avenue, Cumbernauld, Glasgow G67 4RB
☎ 01236 780136
ckrambler.info@blueyonder.co.uk

Cunninghame ● Mrs C Jeffers, 12 Thornhouse Avenue, Irvine, Ayrshire, Scotland KA12 0LT
christine.jeffers@tesco.net
www.cunninghameramblers.org.uk
Dumfries & Galloway Ms Jean Snary, 7 Birchwood Place, Lockerbie Road, Dumfries DG1 3EB
☎ 01387 267450
Eastwood Mrs AP Fulton, 132 Greenwood Road, Clarkston, Glasgow G76 7LQ
apfulton@hotmail.com
www.eastwood-ramblers.org.uk
Glasgow Ms Denise Connell, 14a Carment Drive, Shawlands, Glasgow G41 3PP ☎ 0141 632 0832 [after 5pm]
Glasgow Region Under 40 First Footers (GRUFF) www.geocities.com/GRUFF_RAMBLERS or see www.ramblers.org.uk/info/localgroups or contact our central office for current details
Helensburgh & West Dunbartonshire Ms Una Campbell, 5 Dalmore House, Dalmore Crescent, Helensburgh G84 8JP
☎ 01436 673726
www.hwdramblers.me.uk
Inverclyde ● Mr Alex Wooler, 37 Margaret Street, Greenock PA16 8BU
☎ 01475 727849
awooler@hotmail.com
www.inverclyderamblers.org.uk
Isle of Bute Ms Ellen McKenzie, 14 Bishop Street, Rothesay, Isle of Bute PA20 9DG
Kilmarnock & Loudoun Ms M Bush, 14 Goatfoot Road, Galston, Ayrshire KA4 8BJ ☎ 01563 821331
www.freewebs. com/kilmarnockandloudounramblers
Mid Argyll & Kintyre Mrs Brenda Nicholson, 14 Wilson Road, Lochgilphead, Argyll PA31 8TR ☎ 01546 603026
Moffat Mrs Sheila Bowman, Victoria Cottage, Victoria Place, Moffat DG10 9AG
☎ 01683 221440
Monklands Ms C McMahon, 4 Blackmoor Place, New Stevenston, Motherwell ML1 4JX
☎ 01698 833983
christine.mcmahon@scott-moncrieff.com
www.monklandsramblers.org.uk
Paisley Ms M Docherty, 22 Douglas Road, Renfrew PA4 8BB ☎ 0141 561 4416 m.docherty363@ntlworld.com
SLOW – S Lanark Older Walkers Ms MA Rankin, 18 Cherrytree Crescent, Larkhall, Lanarkshire ML9 2AP
☎ 01698 885995
South Ayrshire Mrs K Graham, 113 Logan Drive, Troon KA10 6QE
☎ 01292 311704
Stranraer & The Rhins Mr James Kelly, 1d McCormack Gardens, Stranraer, Wigtownshire DG9 7JB
Strathkelvin Miss M Lang, 69 Redbrae Road, Kirkintilloch, Glasgow G66 2DE
☎ 0141 776 4161

LOCAL RAMBLERS PUBLICATIONS

The books and guides listed – by country, then county – cover a huge range of walks, from short circular strolls to long distance paths. All are written and published by local Ramblers Groups with local walking knowledge, and are available by mail order directly from the addresses shown.

Where no p&p charge is shown, this is included in the price. Publications specifically about long distance paths can be found listed in the section on p25.

Titles published in 2006 are highlighted as *NEW* and where possible we've included the new 13-digit ISBNs.

ENGLAND

Walk East Midlands
edited by Chris Thompson of Nottinghamshire Area. ISBN 1-850588-24-4. This book brings together the expertise of six Ramblers Areas to create the definitive volume of circular walks in an English region that, as the preface admits, 'has a recognition problem'. A substantial book offering 50 walks, most with short and long options, all with public transport links, avoiding the obvious honeypots of the Peak District and exploring instead the varied landscapes of Derbyshire, Leicestershire, Nottinghamshire, Rutland, Lincolnshire and Northamptonshire, from flat fens to limestone uplands. Even the shorter options can be on the long side (up to 16km/10 miles) but otherwise this is a laudable enterprise, published jointly with Sigma Leisure ☎ 01625 531035, www.sigmapress.co.uk. *£8.95, order from bookshops or Sigma Leisure.*

BEDFORDSHIRE

Leighton Buzzard Millennium Walks
(Leighton Buzzard Group). Ten tried and tested walks from gentle strolls to day treks, illustrated in full colour with OS map extracts. *Free + first class stamp from 8 Carlton Grove, Leighton Buzzard LU7 3BR.*

BERKSHIRE

The Chairman's Walk around the perimeter of West Berkshire
edited by Geoff Vince, ISBN 1-901184-59-5. A series of 25 linear walks, each of about 7km/4 miles, grouped in 10 sections and completing a 158km/98-mile circuit. Guide contains maps, route guides, public transport and local interest information and photographs. *£7 + £1 p&p from West Berks Ramblers, 38 Kipling Close, Thatcham RG18 3AY. Cheques to West Berks Ramblers.*

Rambling for Pleasure Footpath Maps for East Berkshire:

Cookham & District
ISBN 1-874258-11-2. A superb area of walking country in the Thames Valley easily accessible by rail. *50p + 40p p&p.*

Hurley & District
ISBN: 1-874258-14-7. Highlights the dense network of footpaths linking the Thames Path with the quiet meadows and wooded slopes surrounding Warren Row and Knowl Hill. *50p + 40p p&p.*
NEW **Windsor & The Great Park, revised full-colour 6th edition.**
ISBN 1-874258-18-X. The only guide to show all the paths and areas open to the public on foot in the Park, plus footpaths in surrounding areas and other features of interest.
50p + 40p p&p.

Rambling for Pleasure Guides:

NEW **Along the Thames, revised 6th edition**
ISBN 1-874258-19-8. 24 walks of 3km/2 miles to 9.5km/6 miles between Runnymede and Sonning.
£2.95 + 60p p&p.
Around Reading – 1st Series,
ISBN 1-874258-12-0, and 2nd Series ISBN 1-874258-16-3. Two books each of 24 easy country walks of 5km/3 miles to 16km/10 miles through Berkshire, Oxfordshire and north Hampshire, within an 11km/7-mile radius of Reading.
£2.95 + 60p p&p.

NEW **In East Berkshire, revised 2nd edition**
ISBN 978-1-874258-19-3. 24 mainly flat walks of 5km/3 miles to 12km/7.5 miles around Maidenhead, Wokingham, Bracknell and Ascot, including 6 from stations.
£2.95 + 60p p&p.
Kennet Valley & Watership Down
ISBN 1-874258-13-9. 24 walks of 4km/2.5 miles and 11km/7 miles exploring the hidden countryside between Reading, Newbury and Basingstoke. Some modest hills.
£2.95 + 60p p&p.
All Rambling for Pleasure Guides and Maps from East Berks RA Publications, PO Box 1357, Maidenhead SL6 7FP. Cheques to East Berks RA Publications.

NEW **The Secrets of Countryside Access**
by Dave Ramm, ISBN 978-1-874258-20-9. A new illustrated guide to finding, using and enjoying country paths. A mine of information, full of practical advice, explained in simple terms and attractively presented with over 200 illustrations.
£4.95 + £1 p&p.
Three Castles Path
ISBN 1-874258-08-2. A 96km/60-mile route from Windsor to Winchester with six circular walks.
£4.95 + 60p p&p.
Both from East Berks RA Publications, PO Box 1357, Maidenhead SL6 7FP. Cheques to East Berks RA Publications.

21 Walks for the 21st Century
Walks on the Berkshire/Wiltshire border of between 8km/5 miles and 14.5km/9 miles, on a set of colour laminated cards with maps, directions, points of interest and transport details .
£6 + £1 p&p from West Berks Group, 38 Kipling Close, Thatcham RG18 3AY. Cheques to West Berks Ramblers.

BIRMINGHAM & THE BLACK COUNTRY
Birmingham Greenway
by Fred Willits. ISBN 1-869922-40-9. From the southern to the northern boundary of Birmingham using footpaths, riversides and towpaths.
£4.95 + £1 p&p.
Waterside Walks in the Midlands
by Birmingham Ramblers, ISBN 1-869922-09-3. Twenty-two walks by brooks, streams, pools, rivers and canals in Derbyshire, Shropshire, Staffordshire, Warwickshire and Worcestershire.
£4.95 + £1 p&p.
More Waterside Walks in the Midlands
by Birmingham Ramblers, ISBN 1-869922-31-X. A second collection of Midlands walks.
£5.95 + £1 p&p.
All from Meridian Books, 40 Hadzor Road, Oldbury B68 9LA.

BUCKINGHAMSHIRE
Best Walks in Bucks by Bus and Train
Although the printed edition is no longer available, up-to-date detailed route descriptions are now available online at www.bucks-wmiddx-ramblers.org.uk

Walks in South Bucks
by West London Ramblers. Seventeen short walks. £1.50 from 128 Park Lane, Harrow HA2 8NL. Cheques to West London Group Ramblers' Association.

CAMBRIDGESHIRE
Guide to the Fen Rivers Way
Describes this 80km/50-mile route, part of E2 (see p39), from Cambridge to Ongar Hill, on the Wash north of King's Lynn, with some circular walks of 6.5km/4 miles to 13km/8 miles linked to the main route.
£4.50 from 52 Maids Causeway, Cambridge CB5 8DD. Cheques to Cambridge Group of the Ramblers' Association.

Twenty Rambles in Huntingdonshire
Revisited by Huntingdonshire Ramblers, ISBN 1-901184-77-3. Walks in lowland countryside in the former county, 8km/5 miles to 21km/13 miles, spiral bound in handy pocket size, sketch maps, no public transport details. Revised and updated second edition of a book first published in1998. £4 + 50p p&p from 8 Park View, Needingworth, St Ives PE27 4TJ. Cheques to Huntingdonshire Group Ramblers.

Walks in East Cambridgeshire
ISBN 0-952251-80-9: circular lowland walks from 9.5km/6 miles to 19km/12 miles.
Walks in South Cambridgeshire
ISBN 0-952251-83-3: circular lowland walks from 8km/5 miles to 19km/12 miles.
Walks on the South Cambridgeshire Borders
ISBN 0-952251-82-5. 20 easy to moderate walks of from 8km/5 miles to 19km/12 miles along the boundaries with Essex, Hertfordshire and Bedfordshire.
All £4.50 each from 52 Maids Causeway, Cambridge CB5 8DD.Cheques to Cambridge Group of the Ramblers' Association.

CORNWALL
The Maritime Line: Trails from the Track Walk
Card pack detailing nine walks, 3km/2 miles to 11km/7 miles, with most 8km/5 miles or under, generally easy-going, and all connecting with the Maritime Line, one of Cornwall's attractive branch lines running from Truro on the Great Western main line to Falmouth Docks. Includes linear walks linking all the stations between Truro and Penmere, and some circular options. Attractive and clear mapping, route

descriptions and background information. A joint project of Carrick Group and the Devon & Cornwall Rail Partnership.
Free from local stations and information centres, or send an SAE to Carrick Ramblers, 7 Moresk Close, Truro TR1 1DL.

Rambles in the Roseland
(six walks 4km/2.5 miles to 9km/5.5miles)
Six Circular Coast and Country Walks on the Lizard
(6.5km/4 miles to 11km/7 miles)
Six Coastal Walks with Inland Returns in or on The Lizard
(5.5km/3.5 miles to 13km/8 miles)
Six Coastal Walks with Inland Returns in Penwith Book 1
(3km/2 miles to 11km/7 miles)
Six Coastal Walks with Inland Returns in Penwith Book 2
(3km/2 miles to 11km/7 miles)
Six Walks around Falmouth 1
(3km/2 miles to 11km/7 miles)
Six Walks around Falmouth 2
(3km/2 miles to 11km/7 miles)
Six North Cornwall Walks 1
(5km/3 miles to 9.5km/6 miles)
Six North Cornwall Walks 2
(5.5km/3.5 miles to 13km/8 miles)
Six Walks from Truro
(6.5km/4 miles to 11km/7 miles)
Wendron's Church and Chapels Walks
(six walks 6.5km/4 miles to 8km/5 miles)
All £1.25 each from Publicity Officer, 2 Lanaton Road, Penryn TR10 8RB. Cheques to Cornwall Area, Ramblers' Association.Penwith and Lizard booklets also available from Trebant, Ludgvan Churchtown, Penzance TR20 8HH. Cheques to Penwith/Kerrier Ramblers.

Six North Cornwall Walks Book 1
Six North Cornwall Walks Book 2
Six short walks in each. Mainly around 6.5km/4 miles to 9.5km/6 miles.
Each £1.50 from Pridham House, Molesworth Street, Wadebridge PL27 7DS. Cheques to Ramblers' Association Camel District.

CUMBRIA
The Cumbria Way
by John Trevelyan. ISBN 1-855681-97-8 (Lake District Ramblers/Dalesman). Concise guide to this popular 112km/70-mile route from Ulverston to Carlisle, with sketch maps, route description and background information.
£2.99 from Lakeing, Grasmere, Ambleside LA22 9RW, cheques to Lake District RA.

More Walks Around Carlisle and North Cumbria
ISBN 1-904350-43-6 (Carlisle Ramblers). Well-stuffed book of 37 circular and linear walks including countryside, coast and Hadrian's Wall. From 4km/2.5 miles to 23km/14 miles, with quite a few options

under 8km/5 miles. Some public transport walks, several starting from Carlisle and several of the walks interconnect for more options. Sketch maps, background details.
£4 from Little Gables, Brampton CA8 2HZ. Cheques to Ramblers' Association.

Walks Around Carlisle & North Cumbria
ISBN 0-9521458-0-4 (Carlisle Ramblers). Seventeen fairly easy walks of between 8km/5 miles and 14.5km/9 miles in the lowland countryside around Carlisle, including Eden Valley and Hadrian's Wall.
£3.50 post free to members, + 50p p&p to non-members from 24 Currock Mount, Carlisle CA2 4RF. Cheques to Carlisle Ramblers.

Walks from the Limestone Link
ISBN 0-904350-41-X. Seventeen easy walks of between 2km/1.5 miles and 16km/10 miles in the beautiful limestone area north of Lancaster, and the 19km/12-mile Limestone Link path. Includes maps and sketches.
£2.95 + 45p p&p each from 116 North Road, Carnforth LA5 9LX. Cheques to Ramblers' Association Lancaster Group.

Walks in the Kendal Area Book 1
3rd edition. ISBN 0-904350-40-1. Eighteen low level walks within 16km/10 miles of Kendal.
Walks in the Kendal Area Book 3
2nd edition. ISBN 0-904350-37-1. Mostly lower level walks of between 6.5km/4 miles and 24km/15 miles within 16km/10 miles of Kendal.
Each £2.95 post free from 6 Orchard Close, Sedgwick, Kendal LA8 0LJ. Cheques to RA Kendal Group

DERBYSHIRE
Chesterfield Round Walk
Devised by Chesterfield and Northeast Derbyshire Group and written by Rob Haslam. A colour leaflet, including maps, of this new 55km/34-mile walk around Chesterfield, launched in June 2005.
£1.50 + 50p p&p from membership secretary, 195 Old Road, Chesterfield S40 3QH. Chequest to Chesterfield and North East Derbyshire Ramblers' Group.

Walks Through Derbyshire's Gateway
Favourite walks of the Bolsover Group in their own backyard. Five leaflets with clear maps and route descriptions, each describing a single circular walk of between 6.5km/4 miles and 13km/8 miles.
Free from local outlets or send an SAE to 34 Lime Tree Avenue, Glapwell, Chesterfield S44 5LE.

Our Favourite Walks
See under Staffordshire.

DEVON

NEW John Musgrave Heritage Trail
56km/35-mile route created from a generous legacy left by former South Devon Group chairman John Musgrave. The Trail is split into four managable sections of between 9km/5.5 miles to 18km/11 miles each. The guide provides detailed commentary of local heritage, maps and transport links along the way.
£3 from the secretary of the South Devon Ramblers, The Lodge, 43 Seymour Drive, Watcombe, Torquay, Devon TQ2 8PY. Cheques to Ramblers' Association South Devon Group.

Walks Around Dawlish
by Teignmouth and Dawlish Ramblers, published with Dawlish Town Council. Leaflet pack of seven illustrated walks around the town. *£2 from Dawlish Town Council, The Manor House, Old Town Street, Dawlish EX7 9AP ☎ 01626 863388. Cheques to Dawlish Town Council*

DORSET

A Rambler's Guide to the Dorset Jubilee Trail
A comprehensive guide with maps to this 145km/90-mile walk across Dorset from Forde Abbey to Bokerley Dyke. ISBN 1-901184-04-8.
£4.50 + 50p p&p from Jubilee Trail Contact, 19 Shaston Crescent, Dorchester DT1 2EB. Cheques to Ramblers' Association Dorset Area.

Channel to Channel
See under Somerset.

ESSEX

Camuplodunum
by Colchester Ramblers. 40km/25 miles around Colchester via Great Horkesley and Mersea Road. No printed guide but a full route description, updated in 2004, is available at www.colchester-ramblers.ccom.co.uk.

The Ramblers Millennium Walk
37km/23-mile walk around Southend-on-Sea and district.
£1 + A5 SAE from Southend Borough Council Leisure Services Department, Civic Centre, Victoria Avenue, Southend-on-Sea SS2 6ER. Cheques to Southend Borough Council.

15 Walks in South East Essex for all the Family
ISBN 1-901184-17-X
17 More Walks in and around South East Essex
ISBN 1-901184-50-1

Short Walks in the area of Southend-on-Sea
Walks of 6.5km/4 miles to 14.5km/9 miles.
£2.25 each including postage from 146 Kenneth Road, Thundersley SS7 3AN. Cheques to SE Essex Group RA.

GLOUCESTERSHIRE AND BRISTOL

Bristol Backs: Discovering Bristol on Foot
compiled by Peter Gould, jointly published with Bristol City Council, ISBN 1-901184-52-8. 27 walks of between 3km/2 miles and 17.5km/11 miles in the city including street-based heritage walks, green trails, waterside strolls and a sculpture trail, with plentiful background descriptions.
£6.99 + £1.50 p&p.

Bristol Triangular City Walk
A 28km/18-mile circuit of the city starting at Temple Meads station, easily walked as three sections of between 6km/4 miles and 13km/8 miles connected by public transport. Includes the waterfront, Durdham Downs, Avon Gorge and Blaise Castle Estate as well as the heart and history of the city, developed by Bristol Group in association with the City Council. Connects with South Bristol Circular Walk (see below). *Colour leaflet £1.50. Both from 57 Somerset Road, Bristol BS4 2HT. Cheques to Bristol Group Ramblers' Association. (Leaflet is free from local outlets.)*

Cirencester Circuit
A moderate 16km/10 mile walk around Cirencester. *£1 + 40p p&p;* and
Walks Around Cirencester
Three A4 leaflets of moderate local walks, each starting from the Market Place.
Walk 1: Stratton and Baunton
Walk 2: Preston and Siddington
Walk 3: Duntisbourne Valley (linear walk)
A fourth leaflet was in production at the time of going to press.
20p each + SAE from 80 Melmore Gardens, Cirencester GL7 1NS. Cheques to Cirencester Ramblers.

Cotswold Way Handbook & Accommodation List
ISBN 1-901184-62-5. *£2.95 + 50p p&p from Mail Order Secretary, Tudor Cottage, Berrow, Malvern WR13 6JJ. Cheques to Ramblers' Association Gloucestershire Area.*

Favourite South Cotswold Walks Book One
by South Cotswold Ramblers. Eighteen attractive half-day walks, several of which can be combined into day walks, in the Cotswolds Area of Outstanding Natural Beauty. A fully revised and extended issue of a best selling book first published in 1995. *£3 + 95p p&p.*

More Favourite Walks in the South Cotswolds
Fifteen fully graded and illustrated walks of between 3km/2 miles and 22.5km/14 miles in the Cotswolds Area of Outstanding Natural Beauty.
Special offer price £3 + 50p p&p. Both from Southcot, The Headlands, Stroud GL5 5PS. Cheques to South Cotswold Ramblers. See also www.southcotswold ramblers.org.uk/books for further information and updates.

Forest of Dean East
40p + 30p p&p from Mail Order Secretary, Tudor Cottage, Berrow, Malvern WR13 6JJ. Cheques to Ramblers' Association Gloucestershire Area.

NEW The Glevum Way
by Gloucester Ramblers. A 38.5km/24-mile circular route around Gloucester originally launched in 1995. New colour leaflet now available, dividing the Way into five sections with transport connections *available free from Gloucester TIC ☎ 01452 396572.*

North Cotswold Diamond Way
Thirty sparkling short walks by Elizabeth Bell (North Cotswold Group). Revised edition presenting this 96km/60-mile circular route via Moreton-on-Marsh, devised to celebrate the Ramblers' diamond jubilee in 1975, as 30 linked shorter (around 8km/5 miles) circular walks. Varied terrain, gently undulating with no steep hills, stone villages, open fields, streams and pleasant rural views. *£6.95 + £2 p&p from Holly Tree House, Evenlode GL56 0NT. Cheques to Ramblers' Association North Cotswold Group.*

Samaritans Way South West
A Walk from Bristol to Lynton by Graham Hoyle. Linking Bristol with the Cotswold Way National Trail at Bath, the Mendips, Cheddar, the Quantocks, Exmoor National Park and the South West Coast Path at Lynton, 160km/100 miles. Pocket guide with overprinted old OS map extracts.
£5.45 from Samaritans Way SW Association, 6 Mervyn Road, Bristol BS7 9EL or email samaritansway@aol.com Cheques to Samaritans Way SW.

Six Walks in Chipping Sodbury
by South Gloucestershire Council and Southwold Ramblers. Leaflets are Work and Play, Golf Course and Common, The Sodbury Round, Old Sodbury and Kingrove Common, Kingrove Common and Codrington, Paddocks and Ponds. *Free from Chipping Sodbury Tourist Information Centre, The Clock Tower, Chipping Sodbury BS37 6AH ☎ 01454 888686.*

South Bristol Circular Walk
devised by Neil Buriton. A 37km/23-mile route following quiet streets and paths around the south of the city, from Temple Meads station via Troopers Hill, Whitchurch, Dundry and Clifton Bridge. The route offers beautiful views of the city centre, the Avon Valley, Stockwood Nature Reserve, Dundry Hill and Ashton Court. Lots of opportunities to split the walk into smaller sections via public transport, and a connection with the Bristol Triangular City Walk (see above). Developed by Bristol Group and Bristol council. Excellent free colour booklet with maps, route description, photos.
Free from Bristol TIC.

Waymarked Trails in the Forest of Dean and Highmeadow Woods
Attractive leaflet describing two circular walks, the Beechenhurst Trail and the Highmeadow Trail.
60p + 30p p&p as North Cotswold Diamond Way above.

Walk West
by Geoff Mullett (Avon Area). Thirty country walks of between 6.5km/4 miles and 22.5km/14 miles within easy reach of Bristol and Bath, including south Wales.
Walk West Again
by Geoff Mullett, ISBN 1-901184-61-7. A second volume of walks from 6.5km/4 miles to 19km/12 miles, within easy reach of Bristol and Bath.
£7.99 each from 12 Gadshill Drive, Stoke Gifford, Bristol BS34 8UX. Cheques to Geoff Mullett. For information and updates visit walk-west.members.beeb.net

Yate Walks Leaflets
by Yate Town Council and Southwold Ramblers. Three leaflets: Brimshaw Manor Walk, Stanshawes Walk and Upstream & Downstream Walk.
Free from Yate Town Council, Poole Court, Poole Court Drive, Yate BS37 5PP, ☎ 01454 866506.

HAMPSHIRE
Avon Valley Path
55km/34-mile route from Salisbury to Christchurch.
£2.99 from 9 Pine Close, Dibden Purlieu, Southampton SO45 4AT. Cheques payable to Ramblers' Association New Forest Group.

King's Way
by Pat Miles, ISBN 0-861460-93-X (Meon Group). A 72km/45-mile walk from Portchester to Winchester, divided into easy stages.
£3.25 + £1 p&p from 19 New Road, Fareham PO16 7SR. Cheques to Ramblers' Association Meon Group.

More Than the New Forest
by New Forest Ramblers, ISBN 1-901184-75-7. Not a guide book, but a collection of forest lore and walking anecdotes, from prehistory to the National Park, illustrated with cartoons. *£1.*
More Walks Around the New Forest
Seventeen walks between 5km/3 miles and 13km/8 miles covering the whole of the proposed National Park, with detailed maps, route descriptions, points of special interest and colour photos. *£2.50.*
Walking the Wessex Heights
Detailed maps and route descriptions for a 123km/77-mile route and 14 circular walks. *£1.99.*
NEW Walks Around the New Forest
National Park 17 newly surveyed and updated short and medium length routes into the heart of the new National Park and along its borders, plus carefully researched route maps, times and walk directions.
£3.50 + 50p p&p.
All from 9 Pine Close, Dibden Purlieu, Southampton SO45 4AT. Cheques payable to Ramblers' Association New Forest Group.

Rural Rambles from the villages around Alton
by Alton and District Ramblers. Ten circular walks from 9.5km/6 miles to 16km/10 miles starting from villages, including details of places of interest, pubs and public transport. Ideal for visitors to east Hampshire and Jane Austen's house at Chawton.
Walks From Alton
10 walks from 6km/4 miles to 14km/9 miles through typical Hampshire landscapes, all starting in the town.
£3.50 for both from Green Bank, Wilsons Road, Headley Down, Bordon GU35 8JG. Cheques to Alton and District Ramblers.

 ## NEW 12 Walks in and Around Winchester
Updated edition. Moderate-level walks in town and countryside varying from 3km/2 miles to 14.5km/9 miles. *£2 + 50p p&p from Underhill House, Beech Copse, Winchester SO22 5NR. Cheques to Winchester Ramblers.*

HEREFORDSHIRE
The Herefordshire Trail
by Hereford Ramblers, ISBN 1-901184-73-0. A 246km/154-mile circuit of Herefordshire visiting all eight market towns in the county, some delightful villages and attractive countryside. Ringbound colour guide dividing the route into 15 manageable sections of around 16km/10 miles each, most with public transport connections, with detailed route descriptions, tempting photos and very clear maps. *£5.95 + £2 p&p from The*

Book Secretary, 98 Gorsty Lane, Hereford HR1 1UN. Cheques to the Hereford Group of the Ramblers' Association.

HERTFORDSHIRE
Ten Walks in North Herts
by North Hertfordshire Ramblers, ISBN 0-900613-90-4. Ten mainly easy walks of 9.5km/6 miles for enjoyment in all seasons, most accessible by public transport and each a personal favourite.
£2.50 + 21p p&p from 55 Derby Way, Stevenage SG1 5TR. Cheques to North Herts Ramblers Group.

ISLE OF WIGHT
12 Favourite Walks on the Isle of Wight
12 More Favourite Walks on the Isle of Wight
12 Walks from Country Towns on the Isle of Wight
Walks of between 5km/3 miles and 14.5km/9 miles, with simple maps and route descriptions, all suitable for the infrequent walker.
All £2 + 40p p&p each from Dibs, Main Road, Rookley, Ventnor PO38 3NQ. Cheques payable to Mrs Joan Deacon.

 ## NEW Vectis Trail
by Isle of Wight Ramblers, originally devised by Barbara Aze and Iris Evans. A 120km/75-mile mainly inland exploration of the Isle of Wight devised by local Ramblers, this route predates many of the excellent signed walking routes that now crisscross this well-loved island. This fully revised and updated guide splits the route into six sections between transport points with sketch maps, full route descriptions and plenty of helpful practical information.
£2.50 including postage and packaging from Mike Marchant, Merry Meeting, Ryde House Drive, Binstead Road, Ryde, Isle of Wight PO33 3NF. Cheques to Isle of Wight Ramblers' Association.

KENT
Ashford Ring Walk and 7 Loop Walks
by Fred Wright (Ashford Group). A 35km/22-mile loop circling Ashford, linking outer villages, and connected by loops of around 13km/8 miles to the town centre. *£2.50 from 93 Rylands Road, Kennington, Ashford TN24 9LR. Cheques to Ashford Ramblers.*

Maidstone Circular Walk Part 1 and Part 2
Two sets of six walk cards describing a circular route around Maidstone. *Each £1.80 + 50p p&p from Little Preston Lodge, Coldharbour Lane, Aylesford ME20 7NS. Cheques to Ramblers' Association – Maidstone Group.*

PLANNING A BREAK?
FREE VISITOR GUIDES
FROM THE HOLIDAY GUIDE FINDER

Free Visitor Guides can be ordered all year round. These colourful guides contain a wealth of information on accommodation and places to visit and are delivered to your home completely free of charge. Guides can be ordered online now at www.guidefinder.co.uk or send for our free directory showing the guides available with a free reader reply coupon.

The Holiday Guide Finder
PO BOX 132 LUDLOW SY8 9AD

www.guidefinder.co.uk

Walks to Interesting Places in Sussex & Kent and Walks in the Weald
(Heathfield & District Group): see Sussex.

LANCASHIRE & MANCHESTER

Cown Edge Way (Manchester Area)
32km/20-mile walk in six sections from Hazel Grove, Stockport to Gee Cross, Woodley, with notes on history, fauna and flora, maps and drawings.
£1 from 31 Wyverne Road, Manchester M21 0ZW. Cheques to RA Manchester Area.

NEW The Hodder Way With Circular Walks Along The Hodder
by Clitheroe Ramblers, ISBN 1-901184-86-2. A new medium distance walk (43km/27 miles) from the source of the Hodder to its confluence with the Ribble, described as eight circular walks (mainly around 11km/7 miles) and two walks to the centre of Great Britain.
£4.50.

25 Walks in the Ribble and Hodder Valleys
by Clitheroe Ramblers, ISBN 1-901184-72-2. 25 walks from 6.5km/4 miles to 9.5km/6 miles all selected by members of the Group.
£5.99.
Both from 1 Albany Drive, Salesbury, Blackburn BB1 9EH. Cheques to The Ramblers' Association Clitheroe Group Social Account.

Rambles Around Oldham
by Oldham Ramblers. 20 easy walks of between 6.5km/4 miles and 16km/10 miles, all connecting with bus services, including Sites of Biological Importance.
£3.50 + 50p p&p from 682 Ripponden Road, Oldham OL4 2LP. Cheques to Oldham Ramblers Book Account.

Walks Around Heywood
by S Jackson and DM Williams (Rochdale Group). 20 easy to moderate walks of 5km/3 miles to 10km/6 miles in Heywood and surrounding area, with public transport details and local information.
£3 + 50p p&p from 152 Higher Lomax Lane, Heywood OL10 4SJ. Cheques to Ramblers' Association Rochdale Group.

Walks from the Limestone Link
ISBN 0-904350-41-X. 17 easy walks of between 2km/1.5 miles and 16km/10 miles in the beautiful limestone area north of Lancaster, and the 19km/12-mile Limestone Link path. Includes maps and sketches.
£2.95 + 45p p&p.

Walks in the Lune Valley
ISBN 0-904350-39-8. Fourteen walks of between 4km/2.5 miles and 24km/15 miles, and the Lune Valley Ramble, 37km up the north bank of the river and 38.5km/24 miles down the south bank. Includes maps and sketches.
£2.95 + 45p p&p.

Walks in North West Lancashire
15 easy walks of between 6.5km/4 miles and 14.5km/9 miles in the areas surrounding the rivers Lune, Keer and Wyre and parts of Silverdale and Arnside and Forest of Bowland AONBs, including sketch maps and notes on public transport.
£2.95 + 45p p&p.

NEW More Walks in North West Lancashire
ISBN 0-904350-46-0. 21 walks of between 5km/3 miles and 14.5km/9 miles in the areas surrounding the rivers Lune, Keer and Wyre and parts of Silverdale and Arnside and Forest of Bowland AONBs, including sketch maps and notes on public transport. Most are easy but nine are in access areas and include rough walking.
£2.95 + 45p p&p.

NEW Walks Round Lancaster City
ISBN 0-904350-45-2. Five easy walks between 7km/4 miles and 8km/5 miles from the city centre which can be combined into one 24km/15 mile walk through the surrounding countryside. *£1.50 + 40p p&p.*
All from 116 North Road, Carnforth LA5 9LX. Cheques to Ramblers' Association Lancaster Group.

LINCOLNSHIRE

Country Walks in Kesteven
by NSP Mitchell (new for 2002). 30 circular walks, many with shorter options, from 2.5km/1.5 miles to 14.5km/9 miles, within a 24km/15-mile radius of Grantham. Walk descriptions and sketch maps. This book has been revised and expanded many times since its original appearance in 1975.
£3.50 post free from Tweedsdale, Aviary Close, Grantham NG31 9LF. Cheques to Grantham Ramblers.

Danelaw Way
by Brett Collier. A 100km/60-mile walk in five stages between Lincoln and Stamford, the 'burghs' of the ancient Danelaw, plus a circular route from Ryhall. The spiral bound guide has a detailed route description, sketch maps, background and extracts from poetry related to the route. *£5.95 + 80p p&p from 39 Fiskerton Rd, Reepham, Lincoln LN3 4EF. Cheques to Lincoln Group Ramblers' Association.*

Gingerbread Way
A Grantham Perimeter Country Walk (Grantham Group). 40km/25 mile challenging circuit developed to celebrate the Ramblers' Golden Jubilee in 1985. The name of the path refers to the gingerbread biscuit, a Grantham speciality. Booklet with route description and OS 1:50 000 map.
£1.20 post free from Tweedsdale, Aviary Close, Grantham NG31 9LF. Cheques to Grantham Ramblers.

Lindsey Loop
by Brett Collier, ISBN 1-901184-13-7 (2nd edition). 154km/96 miles through the Lincolnshire Wolds Area of Outstanding Natural Beauty between Market Rasen and Louth, in eight stages.
£5.95 + 70p p&p.
Sew-on badge for this route
£1.25 + p&p.
Plogsland Round
by Brett Collier, ISBN 1-901184-41-2. A 75km/47 mile circular walk around Lincoln.
£5.50 + 60p p&p
Viking Way and Danelaw Way and Plogsland Round sew-on badges
£1.25 each + SAE.
All from 2 Belgravia Close Lincoln LN6 0QJ. Cheques to Lincoln Group Ramblers' Association.

Our Favourite Walks:
See under Staffordshire.

The Silver Lincs Way Linking Grimsby & Louth
A 40km/25-mile walk through the Lincolnshire Wolds via Ludborough using footpaths, bridleways and quiet lanes. A parallel bus service offers good public transport connections. Established by Grimsby/Louth Ramblers to mark their 25th anniversary, in conjunction with the Lincolnshire Wolds countryside service and with funding from Awards for All.
Circular Walks from the Silver Lincs Way
Linking paths and circular options from the Silver Lincs Way, giving a choice of walks from 3km/2 miles up to 21.5km/13.5 miles. *Both colour leaflets with maps, points of interest and route descriptions, free from local information outlets or by sending an SAE to 50 Gayton Road, Cleethorpes DN35 0HN.*

Towers Way
by Alan Nash, Janet Nash, Tony Broad. A meandering 160km/100-mile route linking 40 churches between Barton-upon-Humber and Lincoln Cathedral, as an alternative to the Viking Way. Route description available from 39 Fiskerton Road, Reepham, Lincoln LN3 4EF; publication to follow.

LONDON

Highlights of Surrey
Includes some walks in south London:
see under Surrey.

Rural Walks around Richmond
by Ramblers' Association Richmond
Group. 21 walks of between 3km/2 miles
and 24km/15 miles, many with various
short options, in a London borough rich in
green space, including Richmond Park,
Bushey Park, Barnes and the Thames. Eight
walks have details of wheelchair-accessible
sections, including one route that is
accessible throughout. £1.80 + 45p p&p
from 59 Gerard Road, London SW13 9QH.
Cheques to Margaret Sharp.

NORFOLK

Angles Way
edited by Sheila Smith, ISBN 1-901184-
84-6. 125km/78mile route following the
Waveney Valley along the Norfolk/Suffolk
border from Great Yarmouth in the
Norfolk Broads to Knettishall Heath in the
Suffolk Brecks, and completing the circuit of
the Peddars Way National Trail and
Weavers Way. Includes maps, public
transport information and accommodation.
Iceni Way
edited by Sheila Smith, ISBN 1-901184-
64-1.134.5km/84-mile route from
Knettishall Heath in Breckland to the coast
at Hunstanton along the Little and Great
Ouse Valleys. First 24km/15 miles from
Knettishall to Thetford is a useful footpath
link for Peddars Way or Angles Way with
transport and other facilities in Thetford.
Guide includes maps, accommodation
details and transport information.
North Norfolk Rambles
edited by Allan Jones, ISBN 1-901184-88-
9. 16 walks covering coast, country and
city in the area around Hunstanton,
Cromer and Norwich, 9km/5.5 miles to
17km/10.5 miles and all from car parks,
with sketch maps.
Southern Norfolk Rambles
edited by Allan Jones, ISBN 1-901184-87-
0. 16 walks in the Broads and Brecks,
9.5km/6 miles to 17.5km/11 miles and all
from car parks, with sketch maps.

 **NEW Walking the
Peddars Way & Norfolk
Coast Path with Weavers
Way**
edited by Ian Mitchell, ISBN
978-901184-95-2. Concise
guide covering a total distance of
239km/149 miles of the national trail from
Knettishall Heath to Holme-next-the Sea
then along the coast to Cromer, and an
inland route from Cromer to Great
Yarmouth. Combined with the Angles Way
they provide a circular route of 364km/
227 miles. Guide includes maps, public
transport information and accommodation.

West Norfolk Walkaway 3
edited by Allan Jones, ISBN 1-901184-89-
7.16 easy circular walks between 8km/
5 miles to 15km/9.5 miles in the area of
the Peddars Way, between King's Lynn and
Fakenham. Sketch maps, route descriptions
and details of local features, with sketch
maps and details of local features.
All £2.70 each + 30p p&p (1st class post –
add 10p) each from Caldcleugh, Cake
Street, Old Buckenham, Attleborough NR17
1RU. Postage is free if three or more guides
are ordered together. Cheques to Ramblers'
Association, Norfolk Area.

NORTHUMBERLAND
**NEW A Walk Round Berwick
Borough**
by Arthur Wood. ISBN 978-0-
9545331-1-3. A 120-mile circuit of
Berwick Borough, through beautiful
scenery in a land bearing witness to a
turbulent history. It passes five castles, a
palace and a mountain. A hand-drawn and
lettered pocket book. £4.95.
Berwick Walks
by Arthur Wood. ISBN 978-0954533-0-6.
A beautifully hand-drawn and calligraphed
pocket book with 24 town, coastal,
countryside and riverside walks within a
19km/12-mile radius of Berwick upon
Tweed, many of them shorter walks. £4.95.
Both from Berwick Group, 5 Quay Walls,
Berwick-upon-Tweed TD15 1HB. Cheques to
Ramblers' Association.

**Walking the Tyne: Twenty-five Walks
from Mouth to Source**
by J B Jonas (Northumbria Area). ISBN
1-901184-70-6. A route along all
133km/83 miles of this great river, divided
into 25 linked, mainly circular walks of
8km/5 miles to 14.5km/9 miles, with
suggestions for lunch stops, time estimates,
public transport details, and notes on stiles,
terrain and places of interest. Follows the
North Tyne from Hexham to the source.
£5.50.
**Walking the North Tyne: Seventeen
Walks from Hexham to the Source**
by JB Jonas (Northumbria Area). ISBN
1-901184-82-X. Complementing
Walking the Tyne by the same author, this
volume follows the North Tyne branch of
the river through remote northern
countryside from Hexham to the source
near Deadwater in the Kielder Forest
area, including a walk alongside Kielder
Water. Divided into sections, most of
which are circular (3km/2 miles to
12km/7.5 miles). Total length of the walk is
76km/47.5 miles. Sketch maps, photos,
route description and practical information.
£5.
Both from 8 Beaufront Avenue, Hexham
NE46 1JD. Cheques to J B Jonas, profits to
Ramblers' Association.

SHROPSHIRE
**Ramblers Guide to the Shropshire
Way**
by Shropshire Ramblers. ISBN 1-946679-
44-4. Guidebook with useful background
information and clear sketch maps.
£6.99 + £1.50 p&p from Pengwern Books,
23 Princess St, Shrewsbury SY1 1LW.
Cheques to Pengwern Books.

SOMERSET
Channel to Channel Seaton-Watchet
by Ken Young: 80km/50-mile rural walk
across the southwest peninsula at its
narrowest point, via the Blackdown Hills.
£2 + 50p p&p from K Young, 14 Wilton
Orchard, Taunton TA1 3SA. Cheques to
Somerset Area Ramblers' Association.

Somerset Walks
by Taunton Deane Ramblers, illustrated by
Ann Sharp, ISBN 1-901184-69-2. 16
circular walks 6.5km/4 miles to 22.5km/
14 miles, including the Quantocks,
Blackdown Hills, Brendon Hills, Somerset
Levels and Exmoor, with notes on things to
look out for, tea shops and pubs, but all
from car parks. £2.95 + 50p p&p from
Greenway Thatch, North Curry, Taunton TA3
6NH. Cheques to Taunton Deane Ramblers.

Walking for Pleasure
edited by Mike Emmett (Taunton Deane
Group). 14 circular walks exploring the
hidden countryside in and around Taunton
Deane, 6.5km/4 miles to 10.5km/
6.5 miles. £2 + 50p p&p from Fairacre,
West Hatch, Taunton TA3 5RJ. Cheques to
Mike Emmett.

 **NEW Walks Around
Shepton Mallet**
compiled by Mendip Group
and published by Shepton
Mallet Town Council.
Thirteen circular walks of
between walks of 5km/3 miles to 18km/11
miles, all starting at Mendip District Council
car park. Includes colour photographs, OS
map extracts, clear route descriptions and
historical reference. £3.95 from Shepton
Mallet Town Council, 1 Park Road, Shepton
Mallet BA4 5BS, ☎ 01749 343984.
Cheques to Shepton Mallet Town Council.

 NEW Yeovil's Green Bypass
Free leaflet guide to a 2km/
1.5 mile fully accessible traffic-free
walking and cycling route across
town linking Pen Mill Station with
Yeovil Country Park and the
Westlands Area. Produced by the Heart
of Wessex Rail Partnership in collaboration
with South Somerset Group.
Free from Yeovil Visitor Information Centre
☎ 01935 845946 or download at
www.heartofwessex.org.uk

STAFFORDSHIRE
Our Favourite Walks
Twelve walks of between 11km/7 miles and 22.5km/14 miles, mainly in Staffordshire but venturing into Derbyshire and Shropshire.
£2.95 + 35p p&p or A5 SAE from Liz Charlton at 48, Bluebell Hollow, Walton on the Hill, Stafford ST17 0JN. Cheques to Ramblers' Association, Mid Staffs Group.

Walks Around Stone
by Stone Ramblers. Twelve walks each from Westridge Port and from Downs Banks, between 1.5km/1 mile and 11km/7 miles with route descriptions, maps and guidance on healthy walking in plastic cover.
£3 + 50p p&p from 1 Vanity Close, Oulton, Stone ST15 8TZ. Cheques to Ramblers' Association Stone Group.

SUFFOLK
Cornard and Beyond
by Laurie Burroughs, ISBN 1-901194-65-X (Sudbury Group). Four short easy walks of 6.5km/4 miles or less through the countryside around Cornard.
Glemsford and Beyond
by Lesley Pilbrow (Sudbury Group). A4 route cards with three walks of 6.5km/4 miles to 9.5km/6 miles, all starting at Glemsford's fifteenth century church.
Both £1.20 + 50p p&p each from 6 Chaplin Walk, Great Cornard, Sudbury CO10 0YT. Cheques to Sudbury and District Ramblers.

East Suffolk Line Walks: Station to Station Ipswich to Lowestoft
by Roger Wolfe, ISBN 0-9547865-0-5. 11 varied and attractive walks linking the stations along the East Suffolk Line through both remote rural areas and parkland on the urban fringe, ranging from a short stroll beside a tidal estuary (2.5km/1.5 miles) to a lengthy field path and woodland walk (16km/10 miles). All the walks link together so you can join together sections to taste or even treat the route as a single long distance path of over 112km/70 miles. Jointly published by the East Suffolk Travellers Association, Suffolk Area and Railfuture.
£2 from East Suffolk Travellers Association, 15 Clapham Road South, Lowestoft NR32 1RQ, or downloadable at www.eastsuffolklinewalks.co.uk

Rural Rambles Round Beccles
(Waveney Ramblers) 12 walks, 5.5km/3.5 miles to 13km/8 miles.
Rural Rambles Round Lowestoft
(Waveney Ramblers) 11 walks, 6.5km/4 miles to 16km/10 miles.
Rural Rambles Round Southwold
(Waveney Ramblers) 12 walks, 8km/5 miles to 13km/8 miles.
All £1.80 + 35p p&p each, address as

Waveney Way below.
Waveney Way
(Waveney Ramblers). 115km/72 mile circular walk from Lowestoft.
£2.10 + 35p p&p from 1 Church Close, Redenhall, Harleston IP20 9QS. Cheques to Ramblers' Association.

SURREY
Four Stations Way
18.5km/11 mile route via stations from Godalming to Haslemere. Illustrated in both directions on two laminated A4 cards
£1.50 + 50p p&p from Kate Colley, 6 Hill Court, Haslemere GU27 2BD. Cheques to Godalming and Haslemere RA Group.

The Highlights of Surrey
A series of 48 online walks originally devised by members of Surrey Area to mark the Millennium. Lengths from 3km/2 miles to 13.5km/8.5 miles with some linking walks, and 30 of the walks starting from train stations. The walk descriptions are in simple route card style and you will need to be able to use an OS map.
surreyhilitewalks.mysite.wanadoo-members.co.uk

Twenty-five Favourite Walks in West Surrey & Sussex
by Godalming & Haslemere Ramblers, revised edition, ISBN 1-901184-63-3. Variety of circular walks offering both short and long options between 5.5km/3.5 miles and 25.5km/16 miles.
£4.95 + 60p p&p from Elstead Maps UK Ltd, 11 The Bramley Business Centre, Station Road, Bramley, Guildford GU5 0AZ, ☎ 01483 898099. Cheques to Elstead Maps.

NEW Another Twenty-five Favourite Walks in Surrey, Sussex & Hampshire
by Godalming & Haslemere Ramblers, ISBN 978-1-901184-81-5. A new book of 25 circular walks offering longer and shorter options, available 2007.
£4.95 + 60p p&p. Visit www.godalmingand haslemereramblers.org.ukGuides.htm for up-to-date details or contact Godalming & Haslemere Group secretary (p79).

SUSSEX
Sussex Diamond Way
Midhurst–Heathfield. 96km/60 mile walk across the county.
Free + £1 p&p.
Walks to Interesting Places in Sussex & Kent
by Heathfield Ramblers, ISBN 0-900613-99-8. Twenty-one walks from 4km/2.5miles across easy terrain, including some linear walks returning on preserved railways.

£3.50
Walks in the Weald
Revised 2nd edition. Thirty-six walks from 5km/3 miles to 16km/10 miles (average 10km) across varied terrain. £3.50.
All from Cobbetts, Burnt Oak Road, High Hurstwood, Uckfield TN22 4AE. Cheques to Heathfield and District RA Group.

Twenty-five Favourite Walks in West Surrey & Sussex
NEW Another Twenty-five Favourite Walks in Surrey, Sussex & Hampshire
See under Surrey.

WILTSHIRE
Avon Valley Path
See under Hampshire.

The Kennet & Avon Wiggly Walks Guide
Three walks 3km/2 miles to 19km/12 miles, along the beautiful Vale of Pewsey and the Kennet and Avon Canal, connecting with Wigglybus services from Devizes. Produced by the Kennt and Avon Canal Rural Transport Partnership with assistance from the Ramblers.
Free from ☎ 01249 460600.

Northeast Wiltshire Group Publications:
Nine Downland Walks between Swindon and Marlborough
between 5km/3 miles and 12km/7.5 miles on the Downs. £2.20.
Ten walks from village pubs near Swindon
by Pat Crabb. Short circular walks of 2km/1.5 miles to 8km/5 miles with bus options given where appropriate. £2.20.
11 Short Walks in North East Wiltshire
by Phil Claridge. Circular walks of 7km/4.5 miles to 9km/5.5 miles. £2.20.
12 Walks around Marlborough:
between 5.5km/3.5 miles and 14.5km/9 miles. £2.20.
20 Walks around Swindon
by Northeast Wiltshire Ramblers: between 3km/2 miles and 12km/7.5 miles, within a 30km/20-mile radius of Swindon. £2.50.
All from 21 Brynards Hill, Wootton Bassett, Swindon SN4 7ER. Cheques to Ramblers' Association NE Wilts Group.

Sarum Way
A circular walk around Salisbury and Wilton. Booklet £3.50 from 27 Richard Way, Salisbury SP2 8NT. Cheques to South Wilts Ramblers Group.

South Wiltshire Group Publications:
Eight easy walks in the Salisbury

Area route card pack
Ten shorter walks in the Salisbury Area booklet
Ten longer walks in the Salisbury Area route card pack
£3.50 each from 27 Richard Way, Salisbury SP2 8NT. Cheques to Ramblers' Association W3.

Ten Walks Around Devizes
Varied walks of between 6.5km/4 miles and 11km/7 miles starting at Devizes market place, with maps, illustrations and historical notes. *£1.50 + 40p p&p from 1 Copings Close, Devizes SN10 5BW. Cheques to Ramblers' Association Mid Wilts Group.*

12 Walks Around Chippenham
by Chippenham Ramblers, ISBN 1-00033-88-6. Varied selection of 4km/2.5 mile to 11km/8-mile walks in excellent walking country, all using public transport. *£2*

 NEW 12 More Walks Around Chippenham
by Chippenham Ramblers. A selection of 5km/3-mile to 14.5km/9-mile walks. £2.50. *Both from 11A High Street, Sutton Benger SN15 4RE. Cheques to RA Chippenham Group.*

West Wiltshire Group Publications:
Ten Walks in West Wiltshire
Ten circular walks between 6.5km/4 miles and 17.5km/11 miles, including some near railway stations, with OS maps. £2.50.
Walking in West Wiltshire Book 2
10 circular walks between 6.5km/4 miles and 11km/7 miles, including some near railway stations, with sketch maps. £1.25.
Walking in West Wiltshire Book 3
10 circular walks between 8km/5 miles and 16km/10 miles, including some near railway stations, with sketch maps. £1.25.
All from 68 Savernake Avenue, Melksham SN12 7HE. Cheques to West Wilts Ramblers' Association.

21 Walks for the 21st Century
See under Berkshire.

WORCESTERSHIRE
Bromsgrove Ramblers
48km/30-mile circuit around Bromsgrove from Wychbold via Chaddesley Corbett and Alvechurch, devised to celebrate the 30th anniversary of the Group. Leaflet has route description and overview map and would need to be used in conjunction with the local OS map. *£1.50 from 13 Victoria Road, Bromsgrove B61 0DW. Cheques to Ramblers' Association Bromsgrove Group.*

Walks in the Vale of Evesham
2nd edition. Twelve walks, all reasonably easy, of between 2.5km/1.5 miles and 11.5km/7 miles, in and around Evesham.

£3 + A5 1st class SAE, from 12 Queens Road, Evesham WR11 4JN. Cheques to RA Vale of Evesham Group.

YORKSHIRE
Airedale Way
by Douglas Cossar. ISBN 0-900613-95-5. An 80km/50-mile riverside walk from Leeds to Malham Tarn in the Dales, in 11 sections, 10 of them walkable as circular walks, with additional walks in Airedale. *£4.50 + £1 p&p from 11 Woodroyd Avenue, Honley, Holmfirth HD9 6LG. Cheques to West Riding Area Ramblers' Association.*

Car-Free Countryside Walks accessible from York
by Patsy Pendegrass, ISBN 1-904446-04-3 (East Yorkshire and Derwent Area). Fifteen walks from stations or bus stops over a wide area within easy reach of York, all 8km/5 miles to 19.5km/12 miles, some with shorter options.
£4.99 from local bookshops or from the author (+ 50p p&p) at 92 The Village, Haxby, York YO32 2JL. Cheques to PM Pendegrass. All profits to Ramblers' Association.

Chalkland Way
by Ray Wallis (Hull RA). 66km/40-mile circular walk through the chalk hills of the Yorkshire Wolds from Pocklington, including chalk wolds, arable land and woodland. A few steep hills but not too strenuous.
Colour leaflet free + A5 SAE to R Wallis, 75 Ancaster Avenue, Kingston upon Hull HU5 4QR. Badge available from the same source.

Country Walks in Mirfield, Emley, Thornhill and Denby Dale
by Douglas Cossar and John Lieberg, ISBN 1-901184-30-7. 17 circular walks of between 6km/4 miles and 12km/7.5 miles, with sketch maps, route descriptions, photos and public transport details.
£4.75 + £1 p&p, as Airedale Way (above).

Dales Way Handbook
edited by West Riding RA. An annually updated guide to accommodation and transport along the path between Ilkley and Windermere.
£1.50 + £1 p&p, as Airedale Way (above).

Danum Trail
A series of walks linking villages and towns in Doncaster borough, readily accessible by public transport and creating a 80km/50-mile walk from Dome Leisure Park Doncaster to the Glass Park, Kirk Sandall, taking in the Earth Centre, short sections of the Trans Pennine Trail, historic villages and open countryside. Colour foldout leaflet with map of the route and notes on places

of interest.
£1.30 from 31 Broom Hill Drive, Doncaster DN4 6QZ. Cheques to Ramblers' Association Doncaster Group.

Dearne Valley Group Walks
(Dearne Valley Ramblers). Seven free walks leaflets: Conisborough to Sprotbrough (9.5km/6 miles easy); River Don Walk from Sprotbrough via Cusworth (13km/8 miles easy); Elsecar and Wentworth (12km/7.5 miles easy); Swinton and Rawmarsh (8km/5 miles easy to moderate); Dearne Valley Ramble (11km/7 miles easy to moderate); Broomhill, Bolton & Wath (6.5km/4 miles easy); Swinton & Wath (8km/5 miles easy to moderate). Each has sketch map and route description.
Free + SAE from 6 Ruskin Avenue, Mexborough S64 0AU, or downloadable from www.dearnevalleyramblers.org.uk

East Riding Walks
(East Yorkshire and Derwent Ramblers). Four circular routes of around 14.5km/9 miles each with full description and photo, in a plastic case.
£2 from 2 Spellowgate, Driffield YO25 7BB. Cheques to J Jefferson.

Harrogate Dales Way Link
32km/20 miles from Valley Gardens, Harrogate to Bolton Abbey, linking to the Dales Way. A5 leaflet.
30p + SAE.
Sew-on badge available on completion.
£1.50 + SAE.
Harrogate Ringway
(Harrogate Ramblers). 33.5km/21 miles circular trail around this spa town, starting from Pannal via Knaresborough, in easy stages with public transport connections. A5 leaflet.
30p + SAE.
Sew-on badge available on completion.
£1.50 + SAE
Both from 20 Pannal Ash Grove, Harrogate HG2 0HZ. Cheques to Harrogate RA Group.

Kirklees Way. Circular walk around Huddersfield and Dewsbury
£2.70 + £1 p&p, as Airedale Way (above).

Knaresborough Round
32km/20 mile circular walk round this ancient town, in two stages with bus connections. A5 leaflet.
30p + SAE.
Sew-on badge available on completion.
£1.50, as Harrogate Dales Way (above).

Minster Way
by Ray Wallis (Hull RA). An 83km/50-mile signed walk established in 1980 between the Minsters of Beverley and York, crossing

the Yorkshire Wolds and Vale of York. A good variety of countryside, not too strenuous but with hills up to 180m. Guidebook with maps and colour photos, dividing the route into three sections. £4 + 55p p&p from 75 Ancaster Avenue, Hull HU5 4QR. Cheques payable to R Wallis. Badge and accommodation list available from same source.

Penistone Line Trail Sheffield to Huddersfield

by the Penistone Line Partnership, supported by South Yorkshire and North Derbyshire Area. 95km/60 miles divided into several sections ranging from 2.5km/1.5 miles to 7.5km/5 miles, all between stations on this attractive railway branch through the south Pennines, linking Lincoln and Huddersfield. Route descriptions, background on the line, overprinted OS maps.
£4.95 + 55p (or £2.95 + 55p p&p for RA or Partnership members) from PLP, St Johns Community Centre, Church Street, Penistone S36 9AR. Cheques to Penistone Line Partnership.

The Ramblers' Association Book of Kiddiwalks

Thirty short family rambles in and near West Yorkshire 70th Jubilee Edition, by West Riding Ramblers, ISBN 0-900613-88-2. Easy walks 1.5km/1 mile to 6.5km/4 miles, devised principally with young families in mind, with lots of interest along the route, including some suitable for pushchairs. The book includes sketch maps, route descriptions, background notes and photos. All walks are accessible by public transport, with details included. A welcome new edition for this popular guide covering every part of West Yorkshire as well as the southern Yorkshire Dales.
£5.99 + £1 p&p, as Airedale Way (above).

Ramblers' Bradford Volume 1

by Douglas Cossar, ISBN 1-901184-22-6. 20 circular walks 3km/2 miles to 16km/10 miles, covering the whole of the district, accessible by public transport.
£4.95 + £1 p&p.

Ramblers' Leeds Volume 1 East of Leeds

by Douglas Cossar, ISBN 1-901184-23-4. 25 mostly circular walks, 5.5km/3.5 miles to 18.5km/11.5 miles, accessible by public transport.
£4.95 + £1 p&p.

Ramblers' Leeds Volume 2 West of Leeds

by Douglas Cossar, ISBN 1-901184-24-2. 24 mainly circular walks, 4km/2.5 miles to 14.5km/9 miles, using the extensive footpath network in the area, accessible by public transport.
£5.95 + £1 p&p.
All as Airedale Way (above).

Rambles Around Ripon

by Ripon Ramblers. Fifteen varied countryside walks 2km/1.5 miles to 20km/13 miles.
£3.60 + 70p p&p. Cheques to Rambles Around Ripon.

Ripon Rowel Walk

by Les Taylor. 80km/50 mile circular route from Ripon Cathedral via Masham, with 12 circular walks of between 5km/3 miles and 24km/15 miles along the way.
£4.95 + 70p p&p. Cheques to The Ripon Rowel.
Both from 10 Pine Walk, Ripon, HG4 2LW. Order both at the same time and get them for £8 + 70p p&p.

Rotherham Ring Route

by Rotherham Metro Ramblers. An 80km/50-mile circular walk through the gently rolling landscape around the boundary of Rotherham borough including many fine country parks. Pack of 10 leaflets in a plastic wallet plus bus details and additional useful information for beginners.
£2 + £1 p&p from Rotherham Visitor Centre, 40 Bridge Gate, Rotherham S60 1PQ, ☎ 01709 835904. Cheques to Rotherham TIC. Badges and completion cards from same source.

Sheffield Country Walk

3rd edition by Sheffield Group and Sheffield City Council. 87km/54.5 miles through the countryside round Sheffield via Eckington, Dronfield, Burbage, Grenoside and Meadowhall, in ten sections of around 8km/5 miles each, linked by public transport, all with separate colour route cards in an attractive folder.
£3.95 + 55p p&p from Ramblers' Association Sheffield Group, 33 Durvale Court, Sheffield S17 3PT. Cheques to Ramblers' Association Sheffield Group.

Sheffield Walks:
NEW Sheffield Walking Map

Complete fold-out colour map of Sheffield city showing a wide range of walking routes in both the urban areas and surrounding countryside.
Published by Sheffield City Council in partnership with Sheffield Ramblers, a vailable free from Sheffield Visitor Information Centre ☎ 0114 221 1900, or downloadable from the council website (under Roads and Transport/Cycling and Walking/Walking) see p113.
Inner City Round Walk of Sheffield

by Terry Howard. 19km/12-mile circuit through urban streets and parks from Broomhill via Crookesmoor, Pitsmoor, Attercliffe, Sheffield Park, Heeley, Sharrow and the Botanical Gardens.

Iron Age to Steel Age (City Walk)

by Terry Howard. Meadowhall to Doncaster Street (edge of Sheffield city centre), 8km/5 miles.
All leaflets published by Sheffield Ramblers and Sheffield City Council, free from Sheffield Visitor Information Centre ☎ 0114 221 1900.

Wakefield Way

by Douglas Cossar, ISBN 1-901184-74-9 (West Riding Ramblers). Describes a 120km/75-mile loop around the boundary of Wakefield district in West Yorkshire, from Anglers Country Park via Gawsthorpe, Castleford, Pontefract and South Kirkby. Easily walked as 24 shorter walks (5.5km/3.5 miles to 13.5km/8.5 miles), both circular and linear, with public transport connections.
£5.99 + p&p, as Airedale Way above.

NEW Walking with the Ramblers in Sheffield

Free colour leaflets with local walks around Sheffield, all accessible by public transport.
1. Deepcar Circular 11km/7 miles
2. Mayfield and Porter Valleys 6.5km/4 miles, easy.
3. Iron Age to Steel Age (Meadowhall to Crabtree Pond) 5km/3 miles, mainly surfaced paths with no obstructions.
4. Herdings Circular 6.5km/4 miles, easy but numerous stiles, recommended for families.
5. Lodge Moor Circular 13km/8 miles. Includes open country and access land.
6. Moscar Moor 8km/5 miles. Includes open moorland and access land.
From local outlets or contact Sheffield Group ☎ 01709 586870 or download from www.sheffield.ramblers.care4free.net

NEW Walks in and around Kirklees

ISBN 978-1-901184-93-8 Twelve varied, hand-illustrated walks in Huddersfield/Holmfirth area by Huddersfield Group.
£2.40 + £1 p&p.

NEW More Walks in and around Kirklees

ISBN 978-1-901184-94-5 Fifteen varied, hand-illustrated walks in Huddersfield/Holmfirth area by Huddersfield Group.
£2.40 + £1 p&p.
Both from 11 Woodroyd Avenue, Honley, Holmfirth HD9 6LG. Cheques to West Riding Area Ramblers' Association.

Yorkshire Wolds Way Accommodation Guide
(E Yorks & Derwent Area).
95p + SAE from Mrs S M Smith, 65 Ormonde Avenue, Kingston upon Hull HU6 7LT.

WALES

The Pioneer Ramblers
1850-1940 by David Hollett (North Wales Ramblers). ISBN 1-901184-54-4. The history of walking is full of vivid incidents and striking characters, many of them captured in this new book.
£8.95 + £1 p&p from 69 Wethersfield Road, Prenton CH43 9YF. Cheques to North Wales Area RA.

CEREDIGION
Cardigan Centre for Walkers – Aberteifi Canolfan Cerddwyr
by Cardigan and District Ramblers. Collection of 11 graded walks of between 5km/3 miles and 16km/10 miles in and around Cardigan, with connecting bus service information, on attractive cards in a pack. Bilingual Welsh/English.
£5.50 + 50p p&p from G Torr, Parc-y-Pratt, Cardigan SA43 3DR. Cheques to Cardigan and District Ramblers.

Lampeter Walks – Llwybrau Llanbed
by Lampeter Ramblers. ISBN 1-901184-58-7. Revised edition of this book of 16 walks 2.5km/1.5 miles to 13km/8 miles, with route maps, background notes on geographical and historical context and accommodation listings, with colour illustrations and line drawings by Robert Blayney. Bilingual Welsh/English.
£2.50 + £1 p&p from Lampeter Bookshop, 21 Bridge Street, Lampeter SA48 7AA. Cheques to Lampeter Ramblers. Alternatively you can order from www.lampeter.org/english/walks/index.html

DENBIGHSHIRE
Clwydian Way
by David Hollett. ISBN 1-901184-36-6. Circular route around Denbighshire, looping through some of the best walking country in the region, including details of 12 short circular walks.
£5.95 + £1.55 p&p from PO Box 139, Llanfairpwllgwyngyll LL61 6WR . Cheques to The Ramblers' Association North Wales Area.

GLAMORGAN

NEW **Bunny Walk Leaflets.**
Free. Produced by the Taff Ely (Llantrisant) Group. Six A4 sized leaflets with details of short 4km/2.5 mile to 6.5km/4-mile walks around the Llantrisant area in Rhondda Cynon Taf.

PDF electronic copies of the walks are available for download at www.apyule.demon.co.uk/walkindex.htm or contact Marvi Yule ☎ 029 2089 0621 to order.

Capital Walks and **The Capital Walk**
Cardiff Group have produced two books of countryside walks around Cardiff, with a total of 30 short circular walks between about 5km/3 miles and 18km/11.5 miles. These link up into a circular Capital Walk around the city of 61km/38 miles starting from Swanbridge.
Both books are out of print, but walk descriptions are available to download from the website at www.btinternet.com/~cardiff.ramblers

Valeways Millennium Heritage Trail
by B Palmer and G Woodnam (Vale of Glamorgan Group). Fascinating 99km/62-mile circular walk with various spurs linking up many places of historical, geographic and geological interest, developed by a partnership of the Ramblers' Association, Vale of Glamorgan Council and other organisations. Pack with attractive descriptive booklet and 16 route cards with map and route details in easy sections.
£6.99 + £1.50 p&p from Valeways, Unit 7 BCEC, Skomer Road, Barry CF62 9DA. Cheques to Valeways.

Walk West
See under Gloucestershire and Bristol.

Walking Around Gower
4th edition by Albert White. ISBN 0-951878-01-8 (West Glamorgan Ramblers). 10 circular walks of between 8km/5 miles and 21km/13 miles around the Gower peninsula, going out along the coast and returning inland, including extensive notes on scenery, wildlife and history.
Walking Around Northern Gower and the Swansea Valley
by Peter Beck and Peter J Thomas, based on an original work by Albert White. ISBN 0-951878-11-5. Ten circular walks that can be split into 25 shorter circuits, giving options of between 8km/5 miles and 21km/13 miles.in the former mining area north of Swansea and the Gower peninsula. Includes overprinted OS maps and extensive background notes.
Both £7.50 each post free from Peter Beck, 24 Hazelmere Road, Sketty, Swansea SA2 0SN. Cheques to The Ramblers' Association.

MONMOUTHSHIRE
Lower Wye Rambles
2nd edition, edited by Allan Thomas and Gill Nettleship. 16 walks in the Lower Wye Valley, part of the Wye Valley Area of Outstanding Natural Beauty, between

Chepstow and Monmouth, 4-14km/2.5 to 9 miles, some linking together to make longer walks and including parts of the Wye Valley Walk, with clear colour maps.
£3.75 from 3 Mount Way, Chepstow NP16 5EG. Cheques to Lower Wye Group RA.

POWYS
Walks you will enjoy
Pack of 18 walks in east Radnorshire and northwest Herefordshire on laminated pocket-sized cards.
£4.50 (£3.75 to Ramblers members) from East Radnor Publications, 1 Heyope Road, Knucklas LD7 1PT. Cheques to East Radnor Publications.

SCOTLAND

DUNBARTONSHIRE AND LANARKSHIRE
Explore and Enjoy East Dunbartonshire Area Walks
by Bearsden and Milngavie Ramblers and East Dunbartonshire Council. Eight local walks including short, easy options, with OS map extracts.
Free leaflet available from council's access officer ☎ 0141 578 8520 or www.eastdunbarton.gov.uk

Walk Strathkelvin
by John Logan (Strathkelvin Ramblers) with introduction by Cameron McNeish, historical essays by Don Martin and nature notes by Ian McCallum. ISBN 1-901184-44-7. Handsome book of over 70 walks, mainly short and easy walks taking half an hour to two hours, plus longer walks in the Campsies, canalside and disused railway line trails, illustrated with over 40 maps.
£7.99 from Strathkelvin Ramblers, 25 Anne Crescent, Lenzie, Kirkintilloch G66 5HB. Cheques to Strathkelvin Ramblers.

FIFE
Cupar Walks: Explore Fife's Farming Heritage
by St Andrews Ramblers. Free colour leaflet offering a large variety of walks around this historic market town and out into the surrounding countryside. 14 different walks, ranging from 3km/2 miles to 14km/9 miles, and from surfaced paths in parks to rough country and woodland tracks. Maps, detailed route descriptions, photos. Produced in association with ScotWays and funded by Scottish Natural Heritage and Sport Scotland.
Send 22cm x 11cm SAE to 63 St Michaels Drive, Cupar KY15 5BP, or contact St Andrews Tourist Information Centre ☎ 01334 472021.

PUBLISHERS OF WALKS GUIDES

Aurum Press
☎ 020 7637 3225
www.aurumpress.co.uk

Cicerone Press
☎ 01539 562069
www.cicerone.co.uk

Countryside Books
☎ 01635 43816
www.countrysidebooks.co.uk

Frances Lincoln
☎ 020 7284 4009
www.franceslincoln.com

Harvey Maps
☎ 01786 841202
www.harveymaps.co.uk

Jarrold
☎ 01264 409206
www.totalwalking.com

Kittiwake
☎ 01650 511314
www.kittiwake-books.com

memory-map
☎ 0870 740 9040
www.memory-map.co.uk

Rucksack Readers
☎ 01786 824 696
www.rucsacs.com

Sigma Leisure
☎ 01625 531035
www.sigmapress.co.uk

RAMBLERS BOOKSHOP

WALKING IN BRITAIN

walk BRITAIN 2007
The indispensable guide for walkers, packed with useful
information and details of over 2,000 places to stay
£5.99 (free to members)

Ramblers' Regional Guides Directories of places to walk
London (all of Greater London)   FREE
West Midlands (Hereford, Worcs, Shrops, Staffs, Warks) FREE
Yorkshire (including Dales and Moors)   FREE
An older series of guides is available covering other areas: please enquire for details.
Collins Rambler's Guides 30 walks in each colour volume
Ben Nevis and Glen Coe by Chris Townsend   £9.99
Connemara by Paddy Dillon   £9.99
Dartmoor by Richard Sale   £9.99
Isle of Skye by Chris Townsend   £9.99
Yorkshire Dales by David Leather   £9.99
Walking in Britain (FS1) Outline of access arrangements,
transport, accommodation, parks etc   FREE
Walk South East England Colour booklet   FREE

PATHS AND ROUTES

Angles Way Norfolk Broads–Suffolk Broads
Route guide with accommodation by RA Norfolk/Suffolk £2.70
Battlefields Trail Edgcote–Cropredy Bridge–Edgehill FREE
Capital RING Inner London Circular
Official guide to whole route by Colin Saunders £12.99
Walking the Ceredigion Coast   FREE
Cleveland Way Around North York Moors and coast
Accommodation and information guide   FREE

Cotswold Way Chipping Campden to Bath
Handbook: Accommodation list and practical info £2.95
Cumbria Way Ulverston to Carlisle
Official RA Guide by John Trevelyan   £2.99
Dales Way Leeds, Bradford or Ilkley to Bowness
Handbook and accommodation list   £1.50
Great Glen Way Fort William to Inverness
Accommodation and services guide   FREE
Green Chain Walk Thames Barrier, Thamesmead, Erith to
Chislehurst, Crystal Palace   £3.50
Gritstone Trail Disley to Kidsgrove   FREE
Hadrian's Wall Path Wallsend to Bowness
Accommodation guide   FREE
Heart of England Way Stafford to Bourton on the Water
Accommodation list   FREE
Icknield Way See under Ridgeway
John Musgrave Heritage Trail Maidencombe–Brixham £2.50
Jubilee Walkway Central London map/guide   FREE
London Loop near-circular walk around outer London
Official guide to whole route by David Sharp   £12.99
New River Path Islington–Hertford   FREE
**Walking the Peddars Way & Norfolk Coast Path with
Weavers Way** Guidebook with accommodation   £2.70
Pennine Bridleway Derbyshire to the South Pennines National
Accommodation and information guide   FREE
Pennine Way Edale to Kirk Yetholm
Accommodation and transport pack   FREE
Ridgeway/Greater Ridgeway (see also Peddars Way)
Wessex Ridgeway Marlborough to Shaftesbury   £2.00
Icknield Way Ivinghoe to Knettishall Heath   £8.50
Icknield Way accommodation list   £1.00

Sandstone Trail Frodsham to Whitchurch   FREE
Solent Way outline leaflet   FREE
South Downs Way Eastbourne to Winchester
Along the South Downs Way in both directions   £6.00
Southern Upland Way Portpatrick to Cockburnspath
Accommodation leaflet   FREE
Speyside Way Buckie to Craigelachie, Tomintoul, Aviemore
Accommodation and information   FREE
Staffordshire Way Mow Cop to Kinver Edge
Accommodation list (with Way for Millennium)   FREE
Test Way Inkpen Beacon to Totton   FREE
Thames Path Thames Barrier to Source
Official National Trail Guide by David Sharp   £12.99
Thames Path Companion: accom, practical info   £4.75
Three Castles Path Windsor to Winchester
Accommodation guide   FREE
Vanguard Way Croydon to Newhaven: Route guide by
Vanguards Rambling Club   £2.95
Way for the Millennium (Staffs) Newport to Burton upon Trent
For accommodation guide see Staffordshire Way
Weavers Way See under Peddars Way
Wessex Ridgeway See under Ridgeway
West Highland Way Glasgow to Fort William
Accommodation, practical information   FREE
Yorkshire Wolds Way Filey to Hull
Accommodation and information guide   FREE

WALKING FOR EVERYONE

Walking for Health by Dr W Bird & V Reynolds.
Comprehensive and accessible full-colour guide   £14.99
Take 30 Practical booklet on walking for health   FREE
Take 30 Poster 10-week healthy walking plan   FREE
Walking for health factsheet (FS18)   FREE
Walking for everyone (FS11) Includes advice on finding easier
walks, walking with children and access to the outdoors for
people with disabilities   FREE
The Walker's Companion A miscellany of walking facts, tit-bits
and information   £9.99
Walking: getting started (FS16)   FREE
Walking: a useful guide Booklet answering common questions
about walking, with useful addresses and contacts   FREE
Walking facts and figures (FS12)   FREE
Preparing Walks Guidebooks   FREE
Discovering new routes A report of the Volunteers'
Conference 2000 on outreach work   FREE

TECHNICAL & LEADERSHIP ADVICE

Navigation and Leadership Practical official Ramblers' guide for
planning and navigating group walks   £4.00
Navigation for Walkers by Julian Tippett, with colour
illustrations & OS map extracts, ideal for beginners   £8.99
Maps and navigation (FS2)   FREE
Clothing, equipment and safety (FS3)   FREE
Leading group walks (FS6)   FREE
Leading group walks in remote areas or demanding
conditions (GWSP1)   FREE
Walk leader's checklist on laminated card   FREE
Let's Get Going Advice on leading group walks for people with
disabilities and other special needs   FREE

FOOTPATHS, ACCESS, COUNTRYSIDE

Rights of Way: A guide to law and practice ('Blue Book')
3rd edition. Full guide to law in England & Wales (see p40) £10
4th edition available March 2007   £25

Footpath Worker Authoritative Journal on footpath law and
related matters, including regular updates to Rights of Way
                            4 issues £12 (free to RA Groups/Areas)
Animals and Rights of Way (CAN4) Walking with your dog,
dangerous animals on paths etc   FREE
Basics of Footpath Law (FS7) Introduction in question and
answer form   FREE
Defending public paths What the RA does to defend public
paths and how you can help.   FREE
The Economic and Social Value of Walking in England
A report for the Ramblers   FREE
Footpath erosion (FS14) How serious is the problem, and what
can walkers do about it?   FREE
The Secrets of Countryside Access by Dave Ramm (p84)   £4.95
Freedom to Roam Walker's Guides edited by Andrew Bibby
Forest of Bowland   £7.99
Peak District East & South   £7.99
Peak District West & North   £7.99
Pennine Divide   £7.99
South Pennines & the Bronte Moors   £7.99
Wharfedale and Nidderdale   £8.99
Wensleydale & Swaledale   £8.99
Three Peaks & Howgill Fells   £8.99
North York Moors   £8.99
Freedom to Roam in England and Wales (FS8) The
Countryside & Rights of Way Act explained   FREE
Golf Courses (CAN2): their impact on paths   FREE
Managing conflict over access to open country
A case study of the Peak National Park   FREE
Meeting the challenges of the new millennium
A proposal for a wider New Forest National Park   FREE
Paths for People for parish and community councils. Also in
bilingual Welsh/English version.   FREE
Reporting path problems Includes a report form and general
guidance. Also available in Welsh.   FREE
Rights of Way and Development (CAN3) Planning permission
and proposed path changes   FREE
Roads used as Public Paths and Byways Open To All Traffic
(CAN1) A detailed guide   FREE
You're Either Quick or Dead Locations where walkers need
safe, convenient road crossings   FREE

ABOUT THE RAMBLERS

About the Ramblers' Association (FS4)   FREE
Annual report 2004/5   FREE
Legacies How to remember the RA in your will   FREE
Waymarking the future A strategic framework for the growth
and development of the RA 2002–2007   FREE
Tom Stephenson a 1970s photographic tribute   FREE
A Tribute to Adrian Ritchie Privately-funded book written by
staff and volunteers in tribute to the unsung hero of the Ramblers
– please donate £10.99 or whatever you can afford   FREE

Ramblers' Association Cloth Badge
                              50p, free with orders over £15.00

MAPS

We don't sell walkers' maps, but we do maintain a map library
which members can use for a small fee. Please contact us for
details on 020 7339 8500.

WALKING INFORMATION ONLINE

An expanded range of the material listed on this page, and more,
is available to download from www.ramblers.org.uk/info

ORDER FORM

Item	Quantity	Price

Continue on a plain piece of paper if necessary

POSTAGE CHARGES

Please add these as follows:

● **UK Addresses**
Orders up to £4, add £1.60
Orders over £4 add £2.00 for first item, then £1.50 per item
Orders including Rights of Way (the 'Blue Book'): Minimum p&p charge £5.50

● **Other European addresses**
Orders up to £4, add £2.50
Orders over £4 add £3.00 for first item, then £2.00 per item
Orders including Rights of Way (the 'Blue Book'): Minimum shipping charge £7.50

● **All other addresses**
Orders up to £4, add £4.00
Orders over £4 add £4.50 for first item, then £2.00 per item
Orders including Rights of Way (the 'Blue Book'): Minimum shipping charge £12

FREE PUBLICATIONS

● 1 free publication may be sent free of charge.
● Otherwise postage charges for 3–5 items are: UK addresses £2.00, Europe £3.00, all other addresses £4.00. For over 5 items: £3.50 (UK), £4.50 (Europe), £5.50 (all other).

PAYMENT METHODS

We accept **cheques** or **postal orders** in UK pounds, made payable to the Ramblers' Association. We cannot accept cheques in any other currency, including Euro. Please don't send cash in the post.

We accept **credit** or **debit cards**: Visa, Mastercard, Switch and Delta only. Please note: we must have the card's security code to process the order.

Telephone orders
Please ☎ 020 7339 8500 (international +44 20 7339 8500) on Mondays to Fridays 10:00–17:00hrs. You can also take out a membership subscription by telephone.

Internet shopping
Download an order form, make donations and join the Ramblers by credit or debit card at our website, www.ramblers.org.uk. You can also view a range of our free literature online at the site.

Total cost of items _____
Total postage (shipping) charges _____
Donation to Ramblers' Association _____
Grand total _____

Name _____
Address _____
_____
_____
Postcode _____ Country _____

Send this form and your payment to:
Ramblers' Association (Sales), 2nd Floor Camelford House, 89 Albert Embankment, London SE1 7TW, UK
Please allow 14 days for delivery to UK, 28 days to rest of the world.

RAMBLERS GROUPS & PUBLICATIONS

Walk Britain in Páramo

Voted one of the Ramblers' Association members' favourite waterproof jackets for two consecutive years, Páramo garments make the ideal addition to your walking wardrobe.

Here are five reasons why Páramo will keep you comfortable this year...

1. The professional touch
Rescue teams and outdoor instructors were Páramo's earliest converts and remain the focus of our development. By meeting their needs, all outdoor enthusiasts benefit from garment improvements. That's why more than 30 mountain rescue teams routinely choose Páramo to go on the hill.

2. 'On the Hill' experience
Páramo's designs work because they are born 'on the hills' by people who understand what it's like to be in the great outdoors. Months are spent trialling garments and great emphasis is placed on comfort and function. Intelligent ventilation means garments stay comfortable, pockets are sited for maximum convenience, and hoods even move with you.

3. Whatever the weather
Páramo clothing complements the body's physiological capacity to warm up and cool down. Our designs provide the ultimate in temperature control and comfort, outperforming other outdoor products. Our innovative Nikwax fabrics have Directional water repellency, to actively push moisture away from the body, and the weatherproof protection of Nikwax Analogy mimics the action of mammal fur, making it better than 'breathable', more comfortable than 'hard shell' and as soft and rustle-free as 'soft shell'.

4. Handled with care
Páramo is not just about comfort but about making garments in an ethical way. Our production facility in Bogotá, Colombia is part of a valuable social programme with the Miquelina Foundation, providing employment and skills to 'at risk' women. Thousands of women and children gain in practical ways, and profits from the facility are used to fund housing projects, a kindergarten and a canteen for local children.

5. Built to last
With Páramo comes a lifetime guarantee. With no membranes to break down in our waterproofs, your jacket won't pack up after a couple of seasons. Its waterproof performance can be renewed indefinitely with straightforward Nikwax aftercare. Any manufacturing defects will be rectified free of charge

PÁRAMO – *Leaders in comfort and performance*

For more information on Páramo's unique advantages telephone **01892 786444** or visit **www.paramo.co.uk**

NATIONAL PARKS

Association of National Park Authorities
☎ 029 2049 9966
www.nationalparks.gov.uk

Council for National Parks
☎ 020 7924 4077
Wales office:
☎ 029 2049 9966
www.cnp.org.uk
Works to protect and enhance the national parks of England and Wales, and areas that merit national park status and promote understanding and quiet enjoyment of them for the benefit of all.

Scottish Council for National Parks
☎ 01505 682447
www.scnp.org.uk
Works to protect and enhance national parks in Scotland and to promote the case for new national parks.

Brecon Beacons
☎ 01874 624437
Brecon Beacons Visitor Centre (Mountain centre)
☎ 01874 623366
Brecon Beacons Park Society – Cymdeithas Parc Bannau Brycheiniog
☎ 01639 730179
www.breconbeaconsparksociety.org
Organise a programme of free led walks in the Park.

The Broads
☎ 01603 610734
www.broads-authority.gov.uk

Cairngorms
☎ 01479 873535
www.cairngorms.co.uk

Dartmoor
☎ 01626 832093
High Moorland Visitor Centre
☎ 01822 890414
www.dartmoor-npa.gov.uk

Dartmoor Preservation Association
☎ 01822 890646
www.dartmoorpreservation.com
Aims to protect, preserve and enhance the natural beauty, cultural heritage and scientific interest of Dartmoor, and to preserve public access and commoners' rights.

Exmoor
☎ 01398 323665
Dulverton Visitor Centre
☎ 01398 323841
www.exmoor-nationalpark.gov.uk

Lake District
☎ 01539 724555
www.lake-district.gov.uk
Brockhole Visitor Centre
☎ 01539 446601
Friends of the Lake District
Murley Moss
☎ 01539 720788
www.fld.org.uk
Cares for the countryside and wildlife of the Lake District.

Loch Lomond & The Trossachs
☎ 01389 722600
National Park Gateway Centre
☎ 0845 345 4978
www.lochlomond-trossachs.org

New Forest
☎ 01590 646600
www.newforestnpa.gov.uk
Lymington Visitor Information Centre
☎ 01590 689000
www.thenewforest.co.uk

Northumberland
☎ 01434 605555
Once Brewed Visitor Centre
☎ 01434 344396
www.northumberland-national-park.org.uk

North York Moors
☎ 01439 770657
Moors Information Centre
☎ 01439 772737
Park Information Centre
☎ 01845 597426
www.moors.uk.net

Peak District
☎ 01629 816200
www.peakdistrict.org
Visitor information
www.visitpeakdistrict.com

Pembrokeshire Coast – Arfordir Penfro
☎ 0845 345 7275
www.pcnpa.org.uk

Visitor Centre
☎ 01437 720392
stdavids.pembrokeshirecoast.org.uk

Snowdonia – Eryri
☎ 01766 770274
www.eryri-npa.gov.uk
Information Centre
☎ 01690 710426

Cymdeithas Eryri – Snowdonia Society
☎ 01690 720287
www.snowdonia-society.org.uk
Works to protect Snowdonia National Park.

South Downs
☎ 01243 558700
www.southdownsonline.org
Works to protect, conserve and enhance the natural beauty of the South Downs. A public consultation is currently being carried out on government proposals to designate this area as a national park, with a decision expected in 2007.

South Downs Campaign
☎ 01273 563358
www.southdownscampaign.org.uk
Grouping of organisations including the Ramblers campaigning for the adoption of the South Downs as a National Park.

South Downs Society
☎ 01798 875073
www.southdownssociety.org.uk
Aims to preserve and protect the South Downs.

Yorkshire Dales
☎ 0870 1 666333
www.yorkshiredales.org.uk
Visitor centre
☎ 01969 667450
www.destinationdales.org

USEFUL CONTACTS

AONBs & FOREST PARKS

**Association for AONBs –
Cymdeithas dros AoHNE**
☎ 01451 862007
www.aonb.org.uk

Arnside/Silverdale
☎ 01524 761034
www.arnsidesilverdaleaonb.org.uk

Blackdown Hills
☎ 01823 680681
www.blackdown-hills.net

Cannock Chase
☎ 01889 882613
Visitor Centre
☎ 01543 876741
www.cannockchasedc.gov.uk/cannockcha
se/countryside.htm
Forest Centre
☎ 01889 586593

Chichester Harbour
☎ 01243 512301
www.conservancy.co.uk

Cornwall
☎ 01872 322350
www.cornwall-aonb.gov.uk

Chilterns
☎ 01844 355500
www.chilternsaonb.org

Chiltern Society
☎ 01494 771250
www.chilternsociety.org.uk

**Clwydian Range – Bryniau
Clwyd**
☎ 01352 810614
www.clwydianrangeaonb.org.uk

Cotswolds
☎ 01451 862000
www.cotswoldsaonb.com

**Cranborne Chase & West
Wiltshire Downs**
☎ 01725 517417
www.dorsetcc.gov.uk/cranbornechase

Dedham Vale & Stour Valley
☎ 01473 264263
www.dedhamvalestourvalley.org

Dorset
☎ 01305 756782
www.dorsetaonb.org.uk

East Devon
☎ 01404 46663
www.eastdevonaonb.org.uk

East Hampshire
See South Downs under National Parks

Forest of Bowland
☎ 01772 534140
www.forestofbowland.com

Gower
☎ 01792 635741
www.swansea.gov.uk
(under Environment)

High Weald
☎ 01580 879500
www.highweald.org

Howardian Hills
☎ 01653 627164
www.howardianhills.org.uk

Isle of Anglesey – Ynys Môn
☎ 01248 752429
www.anglesey.gov.uk

Isle of Wight
☎ 01983 823855
www.wightaonb.org.uk

Isles of Scilly
☎ 01720 423486
www.ios-aonb.org.uk

Kent Downs
☎ 01303 815170
www.kentdowns.org.uk

Kielder
☎ 01434 220643
www.kielder.org

Lincolnshire Wolds
☎ 01507 609740
www.lincswolds.org.uk

Llyn
☎ 01758 704155
www.gwynedd.gov.uk

Malvern Hills
☎ 01684 560616
www.malvernhillsaonb.org.uk

Mendip Hills
☎ 01761 462338
www.mendiphillsaonb.org.uk

Nidderdale
☎ 01423 712950
www.nidderdaleaonb.org.uk

Norfolk Coast
☎ 01328 850530
www.norfolkcoastaonb.org.uk

North Devon
☎ 01237 423655
www.northdevon-aonb.org.uk
Includes Braunton Burrows Biosphere
Reserve.

North Pennines
☎ 01388 528801
www.northpennines.org.uk

North Wessex Downs
☎ 01488 685440
www.northwessexdowns.org.uk

Northumberland Coast
☎ 01670 534088
www.northumberlandcoastaonb.org

Quantock Hills
☎ 01278 732845
www.quantockhills.com

Shropshire Hills
☎ 01588 674080
www.shropshirehillsaonb.co.uk

Solway Coast
☎ 016973 33055
www.solwaycoastaonb.org.uk

South Devon
☎ 01803 861384
www.southdevonaonb.org.uk

Suffolk Coast and Heaths
☎ 01394 384948
www.suffolkcoastandheaths.org

Surrey Hills
☎ 01372 220653
www.surreyhills.org

Sussex Downs
See South Downs under National Parks

Tamar Valley
☎ 01579 351681
www.tamarvalley.org.uk

Wye Valley
☎ 01600 713977
www.wyevalleyaonb.co.uk

COMMUNITY FORESTS

England's Community Forests
☎ 01684 274811
www.communityforest.org.uk
Umbrella organisation for England's 12 community forests partnerships, regenerating large areas on the urban fringe for forestry, conservation and recreation.

Forest of Avon
☎ 0117 953 2141
www.forestofavon.org.uk

Central Scotland Forest
☎ 01501 822015
www.csct.co.uk

Forest of Marston Vale
☎ 01234 767037
www.marstonvale.org
Let's Go website promoting walks and sites

in the Forest and in the rest of Bedfordshire
www.letsgo.org.uk

Forest of Mercia
☎ 01543 370737
www.forestofmercia.co.uk

Great North Forest
☎ 0191 460 6200
www.greatnorthforest.co.uk

Great Western Community Forest
☎ 01793 466324
www.forestweb.org.uk

The Greenwood Community Forest
☎ 01623 758231
www.greenwoodforest.org.uk

Mersey Forest
☎ 01925 816217
www.merseyforest.org.uk

National Forest
☎ 01283 551211
www.nationalforest.org

Red Rose Forest
☎ 0161 872 1660
www.redroseforest.co.uk

South Yorkshire Forest
☎ 0114 257 1199
www.syforest.co.uk
Greensites website:
www.greensites.co.uk
South Yorkshire interactive environmental website with walking information.

Tees Forest
☎ 01642 300716
www.teesforest.org.uk

Thames Chase
☎ 01708 641880
www.thameschase.org.uk

Watling Chase
☎ 01992 555256
http://enquire.hertscc.gov.uk/cms/wccf/default.htm

ENVIRONMENT AND COUNTRYSIDE

BEN (Black Environment Network)
☎ 01286 870715
www.ben-network.org.uk
Promotes equality of opportunity with respect to ethnic communities in the preservation, protection and development of the environment.

BTCV (British Trust for Conservation Volunteers)
☎ 01302 388888
www.btcv.org
The UK's largest practical conservation

charity helping volunteers take hands-on action to improve the rural and urban environment including improving access to the outdoors. Also runs Natural Breaks conservation holidays.

Campaign to Protect Rural England (CPRE)
☎ 020 7981 2800
www.cpre.org.uk
Promotes the beauty, tranquillity and diversity of rural England by encouraging the sustainable use of land and other natural resources in town and country.

See also CPRW/YDCW, ruralScotland

CPRW/YDCW (Campaign for the Protection of Rural Wales – Ymgyrch Diogelu Cymru Wledig)
☎ 01938 552525
www.cprw.org.uk
Aims to help the conservation and enhancement of the landscape, environment and amenities of the countryside, towns and villages of rural Wales.
See also CPRE, ruralScotland

USEFUL CONTACTS

ENCAMS (Envrionmental Campaigns)
☎ 01942 612621
www.encams.org.uk
Environmental charity aiming to achieve litter-free and sustainable environments by working with community groups, local authorities, businesses and other partners.

Environmental Transport Association (ETA)
☎ 0845 389 1010
www.eta.co.uk
Campaigns for a sound and sustainable transport system and provides an environmental alternative to the other motoring organisations.

Everyone Campaign
see *Scottish Environment LINK*

Friends of the Earth
☎ 020 7490 1555
www.foe.co.uk
Scotland: ☎ 0131 554 9977
www.foe-scotland.org.uk
The world's largest federation of environmental campaigning groups.

Greenpeace UK
☎ 020 7865 8100
www.greenpeace.org.uk
Researches and campaigns on the environment using non-violent direct action.

Green Space
☎ 0118 946 9060
www.green-space.org.uk
Helps those committed to the planning, design, management and use of public parks and open spaces.

Groundwork UK
☎ 0121 236 8565
www.groundwork.org.uk
Federation of trusts working in poor areas to help build sustainable communities through joint environmental action.

PHILIP ROXBY

IWA (Inland Waterways Assciation)
☎ 01923 711114
www.waterways.org.uk
Campaigns for the conservation, use, maintenance, restoration and development of inland waterways in England and Wales.
See also Scottish Inland Waterways Association

John Muir Trust
☎ 0131 554 0114
www.jmt.org
Conserves and protects wild places by acquisition; currently owns seven areas in the Scottish Highlands and Islands totalling 20,000ha/50,000 acres.

Keep Britain Tidy
See *ENCAMS*

National Trust
☎ 0870 458 4000
Wales: ☎ 01492 860123
www.nationaltrust.org.uk
Protects, through ownership, countryside, coastline and historic buildings in England, Wales and Northern Ireland.

National Trust for Scotland
☎ 0131 243 9300
www.nts.org.uk
Protects, through ownership, countryside, coastline and historic buildings.

Open Spaces Society
☎ 01491 573535
www.oss.org.uk
Works to protect common land and footpaths in England and Wales.

RSPB (Royal Society for the Protection of Birds)
☎ 01767 680551
Scotland: ☎ 0131 311 6500
Wales: ☎ 029 2035 3000
www.rspb.org.uk
Works for a healthy environment rich in birds and wildlife, including managing over 150 nature reserves.

ruralScotland (Association for the Protection of Rural Scotland)
☎ 0131 225 7012
www.aprs.org.uk
Scotland's rural champion.
See also Campaign for the Protection of Rural Wales, CPRE

Scottish Environment LINK
☎ 01738 630804
www.scotlink.org
Everyone campaign:
www.everyonecan.org

Voluntary organisations working together to care for and improve Scotland's heritage for people and nature. Also manages the LEARN project.
See also Wildlife and Countryside Link

Scottish Inland Waterways Association
www.siwa.org.uk
Coordinates the conservation and use of the waterway network. See also *IWA*

Scottish Wildlife Trust
☎ 0131 312 7765
www.swt.org.uk
Protects all forms of wildlife and the environment, with over 120 reserves. Part of The Wildlife Trusts network.

Transport 2000
☎ 020 7613 0743
www.transport2000.org.uk
National campaign for environmental and sustainable transport.

Wildlife and Countryside Link
☎ 020 7820 8600
www.wcl.org.uk
Liaison service for all the major non-governmental organisations in the UK concerned with the protection of wildlife and the countryside.
See also Scottish Environment LINK

Wildlife Helpline National Service
☎ 01522 544245
www.wildlifehelpline.org.uk
Information on the identification of British wildlife and wild flowers and contacts for wildlife organisations.

Wildlife Trusts
☎ 0870 036 7711
www.wildlifetrusts.org
Partnership of 46 local groups throughout Britain and junior group Wildlife Watch protecting wildlife in town and countryside, and maintaining 2,400 nature reserves.

Woodland Trust
☎ 01476 581135
Scotland: ☎ 01764 662554
Wales: ☎ 01686 412508
www.woodland-trust.org.uk
Protects Britain's native woodland heritage by conserving and managing over 1,000 sites, all with public access, and creating new woodlands.

WWF-UK
☎ 01483 426444
www.wwf-uk.org
Aims to conserve and protect endangered species and address global threats to nature.

WALKING AND OUTDOOR ACTIVITIES

DAVE SIMMS

Camping and Caravanning Club
☎ 0845 130 7631
www.campingandcaravanningclub.co.uk
Runs 90 members' sites throughout the
UK, offers technical advice and
membership benefits.

Countrygoer
☎ 01943 607868
www.countrygoer.org
Promotes the use of public transport
for countryside visits and publicises
information about services through the
website.

CTC (Cyclists' Touring Club)
☎ 0870 873 0060
www.ctc.org.uk
Campaigning for cyclists' rights, lobbying
government and other agencies to
promote, invest in and facilitate cycling,
also organises club activities.

Disabled Ramblers
www.disabledramblers.co.uk
Aims to improve countryside access for
disabled people and organises regular
rambles and visits.

Duke of Edinburgh's Award
☎ 01753 727400
www.theaward.org
Operates a challenging and rewarding
personal development programme for
people aged 14–25.

Fieldfare Trust
☎ 01334 657708
www.fieldfare.org.uk
Works with people with disabilities and
countryside managers to improve access
to the countryside for everyone.

Gay Outdoor Club (GOC)
☎ 01673 861962
http://goc.uk.net
Organises walking and other outdoor
activities for lesbian, gay, bisexual and
transgender people across the UK.

Go Outdoors
☎ 020 8842 1111
www.go-outdoors.org.uk
Trade body for manufacturers and
retailers of outdoor clothing and
equipment in Britain and Ireland.

Hillphones
www.hillphones.info
Information on deer stalking between
August and October in selected areas to
assist those planning walks and climbs.

IBHS (Independent
Backpackers Hostels Scotland)
www.hostel-scotland.co.uk

Backpackers Club
www.backpackersclub.co.uk
Promotes and encourages backpacking
for the benefit of its members.

BMC (British Mountaineering
Council)
☎ 0870 010 4878
www.thebmc.co.uk
Protects the freedoms and promotes the
interests of climbers, hillwalkers and
mountaineers.

British Horse Society
☎ 0870 120 2244
www.bhs.org.uk
Works to improve the welfare of
horses through education, training and
promoting the interests of horse riders
and owners, including defending
bridleways.

British Orienteering
Federation
☎ 01629 734042
www.britishorienteering.org.uk

British Upland Footpath Trust
(BUFT)
☎ 0870 010 4878
Aims to improve the quality and standard
of footpath works and deal with erosion
problems on upland paths.

British Walking Federation
(BWF)
www.bwf-ivv.org.uk
British affiliate of the International
Volkssport Federation, organising non-
competitive walking events.

British Waterways
☎ 01923 201120
www.britishwaterways.co.uk
Leisure information on waterways
including walking:
www.waterscape.com

Byways and Bridleways Trust
www.bbtrust.org.uk
Aims to protect Britain's ancient minor
highways.

Institute of Public Rights of Way Officers (IPROW)
☎ 0700 078 2318
www.iprow.co.uk
Professional body for local authority rights of way officers in England and Wales; also run a variety of training courses.

Living Streets
☎ 020 7820 1010
www.livingstreets.org.uk
Defends the rights of pedestrians and campaigns for living streets.
See also Walk to School, Walking Bus

Long Distance Walkers Association
www.ldwa.org.uk
Works to further the interests of those who enjoy long distance walking.

Mountain Bothies Association (MBA)
www.mountainbothies.org.uk
Maintains around 100 simple, unlocked shelters in remote country.

Mountaineering Council of Scotland (MCS)
☎ 01738 493942
www.mountaineering-scotland.org.uk
Representative body for climbers, walkers and others who enjoy the Scottish mountains.
Boots Across Scotland:
www.bootsacrossscotland.org.uk
Provides support for injured hillwalkers

and climbers, and promotes mountain safety.

NNAS (National Navigation Award Scheme)
☎ 01786 451307
www.nnas.org.uk
National body which offers navigation training via independent accredited outdoor centres.

Paths for All Partnership
☎ 01259 218888
Paths to Health:
www.pathstohealth.org.uk
Partnership of 17 Scottish organisations working to create path networks for walkers of all abilities to walk, cycle and ride for recreation, health and sustainable transport. Also coordinates local Paths to Health schemes in Scotland.

Railway Ramblers
www.railwayramblers.org.uk
Discovers and explores old railway lines and promotes their use as footpaths and cycleways.

Red Rope
☎ 01274 493995
www.redrope.org.uk
The socialist walking and climbing club.

Scottish Avalanche Information Service
www.sais.gov.uk
Forecasts for five key climbing areas in Scotland during the winter season.

ScotWays
☎ 0131 558 1222
www.scotways.com
Works for the preservation, defence, restoration and acquisition of public rights of over land in Scotland, including publc rights of way.

Sensory Trust
☎ 01726 222900
www.sensorytrust.org.uk
Works to make green space accessible to as many people as possible.

SYHA (Scottish Youth Hostels)
☎ 0870 155 3255
www.syha.org.uk
Providers of budget accommodation and countryside activities. *See also YHA*

Wainwright Society
www.wainwright.org.uk
Set up in commemoration of renowned hillwalker and author A Wainwright.

Walk to School
www.walktoschool.org.uk
Encourages walking to school and promotes National Walk to School Week. Partnership of TravelWise, Living Streets and Dorset County Council.

Walking Bus
☎ 01932 832 073
www.walkingbus.org
Information about walking buses – groups of children who walk to school together according to a set route and timetable.

Walking-Routes website
www.walking-routes.co.uk
Extensive links to sites with online route descriptions.

Walking the way to Health Initiative – Cerdded Llwybr Iechyd
Joint initiative of the Countryside Agency, CCW and British Heart Foundation using walking to improve the health of people who currently get little exercise.

England: contact the WHI team at the Countryside Agency
☎ 01242 533258
www.whi.org.uk

Wales: contact the WW2H team at the Countryside Council for Wales
☎ 0845 130 6229
www.ww2h.org.uk

Scotland: see *Paths for All Partnership (Paths to Health)*

YHA England & Wales
☎ 0870 770 8868
www.yha.org.uk
Edale Activity Centre:
☎ 0870 770 5808
Providers of budget accommodation and countryside activities. *See also SYHA*

FIRST AID AND EMERGENCIES

Mountain Rescue Committee of Scotland
☎ 01360 770431
www.mrc-scotland.org.uk
Representative and coordinating body for mountain rescue in Scotland.

Mountain Rescue Council
www.mountain.rescue.org.uk
Official coordinating body for mountain rescue in England and Wales.

NHS Direct
(medical information and advice)
☎ 0845 4647
www.nhsdirect.nhs.uk

RNLI (Royal National Lifeboat Institution)
☎ 0845 122 6999
www.mli.org.uk
Aims to save lives at sea by operating lifeboats and search and rescue facilities in Britain and Ireland.

St Andrew's Ambulance Association
☎ 0141 332 4031
www.firstaid.org.uk
Scotland's premier provider of first aid training and services. See also St John Ambulance.

St John Ambulance
☎ 0870 010 4950
www.sja.org.uk
St John Ambulance Wales:
www.stjohnwales.co.uk
St John Supplies (trading arm):
☎ 020 7278 7888
www.stjohnsupplies.co.uk
Leading first aid, transport and care charity in in England, Wales, Northern Ireland, Channel Islands and Isle of Man.

TOURISM

Tourist Information Centres
For your local tourist or visitor information centre, see your phonebook. The local centre can give you contact details of centres in other areas, or search the full list at www.visitbritain.com

VisitBritain
☎ 020 8846 9000 (not an information line: for Tourist Information please visit the Visit Britain website and look up your nearest centre)

Wales Tourist Board – Bwrdd Croeso Cymru
☎ 029 2049 9909
Information and booking line:
☎ 0870 830 0306
Minicom ☎ 0870 121 1255
www.visitwales.com
Walking website:
www.walking.visitwales.com

VisitScotland
☎ 0845 225 5121 or 01506 832121
www.visitscotland.com
Walking in Scotland website:
http://walking.visitscotland.com

NATIONAL GOVERNMENT ORGANISATIONS

CABE
(Commission for Architecture and the Built Environment)
☎ 020 7070 6700
www.cabe.org.uk
CABE Space
(Parks and public open spaces)
www.cabespace.org.uk
Non-departmental public body championing the creation of great buildings and public spaces.

CADW – Welsh Historic Monuments
☎ 01443 33 6000
www.cadw.wales.gov.uk
Guardian of built heritage in Wales.

Countryside Council for Wales – Cyngor Cefn Gwylad Cymru
☎ 0845 130 6229
www.ccw.gov.uk
Wildlife conservation authority and advisor on sustaining natural beauty, wildlife and the opportunity for outdoor enjoyment in Wales and its inshore waters, including overseeing National Trails.
Countryside Code website:
www.codcefngwlad.org.uk

Directgov
www.direct.gov.uk
Principal internet portal for government departments and services.

DCMS
(Department for Culture, Media and Sport)
☎ 020 7211 6200
www.culture.gov.uk

Defence Estates
(manages MoD lands)
☎ 0121 311 2140
www.defence-estates.mod.uk
Information on access to MoD lands and contact telephone numbers for details of firing times.

DEFRA
(Department for Environment, Food & Rural Affairs)
☎ 0845 933 5577
www.defra.gov.uk
Conservation Walks register:
countrywalks.defra.gov.uk
Lists walks in England on countryside managed under environmental schemes providing public access.

Department for Communities and Local Government (DCLG)
(Formerly ODPM)
☎ 020 7944 4400
www.communities.gov.uk
Deals with planning, regional and local government.

Department for Transport (DfT)
☎ 020 7944 8300
www.dft.gov.uk
In Town Without My Car (Car-free day):
www.itwmc.gov.uk
Highway Code online (rules and advice for all road users):
www.highwaycode.gov.uk

English Heritage
☎ 0870 333 1181
www.english-heritage.org.uk
Responsible for protecting many of England's historic buildings, landscapes and archaeological sites, including many properties open to the public.

Environment Agency
☎ 0870 850 6506
www.environment-agency.gov.uk
Responsible for protecting and enhancing the environment, including maintaining flood defences and rivers.

Forestry Commission
☎ 0845 604 0845
www.forestry.gov.uk
Protects and expands Britain's forests and woodlands and increases their value to society and the environment, both by managing its own woodlands and making grants to other landowners.

Historic Scotland
☎ 0131 668 8600
www.historic-scotland.gov.uk
Agency of the Scottish Executive that safeguards Scotland's built heritage.

MAGIC (Multi-Agency Geographic Information for the Countryside)
www.magic.gov.uk
Project to create a single website for rural and countryside information about England on the web, including mapping boundaries of protected areas. Partnership of Natural England, DEFRA, English Heritage, the Environment Agency, Forestry Commission, ODPM.

USEFUL CONTACTS

**National Assembly for Wales –
Cynulliad Cenedlaethol Cymru**
☎ 029 2082 5111
www.wales.gov.uk

Natural England
☎ 01733 455100
www.naturalengland.org.uk
New body replacing the functions of the
Countryside Agency and English Nature.
Countryside access helpline:
☎ 0845 100 3298
www.countrysideaccess.gov.uk

ODPM
*See Department for Communities and
Local Government (DCLG)*

Planning Inspectorate (PINS)
☎ 0117 372 6372
www.planning-inspectorate.gov.uk
Deals with appeals against local
government planning decisions including
cases involving footpaths and access.

Scottish Executive
☎ 0845 774 1741
www.scotland.gov.uk

Scottish Natural Heritage
☎ 01463 725000
www.snh.org.uk
Responsible for the care, improvement
and responsible enjoyment of Scotland's
natural heritage.
Outdoor Access Scotland:
www.outdooraccess-scotland.com

Details of Statutory Access Rights and the
Scottish Outdoor Access Code.

**Sports Council for Wales –
Cyngor Chwaraeon Cymru**
and Welsh Institute for Sport
☎ 0845 045 0904
www.sports-council-wales.co.uk

Sport England
☎ 0845 850 8508
www.sportengland.org

SportScotland
☎ 0131 317 7200
www.sportscotland.org.uk
Outdoor Training Centre:
☎ 01479 861256
www.glenmorelodge.org.uk

LOCAL AUTHORITIES

In this section we list councils in Britain with primary
responsibility for footpaths and access to whom
problems should be reported. Many of them also
promote walking locally and can provide information
about walking routes, parks and countryside areas.

You can send your report either to our central
office, or report the problem directly to the local
authority – but please send us a copy too.

A Path/Access Problem Report Form is on p49.
Further forms are available on request from Ramblers'

Association offices. You can also report problems on
our website at www.ramblers.org.uk/footpaths. Don't
forget to report what the problem is, where it is and
when you noticed it (see p48 for more detailed
instructions).

Alphabetical order
Councils covering only part of an historic county are
listed under the council area's name, not the county's
name – eg West Dunbartonshire is listed under 'W'.

ENGLAND

Barking and Dagenham
(Outer London Borough) Civic Centre,
Dagenham RM10 7BN
☎ 020 8592 4500
www.barking-dagenham.gov.uk

Barnet
(Outer London Borough) Hendon Town
Hall, The Burroughs, London NW4 4BG
☎ 020 8359 2000
www.barnet.gov.uk

Barnsley
(Metropolitan Borough) Town Hall,
Barnsley S70 2TA
☎ 01226 770770
www.barnsley.gov.uk

Bath & North East Somerset
(Unitary Authority) The Guildhall,
High Street, Bath BA1 5AW
☎ 01225 477000
www.bathnes.gov.uk

Bedfordshire
(County Council) County Hall,
Cauldwell Street, Bedford MK42 9AP
☎ 01234 363222
www.bedfordshire.gov.uk

Bexley
(Outer London Borough) Civic Offices,
Broadway, Bexleyheath DA6 7LB
☎ 020 8303 7777
www.bexley.gov.uk

Birmingham
(Metropolitan Borough) The Council
House, Victoria Square,
Birmingham B1 1BB
☎ 0121 303 9944
www.birmingham.gov.uk

Blackburn with Darwen
(Unitary Authority) King William Street,
Town Hall, Blackburn BB1 7DY
☎ 01254 585585
www.blackburn.gov.uk

Blackpool
(Unitary Authority) Municipal Buildings,
PO Box 77, Town Hall,
Blackpool FY1 1AD
☎ 01253 477477
www.blackpool.gov.uk

Bolton
(Metropolitan Borough) Town Hall,
Victoria Square, Bolton BL1 1RU
☎ 01204 333333
www.bolton.gov.uk

Bournemouth
(Unitary Authority) Town Hall,
Bourne Avenue, Bournemouth BH2 6DY
☎ 01202 451451
www.bournemouth.gov.uk

Bracknell Forest
(Unitary Authority) Market Street,
Bracknell RG12 1JD
☎ 01344 352000
www.bracknell-forest.gov.uk

Bradford City
(Metropolitan Borough) City Hall,
Channing Way, Bradford BD1 1HY
☎ 01274 431000
www.bradford.gov.uk

Brent
(Outer London Borough) Town Hall,
Forty Lane, Wembley HA9 9HD
☎ 020 8937 1234
www.brent.gov.uk

Brighton & Hove
(Unitary Authority) King's House,
Grand Avenue, Hove BN3 2LS
☎ 01273 290000
www.brighton-hove.gov.uk

Bristol City
(Unitary Authority) The Council House,
College Green, Bristol BS1 5TR
☎ 0117 922 2000
www.bristol-city.gov.uk

Bromley
(Outer London Borough) Civic Centre,
Stockwell Close, Bromley BR1 3YH
☎ 020 8464 3333
www.bromley.gov.uk

Buckinghamshire
(County Council) County Hall,
Walton Street, Aylesbury HP20 1UA
☎ 01296 395000
www.buckscc.gov.uk

Bury
(Metropolitan Borough) Town Hall,
Knowsley Street, Bury BL9 0SW
☎ 0161 253 5000
www.bury.gov.uk

Calderdale
(Metropolitan Borough) Town Hall,
Crossley Street, Halifax HX1 1UJ
☎ 01422 357257
www.calderdale.gov.uk

Cambridgeshire
(County Council) Shire Hall, Castle Hill,
Cambridge CB3 0AP ☎ 01223 717111
www.cambridgeshire.gov.uk

Camden
(Inner London Borough) Camden Town
Hall, Judd Street, London WC1H 9JE
☎ 020 7278 4444
www.camden.gov.uk

Cheshire
(County Council) County Hall,
Chester CH1 1SE
☎ 0845 11 333 11
www.cheshire.gov.uk

Cornwall
(County Council) County Hall,
Treyew Road, Truro TR1 3AY
☎ 01872 322000
www.cornwall.gov.uk

Corporation of London
PO Box 270, Guildhall,
London EC2P 2EJ
☎ 020 7606 3030
www.cityoflondon.gov.uk

Coventry
(Metropolitan Borough) Council House,
Earl Street, Coventry CV1 5RR
☎ 024 7683 3333
www.coventry.gov.uk

Croydon
(Outer London Borough) Taberner
House, Park Lane, Croydon CR9 3JS
☎ 020 8686 4433
www.croydon.gov.uk

Cumbria
(County Council) The Courts,
Carlisle CA3 8NA
☎ 01228 606336
www.cumbriacc.gov.uk

Darlington
(Unitary Authority) Town Hall, Feethams,
Darlington DL1 5QT ☎ 01325 380651
www.darlington.gov.uk

Derby
(Unitary Authority) The Council House,
Corporation Street, Derby DE1 2FS
☎ 01332 293111
www.derby.gov.uk

Derbyshire
(County Council) County Hall,
Matlock DE4 3AG
☎ 0845 605 8058
www.derbyshire.gov.uk

Devon
(County Council) County Hall,
Topsham Road, Exeter EX2 4QD
☎ 01392 382000
www.devon.gov.uk

Doncaster
(Metropolitan Borough) 2 Priory Place,
Doncaster DN1 1BN
☎ 01302 734444
www.doncaster.gov.uk

Dorset
(County Council) County Hall,
Colliton Park, Dorchester DT1 1XJ
☎ 01305 251000
www.dorsetforyou.com

Dudley
(Metropolitan Borough) Council House,
Priory Road, Dudley DY1 1HF
☎ 01384 818181
www.dudley.gov.uk

Durham
(County Council) County Hall,
Durham DH1 5UB
☎ 0191 383 3000
www.durham.gov.uk

Ealing
(Outer London Borough) Perceval House,
14-16 Uxbridge Road, London W5 2HL
☎ 020 8825 5000
www.ealing.gov.uk

East Riding of Yorkshire
(Unitary Authority) County Hall,
Beverley HU17 9BA
☎ 01482 393939
www.eastriding.gov.uk

East Sussex
(County Council) County Hall,
St Anne's Crescent, Lewes BN7 1SF
☎ 01273 481000
www.eastsussexcc.gov.uk

Enfield
(Outer London Borough) Civic Centre,
Silver Street, Enfield EN1 3XY
☎ 020 8379 1000
www.enfield.gov.uk

Essex
(County Council) County Hall,
Market Road, Chelmsford CM1 1LX
☎ 08457 430430
www.essexcc.gov.uk

Gateshead
(Metropolitan Borough) Civic Centre,
Regent St, Gateshead NE8 1HH
☎ 0191 433 3000
www.gateshead.gov.uk

Gloucestershire
(County Council) Shire Hall, Westgate St,
Gloucester GL1 2TG
☎ 01452 425000
www.gloucestershire.gov.uk

Greenwich
(Inner London Borough) Woolwich Town
Hall, Wellington St, London SE18 6PW
☎ 020 8854 8888
www.greenwich.gov.uk

Hackney
(Inner London Borough) Town Hall,
Mare Street, London E8 1EA
☎ 020 8356 3000
www.hackney.gov.uk

USEFUL CONTACTS

Halton
(Unitary Authority) Municipal Building,
Kingsway, Widnes WA8 7QF
☎ 0151 424 2061
www.halton.gov.uk

Hammersmith and Fulham
(Inner London Borough) Town Hall,
King Street, London W6 9JU
☎ 020 8748 3020
www.lbhf.gov.uk

Hampshire
(County Council) The Castle,
Winchester SO23 8UJ
☎ 01962 870 500
www.hants.gov.uk

Haringey
(Outer London Borough) Civic Centre,
High Road, London N22 8LE
☎ 020 8489 0000
www.haringey.gov.uk

Harrow
(Outer London Borough) Civic Centre,
Station Road, Harrow HA1 2XF
☎ 020 8863 5611
www.harrow.gov.uk

Hartlepool
(Unitary Authority) Civic Centre,
Hartlepool TS24 8AY
☎ 01429 266522
www.hartlepool.gov.uk

Havering
(Outer London Borough) Town Hall,
Main Road, Romford RM1 3BD
☎ 01708 434343
www.havering.gov.uk

Herefordshire
(Unitary Authority) Brockington,
35 Hafod Road,
Hereford HR1 1SH
☎ 01432 260000
www.herefordshire.gov.uk

Hertfordshire
(County Council) County Hall, Pegs Lane,
Hertford SG13 8DQ
☎ 01438 737555
www.hertsdirect.org

Hillingdon
(Outer London Borough) Civic Centre,
High Street, Uxbridge UB8 1UW
☎ 01895 250111
www.hillingdon.gov.uk

Hounslow
(Outer London Borough) Civic Centre,
Lampton Road, Hounslow TW3 4DN
☎ 020 8583 2000
www.hounslow.gov.uk

Hull: see *Kingston upon Hull*

Isle of Wight
(Unitary Authority) County Hall,
Newport PO30 1UD
☎ 01983 821000
www.iwight.com

Isles of Scilly
Town Hall, St Mary's TR21 0LW
☎ 01720 422537
www.scilly.gov.uk

Islington
(Inner London Borough)
222 Upper Street,
London N1 1XR
☎ 020 7527 2000
www.islington.gov.uk

Kensington and Chelsea
(Inner London Borough) Town Hall,
Hornton Street,
London W8 7NX
☎ 020 7937 5464
www.rbkc.gov.uk

Kent
(County Council) County Hall,
Maidstone ME14 1XQ
☎ 0845 824 7247
www.kent.gov.uk

Kingston upon Hull
(Unitary Authority) Guildhall,
Hull HU1 2AA
☎ 01482 300300
www.hullcc.gov.uk

Kingston upon Thames
(Outer London Borough) Guildhall,
High Street,
Kingston upon Thames KT1 1EU
☎ 020 8547 5757
www.kingston.gov.uk

Kirklees
(Metropolitan Borough) Civic Centre 3,
Market Street, Huddersfield HD1 1WG
☎ 01484 221000
www.kirkleesmc.gov.uk

Knowsley
(Metropolitan Borough) Muncipal
Buildings, Archway Rd, Huyton L36 9UX
☎ 0151 489 6000
www.knowsley.gov.uk

Lambeth
(Inner London Borough) Town Hall,
Brixton Hill, London SW2 1RW
☎ 020 7926 1000
www.lambeth.gov.uk

Lancashire
(County Council) PO Box 78, County
Hall, Fishergate, Preston PR1 8XJ
☎ 0845 053 0000
www.lancashire.gov.uk

Leeds
(Metropolitan Borough) Civic Hall,
Calverley Street, Leeds LS1 1UR
☎ 0113 234 8080
www.leeds.gov.uk

Leicester
(Unitary Authority) New Walk Centre,
Welford Place, Leicester LE1 6ZG
☎ 0116 254 9922
www.leicester.gov.uk

Leicestershire
(County Council) County Hall, Glenfield,
Leicester LE3 8RA
☎ 0116 232 3232
www.leics.gov.uk

Lewisham
(Inner London Borough) Town Hall,
London SE6 4RU
☎ 020 8314 6000
www.lewisham.gov.uk

Lincolnshire
(County Council) County Offices,
Newland, Lincoln LN1 1YL
☎ 01522 552222
www.lincolnshire.gov.uk

Liverpool
(Metropolitan Borough) Municipal
Buildings, Dale St, Liverpool L69 2DH
☎ 0151 233 3000
www.liverpool.gov.uk

London
Greater London Authority and Mayor of
London (strategic only): City Hall, The
Queen's Walk, London SE1 2AA
☎ 020 7983 4100
www.london.gov.uk

Luton
(Unitary Authority) Town Hall,
George Street, Luton LU1 2BQ
☎ 01582 546000
www.luton.gov.uk

Manchester
(Metropolitan Borough) Town Hall,
Albert Sq, Manchester M60 2LA
☎ 0161 234 5000
www.manchester.gov.uk

Medway
(Unitary Authority) Civic Centre, Strood,
Rochester ME2 4AU
☎ 01634 306000
www.medway.gov.uk

Merton
(Outer London Borough) Civic Centre,
London Road, Morden SM4 5DX
☎ 020 8274 4901
www.merton.gov.uk

Middlesbrough
(Unitary Authority) PO Box 99A, Town
Hall, Middlesbrough TS1 2QQ
☎ 01642 245432
www.middlesbrough.gov.uk

Milton Keynes
(Unitary Authority) Civic Offices,
1 Saxon Gate, Milton Keynes MK9 3HG
☎ 01908 691691
www.miltonkeynes.gov.uk

Newcastle
(Metropolitan Borough) Civic Centre,
Barras Bridge, Newcastle upon Tyne
NE99 1RD
☎ 0191 232 8520
www.newcastle.gov.uk

Newham
(Outer London Borough) Town Hall,
London E6 2RP
☎ 020 8430 2000
www.newham.gov.uk

Norfolk
(County Council) County Hall,
Martineau Lane, Norwich NR1 2DH
☎ 0844 800 8020
www.norfolk.gov.uk

North East Lincolnshire
(Unitary Authority) Municipal Offices,
Town Hall Square, Grimsby DN31 1HU
☎ 01472 313131
www.nelincs.gov.uk

North Lincolnshire
(Unitary Authority) Pittwood House,
Ashby Road, Scunthorpe DN16 1AB
☎ 01724 296296
www.northlincs.gov.uk

North Somerset
(Unitary Authority) Town Hall, Walliscote
Grove Road, Weston-super-Mare
BS23 1UJ ☎ 01934 888888
www.n-somerset.gov.uk

North Tyneside
(Metropolitan Borough) Strategic
Services, Pametrada Building,
Davy Bank, Wallsend NE28 6WJ
☎ 0191 200 5000
www.northtyneside.gov.uk

North Yorkshire
(County Council) County Hall,
Northallerton DL7 8AD
☎ 01609 780780
www.northyorks.gov.uk

Northamptonshire
(County Council) County Hall,
Northampton NN1 1DN
☎ 01604 236236
www.northamptonshire.gov.uk

Northumberland
(County Council) County Hall,
Morpeth NE61 2EF
☎ 01670 533000
www.northumberland.gov.uk

Nottingham
(Unitary Authority) The Guildhall, South
Sherwood Street, Nottingham NG1 4BT
☎ 0115 915 5555
www.nottinghamcity.gov.uk

Nottinghamshire
(County Council) County Hall, West
Bridgford, Nottingham NG2 7QP
☎ 0115 982 3823
www.nottinghamshire.gov.uk

Oldham
(Metropolitan Borough) Civic Centre,
West Street, Oldham OL1 1UG
☎ 0161 911 3000
www.oldham.gov.uk

Oxfordshire
(County Council) County Hall,
New Road, Oxford OX1 1ND
☎ 01865 792422
www.oxfordshire.gov.uk

Peterborough
(Unitary Authority) Town Hall,
Peterborough PE1 1PJ
☎ 01733 747474
www.peterborough.gov.uk

Plymouth
(Unitary Authority) Civic Centre,
Plymouth PL1 2AA ☎ 01752 668000
www.plymouth.gov.uk

Poole
(Unitary Authority) Civic Centre,
Poole BH15 2RU ☎ 01202 633633
www.boroughofpoole.com

Portsmouth
(Unitary Authority) Civic Offices, Guildhall
Square, Portsmouth PO1 2BG
☎ 023 9283 4092
www.portsmouth.gov.uk

Reading
(Unitary Authority) Civic Centre,
Reading RG1 7TD
☎ 0118 939 0900
www.reading.gov.uk

Redbridge
(Outer London Borough) PO Box 2,
Town Hall, 128-142 High Road,
Ilford IG1 1DD
☎ 020 8854 5000
www.redbridge.gov.uk

Redcar and Cleveland
(Unitary Authority) Redcar and
Cleveland House, Kirkleatham Street,
Redcar TS10 1YA ☎ 0845 612 6126
www.redcar-cleveland.gov.uk

Richmond upon Thames
(Outer London Borough) Civic Centre,
44 York Street, Twickenham TW1 3BZ
☎ 020 8891 1411
www.richmond.gov.uk

Rochdale
(Metropolitan Borough) PO Box 39,
Municipal Offices, Smith St,
Rochdale OL16 1LQ
☎ 01706 647474
www.rochdale.gov.uk

Rotherham
(Metropolitan Borough) Civic Building,
Walker Place, Rotherham S65 1UF
☎ 01709 382121
www.rotherham.gov.uk

Rutland
(Unitary Authority) Catmose,
Oakham LE15 6HP
☎ 01572 722577
www.rutland.gov.uk

Salford
(Metropolitan Borough) Civic Centre,
Chorley Road, Swinton,
Salford M27 5DA
☎ 0161 794 4711
www.salford.gov.uk

Sandwell
(Metropolitan Borough) Sandwell Council
House, PO Box 2374, Oldbury B69 3DE
☎ 0121 569 2200
www.sandwell.gov.uk

Sefton
(Metropolitan Borough) Balliol House,
Balliol Road, Bootle L20 3AH
☎ 0151 934 4040
www.sefton.gov.uk

Sheffield
(Metropolitan Borough) Town Hall,
Surrey Street, Sheffield S1 2HH
☎ 0114 272 6444
www.sheffield.gov.uk

Shropshire
(County Council) Shirehall, Abbey
Foregate, Shrewsbury SY2 6ND
☎ 0845 678 9000
www.shropshire.gov.uk

Slough
(Unitary Authority) Town Hall, Bath Road,
Slough SL1 3UQ
☎ 01753 552288
www.slough.gov.uk

Solihull
(Metropolitan Borough) PO Box 18,
Solihull B91 3QS
☎ 0121 704 6000
www.solihull.gov.uk

Somerset
(County Council) County Hall,
Taunton TA1 4DY
☎ 0845 345 9166
www.somerset.gov.uk

South Gloucestershire
(Unitary Authority) The Council Offices,
Castle Street, Thornbury BS35 1HF
☎ 01454 868686
www.southglos.gov.uk

South Tyneside
(Metropolitan Borough) Town Hall &
Civic Offices, Westoe Road,
South Shields NE33 2RL
☎ 0191 427 7000
www.southtyneside.info

Southampton
(Unitary Authority) Civic Centre,
Southampton SO14 7LY
☎ 023 8022 3855
www.southampton.gov.uk

Southend on Sea
(Unitary Authority), Civic Centre, Victoria
Ave, Southend-on-Sea SS2 6ER
☎ 01702 215000
www.southend.gov.uk

Southwark
(Inner London Borough) Town Hall,
Peckham Road, London SE5 8UB
☎ 020 7525 5000
www.southwark.gov.uk

St Helens
(Metropolitan Borough) Town Hall,
Victoria Square, St Helens WA10 1HP
☎ 01744 456000
www.sthelens.gov.uk

Staffordshire
(County Council) County Buildings,
Martin Street, Stafford ST16 2LH
☎ 01785 223121
www.staffordshire.gov.uk

Stockport
(Metropolitan Borough) Town Hall,
Edward Street, Stockport SK1 3XE
☎ 0161 480 4949
www.stockport.gov.uk

Stockton-on-Tees
(Unitary Authority) Municipal Buildings,
PO Box 11, Church Road,
Stockton-on-Tees TS18 1LD
☎ 01642 393939
www.stockton.gov.uk

Stoke-on-Trent
(Unitary Authority) Civic Centre,
Glebe Street,
Stoke-on-Trent ST4 1RN
☎ 01782 234567
www.stoke.gov.uk

Suffolk
(County Council) Endeavour House,
Russell Road, Ipswich IP1 2BX
☎ 01473 583000
www.suffolk.gov.uk

Sunderland
(Metropolitan Borough) Civic
Centre, Burdon Road,
Sunderland SR2 7DN
☎ 0191 520 5555
www.sunderland.gov.uk

Surrey
(County Council) Contact Centre,
Floor 3, Conquest House, Wood St,
Kingston upon Thames KT1 1AB
☎ 0845 600 9009
www.surreycc.gov.uk

Sutton
(Outer London Borough) Civic Offices,
St Nicholas Way, Sutton SM1 1EA
☎ 020 8770 5000
www.sutton.gov.uk

Swindon
(Unitary Authority) Civic Offices,
Euclid Street, Swindon SN1 2JH
☎ 01793 463725
www.swindon.gov.uk

Tameside
(Metropolitan Borough) Council Offices,
Wellington Road, Ashton-under-Lyne,
Tameside OL6 6DL
☎ 0161 342 8355
www.tameside.gov.uk

Telford & Wrekin
(Unitary Authority) Civic Offices,
Telford TF3 4LD
☎ 01952 202100
www.telford.gov.uk

Thurrock
(Unitary Authority) Civic Offices, New
Road, Grays RM17 6SL
☎ 01375 652652
www.thurrock.gov.uk

USEFUL CONTACTS

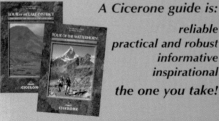

Torbay
(Unitary Authority) Town Hall,
Castle Circus, Torquay TQ1 3DR
☎ 01803 201201
www.torbay.gov.uk

Tower Hamlets
(Inner London Borough) Town Hall,
5 Clove Crescent, London E14 2BG
☎ 020 7364 5000
www.towerhamlets.gov.uk

Trafford
(Metropolitan Borough) Town Hall,
Talbot Road, Stretford M32 0YT
☎ 0161 912 2000
www.trafford.gov.uk

Wakefield
(Metropolitan Borough) Town Hall,
Wood Street, Wakefield WF1 2HQ
☎ 01924 306090
www.wakefield.gov.uk

Walsall
(Metropolitan Borough) Civic Centre,
Walsall WS1 1TP ☎ 01922 650000
www.walsall.gov.uk

Waltham Forest
(Outer London Borough) Town Hall,
Forest Road, London E17 4JF
☎ 020 8496 3000
www.lbwf.gov.uk

Wandsworth
(Inner London Borough) Town Hall,
Wandsworth High Street, London
SW18 2PU ☎ 020 8871 6000
www.wandsworth.gov.uk

Warrington
(Unitary Authority) Town Hall,
Warrington WA1 1UH
☎ 01925 444400
www.warrington.gov.uk

Warwickshire
(County Council) Shire Hall,
Warwick CV34 4RA
☎ 0845 090 7000
www.warwickshire.gov.uk

West Berkshire
(Unitary Authority) Council Offices,
Market Street, Newbury RG14 5LD
☎ 01635 42400
www.westberks.gov.uk

West Sussex
(County Council) County Hall,
West Street, Chichester PO19 1RQ
☎ 01243 777100
www.westsussex.gov.uk

Westminster
(Inner London Borough) PO Box 240,
City Hall, 64 Victoria Street,
London SW1E 6QP
☎ 020 7641 6000
www.westminster.gov.uk

Wigan
(Metropolitan Borough) Town Hall,
Library Street, Wigan WN1 1YN
☎ 01942 244991
www.wiganmbc.gov.uk

Wiltshire
(County Council) County Hall,
Bythesea Road, Trowbridge BA14 8JN
☎ 01225 713000
www.wiltshire.gov.uk

Wirral
(Metropolitan Borough) Town Hall,
Brighton Street, Wallasey CH44 8ED
☎ 0151 606 2000
www.wirral.gov.uk

Windsor and Maidenhead Royal Borough
(Unitary Authority) Town Hall,
St Ives Road, Maidenhead SL6 1RF
☎ 01628 798888
www.rbwm.gov.uk

Wokingham
(Unitary Authority) Civic Offices,
Shute End, Wokingham RG40 1BN
☎ 0118 974 6000
www.wokingham.gov.uk

Wolverhampton
(Metropolitan Borough) Civic Centre,
St Peter's Square,
Wolverhampton WV1 1SH
☎ 01902 556556
www.wolverhampton.gov.uk

Worcestershire
(County Council) County Hall,
Spetchley Road, Worcester
WR5 2NP
☎ 01905 763763
www.worcestershire.gov.uk

York City
(Unitary Authority) The Guildhall,
York YO1 9QN
☎ 01904 613161
www.york.gov.uk

WALES

Blaenau Gwent
Municipal Offices, Civic Centre,
Ebbw Vale NP23 6XB
☎ 01495 350555
www.blaenau-gwent.gov.uk

Bridgend – Pen y Bont
Civic Offices, Angel Street,
Bridgend CF31 4WB
☎ 01656 643643
www.bridgend.gov.uk

Caerphilly – Caerffilli
Council Offfices, Nelson Road,
Tredomen, Ystrad Mynach CF82 7WF
☎ 01443 815588
www.caerphilly.gov.uk

Cardiff – Caerdydd
County Hall, Atlantic Wharf,
Cardiff CF10 4UW
☎ 029 2087 2000
www.cardiff.gov.uk

Carmarthenshire – Caerfyrddin
County Hall, Carmarthen SA31 1JP
☎ 01267 234567
www.carmarthenshire.gov.uk

Ceredigion
Penmorfa, Aberaeron SA46 0PA
☎ 01545 570881
www.ceredigion.gov.uk

Conwy
Bodlondeb, Conwy LL32 8DU
☎ 01492 574000
www.conwy.gov.uk

Denbighshire – Sir Ddinbych
County Hall, Wynnstay Road,
Ruthin LL15 1YN
☎ 01824 706000
www.denbighshire.gov.uk

Flintshire – Sir y Fflint
County Hall, Mold CH7 6NB
☎ 01352 752121
www.flintshire.gov.uk

Gwynedd
Council Offices, Shirehall Street,
Caernarfon LL55 1SH
☎ 01286 672255
www.gwynedd.gov.uk

Isle of Anglesey – Ynys Môn
Council Offices, Llangefni LL77 7TW
☎ 01248 750057
www.anglesey.gov.uk

Merthyr Tydfil
Civic Centre, Castle Street,
Merthyr Tydfil CF47 8AN
☎ 01685 725000
www.merthyr.gov.uk

USEFUL CONTACTS

Monmouthshire – Sir Fynwy
County Hall, Cwmbran NP44 2XH
☎ 01633 644644
www.monmouthshire.gov.uk

Neath Port Talbot – Castell-nedd
Civic Centre, Neath SA13 1PJ
☎ 01639 763333
www.neath-porttalbot.gov.uk

Newport – Casnewydd
Civic Centre, Newport NP20 4UR
☎ 01633 656656
www.newport.gov.uk

Pembrokeshire – Sir Benfro
County Hall,
Haverfordwest SA61 1TP
☎ 01437 764551
www.pembrokeshire.gov.uk

Powys
County Hall, Llandrindod Wells LD1 5LG
☎ 01597 826000
www.powys.gov.uk

Rhondda Cynon Taff
The Pavillions, Cambrian Park,
Clydach Vale CF40 2XX
☎ 01443 424000
www.rhondda-cynon-taff.gov.uk

Swansea – Abertawe
County Hall, Oystermouth Road,
Swansea SA1 3SN
☎ 01792 636000
www.swansea.gov.uk

Torfaen
Civic Centre, Pontypool NP4 6YB
☎ 01495 762200
www.torfaen.gov.uk

Vale of Glamorgan – Bro Morgannwg
Civic Offices, Holton Road,
Barry CF63 4RU
☎ 01446 700111
www.valeofglamorgan.gov.uk

Wrexham – Wrecsam
The Guildhall, Wrexham LL11 1WF
☎ 01978 292000
www.wrexham.gov.uk

SCOTLAND

Aberdeen
The Point, Ground Floor,
St Nicholas House, Broad Street,
Aberdeen AB10 1BX
☎ 01224 522000
www.aberdeencity.gov.uk

Aberdeenshire
Woodhill House, Westburn Road,
Aberdeen AB16 5GB
☎ 0845 606 7000
www.aberdeenshire.gov.uk

Angus
The Cross, Forfar DD8 1BX
☎ 0845 277 7778
www.angus.gov.uk

Argyll and Bute
Kilmory Castle, Lochgilphead,
Argyll PA31 8RT
☎ 01546 602127
www.argyll-bute.gov.uk

Clackmannanshire
Council Offices, Greenfield,
Alloa FK10 2AD
☎ 01259 450000
www.clacks.gov.uk

Dumfries & Galloway
Council Offices, English Street,
Dumfries DG1 2DD
☎ 01387 260000
www.dumgal.gov.uk

Dundee
Council Offices, 21 City Square,
Dundee DD1 3DB ☎ 01382 434800
www.dundeecity.gov.uk

East Ayrshire
Council Headquarters, London Road,
Kilmarnock KA3 7BU
☎ 0845 724 0000
www.east-ayrshire.gov.uk

East Dunbartonshire
Council Offices, Tom Johnston House,
Civic Way, Kirkintilloch G66 4TJ
☎ 0141 578 8000
www.eastdunbarton.gov.uk

East Lothian
John Muir House,
Haddington EH41 3HA
☎ 01620 827827
www.eastlothian.gov.uk

East Renfrewshire
Council Offices, Eastwood Park, Rouken
Glen Road, Giffnock G46 6UG
☎ 0141 577 3001
www.eastrenfrewshire.gov.uk

Edinburgh
City Chambers, High St, Edinburgh EH1 1YJ
☎ 0131 200 2000
www.edinburgh.gov.uk

Eilean Siar – Western Isles
Sandwick Road, Stornoway HS1 2BW
☎ 01851 703773
www.w-isles.gov.uk

Falkirk
Municipal Buildings, Falkirk FK1 5RS
☎ 01324 506070
www.falkirk.gov.uk

Fife
Fife House, North Street,
Glenrothes KY7 5LT
☎ 01592 414141
www.fife.gov.uk

Glasgow
City Chambers, George Sq,
Glasgow G2 1DU
☎ 0141 287 2000
www.glasgow.gov.uk

Highland
Glenurquhart Road, Inverness
IV3 5NX
☎ 01463 702000
www.highland.gov.uk

Inverclyde
Municipal Buildings, Clyde Square,
Greenock PA15 1LY
☎ 01475 717171
www.inverclyde.gov.uk

Midlothian
Midlothian House, 40 Buccleuch Street,
Dalkeith EH22 1DN
☎ 0131 270 7500
www.midlothian.gov.uk

Moray
Council Offices, High St, Elgin
IV30 1BX
☎ 01343 543451
www.moray.gov.uk

North Ayrshire
Cunninghame House, Friar's Croft,
Irvine KA12 8EE
☎ 01294 324100
www.north-ayrshire.gov.uk

North Lanarkshire
PO Box 14, Civic Centre,
Motherwell
ML1 1TW
☎ 01698 403200
www.northlan.gov.uk

Orkney Islands
Council Offices, School Place,
Kirkwall, Orkney
KW15 1NY
☎ 01856 873535
www.orkney.gov.uk

Perth & Kinross
Council Offices, 2 High Street,
Perth PH1 5PH
☎ 01738 475000
www.pkc.gov.uk

Renfrewshire
North Building, Cotton St, Paisley PA1 1BU
☎ 0141 842 5000
www.renfrewshire.gov.uk

Scottish Borders
Council Headquarters, Newtown St
Boswells, Melrose TD6 0SA
☎ 01835 824000
www.scotborders.gov.uk

Shetland Islands
Town Hall, Lerwick ZE1 0HB
☎ 01595 693535
www.shetland.gov.uk

South Ayrshire
County Buildings, Wellington Square,
Ayr KA7 1DR ☎ 00845 601 2020
www.south-ayrshire.gov.uk

South Lanarkshire
Council Offices, Almada Street,
Hamilton ML3 0AA
☎ 01698 454444
www.southlanarkshire.gov.uk

Stirling
Council Offices, Viewforth,
Stirling FK8 2ET
☎ 0845 277 7000
www.stirling.gov.uk

West Dunbartonshire
Council Offices, Garshake Road,
Dunbarton G82 3PU
☎ 01389 737000
www.west-dunbarton.gov.uk

West Lothian
West Lothian House, Almondvale
Boulevard, Livingston EH54 6QG
☎ 01506 775000
www.westlothian.gov.uk

Western Isles
See Eilean Siar

OUTSIDE BRITAIN

EUROPE

European Ramblers Association (ERA)
c/o Klub âesk˘ch TuristÛ, Archeologická
2256, CZ-155 00 Praha 5 - Luïíny,
☎ +420 2 5162 7356
www.era-ewv-ferp.com
Federation of 26 national organisations,
including the Ramblers' Association,
working for walking and climbing,
protecting the countryside and creating
international long distance paths (E-Paths,
see p39). The website is a good source of
information on walking in Europe and
member organisations' contact details.

Hostelling International
(International Youth Hostels Federation)
☎ 01707 324170
www.iyhf.org

CHANNEL ISLANDS

Alderney Tourist Information
☎ 01481 822333
www.visitaldemey.com

Guernsey Tourist Board
☎ 01481 723552
www.visitguernsey.com

Herm Tourist Information Herm
☎ 01481 722377
www.herm-island.com

Jersey Tourist Information
☎ 01534 500700
www.jersey.com

Sark Tourist Information
☎ 01481 832345
www.sark.info

NORTHERN IRELAND

Countryside Access and Activities Network for Northern Ireland
☎ 028 9030 3930
www.countrysiderecreation.com
Responsibilities include the province's
network of 14 Waymarked Ways.

Northern Ireland Tourist Board
☎ 029 9024 6609
www.discovernorthernireland.com
*London: information available from Fáilte
Ireland (see below)*

Ordnance Survey of Northern Ireland
☎ 028 9025 5755
www.osni.gov.uk

Translink
☎ 028 9089 9400
Enquiry line: ☎ 028 9066 6630
www.translink.co.uk
Operates integrated public transport
services including Northern Ireland
Railways, Citybus and Ulsterbus.

Ulster Federation of Rambling Clubs
☎ 028 9066 6358
www.ufrc-online.co.uk

REPUBLIC OF IRELAND

Fáilte Ireland (Tourism Ireland)
☎ +353 (0)1 850 230 330
www.ireland.ie
Walking website:
www.walking.travel.ie

CIE
(Córas Iompair Éireann)
☎ +353 (0)1 703 2358
Rail enquiries: ☎ +353 (0)1 836 6222
Bus enquiries: ☎ +353 (0)1 836 6111
www.cie.ie
Operates integrated public transport
services including Iamród Éireann (Irish
Rail), Bus Éireann and Dublin Bus.

Mountaineering Council of Ireland
☎ +353 (0)1 625 1115
www.mountaineering.ie

National Waymarked Ways Advisory Committee
Irish Sports Council
☎ +353 (0)1 860 8823
www.walkireland.ie

Ordnance Survey Ireland
☎ +353 (0)1 802 5300
www.osi.ie

ISLE OF MAN

VisitIsleofMan
☎ 01624 686801
www.visitisleofman.com

USEFUL CONTACTS

Accommodation

HOW TO USE THE ACCOMMODATION GUIDE

The accommodation guide is divided into eight English regions, Wales and Scotland. Each section contains:

- an introduction with lots of **ideas for walks** and places to visit, including details of long distance paths and national parks in the region, plus news of local Ramblers Group activities
- a **map** of the area showing the locations of all B&Bs listed, long distance paths and national parks
- and the accommodation **listings**.

NB - All locations of the accommodation are indexed at the back of the book (see pp310-317).

Accommodation

The listings are organised by country/region then alphabetically by county or unitary authority. Some with fewer listings are banded together – see the key map overleaf for a complete breakdown. Many entries come from members' recommendations and since we are unable to independently assess establishments, this is a vital resource for us. Please keep them coming using the Recommendation/Feedback form on p123.

Bed & Breakfast

Entries are all listed under a 'place' – a village, town or hamlet. If the place is situated within two miles of a long distance path listed on p25 or in a national park, the path or national park is cross-referenced after the place name.

Self-catering

Prices for self-catering vary by season – we give the lowest and highest cost per week. Where a proprietor lets more than one property, the price of the cheapest in low season and the most expensive in high season is given. Tourist board awards may be different for each property let, so we give the range of classifications awarded.

Group Accommodation

There is a variety of types, standards, prices and sizes – many tested by Ramblers Groups. Some are self-catering (SC), others provide meals (BB, DBB, FB), and include hotels, hostels, university halls of residence, cabins in the woods and farmhouses.

Hostels, Bunkhouses and Campsites

Some centres listed are primarily for groups but should all be open to individuals too. For each we state prices per night and whether meals and/or self-catering facilities are available. Many hostels accept children at a reduced rate. Categories of establishments are:

BHB = Bunkhouse Barn A converted farm building, better equipped than a camping barn. Stoves and cooking

facilities provided. Toilets may be chemical. Separate sleeping areas for males and females but little privacy. Bunkbeds provided.

B = Bunkhouse Other kinds of converted buildings, simply furnished. Cooking facilities and utensils provided. Separate sleeping areas for males and females with beds or bunks. Showers and drying facilities provided.

C = Campsite May be for tents only, plus tourers, or have hook-up facilities for caravans. In some sites static caravans are available. Some provide meals on-site.

CB = Camping Barn A redundant farm building converted to provide basic shelter. Little or no privacy. Limited facilities. Toilets may be chemical. Sleeping areas usually not divided between the sexes and there are wooden sleeping platforms.

IH = Independent Hostel A privately run hostel. Standards and conditions will vary. Some provide meals but most are self-catering. Sheet sleeping-bag liners are usually required.

OC = Outdoor Centre Often for groups only. See also Group Accommodation.

YHA = Youth Hostel A hostel which is a member of the Youth Hostels Association.

Tourist Board classifications

The AA, RAC, VisitBritain, VisitScotland and the Wales Tourist Board rate serviced accommodation using a common set of standards: '★-★★★★★' for hotels and '◆-◆◆◆◆◆' (in England and Wales) for smaller guest accommodation. Self-catering establishments are rated ★-★★★★★. Each organisation has its own special award scheme: we only display VisitBritain's Silver Ⓢ and Gold Ⓖ awards in this guide.

In 2004, VisitBritain produced a national rating for meeting the needs of walkers and cyclists in consultation with the Ramblers and others. Ⓦ indicates a Walkers Welcome or Cyclists Welcome award. However, all the accommodation listed here should welcome walkers.

Further Information

Six-figure grid references are given for each entry referring to OS Landranger maps, scale 1:50,000. Most are generated from the postcode and can be inaccurate in sparsely populated areas.

Any deposit paid to establishments is non-refundable in all circumstances, and any amount paid by credit card may be non-returnable.

Finally, a disclaimer. The information in the guide is based on details received from proprietors during 2006. The Ramblers' Association cannot be held responsible for errors or omissions.

SCOTLAND
p 286

HIGHLAND

NORTH EAST
SCOTLAND

PERTH & KINROSS

ARGYLL
& BUTE
STIRLING

CENTRAL BELT

SCOTTISH
BORDERS

DUMFRIES &
GALLOWAY

NORTHUMBERLAND

**NORTH
EAST**
p 254

TYNE & WEAR

DURHAM

CUMBRIA

NORTH YORKS

YORKSHIRE
p 238

EAST
YORKS &
HUMBERSIDE

**NORTH
WEST**
p 218

LANCS

WEST
YORKS

SOUTH
YORKS

**EAST
MIDLANDS**
p 190

ANGLESEY

CHESHIRE

DERBYSHIRE

N.E.
CONWY WALES

NOTTS

LINCS

GWYNEDD

STAFFS

NORFOLK

WEST MIDLANDS
p 204

BIRMINGHAM
& BLACK COUNTRY

LEICS

RUTLAND

CAMBS

SUFFOLK

WALES
p 264

POWYS

SHROPSHIRE

CEREDIGION

WORCS

HEREFORD

WARKS

NORTHANTS

BEDS

HERTS

ESSEX

EAST
p 180

CARMARTHENSHIRE

PEMBROKESHIRE

MONMOUTH-
SHIRE

GLOS

OXFORDSHIRE

BUCKS

LONDON

SOUTH WALES

BERKS

KENT

WILTS

SURREY

SOUTH WEST
p 126

SOMERSET

HAMPSHIRE

WEST
SUSSEX

EAST
SUSSEX

DEVON

DORSET

ISLE OF
WIGHT

SOUTH
p 160

CORNWALL

RAMBLERS DISCOUNT VOUCHERS

All establishments marked with a ⚫◄ in the 2007 edition of **walk BRITAIN** accept the vouchers overleaf. The discount is for a maximum of £1 per night. Vouchers may be combined for a longer stay, or higher value vouchers used for shorter stays. For example, a £4 voucher can be used for one, two, three or four nights at a discount of £1 per night. Each voucher can only be used once and cannot be exchanged for services other than bed and breakfast. Photocopies will not be accepted. Proprietors have the right to withhold the reduction in price if the visitor is already in receipt of another discount or they booked through means other than **walk BRITAIN** 2007.

Discounts shown in **walk BRITAIN** are wholly at the discretion of the retailer and are not an entitlement to Ramblers members.

The Ramblers walk BRITAIN 2007 DISCOUNT VOUCHER

VALID FOR ONE NIGHT...

£1

...AT ANY B&B MARKED WITH A ▶ in walk BRITAIN 2007

Please refer to the terms and conditions left

The Ramblers walk BRITAIN 2007 DISCOUNT VOUCHER

VALID FOR UP TO TWO NIGHTS...

£2

...AT ANY B&B MARKED WITH A ▶ in walk BRITAIN 2007

Please refer to the terms and conditions left

The Ramblers walk BRITAIN 2007 DISCOUNT VOUCHER

VALID FOR UP TO THREE NIGHTS...

£3

...AT ANY B&B MARKED WITH A ▶ in walk BRITAIN 2007

Please refer to the terms and conditions left

The Ramblers walk BRITAIN 2007 DISCOUNT VOUCHER

VALID FOR UP TO FOUR NIGHTS...

£4

...AT ANY B&B MARKED WITH A ▶ in walk BRITAIN 2007

Please refer to the terms and conditions left

polartec.com

FABRIC ENGINEERS. WE MIGHT NOT BE THE BEST FOR CASUAL CONVERSATION, BUT WHEN YOU'RE RUNNING THROUGH A COLD RAIN, THERE'S NO BETTER COMPANY. SO WE'RE STICKING TO WHAT WE KNOW – CREATING THE WORLD'S MOST ADVANCED FABRICS. WE'LL LEAVE THE WHOLE "TALK-ING" THING TO YOU.

POLA
FORWARD FA

RECOMMENDATION/FEEDBACK FORM

FOUND SOME GOOD DIGS
THAT AREN'T IN THE GUIDE?

☐

or

HAVE A COMPLAINT ABOUT
ACCOMMODATION IN THIS EDITION?

☐

Your name and address _____

_____

Name and full postal address of the establishment _____

_____

Email (if known) _____

Comments

WHAT DO YOU THINK OF walk BRITAIN 2007?

ANY SUGGESTIONS TO IMPROVE FUTURE EDITIONS?

THANK YOU. PLEASE RETURN THIS FORM TO THE PUBLICATIONS TEAM:

RAMBLERS' ASSOCIATION, 2ND FLOOR CAMELFORD HOUSE
87-90 ALBERT EMBANKMENT, LONDON SE1 7TW

insurance with principles

Ramblers' Association supporters like our principled approach to home insurance.

Our mutual status is something we are very proud of. But it would count for little if we couldn't deliver where it matters most – with low prices.

Happily, as a Ramblers' Association member you and your family get the best of both worlds with UIA. Solid principles, together with home insurance premiums that really will suit your pocket.

All-round great value

Home insurance from UIA offers you all this:
- Interest-free monthly payments at no extra charge
- Up to £25 if your mortgage lender charges you for switching your buildings insurance to UIA
- 5% discount for combined buildings and contents cover
- Free accidental damage cover for audio and computer equipment at home
- Free emergency helplines
- Friendly paperless claims
- We also offer travel and motor insurance

Go online and save an extra 15%†

Now Ramblers' supporters can save time and money by buying insurance online. Visit www.ramblersinsurance.co.uk to see how quick and easy it is.

Yes. That and the 15% online discount!

Helping the Ramblers' Association

For every insurance policy taken out we will make a generous donation to the Rambers' Association* to help fund vital charity work. You can be sure you are helping the Rambler's Association achieve their core aims – and getting a great deal.

See how much you could save

	Liverpool L16 7	Bristol BS1 3	Croydon CR5 3	Sheffield S12 3
Average Market Premium	£404.64	£435.10	£360.96	£336.91
UIA Premium	£266.80	£339.26	£261.68	£228.60
UIA Premium with 15% online discount	£226.78	£288.37	£222.42	£194.31
Online savings with UIA	£177.86	£146.73	£138.54	£142.60

Premiums illustrated (including Insurance Premium Tax at the current rate) are for standard cover for combined buildings and contents insurance for a buildings sum insured of £110,000 and a contents sum insured of £25,000. These premiums are calculated for a 37 year old, living in a 3 bedroom, semi-detached house, built in 1970. Market average is based on a selection of five leading companies (Source: ISI, Whatif August 2006). Prices are correct at the time of print (August 2006). But may be subject to change.

This is an estimate and your actual premium will depend on individual circumstances.

Call for a free quote today

0800 013 0064**

or buy online at www.ramblersinsurance.co.uk

Please quote ref. Yearbook 07

The Ramblers

†Compared to the standard price you would be quoted if you called us. This only applies to home (buildings and contents) and travel insurances. *Subject to our usual acceptance criteria. **Lines are open from 8.30am - 8pm Mon - Fri, 9am - 1pm Sat. For quality and protection, your call will be recorded. We exchange information with other insurance companies and the police to prevent fraud.
The Ramblers' Association is an Introducer Appointed Representative of UIA (Insurance) Ltd and UIA (Insurance Services) Ltd who are both authorised and regulated by the Financial Services Authority. Travel insurance is arranged by Fortis Insurance Ltd. Motor insurance is promoted and administered by BDML Connect Ltd. All these companies are authorised and regulated by the Financial Services Authority.

SOUTH WEST

Long Distance Paths

See Paths & Access p25 for full details of LDPs and waymarks

National Parks

Dartmoor

Exmoor

See Useful Contacts p99 for full details of national parks

KILMAR TOR ON BODMIN MOOR, NORTH CORNWALL

WALK...
...THE JOHN MUSGRAVE HERITAGE TRAIL

This new 56km/35-mile trail through the beautiful South
Hams connects Maidencombe, near Torquay, with Brixham
harbour, going via Totnes and some spectacular views of
the River Dart. Named after the former chairman of the
South Devon Group, whose generous legacy to the
Ramblers' Association helped create it, the route is divided
into four sections of 9km/5.5 miles and 18km/11 miles.

A guidebook and free leaflet are available from local
TICs, or contact Torbay Coast and Countryside Trust
☎ 01803 606035, or South Devon Ramblers (see p86).

VISIT...   ...THE CORNISH TIN MINES

Cornwall and West Devon's unique tin-mining
heritage now ranks alongside Stonehenge and the
Great Wall of China as a cultural landmark of global
significance, after being designated a UNESCO World
Heritage Site last year. The 'deep mining' techniques
and technology pioneered in the mines during the
18th and 19th centuries left a plethora of industrial
archaeology across the Cornish peninsula, familiar to
many walkers of the South West Coast Path. Ten sites
were awarded protected status, from St Just in the
west to the Tamar Valley.

For full details, visit www.cornish-mining.org.uk

SEE...
...WEMBURY POINT AND THE GREAT MEWSTONE

Used by the Ministry of Defence as a naval gunnery training
school since 1940, the National Trust successfully bid £1.4m
for this 56-acre stretch of majestic south Devon coastline and
opened it to the public last year. Wembury Point guards the
eastern side of Plymouth Sound in the South Devon AONB
and looks out over the bay where the Great Mewstone lies.
Free from gunfire, the island has become an important site for
cliff-nesting seabirds.

Visit www.nationaltrust.org.uk for further information.

LOCAL RAMBLERS GROUPS... The previously off-limits Coombe Martin, near Newton
Abbot in Dartmoor, is now open for walkers following Devon Area's petitions... **The Glevum
Way has been newly waymarked by Gloucester Group and a new leaflet for the scenic
circular route is available (see Local Ramblers Publications, p86)**... A series of walks
led by Ramblers volunteers from rural locations along the Bristol-to-Weymouth train line are
running throughout the summer as part of the Wessex Rail Partnership. ☎ 01305 263759
for a leaflet or download it from www.heartofwessex.org.uk

MAP 129

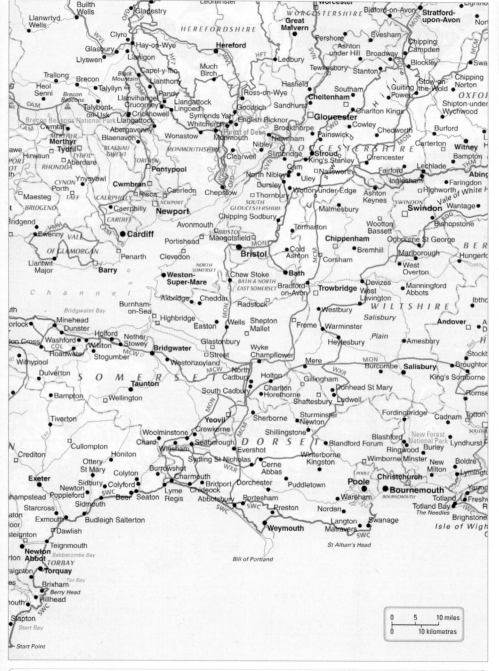

BED & BREAKFAST

CORNWALL

● Altarnun (Launceston)

Trenarrett House, PL15 7SY ☎ 01566 86203 (Mrs Linda Sanders)
lotcflybybroom@tesco.net Map 201/245826
BB **B** ✕ book first £10, 7pm D1 T1
Ⓥ Ⓑ Ⓓ ⊗ 🛏️🦴🚗!🍴

● Boscastle
SOUTH WEST COAST PATH

The Old Coach House, Tintagel Road, PL35 0AS ☎ 01840 250398
www.old-coach.co.uk Map 190/098906
BB **B/C** ✕ nearby D4 T1 F3 Closed Xmas
Ⓑ Ⓓ ⊗ 🛏️🦴🚗!🍴 ◆◆◆◆

Trerosewill Farm, Paradise , PL35 0BL ☎ 01840 250545
(Mrs Cheryl Nicholls) www.trerosewill.co.uk Map 190/098904
BB **D** ✕ nearby D3 T1 F2 Closed Xmas
Ⓑ Ⓓ ⊗ 🛏️🦴🚗!🍴Ⓜ ◆◆◆◆◆Ⓢ

Lower Meadows, Penally Hill, PL35 0HF ☎ 01840 250570
(Anne & Adrian Prescott) www.lowermeadows.co.uk Map 190,200/101913
BB **D** ✕ nearby D4 T1 Closed Xmas Ⓑ Ⓓ ⊗ 🛏️🦴🚗! ◆◆◆◆

● Bude
SOUTH WEST COAST PATH

Pencarrol Guest House, 21 Downs View, EX23 8RF ☎ 01288 352478
(M & E Payne) pencarrolbude@aol.com Map 190/207071
BB **B/C** ✕ nearby S2 D3 T1 F1 Closed Dec
Ⓑ Ⓓ ⊗ 🛏️🦴🚗! ◆◆◆◆

☆ **Harefield Cottage**
Upton, EX23 0LY ☎ 01288 352350 (Sally-Ann Trewin)
www.coast-countryside.co.uk Map 190/202048
BB **C** ✕ book first £15, 6.30pm S2 D2 T1 Closed Xmas
Ⓥ Ⓑ Ⓓ ⊗ 🛏️🦴🚗!🍴 ◆◆◆◆Ⓢ

Harefield Cottage is only 250 yards from
the South West Coast Path.
Luxurious bedrooms. A hot tub in the
garden to relax those weary muscles.
Excellent homecooked meals on request.
We offer a pick-up and drop service with
luggage carried forward.

Tee-side Guest House, 2 Burn View, EX23 8BY ☎ 01288 352351
(June Downes) www.tee-side.co.uk Map 190/208066
BB **C** ✕ nearby S1 D2 T3 Closed Xmas
Ⓑ Ⓓ ⊗ 🛏️🦴🚗! ★★★★

Surf Haven, 31 Downs View, EX23 8RE ☎ 01288 353923 (Jan Penn)
www.surfhaven.co.uk Map 190/210070
BB **B** ✕ nearby D7 T2 Ⓥ Ⓑ Ⓓ ⊗ 🛏️🦴🚗!🍴 ◆◆◆◆

● Carbis Bay (St Ives)
SOUTH WEST COAST PATH

Coast Vegetarian B&B, St Ives Rd, TR26 2RT ☎ 01736 795918
www.coastcornwall.co.uk Map 203/524385
BB **D** ✕ book first £7.95-£15, 6-8pm D5 T1 F2 Closed Xmas
🚌(Carbis Bay) Ⓥ Ⓑ ⊗ 🛏️🦴

● Coverack (Helston)
SOUTH WEST COAST PATH

Mellan House, TR12 6TH ☎ 01326 280482 (Muriel Fairhurst)
hmfmelcov@aol.com Map 204/780186
BB **B** ✕ nearby S1 D1 T1 Closed Xmas Ⓑ Ⓓ ⊗ 🛏️🦴🚗!🍴

● Cury (Mullion)
SOUTH WEST COAST PATH

☆ **Cobblers Cottage**
Nantithet, TR12 7RB ☎ 01326 241342 (Mrs Hilary Lugg)
Map 203/681223
BB **C** ✕ book first £15, 6:30pm D2 T1 Closed Nov-Mar
Ⓑ Ⓓ ⊗ 🦴🛏️ ◆◆◆◆◆Ⓢ

This picturesque 17th-century
riverside cottage, set in an acre
of beautiful gardens is situated
just 2½ miles from the SW Coast
Path. All bedrooms en-suite.
Evening dinner optional.
Colour brochure available.

● Falmouth
SOUTH WEST COAST PATH

Lerryn Hotel, De Pass Road, TR11 4BJ ☎ 01326 312489 (Ann Picken)
www.thelerrynhotel.co.uk Map 204/813319
BB **D** ✕ book first £9, 6:30-8pm S4 D6 T8 F2 🚌(Falmouth Town)
Ⓥ Ⓑ Ⓓ ⊗ 🛏️🦴🚗!🍴 ★★

Wickham, 21 Gyllyngvase Terrace, TR11 4DL ☎ 01326 311140
(Steve & Jenny Lake) www.wickham-hotel.co.uk Map 204/810318
BB **C** ✕ nearby S2 D2 T/F2 Closed Nov-Mar 🚌(Falmouth Town)
Ⓑ ⊗ 🛏️🦴 ◆◆◆

● Fowey
SOUTH WEST COAST PATH & SAINTS' WAY

4 Daglands Road, PL23 1JL ☎ 01726 833164 (John & Carol Eardley)
www.jabedesign.co.uk/keverne Map 200/123518
BB **C** ✕ nearby D2 Closed Dec Ⓑ Ⓓ ⊗ 🛏️🦴!🍴Ⓜ

☆ **Wringford**
Golant, PL23 1LA ☎ 01726 832205 (Liz Barclay)
Map 200/114548
BB **C** ✕ book first £12, 7-8pm S1 T1 Closed Xmas
Ⓥ Ⓑ Ⓓ ⊗ 🛏️🚗!🍴

Organically run smallholding in the
Fowey River Valley, on the Saints' Way,
3 miles from the south coast. No
television. Evening meals for walkers
only and by arrangement. Privacy and
atmosphere. 1 twin en-suite £30pp,
1 single £27pp. The kettle is always on!

Magnolia Cottage, Lankelly Lane, PL23 1HN ☎ 01726 832950
(Suzanne Bugano) suzanne_bugano@hotmail.co.uk Map 204,200/113518
BB **C** ✕ book first £ S1 D1 🚌(Par) Ⓥ Ⓑ Ⓓ ⊗ 🛏️🦴

● Golberdon (Callington)

Keadeen, PL17 7LT ☎ 01579 384197 (Geraldine Parkyn)
family@parkyn.charitydays.co.uk Map 201/329714
BB **B** ✕ nearby S1 D1 T1 Ⓑ Ⓓ ⊗ 🛏️🦴🍴

● **Hayle**
SOUTH WEST COAST PATH

54 Penpol Terrace, TR27 4BQ ☎ 01736 752855 (Anne Cooper)
annejohn@cooper827.fsnet.co.uk Map 203/558374
BB **C** ✗ nearby S1 D1 T1 Closed Xmas-Jan ⋙(Hayle) Ⓓ ⊛🐾♨🚗!Ⓜ

● **Lanivet (Bodmin)**
SAINTS' WAY

Willowbrook, Old Coach Road, Lamorick, PL30 5HB
☎ 01208 831670 (Tony & Elaine Barnaby)
www.welcomingyou.co.uk/willowbrook Map 200/037646
BB **C** ✗ book first £13 S1 D2 T1 Ⓥ Ⓓ ⊛🐾♨🚗! ◆◆◆◆

● **Lewannick (Launceston)**

Trevadlock Manor, PL15 7PW ☎ 01566 782227 (M & C Bruton)
www.trevadlockmanor.co.uk Map 201/265791
BB **B/D** ✗ book first £25, 8pm D1 T2 Closed: please call
Ⓥ Ⓑ Ⓓ ⊛🐾♨🚗!🐾 Private fishing. See SC also.

● **Liskeard**

🏠⋙ Elnor Guest House, 1 Russell Street, PL14 4BP ☎ 01579 342472
(Mr & Mrs B J Slocombe) www.elnorguesthouse.co.uk Map 201/250642
BB **B/C** ✗ nearby S4 D1 T1 F3 Closed Xmas ⋙(Liskeard)
Ⓑ Ⓓ🐾♨ ◆◆◆

● **Looe**
SOUTH WEST COAST PATH

Marwinthy Guest House, East Cliff, PL13 1DE ☎ 01503 264382 (Eddie Mawby)
www.marwinthy.co.uk Map 201/256533
BB **B** ✗ nearby D2 T1 F1 Closed Jan ⋙(Looe) Ⓑ Ⓓ♨🐾

☆ 🏠⋙ **Schooner Point**
1 Trelawney Terrace, PL13 2AG ☎ 01503 262670 (Paul & Helen Barlow)
www.schoonerpoint.co.uk Map 201/252536
BB **B** ✗ nearby S2 D3 T1 F0 Closed Xmas ⋙(Looe)
Ⓥ Ⓑ Ⓓ⊛🐾 ◆◆◆

Relaxed B&B offering clean, fresh rooms in a happy
family house with splendid river views.
Set only 150m from South West Coast Path and
Looe bridge
Non-smoking throughout. Widely appreciated
breakfasts, including vegetarian.
One-night stays accepted. Limited parking.

Kantana Guest House, 7 Trelawney Terrace, PL13 2AG
☎ 01503 262093 (Rick Blanks) www.kantana.co.uk Map 201/252536
BB **B** ✗ nearby S1 D2 T1 F1 ⋙(Looe) Ⓥ Ⓑ Ⓓ🐾♨

🏠⋙ Haven House, Barbican Hill, PL13 1BQ ☎ 01503 264160 (Edwina Arkell)
www.visitlooe.co.uk Map 201/255533
BB **B** ✗ book first £15, 7-9pm D2 F1 ⋙(Looe)
Ⓥ Ⓓ⊛🐾♨🚗! ★★★

🏠⋙ The Hill House, St Martins Road, PL13 1LP ☎ 01503 262556
(Liz Ferguson) www.thehillhouse.webeden.co.uk Map 201/254542
BB **D** ✗ nearby D4 Closed Xmas ⋙(Looe) Ⓥ Ⓑ Ⓓ⊛🐾♨!

● **Mevagissey (St Austell)**
SOUTH WEST COAST PATH

🏠⋙ The Spa Hotel, Polkirt Hill, PL26 6UY ☎ 01726 842244
(Mr & Mrs Schofield) www.spahotel-cornwall.co.uk Map 204/015443
BB **C** ✗ £15, 6:30-7pm S1 D4 T2 F4 Closed 12-2
Ⓥ Ⓑ Ⓓ🐾♨🐾 ★★

🏠⋙ Honeycombe House, 61 Polkirt Hill, PL26 6UR
☎ 01726 843750 (Ian & Val Soper)
www.honeycombehouse.com Map 204/015446
BB **C** ✗ nearby S1 D3 T1 Closed Xmas Ⓥ Ⓑ ·Ⓓ⊛🐾🚗!

● **Morwenstow (Bude)**
SOUTH WEST COAST PATH

☆ **Cornakey Farm**
EX23 9SS ☎ 01288 331260 (Monica Heywood)
Map 190/208157
BB **B** ✗ book first £12, 6:30pm D1 T1 F1 Closed Xmas
Ⓥ Ⓑ Ⓓ⊛🐾♨🚗! ◆◆◆

Cornakey Farm is in the far north-east
of Cornwall, directly overlooking the
Atlantic Ocean.
The farm consists of 220 acres, some of
which forms part of the coastal
footpath. Good home cooking.
Guests welcome to wander around farm.

☆ 🏠⋙ **The Bush Inn**
Crosstown, EX23 9ST ☎ 01288 331242
www.bushinn-morwenstow.co.uk Map 190/216167
BB **D** ✗ £10, 6-9pm D1 T2
Ⓥ Ⓑ Ⓓ⊛♨🐾

A 13th-century
freehouse in a
stunning
location just
off the South
West Coast
Path.

Once a haunt
for smugglers
and wreckers,
this historic pub has provided sustenance for weary travellers for hundreds of
years and is situated halfway between Bude and Hartland on one of the most
dramatic stretches of the north Cornish coast.

Open all day serving home-cooked food and Cornish real ales. Children and dogs
welcome. A quarter of a mile from the coast.

● **Mullion (Helston)**
SOUTH WEST COAST PATH

Campden House, The Commons, TR12 7HZ ☎ 01326 240365 (Joan Hyde)
campdenhouse@aol.com Map 203/677194
BB **B** ✗ £8, 6:30pm onwards S2 D2 T1 F2 Closed Xmas
Ⓥ Ⓑ Ⓓ⊛🐾♨🚗

Criggan Mill, Mullion Cove, TR12 7EU ☎ 01326 240496 (Mike & Jackie Bolton)
www.crigganmill.co.uk Map 203/667180
BB **C** ✗ book first £9 S4 D4 T4 F4 Closed Nov-Mar
Ⓥ Ⓑ Ⓓ⊛🐾♨ ★★★★★ See SC also.

🏠⋙ Trenance Farmhouse, TR12 7HB ☎ 01326 240639
www.trenancefarmholidays.co.uk Map 203/673185
BB **C/D** ✗ nearby D4 T1 Closed Nov-Feb
Ⓑ Ⓓ⊛🐾♨!🐾 ◆◆◆◆

● Newquay
SOUTH WEST COAST PATH

Chichester, 14 Bay View Terrace, TR7 2LR ☎ 01637 874216 (S R Harper)
http://freespace.virgin.net/sheila.harper Map 200/813614
BB **B** ✗ nearby S1 D3 T2 F1 Closed Dec-Feb ∿(Newquay)
🅱 🅳 ⊗ Ⓜ ◆◆◆ Organised spring/autumn walking weeks.

Roma Guest House, 1 Atlantic Road, TR7 1QJ ☎ 01637 875085
(Mrs P Williams) www.romaguesthouse.co.uk Map 200/803616
BB **B** ✗ book first £10, 6pm S1 D2 T1 F2 Closed Xmas ∿(Newquay)
Ⓥ 🅱 🅳 ⊗ 🐾 ♨ ! ★★★★

🏨 The Three Tees Hotel, 21 Carminow Way, TR7 3AY
☎ 01637 872055 (Greg & Fiona Dolan) www.3tees.co.uk Map 200/823622
BB **C/D** ✗ nearby D4 T1 F4 Closed Nov-Feb ∿(Newquay)
🅱 🅳 ⊗ 🐾 ♨ ! 🕯 ◆◆◆

🏨 Dewolf Guest House, 100 Henver Rd, TR7 3BL ☎ 01637 874746
www.dewolfguesthouse.com Map 200/828620
BB **B/C** ✗ nearby S2 D2 F2 ∿(Newquay)
🅱 ⊗ 🐾 ♨ ! 🕯 Ⓜ ★★★★

● Padstow
SOUTH WEST COAST PATH & SAINTS' WAY

☆ 🏨 **Trevorrick Farm**
St Issey, PL27 7QH ☎ 01841 540574 (Mr & Mrs M Benwell)
www.trevorrick.co.uk Map 200/922732
BB **C** ✗ nearby D2 T1 Closed Xmas
🅱 🅳 ⊗ 🐾 ♨ ! ◆◆◆

Magnificent location near Padstow. Warm welcome – tea and homemade cake. Pub/restaurant half a mile. Ideal walking/touring base; visiting Eden. Easy footpath access to Camel Trail, Padstow and coast path. Heated swimming pool (seasonal).

● Par
SOUTH WEST COAST PATH & SAINTS' WAY

🏨 Palm Garden House, 3 Tywardreath Highway, PL24 2RW
☎ 01726 816112 (Pat Taylor)
roytaylor49@yahoo.co.uk Map 200/077556
BB **B** ✗ book first £7.50-£14.50, 6:30pm onwards S1 D1 T1 F1 ∿(Par)
Ⓥ 🅳 ⊗ 🐾 ♨ � ! 🕯

● Pendoggett (Port Isaac)
SOUTH WEST COAST PATH

🏨 Lane End Farm, PL30 3HH ☎ 01208 880013 (Linda Monk)
nabmonk@tiscali.co.uk Map 200/026793
BB **C** ✗ nearby S1 D1 T1 Closed Xmas
Ⓥ 🅱 🅳 ⊗ 🐾 ♨ � ! Ⓜ ◆◆◆◆ See SC also.

● Penryn (Falmouth)
SOUTH WEST COAST PATH

🏨 62 St Thomas Street, TR10 8JP
☎ 01326 374473 (Brian & Penny Ward) Map 204/786341
BB **A** ✗ nearby S1 D2 T1 F1 Closed Nov-Feb ∿(Penryn)
🅳 🐾 ♨ Ⓜ

● Penzance
SOUTH WEST COAST PATH

☆ 🏨 **Torre Vene**
Lescudjack Terrace, TR18 3AE ☎ 01736 364103 (Mrs G Ash)
Map 203/475308
BB **C** ✗ nearby S2 D4 T4 F4 Closed Xmas ∿(Penzance)
🅳 ⊗ 🐾 ♨

Well-appointed guesthouse, delightful views of harbour, Mount's Bay.
Friendly "home from home" atmosphere.
Ideal overnight stop for Isles of Scilly.
Close to railway, coach stations and coastal paths.
Good home cooking.
A warm welcome awaits you.

🏨 Woodstock Guest House, 29 Morrab Road, TR18 4EZ
☎ 01736 369049 (Anne & David Peach) www.woodstockguesthouse.co.uk
Map 203/472300 BB **C/D** ✗ nearby S4 D2 T1 F1 Closed Xmas-Jan
∿(Penzance) 🅱 🅳 ⊗ 🐾 ♨ ! Ⓜ ◆◆◆

☆ 🏨 **Trewella Guest House**
18 Mennaye Road, TR18 4NG ☎ 01736 363818 (Shan & Dave Glenn)
www.trewella.co.uk Map 203/469298
BB **B** ✗ nearby S2 D4 T1 F1 Closed Nov-Feb ∿(Penzance)
🅱 ⊗ ♨ ◆◆◆

A warm welcome awaits you at Trewella.
Fully non-smoking, single to triple en-suite rooms.
One mile from main bus/train station, town centre 10 mins walk. Ideal centre for west Cornwall and South West Coast Path.
Discount for 4 or more days.
Email: shan.dave@lineone.net

Penrose Guest House, 8 Penrose Terrace, TR18 2HQ
☎ 01736 362782 (Marc White) www.penrosegsthse.co.uk Map 203/475307
BB **C** ✗ nearby S1 D1 T1 F1 ∿(Penzance) Ⓥ 🅱 🅳 ⊗ 🐾 ♨ ◆◆◆

🏨 Glencree House, 2 Mennaye Road, TR18 4NG ☎ 01736 362026
(Helen Cahalane) www.glencreehouse.co.uk Map 203/469297
BB **A/C** ✗ nearby S3 D4 T2 F2 Closed Xmas ∿(Penzance)
🅱 🅳 ⊗ 🐾 ♨ ! 🕯 Ⓜ ◆◆◆◆

● Perranporth
SOUTH WEST COAST PATH

Chy An Kerensa, Cliff Road, TR6 0DR ☎ 01872 572470 (W Woodcock)
Map 200,203/754543 BB **B/C** ✗ nearby S2 D2 T2 F3 Closed Xmas
🅱 🅳 ⊗ 🐾 ♨ ! 🕯 ◆◆◆

🏨 Cliffside Hotel, Cliff Rd, TR6 0DR ☎ 01872 573297 (Maureen Burch)
www.cliffsideperranporth.co.uk Map 200/754544
BB **B** ✗ nearby S3 D5 T1 F2 Closed Xmas Ⓥ 🅱 🅳 ♨ 🕯

🏨 Penarth Guest House, 26 St Pirans Road, TR6 0BH ☎ 01872 573186
(Peter & Diana Freckleton) www.penarthperranporth.co.uk Map 200/758542
BB **C** ✗ nearby S3 D3 T1 F/D1 Closed Dec-Feb 🅱 🐾 ♨ 🕯

● Polgooth (St Austell)
SOUTH WEST COAST PATH

🏨 Hunter's Moon, Chapel Hill, PL26 7BU
☎ 01726 66445 (Richard & Pauline Scott)
www.huntersmooncornwall.co.uk Map 204,200/994505
BB **C** ✗ nearby D/T/F4 ∿(St Austell) 🅱 🅳 ⊗ 🐾 ♨ 🚗 ◆◆◆◆

● Port Isaac
SOUTH WEST COAST PATH

☆ **Anchorage**
The Terrace, PL29 3SG ☎ 01208 880629 (Colin & Maxine Durston)
www.anchorageportisaac.co.uk Map 200/999807
BB **C** ✕ nearby SI D3 TI FI Closed Xmas-Jan
Ⓥ Ⓑ Ⓓ ⊛ ⏰ ♨ ! ◆◆◆◆

Stunning sea views.

Perfectly situated on the North Cornwall
Coast Path.

Contact Colin and Maxine Durston.

● Porthcurno (Penzance)
SOUTH WEST COAST PATH

🏠 Sea View House, The Valley, TR19 6JX ☎ 01736 810638 (Susan Davis)
www.seaviewhouseporthcurno.com Map 203/383227
BB **C** ✕ book first £13, 7:30pm SI D3 T/D2 Closed Nov-Feb
Ⓥ Ⓑ Ⓓ ⊛ ⏰ ♨ ! ♨ Ⓜ

🏠 Porthcurno Hotel, The Valley, TR19 6JX ☎ 01736 810119
www.porthcurnohotel.co.uk Map 203/383227
BB **D** ✕ book first £24.50, 6-8pm D/S4 T/S3 FI
Ⓥ Ⓑ Ⓓ ⊛ ⏰ ♨ ! ◆◆◆◆ Guide dogs welcome.

● Ruan-High-Lanes (Truro)
SOUTH WEST COAST PATH

☆ **New Gonitor Farm**
TR2 5LE ☎ 01872 501345
newgonitorfarm.wanadoo.co.uk Map 204/905416
BB **C** ✕ nearby DI TI Closed Dec-Jan
Ⓑ Ⓓ ⊛ ⏰ ♨ ♨

Stay at our comfortable
farmhouse in the beautiful Roseland.
Wonderful coastal walks and NT
gardens within the local area.
Also, Lost Gardens of Heligan and
Eden Project. En-suite rooms,
traditional farmhouse fare.

● Sennen (Penzance)
SOUTH WEST COAST PATH

Treeve Moor House, TR19 7AE ☎ 01736 871284 (Liz Trenary)
www.firstandlastcottages.co.uk Map 203/353251
BB **C** ✕ nearby D2 TI Closed Xmas Ⓑ Ⓓ ♨ ! ◆◆◆◆

● St Agnes
SOUTH WEST COAST PATH

Penkerris, Penwinnick Road, TR5 0PA ☎ 01872 552262 (Gill-Carey)
www.penkerris.co.uk Map 204/720501
BB **B/C** ✕ nearby SI D2 TI Ⓑ Ⓓ ⏰ ♨ ♨ ★★

● St Austell

🏠 Spindrift, London Apprentice, PL26 7AR ☎ 01726 69316 (Linda Mcguffie)
www.spindrift-guesthouse.co.uk Map 204/007501
BB **C** ✕ nearby DI F2 Closed Xmas Ⓑ ⊛ ♨ ♨ ◆◆◆ See SC also.

● St Breward (Bodmin)

🏠 Tremorcoombe Guest House, Row, PL30 4LN ☎ 01208 851744
(Cathy & Peter Glaser) www.tordownholidays.co.uk Map 109/096766
BB **B** ✕ nearby S/DI FI Ⓥ Ⓑ Ⓓ ⊛ ⏰ ♨ ! Ⓜ

● St Cleer (Liskeard)
COPPER TRAIL

☆ 🏠 **Redgate Smithy**
Redgate, PL14 6RU ☎ 01579 321578 (Clive & Julie Ffitch)
www.redgatesmithy.co.uk Map 201/227685
BB **D** D2 TI Closed Xmas
Ⓑ Ⓓ ⊛ ♨ ! ♨ ◆◆◆◆

Welcoming B&B situated above beautiful
Golitha Falls on southern edge of Bodmin
Moor. Excellent walking, on moor or coast.
On the Copper Trail.
Area abounds with Cornish mining heritage
and birds and wildlife on the moor. Lovely
woodland garden. Brochure available.

● St Gennys (Bude)
SOUTH WEST COAST PATH

Bears & Boxes Country Guest House, Penrose, Dizzard, EX23 0NX
☎ 01840 230318 (Robert & Francoise Holmes) www.bearsandboxes.com
Map 190/170986 BB **C/D** ✕ book first £13, 6:30-8pm D2 TI FI
Ⓥ Ⓑ Ⓓ ⊛ ⏰ ♨ ! ♨ ◆◆◆◆

● St Ives
SOUTH WEST COAST PATH

🏠 Ten Steps, Fish St, TR26 1LT ☎ 01736 798222 (Lydia Dean-Barrows)
www.tenstepsbandb.co.uk Map 203/519408
BB **C/D** ✕ nearby SI DI TI FI ⋀⋀(St Ives)
Ⓥ Ⓑ Ⓓ ⊛ ⏰ ♨ ! ♨ ◆◆◆◆

🏠 Ocean Rooms, Above Ocean Grill, Wharf Road, TR26 1LG
☎ 01736 798024 www.ocean-rooms.co.uk Map 203/518407
BB **D** ✕ nearby D4 Closed Nov-Jan ⋀⋀(St Ives) Ⓥ Ⓑ ⊛ ♨

Pebble Private Hotel, 4 Park Avenue, TR26 2DN
☎ 01736 794168 (Jenny & Ricky) www.pebble-hotel.co.uk Map 203/516402
BB **D** ✕ nearby S2 D5 TI FI Closed Dec-Jan ⋀⋀(St Ives)
Ⓑ Ⓓ ⊛ ⏰ ♨ ◆◆◆◆

🏠 Turning Tide, 28 Trenwith Place, TR26 1QD
☎ 01736 799267 (Imi Mulqueen) mrsshantyb@aol.com Map 203/516403
BB **C** ✕ book first £10, 7pm DI ⋀⋀(St Ives)
Ⓥ Ⓓ ⊛ ⏰ ♨ ⛟ ! Ⓜ Vegetarian food only.

● St Just (Penzance)
SOUTH WEST COAST PATH

☆ 🏠 **Bosavern House**
TR19 7RD ☎ 01736 788301 (Mrs C Collinson)
www.bosavern.com Map 203/371305
BB **C/D** ✕ nearby SI D3 T2 F2 Closed Xmas
Ⓑ Ⓓ ⊛ ⏰ ♨ ! ◆◆◆◆

17th-century country house offering
centrally heated, comfortable
accommodation. Most bedrooms have sea or
moorland views; en-suite or private
facilities. Lounge with log fire, TV & bar.
Drying facilities. Home cooking using local
produce. Half mile from the SW Coast Path.

SOUTH WEST

The Old Fire Station, 2 Nancherrow Terrace, TR19 7LA ☎ 01736 786463 (Angus & Liz Baxter) www.oldfirestationstjust.com Map 203/369315
BB C ✗ nearby D2 TI Ⓥ Ⓑ Ⓓ ⊗ 🐾 👜 🚗 ❗

● St Wenn (Bodmin)
SAINTS' WAY

☆ Tregolls Farm
PL30 5PG ☎ 01208 812154 (Marilyn Hawkey)
www.tregollsfarm.co.uk Map 200/983661
BB C ✗ book first £13, 7pm D2 TI Closed Xmas
Ⓥ Ⓑ Ⓓ ⊗ 🐾 👜 🚗 ❗ ◆◆◆◆ See SC also.

Grade II listed farmhouse with beautiful countryside views from all windows. 2 guest bedrooms. Farm trail links up to Saints' Way footpath. Pets' corner. Eden, Helligan, Fowey and Padstow all within 25 minutes drive.

Treliver Farm, PL30 5PQ ☎ 01726 890286 (Jenny Tucker)
jenny@tucker600.freeserve.co.uk Map 200/980655
BB D ✗ £17, until 8:30pm DI TI FI
Ⓥ Ⓑ Ⓓ ⊗ 🐾 👜 🚗 ❗ ◆◆◆◆

● Stithians (Falmouth)
Tregolls Cottage B&B, Tregolls, TR3 7BX ☎ 01209 861749 (Fay Badcock)
tregollscottage@tesco.net Map 204/730359
BB B ✗ £12, 7:30pm D2 TI FI Ⓥ Ⓓ 🐾 👜 🚗 ❗ 🏠

● The Lizard (Helston)
SOUTH WEST COAST PATH

Carmelin, Pentreath Lane, The Lizard, TR12 7NY ☎ 01326 290677 (Mrs Jane Grierson) www.bedandbreakfastcornwall.co.uk Map 203/699126
BB C ✗ £15, 7-8pm SI DI Ⓥ Ⓑ Ⓓ ⊗ 🐾 👜 🚗 ❗ 🏠

● Tintagel
SOUTH WEST COAST PATH

Bosayne Guest House, Atlantic Road, PL34 0DE
☎ 01840 770514 (Julie & Keith Walker) www.bosayne.co.uk Map 200/050890
BB B/C ✗ nearby S3 D2 TI F2 Closed Xmas Ⓑ Ⓓ ⊗ 🐾 👜 ❗ ◆◆◆

● Treknow (Tintagel)
SOUTH WEST COAST PATH & COPPER TRAIL

Michael House Vegetarian Guest House, Trelake Lane, PL34 0EW
☎ 01840 770592 (Vanessa Lackford) www.michael-house.co.uk
Map 200/057866 BB C ✗ book first £17.50, 7:30pm D2 TI
Ⓥ Ⓑ Ⓓ ⊗ 🐾 👜 🚗 ❗ 🏠

☆ Tregosse House
PL34 0EP ☎ 01840 779229 (Richard Hart)
www.tregossehouse.co.uk Map 200/052866
BB D ✗ nearby D2 TI
Ⓥ Ⓑ Ⓓ 🐾 👜 🚗 ❗

A beautiful Victorian detached property only 150 yards from the South West Coast Path – ideal location to explore the north Cornwall coast.

Every room has panoramic sea views, en-suites, colour TV/DVDs and tea/coffee making facilities.

● Truro
The Bay Tree, 28 Ferris Town, TR1 3JH ☎ 01872 240274 (Ann Talbot)
Map 204/821448 BB C ✗ nearby SI DI T2 FI �／(Truro) ⊗ 👜 🏠

Cliftons, 46 Tregolls Road, TR1 1LA ☎ 01872 274116
(Peter & Sarah Conisbee) www.cliftonsguesthouse.co.uk Map 204/833451
BB C ✗ nearby SI D2 T2 FI �／(Truro)
Ⓥ Ⓑ Ⓓ ⊗ 🐾 👜 🚗 ❗ ◆◆◆

● Whitecross (Wadebridge)
SOUTH WEST COAST PATH

The Old Post Office, Atlantic Highway, PL27 7JD ☎ 01208 812620
www.byways activity holidays.co.uk Map 200/966722
BB B ✗ book first £7 DI T2 Ⓑ Ⓓ 🐾 👜 🚗 ❗ 🏠 ◆◆◆

● Zennor (St Ives)
SOUTH WEST COAST PATH

Trewey Farm, TR26 3DA ☎ 01736 796936 (Mrs N I Mann) Map 203/454384
BB C ✗ nearby SI D2 TI F2 Closed Dec Ⓥ Ⓓ ⊗ 🐾 👜 🏠

Boswednack Manor, TR26 3DD ☎ 01736 794183 (Dr E Gynn)
www.boswednackmanor.co.uk Map 203/442378
BB B ✗ nearby SI D2 TI FI Closed Nov-Mar Ⓥ Ⓑ Ⓓ ⊗ 🐾 👜 ❗

The Tinners Arms, TR26 3BY ☎ 01736 796927
www.tinnersarms.com Map 203/454385
BB D ✗ £12, 6:30-9pm S2 D2 Ⓥ Ⓑ Ⓓ ⊗ 🐾 👜 🚗 ❗

DEVON

● Ashburton (Newton Abbot)
DARTMOOR

☆ Gages Mill Country Guest House
Buckfastleigh Road, TQ13 7JW ☎ 01364 652391 (Lynda Richards)
www.gagesmill.co.uk Map 202/748689
BB C ✗ nearby D6 TI Closed Nov-Feb
Ⓥ Ⓑ Ⓓ 🐾 👜 ◆◆◆◆

Gages Mill is a former 14th-century woolmill set in an acre of gardens on the edge of the Dartmoor National Park. This family-run house offers a warm home-from-home atmosphere once you have visited the beautiful countryside.

● Bampton (Tiverton)
Rows Farmhouse, EX16 9LD ☎ 01398 331579 (Mr & Mrs H Brooks)
suzannah@dircon.co.uk Map 181/946227
BB C ✗ book first £10 DI TI FI Closed Xmas Ⓥ Ⓑ Ⓓ 🐾 👜 🚗 ❗ 🏠

● Beer
SOUTH WEST COAST PATH

Bay View Guest House, Fore Street, EX12 3EE
☎ 01297 20489 (Mr & Mrs R Oswald) Map 192/230891
BB B/C ✗ nearby SI D5 TI FI Ⓑ Ⓓ ⊗ 🐾 👜 ◆◆◆

● Belstone (Okehampton)
DARTMOOR

Moorlands House, EX20 1QZ ☎ 01837 840549
www.moorlands-house.co.uk Map 191/620935
BB B/C ✗ nearby D2 Closed Xmas Ⓑ Ⓓ 🐾 👜 🚗 🏠

● **Bideford**

SOUTH WEST COAST PATH

The Mount, Northdown Road, EX39 3LP ☎ 01237 473748
(Heather & Andrew Laugharne) www.themount1.cjb.net Map 190/449269
BB **D** ✕ nearby S2 D3 T1 F2 Closed Xmas
B D ⊗ 🐾 🛏 🚗 ! ◆◆◆◆

Corner House, The Strand, EX39 2ND ☎ 01237 473722
(Chris & Sally Stone) www.cornerhouseguesthouse.co.uk Map 190,180/452268
BB **B** ✕ nearby S1 D2 T1 F2 Closed Xmas V D ⊗ 🐾 🛏 🚲

● **Braunton**

SOUTH WEST COAST PATH

North Cottage, 14 North Street, EX33 1AJ ☎ 01271 812703 (Jean Watkins)
north_cottage@hotmail.com Map 180/485367
BB **B** ✕ nearby S2 D1 T1 F1 B D 🐾 🛏 ! 🚲 Ⓜ

The Firs, Higher Park Road, EX33 2LG ☎ 01271 814358 (Alison Benning)
www.bennings.co.uk Map 180/498364
BB **C** ✕ nearby D1 T1 B D ⊗ 🐾 🛏 🚗 ! 🚲

● **Brixham**

SOUTH WEST COAST PATH

Nods Fold B&B, Mudstone Lane, TQ5 9EQ ☎ 01803 856138
www.nodsfold.co.uk Map 202/930555
BB **B** ✕ nearby D1 V B D ⊗ 🐾 🛏 🚗 !

● **Budleigh Salterton**

SOUTH WEST COAST PATH

Ropers Cottage, Ropers Lane, Otterton, EX9 7JF ☎ 01395 568826 (Mrs Earl)
Map 192/081851 BB **B** ✕ nearby T1 Closed Xmas B D 🛏 🚲

● **Chagford (Newton Abbot)**

DARTMOOR

TWO MOORS WAY

Cyprian's Cot, 47 New Street, TQ13 8BB ☎ 01647 432256 (Shelagh Weeden)
www.cyprianscot.co.uk Map 191/701874
BB **C** ✕ nearby S1 D1 T1 Closed Xmas
B D 🛏 🚗 ! 🚲 Luggage transfer off-season only.

● **Clovelly (Bideford)**

SOUTH WEST COAST PATH

The New House, EX39 5TQ ☎ 01237 431303 www.clovelly.co.uk
Map 190/317248 BB **B** ✕ book first £20, 7-8:30pm D2 T3 F2 Closed Xmas
V ⊗ 🐾 🛏 Ⓜ ★★

☆ **I Southdown Cottage**
Higher Clovelly, EX39 5SA ☎ 01237 431504 (Mary McColl)
maryfmcoll@hotmail.com Map 190/297236
BB **B** ✕ book first £12 S1 D1 T1 F1
V B D 🐾 🛏 🚗 ! 🚲 Ⓜ

Lovely cosy cottage. Bright en-suite
& standard rooms with TV,
tea/coffee and wonderful views.
Lifts to/from South West Coast Path
anywhere between Barnstaple and
Bude, so make us your base for a
while. Breakfast a speciality.

● **Colebrooke (Crediton)**

TWO MOORS WAY

The Oyster, EX17 5JQ ☎ 01363 84576 (Pearl Hockridge) Map 191/770008
BB **B** ✕ nearby D2 T1 🚌(Yeoford) B D 🐾 🛏 🚗 ! 🚲

● **Colyton**

Sunnyacre, Rockerhayne Farm, Northleigh, EX24 6DA
☎ 01404 871422 (Norma Rich) sunnyacre@tesco.net Map 192,193/213963
BB **B** ✕ book first £7, 6:30pm D1 T1 F1 V D ⊗ 🐾 🛏 ! 🚲 ◆◆◆

The Cobblers, Dolphin Street, EX24 6NA ☎ 01297 552825 (Caroline Galt)
www.colyton.net Map 192,193/246940
BB **C** ✕ £14, 7-9pm S1 D1 T1 Closed Jan V B D ⊗ 🐾 🛏

● **Combe Martin**

EXMOOR

SOUTH WEST COAST PATH

☆ **The Royal Marine Public House Hotel**
Seaside, EX34 0AW ☎ 01271 882470 (M J Lethaby)
www.theroyalmarine.co.uk Map 180/576472
BB **C** ✕ book first £5-£10, 6-10pm D4 T1 F1
V B D 🐾 🛏 🚗 !

A warm welcome by the sea awaits you from
resident proprietors Pat and Merv.
Five beautiful en-suite rooms with beach views.
Award-winning licensee for food and service.
We specialise in home cooked food.
Mini breaks 1, 2, 3, 4 days, mid-week/weekends.
theroyal.marine@btconnect.com

Mellstock House, Woodlands, EX34 0AR ☎ 01271 882592
(Mary Burbidge) www.mellstockhouse.co.uk Map 180/575473
BB **C** ✕ book first £12, 7pm S1 D4 T1 F1 Closed Xmas
V B D ⊗ 🐾 🛏 🚗 ! ◆◆◆◆

● **Dartmouth**

DARTMOOR

SOUTH WEST COAST PATH

Hill View House, 76 Victoria Road, TQ6 9DZ ☎ 01803 839372
(Suzanne White) www.hillviewdartmouth.co.uk Map 202/872512
BB **D** D3 T2 Closed Jan 🚌(Kingswear) B D ⊗ 🛏 🚗 ! ◆◆◆◆Ⓖ

● **Exeter**

Park View Hotel, 8 Howell Road, EX4 4LG ☎ 01392 271772
www.parkviewexeter.co.uk Map 192/917933
BB **C** ✕ nearby S1 D7 T3 F2 Closed Xmas 🚌(Exeter Central)
B D ⊗ 🐾 🛏 ◆◆◆

The Old Mill, Mill Lane, Alphington, EX2 8SG ☎ 01392 259977
www.smoothhound.co.uk/hotels/oldmillg.html Map 192/915903
BB **A** ✕ nearby S1 D1 T1 F2 🚌(Exeter St Davids)
D ⊗ 🛏 Wheelchair access.

● **Exmouth**

SOUTH WEST COAST PATH

Sholton Guest House, 29 Morton Road, EX8 1BA ☎ 01395 277318 (Ann Jones)
Map 192/999807 BB **B** ✕ nearby S1 D3 T2 F1 🚌(Exmouth) B D ⊗ 🛏

● **Halwill Junction (Holsworthy)**

Market House, EX21 5TN ☎ 01409 221339 (Caroline Halliwell)
ctandf@aol.com Map 190/447990
BB **C** ✕ book first £12, 7pm D1 T1 Closed Xmas V B D 🐾 🛏 🚗 🚲

● **Hartland (Bideford)**

SOUTH WEST COAST PATH

West Titchberry Farm, Hartland Point, EX39 6AU
☎ 01237 441287 (Mrs Y Heard) Map 190/242272
BB **B** ✕ book first £12, 6:30pm D1 T1 F1 V B D ⊗ 🐾 🛏 🚗 !

Elmscott Farm, EX39 6ES ☎ 01237 441276 (Thirza Goaman)
Map 190/231215 BB **B** ✕ book first £12, 6pm D1 T1 F1 Closed Xmas
Ⓥ Ⓑ Ⓓ ⊗ 🐾 ⛶ 🚗 ! ◆◆◆◆

☆ **Gawlish Farm**
EX39 6AT ☎ 01237 441320 (Jill George)
Map 190/256263
BB **B** ✕ book first £12, 6:30pm D1 T2 Closed Xmas
Ⓥ Ⓑ Ⓓ ⊗ 🐾 ⛶ 🚗 ! 🏠 ◆◆◆◆

You will be warmly welcomed to this tastefully furnished farmhouse. Beautifully quiet countryside on route to the South West Coast Path.

● Hillhead (Brixham)
SOUTH WEST COAST PATH

☆ 🛏🍴 **Raddicombe Lodge**
Kingswear Road, TQ5 0EX ☎ 01803 882125 (Kay Sowerby)
www.raddicombelodge.co.uk Map 202/905539
BB **C** ✕ book first £15 S1 D4 T2 F2
Ⓥ Ⓑ Ⓓ ⊗ 🐾 ⛶ 🚗 ! 🏠 ◆◆◆◆

Luxury ensuite guesthouse in quiet situation between Dartmouth and Brixham, close to South West Coast Path OL20 905539.

Private car park. Sea/countryside views.

Delicious food — evening meals by arrangement.
In room tea/coffee facilities. Relaxing garden, comfortable dining room and guests' sitting room. Drying room for kit. Walkers' packed lunches.

Collection from train/bus station or Exeter airport. Bus route from Brixham/Dartmouth. Ideal base for your walking holiday in South Devon.

● Holne (Ashburton)
DARTMOOR & TWO MOORS WAY

Chase Gate Farm, TQ13 7RX ☎ 01364 631261 (Anne & David Higman)
www.chasegatefarm.com Map 202/716703
BB **B** D2 T1 Closed Xmas Ⓑ Ⓓ 🐾 ⛶ 🚗 ! 🏠

● Holsworthy

☆ **Leworthy Farmhouse**
Pyworthy, EX22 6SJ ☎ 01409 259469 (Pat Jennings)
www.leworthyfarmhouse.co.uk Map 190/322012
BB **D** ✕ nearby D4 T2 F1
Ⓑ Ⓓ ⊗ 🐾 ⛶ 🚗 ! ◆◆◆◆Ⓢ

Charming Georgian farmhouse in idyllic backwater. Delightful ensuite rooms, fresh milk, fresh flowers, pretty china. Peaceful lounge with books, ticking clocks, comfy old sofas, Chinese carpets. Scrumptious breakfasts: porridge, kippers, haddock, free-range eggs, local bacon. Warm welcome assured.

● Hope Cove (Kingsbridge)
SOUTH WEST COAST PATH

☆ 🛏🍴 **The Cottage Hotel**
TQ7 3HJ ☎ 01548 561555
www.hopecove.com Map 202/676401
BB **C/D** ✕ book first £17.45, 7:30-8:30pm S10 D/T20 F5 Closed Jan
Ⓥ Ⓑ Ⓓ ⊗ 🐾 ⛶ 🚲 ★★Ⓢ Price includes dinner!

The hotel enjoys a magnificent position in this pretty and secluded fishing village. By heritage coastline and National Trust land. Ideally situated for walks. Log fire in winter. Drying facilities. Group rates available. Friendly & efficient service. Good food & wine.

● Horrabridge (Yelverton)
DARTMOOR

☆ 🛏🍴 **Overcombe Guest House**
Old Station Road, PL20 7RA ☎ 01822 853501
www.overcombehotel.co.uk Map 201/511693
BB **D** ✕ nearby S1 D3 T2 F2
Ⓥ Ⓑ Ⓓ ⊗ 🐾 ⛶ 🚗 ◆◆◆◆Ⓦ NAS mobility 1 & 2.

Located within Dartmoor National Park, offering quality facilities and a personal service in a relaxed, homely atmosphere.

All guests can be assured of receiving a friendly welcome, comfortable en-suite accommodation, and a substantial breakfast using local and home-made produce.

Some rooms enjoy stunning views of Dartmoor. Conveniently located for exploring the national park and the adjacent Tamar Valley.

● Ilfracombe
SOUTH WEST COAST PATH

🛏🍴 The Woodlands, Torrs Park, EX34 8AZ ☎ 01271 863098 (Mark O'Brien)
www.thewoodlands-hotel.co.uk Map 180/511472
BB **C/D** ✕ nearby S2 D6 T1 F1 Closed Xmas
Ⓑ Ⓓ ⊗ 🐾 🚗 ! ◆◆◆◆Ⓢ

Lyncott House, 56 St Brannock's Road, EX34 8EQ ☎ 01271 862425
(John & Carol Pearson) www.lyncotthouse.co.uk Map 180/515468
BB **C** ✕ book first £15, 7-8pm D4 F1 Ⓥ Ⓑ Ⓓ ⊗ 🐾 ⛶ ★★★★

● Ivybridge
DARTMOOR
TWO MOORS WAY

🛏🍴 Hillhead Farm, Ugborough, PL21 0HQ ☎ 01752 892674 (Jane Johns)
www.hillhead-farm.co.uk Map 202/674564
BB **C** ✕ nearby D2 T1 Closed Oct-Dec
Ⓑ Ⓓ ⊗ 🐾 ⛶ 🚗 ! 🏠 ★★★★Ⓢ

Kevela, 4 Clare Street, PL21 9DL ☎ 01752 893111 (Ray & May Dunn)
www.kevela.co.uk Map 202/632559
BB **C** ✕ nearby D2 T1 🚌(Ivybridge) Ⓑ Ⓓ ⊗ 🐾 ⛶ ! 🏠

● Kingsbridge

SOUTH WEST COAST PATH

▪◨◀ Ashleigh House, Ashleigh Road, TQ7 1HB ☎ 01548 852893
(Nick & Jan Alen) www.ashleigh-house.co.uk Map 202/731439
BB **C** ✕ nearby D5 T1 F2 Closed Dec Ⓥ Ⓑ Ⓓ ⊛ ♨ ☺ ⛟ Ⓜ ◆◆◆◆

● Knowstone (South Molton)

TWO MOORS WAY

West Bowden Farm, EX36 4RP ☎ 01398 341224 (Mrs J Bray)
www.westbowden.ukf.net Map 181/833224 BB **C** ✕ book first £12, 6:30pm
S1 D3 T2 F2 Closed Xmas Ⓥ Ⓑ Ⓓ ⛟♨☺⛟!⛺ ◆◆◆

● Leworthy Barton (Woolsery)

The Stables, EX39 5PY ☎ 01237 431140 (Kim Woodward)
kim@westcountrylife.co.uk Map 190/352191
BB **D** ✕ book first £12 D1 Ⓥ Ⓑ Ⓓ ⊛ ⛟♨⛟!⛺

● Lydford (Okehampton)

DARTMOOR

☆ ▪◨◀ **Lydford House**
EX20 4AU ☎ 01822 820347
www.lydfordhouse.com Map 201,191/517852
BB **D** ✕ nearby S2 D3 T2 F2
Ⓥ Ⓑ Ⓓ ⊛ ⛟♨⛟⛺ ◆◆◆◆

Set amidst the spectacular
scenery of Dartmoor National
Park near to Lydford Gorge, an
ideal location for walking or
cycling.
A warm relaxed atmosphere. Beautifully appointed, spacious rooms, licensed
tearooms, cycle hire and walks in every direction. Excellent local restaurants.

● Lynmouth

EXMOOR

SOUTH WEST COAST PATH & TWO MOORS WAY

☆ **Tregonwell & The Olde Sea-Captain's House**
1 Tors Road, EX35 6ET ☎ 01598 753369 (Mr & Mrs C & J Parker)
www.smoothhound.co.uk/hotels/tregonwl.html Map 180/727494
BB **C/D** ✕ nearby S1 D5 T1 F2 Closed Xmas
Ⓑ Ⓓ ⊛ ⛟♨⛟!⛺ ◆◆◆

Awarded 'England's B&B of the Year' (IV).
Warm welcome guaranteed at the best
place for you Exmoor ramblers. Our
elegant Victorian riverside guesthouse
is snuggled in wooded valleys,
waterfalls, England's highest clifftops & most enchanting harbour. Pretty en-suite
bedrooms with dramatic views. Log fires. Garaged parking. Group discounts.

☆ **Glenville House**
2 Tors Road, EX35 6ET ☎ 01598 752202 (Tricia & Alan Francis)
www.glenvillelynmouth.co.uk Map 180/727494
BB **C** ✕ nearby S1 D4 T1 Closed Dec-Feb
Ⓑ Ⓓ ⊛ ⛟♨⛟!Ⓜ ◆◆◆◆

Elegant Victorian house in idyllic
riverside setting. Lovely licensed B&B.
Tastefully decorated bedrooms.
Picturesque harbour and village.
Dramatic Exmoor scenery & spectacular
valley/coastal walks. Peaceful, tranquil,
romantic – a very special place.

☆ ▪◨◀ **The Bath Hotel**
EX35 6EL ☎ 01598 752238 (Mrs S L Hobbs)
www.torslynmouth.co.uk Map 180/723496
BB **D** ✕ book first £18, 7-8:30pm S1 D10 T7 F4 Closed Dec-Jan
Ⓥ Ⓑ Ⓓ ⊛ ⛟♨☺⛺ ★★

Friendly, family-run two-star
establishment with good facilities
and excellent food. 22 bedrooms,
all ensuite with TV, tea & coffee.
Situated on edge of Exmoor, an
ideal location for a walking holiday.
Special group rates available.

☆ **River Lyn View**
26 Watersmeet Road, EX35 6EP ☎ 01598 753501 (Carol Sheppard)
www.riverlynview.com Map 180/725493
BB **B** ✕ nearby D4 T1
Ⓑ Ⓓ ⊛ ⛟♨⛟!⛺

River Lyn View offers comfortable B&B.
Rooms are en-suite & overlook the East Lyn
River situated on the edge of Exmoor near the
picturesque harbour in Lynmouth with its
spectacular coastal views. Ideal for walking
holidays. Major credit cards accepted.
Email: riverlynview@aol.com

● Lynton

EXMOOR

SOUTH WEST COAST PATH & TWO MOORS WAY

▪◨◀ Lee House, 27 Lee Road, EX35 6BP ☎ 01598 752364
(Mike & Lesley Tucker) www.leehouselynton.co.uk Map 180/717495
BB **C** ✕ nearby D6 T2 F1 Closed Xmas Ⓑ Ⓓ ⊛ ⛟♨☺! ◆◆◆◆

▪◨◀ Longmead House, EX35 6DQ ☎ 01598 752523 (Jacqueline & Nigel)
www.longmeadhouse.co.uk Map 180/715493
BB **C** ✕ nearby S1 D4 T2 F1 Ⓑ Ⓓ ⊛ ⛟♨⛟! ◆◆◆◆

☆ **The Denes**
15 Longmead, EX35 6DQ ☎ 01598 753573 (John McGowan)
www.thedenes.com Map 180/715495
BB **B/C** ✕ book first £15, 6:30-8pm D3 T2 FT/3 Closed Xmas
Ⓥ Ⓑ Ⓓ ⊛ ⛟♨⛟! ◆◆◆◆

Glorious place, Good food, Great value. An
ideal base for exploring Exmoor or stopover for SW Coast Path trekkers. Drying
facilities. Car parking. Licensed. Evening
meals. En-suites rooms available. From
£21-27.50pppn. Open all year.
Major credit cards accepted.

☆ ▪◨◀ **Meadpool House**
Brendon, EX35 6PS ☎ 01598 741215 (Nigel & Vivienne Wood)
www.whatsonexmoor.co.uk/meadpool Map 180/771482
BB **B** ✕ nearby D2 T1 Closed Xmas
Ⓑ Ⓓ ⊛ ⛟♨⛟!

Luxury, smoke-free B&B on East Lyn
river. 4-mile walk to Lynmouth via
wooded gorge. Upstream to open moor
through Doone Valley. Coast Path 2
miles, pub ¼ mile. Bedrooms (with TVs)
are en-suite or with private bathroom.
Lounge. From £20pppn.

● Manaton (Newton Abbot)
DARTMOOR
TWO MOORS WAY

Hazelcott B&B, TQ13 9UY ☎ 01647 221521 (Nigel Fisher)
www.dartmoordays.com Map 191/751822
BB **C** ✕ book first £17.50, 7:30pm D2 T1 F1
Ⅴ B D ⊗ 🛏🍵☕🚗🚇!⚘ ◆◆◆◆

Wingstone Farm, TQ13 9UL ☎ 01647 221215 (Juliette Rich)
www.wingstonefarm.co.uk Map 191/747811
BB **B** ✕ nearby S1 D2 Closed Xmas D ⊗ 🛏☕🚇!⚘

● Mary Tavy (Tavistock)
DARTMOOR

Dowerland Farm, PL19 9PR ☎ 01822 810345 (Doreen Rogers)
www.dowerlandfarm.co.uk Map 201,191/506791
BB **C** ✕ nearby D2 T1 Ⅴ B D ⊗ 🛏☕🚗!

● Moretonhampstead (Newton Abbot)
DARTMOOR
TWO MOORS WAY

Great Slon Combe Farm, TQ13 8QF ☎ 01647 440595
(Mrs Trudie Merchant) www.greatsloncombefarm.co.uk Map 191/736862
BB **C** D2 T1 Ⅴ B D ⊗ 🛏☕🚇!⚘ ◆◆◆◆Ⓢ

Little Wooston Farm, TQ13 8QA ☎ 01647 440551 (Jeanne Cuming)
jeannecuming@tesco.net Map 191/760887
BB **A** ✕ book first £6-8, 6:30-7pm S1 D1 F1 Ⅴ D 🛏☕🚗⚘ ★★★

☆ **Cookshayes Country Guest House**
33 Court Street, TQ13 8LG ☎ 01647 440374 (Tracy Williams)
www.cookshayes.co.uk Map 191/751860
BB **B** ✕ book first £16, 6:30pm S1 D5 T1 F1
Ⅴ B D 🛏☕!⚘ ◆◆◆

Beautiful mid-Victorian house set in large gardens on the edge of Dartmoor. Minutes away from village centre. Most rooms en-suite.

Email:cookshayes@aol.com

● Newton Abbot (Torquay)

Branscombe House B&B, 48 Highweek Village, TQ12 1QQ
☎ 01626 356752 (Miles Opie) www.branscombe-house.co.uk Map 191/845721
BB **D** ✕ nearby D2 T1 ⚘(Newton Abbot) B D ⊗ 🛏☕!

● Newton Popplford (Sidmouth)
SOUTH WEST COAST PATH

Milestone, High ST., EX10 0DU ☎ 01395 568267 Map 192/081896
BB **C** ✕ nearby S2 D1 T/D1 B D ⊗ 🛏☕🚗 ★★★

● North Bovey
DARTMOOR
TWO MOORS WAY

Lower Hookner Barn, TQ13 8RS ☎ 01647 221282 (Jenny Pryce-Davies)
lowerhookner@hotmail.com Map 191/714825
BB **B** ✕ book first £11, 7:30pm onwards D1 T1 F1 Closed Xmas
Ⅴ B D ⊗ 🛏☕🚇!⚘

● Northam (Bideford)
SOUTH WEST COAST PATH

Riversford Hotel, Limers Lane, EX39 2RG
☎ 01237 474239 (Antony Jarrad) www.riversford.co.uk Map 180/452281
BB **D** ✕ £15, 6-9:30pm S4 D8 T2 F1 Ⅴ B D 🛏☕🚗!⚘ ★★

● Okehampton
DARTMOOR

Northlake, Stockley, EX20 1QH ☎ 01837 53100 (Pam Jeffrey)
www.northlakedevon.co.uk Map 191/610953
BB **B** ✕ book first £8 S1 D1 T1 Closed Jan Ⅴ B D ⊗ 🛏☕🚗!⚘

● Ottery St Mary

Fluxton Farm, EX11 1RJ ☎ 01404 812818 (Mrs E A Forth)
www.fluxtonfarm.co.uk Map 192/086934
BB **C** ✕ nearby S2 D2 T3 Closed Xmas
B D ⊗ 🛏⚘ ◆◆ Oct-May weekend stays only. Must be cat lovers!

● Paignton
SOUTH WEST COAST PATH

Culverden Hotel, 4 Colin Road, TQ3 2NR ☎ 01803 559786
www.culverdenhotel.co.uk Map 202/893614
BB **B** ✕ nearby S2 D2 T2 F2 ⚘(Paignton) Ⅴ B ⊗ 🛏☕⚘ ◆◆◆

Norbreck Guest House, 35 New Street, TQ3 3HL
☎ 01803 558033 (A & B Hopes) www.norbreck.com Map 202/885605
BB **B** ✕ book first £10, 6-7pm S2 T1 F4 ⚘(Paignton)
Ⅴ B D 🛏☕⚘ ◆◆◆

Harbour Lodge Guest House, 4 Cleveland Road, TQ4 6EN
☎ 01803 556932 www.harbourlodge.co.uk Map 202/893601
BB **B** ✕ nearby D3 T1 F1 ⚘(Paignton) Ⅴ B ⊗ 🛏☕ ◆◆◆

☆ **Roslyn Hotel**
Beach Road, TQ4 6AY ☎ 01803 665634 (Terry Chamberlain)
www.roslynhotel.org.uk Map 202/892608
BB **B** ✕ book first £10, 6-7pm S2 D4 T1 F1 ⚘(Paignton)
Ⅴ B D ⊗ 🛏☕!⚘

Attractive Victorian townhouse only 80 yards from coastal path.
5-mile coast walk to Brixham via wooded coves, stop-over coast path trekkers with east Dartmoor walks within easy reach.
Colour TV in all rooms.
Full English or vegetarian breakfast.

● Plymouth
SOUTH WEST COAST PATH

Old Pier Guest House, 20 Radford Road, West Hoe, PL1 3BY
☎ 01752 268468 (Steve Jones) www.oldpier.co.uk Map 201/472537
BB **B** ✕ nearby S1 D3 T3 ⚘(Plymouth) B D ⊗ 🛏☕Ⓜ ◆◆◆

Mount Batten Centre, 70 Lawrence Rd, Mount Batten, PL9 9SJ
☎ 01752 404567 www.mount-batten-centre.com Map 201/487532
BB **D** ✕ nearby T20 F3 Closed Xmas ⚘(Plymouth)
Ⅴ B D ⊗ 🛏☕Ⓜ Booking advisable Nov-Feb.

4 Garden Crescent, West Hoe, PL1 3DA ☎ 01752 250128 (Franca Burge)
francaburge@hotmail.com Map 201/471537
BB **C** ✕ nearby S2 D4 T2 F/T2 Closed Xmas ⚘(Plymouth) B D 🛏☕Ⓜ

The Rusty Anchor, 30 Grand Parade, West Hoe, PL1 3DJ
☎ 01752 663924 (Jan Taylor)
www.therustyanchor-plymouth.co.uk Map 201/472536
BB **C** ✕ nearby S2 D4 T1 F2 ⚘(Plymouth) Ⅴ B D ⊗ 🛏☕⚘

The Caledonia, 27 Athenaeum Street, The Hoe, PL1 2RQ ☎ 01752 229052
(David & Karen Marshall) www.thecaledonia.co.uk Map 201/474541
BB **C** ✕ nearby S1 D5 T4 F1 Closed Xmas ⚘(Plymouth)
Ⅴ B D ⊗ 🛏☕! ◆◆◆

● Seaton
SOUTH WEST COAST PATH

Beach End, 8 Trevelyan Road, EX12 2NL
☎ 01297 23388 (Hilary Bevis)   Map 192/251899
BB **D** ✗ nearby D2 T1 Ⓥ Ⓑ Ⓓ ☺ ♨ ! Ⓜ ◆◆◆◆Ⓢ

● Shirwell (Barnstaple)
The Spinney Guest House, EX31 4JR ☎ 01271 850282 (Mrs Janet Pelling)
www.thespinneyshirwell.co.uk Map 180/590370
BB **B/C** ✗ book first £16, 7pm S1 D2 T1 F1 Closed Xmas
Ⓥ Ⓑ Ⓓ ☺ ♨ ⅚ ◆◆◆◆Ⓢ

● Sidbury (Sidmouth)
Rose Cottage, Greenhead, EX10 0RH ☎ 01395 597357 (Roslyn Kendall)
www.rosecottagesidbury.co.uk Map 192,193/137916
BB **D** ✗ book first £12.50, 6:30pm D2 T1
Ⓥ Ⓑ Ⓓ ☺ 🐾♨ ◆◆◆◆Ⓢ

● Sidmouth
SOUTH WEST COAST PATH

Canterbury House, Salcombe Road, EX10 8PR ☎ 01395 513373 (Ms A Garton)
anny@agarton8.wanadoo.co.uk Map 192/127878
BB **B** ✗ book first £12, 6pm S1 D4 T2 F3 Closed Xmas
Ⓥ Ⓑ Ⓓ ☺ ♨ ⅚ ◆◆◆

Ryton Guest House, 52-54 Winslade Road, EX10 9EX ☎ 01395 513981
(Mrs G Bradnam) www.ryton-guest-house.co.uk Map 192/126885
BB **B/C** ✗ nearby S3 D1 T2 F4 Closed Nov-Jan
Ⓥ Ⓑ Ⓓ ☺ 🐾♨ 🚗 ! ⅚ ◆◆◆

● Slapton (Kingsbridge)
SOUTH WEST COAST PATH

Old Walls, TQ7 2QN ☎ 01548 580516 (V J Mercer)   Map 202/823449
BB **B** ✗ nearby S1 D2/F2 T1 Closed Xmas Ⓥ Ⓑ Ⓓ ☺ 🐾♨ 🚗 ! ⅚ Ⓜ

● South Brent (Torquay)
DARTMOOR

Winsford, Totnes Road, TQ10 9JN ☎ 01364 72236 (Anne Halliday)
winsford_99@yahoo.com Map 202/700599
BB **B** ✗ book first £12 D1 T1 Ⓥ Ⓑ Ⓓ ☺ 🐾♨ 🚗 ! ⅚

● Starcross (Exeter)
Stile Farm, EX6 8PD ☎ 01626 890268 (Karen Williams)
www.stile-farm.co.uk Map 192/973825
BB **C** ✗ nearby S1 D1 T1 Closed Dec-Feb ⋙(Starcross) Ⓥ Ⓑ ☺ ♨

● Teignmouth
SOUTH WEST COAST PATH

Brunswick House, 5 Brunswick Street, TQ14 8AE
☎ 01626 774102 (Margrethe & Pete Hockings)
margrethehockings@hotmail.com Map 192/941727
BB **B/C** ✗ nearby S1 D4 T/F3 F1 ⋙(Teignmouth) Ⓑ Ⓓ ☺ 🐾♨ ⅚

● Tiverton
Bridge Guest House, 23 Angel Hill, EX16 6PE ☎ 01884 252804
www.smoothhound.co.uk/hotels/bridgegh.html Map 181/953125
BB **C** ✗ book first £16, 6:30-7pm S6 D2 F2 Closed Xmas
Ⓥ Ⓑ Ⓓ ☺ 🐾♨ ◆◆◆

Angel Guest House, 13 St Peter Street, EX16 6NU ☎ 01884 253392
(Gary & Angela Mulligan) www.angelguesthouse.com Map 181/954126
BB **C** ✗ nearby S1 D3 T1 F2 Ⓑ Ⓓ ☺ 🐾♨

● Torquay
SOUTH WEST COAST PATH

☆ ☆ **Meadfoot Bay Hotel**
Meadfoot Sea Road, TQ1 2LQ ☎ 01803 294722 (Chris Waters)
www.meadfoot.com Map 202/926632
BB **D** ✗ book first £15, 7-7:30pm S3 D12 T5 ⋙(Torquay)
Ⓥ Ⓑ ☺ 🐾♨ ◆◆◆◆

This comfortable, quiet and friendly hotel is close to the harbour, beaches and
local amenities. We are in an ideal location for exploring the South West Coast
Path which is just 200 yards from the hotel as well as other local walks in
Torbay and the surrounding area.
All bedrooms are en-suite with colour television and beverage making facilities.
Towels and complimentary toiletries are provided.
Email: stay@meadfoot.com

Westbourne Hotel, 106 Avenue Road, TQ2 5LQ ☎ 01803 292927
(Marjorie Riley) www.westbournehoteltorquay.co.uk Map 202/904646
BB **D** ✗ book first £13.50, 6-7pm S1 D3 T2 F2 Closed Xmas ⋙(Torre)
Ⓥ Ⓑ Ⓓ ☺ 🐾♨ 🚗 ! ◆◆◆◆

● Welcombe (Bideford)
SOUTH WEST COAST PATH

Cranham House, EX39 6ET ☎ 01288 331351 (Jennifer Jones)
www.cranhamhouse.co.uk Map 190/224192
BB **D** ✗ book first £15-£18.50, 6-8pm D2 T1 Closed Xmas
Ⓥ Ⓑ Ⓓ ☺ 🐾🚗 !

● West Buckland (Barnstaple)
MACMILLAN WAY WEST

Huxtable Farm, EX32 0SR ☎ 01598 760254 (Jackie & Antony Payne)
www.huxtablefarm.co.uk Map 180/665308
BB **D** ✗ book first £22, 7:30pm D3 T1 F2 Closed Dec-Jan
Ⓥ Ⓑ Ⓓ ☺ 🐾♨ 🚗 ! ◆◆◆◆Ⓢ

● Westward Ho! (Bideford)
SOUTH WEST COAST PATH

Culloden House, Fosketh Hill, EX39 1UL ☎ 01237 479421 (Graham Gent)
www.culloden-house.co.uk Map 180/432289
BB **D** ✗ nearby D2 T1 F2 Ⓥ Ⓑ Ⓓ ☺ 🐾♨ ! ⅚

● Widecombe-in-the-Moor (Newton Abbot)
DARTMOOR
TWO MOORS WAY

The Old Rectory, TQ13 7TB ☎ 01364 621231
rachel.belgrave@care4free.net Map 191/717767
BB **C** ✗ nearby D2 T/F1 F1 Closed Nov-Feb Ⓑ Ⓓ ☺ 🐾♨ 🚗 ! ⅚

Lower Blackaton, TQ13 7UB ☎ 01364 621369 (Judy Lomax)
www.lowerblackaton.co.uk Map 191/694780
BB **B** ✗ book first £10, 7:30pm S1 T2 F2 Closed June-Aug
Ⓥ Ⓑ Ⓓ ☺ 🐾♨ ! ⅚ See SC also.

● Woolacombe
SOUTH WEST COAST PATH
Clyst House, Rockfield Road, EX34 7DH
☎ 01271 870220 (Ann Braund) Map 180/455441
BB **C** ✕ nearby SI DI TI FI Closed Nov-Feb Ⓓ ⊛ 🐾 🐾

● Yealmpton
SOUTH WEST COAST PATH
Kitley House Hotel, Kitley Estate, PL8 2NW ☎ 01752 881555
www.kitleyhousehotel.com Map 202/559514
BB **D** ✕ £30, 7-9pm SI D9 T2 F7 Ⓥ Ⓑ Ⓓ 🐾 ⚓ ! 🐾 Ⓜ ★★★

DORSET

● Abbotsbury (Weymouth)
SOUTH WEST COAST PATH & MACMILLAN WAY
Swan Lodge, DT3 4JL ☎ 01305 871249 Map 194/578852
BB **D** ✕ £8, 6-9:30pm D3 T2 Ⓥ Ⓑ Ⓓ 🐾 ⚓ 🐾 ◆◆◆

● Bournemouth
SOUTH WEST COAST PATH
St Michaels Guest House, 42 St Michaels Road, Westcliff, BH2 5DY
☎ 01202 557386 (Mrs E Davies) www.stmichaelsfriendlyguesthouse.co.uk
Map 195/082910 BB **B** ✕ £6, 6pm SI D2 T2 FI Closed Xmas
🚂(Bournemouth) Ⓥ Ⓓ 🐾 ⚓ 🐾

Devonshire Guest House, 40 St Michaels Road, BH2 5DY
☎ 01202 291610 (Mrs K Ferns) Map 195/082910
BB **B** ✕ nearby SI D3 T2 FI 🚂(Bournemouth) Ⓥ Ⓓ 🐾 ⚓ 🐾

● Bridport
SOUTH WEST COAST PATH & MONARCH'S WAY

☆ **Britmead House**
154 West Bay Road, DT6 4EG ☎ 01308 422941
www.britmeadhouse.co.uk Map 193/465912
BB **D** ✕ nearby D4 T2 F2 Closed Xmas
Ⓑ Ⓓ ⊛ 🐾 ⚓ ! 🐾 ◆◆◆◆

An elegant Edwardian house, situated within walking distance of West Bay harbour and the SW Coast Path, part of the World Heritage Site. We offer comfortable en-suite accommodation with many thoughtful extras. Parking, non-smoking. Dogs welcome by arrangement.

Fleet Cottage, 152 West Bay Road, DT6 4AZ ☎ 01308 458698
(Janice Warburton) janice_warburton@supanet.com Map 193/465915
BB **C** ✕ book first £7, 6:30pm D/S2 TI FI Closed Xmas
Ⓥ Ⓑ Ⓓ 🐾 ⚓ 🐾

Green Lane House, Dorchester Road, DT6 4LH ☎ 01308 422619
(Christine Prideaux) greenlanehouse@aol.com Map 193/483932
BB **B** ✕ book first £12 SI DI TI FI Closed Xmas
Ⓥ Ⓑ Ⓓ ⊛ 🐾 ⚓ 🐾

🚻 Eypeleaze Bed & Breakfast, 117 West Bay Road, DT6 4EQ
☎ 01308 423363 (Ann Walker) www.eypeleaze.co.uk Map 193/467912
BB **A/B/C** ✕ nearby DI TI Ⓑ Ⓓ ⊛ 🐾 ! ◆◆◆◆

🚻 At Home, 134 West Bay Road, DT6 4AZ ☎ 01308 458880 (Linda Bane)
www.dorset-coast.co.uk Map 193/465914
BB **D** ✕ nearby D2 TI Ⓥ Ⓑ Ⓓ ⊛ 🐾 ⚓ ! ◆◆◆◆Ⓦ

☆🚻 **Eypes Mouth Country Hotel**
Eype, DT6 6AL ☎ 01308 423300 (Kevin & Glenis French)
www.eypesmouthhotel.co.uk Map 193/448914
BB **D** ✕ book first £23, 7-9pm S2 DI2 T3 FI
Ⓥ Ⓑ Ⓓ 🐾 ⚓ ! 🐾 ★★

The hotel nestles between the clifftops and downland that form the Heritage Coastline. Close to SW Coast Path, the hotel enjoys stunning seaviews, peace and tranquility, superb food using the best of local produce and offers a high standard of hospitality.

● Cerne Abbas (Dorchester)
WESSEX RIDGEWAY
🚻 Badger Hill, 11 Springfield, DT2 7JZ
☎ 01300 341698 (Patricia Hammett) Map 194/663014
BB **C** ✕ nearby DI TI Ⓑ Ⓓ ⊛ 🐾 ⚓ 🐾 Ⓜ ◆◆◆◆

● Charmouth (Bridport)
SOUTH WEST COAST PATH
🚻 Cliffend B&B, Higher Sea Lane, DT6 6BD ☎ 01297 561047
www.cliffend.org.uk Map 116/364931
BB **C** ✕ nearby D2 Closed Dec-Feb Ⓑ Ⓓ ⊛ 🐾 ⚓ ! ◆◆◆◆

● Chideock (Bridport)
SOUTH WEST COAST PATH & MONARCH'S WAY
🚻 Rose Cottage, Main Street, DT6 6JQ ☎ 01297 489994 (Sue & Mick Kelson)
www.rosecottage-chideock.co.uk Map 193/423927
BB **D** ✕ nearby DI T/DI Closed Xmas
Ⓑ Ⓓ ⊛ 🐾 🐾 ◆◆◆◆ Closed Sun-Tues.

☆ **Bay Tree House**
Duck Street, DT6 6JW ☎ 01297 489336
www.baytreechideock.co.uk Map 193/419929
BB **D** ✕ nearby DI TI
Ⓥ Ⓑ Ⓓ ⊛ 🐾 🐾 ★★★★Ⓢ

Bay Tree House is just a ten-minute walk from the Coast Path at Seatown. Both rooms have en-suite facilities and are extremely comfortable. There are three pubs and a hotel within walking distance for evening meals. Stunning views and walking.

● Dorchester

☆🚻 **Churchview Guest House**
Winterbourne Abbas, DT2 9LS ☎ 01305 889296
www.churchview.co.uk Map 194/618905
BB **D** ✕ £15, 7pm SI D4 T3 FI Closed Xmas
Ⓥ Ⓑ Ⓓ ⊛ 🐾 ⚓ ! 🐾 ◆◆◆◆Ⓢ See Groups also.

Our beautiful 17th-century guest house set in picturesque countryside makes an ideal rambling base. Period dining room, two lounges, licensed bar. Delicious evening meals. Non-smoking. Groups are our speciality. Call Michael & Jane Deller. Email: stay@churchview.co.uk

◼◼ Cowden House, Fry's Lane, Godmanstone, DT2 7AG
☎ 01300 341377 (Tim Mills) www.cowdenhouse.co.uk Map 194/666970
BB **C** ✕ book first £16.50, 7pm D1 T2 F1 Closed Xmas
Ⓥ Ⓑ Ⓓ ⊗ 🍴☕ ⊕ 🚗 !

● Evershot
MACMILLAN WAY, MONARCH'S WAY & WESSEX RIDGEWAY

☆ ◼◼ **Rectory House**
2 Fore Street, DT2 0JW ☎ 01935 83976 (Jan & Barry Delves)
www.rectoryhouse.com Map 194/576045
BB **D** ✕ nearby D2 T2
Ⓥ Ⓑ Ⓓ ⊗ 🍴☕ ⊕ 🚗 ! 🛏 ★★★★

Attactive former rectory set in the heart of Hardy country. Spacious bedrooms, all en-suite with colour TVs and tea/coffee making facilities. Large guest lounge with real log fire. Excellent walking. A warm welcome awaits.

● Langton Matravers (Swanage)
SOUTH WEST COAST PATH

◼◼ Kamloops, Haycrafts Lane, BH19 3EE ☎ 01929 439193 (Mr D V Joseph)
info@kamloops.co.uk Map 195/983792
BB **D** ✕ nearby D/T3 Closed Xmas Ⓑ Ⓓ ⊗ 🍴☕ ⊕ 🚗 !

● Ludwell (Shaftesbury)
WESSEX RIDGEWAY

◼◼ Cedar Lodge, 5 Dewey's Place, SP7 9LW ☎ 01747 829240
(Lorraine Dewey) www.cedarlodge.org.uk Map 183/902227
BB **D** ✕ nearby D1 T2 Closed Nov-Feb
Ⓑ Ⓓ ⊗ 🍴☕ ⊕ ! ◆◆◆Ⓦ

● Lyme Regis
SOUTH WEST COAST PATH, WESSEX RIDGEWAY & MONARCH'S WAY

Lucerne, View Road, DT7 3AA ☎ 01297 443752 (Owen Keith Lovell)
http://lymeregis.com/lucerne Map 193/338923
BB **C** S1 D3 T1 Closed Xmas Ⓑ Ⓓ ⊗ ☕ ⊕ ! ★★★★

The Orchard Country Hotel, Rousdon, DT7 3XW ☎ 01297 442972
(Mr P Wightman) www.orchardcountryhotel.com Map 193/296916
BB **D** ✕ book first £17, 7:15pm S1 D6 T4 Closed Dec-Feb
Ⓥ Ⓑ Ⓓ ⊗ 🍴☕ 🚗 ◆◆◆◆

Charnwood Guest House, 21 Woodmead Road, DT7 3AD ☎ 01297 445281
(Wayne & Ann Bradbury) www.lymeregisaccommodation.com Map 193/339924
BB **C** ✕ nearby S1 D4 T2 Closed Xmas Ⓑ Ⓓ ⊗ ☕ Ⓜ ◆◆◆◆

◼◼ Thatch, Uplyme Rd, DT7 3LP ☎ 01297 442212 (Frank & Wendy Rogers)
thatchbb@aol.com Map 193/335924
BB **C** ✕ nearby S1 D1 T1 Ⓑ Ⓓ ⊗ 🍴☕ ⊕ ! 🛏 ◆◆◆◆

● Norden (Wareham)
Three Barrows Farm, BH20 5DU ☎ 01929 480797 (Valerie Bull)
Map 195/938841
BB **C** ✕ nearby D1 T1 F1 Closed Xmas Ⓑ Ⓓ ⊗ 🍴☕ ⊕ 🚗 ! 🛏

● Poole
SOUTH WEST COAST PATH

The Laurels, 60 Britannia Road, BH14 8BB ☎ 01202 265861 (Mrs North)
www.thelaurelsbandb.freeservers.com Map 195/033913
BB **C** ✕ nearby S1 D1 T1 F1 🚌(Parkstone) Ⓑ Ⓓ ⊗ ☕

● Portesham (Weymouth)
SOUTH WEST COAST PATH

◼◼ Lavender Cottage, 9 Malthouse Meadow, DT3 4NS ☎ 01305 871924
(Mrs Joan Haine) joanhaine@sagainternet.co.uk Map 194/599856
BB **B** ✕ nearby D1 T1 Closed Dec-Jan Ⓓ ⊗ ☕ 🚗 !

◼◼ Bridge House, 13 Frys Close, DT3 4LQ ☎ 01305 871685 (Thea Alexander)
www.bridgehousebandb.co.uk Map 194/602858
BB **B/C** ✕ nearby D2 Closed Xmas Ⓑ Ⓓ ⊗ ☕ 🚗 ! ★★★★

● Puddletown (Dorchester)
◼◼ Zoar House, DT2 8SR ☎ 01305 848498 (Mrs J Stephens)
Map 194/762942 BB **B** ✕ nearby S1 D1 T1 F1 Ⓓ ⊗ 🍴☕ 🛏

● Seaborough (Beaminster)
MONARCH'S WAY & WESSEX RIDGEWAY

Seaborough Manor Farm, DT8 3QY ☎ 01308 868272 (Mrs V Barber)
www.seaboroughmanor.co.uk Map 193/431060
BB **D** ✕ book first £12, 6-8pm S1 D2 Closed Xmas Ⓥ Ⓑ Ⓓ 🍴☕ 🚗 !

● Sherborne
MACMILLAN WAY

◼◼ Honeycombe View, Lower Clatcombe, DT9 4RH ☎ 01935 814644
(Mrs D Bower) honeycombower@talktalk.net Map 183/637179
BB **B** ✕ nearby T1 Closed Xmas 🚌(Sherborne) Ⓑ Ⓓ ⊗ ☕

● Shillingstone (Blandford Forum)
WESSEX RIDGEWAY

Pennhills Farm, Sandy Lane, Off Lanchards Lane, DT11 0TF
☎ 01258 860491 (Rosemary Watts) Map 194/819102
BB **B** ✕ nearby D/F1 T/S1 Closed Xmas Ⓑ Ⓓ ⊗ 🍴☕ ⊕ 🚗 ! 🛏 ◆◆◆

● Sturminster Newton
◼◼ Newton House, DT10 2DQ ☎ 01258 472783 (Margie Fraser)
www.newtonhousedorset.co.uk Map 194/783135
BB **C/D** ✕ nearby S2 D2 T1 Closed Xmas Ⓑ Ⓓ ⊗ 🍴!

● Swanage
SOUTH WEST COAST PATH

Hermitage Guesthouse, 1 Manor Road, BH19 2BH ☎ 01929 423014
(Susan Pickering) www.hermitage-online.co.uk Map 195/031785
BB **B** ✕ nearby D2 T1 F4 Closed Dec-Feb Ⓓ ⊗ ☕ 🛏 Ⓜ

☆ ◼◼ **The Limes Hotel**
48 Park Road, BH19 2AE ☎ 01929 422664
www.limeshotel.net Map 195/033783
BB **D** ✕ nearby S3 D2 T4 F3
Ⓑ Ⓓ ⊗ 🍴☕ ⊕ 🚗 ! 🛏 ◆◆◆◆

Swanage – just off Coast Path. Close to town and the beach. Wonderful for walking. Car park, bar, laundry. Open all year for B&B. Families, groups and pets are welcome. Email: info@limeshotel.net

Beachway Private Hotel, 19 Ulwell Road, BH19 1LF ☎ 01929 423077
(Helen Holt) beachway.19ulwellroad@fsmail.net Map 195/030799
BB **B/C** ✕ nearby S2 D2 T2 F2 Closed Xmas Ⓥ Ⓑ Ⓓ 🍴☕ 🛏

The Oxford, 3-5 Park Road, BH19 2AA ☎ 01929 422247 (Robin Creed)
www.theoxfordswanage.co.uk Map 195/032784
BB **C** ✕ nearby S2 D6 T1 F3 Ⓑ ⊗ 🍴☕ ◆◆◆

Sandhaven, 5 Ulwell Rd, BH19 1LE ☎ 01929 422322 (Janet Foran)
www.sandhaven-guest-house.co.uk Map 195/030798
BB **C** ✕ nearby S1 D4 T2 F2 Closed Xmas
Ⓥ Ⓑ Ⓓ ⊛ 🖐🛁🐾 ★★★ See SC also.

Perfick Piece, Springfield Road, BH19 1HD ☎ 01929 423178 (Elaine Hine)
www.perfick-piece.co.uk Map 195/028788
BB **B** ✕ book first £8.50, 6pm S1 D1 T1 F1
Ⓥ Ⓑ Ⓓ 🖐🛁 ◆◆◆ Evening meals in winter only.

Sandringham Hotel, 20 Durlston Rd, BH19 2HX ☎ 01929 423076 (Mr & Mrs T
Silk) www.smoothhound.co.uk/hotels/sandringham.html Map 195/033782
BB **D** ✕ book first £17 (groups only), 6:30-7pm S2 D3 T2 F4 Closed Xmas
Ⓥ Ⓑ 🛁🐾 ◆◆◆ See Groups also.

☞◄ Grace Gardens Guest House, 28 Victoria Avenue, BH19 1AP
☎ 01929 422502 (Lorraine White) www.gracegardens.co.uk Map 195/025791
BB **C** ✕ book first £13.50, 6:30-7pm S1 D2 F2
Ⓥ Ⓑ Ⓓ ⊛ 🖐🛁🚗🐾 ◆◆◆◆Ⓢ

● Sydling St Nicholas (Dorchester)
WESSEX RIDGEWAY

City Cottage, DT2 9NX ☎ 01300 341300 (Mrs J Wareham) Map 194/632994
BB **B** ✕ nearby S1 D1 Closed Xmas Ⓓ 🖐

Magiston Farm, DT2 9NR ☎ 01300 320295 (Mrs Barraclough)
Map 194/637967 BB **B** ✕ book first £12, 7pm S1/2 D1 T3 Closed Xmas
Ⓥ Ⓑ Ⓓ 🛁🐾 ◆◆◆

● Wareham
☞◄ Hyde Cottage, Furzebrooke Rd, Stoborough, BH20 5AX
☎ 01929 553344 (D & J Bryer) hydecottbb@yahoo.co.uk Map 195/927853
BB **C** ✕ book first £10, 6:30-7:30pm S1 D1 T1 F2 Closed Xmas
➜(Wareham) Ⓥ Ⓑ Ⓓ ⊛ 🖐🛁🚗! ◆◆◆◆

☞◄ Birchfield, 2 Drax Ave, BH20 4DJ ☎ 01929 552462 (Diana Hutton)
www.birchfieldbedandbreakfast.co.uk Map 195/922885
BB **B** ✕ nearby S1 D1 T1 Closed Dec-Feb ➜(Wareham)
Ⓑ Ⓓ ⊛ 🖐🛁🚗! ◆◆◆

● Weymouth
SOUTH WEST COAST PATH

☞◄ Cunard Guest House, 45/46 Lennox Street, DT4 7HB ☎ 01305 771546
(Mr & Mrs Harris) www.cunardguesthouse.co.uk Map 194/681798
BB **B/C** S1 D5 T2 F1 ➜(Weymouth) Ⓑ Ⓓ ⊛ 🖐🛁🚗!🛁Ⓜ ◆◆◆

☞◄ Harbour Lights Guesthouse, 20 Buxton Rd, DT4 9PJ ☎ 01305 783273
(Diane Quick) http://harbourlights-weymouth.co.uk Map 194/672779
BB **D** ✕ nearby S2 D5 T1 F2 Closed Nov-Feb ➜(Weymouth)
Ⓥ Ⓑ Ⓓ ⊛ 🛁 ◆◆◆◆

☞◄ Channel View Guest House, 10 Brunswick Terrace, DT4 7RW
☎ 01305 782527 (Martin & Alison Weller) www.channelviewweymouth.co.uk
Map 194/682799 BB **C** ✕ nearby S2 D3 T1 F1 Closed Xmas ➜(Weymouth)
Ⓑ Ⓓ ⊛ 🛁! ◆◆◆◆

☞◄ Greenwood Guest House, 1 Holland Rd, DT4 0AL ☎ 01305 775626
(Sharon Arnold) www.greenwoodguesthouse.co.uk Map 194/674793
BB **C** ✕ nearby D3 T2 F1 ➜(Weymouth) Ⓑ Ⓓ ⊛ 🖐🛁🚗!🛁

☞◄ Sunningdale House, 52 Preston Road, DT3 6QD ☎ 01305 832179
(Mrs G L Flux) flux@sunningdale52.freeserve.co.uk Map 194/696822
BB **C** ✕ nearby S1 D3 Closed Xmas ➜(Weymouth) Ⓑ Ⓓ ⊛ 🛁

● Winterborne Kingston
☞◄ West Acres, West Street, DT11 9AT ☎ 01929 471293 (Mr & Mrs Jenkins)
www.westacres-bedandbreakfast.co.uk Map 194/854976 BB **C** ✕ book first
£10, 7:30pm D1 T1 Closed Xmas Ⓥ Ⓓ ⊛ 🖐🛁🚗!🛁

GLOUCESTERSHIRE

● Blockley (Moreton-in-Marsh)
MONARCH'S WAY & HEART OF ENGLAND WAY

☆ ☞◄ **Lower Brook House**
Lower Street, GL56 9DS ☎ 01386 700286 (Julian Ebbitt)
www.lowerbrookhouse.com Map 151/165348
BB **D** ✕ £25, 7:30-9pm D4 T2 ➜(Moreton-in-Marsh)
Ⓥ Ⓑ Ⓓ ⊛ 🖐🛁! ◆◆◆◆◆

17th-century Lower Brook House
is at the heart of the village of
Blockley. We offer home-cooked
dinners and breakfasts, all the
modern comforts you would
expect and a location ideal for
exploring the Cotswolds.

● Brookthorpe (Gloucester)
COTSWOLD WAY

☆ ☞◄ **Brookthorpe Lodge**
Stroud Road, GL4 0UQ ☎ 01452 812645 (Robert & Diana Bailey)
www.brookthorpelodge.demon.co.uk Map 162/835128
BB **D** ✕ book first £14.95, until 7pm S3 D2 T3 F2 Closed Xmas
Ⓥ Ⓑ Ⓓ ⊛ 🖐🛁🚗!🛁 ◆◆◆

Elegant Georgian house set in lovely
countryside at the foot of the Cotswold
escarpment between Gloucester & Stroud.
Family run, traditional service and
delicious breakfasts. Excellent walking
country & ideal base for Cotswolds,
Cheltenham and Bath. Good access to M5.

● Cam (Dursley)
COTSWOLD WAY

☆ **Foresters**
31 Chapel Street, GL11 5NX ☎ 01453 549996 (Victoria Jennings)
www.foresters-inn.co.uk Map 162/750002
BB **C** ✕ book first £10-14, 6-8:30pm D2 T2 F1 ➜(Cam & Dursley)
Ⓥ Ⓑ Ⓓ ⊛ 🖐🛁🚗🛁 ◆◆◆◆

18th-century cosy
former village inn
with pretty walled
garden. Spacious
en-suite beamed
bedrooms and visitor
lounge with open fire
and central heating.
Drying facilities
available.

Excellent walking on our doorstep and a wealth of attractions/villages and cities
to visit: Westonbirt, Slimbridge, Bath, Cotswold Way, Berkeley Castle,
Gloucester, Bristol, Cheltenham, Tetbury. Village pub, evening meals – 2 mins.
Close to Jct 13/14 M5. Dogs welcome by arrangement.
10% reduction for 7 nights stay. Discounts for 2 nights or more.
Colour TVs/tea/coffee facilities. Four-poster bed/2 twins.

● Charlton Kings (Cheltenham)
COTSWOLD WAY

☆ ▄◄ **Charlton Kings Hotel**
London Road, GL52 6UU ☎ 01242 231061
www.charltonkingshotel.co.uk Map 163/977201
BB **D** ✕ £18-£23, 7-9pm S2 D5 T5 F1
Ⓥ Ⓑ Ⓓ ⊗ 🛁 ⛽ 🎣 ★★★

Ideally situated on edge of town, ½ mile from Cotswold Way. All rooms refurbished with bath/shower, most have views of the Cotswold Hills. Set in an acre of gardens, ample parking. Restaurant open every night. Conde Nast Johansens Recommended.
enquiries@charltonkingshotel.co.uk.

22 Ledmore Road, GL53 8RA ☎ 01242 526957 (Geraldine White)
www.cotswoldstudio.co.uk Map 163/967207
BB **B** ✕ nearby S1 D1 T1 Closed Xmas ⋙(Cheltenham)
Ⓑ Ⓓ ⊗ 🛁 ⛽ ! Ⓜ

California Farm, Capel Lane, GL54 4HQ
☎ 01242 244746 Map 163/979188
BB **C** ✕ book first £12-£15, 7pm D2 T2 Closed Xmas
Ⓥ Ⓑ Ⓓ ⊗ 🛁 ⛽

● Chedworth (Cheltenham)
MONARCH'S WAY & MACMILLAN WAY

▄◄ The Vicarage, GL54 4AA ☎ 01285 720392 (George & Pattie Mitchell)
canongeorgemitchell@btinternet.com Map 163/052118
BB **B** ✕ nearby S1 T1 Closed Xmas Ⓑ Ⓓ ⊗ 🛁 ⛽ ◆◆◆

● Chipping Campden
COTSWOLD WAY & HEART OF ENGLAND WAY

Weston Park Farm, Dovers Hill, GL55 6UW ☎ 01386 840835
(Mrs J Whitehouse) www.cotswoldcottages.uk.com Map 151/130390
BB **D** ✕ nearby D1 F1 Closed Xmas
Ⓑ Ⓓ 🛁 ⛽ ! ◆◆◆ See SC also.

▄◄ Lygon Arms Hotel, High Street, GL55 6HB ☎ 01386 840318
www.lygonarms.co.uk Map 151/153394
BB **D** ✕ book first £6-£20, 6-10pm S2 D/T5 T2 F2 Closed Xmas
Ⓥ Ⓑ Ⓓ 🛁 ⛽ ! 🎣 ◆◆◆◆

Green Cottage Bed & Breakfast, Park Road, GL55 6EB ☎ 01386 841428
(Vanessa Ryle) www.greencottagebandb.co.uk Map 151/146389
BB **C** ✕ nearby S1 D1 Ⓥ Ⓓ ⊗ 🛁

● Chipping Sodbury
MONARCH'S WAY & COTSWOLD WAY

The Moda Hotel, 1 High St, BS37 6BA ☎ 01454 312135 (Jo Macarthur)
www.modahotel.com Map 172/726822
BB **D** ✕ nearby S4 D4 T1 F1 ⋙(Yate)
Ⓑ Ⓓ ⊗ 🛁 ⛽ ◆◆◆◆

● Cirencester
MONARCH'S WAY

Royal Agricultural College, GL7 6JS
☎ 01285 652531 (Conference Department) www.rac.ac.uk Map 163/004011
BB **D** ✕ book first £19, 7pm S12 T7 Closed Xmas
Ⓥ Ⓑ Ⓓ 🛁 ⛽ ★★★

● Clearwell (Coleford)
WYE VALLEY WALK

☆ ▄◄ **Tudor Farmhouse Hotel**
High Street, GL16 8JS ☎ 01594 833046
www.tudorfarmhousehotel.co.uk Map 162/573080
BB **D** ✕ £25, 7-9pm S4 D14 T2 F2 Closed Xmas
Ⓥ Ⓑ Ⓓ 🛁 ⛽ ! 🎣 ★★★

A cosy 13th-century stone built hotel with 2 AA Rosettes restaurant in the historic & pretty village of Clearwell in the Forest of Dean is the ideal setting for a relaxed or active holiday. Near the Wye Valley Walk & Offa's Dyke with walking also available from the hotel.
All rooms en-suite with some having jacuzzi baths and four-poster beds. Drying room & cycle storage available. Pets welcome.

● Cold Ashton (Bristol)
COTSWOLD WAY

Toghill House Farm, BS30 5RT ☎ 01225 891261 (D Bishop)
www.toghillhousefarm.co.uk Map 172/731724
BB **D** ✕ nearby D/S5 T/S3 F/S3 Ⓑ Ⓓ ⊗ 🛁 ⛽ 🎣 ◆◆◆◆

● Cowley (Cheltenham)
COTSWOLD WAY

▄◄ Greenhatch Farm, GL53 9NJ ☎ 01242 870237
lindsaybaker@waitrose.com Map 163/962147
BB **D** ✕ book first £15, 7pm D1 Closed Xmas Ⓥ Ⓑ Ⓓ ⊗ 🛁 ⛽ !

● English Bicknor (Coleford)
WYE VALLEY WALKX

▄◄ Dryslade Farm, GL16 7PA ☎ 01594 860259 (Daphne Gwilliam)
www.drysladefarm.co.uk Map 162/579149
BB **C/D** ✕ nearby D1 T1 F1 Closed Xmas
Ⓑ Ⓓ ⊗ 🛁 ⛽ ! ◆◆◆◆

● Fairford
THAMES PATH

▄◄ Kempsford Manor, GL7 4EQ ☎ 01285 810131
www.kempsfordmanor.co.uk Map 163/158969
BB **D** ✕ book first £17.50, 7:30-8:30pm S2 D2 F1
Ⓥ Ⓑ Ⓓ ⊗ 🛁 ⛽ 🎣 ◆◆◆

● Guiting Power
Guiting Guest House, GL54 5TZ ☎ 01451 850470 (Barbara Millar)
www.guitingguesthouse.com Map 163/099245
BB **D** ✕ book first £28, 7pm S1 D6 T1 F1
Ⓥ Ⓑ ⊗ 🛁 ⛽ ! 🎣 ◆◆◆◆◆Ⓢ

● Hasfield (Gloucester)
SEVERN WAY

▄◄ Rural Cottage B&B, Rust's Meadow, Hasfield Road, GL19 4LL
☎ 01452 700814 (Liz Dawson) Map 162/809279
BB **B** ✕ book first £7.50 D1 T1 Ⓥ Ⓑ Ⓓ ⊗ 🛁 ⛽ ! 🎣

● King's Stanley (Stonehouse)
COTSWOLD WAY

Old Chapel House, Broad Street, GL10 3PN ☎ 01453 826289 (Jean Hanna)
www.geocities.com/bandbinuk Map 162/813033
BB **B/C** ✗ book first £6 upwards, 6:30-7:30pm S2 D1 T1 F1 Closed Xmas
ᗡᗡ(Stonehouse) ⓥ Ⓑ Ⓓ 🐕🛏☺!

▦◀ Valley Views, 12 Orchard Close, Middleyard, GL10 3QA
☎ 01453 827458 (Pam White) www.valley-views.com Map 162/819032
BB **C** ✗ book first £5+, 7pm D2 T1 Closed Xmas ᗡᗡ(Stonehouse)
ⓥ Ⓑ Ⓓ 🐕🛏☺🚗! ★★★★ⓦ

● Lechlade
THAMES PATH

Cambrai Lodge, Oak Street, GL7 3AY ☎ 01367 253173 (John Titchener)
www.cambrailodgeguesthouse.co.uk Map 163/214998
BB **C** ✗ nearby S2 D3 T2 Ⓑ Ⓓ☺ 🐕🛏🌸 ◆◆◆◆Ⓢ

● Newnham
SEVERN WAY

☆ ▦◀ **Swan House**
The High Street, GL14 1BY ☎ 01594 516504
www.swanhousenewnham.co.uk Map 162/701117
BB **D** ✗ book first £14, 7:30pm S2 D3 T2 F1 Closed Dec
ⓥ Ⓑ Ⓓ☺ 🐕🛏🚗!🌸 ◆◆◆◆

Swan House provides a haven for walkers within the attractive riverside village of Newnham. Delicious breakfasts served, 6 en-suite bedrooms, guest lounge, relaxing sit-out garden and easy parking. Evening meals by arrangement. Drying Room. Packed Lunches. Pets welcome. On bus routes.

● Nibley (Blakeney)
SEVERN WAY

☆ ▦◀ **Old Nibley Farmhouse B&B**
Nibley Hill, GL15 4DB ☎ 01594 516770 (Marian Buckmaster)
www.oldnibleyfarmhouse.co.uk Map 162/667066
BB **D** ✗ book first £16, 7:30-9pm S1 D4 T2
ⓥ Ⓑ Ⓓ☺ 🐕🛏🚗!🌸 ◆◆◆◆

300-year-old former farmhouse ideally situated for exploring the Forest of Dean and surrounding areas, including Symonds Yat and the Wye Valley Walk. Extremely comfortable bedrooms. Facilities include hot/cold beverages, dressing gowns, toiletries and other touches of luxury.

● North Nibley (Dursley)
COTSWOLD WAY

☆ **Nibley House**
GL11 6DL ☎ 01453 543108 (Diana A Eley)
www.nibleyhouse.co.uk Map 162/737958
BB **C** ✗ nearby D2 T2 F1 Closed Xmas
ⓥ Ⓑ Ⓓ☺ 🐕🛏🚗!🌸

Relax... Splendid views.
Relax... 2½ acres of garden.
Relax... 400 years of history.
Relax... Hospitality.
Relax... Where to stay on the Cotswold Way?
Relax... You've found it.

Burrows Court, Nibley Green, GL11 6AZ ☎ 01453 546230 (Peter Rackley)
www.burrowscourt.co.uk Map 162/732967
BB **D** D3 T2 F1 Closed Dec-Jan ⓥ Ⓑ Ⓓ☺ 🐕🛏🚗🌸 ◆◆◆

● Painswick (Stroud)
COTSWOLD WAY

▦◀ Skyrack, The Highlands, GL6 6SL ☎ 01452 812029 (Wendy Hodgson)
wendyskyrack@hotmail.com Map 162/868105
BB **C** ✗ nearby S2 D/T/F1 F2 Closed Xmas
Ⓑ Ⓓ☺ 🐕🛏🚗!🌸 ◆◆◆

Orchard House, 4 Court Orchard, GL6 6UU ☎ 01452 813150 (Barbara Harley)
www.painswick.co.uk Map 162/866095
BB **B/C/D** ✗ nearby D1 T1 Closed Xmas Ⓑ☺ 🐕🛏🚗!Ⓜ

The Falcon Inn, New Street, GL6 6UN ☎ 01452 814222 (Fiona Layfield)
www.falconinn.com Map 162/866097
BB **D** ✗ book first £9, 7-9:30pm D4 T4 F4 ⓥ Ⓑ Ⓓ🐕🛏🚗!🌸 ★★

Cardynham House, The Cross, GL6 6TX ☎ 01452 814006 (John Paterson)
www.cardynham.co.uk Map 162/868098
BB **D** ✗ book first £24.50, 7pm onwards D6 F3 ⓥ Ⓑ☺ ◆◆◆◆

▦◀ Wren's Nest, 3 Painswick Heights, Yokehouse Lane, GL6 7QS
☎ 01452 812347 (Patricia Moroney)
bsimplybetter@tiscali.co.uk Map 162/873086
BB **C** ✗ book first £15, 7-9pm D1 T1 ⓥ Ⓑ Ⓓ☺ 🐕🛏🚗

● Sandhurst (Gloucester)
SEVERN WAY

☆ ▦◀ **Moat Farm**
Base Lane, GL2 9NU ☎ 01452 739408 (Julie Royle)
Map 162/830227
BB **B** ✗ nearby F1 ᗡᗡ(Gloucester)
Ⓑ Ⓓ☺ 🐕🛏🚗!🌸

Moat Farm is a working family farm, medieval/Victorian house set in half-an-acre of gardens and 138 acres of farmland with many footpaths. Access to the River Severn. Gloucester city 2 miles away. Quiet location, friendly atmosphere, pets welcome.

● Slimbridge
SEVERN WAY

May Cottage, Shepherd's Patch, GL2 7BP ☎ 01453 890820
(Peter & Sue Gibson) www.smoothhound.co.uk/hotels/maycottage1
Map 162/721044 BB **C** ✗ nearby T1 Closed Xmas Ⓑ Ⓓ☺ 🐕🛏

● Southam (Cheltenham)
COTSWOLD WAY

Pigeon House Cottage, next Tithe Barn, Southam Lane, GL52 3NY
☎ 01242 584255 (BJ Holden)
www.pigeonhousecottage.co.uk Map 163/973255
BB **D** ✗ nearby D1 T2 Closed Xmas Ⓑ Ⓓ☺ 🐕🛏🚗!

● Stanton (Broadway)
COTSWOLD WAY

Shenberrow Hill, WR12 7NE ☎ 01386 584468 (Angela Neilan)
michael.neilan1@btopenworld.com Map 150/071342
BB **D** ✗ nearby D2 T2 F2 Closed Xmas
Ⓑ Ⓓ☺ 🐕🛏🚗!🌸 ◆◆◆◆

● Stow-on-the-Wold (Cheltenham)
HEART OF ENGLAND WAY, MONARCH'S WAY & MACMILLAN WAY

The Limes, Evesham Road, GL54 1EJ ☎ 01451 830034
(Helen & Graham Keyte)   thelimes@zoom.co.uk Map 163/181264
BB **B** ✗ nearby D3 T1 F1 Closed Xmas Ⓑ Ⓓ ♨ ! 🐾

Corsham Field Farm House, Bledington Road, GL54 1JH ☎ 01451 831750
(Robert Smith) www.corshamfield.co.uk Map 163/217250
BB **B/C** ✗ nearby D2 T2 F3 Closed Xmas Ⓑ Ⓓ ⊛ ♨ ◆◆◆

● Stroud
COTSWOLD WAY

Pretoria Villa, Wells Road, Eastcombe, GL6 7EE ☎ 01452 770435
(Glynis Solomon) www.bedandbreakfast-cotswold.co.uk Map 163/891044 BB
C ✗ book first £20, 7-8:30pm S1 D1 T1 Closed Xmas
Ⓥ Ⓑ Ⓓ ⊛ 🐾 ♨ ! ◆◆◆◆Ⓢ

Braemar, Selsley West, GL5 5LG ☎ 01453 826102 (Mrs D Wear)
www.cotswoldsbraemarbb.co.uk Map 162/828035
BB **B** S1 D2 T1 F2 Closed Xmas ᐱᐱᐱ(Stroud) Ⓑ Ⓓ ⊛ 🐾 ♨ 🚗 !

Hillenvale Guest House, The Plain, Whiteshill, GL6 6AB
☎ 01453 753441 (Bob & Sue Baker) www.hillenvale.co.uk Map 162/840068
BB **C** ✗ nearby D1 T2 Closed Xmas ᐱᐱᐱ(Stroud)
Ⓑ Ⓓ ⊛ 🐾 ♨ 🚗 ! ◆◆◆◆

● Tormarton (Badminton)
COTSWOLD WAY & MONARCH'S WAY

The Compass Inn, GL9 1JB ☎ 01454 218242
www.compass-inn.co.uk Map 172/760780
BB **D** ✗ £7-£25, until 10pm D11 T8 F6 Ⓥ Ⓑ Ⓓ 🐾 ♨ ! 🐾 ★★

Chestnut Farm, GL9 1HS ☎ 01454 218563
www.chestnut-farm.co.uk Map 172/768790
BB **D** ✗ £10, 8pm D5 T2 Ⓥ Ⓑ Ⓓ ⊛ 🐾 ♨ 🚗 ! 🐾

● Uley (Dursley)
COTSWOLD WAY

Hodgecombe Farm, GL11 5AN ☎ 01453 860365 (Catherine Bevan)
www.hodgecombefarm.co.uk Map 162/790985
BB **C** ✗ book first £16, 7pm D1 T1 Closed Oct-Feb
Ⓥ Ⓑ ⊛ 🐾 ♨ 🚗 ! ◆◆◆◆

● Winchcombe (Cheltenham)
COTSWOLD WAY

Gower House, 16 North Street, GL54 5LH ☎ 01242 602616 (Mrs S Simmonds)
gowerhouse16@aol.com Map 150,163/025284
BB **B** ✗ nearby D1 T2 Closed Xmas Ⓑ Ⓓ ⊛ 🐾 ♨ ! Ⓜ ◆◆◆◆

Cleevely Cottage, Wadfield Farm, Corndean Lane, GL54 5AL
☎ 01242 602059 (Mrs C M Rand) cleevelybxb@hotmail.com
Map 150/025263 BB **B** ✗ book first £16, 6:30pm D1 T1 F1 Closed Xmas
Ⓥ Ⓑ Ⓓ 🐾 ♨ 🚗 ◆◆◆◆

Blair House, 41 Gretton Road, GL54 5EG ☎ 01242 603626 (Mrs S Chisholm)
chissurv@aol.com Map 150,163/023287
BB **C** ✗ nearby S2 D1 T1 Closed Dec-Jan Ⓓ ⊛ ♨ ◆◆◆◆

Glebe Farm, Wood-Stanway, GL54 5PG ☎ 01386 584791
(Ann Flavell-Wood) www.woodstanway.co.uk Map 150/065313
BB **C** ✗ book first £19.50, 6:30pm D1 T2 Closed Xmas
Ⓥ Ⓑ Ⓓ 🐾 🚗 🐾

One Silk Mill Lane, GL54 5HZ ☎ 01242 603952 (Jenny Cheshire)
jenny.cheshire@virgin.net Map 150,163/026284
BB **C** ✗ nearby T2 Closed Xmas Ⓑ Ⓓ ⊛ 🐾 ♨ 🚗 ! ◆◆◆◆

Wood Stanway Farmhouse, Wood Stanway, GL54 5PG ☎ 01386 584318
(Maggie Green) www.woodstanwayfarmhouse.co.uk Map 150/062311
BB **C** ✗ book first £12, 6-7pm D1 T1 F1 Closed Xmas
Ⓥ Ⓑ Ⓓ 🐾 ♨ 🚗 !

Gaia Cottage, 50 Gloucester St, GL54 5LX ☎ 01242 603495
(Brian & Sally Simmonds) briansimmonds@onetel.com Map 150,163/022282
BB **D** ✗ nearby D1 T1 Ⓑ Ⓓ ⊛ 🐾 ♨ ! ◆◆◆◆

● Wotton-under-Edge
COTSWOLD WAY & MONARCH'S WAY

Cotswold Way B&B, Holywell Farm, Valley Road, GL12 7NP
☎ 07887 520890 (Maggie Sampson)
www.webspawner.com/users/cotswoldwaybb Map 172,162/761935
BB **C/D** ✗ nearby D1 F1 Ⓑ Ⓓ ⊛ 🐾 ♨ 🚗 ! 🐾 See SC also.

SOMERSET

● Axbridge
Waterside, Cheddar Road, BS26 2DP ☎ 01934 743182 (Gillian Aldridge)
www.watersidecheddar.co.uk Map 182/438545
BB **B** ✗ book first £10, 6pm S1 D2 T1 Ⓥ Ⓑ Ⓓ ⊛ 🐾 ♨ 🐾 ◆◆◆

● Bath
COTSWOLD WAY

Cranleigh, 159 Newbridge Hill, BA1 3PX ☎ 01225 310197
www.cranleighguesthouse.com Map 172/724656
BB **D** ✗ nearby D4 T2 F2 Closed Xmas ᐱᐱᐱ(Bath Spa)
Ⓑ Ⓓ ⊛ ♨ 🚗 ◆◆◆◆

Brocks, 32 Brock Street, BA1 2LN ☎ 01225 338374 (Marion Dodd)
www.brocksguesthouse.co.uk Map 172/746652
BB **D** ✗ nearby D3 T1 F2 Closed Xmas ᐱᐱᐱ(Bath Spa)
Ⓑ Ⓓ ⊛ ♨ ◆◆◆◆

Flaxley Villa, 9 Newbridge Hill, BA1 3PW ☎ 01225 313237 (M A Cooper)
flaxleyvilla@fsmail.net Map 172/731651
BB **B** ✗ nearby S1 D1 T2 F1 ᐱᐱᐱ(Bath Spa) Ⓑ ⊛ ♨

☆ **Marlborough House**
1 Marlborough Lane, BA1 2NQ ☎ 01225 318175
www.marlborough-house.net Map 172/742651
BB **D** S7 D7 T1 F2 ᐱᐱᐱ(Bath Spa)
Ⓥ Ⓑ ⊛ 🐾 ♨ 🐾 Ⓜ ◆◆◆◆ Vegetarian & organic food only.

Elegant vegetarian B&B in Bath. Rambler friendly with knowledgable hosts who are walkers themselves. Happily enlighten our guests on Bath's many fabulous walks as well as heritage sites. Beautiful en-suite rooms furnished with antiques. Children and pets welcome.

Athole Guest House, 33 Upper Oldfield Park, BA2 3JX ☎ 01225 320000
www.atholehouse.co.uk Map 172/742641
BB **D** ✗ nearby S2 D3 T1 F1 ᐱᐱᐱ(Bath Spa)
Ⓥ Ⓑ Ⓓ ⊛ ♨ ! ◆◆◆◆◆ⒼⓌ

Lindisfarne Guest House, 41a Warminster Road, BA2 6XJ ☎ 01225 466342
(Ian & Carolyn Tiley) www.bath.org/hotel/lindisfarne.html Map 172/776658
BB **C/D** ✗ nearby D2 T1 F1 Closed Xmas-Jan ᐱᐱᐱ(Bath Spa)
Ⓑ ⊛ 🐾 ♨ 🚗 ! ◆◆◆◆

☆🚶🍴 Number 30 Crescent Gardens

BA1 2NB ☎ 01225 337393 (David Greenwood)
www.numberthirty.com Map 172/744650
BB **D** 🍴 nearby S1 D5 T1 Closed Xmas ᨐᨐ(Bath Spa)
Ⓑ Ⓓ⊗🐾👙Ⓜ ◆◆◆◆Ⓢ

4 diamond standards of comfort
and housekeeping in our Victorian
house in Bath city centre.
Non-smoking. Vegetarian options.
All rooms en-suite, light and airy.
No pets. Private parking.
Two nights minimum at weekends.

☆🚶🍴 Crescent Guest House

21 Crescent Gardens, Upper Bristol Rd, BA1 2NA ☎ 01225 425945
(John & Gilly Deacon) www.crescentbath.co.uk Map 172/744650
BB **D** 🍴 nearby S1 D2 T1 Closed Xmas ᨐᨐ(Bath Spa)
Ⓑ Ⓓ⊗👙 ◆◆◆◆Ⓢ

Immaculate en-suite accommodation at
affordable rates in this award-winning
Victorian city centre guest house. High
service standards, generous breakfasts,
including vegetarian options, and just a
five-minute gentle stroll to the shopping
centre and Bath's many attractions.

🚶🍴 Devonshire House, 143 Wellsway, BA2 4RZ ☎ 01225 312495 (Louise Fry)
www.devonshire-house.uk.com Map 172/746631
BB **D** 🍴 nearby S3 D3 T2 F1 ᨐᨐ(Bath Spa)
Ⓥ Ⓑ Ⓓ⊗🐾👙 ◆◆◆◆

● Bridgwater (Wembdon)

MACMILLAN WAY WEST

Cokerhurst Farm, 87 Wembdon Hill, TA6 7QA
☎ 01278 422330 (Mrs D Chappell) www.cokerhurst.co.uk Map 182/280378
BB **C/D** 🍴 nearby D1 T1 F1 Closed Xmas ᨐᨐ(Bridgwater)
Ⓑ Ⓓ⊗🐾👙🚗! ◆◆◆◆

● Bristol

MONARCH'S WAY

Mayfair Lodge, 5 Henleaze Road, Westbury-on-Trym, BS9 4EX
☎ 0117 962 2008 (Mrs A Kitching)
www.smoothhound.co.uk/hotels/mayfairlodge.html Map 172/573761
BB **D** 🍴 nearby S5 D2 T2 Closed Xmas Ⓑ⊗👙 ◆◆◆

● Charlton Horethorne (Sherborne)

MONARCH'S WAY & MACMILLAN WAY

Beech Farm, Sigwells, DT9 4LN ☎ 01963 220524 (Susan Stretton)
stretton@beechfarmsigwells.freeserve.co.uk Map 183/642231
BB **B** 🍴 nearby S1 D1 T1 F1 Closed Xmas Ⓑ Ⓓ⊗🐾👙🚗! Ⓜ

● Cheddar

Constantine, Lower New Road, BS27 3DY
☎ 01934 741339 (Sue & Barry Mitchell) Map 182/450531
BB **B** 🍴 book first £10, 6:30pm S1 D2 T/D1 F1 Closed Dec
Ⓥ Ⓑ Ⓓ🐾👙 ◆◆◆

● Chew Stoke (Bristol)

MONARCH'S WAY

Orchard House, Bristol Road, BS40 8UB ☎ 01275 333143 (Ann Hollomon)
www.orchardhse.ukgateway.net Map 182, 172/561618
BB **C/D** 🍴 nearby S1 D1 T2 F1 Ⓑ Ⓓ🐾👙🚗! ★★★

Breach Hill Farm, BS40 8YD ☎ 01761 462411 (Margaret Wilson)
margaret@jmwilson.fsbusiness.co.uk Map 182,172/539597
BB **B** 🍴 book first £12, 7-8pm D1 Closed Dec-Mar Ⓓ⊗🐾👙🚗!Ⓜ

● Chipping Sodbury (Bristol)

MONARCH'S WAY & COTSWOLD WAY

🚶🍴 Kingrove Farm, BS37 6DY ☎ 01454 312314 (Mary Watson)
Map 172/731813 BB **B** 🍴 nearby S2 D2 T1 Ⓥ Ⓑ Ⓓ⊗🐾👙👝

● Crewkerne

MONARCH'S WAY

🚶🍴 George Hotel and Courtyard Restaurant, Market Square, TA18 7LP
☎ 01460 73650 (Frank E Joyce) www.thegeorgehotelcrewkerne.co.uk
Map 193/441098 BB **C** 🍴 £5-£15, 7-9pm S3 D5 T2 F3 ᨐᨐ(Crewkerne) Ⓥ
Ⓑ Ⓓ🐾👙 ◆◆◆

Honeydown Farm, Seaborough Hill, TA18 8PL
☎ 01460 72665 (Catherine Bacon) www.honeydown.co.uk Map 193/430072
BB **C** 🍴 book first £16, 7pm D2 T1 Closed Xmas ᨐᨐ(Crewkerne)
Ⓥ Ⓑ Ⓓ⊗🐾👙🚗! ★★★★

● Dunster (Minehead)

EXMOOR

SOUTH WEST COAST PATH & MACMILLAN WAY WEST

☆🚶🍴 The Yarn Market Hotel

High Street, TA24 6SF ☎ 01643 821425 (Penny Bale)
www.yarnmarkethotel.co.uk Map 181/992437
BB **D** 🍴 £20, 5:30-8:30pm S6 D12 T3 F3
Ⓥ Ⓑ Ⓓ⊗🐾👙🚗!Ⓜ ★★★

Our family-run hotel provides a friendly atmosphere, home cooking, en-suite
single, double, twin, four-poster and family rooms. Residents' lounge, packed
lunches and drying facilities available. Open all year.
1 night B&B from £45pp (£65 to include evening meal). 3 nights £120pp
(£180). Special offer for walking parties (10-50 people) — 3 nights B&B from
£100pp (£145). An ideal centre for exploring Exmoor.
Email Penny Bale: yarnmarket.hotel@virgin.net

● Easton (Wells)

Beaconsfield Farm, BA5 1DU ☎ 01749 870308 (Carol Lloyd)
www.beaconsfieldfarm.co.uk Map 182,183/514475
BB **D** D3 Closed Xmas Ⓥ Ⓑ Ⓓ⊗🐾👙🚗 ◆◆◆◆◆Ⓖ

● Holford (Bridgwater)

MACMILLAN WAY WEST & COLERIDGE WAY

Forge Cottage, TA5 1RY ☎ 01278 741215 (Susan Ayshford)
Map 181/158413
BB **B** 🍴 book first £8, 6-7pm D2 T1 Closed Xmas Ⓥ Ⓓ🐾👙🚗!Ⓜ

● Holton (Wincanton)

MONARCH'S WAY & MACMILLAN WAY

🚶🍴 Brookleigh, BA9 8AE ☎ 01963 34685 (Sally Clements)
theclementss@hotmail.com Map 183/698274
BB **C** 🍴 nearby S1 D1 T1 Ⓥ Ⓑ Ⓓ⊗🐾👙🚗👝 ◆◆◆◆

SOUTH WEST

● Minehead
EXMOOR
SOUTH WEST COAST PATH & MACMILLAN WAY WEST

The Parks Guesthouse, 26 The Parks, TA24 8BT ☎ 01643 703547
(Jackie & Richard Trott) www.parksguesthouse.co.uk Map 181/964462
BB **D** ✗ nearby D3 T2 F2 Closed Xmas-Jan
🅱 🅳 ⊗ 🐾 🛏 🚗 ! ◆◆◆◆ⓌⓈ

Kenella House, 7 Tregonwell Rd, TA24 5DT ☎ 01643 703128
(Steve and Sandy Poingdestre) www.kenellahouse.co.uk Map 181/972461
BB **D** ✗ book first £15, 7:30pm D4 T2 Closed Xmas
Ⓥ 🅱 🅳 ⊗ 🐾 🛏 🚗 ! ◆◆◆◆

● Nether Stowey (Bridgwater)
MACMILLAN WAY WEST & COLERIDGE WAY

The Old Cider House, 25 Castle Street, TA5 1LN ☎ 01278 732228
www.theoldciderhouse.co.uk Map 181/191397
BB **D** ✗ book first £13.50, approx 7:30pm D2 T3
Ⓥ 🅱 🅳 🐾 🛏 ★★★★

Castle of Comfort Country House, Dodington, TA5 1LE ☎ 01278 741264
(Carol & Nigel Venner) www.castle-of-comfort.co.uk Map 181/173399
BB **D** ✗ book first £28.50, 7-8:30pm S1 D3 T1 F1 Closed Xmas
Ⓥ 🅱 🅳 ⊗ 🐾 🛏 🚗 ! 🏇 ◆◆◆◆◆Ⓢ

● North Cadbury
MACMILLAN WAY & MONARCH'S WAY

Ashlea House, High Street, BA22 7DP ☎ 01963 440891
(Mr & Mrs J Wade) www.ashleahouse.co.uk Map 183/635274
BB **C** ✗ book first £14-£16, 7pm D1 T1 Closed Xmas
Ⓥ 🅱 🅳 ⊗ 🐾 🛏 🚗 ! ◆◆◆◆Ⓢ

● Porlock (Minehead)
EXMOOR
SOUTH WEST COAST PATH & COLERIDGE WAY

Leys — The Ridge, off Bossington Lane, TA24 8HA
☎ 01643 862477 (Mrs J Stiles-Cox) Map 181/892469
BB **B** ✗ nearby S2 D/T1 Closed Xmas 🅳 ⊗ 🐾 🛏 ◆◆◆◆

The Lorna Doone Hotel, High Street, TA24 8PS
☎ 01643 862404 (R G Thornton) porlockld@yahoo.com Map 181/887469
BB **C** ✗ book first £14, 6.15-8.30pm S4 D4 T4 F2 Closed Xmas
Ⓥ 🅱 🅳 🐾 🛏 ! 🏇

Silcombe Farm, Culbone, TA24 8JN
☎ 01643 862248 (Mrs E J Richards) Map 181/833482
BB **B** ✗ book first £11, 7.30pm S1 D1 T2 Closed Xmas
Ⓥ 🅱 🅳 ⊗ 🐾 🛏 🚗 ! 🏇

● Roadwater (Watchet)
EXMOOR
COLERIDGE WAY

☆ Trinity Cottage Bed & Breakfast
TA23 0QY ☎ 01984 641676 (Abigail Humphrey)
www.trinitycottage.co.uk Map 181/031382
BB **D** ✗ £17, 6:30-7pm D2 T1 Closed Xmas
Ⓥ 🅱 🅳 ⊗ 🐾 🛏 🚗 ! 🏇 ◆◆◆◆

Quiet, attractive, comfortable en-suite accommodation on the Coleridge Way and within Exmoor National Park. Excellent local walks. Pick-up and drop-off service available making a convenient base. Delicious breakfasts and a smile to greet you!

● South Cadbury (Yeovil)
MACMILLAN WAY & MONARCH'S WAY

Lower Camelot B&B, Lower Camelot, BA22 7HA ☎ 01963 440581
(Julie Verney) www.southcadbury.co.uk Map 183/633256
BB **D** ✗ nearby S/D/T3 Closed Jan-Feb 🅱 🅳 ⊗ 🐾 🛏 🚗 !

● Stogumber (Taunton)

☆ **The White Horse Inn**
High Street, TA4 3TA ☎ 01984 656277
www.whitehorsestogumber.co.uk Map 181/098373
BB **D** ✗ £6.95, 7-9pm D1 T1
Ⓥ 🅱 🐾 🛏 ◆◆◆ Available for large group bookings.

The White Horse is a Grade II-listed freehouse in the picturesque village of Stogumber in glorious countryside on the slopes of the Quantock Hills. The extensive menu uses fresh local produce and award-winning locally-brewed real ales are a speciality.

Wick House, 2 Brook Street, TA4 3SZ ☎ 01984 656422 (Sheila Gibbs)
www.wickhouse.fsbusiness.co.uk Map 181/097372
BB **C** ✗ book first £12, 6:30-8:30pm D3 T2
Ⓥ 🅱 🅳 ⊗ 🐾 🛏 🚗 ! ◆◆◆ Room equipped for disabled guests.

● Taunton

Blorenge House, 57 Staplegrove Road, TA1 1DG ☎ 01823 283005
(Mr & Mrs Painter) www.blorengehouse.co.uk Map 193/223250
BB **D** ✗ nearby S5 D8 T8 F3 Closed Xmas 🚉(Taunton)
🅱 🅳 🐾 🛏 🏇 ◆◆◆◆

● Washford (Watchet)
MACMILLAN WAY WEST & COLERIDGE WAY

Green Bay B&B, TA23 0NN ☎ 01984 640303 (Ann Morgan)
www.greenbaybedandbreakfast.co.uk Map 181/049410
BB **A/B** ✗ book first £8, 6-7:30pm S2 D1 T1
Ⓥ 🅱 🅳 🐾 🛏 ! 🏇 ◆◆◆

● Wells
MONARCH'S WAY

Cadgwith House, Hawkers Lane, BA5 3JH ☎ 01749 677799
(Elspeth Fletcher) www.cadgwithhouse.co.uk Map 182/559462
BB **D** S1 D1 T1 F1 Closed Xmas 🅱 🅳 ⊗ 🐾 🛏 🚗 ! 🏇 ★★★★

☆ **The Crown At Wells**
Market Place, BA5 2RP ☎ 01749 673457
www.crownatwells.co.uk Map 182,183/550457
BB **D** ✗ book first £15, 6pm onwards S2 D7 T4 F2
Ⓥ 🅱 🅳 🐾 🛏 🏇 Ⓜ ★★

Superbly located 15th-century coaching inn, overlooking Wells Cathedral and Bishop's Palace. The Crown provides comfortable and affordable accommodation. Fabulous food served in popular restaurant, bar and courtyard.
Warm welcome and friendly service, in a relaxed atmosphere.

● Weston-Super-Mare

The Owls Crest, 39 Kewstoke Road, Kewstoke, BS22 9YE ☎ 01934 417672
(Mike & Maura O'Callaghan) www.theowlscrest.co.uk Map 182/335633
BB **D** ✗ book first £12.50, 6:30-8pm D3 T1 Closed Jan 🚉(Parkway)
Ⓥ 🅱 ⊗ 🐾 🛏 🏇 Ⓖ

● Wheddon Cross (Minehead)
EXMOOR
COLERIDGE WAY & MACMILLAN WAY WEST
▪➤◀ Exmoor House, TA24 7DU ☎ 01643 841432
www.exmoorhouse.com Map 181/924388
BB **D** ✕ book first £19.50, 7:30pm D3 T1 F1 Closed Dec-Jan
Ⓥ Ⓑ Ⓓ ⊛ 🐾 ♨ 🚗 ! 🛏 ◆◆◆◆◆Ⓢ

● Winsham (Chard)
MONARCH'S WAY & WESSEX RIDGEWAY
▪➤◀ Fulwood House, Ebben Lane, TA20 4EE ☎ 01460 30163
(Elizabeth & Carl Earl) carleton.earl@virgin.net Map 193/377066
BB **C** ✕ nearby D2 Ⓥ Ⓑ Ⓓ ⊛ 🐾 ♨ 🚗 Ⓜ ◆◆◆◆

● Withypool (Minehead)
EXMOOR
TWO MOORS WAY & MACMILLAN WAY WEST
Hamiltons, TA24 7QP ☎ 01643 831431 (Ina Gage) Map 181/846355
BB **C** ✕ nearby S1 D3 T1 Ⓑ Ⓓ ⊛ 🐾 ♨ ! 🛏

● Wyke Champflower (Bruton)
MACMILLAN WAY, MACMILLAN WAY WEST & MONARCH'S WAY

☆ ▪➤◀ **Steps Farmhouse**
BA10 0PW ☎ 01749 812788
www.stepsfarm.com Map 183/658341
BB **B** ✕ book first £7.50, 7pm S1 D1 T1 Closed Xmas 🚍(Castle Cary)
Ⓥ Ⓑ Ⓓ ⊛ 🐾 ♨ 🚗 ! 🛏 Vegetarian food only.

Smallholding in beautiful south Somerset.
Haven of peace. Excellent vegetarian food enjoyed by
non-vegetarians too. Perfect place to relax.
En-suite rooms and lovely garden.
Leland Trail/Macmillan Way/Stourhead nearby.
Much more information on website or brochure
by request.

WILTSHIRE

● Amesbury (Salisbury)
Mandalay, 15 Stonehenge Road, SP4 7BA
☎ 01980 623733 Map 184/147414
BB **D** ✕ nearby D2 T2 F1 Ⓥ Ⓑ Ⓓ ⊛ 🐾 ♨ 🚗

● Ashton Keynes (Cirencester)
THAMES PATH
▪➤◀ The Firs, High Rd, SN6 6NX ☎ 01285 860169 (Karen Shaw)
thefirsbb@yahoo.co.uk Map 173,163/045941
BB **C** ✕ nearby S2 D2 T1 Ⓑ Ⓓ 🐾 ♨ 🚗 ! 🛏 Ⓜ ◆◆◆

● Bishopstone (Swindon)
▪➤◀ Prebendal Farm, SN6 8PT ☎ 01793 790485 (Jo Selbourne)
www.prebendal.com Map 174/243835
BB **D** ✕ nearby D3 T1 Ⓥ Ⓑ Ⓓ ⊛ 🐾 ♨ 🚗 ! 🛏

● Bremhill (Calne)
Lowbridge Farm, SN11 9HE
☎ 01249 815889 (Elizabeth Sinden) Map 173/987737
BB **C** ✕ book first £10.50, 7-9pm S1 D1 T1 F1
Ⓥ Ⓓ 🐾 ♨ 🚗 ! 🛏 Jacuzzi available.

● Burcombe (Salisbury)
▪➤◀ Burcombe Manor B&B, SP2 0EJ ☎ 01722 744288 (Wendy Combes)
www.burcombemanor.co.uk Map 184/069309
BB **D** ✕ nearby D2 T1 F1 Ⓥ Ⓑ Ⓓ ⊛ 🐾 ♨ 🚗 ◆◆◆◆

● Devizes
WESSEX RIDGEWAY
Rockley, London Road, SN10 2DS ☎ 01380 723209 (Jean & Richard Bull)
www.rockley.org.uk Map 173/003618
BB **C/D** ✕ nearby S3 D1 T2 F1 Closed Xmas Ⓑ Ⓓ ⊛ 🐾 ♨ 🚗

▪➤◀ The Gatehouse, Wick Lane, SN10 5DW ☎ 01380 725283 (Mrs L Stratton)
www.visitdevizes.co.uk Map 173/006605
BB **C** ✕ nearby S1 D1 T1 Closed Xmas Ⓑ Ⓓ ⊛ 🐾 ♨ 🚗 ! 🛏 ◆◆◆

☆ ▪➤◀ **Rosemundy Cottage**
London Road, SN10 2DS ☎ 01380 727122
www.rosemundycottage.co.uk Map 173/014621
BB **D** ✕ nearby D2 T1 F1
Ⓥ Ⓑ Ⓓ ⊛ 🐾 ♨ 🚗 ! ◆◆◆◆

Alongside the Kennet & Avon Canal, just off
Wessex Ridgeway, and a short walk to the town
centre. Facilities include guest office, sitting
room and garden with seasonal heated pool
and BBQ. All rooms en-suite. Four-poster and
ground floor rooms available. Good base for
varied walks. Double/3-night offers.

● Heytesbury (Warminster)
WESSEX RIDGEWAY
▪➤◀ The Resting Post, 67 High Street, BA12 0ED
☎ 01985 840204 (Felicity McLellan)
www.therestingpost.co.uk Map 184/926425
BB **D** ✕ nearby D2 T1 Ⓥ Ⓑ Ⓓ ⊛ 🐾 ♨ 🚗 ! ★★★★

● Inglesham (Swindon)
THAMES PATH
Evergreen, 3 College Farm Cottages, SN6 7QU ☎ 01367 253407
(Mr & Mrs G Blowen) www.evergreen-cotswolds.co.uk Map 163/204959
BB **D** ✕ nearby S2 D1 Closed Xmas Ⓑ Ⓓ ⊛ 🐾 ♨ 🚗 !

● Ludwell (Shaftesbury)
WESSEX RIDGEWAY
Birdbush Farm, SP7 9HH ☎ 01747 828252 (Ann Rossiter)
annrossiter@fsmail.net Map 184/913229
BB **B** ✕ nearby S1 D1 Closed Dec-Feb Ⓓ ⊛ 🐾 ♨ 🚗 !

● Malmesbury
▪➤◀ Mayfield House Hotel, Crudwell, SN16 9EW ☎ 01666 577409
(Chris Marston) www.mayfieldhousehotel.co.uk Map 173,163/954928
BB **D** ✕ £18, 6:30-8:45pm S3 D12 T9 F2
Ⓥ Ⓑ Ⓓ 🐾 ♨ 🚗 ★★ See Groups also.

● Manningford Abbots (Marlborough)
Huntleys Farm, SN9 6HZ ☎ 01672 563663 (Margot Andrews)
meg@gimspike.fsnet.co.uk Map 173/145593
BB **C** ✕ book first £13.50 D1 T/F1 🚍(Pewsey)
Ⓥ Ⓑ Ⓓ ⊛ 🐾 ♨ 🚗 ! 🛏 ★★★

● Marlborough
WESSEX RIDGEWAY

☆ **Browns Farm**
SN8 4ND ☎ 01672 515129 (Hazel J Crockford)
www.marlboroughholidaycottages.co.uk Map 173/198678
BB **B** ✕ nearby D2 T1 F1
Ⓑ Ⓓ ⊗ 🐾🛁🚗🐕 See SC also.

Attractive farmhouse set on the edge of the Savernake Forest. Large comfortable rooms offering views over open farmland. Ideal base for walkers & cyclists. Close to the Ridgeway, Averbury and Wansdyke.

● Mere
MONARCH'S WAY

Castleton House, Castle St, BA12 6JE ☎ 01747 860446 (Gail Garbutt)
www.castletonhouse.com Map 183/811323
BB **C** ✕ book first £15, 7:30-8:30pm D1 T1 F1 Closed Xmas
Ⓥ Ⓑ Ⓓ 🐾🛁🚗! ◆◆◆◆

● Ogbourne St George (Marlborough)
RIDGEWAY

Foxlynch, Bytham Road, SN8 1TD
☎ 01672 841307 (Mr G H Edwins) Map 173/190740
BB **B** ✕ nearby S1 F1 Ⓑ Ⓓ 🐾🛁🚗! 🛁 Bunkroom only.

☆🍴 **Parklands Hotel & Restaurant**
High Street, SN8 1SL ☎ 01672 841555 (Mark Bentley)
www.parklandshoteluk.co.uk Map 174/200744
BB **D** ✕ book first £14.75, 7-9pm S2 D3 T7
Ⓥ Ⓑ Ⓓ 🐾🛁🚗!🛁 ◆◆◆◆

Set in the tiny Wiltshire village of Ogbourne St George, Parklands Hotel offers comfortable, peaceful accommodation and an excellent restaurant in a family run hotel. Conveniently located for the Ridgeway path.

To see more details, please visit our website.

● Salisbury

🍴 Hayburn Wyke Guest House, 72 Castle Road, SP1 3RL ☎ 01722 412627
www.hayburnwykeguesthouse.co.uk Map 184/142309
BB **B/C** ✕ nearby D3 T2 F2 ⚑(Salisbury) Ⓑ Ⓓ🛁 ◆◆◆

🍴 Byways House, 31 Fowler's Rd, SP1 2QP ☎ 01722 328364
(Barbara Bouffard) www.bywayshouse.co.uk Map 184/149299
BB **D** ✕ nearby S4 D7 T7 F5 Closed Xmas ⚑(Salisbury)
Ⓑ 🐾🛁🛁 ◆◆◆

● Warminster
WESSEX RIDGEWAY

🍴 Farmers' Hotel, 1 Silver Street, BA12 8PS ☎ 01985 213815
www.farmershotel.yahoo.uk Map 183/871451
BB **B/C** ✕ £9, 6-10pm S9 D6 T7 F3 ⚑(Warminster)
Ⓥ Ⓑ Ⓓ 🐾🛁🛁 ◆

● West Lavington (Devizes)
WESSEX RIDGEWAY

Littleton Lodge (A360), Littleton Panell, SN10 4ES
☎ 01380 813131 (May Linton) www.littletonlodge.co.uk Map 184/997543
BB **C/D** ✕ nearby D2 T1 Ⓑ Ⓓ ⊗ 🐾🛁 ◆◆◆◆

● West Overton (Marlborough)
RIDGEWAY & WESSEX RIDGEWAY

🍴 Cairncot, SN8 4ER ☎ 01672 861617 (Rachel Leigh)
www.cairncot.co.uk Map 173/131680
BB **B** ✕ nearby S1 D1 Ⓓ ⊗ 🐾🛁🛁🚗!🛁 ◆◆◆

● Westbury
WESSEX RIDGEWAY

Redwood Lodge, The Ham, BA13 4HE ☎ 01373 823949 (Sandy Newbury)
www.redwoodlodgeuk.com Map 183/863524
BB **C** ✕ nearby S3 D4 T4 F2 ⚑(Westbury)
Ⓥ Ⓑ Ⓓ ⊗ 🐾🛁🚗! Wheelchair access.

SELF-CATERING

CORNWALL

☆ **Cornish Traditional Cottages**
☎ 01208 821666
www.corncott.com
£196-£1550 Sleeps 2-12. 400 houses, cottages & bungalows.
Some properties allow dogs and are non-smoking.

Cornish Traditional Cottages has provided quality self-catering accommodation throughout Cornwall for over 40 years, with approximately 400 houses, cottages, bungalows and a few apartments in both coastal and inland areas.

In Cornwall you are never far from our spectacular coastal footpath and lovely rural walks. Out of season there are the wonderful spring gardens to see as well as the multitude of hedgerow and field wild flowers.

Inspected annually and monitored continuously via our questionnaires, the quality and value for money of our properties are all important, as is the friendly and efficient service we provide to our guests.

● Ashton

Chycarne Farm Cottages ☎ 01736 762473 (Pauline & Graham Ross)
www.chycarne-farm-cottages.co.uk
£100-£440 Sleeps 1-4. 9 cottages. Closed Nov, Feb, Mar
Beautiful rural location, overlooks Mounts Bay. ⊗ 🛁 ★★★

● Bodmin

☆ Ruthern Valley Holidays
☎ 01208 831395 (Andrew & Nicola Johnston) www.self-catering-ruthern.co.uk
£220-£630 Sleeps 4-6.
8 lodges, 4 bungalows, 6 static caravans, camping pitches. Closed Jan-Feb
David Bellamy Gold Award for conservation. 🌱 ♿ ★★★★

Mid Cornwall.
A small holiday retreat in 7.5 acres of park
and woodland. Lodges/caravans. 10 miles to
the north or south coasts – Eden Project.
Close to Camel Trail and Saints' Way.
No bar, no disco, no bingo!
Email: ruthern.valley@btconnect.com

● Bude

Flexbury House ☎ 01600 772918 (Sarah Watkins)
www.flexburyhouse.com
£350-£1,050 Sleeps 2-10 + 2 cots. 1 detached house.
5 minutes from coast, town, pub. 🌱 ★★★★

Honeysuckle Cottage ☎ 01288 355496 (Dennis Mobbs)
www.honeysucklecottage.co.uk
£180-£400 Sleeps 2. 1 cottage. Indoor pool. Laundry. ♿ ★★★★

● Callington

Berrio Mill ☎ 01579 363252 (Ivan & Carolyn Callanan)
www.berriomill.co.uk
£210-£660 Sleeps 2-4. 2 cottages.
Peaceful farm, millstream, fishing, superb countryside.
🌱 ★★★★Ⓦ Access scheme M1.

● Camelford

Roughtor Cottage ☎ 01840 211242 (Mrs Ashton)
www.roughtorcottage.co.uk
£150-£295 Sleeps 2-4. 1 cottage.
Near Bodmin Moor, South West Coast Path. 🌱

● Crackington Haven

Crackington Manor ☎ 01840 230397
crackington.manor@virgin.net
£115-£390 Sleeps 2-6. 2 flats. 1 min beach, South West Coast Path. ♿

● Fowey

Fowey Harbour Cottages ☎ 01726 832211 (David Hill)
www.foweyharbourcottages.co.uk
£150-£1,000 Sleeps 2-6. 10 cottages & flats.
On Cornish Coast Path & Saints' Way. ♿ ★★-★★★★

Izzy Minx Cottage ☎ 07813 890768 (Julie Yardley)
www.izzyminx.co.uk
£160-£430 Sleeps 5. 1 cottage.
Fabulous cottage on South West Coast Path. 🌱 ♿

● Helford

Helford River Cottages ☎ 01326 231666 (Pam Royall)
www.helfordcottages.co.uk
£165-£945 Sleeps 2-9. 12 cottages. Enchanting creekside cottages on
coastal footpath. 🌱 ♿ Ⓜ ★★★-★★★★

● Helford Passage

☆ Helford Passage
☎ 0118 9343310 (Linda James)
www.helfordriver.com/accommodation/15d
£210-£640 Sleeps 6. 1 flat.
Scenic walks, pub/restaurant, sheltered beach.

Three bedroom flat ideally situated on the
Cornish coastal path, enjoying the
outstanding beauty of the Helford River.
Swimming, boating, Ferry Boat Inn on site.
Sheltered beautiful beach. Pedestrian ferry
to Helford village. Golf, Trebah and
Glendurgan gardens nearby.

● Holywell

☆ Trenwith House
☎ 01637 830864 (Mr Keogh)
www.trenwithhouse.co.uk
£213-£606 Sleeps 3-6. 4 chalets, 3 caravans. Closed Oct-Apr
♿

Situated in 600 acres of very peaceful
National Trust land, designated an AONB
and SSSI, with coastal walks. Breathtaking
views down to a small sandy beach from
our accommodation which we keep to a
very high standard.
Dogs welcome.

● Launceston

Eastgate Barn ☎ 01566 782573 (Jill Goodman) www.eastgatebarn.co.uk
£250-£460 Sleeps 2-4. 1 barn conversion.
Self-guided local walks to Bodmin Moor. 🌱 Ⓜ ★★★★

☆ Ta Mill
☎ 01840 261797 (Helen Shopland)
www.tamill.co.uk
£195-£1,100 Sleeps 2-9. 12 cottages & lodges.
Tranquil, AONB, nature thrives, stunning location. ♿ ★★★-★★★★

A secluded rural hideaway of Cornish cottages and lodges nestling in a peaceful
hollow of 45 acres on the fringes of Bodmin Moor. Surrounded by rolling
countryside, an idyllic place to relax and unwind. Our peaceful nature trail
follows a babbling brook meandering through the grounds and down the
picturesque valley. Within easy reach of North Cornish coastline and untamed
beauty of Bodmin Moor and Dartmoor. Birdwatchers and walkers paradise.

Trevadlock Manor ☎ 01566 782227 (Mr & Mrs Bruton)
www.trevadlockmanor.co.uk
£272-£621 Sleeps 4-6. 5 cottages. Private fishing. Bodmin Moor 2 miles.
Stunning scenery. 🌱 ♿ See B&B also.

● Liskeard

Cutkive Wood Holiday Lodges ☎ 01579 362216 (Andy Lowman)
www.cutkivewood.co.uk
£120-£440 Sleeps 1-6. 6 lodges.
Idyllic rural location, moors, coasts, countryside. 🛁 See Groups also.

☆ **Butterdon Mill Holiday Homes**
☎ 01579 342636 (Mr & Mrs Turner)
butterdonmill@btconnect.com
£175-£450 Sleeps 2-6. 12 bungalows.
Close to coastal paths and moors. Pets welcome. 🛁

Idyllic rural site near Looe. Two-bedroom detached bungalows set in a peaceful 2.5 acres. Games barn and children's play area. Ideal touring area for both coasts and moors of Cornwall/Devon. Open all year. Discounts couples/OAPs Sept-June. Brochure available.

● Marazion

☆ **Tregew Holiday Bungalows**
☎ 01736 710247 (Mr Pool)
£200-£525 Sleeps 2-3. 2 bungalows.
Breathtaking views of St Michael's Mount.
🚶(Penzance) ★★★

The bungalows are situated on the hillside overlooking St Michael's Mount, Mounts Bay and the Atlantic Ocean, only a few minutes walk to Marazion village, beach and coastal path/walks. Ideal base for walking and touring. Fully equipped. Brochure on request.

● Mullion

Criggan Mill ☎ 01326 240496 (Mike & Jackie Bolton) www.crigganmill.co.uk
£180-£715 Sleeps 2-6. 25 timber lodges.
Coastal path 200yds, village 1 mile. 🛁 ★★★★★ See B&B also.

Trenance Farm Cottages ☎ 01326 240639 (Tamara)
www.trenancefarmholidays.co.uk
£195-£700 Sleeps 2-6. 9 cottages.
Within 5 mins walk of SW Coast Path. 🛁 ★★★

● Padstow

☆ **Bosca Brea**
☎ 01208 814472 (Mrs Alison Mitchell)
alisonm.trevalsa@btinternet.com
£170-£360 Sleeps 1-4. 1 bungalow.
Saints' Way and coastal path nearby. 🛁

Detached bungalow in peaceful hamlet of Tregonce. Views across Little Petherick Creek and towards Padstow from ½ acre private grounds. Close access to Saints' Way, Camel Trail and South West Coast Path. Wadebridge, Padstow, surfing and sandy beaches approx. 5 miles by road.

Yellow Sands Cottages ☎ 01637 881548 (Sharon Keast) www.yellowsands.co.uk
£220-£750 Sleeps 1-6. 6 cottages.
Harlyn Bay, coastal footpath close by – bliss! 🛁 ★★★★

☆ **Pols Piece Holidays**
☎ 01841 520372 (Jo Olivey)
www.polspieceholidays.co.uk
£255-£815 Sleeps 4-7. Apartments & bungalows. Closed Oct-Apr
Child's play equipment, laundry room. 🛁 ★★★-★★★★

Delightful, well equipped apartments set in own grounds, enjoying wonderful sea views. A short walk to natural swimming pool and Trevone beach. Swimming, surfing, sailing, rambling, golfing nearby. Parking, laundry room, tabletennis, children's play area, wendy house. Pets welcome.

Raintree House Holidays ☎ 01841 520228 (Rosemary)
www.raintreehouse.co.uk
£295-£2950 Sleeps 2-16. Cottages & flats. Closed Nov
Close to Camel Trail, beaches & cliff walks. 🛁

Yellow Sands ☎ 01841 520376 (Mr M Dakin)
www.yellowsands.net
£220-£1,200 Sleeps 1-8. 3 flats, 1 house.
Sea views. 200 yards from coastal footpath. ⊗ 🛁 ★★★-★★★★

● Port Isaac

Lane End Farm ☎ 01208 880013 (Linda Monk) nabmonk@tiscali.co.uk
£180-£475 Sleeps 4. 1 bungalow.
Beautiful views. Convenient coast path, moors. ⊗ 🛁 Ⓜ ★★★ See B&B also.

The Scuppers ☎ 020 8891 3293 (Lynne Lightman)
www.scuppers.co.uk
£350-£750 Sleeps 6. 1 cottage.
Stunning views, adjacent to coastal path. ⊗ Ⓜ

● Saltash

Crylla Valley Cottages ☎ 01752 851133
www.cryllacottages.co.uk
£168-£1,096 Sleeps 2-8. 35 cottages.
Close to national parks/coastal walks. ⊗ 🛁 ★★★★

● St Austell

Spindrift ☎ 01726 69316 (Mrs McGuffie)
www.spindrift-guesthouse.co.uk
£200-£550 Sleeps 2-4. 3 varying types.
Close to Eden-Heligan-Mevagissey. ⊗ 🛁 ★★★ See B&B also.

● St Dennis

Ginny ☎ 01726 821715 b&g@bazinny.plus.com
£100-£500 Sleeps 2-6. 1 studio flat, 1 cabin. Closed Jan-Feb (cabin) ⊗

● St Ives

St Ives Cottage ☎ 020 8870 3228 (Sue Kibby)
www.btinternet.com/~stives.cottage
£200-£500 Sleeps 4. 1 cottage.
Self-guided walking pack available. ⊗ 🚶(St Ives) ★★★

☆ Dolphins
☎ 07985 225018 (Jill & Steve Lane)
www.dolphins.uk.com
£250-£600 Sleeps 4-6 + child. 1 cottage.
Overlooks beach, near Tate, adjoins SW coast path. 🚶(St Ives) ⊗

'Dolphins' is our lovely seaside family home, overlooking Porthmeor Beach, with far-reaching sea and coastal views. Peaceful relaxing location. Garden & sheltered south-facing courtyard, for 'al fresco' dining. Comfortable, well equipped. Short walk to beaches, harbour, restaurants, galleries & Tate. Available all year, central heating, large drying cupboard, porch for boots & surfboards. Perfect for walking the coast path. Short breaks & discounts available. Fellow ramblers very welcome!

● St Just
Dowran Cottage ☎ 01865 774166 (Virginia Walker)
evwalker2000@yahoo.co.uk £180-£375 Sleeps 2-3. 1 cottage.
Rural hamlet, superb walking, views Scillys. ⊗

Grenfells Cottage ☎ 07962 235926 (Sue Craythorne)
suecraythorne@hotmail.com £150-£556 Sleeps 5 + cot. 1 cottage.
Sea views, half-mile to coast path. ⊗ 🛏

● St Wenn

☆ Tregolls Farm
☎ 01208 812154 (Marilyn Hawkey)
www.tregollsfarm.co.uk
£225-£850 Sleeps 2-8. 4 converted barns.
Clothes drying facilities. Saints' Way. ⊗ ★★★★ See B&B also.

Quality barn conversion in a picturesque valley overlooking fields of cows and sheep. Farm trail links up with Saints' Way footpath. Pets corner. Games room. BBQs. Central heating and log burners. Only 20 minutes drive from Eden or Padstow.

● The Lizard
Most Southerly House ☎ 01326 290300 (Mr G Sowden)
georgesowden@tiscali.co.uk
£180-£250 Sleeps 2-3. 1 clifftop chalet. Closed Nov-Mar
On coastal path, magnificent sea views. ⊗

● Tintagel
Hendra Farm ☎ 01726 72091 (Mrs A Boyd) alixboyd@tiscali.co.uk
£220-£565 Sleeps 4. 1 cottage.
Mediaeval cottage, sea 500m away, on footpath. ⊗ 🛏 ★★★

● Tregony
Tucoyse Farm Holiday Cottages ☎ 01726 843836 (Penny Blamey)
www.tucoyse.co.uk £265-£535 Sleeps 4 + cot. 2 cottages.
Close to coastal path, Eden, Heligan. ⊗ ★★★ Guide dogs welcome.

DEVON

● Appledore
Number 5 Hillcliff Terrace ☎ 01600 716418 (Jennifer Frecknall)
www.appledore-holiday.co.uk
£225-£495 Sleeps 6. 1 terraced house.
Comfortable family home on waterfront. 🛏

● Berrynarbor

☆ Smythen Farm Coastal Cottages
☎ 01271 882875 (Jayne Elstone)
www.smythenfarmholidaycottages.co.uk
£110-£930 Sleeps 2-8. 5 cottages. Closed Nov-Feb
Heated covered swimming pool. Pony rides. 🛏 ★★★-★★★★

The five cottages, 2-8 berth, set in an area of outstanding natural beauty overlooking the sea.

Heated covered swimming pool in a suntrap enclosure. Spacious lawns and gardens. Children's play area with 12m x 5m all-weather games room with full-size pool, tabletennis, darts and football machine. Also, for younger children, inflatable bouncy castle and ball-pond.

Free pony rides. 14-acre recreation field and dog walk.

The village of Berrynarbor is 2 miles with store, an inn welcoming children and quality eating places. 2, 3, 4 and 5-night breaks available.

● Brixham
Devoncourt ☎ 01803 853748
www.devoncourt.info
£199-£599 Sleeps 5-6. 24 flats.
Overlooking Torbay. Panoramic sea views. 🛏 ★★

● Combe Martin
EXMOOR
Northcote Manor Farm ☎ 01271 882376 (Pat Bunch)
www.northcotemanorfarm.co.uk
£250-£945 Sleeps 4-6. 5 cottages. Closed Nov
Tranquil location. Indoor pool. Games barn. ⊗ 🛏 ★★★★

● Dartmouth
Norton Park ☎ 07802 308030 (Julie Nesbit-Bell)
www.chalets-dartmouth.co.uk £120-£425 Sleeps 4-5. Chalets.
Fully modernised, wonderful views, great walks. ⊗

● Down Thomas

☆ Becalmed
☎ 01989 770725 (Mrs J Davis)
jackienicholsonx@yahoo.co.uk
£150-£425 Sleeps 4. 1 chalet.   Closed Jan-Feb
Stunning position on South West Coast Path. ⊛

'Becalmed' (photo shows view from chalet).

Cosy, modern chalet on the cliffs of the South West Coast Path ovelooking the waters of Plymouth Sound. West facing, the chalet windows and patio enjoy glorious sunsets. Within minutes of the beaches, the position of the chalet provides ample opportunity for walking the footpaths of both the South Hams and Dartmoor.

Completely refurbished with all modern facilities, the chalet has two bedrooms (one double, one twin), lounge with dining area, new shower room and fully equipped fitted kitchen with washer/dryer. Charges are inclusive of heating and electricity. Food baskets can be arranged for walkers on request for a small extra charge. Brochure on request.

● Dunsford
DARTMOOR

Mrs Jean May ☎ 01647 252784 lesjmay@aol.com
£170-£320 Sleeps 2-4. 2 cottages.
Peaceful farmland, lovely views, woodland walks. ⊛

● Hartland

☆ Yapham Cottages
☎ 01237 441916 (Jane Young)
www.yaphamcottages.com
£260-£630 Sleeps 2-4. 3 cottages.
Wonderful walks, tranquil coastal location. Central heating. ⊛ ★★★★

3 beautiful 4-star cottages sleeping 2-4.

Stunning coastal location. Set in landscaped gardens within seven acres of lovely grounds, including an ancient woodland walk. Only 1 mile from South West Coast Path and guided walks can be arranged.

Situated on the breathtaking and unspoilt Hartland Peninsula, Yapham enjoys complete tranquillity yet is perfect for visiting nearby tourist attractions; Exmoor, Dartmoor, The Eden Project, Lundy Island.

Our cottages are beautifully furnished and include central heating. Excellent home cooked meals and dishes can be provided. Delicious cream tea on arrival, plus chocolates and flowers. 'Taxi' service available. Also short breaks.

● Honiton

Twistgates Farm ☎ 01404 861173 (Mrs Gray)
www.twistgatesfarm.co.uk
£185-£650 Sleeps 2-5. 3 cottages.
Woodburner, laundry area, meals available. Rural. ⊛ 🐾 ★★★★

☆ Odle Farm Holiday Cottages
☎ 01404 861105 (Karen Marshallsay)
www.odlefarm.co.uk
£220-£815 Sleeps 2-6. 4 cottages.
Stunning views, AONB, quiet, tranquil setting. ⊛ 🐾

Set in 10 acres of the unspoilt Otter Valley, an excellent area for walking & cycling. Very comfortable accommodation. New commercial hydrotherapy spa and games room for 2007. Other facilities are available a short walk down a leafy lane.

● Ilfracombe

☆ Dune Cottage Holidays
☎ 01271 867395 (Sally Parsons)
www.dunecottageholidays.co.uk
£230-£1429 Sleeps 4-10. 3 cottages.
High quality rural SC accommodation. ⊛ 🐾

All our cottages have a wealth of character, underfloor heating and their own private gardens. This peaceful farm setting offers an opportunity to relax and unwind. The location is perfect for exploring north Devon's coast and countryside, including Exmoor.

● Lyme Regis

Symondsdown Cottages ☎ 01297 32385 (Stuart & Jenny Hynds)
www.symondsdownholidaycottages.co.uk
£175-£600 Sleeps 2-6. 6 cottages.
Close to coastal & country footpaths. ₩(Axminster) 🐾

● Lynton
EXMOOR

South Dean Cottage ☎ 01598 763732 (Trevor & Vicki)
www.southdeancottage.co.uk
£400-£500 Sleeps 6. 1 cottage.
Half a mile from cliff walk. ⊛ 🐾

☆ Martinhoe Cleave Cottages
☎ 01598 763313 (Bob & Heather Deville)
www.exmoorhideaway.co.uk
£290-£435 Sleeps 2. 3 cottages.
Ramblers' paradise for coast and country! 🐾 ★★★★

Three delightful cottages within the Exmoor National Park and adjoining the South West Coast Path. Perfect for exploring this spectacular area of coast and countryside. Of the highest standard throughout, with many extras included. Dogs welcome at no extra cost.

● Moretonhampstead
DARTMOOR

☆ Budleigh Farm
☎ 01647 440835 (Judith Harvey)
www.budleighfarm.co.uk
£150-£510 Sleeps 2-6. 7 varying types.
Heated outdoor swimming pool (summer only). ⊛ 🐾 ★★-★★★

Climb our hill and admire Dartmoor from the site of an Iron Age fort. There's not much left of the fort, but the view is stunning.
Visit historic cities, secret villages, tumbling streams, superb beaches; admire bluebell woods and wildflowers; roam Dartmoor, and sleep soundly after walking the Tors. Short breaks.

● Oare
EXMOOR

☆ Cloud Farm
☎ 01598 741234 (Jill Harman) www.doonevalleyholidays.co.uk
£235-£895 Sleeps 2-8. 3 cottages.
Idyllic riverside setting. Perfect walking base.
🐾 ★★★★ See Hostels also.

Cloud Farm's idyllic riverside setting in the tranquility of the Exmoor National Park's Doone Valley provides perfect 'away-from-it-all' holidays and short breaks all year round.

Three farmhouse cottage accommodations, all newly refurbished, set in an unspoilt paradise for walking, relaxing, exploring, watching wildlife, or riding from our stables (all ages and levels).

Excellent base for touring nearby villages and walking the South West Coast Path. Shop, off-licence, tearoom, gardens, laundry facilities on-site.

FOUND SOMEWHERE GOOD THAT'S NOT IN THE GUIDE?
Fill in the Recommendation/Feedback Form on p123 and send it to the editor at our central office or email:
yearbook@ramblers.org.uk

● Okehampton
DARTMOOR

☆ East Hook Holiday Cottages
☎ 01837 52305 (Mrs M E Stevens)
www.easthook-holiday-cottages.co.uk
£175-£480 Sleeps 2-6. 3 cottages.
Dartmoor fringe, Tarka Trail, woodland walks. 🐾 ★★-★★★★

Heart of glorious Devon with beautiful panoramic view of Dartmoor. Set in own grounds, three idyllic country cottages with oak beams and log fire. Wonderful charm and ambience. Comfortable, peaceful and relaxing.

● Sidmouth
Ann Bowden ☎ 01392 841984 philann@bowthom.fsnet.co.uk
£130-£460 Sleeps 4. 1 bungalow. Closed Jan
Rural location on Jurassic Heritage coast. ⊛ 🐾

Cornerstone ☎ 01275 392148 (Cliff & Val Bond) www.c4miles.me.uk
£125 Sleeps 6. 1 bungalow.
Sea views, quiet site, indoor pool. ⊛ 🐾 ★★★

● Tavistock
DARTMOOR
Langstone Manor ☎ 01822 613371 (Jane Kellett)
http://langstone-manor.co.uk
£160-£580 Sleeps 2-7. 2 cottages, 2 apts, 7 static caravans. Closed Dec-Feb
Direct access onto Dartmoor. Bar meals. ⊛ 🐾 ★★★★ See Hostels also.

Higher Longford Caravan & Camping Park ☎ 01822 613360
www.higherlongford.co.uk
£180-£395 Sleeps 2-4+cot. 4 cottages & touring caravan park.
All-inclusive costs. Direct access to moors. ⊛ 🐾 ★★★-★★★★

● Teignmouth
Bowden Close House ☎ 01803 328029 (Sarah Farquharson)
www.bowdenclose.co.uk
£195-£560 Sleeps 2-4. 6 cottages/apts.
South West Coast Path on doorstep. ⊛ ★★★

● Torquay
Appletorre Flats ☎ 01803 296430 (Mrs C Moon)
www.appletorreflats.co.uk
£120-£410 Sleeps 1-5. 9 flats. Close to South West Coast Path. ⋙(Torquay)
⊛ ★★★

● Whimple
Lower Southbrook Farm ☎ 01404 822989 (Angela Lang)
www.lowersouthbrookfarm.co.uk
£190-£420 Sleeps 4-6. 3 cottages.
Comfortable accommodation in delightful rural situation. 🐾 ★★★

● Widecombe-in-the-Moor
DARTMOOR
Lower Blackaton ☎ 01364 621369 (Judy Lomax)
www.lowerblackaton.co.uk
£500-£1,400 Sleeps 6-12. 1 farmhouse/cottage.
Renovated farmhouse, superb moorland/farmland scenery. ⊛ 🐾 See B&B also.

☆ **Wooder Manor**
☎ 01364 621391 (Angela Bell)
www.woodermanor.com
£180-£1,050 Sleeps 2-12. 5 varying types. Beautiful quiet location,
with central heating. 🛏 ★★★-★★★★ Access category 2.

Cottages in picturesque valley, surrounded by moors and granite tors. Peaceful location with lovely walks from doorstep. Clean & well equipped. Central heating. Gardens. Easy parking. Open all year. Good food at two local inns. Colour brochure. Sleeps 2-4, 4-6, 8-12. Groups welcome.

☆ **Pitt Park**
☎ 01364 621309 (Hilary Jarvis)
timandhilary@barns2.fsnet.co.uk
£150-£400 Sleeps 2-5. 1 coach house..
Woodburning stove. Weekend/short breaks welcome. 🚭 🛏

Detached property set in 2 acres on a quiet country lane 1.25 miles from village with views of Hamel Down. Direct access onto moors for beautiful scenic walks. Walk to local pubs serving excellent food.

● Witherage

☆ **Newhouse Farm Cottages**
☎ 01884 860266 (Keith Jenkins)
www.newhousecottages.com
£235-£1,550 Sleeps 1-40. 8 cottages.
Peaceful location, stunning views. Swimming pool. 🚭 🛏

Eight beautifully converted well-equipped cosy Grade II-listed stone barns, some with wood-burning stoves. Choice of accommodation from one bedroom with four-poster bed to our five bedroom barn sleeping ten. Set in 23 acres of peaceful meadows with many enjoyable local walks.

DORSET

● Abbotsbury

Gorwell Farm ☎ 01305 871401 (Mrs J M Pengelly) www.gorwellfarm.co.uk
£200-£980 Sleeps 2-8. 6 cottages.
Coastal path, Macmillan Way. Wheelchair access.
🚭 🛏 ★★★★-★★★★★ Access category 2.

● Bridport

☆ **Rudge Farm**
☎ 01308 482630 (Mike Hamer)
www.rudgefarm.co.uk
£270-£795 Sleeps 2-6. 10 cottages.
🚭 ★★★★

Rudge Farm is an ideal walking base for the beautiful Bride Valley and is just over 2 miles from Dorset's World Heritage Coastline.

The old farm buildings have been converted into well equipped, comfortable cottages ranged around a flower decked cobbled yard enjoying views across the valley towards the coast. There are a number of leisure facilities on the farm including a tennis court and games barn.

● Corfe Castle

☆ **Manor Farm Barn**
☎ 07909 533107 (Marc Watton)
www.2manorfarmbarn.co.uk
£550-£1050 Sleeps 8+cot. 1 cottage.
Self-contained garden. ⚑(Wool) 🚭 🛏

Converted Dorset barn offering an extremely high standard of accommodation full of charm and ample space for eight people. Situated 5 miles from Lulworth Cove, the barn is in a hamlet in beautiful Dorset countryside, with views across the river Frome.

● Dorchester

Sandyholme Holiday Park ☎ 01305 852677 (Reception)
www.sandyholme.co.uk
£160-£550 Sleeps 2-6. 25 caravans. Closed Nov-Mar ⚑(Moreton) 🛏

● Langton Matravers

April Cottage ☎ 01929 405520 (Roger & Jo Jupp)
www.aprilcottage-dorset.co.uk
£275-£800 Sleeps 2-8. 1 cottage.
Superb coast and country walking area. 🚭 Ⓜ

● Lyme Regis

The Gables Holiday Apartments ☎ 01297 442536 (Alan Simpson)
www.thegableslymeregis.co.uk
£160-£473 Sleeps 2-6. 10 flats. 50 yards from Heritage Coast. 🚭 ★★★

● Swanage

Alrose Villa Apartments ☎ 01929 426318 (Jacqui Wilson)
www.alrosevilla.co.uk
£180-£460 Sleeps 2-6. 4 apartments. Closed Nov-Feb
100m to beach. Some baconies. Sea views. 🚭 🛏 ★★★

Bayview ☎ 01252 328845 (Sue Johnson)
www.bayviewswanage.co.uk
£180-£760 Sleeps 2-8. 1 house.
Central coast paths/town. Panoramic views. Couples discount. ⊗

☆ Westland Flats
☎ 01929 422637 (Mrs J Hancock)
www.westlandflats.co.uk
£110-£440 Sleeps 2-6. 6 flats, 2 maisonettes.
♿

Westland consists of three flats, two maisonettes and three studio flats, all self-contained with private bathrooms and fully equipped, including colour TV. Well situated to explore the Purbeck peninsular and Jurassic Coast. Private car parking. Bed linen hire available.

☆ Robin's Nest
☎ 07930 304828 (Lorraine Wyatt)
caltra@aol.com Sleeps 4. 1 cottage.
Newly renovated, overlooking Purbeck Hills.
⊗

Grade II-listed two-bedroom cottage commanding good views over the town to the Purbeck Hills. Excellent base for Studland and coastal walks.

Refurbished with GCH, cosy lounge, stone fireplace, TV and DVD. Country-style kitchen with washing machine, cooker and dining facilities. Tiled bathroom with heated towel rail, bath and Mira shower. Delightful and relaxing bedrooms with fitted/double wardrobes. Front paved seating area with mature south-facing garden.

Sandhaven ☎ 01929 422322 (Janet Foran)
www.sandhaven-guest-house.co.uk
£250-£750 Sleeps 4-6. 1 cottage.. Recently refurbished 200-year-old inglenook fireplace. ⊗ ♿ ★★★★ See B&B also.

GLOUCESTERSHIRE

● Chipping Campden
Weston Park Farm ☎ 01386 840835 (Mrs J Whitehouse)
http://cotswoldcottages.uk.com
£175-£575 Sleeps 2-5. 1 coach house flat, 2 cottages.
Magnificently situated on Cotswold Way. ♿ ★★★-★★★★★ See B&B also.

● Dursley
Two Springbank ☎ 01453 543047 (Mrs F A Jones)
lhandfaj32lg@surefish.co.uk
£174-£246 Sleeps 4. 1 cottage.
Tranquil village setting near Cotswold Way. ⊗ ᴡᴡ(Cam & Dursley) ★★★

● Elkstone
The Grannery ☎ 01242 870375 (Lois Eyre)
www.cottageguide.co.uk/grannery
£195-£315 Sleeps 1-2. Wing of country house. Closed Jan
Comfortable, walker-friendly, map loan, optional extras. ⊗ ♿

● Little Drybrook
Middle Cottage ☎ 01594 562736 (Angela Flynn)
www.middlerelax.co.uk
£190-£380 Sleeps 4. 1 cottage. Forest of Dean paths from gate. ⊗

● Mitcheldean

☆ Church Farm
☎ 01594 541211 (Lucy & John Verity)
www.churchfarm.uk.net
£200-£350 Sleeps 2-3. 2 apartments. Closed Feb
Situated on farm in Forest of Dean. ⊗ ♿ ★★★

The apartments are situated in a high-standard converted granary on our farm, offering direct walking in 20,000 acres of the Forest of Dean. Trails lasting from 30mins to three hours take you through oak woodland, tranquil ponds, with magnificent views over the Wye and Severn rivers. Pets welcome.

● Stanton

☆ Charity Farm
☎ 01386 584339 (Mrs V Ryland)
www.myrtle-cottage.co.uk/ryland.htm
£215-£550 Sleeps 2-6. 2 cottages.
Idyllic situation near Cotswold Way. ♿ ★★★

Charming Cotswold stone cottages in picturesque village on the Cotswold Way. Pretty gardens offer 'al fresco' dining. Village pub serves food and Broadway has a selection of pubs and restaurants. Walk the hills or visit National Trust houses and gardens.

● Stroud
Middle Farm ☎ 01453 824659 (Fleur Alvares) www.cotswoldsview.co.uk
£320-£495 Sleeps 6. 1 cottage.
Cotswold Way, wonderful views, real fire. ᴡᴡ(Stonehouse) ⊗ ♿

● Wotton-under-Edge
Hollywell Farm ☎ 07887 520890 (Maggie Sampson)
www.webspawner.com/users/cotswoldwaybb
£150-£300 Sleeps 4. Self-contained annex..
Beautiful views and spacious garden. ⊗ ♿ See B&B also.

SOMERSET

● Burrowbridge
Hillview ☎ 01823 698308 (Ros Griffiths)
£185-£210 Sleeps 2. Bungalow annexe.
Fully equipped, central heating. Rural location. ⊗ ♿ ★★★

● Cheddar

☆ Home Farm
☎ 01934 842078 (Chris & Sue Sanders)
www.homefarmcottages.com
£240-£685 Sleeps 1-8. 4 cottages. Closed Jan
Ⓢ ★★★★

Four beautifully converted stone barns with original beams. Set in two acres of an area of outstanding natural beauty, and surrounded by farm and National Trust land. Many local walks. All cottages are comfortable warm and fully equipped.

Sungate Holiday Apartments ☎ 01934 842273 (Mrs M M Fieldhouse)
http://sungateholidayapartments.co.uk
£140-£185 Sleeps 1-5. 4 apartments.
Fully equipped with laundry facilities available. Ⓢ 🦮 ★★★

☆ Bradley Cross Farm
☎ 01934 741771 (Judy Credland)
www.bradleycrossfarm.org.uk
£150-£210 Sleeps 2. 1 cottage. Closed Oct-Mar
Panoramic views over the Somerset Levels. 🦮

Single room stone-built cottage with bunk-beds and separate kitchen and bathroom, on working farm. Situated high on the Mendip Hills, one mile from Cheddar Gorge, with spectacular views over the Somerset Levels.

Close to the West Mendip Way walk.

Venns Views ☎ 01934 741920 (Lawrence Leigh-Coop & Perry Agate)
www.vennsviews.co.uk
£150-£310 Sleeps 2. 4 studio flats. Closed Dec-Jan
Small apartments, big views, private parking. 🦮

● Crewkerne
Mrs Z Morgan ☎ 01460 77259
zenamorgan@hotmail.co.uk
£100-£150 Sleeps 2-4. 1 property.
Listed building in rural setting. 🚂(Crewkerne) 🦮 Ⓜ

● Exford
EXMOOR

Court Farm ☎ 0845 226 7154 (Mr & Mrs Horstmann)
www.courtfarm.co.uk
£180-£350 Sleeps 2-5. 3 cottages.
Adjacent to river with private gardens. 🦮 ★★★★

● Minehead
EXMOOR

Woodcombe Lodge ☎ 01643 702789 (Nicola Hanson)
www.woodcombelodge.co.uk
£120-£1,150 Sleeps 2-12.
6 pine lodges, 2 cottages. Wonderful views, 2.5 acre gardens. 🦮 ★★★★

● Porlock
EXMOOR

☆ The Pack Horse
☎ 01643 862475 (Linda & Brian Garner)
www.thepackhorse.net
£230-£495 Sleeps 2-6. 4 apartments, 1 cottage.
Located in idyllic National Trust village. 🦮 ★★★-★★★★

Our self-catering apartments and cottage are situated in this unique location alongside the shallow river Aller overlooking the famous Pack Horse Bridge. Enjoy immediate access from our doorstep to the beautiful surrounding countryside, pretty villages, spectacular coast & Exmoor. Open all year. Short breaks. Private parking.

● Roadwater
EXMOOR

Lyndale ☎ 01984 641426 (John Middleton) www.uk-holiday-cottages.co.uk/lyndale
£230-£450 Sleeps 4-6. 1 cottage.
Idyllic varied walking on Coleridge Way. Ⓢ 🦮 Ⓜ

● Shepton Mallet
Knowle Farm Cottages ☎ 01749 890482 (Helen Trotman)
www.knowle-farm-cottages.co.uk
£160-£520 Sleeps 2-6. 4 cottages. Ⓢ ★★★★

● Simonsbath
EXMOOR

Wintershead Farm ☎ 01643 831222 (Jane Styles) www.wintershead.co.uk
£250-£675 Sleeps 2-6. 5 cottages. Closed Jan-Feb
Ideal base for a walking holiday. 🦮 ★★★★

● Watchet
Croft Holiday Cottages ☎ 01984 631121 (Andrew & Kirsten Musgrave)
www.cottagessomerset.com
£140-£690 Sleeps 2-8. 7 cottages & bungalows.
Heated indoor swimming pool. Steam railway nearby. 🦮 ★★★★

WILTSHIRE

● Devizes
Tichborne's Farm Cottages ☎ 01380 862971 (Jon & Judy Nash)
www.tichbornes.co.uk
£266-£476 Sleeps 4. 3 cottages.
Converted stables in rural Wiltshire. Ⓢ 🦮 ★★★★

● Marlborough

☆ Dairy Cottage
☎ 01672 515129 (Hazel & Mark Crockford)
www.marlboroughholidaycottages.co.uk
£300-£650 Sleeps 6-8. 1 cottage. Ⓢ 🦮 ★★★
Peaceful bungalow on edge of Savernake Forest. See B&B also.

Dairy Cottage is situated on Brown's Farm, which is a working dairy/arable farm. Set on the edge of Savernake Forest overlooking open farmland, Dairy Cottage offers peace and tranquility for a true north Wiltshire holiday. A modern spacious, well-equipped bungalow with open fire awaits your arrival.

● Warminster
St James Court ☎ 01985 840568 (Anna Giddings) www.wiltscottages.com
£250-£590 Sleeps 5-6. 3 cottages. Closed Feb Ⓢ ★★★★

GROUPS

CORNWALL

Cutkive Wood Holiday Lodges (SC) St Ive, Liskeard PL14 3ND
☎ 01579 362216 (Andy & Jackie Lowman)
www.cutkivewood.co.uk Grid Ref: SX 292676
SC £120-£440 Min 1, max 30. 6 lodges. D ⊗ See SC also.

DEVON

☆ **Royal York & Faulkner Hotel** (BB)
Sidmouth ☎ Freephone 0800 220714
www.royalyorkhotel.co.uk
DBB £35.25-£52.60 Min 30, max 90. Closed Jan
✗ 🐾 B D ★★⑤

Beautifully appointed Regency hotel in centre of Sidmouth's elegant esplanade, adjacent to picturesque town centre. Family-run with excellent amenities and facilities. On the Jurassic Coast World Heritage site, ideally situated for walking the superb coastal paths and inland walks with stunning flora, fauna and views. Regular host to Ramblers Groups.

DORSET

☆ **Churchview Guesthouse** (BB)
Winterbourne Abbas, Dorchester DT2 9LS ☎ 01305 889296
(Michael & Jane Deller) www.churchview.co.uk Map 194/618905
BB £34-£42 Max 17.
✗ 🐾 B D ! 🚗 ◆◆◆◆ See B&B also.

Our beautiful 17th century guest house is ideal for groups wishing to explore west Dorset. We cater for up to 17 (more by arrangement with local B&Bs). Delicious evening meal. Two lounges and bar. Group rates. Call Michael & Jane Deller. Email: stay@churchview.co.uk

HOSTELS, BUNKHOUSES & CAMPSITES

CORNWALL

North Shore Bude (IH) 57 Killerton Road, Bude EX23 8EW
☎ 01288 354256 www.northshorebude.com
Bednight £12 Closed Xmas
✗ nearby B D ⊗ ★★★ Hostel

DEVON   >>

DARTMOOR

Langstone Manor (C) Moortown, Tavistock, PL19 9JZ
☎ 01822 613371 (Jane Kellett)
www.langstone-manor.co.uk Map 201/528734
Camping £8 Closed Nov–mid-Mar
✗ B D ★★★★ See SC also.

SOMERSET

Bowdens Crest Caravan & Camping Park (C) Bowdens, Langport TA10 0DD
☎ 01458 250553 www.bowdenscrest.co.uk
Camping £5 Caravans for hire. ✗ 🐾 B ★★★

Sandringham Hotel (BB) 20 Durlston Rd, Swanage BH19 2HX
☎ 01929 423076 (Mr & Mrs Silk)
www.smoothhound.co.uk/hotels/sandringham.html
Map 195/033782 BB £30-£40 Max 25. Closed mid-July-Aug
✗ 🐾 B D ! 🚗 See B&B also.

WILTSHIRE

☆ **Mayfield House Hotel** (B&B)
Crudwell, Malmesbury SN16 9EW ☎ 01666 577409 (Max or Chris)
www.mayfieldhousehotel.co.uk Map 173/954928
DBB £36 Min 2, max 46.
✗ 🐾 B D See B&B also.

Explore the Cotswolds

Friendly country house hotel in the heart of the Cotswolds. Excellent restaurant. Fresh food and plenty of it! Proprietor run, 26 lovely bedrooms, regularly used by walking groups. Group rates from £36pppn. Dinner, bed and breakfast. Ask for Max or Chris. reception@mayfieldhousehotel.co.uk
AA 3 stars. Award-winning food.

☆ **Cloud Farm** (C)
Oare, Lynton
☎ 01598 741234
www.doonevalleyholidays.co.uk Grid ref: 794468
Bednight £5-7.50 ✗ nearby D See SC also.

Cloud Farm's idyllic riverside setting in the tranquility of the Exmoor National Park's Doone Valley, provides perfect 'away-from-it-all' camping all year.

Three spacious riverside camping/caravan fields, set in an unspoilt paradise for walking, relaxing, watching wildlife, or riding from our stables (all ages and levels). Excellent base for touring nearby villages and walking the South West Coast Path.

Shop, selling food and camping supplies. Laundry facilities and new shower block on-site.

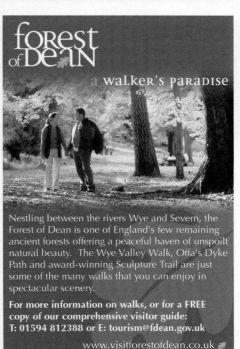

SOUTH

Long Distance Paths

Icknield Way Path ....ICK

Isle of Wight Coastal Path.....IWC

Macmillan Way...................MCM

Midshires Way....................MDS

Monarch's Way.................MON

North Downs Way ....NDN

Ridgeway ....RDG

Solent Way...........................SOL

South Downs Way ....SDN

Thames Path......................THM

Wealdway ....WLD

See Paths & Access p25 for full details of LDPs and waymarks

National Parks

New Forest

South Downs*

See Useful Contacts p99 for full details of national parks

LONG MAN OF WILMINGTON ON WINDOVER HILL, SOUTH DOWNS

WALK...   ...THE FOX WAY

You may spot a few foxes as you go, but this new 63km/39-mile circular route around Guildford is in fact less cunningly named after Richard Fox who established it in conjunction with Surrey Wildlife Trust last year. It's a gentle trail through pretty woodland, quiet villages and verdant canals, briefly visiting the North Downs. Well waymarked with yellow discs and broken into seven easy stages, it offers excellent family-friendly walks of between one and a half to three and a half hours.

A guidebook with details of stop-offs, transport links and historic buildings en route is available from www.thefoxway.com

SOUTH

VISIT...

...THE CHILTERN SCULPTURE TRAIL

High in the Chiltern Hills nestles Cowleaze Wood and the Chiltern Sculpture Trail, where over 20 unique works of art sit among the trees. Each is specially designed to integrate and interact with its natural surrounding – and often in surprising ways. Coin-covered beech trees, beautifully woven hazel-wood structures, and a series of irreverent waymarkers are just some of the exhibits to be discovered. It's a fascinating detour for walkers of the nearby Ridgeway and Oxfordshire Way.

For more information, visit www.chilternsculpturetrail.co.uk

SEE...   ...THE GREAT TREES OF LONDON

The charity Trees for Cities has awarded 'Great Tree' status to 41 specimens around the capital for either being very old, very big, unusually shaped, historically significant or famous. Among them are a mulberry in Charlton planted at Charles I's request to promote a once flourishing silk trade, and a spectacular riverside cut-leaf beech in York House grounds (pictured). Finding these venerable timbers can be a fun game of treasure hunt and makes for some pleasant excursions around London's green spaces.

Each is lovingly documented with directions at www.treesforcities.com

LOCAL RAMBLERS GROUPS... The Valley Gardens at Great Park, Windsor, remain free to the public after Crown Estate plans to fence in the area were successfully opposed by East Berkshire Group. Visit www.thecrownestate.co.uk for details and a downloadable map... **The popular seafront path passing under Southend's famous pier (the longest in Britain) is now unblocked after more than two years of lobbying by Southend Group**... Buckinghamshire and West Middlesex Area offer a series of the best walks in the region on their website (see p69), with detailed route descriptions and maps or DIY instructions.

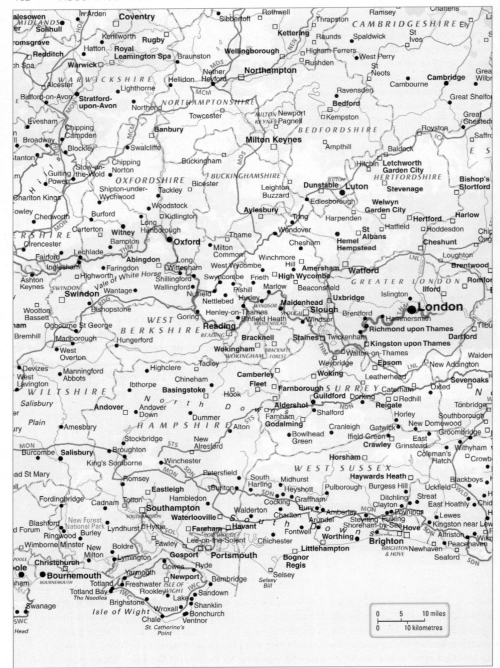

MAP 163

BED & BREAKFAST

BERKSHIRE

● Hurley (Maidenhead)
THAMES PATH & LONDON LOOP
Hurley Bed and Breakfast, The Old Farm House, High St, SL6 5NB
☎ 01628 825446 (Katie Gear)
www.hurleybedandbreakfast.co.uk Map 175/825839
BB **D** ✕ nearby D3 T2 Ⓑ ⊗ 🐾🛁 ◆◆◆◆

● Maidenhead
THAMES PATH
▪️◄ Sheephouse Manor Guest House, Sheephouse Road, SL6 8HJ
☎ 01628 776902 (Mrs C J Street)
www.sheephousemanor.co.uk Map 175/898831
BB **D** S2 D1 Closed Xmas ᴍᴍ(Maidenhead) Ⓑ Ⓓ ⊗ 🐾🛁! 🛏 ◆◆◆

▪️◄ Amerden Lodge, Old Marsh Lane, SL6 0EE ☎ 01628 673458 (Jane Saw)
nigel_saw@lineone.net Map 175/913796
BB **D** ✕ book first £10, 7:30pm D1 T1 ᴍᴍ(Taplow)
Ⓥ Ⓑ Ⓓ ⊗ 🐾🛁🚗

● Windsor
THAMES PATH
▪️◄ The Laurells, 22 Dedworth Road, SL4 5AY
☎ 01753 855821 (Mrs Joyce) Map 175,176/952765
BB **C** ✕ nearby S1 T2 Closed Xmas ᴍᴍ(Central & Riverside) Ⓓ ⊗ 🐾🛁

BUCKINGHAMSHIRE

● Chesham
▪️◄ 49 Lowndes Avenue, HP5 2HH ☎ 01494 792647 (Mrs P Orme)
pageormelowndes@tiscali.co.uk Map 165/957021
BB **C** ✕ nearby S1 T1 ᴍᴍ(Chesham) Ⓓ ⊗ 🛁 🚗 🛏 ★★★

● Edlesborough (Dunstable)
RIDGEWAY & ICKNIELD WAY
Ridgeway End, 5 Ivinghoe Way, LU6 2EL
☎ 01525 220405 (Mr & Mrs Lloyd)
www.ridgewayend.co.uk Map 165/974183
BB **D** ✕ nearby S1 D1 T1 F1 Closed Xmas Ⓑ Ⓓ ⊗ 🐾🛁🚗!

● Marlow
THAMES PATH

☆ ▪️◄ **Merrie Hollow**
Seymour Court Hill, Marlow Road, SL7 3DE
☎ 01628 485663 (Mr & Mrs B Wells) Map 175/837889
BB **C** ✕ book first £12, 7-8pm D1 T1 Closed Xmas ᴍᴍ(Marlow)
Ⓥ Ⓓ ⊗ 🐾🛁🚗 🛏

Secluded country house in
large garden.
150 yards off B428 Marlow
to Stokenchurch Road.
Easy access to M4 and
M25, and also to Heathrow
and Oxford.

● Wendover (Aylesbury)
RIDGEWAY
26 Chiltern Road, HP22 6DB
☎ 01296 622351 (Mrs E C Condie) Map 165/865082
BB **B** ✕ nearby S1 T/F1 Closed Xmas ᴍᴍ(Wendover) Ⓓ ⊗ 🛁 🛏 Ⓜ ◆

● West Wycombe (High Wycombe)
The Swan Inn, HP14 3AE ☎ 01494 527031 Map 175/829945
BB **D** ✕ nearby S1 D2 T1 F1 Closed Xmas ᴍᴍ(Saunderton)

● Winchmore Hill (Amersham)

☆ ▪️◄ **The Potters Arms**
Fognall Lane, HP7 0PH ☎ 01494 722641 (Carol & Irvin Dean)
pottersarms@hotmail.com Map 175/933948
BB **A** ✕ nearby D3
Ⓥ Ⓑ Ⓓ 🐾🛁! 🛏

Picturesque village located in the Chilterns.
Friendly pub atmosphere with B&B facilities,
catering for people who wish to explore
superb locality.
Delicious homemade food available morning,
noon and night. Great base for walkers who
want a memorable experience.

HAMPSHIRE

● Andover Down (Andover)
▪️◄ Forest Edge, SP11 6LJ ☎ 01264 364526
www.forest-edge.co.uk Map 185/400462
BB **D** ✕ book first £15, 7:30pm D2 T2 Ⓥ Ⓑ Ⓓ ⊗ 🐾🛁 ◆◆◆◆Ⓢ

● Blashford (Ringwood)
Fraser House, Salisbury Road, BH24 3PB ☎ 01425 473958 (Mr & Mrs M Burt)
www.fraserhouse.net Map 195/151066
BB **C/D** D3 T2 F1 Ⓥ Ⓑ ⊗ 🐾🛁 🛏 ◆◆◆◆

● Boldre (Brockenhurst)
NEW FOREST
SOLENT WAY
▪️◄ Hilden B&B, Southampton Road, SO41 8PT ☎ 01590 623682
(Mrs A Arnold-Brown) www.newforestbandb-hilden.co.uk Map 196/307989
BB **C** ✕ nearby D/F3 ᴍᴍ(Brockenhurst) Ⓑ Ⓓ 🛁 ! 🛏

● Broughton (Stockbridge)
MONARCH'S WAY
Kings, Salisbury Road, SO20 8BY
☎ 01794 301458 (Ann Heather) Map 185/300336
BB **B** ✕ book first £7.50-£10 D1 T1 Closed Xmas Ⓥ Ⓑ Ⓓ 🐾🛁🚗!

● Buriton (Petersfield)
SOUTH DOWNS*
SOUTH DOWNS WAY
Nursted Farm, GU31 5RW
☎ 01730 264278 (Mrs M Bray) Map 197/754214
BB **B** ✕ nearby D1 T2 F1 Closed Xmas/Mar-Apr ᴍᴍ(Petersfield)
Ⓓ ⊗ 🐾🚗

● Burley (Ringwood)
NEW FOREST
Holmans, Bisterne Close, BH24 4AZ ☎ 01425 402307 (Robin & Mary Ford)
Map 195/229025 BB **D** ✕ nearby D2 T1 Closed Xmas
Ⓑ Ⓓ ⊗ 🛁 ! 🛏 ◆◆◆◆Ⓖ Stabling for horses.

● Cadnam
NEW FOREST

Kingsbridge House, Southampton Road, SO40 2NH ☎ 023 8081 1161
(Linda Goodrich) www.kingsbridgehousebandb.co.uk Map 196/296135
BB **C/D** ✗ nearby D2 F1

🅑 🅓 ⊗ 🐕🛏🚗 ! ◆◆◆◆ See Lyndhurst SC also.

● Chineham (Basingstoke)

☆ 🍴 **The Hampshire Centrecourt**
Centre Drive, Great Binfields Road, RG24 8FY ☎ 01256 319700 (John Cotter)
www.marstonhotels.com Map 185,186/658542
BB **D** ✗ £27.50, 7-9.45pm S27 D55 F1

🅥 🅑 🛏 ★★★★ Wheelchair access.

Conveniently located close to the Basingstoke
Canal and surrounding countryside, the hotel is
the ideal place to relax, with extensive
swimming, tennis, gym, sauna and spa
facilities. Comfortable and stylish bedrooms.
Please ask about our exclusive rates for
walking parties.

● Dummer (Basingstoke)

☆ 🍴 **Oakdown Farm**
RG23 7LR ☎ 01256 397218 (Mrs E Hutton)
Map 185/587472
BB **B** ✗ nearby D1 T2

🅓 ⊗ 🐕🛏🚗 ! 🅗 Ⓜ ◆◆◆

Wayfarers Walk 200 metres.
North of Junction 7 M3.
Secluded position.
Evening meal locally.
Lifts available.
Car parking.

● Fordingbridge (Alderholt)
NEW FOREST

Alderholt Mill, Sandleheath Road, SP6 1PU
☎ 01425 653130 (Mr & Mrs R Harte) www.alderholtmill.co.uk Map 195/119143
BB **C/D** ✗ book first £15, 7-8:30pm S1 D3 T1 Closed Xmas

🅥 🅑 🅓 ⊗ 🐕🛏🚗 ! 🅗 ★★★★ See SC also.

● Hambledon (Waterlooville)
MONARCH'S WAY

🍴 Mornington House, Speltham Hill, PO7 4RU
☎ 023 9263 2704 (Mr & Mrs Lutyens) Map 196/644149
BB **B** ✗ nearby T2 Closed Xmas 🅓 🐕🛏🚗 🅗

● Highclere (Newbury)

Westridge (Open Centre), Star Lane – off A343, RG20 9PJ
☎ 01635 253322 Map 174/436604
BB **A** ✗ nearby T2 Closed Xmas 🅓 🛏 Booking ahead essential.

● Ibthorpe (Andover)

Staggs Cottage, Windmill Hill, Hurstbourne Tarrant, SP11 0BP
☎ 01264 736235 (Mr & Mrs Norton)
www.staggscottage.co.uk Map 185/374536
BB **C** ✗ book first £10, 6-9pm D1 T2 🅥 🅓 🐕🛏🚗 🅗 Ⓜ ◆◆◆◆

● King's Somborne (Stockbridge)
MONARCH'S WAY & TEST WAY

🍴 High View, 12 Nutcher Drove, SO20 6PA ☎ 01794 388626
(Frances Shone) pjshone@btinternet.com Map 185/363313
BB **B** ✗ book first £15, 6-8pm D1 🅥 🅑 🅓 ⊗ 🐕🛏🚗 ! 🅗

● Lymington
NEW FOREST
SOLENT WAY

🍴 Honeysuckle House, 24 Clinton Road, SO41 9EA ☎ 01590 676635
(Mrs P Farrell) www.newforest.demon.co.uk/honeysuckle.htm Map 196/322962
BB **C** ✗ nearby S1 D1 🚋(Lymington Town) 🅥 🅑 🅓 ⊗ 🐕🛏

● Lyndhurst
NEW FOREST

🍴 Stable End, Emery Down, SO43 7FJ ☎ 023 8028 2504
(William & Mary Dibben) dibbenfam@aol.com Map 196/290089
BB **D** ✗ nearby D1 T1 🚋(Ashurst) 🅑 🅓 ⊗ 🛏🚗 ! ◆◆◆◆

☆ 🍴 **Ormonde House Hotel**
Southampton Road, SO43 7BT ☎ 02380 282806 (Paul Ames)
www.ormondehouse.co.uk Map 196/305083
BB **D** ✗ book first £15-£21, 6:30-8pm S1 D17 T4 F1 Closed Xmas
🚋(Ashurst) 🅥 🅑 🅓 ⊗ 🐕🛏 ! 🅗 ★★

Perfect base for
walking; Ormonde
House Hotel &
Pinewood Cottage lie
opposite the open
forest, within walking
distance of Lyndhurst
village. Furnished to a
high standard the hotel
has 19 pretty en-suite
bedrooms with colour
TV & hairdryers.
Pinewood Cottage Suites are self-contained, fully serviced and have full kitchens
with washing machines, dryers & dishwashers.
Pets are welcome. Privately owned & renowned for its excellent home cuisine.
Discounts for midweek 4 day breaks & for parties of min. 6 out of season.
Email: enquiries@ormondehouse.co.uk

☆ **Burwood Lodge**
27 Romsey Road, SO43 7AA ☎ 023 8028 2445
www.burwoodlodge.co.uk Map 196/299083
BB **D** ✗ nearby S1 D3 T1 F2

🅑 🅓 ⊗ 🐕🛏🚗

Burwood Lodge Guest House is a
beautiful Edwardian property
which offers bed & breakfast
accommodation to a high
standard and is set in half an
acre of grounds with ample
private parking to the front.

● New Milton
NEW FOREST

🍴 St Ursula, 30 Hobart Road, BH25 6EG
☎ 01425 613515 (Mr & Mrs M Pearce) Map 195/239947
BB **C** ✗ nearby S2 D1 T2 F1 🚋(New Milton)
🅑 🅓 ⊗ 🐕🛏🚗 ! 🅗 ◆◆◆◆ Access Category 3.

SOUTH

● **Petersfield**
SOUTH DOWNS*
SOUTH DOWNS WAY

🚶🍴 Heath Farmhouse, GU31 4HU ☎ 01730 264709 (Mrs P Scurfield)
www.heathfarmhouse.co.uk Map 197/757224
BB **C** D1 T1 F1 Closed Xmas ⚌(Petersfield)
Ⓑ Ⓓ 🐾🛏🚗!🛁 ◆◆◆◆

🚶🍴 1 The Spain, Sheep St, GU32 3JZ ☎ 01730 263261 (Jennifer Tarver)
allantarver@ntlworld.com Map 197/748232
BB **D** ✗ nearby D2 T1 ⚌(Petersfield) Ⓑ Ⓓ⊗🐾🛏🚗!🛁 ◆◆◆◆

🚶🍴 Copper Beeches, Torberry Farm, Hurst, GU31 5RG ☎ 01730 826662
(Janet Chew) www.visitsussex.org/copperbeeches Map 197/768200
BB **C** D1 F1 Ⓑ Ⓓ⊗🐾🛏🚗!🛁 ◆◆◆

● **Romsey**
MONARCH'S WAY

Berties, 80 The Hundred, SO51 8BX ☎ 01794 830708
www.berties.co.uk Map 185/354211
BB **D** ✗ £11.05, 6:30-10pm S2 D5 T2 F1 ⚌(Romsey) Ⓥ Ⓑ🛁

● **Stockbridge**
MONARCH'S WAY

Carbery Guest House, Salisbury Hill, SO20 6EZ ☎ 01264 810771
Map 185/350351 BB **D** ✗ book first £16, 7pm S4 D4 T2 F1 Closed Xmas-Jan
Ⓥ Ⓑ Ⓓ 🐾🛁 ◆◆◆

● **Winchester**
MONARCH'S WAY & SOUTH DOWNS WAY

🚶🍴 St Margaret's, 3 St Michael's Road, SO23 9JE
☎ 01962 861450 (Brigid Brett) www.winchesterbandb.com Map 185/479290
BB **C** ✗ nearby S2 D1 T1 Closed Xmas ⚌(Winchester) Ⓓ⊗🛁 ◆◆◆

🚶🍴 5 Compton Road, SO23 9SL ☎ 01962 869199 (Gillian Davies)
vicb@csma-netlink.co.uk Map 185/476291
BB **B** ✗ nearby D/T2 F1 ⚌(Winchester) Ⓓ⊗🐾🛏🚗!Ⓜ ◆◆◆

🚶🍴 Brookside, Back St, St Cross, SO23 9SB ☎ 01962 854820 (Jane Harding)
www.brookside-stcross.co.uk Map 185/477279
BB **D** ✗ nearby D1 T1 Closed Xmas ⚌(Winchester)
Ⓑ Ⓓ⊗🛁🚗 ◆◆◆◆Ⓦ

ISLE OF WIGHT

● **Bembridge**
ISLE OF WIGHT COASTAL PATH

Sea Change, 22 Beachfield Road, PO35 5TN ☎ 01983 875558
(Vi & Richard Beet) www.seachangewight.co.uk Map 196/654875
BB **C/D** ✗ nearby D2 T1 Closed Oct-Mar Ⓑ⊗🐾🛏! ◆◆◆◆Ⓢ

● **Bonchurch (Ventnor)**
ISLE OF WIGHT COASTAL PATH

☆ **The Lake Hotel**
Shore Road, PO38 1RF ☎ 01983 852613
www.lakehotel.co.uk Map 196/572778
BB **D** ✗ £12, 6:30-7pm S2 D8 T6 F4 Closed Dec-Jan ⚌(Shanklin)
Ⓥ Ⓑ Ⓓ 🐾🛁🛁 ◆◆◆◆

Visiting beautiful Bonchurch? We offer
comfortable en-suite accommodation in
a country house hotel set in beautiful 2
acre garden. Same family run for last 40
years with assured first-class food and
comfort. Special 4-night break including
car-ferry, dinner/breakfast £175.

● **Brighstone**
ISLE OF WIGHT COASTAL PATH

Buddlebrook Guest House, Moortown Lane, PO30 4AN ☎ 01983 740381
www.buddlebrookguesthouse.co.uk Map 196/426832
BB **C** ✗ nearby D2 T1 Closed Xmas Ⓑ Ⓓ⊗🛁🛏🚗!🛁

● **Chale**
ISLE OF WIGHT COASTAL PATH

Cortina, Gotten Lane, PO38 2HQ
☎ 01983 551292 (Mrs E L Whittington) Map 196/487791
BB **C** ✗ nearby D1 T1 Closed Dec-Jan Ⓓ⊗🐾🚗!

🚶🍴 Butterfly Paragliding, Sunacre, The Terrace, PO38 2HL ☎ 01983 731611
(Miranda Botha) www.paraglide.uk.com Map 196/484774
BB **B** ✗ nearby T2 F1 Closed Xmas
Ⓓ⊗🐾🛏🚗! Organic & vegetarian food.

● **Cowes**
ISLE OF WIGHT COASTAL PATH

🚶🍴 Anchorage Guesthouse, 23 Mill Hill Road, PO31 7EE ☎ 01983 247975
www.anchoragecowes.co.uk Map 196/496956
BB **D** ✗ book first £12, to suit D1 T2 F1
Ⓥ Ⓑ Ⓓ⊗🐾🛏🚗! ★★★★

● **Freshwater**
ISLE OF WIGHT COASTAL PATH

🚶🍴 Rockstone Cottage, Colwell Chine Road, PO40 9NR ☎ 01983 753723
(Bob & Nicky Hurle) www.rockstonecottage.co.uk Map 196/329876
BB **C** ✗ nearby D2 T2 F1
Ⓑ Ⓓ⊗🐾🛏🚗!Ⓜ ◆◆◆◆Ⓢ Guide dogs accepted.

Seahorses, Victoria Road, PO40 9PP ☎ 01983 752574
www.seahorsesisleofwight.com Map 196/341866
BB **C** ✗ nearby D1 T1 F2 Ⓥ Ⓑ Ⓓ⊗🐾🛏🚗!🛁 ◆◆◆◆

🚶🍴 Ruskin Lodge Bed & Breakfast, Guyers Road, Freshwater Bay, PO40 9QA
☎ 01983 756604 www.ruskinlodge.com Map 196/342864
BB **C** ✗ nearby D1 T1 F1 Ⓑ Ⓓ⊗🐾🛏🚗!🛁

● **Lake (Sandown)**

Osterley Lodge, 62 Sandown Road, PO36 9JX ☎ 01983 402017 (Mrs S Horton)
www.netguides.co.uk/wight/basic/osterley.html Map 196/588828
BB **C** ✗ nearby D5 T2 ⚌(Lake) Ⓥ Ⓑ🛁 ◆◆◆◆

● **Rookley**

Sundowner B&B, Niton Rd, PO38 3NX ☎ 01983 721350 (Pauline & Peter Wade)
www.sundowner.iowight.com Map 196/508835
BB **B** ✗ nearby D2 T/F1 Closed Xmas Ⓑ Ⓓ⊗🐾🛏🚗 🛁

● **Sandown**
ISLE OF WIGHT COASTAL PATH

🚶🍴 Heathfield House, 52 Melville St, PO36 8LF ☎ 01983 400002
www.heathfieldhousehotel.com Map 196/595841
BB **C** ✗ nearby S3 D3 T1 F1 Closed Xmas ⚌(Sandown)
Ⓑ Ⓓ⊗🐾🛁 ◆◆◆

🚶🍴 Mount Brocas Guest House, 15 Beachfield Road, PO36 8LT
☎ 01983 406276 www.wightstay.co.uk/brocas.html Map 196/597840
BB **B** ✗ book first £5, 6pm D2 T3 F1 ⚌(Sandown)
Ⓥ Ⓑ Ⓓ⊗🐾🛁!

🚶🍴 Hazelwood Hotel, 19 Carter Street, PO36 8BL ☎ 01983 402536
(Pauline Wright) pwright@btinternet.com Map 196/600845
BB **B** ✗ book first £12, 6pm D2 T2 ⚌(Sandown) Ⓥ Ⓓ⊗🐾🛁🛁

● Shanklin
ISLE OF WIGHT COASTAL PATH

☆ Hambledon Hotel
11 Queens Road, PO37 6AW ☎ 01983 862403 (Bill Grindley)
www.step-by-step.co.uk Map 196/584814 BB **C** ✕ book first £12,
6:30-7pm S1 D5 T2 F2 Closed Nov-Jan ⋙(Shanklin) Ⓥ Ⓑ Ⓓ ⊗ 🍵
🛏 ! Ⓜ ◆◆◆◆ See Walking Holidays and main advert p179 also.

Ideally situated in Shanklin,
The Hambledon has proven to be a
great hotel to enjoy all the great
walking that the island has to offer.
All rooms en-suite with generous
beverage trays and colour TVs. Fully
licensed. Genuine home cooking.

🛏⋘ Atholl Court, 1 Atherley Road, PO37 7AT ☎ 01983 862414
(Chris & Jane Gaskin) www.atholl-court.co.uk Map 196/582818
BB **B/C** ✕ nearby, Xmas S3 D2 T3 ⋙(Shanklin) Ⓑ Ⓓ ⊗ 🍵 ★★★

The Edgecliffe Hotel, Clarence Gardens, PO37 6HA ☎ 01983 866199
(Mick & Dru Webster) www.wightonline.co.uk/edgecliffehotel Map 196/585820
BB **B/C/D** ✕ book first £10.95, 6:30pm S2 D4 T1 F3 ⋙(Shanklin)
Ⓥ Ⓑ Ⓓ ⊗ 🍵 ◆◆◆◆

🛏⋘ Culver View, 24 Upper Hyde Lane, PO37 7PR
☎ 01983 866944 (Pam Johnson) pam52@hotmail.co.uk Map 196/573815
BB **B** ✕ £12, 6:30-9pm D1 ⋙(Shanklin)
Ⓥ Ⓑ Ⓓ ⊗ 🍵 🛏 Ⓜ Vegetarian meals only.

☆ 🛏⋘ The Grange
9 Eastcliff Road, PO37 6AA ☎ 01983 867644
www.thegrangebythesea.com Map 196/582811
BB **D** ✕ book first £15, 7:30-8pm D8 T8 F1 ⋙(Shanklin) Ⓥ Ⓑ Ⓓ
⊗ 🍵 🛏 ◆◆◆◆ Twin room equipped for disabled guests.

Nestled in the heart of Shanklin's old
village, The Grange is friendly and
relaxed and makes the ideal starting
point for exploring the island.
Enjoy local coastline and countryside
walks, and relax with a sauna and
massage on your return!

The Hazelwood, 14 Clarence Road, PO37 7BH ☎ 01983 862824
(Phil Ramage) hazelwoodiow@aol.com Map 196/583820
BB **B** ✕ book first £10, 6pm S1 D3 T2 F2 ⋙(Shanklin) Ⓑ ⊗ 🛏 ◆◆◆

● Totland
ISLE OF WIGHT COASTAL PATH

☆ 🛏⋘ The Hermitage
Cliff Road, Totland Bay, PO39 0EW ☎ 01983 752518 (David & Jane Blake)
www.thehermitagebnb.com Map 196/320864
BB **C** ✕ book first £15, 7-8pm D2 T1 F1
Ⓥ Ⓑ Ⓓ ⊗ 🍵 🛏 ! 🛁

The Hermitage – a beautiful 1880s
Victorian home in the west Wight
(an area of outstanding natural beauty)
is situated between the coastal path
and the cliff edge immediately above
Totland Bay. An ideal centre for enjoying
all the country walks.

● Totland Bay
ISLE OF WIGHT COASTAL PATH

The Golf House, Alum Bay New Road, PO39 0JA ☎ 01983 753293
(Sue Blakemore) sue_blakemore@btinternet.com Map 196/317856
BB **D** ✕ nearby D2 Ⓥ Ⓑ Ⓓ ⊗ 🍵 🛏 🚗 !

● Ventnor
ISLE OF WIGHT COASTAL PATH

☆ Hillside Hotel
151 Mitchell Avenue, PO38 1DR ☎ 01983 852271
hillside-hotel@btconnect.com Map 196/565779
BB **D** ✕ book first £18, 7:30pm onwards S2 D7 T2 F1 Closed Xmas
Ⓥ Ⓑ Ⓓ ⊗ 🍵 🛏 ! 🛁 ★★

Simply delightful in summer & a comfortable
retreat in winter. Built circa 1789, Hillside is
Ventnor's oldest & only thatched hotel. Set in
2 acres of grounds, at the foot of St Boniface
Downs, with sea views. All bedrooms en-suite
with TV. Licensed bar. Extensive choice of
breakfast & evening menu. Dogs welcome.

🛏⋘ Hill House, 22 Spring Hill, PO38 1PF ☎ 01983 854581 (Barbara Roscoe)
www.hillhouse-ventnor.co.uk Map 196/565777
BB **C** ✕ nearby S1 D1 T1 F1 Ⓑ Ⓓ ⊗ 🍵 🛏 🚗 ! ◆◆◆

● Wroxall (Ventnor)
Will-o-Wisp Bed & Breakfast, Castle Road, PO38 3DU
☎ 01983 854241 (Hazel Wood) www.will-o-wisp.co.uk Map 196/552801
BB **B** ✕ book first £12.50, 6pm D1 ⋙(Shanklin)
Ⓥ Ⓑ Ⓓ ⊗ 🍵 🚗 !

● Yarmouth
ISLE OF WIGHT COASTAL PATH

🛏⋘ Wavells B&B & Bike Hire, The Square, PO41 0NP ☎ 01983 760738
www.yarmouthiw.fsworld.co.uk Map 196/355896
BB **C/D** ✕ nearby S1 D3 T1 F1 Ⓑ Ⓓ ⊗ 🛏 ! Ⓜ No children under 8.

The Laurels, Station Road, PO41 0QT ☎ 01983 761201 (Christine Hyland)
www.laurelsbb.com Map 196/357894
BB **D** ✕ nearby D1 T1 Ⓥ Ⓑ Ⓓ ⊗ 🍵 🛏 🚗 ! 🛁

KENT

● Bilsington (Ashford)
Willow Farm, Stone Cross, TN25 7JJ ☎ 01233 721700 (Mrs Hopper)
www.willowfarmenterprises.co.uk Map 189/028366
BB **C/D** ✕ nearby S1 D1 T1 F1 Closed Xmas Ⓓ 🍵 🚗 ! ◆◆◆
Organic establishment.

● Boughton Monchelsea (Maidstone)
🛏⋘ Wierton Hall Farm, East Hall Hill, ME17 4JU ☎ 01622 743535
(Lorraine Curteis) www.wiertonhallfarm.co.uk Map 188/784498
BB **D** ✕ nearby D1 T/D1 Ⓥ Ⓑ Ⓓ ⊗ 🍵 🚗 ! On Greensand Way.

● Charing (Ashford)
NORTH DOWNS WAY

23 The Moat, TN27 0JH ☎ 01233 713141 (Margaret Micklewright)
m.micklewright@btinternet.com Map 189/955492
BB **C** ✕ nearby T1 Closed Nov-Mar ⋙(Charing) Ⓑ Ⓓ ⊗ 🛏 Ⓜ

SOUTH

Timber Lodge B&B, Charing Hill, TN27 0NG
☎ 01233 713641 (Kevin Walters) www.timberlodge.co.uk Map 189/962500
BB **C** ✗ nearby S1 D1 F1 ✻(Charing) V B D ⊗ 🍵 ♨ 🚗 !

● Chartham (Canterbury)
NORTH DOWNS WAY

The Barn Oast, Nickle Farm, CT4 7PF ☎ 01227 731255 (Mary Arnold)
www.thebarnoast.co.uk Map 179/092561
BB **C** ✗ nearby D1 T1 F1 Closed Xmas ✻(Chartham) B D ⊗ ♨

Wisteria Lodge, Newtown Street, Chartham Hatch, CT4 7LT
☎ 01227 738669 (Elizabeth Dyke) www.wisterialodgebedandbreakfast.co.uk
Map 179/104565 BB **D** ✗ nearby S3 D1 T1 F1 ✻(Chartham)
V B D 🍵 ♨ 🚗 ! ★★★★

● Chilham (Canterbury)
NORTH DOWNS WAY

The Old Alma, Canterbury Road, CT4 8DX ☎ 01227 731913 (Jo Niven)
oldalma@aol.com Map 189,179/079538
BB **D** ✗ nearby D1 T2 ✻(Chilham) B D ⊗ 🍵 🚗 ! ◆◆◆

Homelea, Canterbury Road, CT4 8AG ☎ 07951 496836 (Fiona Ely)
www.canterburybnb.co.uk Map 189,179/084543
BB **D** ✗ nearby D/T2 F1 ✻(Chilham) V B D ⊗ 🍵 🚗 !

● Cranbrook
The Hollies, Old Angley Road, TN17 2PN ☎ 01580 713106 (Mrs D M Waddoup)
digs@waddoup.freeserve.co.uk Map 188/775367
BB **C** ✗ book first £10, 7pm S1 T1 F1 Closed Xmas ✻(Staplehurst)
B D ⊗ 🍵 ♨ 🚗 🧺

● Detling (Maidstone)
NORTH DOWNS WAY

Detling Coach House Hotel, Scragged Oak Road, ME14 3HB
☎ 01622 737590 (Emma or Pan Tang)
www.detlingcoachhouse.co.uk Map 188,178/799591
BB **D** ✗ nearby S1 D1 T1 Closed Xmas ✻(Bearsted)
V B D ⊗ 🍵 ♨ 🚗 ★★★

● Dover
NORTH DOWNS WAY

Amanda Guest House, 4 Harold Street, CT16 1SF ☎ 01304 201711
www.amandaguesthouse.homestead.com Map 179/320418
BB **B** ✗ nearby D1 T1 F1 ✻(Dover Priory) D ⊗ ◆◆

Bleriot's, 47 Park Avenue, CT16 1HE ☎ 01304 211394 (M J Casey)
www.bleriots.net Map 179/316422
BB **B/C** ✗ nearby S1 D3 T2 F2 Closed Xmas ✻(Dover Priory)
B ♨ ◆◆◆

● Etchinghill (Folkestone)
NORTH DOWNS WAY

One Step Beyond, Westfield Lane, CT18 8BT ☎ 01303 862637
(John & Jenny Holden) johnosb@rdplus.net Map 189,179/166394
BB **B** ✗ book first £10 S1 D1 Closed Xmas V B D ⊗ 🍵 🚗 !

● Folkestone
NORTH DOWNS WAY

Wycliffe Hotel, 63 Bouverie Road West, CT20 2RN ☎ 01303 252186
(Mike & Kate Sapsford) www.wycliffehotel.com Map 189,179/219357
BB **C** ✗ book first £14, 6:30pm S3 D5 T4 F2 ✻(Folkestone Central)
V B D ♨ 🧺

● Gillingham
Mayfield Guest House, 34 Kingswood Road, ME7 1DZ
☎ 01634 852606 (A Z Sumner) Map 178/776685
BB **C** ✗ nearby S4 D2 T2 F2 ✻(Gillingham) B ♨ ◆◆

● Harrietsham (Maidstone)
NORTH DOWNS WAY

Homestay, 14 Chippendayle Drive, ME17 1AD ☎ 01622 858698
(Barbara Beveridge) www.kent-homestay.info Map 189/870527
BB **C/D** ✗ nearby T2 Closed Xmas ✻(Harrietsham)
B D ⊗ 🍵 ♨ 🚗 ! ◆◆◆◆

● Herne Bay
Hobbit Hole, 41a Pigeon Lane, CT6 7ES ☎ 01227 368155 (Jean Herwin)
hobhole@btinternet.com Map 179/185669
BB **B** ✗ nearby S1 D1 T1 F1 Closed Xmas ✻(Herne Bay)
B D ⊗ 🍵 ♨ ! Ⓜ ◆◆◆

● Hythe

☆ **The Hythe Imperial**
Prince's Parade, CT21 6AE ☎ 01303 267441
www.marstonhotels.com Map 189,179/169344
BB **D** ✗ £32.50, 7-9.30pm S17 D55 T23 F5
V B 🍵 ♨ ★★★★ Wheelchair access.

Victorian splendour on Hythe seafront, convenient for North Downs and Romney Marsh. Fantastic modern leisure facilities and spa. Set in 50 acres with own golf course. Restaurant and two bars.
Please ask about our exclusive rates for walking parties.

● Kingsdown (Deal)
Sparrow Court, Chalk Hill Road, Kingsdown, CT14 8DP
☎ 01304 389253 (Hon Mrs E G Maude)
www.farm-stay-kent.co.uk/popups/sparrowcourt.html Map 179/374481
BB **D** ✗ nearby D1 T1 Closed Xmas ✻(Walmer)
B D ⊗ 🍵 ♨ 🚗 ! 🧺 ◆◆◆◆

☆ **Gardeners' Rest**
Nemesis, Queensdown Road, CT14 8EF ☎ 01304 371449 (Mr & Mrs Upton)
www.holidaysdeal.co.uk Map 179/373477
BB **D** ✗ £15, 6-7pm S1 D1 T1
B D ⊗ 🍵 ♨ ★★★★★Ⓖ

Luxury ensuite accommodation enjoying views over English Channel, acre of Plantsman's Garden, clifftop golf course and area of outstanding natural beauty. Close to national cycle network and Saxon Shore Way. Ideal for walking, cycling, cross-Channel ferries, Eurotunnel and stress-busting breaks.

● Lympne (Hythe)
Corner House, Aldington Road, CT21 4LF ☎ 01303 268108
(Denise Jorgensen) www.cornerhouselympne.co.uk Map 189/119349
BB **B** ✗ book first £8-£10 D2 T1 ✻(Westenhanger)
V B D ⊗ 🍵 🚗 !

● Pluckley (Ashford)

☆ ▦◥◣ **Elvey Farm**
Elvey Lane, TN27 0SU ☎ 01233 840442 (Simon Peek)
www.elveyfarm.co.uk Map 189/914454
BB **D** ✖ nearby D6 F1 ➶(Pluckley)
Ⓥ Ⓑ Ⓓ ⊛ 🐾🐕🚗 ! ⚘ Wheelchair access.

A Grade II-listed farmstead at the foot of the Greensand Way.

Located just outside the delightful village of Pluckley, home to ITV's Darling Buds of May. Enjoy a setting of hop gardens, orchards and oast houses in the 'Garden of England'.

Elvey Farm is surrounded by 75 acres of farmland, and six acres of paddocks are available to guests.

A warm farmhouse welcome to all walkers. Full English or vegetarian breakfast.

Rooms are en-suite, with original timbers and beams. Most rooms are on the ground floor in the converted stables. Own living rooms, private entrance. Wheelchair access.

Dogs especially welcome.

● Rochester
NORTH DOWNS WAY

255 High Street, ME1 1HQ ☎ 01634 842737 (Mrs E Thomas)
thomasbandb@btinternet.com Map 178/748681
BB **B** ✖ nearby D1 T1 F1 Closed Xmas ➶(Rochester) Ⓑ Ⓓ 🐾🐕 ⚘

▦◥◣ St Martin, 104 Borstal Road, ME1 3BD ☎ 01634 848192 (Mrs H Colvin)
jcolvin@stmartin.freeserve.co.uk Map 178/736673
BB **B** ✖ book first £8, To suit. S1 D1 T1 Closed Xmas ➶(Rochester)
Ⓥ Ⓓ ⊛ 🐾🐕🚗 ! Ⓜ ◆◆◆

● Sandwich
▦◥◣ Ilex Cottage, Temple Way, Worth, CT14 0DA
☎ 01304 617026 (Mrs Stobie) www.ilexcottage.com Map 179/335560
BB **D** ✖ nearby D1 T1 F1 Closed Xmas ➶(Sandwich)
Ⓑ Ⓓ ⊛ 🐾🐕🚗 ! ⚘ ◆◆◆◆

Le Trayas, Poulders Road, CT13 0BB ☎ 01304 611056 (Mrs R A Pettican)
www.letrayas.co.uk Map 179/322576
BB **B/C** ✖ nearby D1 T2 Closed Xmas ➶(Sandwich) Ⓑ Ⓓ ⊛ 🐾🐕🚗 !

● Stelling Minnis (Canterbury)
▦◥◣ Great Field Farm, Misling Lane, CT4 6DE ☎ 01227 709223 (Mrs L Castle)
www.great-field-farm.co.uk Map 189,179/134452
BB **D** ✖ nearby D2 T1 F1 Closed Xmas Ⓑ Ⓓ ⊛ 🐾🐕🚗 ! ◆◆◆◆Ⓢ

▦◥◣ Bower Farm House, Bossingham Road, CT4 6BB ☎ 01227 709430
(Anne Hunt) www.bowerfarmhouse.co.uk Map 189,179/147476
BB **C** ✖ nearby D1 T1 Ⓥ Ⓑ Ⓓ ⊛ 🐾🐕🚗 ! ⚘ ◆◆◆◆Ⓢ

● Tenterden
Old Burren, 25 Ashford Rd, TN30 6LL ☎ 01580 764442 (Gill Pooley)
www.oldburren.co.uk Map 189/886337
BB **C** ✖ nearby D2 Closed Xmas Ⓑ Ⓓ ⊛ 🐾🐕 ◆◆◆◆

● Walderslade Woods (Chatham)
NORTH DOWNS WAY

☆ ▦◥◣ **Bridgewood Manor**
Bridgewood Roundabout, ME5 9AX ☎ 01634 201333
www.marstonhotels.com Map 188,178/747634
BB **D** ✖ £32.50, 7-10pm D74 T26
Ⓥ Ⓑ 🐾🐕 ★★★★ Wheelchair access.

Relax at the comfortable Bridgewood Manor. Convenient for North Downs Way and Saxon Shore Way, the hotel offers a restaurant, bar and modern Leisure Club. Well-equipped bedrooms around beautiful courtyard. Please ask about our exclusive rates for walking parties.

● Whitstable
NORTH DOWNS WAY

☆ ▦◥◣ **Windy Ridge**
Wraik Hill, CT5 3BY ☎ 01227 263506 (Hugh & Lynda Scott)
www.windyridgewhitstable.co.uk Map 179/099640
BB **D** ✖ book first £12.50 S2 D6 F2 ➶(Whitstable)
Ⓥ Ⓑ ⊛ 🐾🐕 ! ⚘ ◆◆◆◆

Quirky, unique house in beautiful private garden. Panoramic views of the sea, countryside and famous Whitstable. Local walks – Saxon Shore Way, Viking Coastal Trail, Oare Marshes and South Swale nature reserves, inland to Canterbury along Crab & Winkle Line.

LONDON

● Brentford
THAMES PATH

▦◥◣ Primrose House, 56 Boston Gardens, TW8 9LP ☎ 020 8568 5573
(Garrie & Constance Williams) www.primrosehouse.com Map 176/164786
BB **D** ✖ nearby D2 T1 Closed Xmas ➶(Brentford)
Ⓑ ⊛ 🐕🚗 ! ⚘ ◆◆◆◆

● Central London
THAMES PATH

☆ ▦◥◣ **Cardiff Hotel**
5-9 Norfolk Square, W2 1RU ☎ 020 7723 3513 (Debbie & Andrew Davies)
www.cardiff-hotel.com Map 176/268812
BB **D** ✖ nearby S25 D22 T9 F5 Closed Xmas ➶(Paddington)
Ⓑ 🐕 ◆◆◆

15 minutes from Heathrow Airport by express train, the Cardiff Hotel overlooks a quiet garden square just 2 minutes walk from Paddington station. Rooms have a TV, phone, hairdryer and tea-making facilities. Hearty English breakfast included.

● **Hammersmith**
THAMES PATH

⌖⌖ 91 Langthorne St, SW6 6JU ☎ 020 7381 0198 (Brigid Richardson)
www.londonthameswalk.co.uk Map 176/236770
BB **D** ✕ nearby S1 D2 T1 ⋘(Hammersmith) Ⓑ Ⓓ ⊛ ᛒ ◆◆◆

⌖⌖ The Way to Stay, 67 Rannoch Road, W6 9SS ☎ 020 7385 4904
www.thewaytostay.co.uk Map 176/235775
BB **B** ✕ nearby S2 D2 T2 F2 ⋘(West Brompton) Ⓥ Ⓑ ⊛ ᛒ

● **Islington**
THAMES PATH

☆ ⌖⌖ **Kandara Guest House**
68 Ockendon Road, N1 3NW ☎ 020 7226 5721 (Avril Harmon)
www.kandara.co.uk Map 176,177/327845
BB **D** ✕ nearby S4 D3 T1 F4 Closed Xmas ⋘(Kings Cross)
Ⓥ Ⓓ ⊛ ᛒ ◆◆◆

Family-run guest house in quiet residential road, close
to the Angel, Islington.
Nine bus routes and two tube stations provide good
public transport to all parts of London.
Free overnight street parking and free secure cycle
storage.

● **Richmond-upon-Thames**
THAMES PATH & LONDON LOOP

⌖⌖ Ivy Cottage, Upper Ham Road, Ham Common, TW10 5LA
☎ 020 8940 8601 (David Taylor) www.dbta.freeserve.co.uk Map 176/178717
BB **C** ✕ nearby S1 D1 T2 F1 Closed Xmas Ⓑ Ⓓ ⛺ᛒ 🚗 ! ⅏ ◆◆◆

● **Twickenham**
THAMES PATH & LONDON LOOP

⌖⌖ Arlington B&B, 33 Arlington Road, St Margarets, TW1 2AZ
☎ 020 8287 7492 (David & Silvia Kogan)
www.33arlingtonroad.co.uk Map 176/170744
BB **D** ✕ nearby S1 D1 Closed Xmas ⋘(St Margarets) Ⓓ ⊛ ᛒ Ⓜ ★★★★

OXFORDSHIRE

● **Bampton (Oxford)**
THAMES PATH

⌖⌖ The Talbot Hotel, Market Square, OX18 2HA ☎ 01993 850326
adamr@talbothotel.wanadoo.co.uk Map 164/313030
BB **C** ✕ nearby S3 D4 T2 F1 Ⓑ Ⓓ ⛺ᛒ 🚗 !

● **Binfield Heath (Henley-on-Thames)**
THAMES PATH

⌖⌖ Teapot Cottage, Shiplake Row, RG9 4DR ☎ 01189 470263 (Clare Jevons)
www.teapot-cottage.co.uk Map 175/752784
BB **D** ✕ nearby D2 T1 ⋘(Shiplake) Ⓑ Ⓓ ⊛ ⛺ᛒ 🚗

● **Faringdon**
THAMES PATH

⌖⌖ Sudbury House Hotel, London Street, SN7 8AA ☎ 01367 241272
(Andrew Ibbotson) www.sudburyhouse.co.uk Map 164/294954
BB **D** ✕ £23.50, 7-9:30pm D39 T10 F2 Closed Xmas
Ⓥ Ⓑ Ⓓ ⛺ᛒ 🚗 ! ⅏ Ⓜ ★★★

● **Frieth (Henley-on-Thames)**
⌖⌖ St Katharine's, Parmoor, RG9 6NN ☎ 01494 881037 (Bethan Macleod)
www.srpf.webspace.fish.co.uk Map 175/794893
BB **B** ✕ book first £5, 6-8pm S8 D2 T12 F2 Closed Xmas
Ⓥ Ⓑ Ⓓ ⊛ ⛺ᛒ ⅏

● **Goring-on-Thames (Reading)**
RIDGEWAY & THAMES PATH

⌖⌖ Northview House, Farm Rd, RG8 0AA ☎ 01491 872184 (I Sheppard)
hi@goring-on-thames.freeserve.co.uk Map 175/603808
BB **B/C** ✕ nearby S1 D2 T1 F1 Closed Xmas ⋘(Goring & Streatley)
Ⓓ ⊛ ⛺ᛒ ! ⅏ Ⓜ

● **Henley-on-Thames**
THAMES PATH

⌖⌖ Lenwade, 3 Western Road, RG9 1JL ☎ 01491 573468 (Mrs J Williams)
www.w3b-ink.com/lenwade Map 175/760817
BB **D** ✕ nearby D2 T1 Closed Xmas ⋘(Henley-on-Thames)
Ⓑ Ⓓ ⊛ ⛺ᛒ 🚗 ! Ⓜ ◆◆◆◆◆

● **Long Hanborough (Witney)**
⌖⌖ Wynford House, 79 Main Rd, OX29 8JX ☎ 01993 881402 (Carol Ellis)
www.accommodation.uk.net/wynford.htm Map 164/424142
BB **D** ✕ nearby D1 T1 F1 Closed Xmas ⋘(Hanborough)
Ⓑ Ⓓ ⊛ ⛺ᛒ !

● **Long Wittenham (Abingdon)**
THAMES PATH

⌖⌖ Witta's Ham Cottage, High Street, OX14 4QH
☎ 01865 407686 (Jill Mellor) bandb@wittenham.com Map 174,164/546937
BB **D** ✕ nearby S1 D1 T1 Closed Xmas ⋘(Culham)
Ⓓ ⊛ ⛺ᛒ ! ◆◆◆◆Ⓢ

● **Milton Common (Thame)**

☆ ⌖⌖ **The Oxford Belfry**
OX9 2JW ☎ 01844 279381
www.marstonhotels.com Map 164,165/651035
BB **D** ✕ £32.50, 7-9.30pm S3 D84 T43
Ⓥ Ⓑ ⛺ᛒ ★★★★ Wheelchair access.

Explore Oxford while enjoying the countryside. Set
in 17 acres with excellent leisure facilities. Popular
bar, restaurants and picturesque courtyard.
Close to many attractions including Blenheim
Palace and the Oxfordshire Way.
Please ask about our exclusive rates for walking
parties.

● **Nettlebed (Henley-on-Thames)**
RIDGEWAY

Park Corner Farm House, RG9 6DX ☎ 01491 641450 (Mrs S Rutter)
parkcorner_farmhouse@hotmail.com Map 175/688891
BB **C** S1 T2 Closed Xmas Ⓓ ⊛ ⛺ᛒ 🚗 ! ⅏ ◆◆◆

● **Nuffield (Henley-on-Thames)**
RIDGEWAY

14 Bradley Road, RG9 5SG ☎ 01491 641359 (Diana Chambers)
dianamc@waitrose.com Map 175/681882
BB **C** ✕ nearby D2 T1 Closed Xmas Ⓑ Ⓓ ⊛ ⛺ᛒ 🚗 ! ⅏

● Oxford (Summertown)
THAMES PATH

☆ ◉◀■ **Thames Path Walking Holidays**
Wharf 315, 266 Banbury Road, OX2 7DL ☎ 07970 939725 (Mr RJ Baker)
www.kariuk.com Map 164/508090
BB **D** ✕ book first, 7pm D1 T1 Closed Nov-Feb ⋘(Oxford)
Ⓥ Ⓑ Ⓓ ⊗ 🐄🛁❗🐾 Ⓜ ★★★

We provide comfortable accommodation on the River Thames, especially catering for Thames Path walkers. All rooms en-suite and full-board provided. We cater for all abilities of walkers and operate between Lechlade and Teddington. Call Richard for more information or visit our website.

● Pishill (Henley-on-Thames)
◉◀■ Bank Farm, RG9 6HS ☎ 01491 638601 (Mrs E Lakey)
e.f.lakey@btinternet.com Map 175/713898
BB **B** ✕ nearby D2 T1 Closed Xmas Ⓓ ⊗ 🐄🚗❗ ◆◆

Orchard House RG9 6HH ☎ 01491 638351
joanatpishill@btopenworld.com Map 175/713898
BB **C** ✕ nearby D1 T2 Closed Dec-Jan
Ⓥ Ⓑ Ⓓ ⊗ 🚗❗🐾 Ⓜ ◆◆◆◆ Wheelchair access.

● Shillingford (Wallingford)
THAMES PATH

◉◀■ The Kingfisher Inn, 27 Henley Road, OX10 7EL ☎ 01865 858595
(Alexis or Mayumi) www.kingfisher-inn.co.uk Map 174,164/595928
BB **D** ✕ £10, 7:30-9:30pm D5 T1 Closed Xmas
Ⓥ Ⓑ Ⓓ 🐄🛁❗ ◆◆◆◆

● Shipton-under-Wychwood (Chipping Norton)
Court Farm, Mawles Lane, OX7 6DA ☎ 01993 831515 (Belinda Willson)
enquiries@courtfarmbb.com Map 163/279177
BB **C** ✕ nearby D2 T1 ⋘(Shipton-under-Wychwood)
Ⓥ Ⓑ Ⓓ ⊗ 🐄🚗🐾 ◆◆◆◆Ⓢ

● Swalcliffe
MACMILLAN WAY

☆ **Grange Farm Bed & Breakfast**
Swalcliffe Grange, OX15 5EX ☎ 01295 780206 (Barbara Taylor)
www.swalcliffegrange.com Map 151/372369
BB **C** ✕ nearby D1 T2
Ⓥ Ⓑ ⊗ 🐄🛁

Late 18th-century farmhouse, warm hospitality and comfortable accommodation in a peaceful setting.

● Swyncombe (Henley-on-Thames)
RIDGEWAY

◉◀■ Pathways, Cookley Green, RG9 6EN ☎ 01491 641631 (Ismayne Peters)
ismayne.peters@tesco.net Map 175/695901
BB **C** ✕ book first £9, 7-8pm D1 T2 Closed Xmas
Ⓥ Ⓑ Ⓓ ⊗ 🐄🛁🚗❗

● Tackley (Kidlington)
◉◀■ 55 Nethercote Road, OX5 3AT ☎ 01869 331255 (June Collier)
www.colliersbnb.com Map 164/482206
BB **B/D** ✕ nearby D1 T1/F1 F1 ⋘(Tackley) Ⓓ ⊗ 🐄🛁🚗❗🐾 ◆◆◆

● Wallingford
THAMES PATH & RIDGEWAY

◉◀■ Little Gables, 166 Crowmarsh Hill, OX10 8BG
☎ 01491 837834 (Jill & Tony Reeves) www.stayingaway.com Map 175/627887
BB **C** ✕ nearby S1 D/S2 T/S3 F/S2 ⋘(Cholsey)
Ⓑ Ⓓ ⊗ 🐄🛁❗ ★★★★

◉◀■ Huntington House, 18 Wood Street, OX10 0AX ☎ 01491 839201
(Julie & Mike Huntington) hunting311@aol.com Map 175/607891
BB **D** ✕ nearby D1 T1 Closed Xmas Ⓑ Ⓓ ⊗ 🐄🛁❗ ◆◆◆

● Wantage
RIDGEWAY

Lockinge Kiln Farm, The Ridgeway, Chain Hill, OX12 8PA
☎ 01235 763308 (Stella Cowan) www.lockingekiln.co.uk Map 174/423833
BB **B** ✕ book first £12.50, 7pm D1 T2 Closed Xmas-Jan
Ⓥ Ⓓ ⊗ 🐄🛁❗

SURREY

● Bowlhead Green (Godalming)
Heath Hall Farm, GU8 6NW ☎ 01428 682808 (Susanna Langdale)
www.heathhallfarm.co.uk Map 186/918388
BB **D** ✕ nearby S1 D1 T1 F1 Closed Xmas
Ⓑ Ⓓ ⊗ 🐄🛁🚗🐾 ◆◆◆

● Cranleigh
The White Hart, Ewhurst Road, GU6 7AE ☎ 01483 268647
pasilver@netcomuk.co.uk Map 187/060390
BB **C** ✕ £5-£10, 6-9pm S2 D7 T3 F2 Ⓥ Ⓑ Ⓓ 🐄🛁🐾

● Dorking
NORTH DOWNS WAY

◉◀■ 5 Rose Hill, RH4 2EG ☎ 01306 883127 (Margaret Walton)
www.altourism.com/uk/walt.html Map 187/166491
BB **D** ✕ book first £16, 7:30pm onwards D1 T1 F1 ⋘(Dorking North)
Ⓥ Ⓑ Ⓓ ⊗ 🐄🛁🚗🐾

Fairdene Guest House, Moores Road, RH4 2BG ☎ 01306 888337
(Clive Richardson) zoe.richardson@ntlworld.com Map 187/169496
BB **D** ✕ nearby D2 T2 F2 ⋘(Dorking)
Ⓑ Ⓓ ⊗ 🐄🛁🚗❗🐾 ◆◆◆

☆ **Claremont Cottage**
Rose Hill, RH4 2ED ☎ 01306 885487 (Jan Stammers)
www.claremontcott.co.uk Map 187/164489
BB **D** ✕ nearby S3 D2 T1 ⋘(Dorking)
Ⓥ Ⓑ Ⓓ ⊗ 🐄🛁🚗 ◆◆◆◆ Internet access available.

Olde worlde cottage, formerly coach house and stables, with modern amenities. Very close to town centre yet peaceful location down own lane. Picturesque garden setting. All rooms individually styled and en-suite. Easy access to London, M25 & beauty spots.

SOUTH

● Guildford
NORTH DOWNS WAY

25 Scholars Walk, Ridgemount, GU2 7TR
☎ 01483 531351 Map 186/988498
BB **D** ✕ nearby S2 ᗰ(Guildford) Ⓑ Ⓔ ♨

Highfield House, 18 Harvey Rd, GU1 3SG
☎ 01483 534946 (Mike & Jo Anning)
mj.anning@clara.co.uk Map 186/001494
BB **C** ✕ nearby D1 T1 Closed Xmas ᗰ(Guildford) Ⓑ Ⓓ Ⓔ ♨ ᗰ Ⓜ

● Horley

☆ The Turret Guest House
48 Massetts Road, RH6 7DS ☎ 01293 782490
www.theturret.com Map 187/286426
BB **D** ✕ nearby S2 D3 T2 F3 ᗰ(Horley/Gatwick)
Ⓑ Ⓓ Ⓔ 🏍️🍴♨ Ⓜ ◆◆◆

Situated on the Surrey/Sussex border, The Turret is a 19th Century Victorian guest house which has been recently refurbished and offers superb accommodation ranging from a family room, a triple, double or single rooms.

All rooms are en-suite and centrally heated, with colour TV and tea/coffee making facilities. Guests have the option of full English or Continental breakfast.

Holiday parking is available at £3 per day. Why not take advantage of courtesy transport to and from Gatwick Airport, by arrangement? Information on local attractions and maps are available on request.

So whether you're on 'Business-on-a-Budget' or a 'Traveller-in-Transit' come and enjoy a warm welcome and an enjoyable stay at this award-winning 3-star English Tourist Board house. Book on-line at info@theturret.com

☆ Rosemead Guest House
19 Church Road, RH6 7EY ☎ 01293 784965 (Fiona Stimpson)
www.rosemeadguesthouse.co.uk Map 187/279429
BB **D** ✕ nearby S2 D1 T1 F2 ᗰ(Horley/Gatwick)
Ⓥ Ⓑ Ⓓ Ⓔ 🏍️🍴♨ ᗰ ! Ⓢ

A warm welcome awaits you at this non-smoking Edwardian guesthouse 5 minutes from Gatwick Airport. 24-hour courtesy transfers. Full English breakfast 7:30-8:30am. CTV and full central heating. Private bathrooms in all rooms. Holiday parking available. Families welcome.

☆ ᗰ Southbourne Guest House
34 Massetts Road, Gatwick, RH6 7DS ☎ 01293 771991
www.southbournegatwick.com Map 187/280428
BB **D** ✕ nearby S2 D3 T3 F4 ᗰ(Horley)
Ⓥ Ⓑ Ⓔ ♨ ᗰ ! ★★★★ Wheelchair access.

A warm welcome awaits you in our family-run guesthouse. Ideally located for Gatwick Airport and exploring Surrey, Sussex and London. Five minutes' walk from Horley train station, restaurants, shops and pubs. 30 minutes by train from London and 5 minutes from Gatwick.

☆ ᗰ The Corner House Gatwick
72 Massetts Road, RH6 7ED ☎ 01293 784574
www.thecornerhouse.co.uk Map 187/278427
BB **D** ✕ £6-£8, 6:30-9pm S6 D12 T8 F5 ᗰ(Horley/Gatwick)
Ⓥ Ⓑ Ⓓ 🏍️🍴♨ ᗰ Ⓕ ◆◆◆◆

Family-run guesthouse offering quality accommodation, bar and restaurant. 24hr transfers to Gatwick airport. Holiday car-parking available. Let us take the strain out of getting you to the plane.

The Lawn Guest House, 30 Massetts Rd, RH6 7DF ☎ 01293 775751
(Adrian Grinsted) www.lawnguesthouse.co.uk Map 187/283428
BB **D** ✕ nearby D3 T3 F6 Closed Xmas ᗰ(Horley/Gatwick)
Ⓑ Ⓓ Ⓔ ♨ ᗰ Ⓕ ★★★★Ⓢ

● Oxted
NORTH DOWNS WAY

ᗰ Pinehurst Grange Guesthouse, East Hill (A25), RH8 9AE
☎ 01883 716413 (Laurie Rodgers)
laurie.rodgers@ntlworld.com Map 187/392525
BB **C/D** ✕ nearby S1 D1 T1 Closed Xmas ᗰ(Oxted) Ⓓ Ⓔ 🏍️♨

Meads, 23 Granville Road, RH8 0BX ☎ 01883 730115 (Helen Holgate)
holgate@meads9.fsnet.co.uk Map 187/399530
BB **D** ✕ nearby D2 T1 F1 Closed Jan-Feb ᗰ(Oxted)
Ⓑ Ⓓ Ⓔ 🏍️♨ ᗰ ! ◆◆◆

● Shalford (Guildford)
NORTH DOWNS WAY

ᗰ The Laurels, 23 Dagden Road, GU4 8DD
☎ 01483 565753 (Mrs M J Deeks) Map 186/000475
BB **B** ✕ book first £8, 7-8pm D1 T1 ᗰ(Shalford)
Ⓥ Ⓑ Ⓓ Ⓔ 🏍️♨ ᗰ ! Ⓜ ◆◆◆Ⓦ

EAST SUSSEX

● Alfriston
SOUTH DOWNS WAY & WEALDWAY

Riverdale House, Seaford Road, BN26 5TR ☎ 01323 871038
www.riverdalehouse.co.uk Map 199/516024
BB **D** ✕ nearby D3 T2 ᗰ(Berwick) Ⓑ Ⓓ Ⓔ 🏍️♨ ! ◆◆◆◆

Dacres, BN26 5TP ☎ 01323 870447 (Patsy Embry) Map 199/518028
BB **C** ✕ nearby T1 Closed Xmas ᗰ(Berwick) Ⓑ Ⓓ Ⓔ ♨ !

ᗰ 5 The Broadway, BN26 5XL ☎ 01323 870145 (Janet Dingley)
janetandbrian@dingley5635.freeserve.co.uk Map 199/516030
BB **C** ✕ nearby S1 D1 T1 Closed Xmas Ⓑ Ⓓ Ⓔ 🏍️♨ ᗰ !

ᗰ Martlets, The Broadway, BN26 5XH
☎ 01323 870541 (Mrs R P Danesi) Map 199/516030
BB **C** ✕ nearby D1 T1 Closed Xmas ᗰ(Berwick)
Ⓑ Ⓓ Ⓔ 🏍️♨ ᗰ ! Ⓜ See SC also.

● Blackboys (Uckfield)
WEALDWAY

Rangers Cottage, Terminus Rd, TN22 5LX ☎ 01825 890463
(David & Elizabeth Brown) www.rangerscottage.co.uk Map 199/518207
BB **C/D** ✕ nearby D1 T1 Closed Xmas
Ⓑ Ⓓ Ⓔ 🏍️♨ ᗰ ! ◆◆◆◆

● **Chiddingly (Lewes)**
WEALDWAY

🏠 Hale Farm House, BN8 6HQ ☎ 01825 872619 (David & Sue Burrough)
www.halefarmhouse.co.uk Map 199/555145
BB **D** ✗ book first £7.50, 6-8pm T2 F1 Closed Xmas
Ⓥ Ⓑ Ⓓ ⊗ 🐾 🛆 🚗 ! 🛏 ◆◆◆◆

● **Colemans Hatch (Hartfield)**
WEALDWAY

🏠 Gospel Oak, TN7 4ER ☎ 01342 823840 (Mrs L Hawker)
lindah@thehatch.freeserve.co.uk Map 187/447327
BB **D** ✗ book first £14, 7-8pm D1 T1
Ⓥ Ⓑ Ⓓ ⊗ 🐾 🛆 🚗 ! 🛏 Ⓜ ◆◆◆ Bookings by phone only.

● **East Hoathly (Lewes)**
WEALDWAY

🏠 Aberdeen House B&B, 5 High Street, BN8 6DR
☎ 01825 840219 (Jo Gardiner)
jo@aberdeenhouse.freeserve.co.uk Map 199/522162
BB **D** ✗ nearby S1 D3 T1 F1 Ⓑ Ⓓ ⊗ 🐾 🛆 🚗 ! ◆◆◆◆

● **Eastbourne**
SOUTH DOWNS WAY & WEALDWAY

Ambleside Hotel, 24 Elms Avenue, BN21 3DN ☎ 01323 724991 (J Pattenden)
www.smoothhound.co.uk/hotels/ambleside.html Map 199/616989
BB **B** ✗ nearby S2 D6 T6 ⚍(Eastbourne) Ⓑ Ⓓ 🛆 🛏

Brayscroft House, 13 South Cliff Avenue, BN20 7AH ☎ 01323 647005
www.brayscrofthotel.co.uk Map 199/609980
BB **D** ✗ book first £14, 6pm S1 D3 T2 Closed Xmas ⚍(Eastbourne)
Ⓥ Ⓑ Ⓓ ⊗ 🐾 🛆 🚗 ◆◆◆◆Ⓖ

🏠 The Atlanta Hotel, 10 Royal Parade, BN22 7AR
☎ 01323 730486 (Jason Osbourne)
www.atlantaeastbourne.co.uk Map 199/619993
BB **C** S6 D5 T2 F2 Closed Xmas-Jan ⚍(Eastbourne) Ⓑ ⊗ 🐾 🛆 ! ◆◆◆

🏠 Southcroft, 15 South Cliff Ave, BN20 7AH ☎ 01323 729071
(Andrew Johnson) www.southcrofthotel.co.uk Map 199/609980
BB **D** ✗ book first £12, 6pm S1 D3 T2 Closed Xmas ⚍(Eastbourne)
Ⓥ Ⓑ Ⓓ ⊗ 🐾 🛆 ! ◆◆◆◆

The Cherry Tree Hotel, 15 Silverdale Road, Lower Meads, BN20 7AJ
☎ 01323 722406 (Lynda Couch-Smith)
www.cherrytree-eastbourne.co.uk Map 199/609980
BB **D** ✗ nearby S3 D3 T2 F1 ⚍(Eastbourne) Ⓑ ⊗ 🐾 🛆 ! 🛏 ◆◆◆◆Ⓢ

🏠 Ivydene Hotel, 5/6 Hampden Terrace, Latimer Road, BN22 7BL
☎ 01323 720547 (Carolyn Jane)
www.ivydenehotel-eastbourne.co.uk Map 199/620995
BB **C** ✗ £10, 6-6:30pm S4 D4 T4 F2 ⚍(Eastbourne)
Ⓥ Ⓑ Ⓓ ⊗

🏠 Beach Haven, 61 Pevensey Road, BN21 3HS ☎ 01323 726195
(Christine & Ken Martin) www.beach-haven.co.uk Map 199/617992
BB **C** ✗ book first £10, 6-7pm S2 D3 T2 ⚍(Eastbourne)
Ⓥ Ⓑ Ⓓ ⊗ 🐾 🛆 ◆◆◆

● **Groombridge (Tunbridge Wells)**
WEALDWAY

🏠 Ventura, The Ridge, Withyam Road, TN3 9QU
☎ 01892 864711 (Brenda Horner) Map 188/521369
BB **B** ✗ book first £10, 6:30-7pm S1 D/F1 T1 Closed Xmas
Ⓥ Ⓑ Ⓓ ⊗ 🐾 🛆 🚗 ! 🛏

● **Hailsham**
WEALDWAY

🏠 Longleys Farm Cottage, Harebeating Lane, BN27 1ER
☎ 01323 841227 (David & Jill Hook) Map 199/598105
BB **B** ✗ nearby D1 T1 F1 Ⓑ Ⓓ ⊗ 🐾 🛆 🚗 🛏 ★★★

● **Hastings**

☆ 🏠 **White Cottage**
Battery Hill, Fairlight, TN35 4AP ☎ 01424 812528 (John & June Dyer)
juneandjohn@whitecottagebb.fsnet.co.uk Map 199/873123
BB **D** ✗ nearby D3 T1 Closed Dec
Ⓑ Ⓓ ⊗ 🛆 🚗 ◆◆◆◆

We are a peaceful, friendly B&B with beautiful gardens for our guests to enjoy. We have three doubles and one twin room, all en-suite (two with sea views). Tea/coffee making facilities and TV in all rooms. Extensive breakfast menu.

🏠 Grand Hotel, Grand Parade, St Leonards, TN38 0DD ☎ 01424 428510
(Peter Mann) www.grandhotelhastings.co.uk Map 199/802089
BB **B** ✗ book first £20, 5-7pm S3 D9 T7 F4 ⚍(Warrior Square)
Ⓥ Ⓑ Ⓓ ⊗ 🐾 🛆 🚗 ! ◆◆◆

● **Heathfield**

Spicers Bed and Breakfast, 21 Spicers Cottages, Cade Street, TN21 9BS
☎ 01435 866363 (Graham & Valerie Gumbrell)
www.spicersbb.co.uk Map 199/605212
BB **D** ✗ book first £12-£15, 6-8pm S1 D1 T1
Ⓥ Ⓑ Ⓓ ⊗ 🐾 🛆 🚗 ! 🛏 ★★★★

● **Horam (Heathfield)**
WEALDWAY

🏠 Oak Mead Nursery, Cowden Hall Lane, TN21 9ED
☎ 01435 812962 (Barbara Curtis) Map 199/592171
BB **B/C** ✗ nearby S1 D1 T1 Closed Nov-Mar Ⓑ Ⓓ ⊗ 🐾 🛆

● **Lewes**
SOUTH DOWNS*
SOUTH DOWNS WAY

Settlands, Wellgreen Lane, Kingston, BN7 3NP ☎ 01273 472295 (Diana Artlett)
diana-a@solutions-inc.co.uk Map 198/398082
BB **D** ✗ nearby D1 T1 Closed Xmas ⚍(Lewes)
Ⓓ ⊗ 🐾 🛆 🚗 ! ◆◆◆◆Ⓢ

🏠 Bethel, Kingston Ridge, Kingston, BN7 3JX ☎ 01273 478658 (Tim & Nancy Lear) www.lewes-area-bed-and-breakfast.com/bethel Map 198/387085
BB **D** ✗ nearby D1 T2 Closed Xmas ⚍(Lewes) Ⓑ Ⓓ ⊗ 🐾 🛆 🚗 !

B&B Number 6, Gundreda Rd, BN7 1PX ☎ 01273 472106 (Jackie Lucas)
www.stayinlewes.co.uk Map 198/406105
BB **D** ✗ nearby D2 T1 Closed Xmas ⚍(Lewes)
Ⓑ ⊗ 🐾 🛆 🚗 ◆◆◆◆Ⓢ

🏠 Berkeley House, 2 Albion Street, BN7 2ND ☎ 01273 476057
www.berkeleyhouselewes.co.uk Map 198/418102
BB **D** ✗ nearby D2 T1 ⚍(Lewes) Ⓥ Ⓑ Ⓓ ⊗ 🛆 ! ◆◆◆◆

● **Mayfield**

April Cottage Guest House and Tearoom, West Street, TN20 6BA
☎ 01435 872160 (Miss B Powner) Map 188,199/585269
BB **C** ✗ nearby S1 D/S1 T/S1 Ⓑ Ⓓ 🐾 🛆

● Newhaven
SOUTH DOWNS*
SOUTH DOWNS WAY

▰◢ Newhaven Lodge, 12 Brighton Rd, BN9 9NB
☎ 01273 513736 (Jan Cameron) NewhavenLodge@aol.com Map 198/442013
BB **C** ✕ nearby S2 D1 T1 F3 Closed Xmas ▰▰(Newhaven)
B 🐾⛱️👜❗🏔️ ◆◆◆

● Rye
☆ **Jeake's House**
Mermaid Street, TN31 7ET ☎ 01797 222828 (Mrs J Hadfield)
www.jeakeshouse.com Map 189/919203
BB **D** ✕ nearby D7 T3 F2 ▰▰(Rye)
B D⛱️👜🏔️ ◆◆◆◆◆Ⓢ

Dating from 1534, this listed building stands in Rye's medieval town centre.
Breakfast is served in the elegant galleried hall and features traditional,
vegetarian, devilled kidneys and fish dishes. Stylishly restored bedrooms
combine luxury and modern amenities. After rambling the Romney marshes you
can relax in the book-lined bar with a drink. Bike hire nearby. Private car park.

Flackley Ash Hotel, Peasmarsh, TN31 6YH ☎ 01797 230651
www.flackleyashhotel.co.uk Map 199,189/881233
BB **D** ✕ £25.50, 7-9:30pm D27 T13 F5 Ⓥ 🆕 D 🐾⛱️👜❗🏔️ ★★★

▰◢ Little Saltcote, 22 Military Rd, TN31 7NY ☎ 01797 223210
(Barbara & Denys Martin) www.littlesaltcote.co.uk Map 189/923212
BB **C** ✕ nearby D2 F3 Closed Xmas ▰▰(Rye)
B D⊛🐾👜🚗❗🏔️ ◆◆◆◆

▰◢ The Windmill Guest House, Ferry Road, TN31 7DW
☎ 01797 224027 (Brian Elliott) www.ryewindmill.co.uk Map 189/916203
BB **D** ✕ nearby S1 D/T8 ▰▰(Rye) Ⓥ B D⊛🐾👜🏔️ ◆◆◆◆

● Streat
SOUTH DOWNS* & SOUTH DOWNS WAY

North Acres, BN6 8RX ☎ 01273 890278 (Valerie Eastwood)
www.northacres-streat.co.uk Map 198/353154
BB **C** ✕ nearby S2 D1 T1 Closed Xmas ▰▰(Plumpton) D⊛🐾👜🚗❗

● Wilmington (Polegate)
SOUTH DOWNS WAY & WEALDWAY

▰◢ Crossways Hotel, BN26 5SG ☎ 01323 482455 (David Stott)
www.crosswayshotel.co.uk Map 199/547048
BB **D** ✕ book first £34.95, 7:30-8:30pm S2 D3 T2 Closed Xmas-Jan
▰▰(Polegate) Ⓥ B D⊛🐾👜❗ ◆◆◆◆◆

● Withyham
WEALDWAY

Dorset House, TN7 4BD ☎ 01892 770035 (Meg Stafford)
www.dorset-house.co.uk Map 188/496356
BB **D** ✕ nearby T2 B D⊛🐾👜🚗❗ ★★★

WEST SUSSEX

● Amberley (Arundel)
SOUTH DOWNS*
SOUTH DOWNS WAY & MONARCH'S WAY

▰◢ Woodybanks Cottage, Crossgates, BN18 9NR ☎ 01798 831295
(Mr & Mrs G Hardy) www.woodybanks.co.uk Map 197/041136
BB **C** ✕ nearby D1 T1 Closed Xmas ▰▰(Amberley)
D ⊛🐾👜🚗❗ ◆◆◆◆ Some disabled facilities.

● Arundel
SOUTH DOWNS WAY & MONARCH'S WAY

Arden Guest House, 4 Queen's Lane, BN18 9JN ☎ 01903 882544
carol@short80.fsworld.co.uk Map 197/019068
BB **C/D** ✕ nearby D5 T3 ▰▰(Arundel) B ⊛👜 ◆◆◆

▰◢ Dellfield, 9 Dalloway Road, BN18 9HJ ☎ 01903 882253 (Mrs J M Carter)
jane@heron-electric.com Map 197/006064
BB **B** ✕ nearby S1 T1 Closed Dec ▰▰(Arundel) B D⊛🐾👜🚗

● Burgess Hill
▰◢ The Homestead, Homestead Lane, Valebridge Road, RH15 0RQ
☎ 01444 246899 (Sue & Mike Mundy)
www.burgess-hill.co.uk Map 198/323208
BB **D** ✕ nearby S1 D1 T2 Closed Xmas ▰▰(Wivelsfield)
B D⊛🐾👜🚗 ◆◆◆◆

● Bury (Pulborough)
SOUTH DOWNS*
SOUTH DOWNS WAY & MONARCH'S WAY

▰◢ Harkaway, 8 Houghton Lane, RH20 1PD ☎ 01798 831843 (Carol Clarke)
www.harkaway.org.uk Map 197/012130
BB **B** ✕ nearby S2 D1 T1 Closed Xmas ▰▰(Amberley)
B D⊛🐾👜🚗 ◆◆◆

▰◢ Arun House, RH20 1NT ☎ 01798 831736 (Jan & Chris Briggs)
www.arunhousesussex.co.uk Map 197/010137
BB **B/C** ✕ book first £12, 6:30-8:30pm S1 D1 T1 F1 Closed Xmas
▰▰(Amberley) Ⓥ D⊛🐾👜🚗❗🏔️ ◆◆◆

● Charlton (Chichester)
SOUTH DOWNS*
MONARCH'S WAY & SOUTH DOWNS WAY

☆ **Woodstock House Hotel**
PO18 0HU ☎ 01243 811666 (Aidan F Nugent)
www.woodstockhousehotel.co.uk Map 197/889129
BB **D** ✕ nearby S2 D6 T4 F1 Closed Xmas
B D👜🚗❗🏔️ ◆◆◆◆◆

Situated in magnificent South
Downs just 1 mile from South
Downs Way. Converted from an old
farmhouse our licensed B&B hotel
has 13 en-suite bedrooms with all
modern amenities. Our local inn for
dinner is just 1 minute's walk.

● Clayton (Hassocks)
SOUTH DOWNS* & SOUTH DOWNS WAY

Dower Cottage, Underhill Lane, BN6 9PL ☎ 01273 843363 (Mrs C Bailey)
www.dowercottage.co.uk Map 198/309136
BB **D** ✕ nearby S1 D2 T1 F2 Closed Xmas ▰▰(Hassocks) B D⊛🐾🏔️

● Cocking (Midhurst)
SOUTH DOWNS*
SOUTH DOWNS WAY

Downsfold, Bell Lane, GU29 0HU ☎ 01730 814376 (Malcolm & Janet Hunt)
www.downsfold.co.uk Map 197/876176
BB **C** ✕ nearby D1 T1 Closed Xmas Ⓓ ⊗ 🐾 🚗 !

The Blue Bell, Bell Lane, GU29 0HN ☎ 01730 813449 (Mrs G Bate)
www.thebluebell.org.uk Map 197/877175
BB **D** ✕ £8.95, 6:30-9:30pm D2 T1 Ⓥ Ⓑ 🐾 ♿ 🐾

● Ditchling (Hassocks)
SOUTH DOWNS*
SOUTH DOWNS WAY

South Cottage, 2 The Drove, BN6 8TR
☎ 01273 846636 Map 198/326153
BB **D** ✕ nearby D2 T1 Closed Xmas 🚍(Hassocks)
Ⓓ ⊗ 🐾 ♿ 🚗 🐾

● East Grinstead

Cranston House, Cranston Road, RH19 3HW ☎ 01342 323609
www.cranstonhouse.co.uk Map 187/397385
BB **D** ✕ book first £6 (snacks), 7-8pm S2 D2 T5 F1 Closed Xmas
🚍(East Grinstead) Ⓥ Ⓑ Ⓓ ⊗ 🐾 ♿ ◆◆◆◆

● Fontwell (Arundel)
SOUTH DOWNS*
MONARCH'S WAY

🚍🛌 Woodacre, Arundel Road, BN18 0QP ☎ 01243 814301 (Vicki Richards)
www.woodacre.co.uk Map 197/960068
BB **C** ✕ nearby D1 T2 F1 🚍(Barnham)
Ⓑ Ⓓ ⊗ 🐾 🚗 ♿ ◆◆◆◆

● Fulking (Henfield)
SOUTH DOWNS*
SOUTH DOWNS WAY & MONARCH'S WAY

Knole House, Clappers Lane, BN5 9NH ☎ 01273 857387 (Jill Bremer)
www.knolehouse.co.uk Map 198/249124
BB **D** ✕ book first £15, 7-8pm S2 D1 T1 F1
Ⓥ Ⓑ Ⓓ ⊗ 🐾 ♿ 🚗 !

● Graffham (Petworth)
SOUTH DOWNS* WAY

Brook Barn, GU28 0PU ☎ 01798 867356 (Mr & Mrs S A Jollands)
brookbarn@hotmail.com Map 197/929180
BB **D** ✕ nearby D1 Closed Xmas
Ⓑ Ⓓ ⊗ 🐾 ♿ 🐾 ◆◆◆◆◆Ⓢ

● Heyshott (Midhurst)
SOUTH DOWNS*
SOUTH DOWNS WAY

Little Hoyle, Hoyle Lane, GU29 0DX
☎ 01798 867359 (Robert & Judith Ralph)
www.smoothhound.com/littlehoyle Map 197/906187
BB **D** ✕ nearby D1 Closed Xmas Ⓑ Ⓓ ⊗ 🐾 ♿ 🚗 ◆◆◆◆

● Ifield Green (Crawley)
April Cottage, 10 Langley Lane, RH11 0NA
☎ 01293 546222 (Brian & Liz Pedlow)
www.aprilcottageguesthouse.co.uk Map 187/253379
BB **B/D** ✕ nearby D1 T2 F1 🚍(Ifield)
⊗ 🐾 ♿ 🚗 ! ◆◆◆◆ Guide dogs welcome.

● New Domewood (Copthorne)

☆ 🚍🛌 **Linchens B&B**
Linchens, Herons Close, RH10 3HF ☎ 01342 713085 (Sally Little)
www.linchens.com Map 187/345401
BB **D** ✕ nearby S4 D4 T3 F3 Closed Xmas
Ⓥ Ⓑ Ⓓ ⊗ 🐾 ♿ 🚗

Linchens is situated 10 minutes from Gatwick airport and the South Downs/Worth Way. We offer superb en-suite facilities with 24hr transfer to Gatwick and long-term car parking. We are non-smoking and serve full English breakfasts. Bathrooms have glass bowls and under-floor heating.

● Poynings (Brighton)
SOUTH DOWNS WAY

☆ 🚍🛌 **Cobby Sands Bed & Breakfast**
The Street, BN45 7AQ ☎ 01273 857821 (Mrs Angie Gill)
www.cobbysands.com Map 198/262119
BB **D** ✕ nearby D1 T1
Ⓥ Ⓓ ⊗ 🐾 ♿ 🐾 Ⓜ

Luxury detached country house with direct access to the South Downs Way. Excellent pub (Royal Oak) under two minutes' walk away. Luxury bathroom with jacuzzi and separate shower room.
All bedrooms have views across the South Downs (see picture and website).

● Pulborough
SOUTH DOWNS*
SOUTH DOWNS WAY

Barn House Lodge, Barn House Lane, RH20 2BS ☎ 01798 872682
www.barnhouselodge.co.uk Map 197/052185
BB **C** ✕ nearby D1 T1 🚍(Pulborough) Ⓑ Ⓓ ⊗ 🐾 🚗 ◆◆◆◆

● South Harting (Petersfield)
SOUTH DOWNS*
SOUTH DOWNS WAY

Torberry Cottage, Torberry Farm, GU31 5RG ☎ 01730 826883 (Maggie Barker)
www.visitsussex.org/torberrycottage Map 197/767200
BB **C** ✕ nearby D1 T1 Closed Xmas Ⓑ Ⓓ ⊗ 🐾 ♿ 🚗 ! ◆◆◆◆

● Steyning
SOUTH DOWNS*
MONARCH'S WAY & SOUTH DOWNS WAY

5 Coxham Lane, BN44 3LG ☎ 01903 812286 (Mrs J Morrow) Map 198/176116
BB **A** ✕ nearby S1 T2 Closed Nov-Feb Ⓑ Ⓓ ♿ 🚗 !

🚍🛌 Springwells Hotel, 9 High Street, BN44 3GG ☎ 01903 812446
www.springwells.co.uk Map 198/177112
BB **D** ✕ nearby S2 D3 T4 F1 Closed Xmas Ⓑ Ⓓ 🐾 ♿ 🚗 ! 🐾 ◆◆◆◆

Buncton Manor Farm, Steyning Rd, Wiston, BN44 3DD ☎ 01903 812736
(Nancy Rowland) www.bunctonmanor.supanet.com Map 198/148138
BB **D** D1 T1 Closed Nov Ⓥ Ⓓ ⊗ 🐾 ♿ !

🚍🛌 Uppingham, Kings Barn Villas, BN44 3FH ☎ 01903 812099
(Diana Couling) www.uppingham-steyning.co.uk Map 198/182111
BB **B** ✕ book first £10, 7:30pm S2 D1 T1
Ⓥ Ⓑ Ⓓ ⊗ 🐾 ♿ 🚗 ! 🐾 Ⓜ

SOUTH

● Walderton (Chichester)

SOUTH DOWNS*

MONARCH'S WAY

☆ ▰◀ **Hillside Cottages**
Cooks Lane, PO18 9EF ☎ 02392 631260 (Robina Richter)
www.hillside-cottages.co.uk Map 197/790107
BB **C** ✕ book first £12, 6-8pm D1 T2
Ⓥ Ⓑ Ⓓ ⊗ 🍴🛁☕🚗! ★★★

Hillside Cottages offers a friendly welcome and delicious home cooked food. It has a pretty country garden and downland views. The Monarch's Way, South Downs Way, South Coast Cycle Route and National Nature Reserve of Kingley Vale are nearby.

● Worthing

SOUTH DOWNS WAY

▰◀ Manor Guest House, 100 Broadwater Rd, BN14 8AN ☎ 01903 236028
(Sandy Colbourne) www.manorworthing.com Map 198/147040
BB **D** ✕ book first £7, 5-8pm S1 D2 T1 F2 ⋙(Worthing)
Ⓥ Ⓑ Ⓓ ⊗ 🍴🛁☕🚗!🐾 ◆◆◆◆

SELF-CATERING

HAMPSHIRE

● Alresford

SOUTH DOWNS*

☆ **The Gatekeeper's Lodge**
☎ 01962 732829 (Mary Hide)
www.thegatekeeperslodge.co.uk
£300-£450 Sleeps 4. 1 cottage.
Perfect base for riverside, countryside exploring. ⊗

Beautifully refurbished and spacious two-bedroomed 19th-century cottage. Close to the Wayfarer's Walk and Pilgrim's Way (now St Swithun's Way) and the beautiful South Downs. Stroll along the banks of the Itchen to the ancient capital of England — Winchester.

● East Meon

SOUTH DOWNS*

Church Farm House ☎ 01730 823256 (Christopher Moor)
www.gardenchalet.co.uk
£100-£180 Sleeps 2. 1 chalet. Beautiful village, near South Downs Way. ⊗ 🐾

● Fordingbridge

NEW FOREST

Alderholt Mill ☎ 01425 653130 (Sandra Harte) www.alderholtmill.co.uk
£220-£480 Sleeps 2-6. 3 flats.
Working water mill conversion. Rural setting. ⊗ 🐾 ★★★ See B&B also.

Sandy Balls Holiday Centre ☎ 01425 653042 (Tracey Farmer)
www.sandy-balls.co.uk
£148-£1,113 Sleeps 2-6. 136 lodges/homes. 230 touring/camping pitches.
Closed Jan Set in 120 acres of woodland. 🐾 ★★★★★

● Lymington

NEW FOREST

The Old Exchange ☎ 01590 679228 (Sarah Alborino)
www.newforestretreats.co.uk
£300-£600 Sleeps 2-7. 2 apartments.
Short breaks available all year. ⊗ ⋙(Sway) ★★★

● Lyndhurst

NEW FOREST

Kingsbridge House ☎ 023 8081 1161 (Linda Goodrich)
www.newforest.demon.co.uk/KingsbridgeHouseRetreat.htm
£190-£300 Sleeps 2 + cot. 1 annexe of house.
Comfortable accommodation. Ideal location for the forest. ⊗ See B&B also.

● Petersfield

The Privett Centre ☎ 01730 828238 (Angela Grigsby)
www.privettcentre.org.uk
£150-£200 (per night) Sleeps 20. 1 Victorian schoolhouse.
In Area of Outstanding Natural Beauty. ⊗ See Groups also.

● Romsey

1 Thatched Cottage ☎ 01794 340460 (Mrs R J Crane)
£202-£335 Sleeps 5. 1 cottage.
Thatched country cottage. Bed linen provided. ⊗ ⋙(Dunbridge) 🐾

● Sway

NEW FOREST

Mrs Helen Beale ☎ 01590 682049 hackneypark@tiscali.co.uk
£160-£380 Sleeps 2-6. 1 cottage, 2 flats.
Comfortable accommodation in excellent walking area.
⊗ ⋙(Sway) 🐾 ★★★

● Winchester

SOUTH DOWNS*

Mrs Barbara Crabbe ☎ 01962 777887 crabbesleg@dsl.pipex.com
£200 Sleeps 2 adults 2 children. 1 apartment.
Quiet country lane. Good views. ⊗ 🐾

ISLE OF WIGHT

● Bonchurch

Westfield Lodges & Apartments ☎ 01983 852268 (Toby Brading)
www.westfieldlodges.co.uk
£205-£570 Sleeps 2-6. Lodges and apts.
Indoor heated pool. Tennis court. ⊗ ⋙(Shanklin) 🐾

● Brighstone

☆ **Sea Breeze Cottage**
☎ 01983 740993 (Ginny Peckham)
www.seabreeze-cottage.co.uk
£220-£550 Sleeps 4-5 + cot. 1 cottage.
Sea views, AONB, 250m coastal path. ⊗ ★★★★

Modern, two bedroomed, recently refurbished cottage with sea views. Sleeps 4/5 + cot. In an AONB, 250m from a panoramic coastal path and beach and close to downland trails. Patio. Communal garden. Complimentary ferry collection for foot passengers. Short breaks available.

● Freshwater

Fiona Watson ☎ 020 7274 0394 fiona.watson6@btopenworld.com
£300-£650 Sleeps 6. 1 cottage.
Coastline and river walks on doorstep. ⊗ 🐾

High Edser ☎ 01483 278214 (Carol Franklin-Adams)
www.highedser.co.uk/iowcottage
£250-£600 Sleeps 6. 1 cottage. Situated on beautiful west Wight coastline.

☆ Afton Barns
☎ 01920 822600 (Susan Lankester)
www.aftonbarns.co.uk
£250-£700 Sleeps 5. 1 barn conversion.
Quiet location next to Tennyson Trail. 🚫 🐾

Lovely 3-bedroomed barn conversion at the foot of Afton Down AONB.
Excellent base for walking in west Wight – especially Tennyson Trail and Needles. Well-equipped, bright airy rooms and private west-facing garden.
Freshwater Bay 10 minutes' walk.

Brambles Chine ☎ 01293 528272 (Mrs Sams) brambleschine@aol.com
£150-£450 Sleeps 4. 1 chalet. Closed Dec-Jan
Centrally-heated, comfortably furnished, great location. 🚫

● Godshill
Godshill Park House ☎ 01983 840271 (Nora Down) www.godshillpark.co.uk
£230-£990 Sleeps 2-7 + cot. 2 self-contained annexes..
AONB, immediate access to numerous footpaths. ★★★★

● Kingston

☆ Island Cottage Holidays
☎ 01929 480080 (Honor Vass)
www.islandcottageholidays.com
£189-£1,225 Sleeps 1-12. 65 cottages.
Cottages throughout the Isle of Wight. 🚫 🐾 ★★★-★★★★★

Charming individual cottages in lovely coastal and rural surroundings situated throughout the Isle of Wight.
Close to the coastal paths & the extensive trails that cross the island. Dogs welcome at many cottages. From £185pw.

● Sandown

☆ Rose Holiday Chalets
☎ 01983 403402 (Martin or Dot)
www.sandownbayholidays.co.uk
£110-£400 Sleeps 6. 30+ chalets.
Informal holiday 'village' alongside beach/coast. ᴡᴡ(Sandown)

Fantastic position by coastal path and near Culver Down, Brading Down and nature reserve.
Grid ref: 617853. Well-equipped SC chalets for up to 6, including linen. Hire chalet by week or day. Shop and clubhouse facilities.

● Shanklin
Lyon Court ☎ 01983 865861 (Paul Humphreys)
www.lyoncourtshanklin.co.uk
£190-£710 Sleeps 2-6. 8 apartments.
Overlooks Shanklin Down. Bus and rail links. 🚫 ᴡᴡ(Shanklin) ★★★

☆ YMCA Isle of Wight
☎ 01983 862441
www.ymca-fg.org
£210-£2,100 Sleeps 4-24. 2 properties. Linen included.
Short breaks off season. 🚫 ᴡᴡ(Lake Station, Shanklin) ★★★

In the grounds of a beautiful Victorian house by the sea.
The Lodge, for 10-24; Apartment for 1-4 (both SC or meals in main house). Main house B&B, HB and FB for 1-100+. Mostly twin/group rooms. Close to cliff path and sandy beach. Great base for island walking.

● Ventnor

☆ The Annexe
☎ 01983 855449 (Simon & Anna Wooldridge)
www.isleofwightwalks.co.uk
£250-£590 Sleeps 6. 1 cottage.
Refurbished 2006. Discount for RA members. 🚫 Ⓜ ★★★★

A warm welcome awaits walkers to The Annexe. We have personally put together a series of walks which we can tailor to suit all abilities.

Set in a quiet village location. Ventnor 2 miles, Shanklin 3 miles.

A multitude of walks including the Worsley Trail radiate from the doorstep.

The island has 500 miles of footpaths and half is designated AONB.
Excellent bus service. Free ferry, hover, station pick up.

● Whitwell
Downcourt Manor Farm ☎ 01983 730329 (Mrs Aylwin)
www.downcourtmanorfarm.co.uk £375-£600 Sleeps 6. 1 farmhouse.
Listed building, magnificent views, scenic walks. 🚫

KENT

● Canterbury
Mulberry Cottages ☎ 0870 6092429 www.mulberrycottages.com
£270-£490 Sleeps 4. 1 cottage.
Charming medieval cottage in village square. 🚫 ᴡᴡ(Chilham) 🐾

OXFORDSHIRE

● Shipton-under-Wychwood
King John's Barn ☎ 01993 878075 (Vicky Greves) www.kingjohnsbarn.co.uk
£310-£625 Sleeps 2-4. 2 cottages.
Rural & peaceful with outstanding views. 🐾 ★★★★

● Wallingford
Oxford Holiday Cottage ☎ 01235 512519 (Nigel Ainge)
www.oxfordholidaycottage.com
£330-£365 Sleeps 2-3. 1 cottage. Lovely country cottage near Thames & Ridgeway. ᴡᴡ(Didcot Parkway) ★★★★

SOUTH

SURREY

● **Holmbury St Mary**
Gill Hill ☎ 01306 730210
£250-£410 Sleeps 2-4. 2 units.
Converted farm buildings on Greensand Way.
⊗ 🚲 ★★★ Access Category I.

EAST SUSSEX

● **Alfriston**
SOUTH DOWNS*
Martlets ☎ 01323 870451 (Rosalind Danesi)
£300-£650 Sleeps 4-6. Ground floor of house..
⋙(Berwick) ⊗ Ⓜ See B&B also.

● **Battle**

☆ **Gardners Farm Holidays**
☎ 01323 832219 (Mark & Sue Ward-Smith)
www.gardnersfarmholidays.co.uk
£260-£425 Sleeps 4. 2 chalets.
Panoramic views, family fishing, near beach. 🚲

Two newly converted farm buildings set in the beautiful Sussex countryside. Fitted and furbished to a high standard. There is a large range of walks locally — from country to coastal — with the 1066 Walk passing your front door.

● **Rye**
The Coastguards ☎ 01308 423180 (Mrs Vallor-Doyle)
£275-£495 Sleeps 4. I cottage.
Unique sea/rural retreat. Spacious garden with patio. Ⓜ ★★★

GROUPS

HAMPSHIRE

The Privett Centre (SC) Church Lane, Privett, Petersfield ☎ 01730 828238
www.privettcentre.org.uk
SC £150+pn Max 20. Converted School. Ⅾ ⊗ See SC also.

WEST SUSSEX

Wapsbourne Manor Farm (SC) Sheffield Park, near Uckfield TN22 3QT
☎ 01825 723414 www.wowo.co.uk
SC £60+pppw Min 3, max 170. 10 caravans, I bunkhouse barn, campsite.
✕nearby 🐾 Ⅾ ⊗ 🚗 ! See Hostels also.

HOSTELS, BUNKHOUSES & CAMPSITES

BUCKINGHAMSHIRE

Wendover House School (IH) Church Lane, Wendover HP22 6JZ
☎ 01296 626065 www.wendoverhouse.bucks.sch.uk
Bednight £12 Closed weekdays & school term-time ✕nearby Ⅾ
On the Ridgeway Path.

☆ **Cadborough Farm**
☎ 01424 814823 (Jane Apperly)
www.cadborough.co.uk
£185-£395 Sleeps 2. 5 cottages.
Newly converted. Full GCH. Linen included. ⋙(Rye) ⊗ 🚲 ★★★★

5 newly converted individual farm cottages providing luxurious and spacious accommodation for two people. Located I mile from Rye, close to 1066 Country Walk. Full gas c/h. Linen and towels included. One small, well-behaved dog welcome. ETC 4-star.
Email: cadborough@hotmail.co.uk

WEST SUSSEX

● **Compton**
SOUTH DOWNS*
Yew Tree House ☎ 023 9263 1248 (Mr J Buchanan)
mdrb@dbuchanan.plus.com
£180-£300 Sleeps 2. I flat. Ideal for walking South Downs. ⊗ 🚲 ★★★

● **Henfield**
SOUTH DOWNS*

☆ **New Hall**
☎ 01273 492546 (Mrs M W Carreck)
£260-£420 Sleeps 4-5. I cottage, I flat.
On footpath close to South Downs.
🚲 ★★★

Self-contained flat and 17th-century cottage in two wings of manor house, set in three and a half acres of mature gardens, surrounded by farmland and footpaths. Half a mile from river Adur and Downslink long-distance-footpath. Two and a half miles from the South Downs Way.

KENT

☆ **Palace Farm Hostel** (IH)
Down Court Rd, Doddington ☎ 01795 886200
www.palacefarm.com Grid ref: 935577
Bednight £14+
✕nearby 🐾 Ⓑ Ⅾ ⊗ Ⓜ ★★★Ⓦ

Luxury 30 bed hostel accommodation in the Kent Downs AONB on a family farm in village with pub. Enjoy this beautiful area with many self-guided walks. Ensuite rooms, comfortable beds and bunks, kitchen, garden, BBQ, continental breakfast and linen included.

WEST SUSSEX

Washington Caravan & Camping Park (C) London Rd, Washington RH20 4AJ
☎ 01903 892869 (Max F Edlin) www.washcamp.com
Camping £7.50-£11.50 ⋙ (Worthing) ✕nearby 🐾 Ⅾ ★★★★
Wheelchair access and toilet. On the South Downs Way.

Wapsbourne Manor Farm (C/BHB) Sheffield Park, Uckfield TN22 3QT
☎ 01825 723414 www.wowo.co.uk Bednight £8, camping from £5, caravan
£12 ✕nearby 🐾 Ⅾ ⊗ See Groups also.

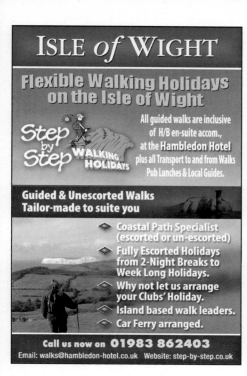
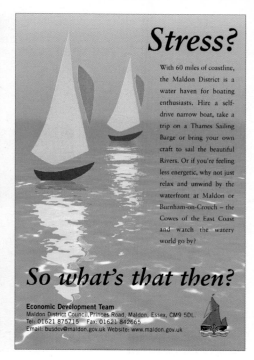

EAST

Long Distance Paths

Essex Way ....ESX

Icknield Way Path...................ICK

London Loop ....LNL

Nene Way ....NEN

Peddars Way and Norfolk
Coast Path............................PNC

Suffolk Coast and
Heaths Path ....SCH

Wherryman's Way...............WRY

See **Paths & Access p25** for full
details of LDPs and waymarks

National Parks

The Broads

See **Useful Contacts p99** for full
details of national parks

TRAIL THROUGH AN OILSEED RAPE FIELD
IN CAMBRIDGESHIRE

WALK...   ...THE ANGLES WAY

Named 'the best waterside walk in Britain' by British Waterways, this little-known but beautiful route trails 125km/ 78 miles from Great Yarmouth, up the Waveney Valley on the Norfolk–Suffolk border. Linking the Broads to the Suffolk Brecks, it takes in numerous historical sites and at one stage borders the RSPB's Breydon Water (pictured) – an important migratory stop for many rare birds, including avocet, dunlin and hen harriers.

A newly updated guidebook with accommodation listings is available from Norfolk Area Ramblers (see Local Ramblers Publications, p90).

EAST

VISIT...   ...THE GREAT FEN PROJECT

East Anglia's wetlands will grow by 3,000 hectares if the aims of this ambitious restoration programme reach their fruition. Based between Huntingdon and Peterborough, the project hopes to return farmland drained as recently as 1850 back to fenland habitat, joining together the Woodwalton and Holme Fens nature reserves. Extensive new footpaths, waterways and facilities are planned. But for now, the 20km/13 miles of walkways and bird hides at Woodwalton, and Holme's birch woodland (the largest in lowland Britain) give a flavour of the future Great Fen, and offer possible glimpses of water vole, bittern or the rare fen violet.

Keep track of developments and visitor information at www.greatfen.org.uk

SEE...   ...SEALS AT BLAKENEY POINT

This spectacular, windswept spit that juts five miles out into the North Sea is home to a colony of 500 common and grey seals. The greys are the larger of the two, but both suckle their pups for up to three weeks on the point's sandbanks, which also act as an important breeding ground for birds, especially terns. Walkers can leave the Peddars Way and Norfolk Coast Path by Cley-next-the-Sea and attempt the slow, arduous journey through marsh and shingle on foot. But the quickest and best way to view the seals is by one of the many boats operating between April and October.

Visit www.nationaltrust.org.uk or ☎ 01263 740241 for more information.

LOCAL RAMBLERS GROUPS... Walkers in Suffolk can get details of all access land in The Sandlings and The Brecks, and download some picturesque path maps not on OS maps (some having been recently saved from deletion) on Suffolk Area's website (see p77)... **South East Essex Group provides a list of pubs and taverns in the locality that are congenial to walkers on their website (see p71)...** West Essex Group offers walks leaders for community projects and schools, including a recent successful walks programme for Asian women in Waltham Forest. Contact Len Banister on ☎ 020 8527 8158 if you would like the Group to help your local organisation.

Explore folklore
Explore Nottinghamshire

Walking

Cycling

Riding

Outdoors

Nottinghamshire
County Council

For walking, cycling and horseriding guides for Nottinghamshire call **0115 9772166** or visit **www.nottinghamshire.gov.uk/countryside**

MAP 183

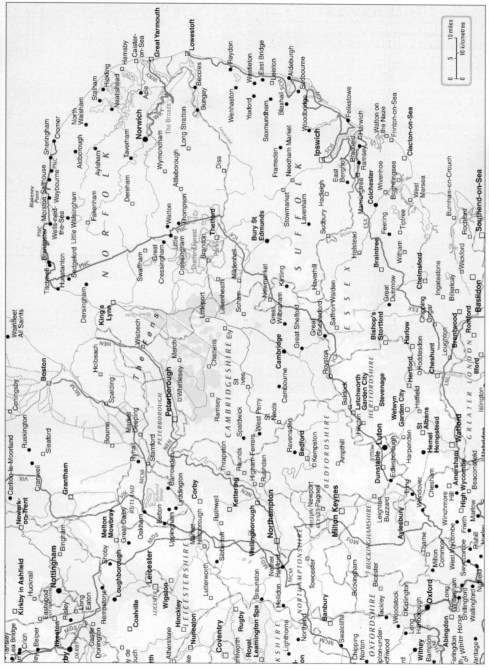

EAST

BED & BREAKFAST

BEDFORDSHIRE

● Ravensden (Bedford)

Tree-Garth, Church End, MK44 2RP ☎ 01234 771745 (Sue & Bruce Edwards)
treegarth@ukonline.co.uk Map 153/079547
BB **C** ✕ nearby SI DI TI Closed Xmas ⊡ ⊗ 🛏🖒🚗 ★★★

CAMBRIDGESHIRE

● Cambourne (Cambridge)

☆ ⌂🛶 **The Cambridge Belfry**
CB3 6BW ☎ 01954 714600
www.marstonhotels.com Map 153/TL 319601
BB **D** ✕ £32.50, 7-9:30pm D96 T24
Ⓥ Ⓑ 🛏🖒 ★★★★ Wheelchair access.

A comfortable, modern four-star hotel with excellent facilities, The Cambridge Belfry is located in Cambourne, just 8 miles from Cambridge, a city itself offering enjoyable walks amongst the colleges and beside the River Cam.

With choice of dining in the main Bridge restaurant or the separate brasserie and bar area, this hotel is the place to stay when exploring the Cambridgeshire countryside with its woods and ridges.

Relax in the Reflections Leisure Club, with its heated indoor swimming pool, body treatments and massages in the spa, gym, sauna and steam room.

Please ask about our exclusive rates for walking parties.

● Cambridge

145 Gwydir Street, CBI 2LJ ☎ 01223 356615 (Mrs M Sanders)
www.thegwydirhouse.co.uk/index.php Map 154/462579
BB **B** ✕ nearby TI Closed Xmas ⋙(Cambridge) ⊡ ⊗ 🛏🖒🚗 !

● Great Shelford (Cambridge)

Norfolk House, 2 Tunwells Lane, CB2 5LJ
☎ 01223 840287 (Janet Diver) Map 154/463521
BB **D** ✕ nearby DI T2 Closed Xmas ⋙(Great Shelford) Ⓑ ⊡ ⊗ 🖒

● Great Wilbraham (Cambridge)

The Sycamore House, 56 High Street, CBI 5JD ☎ 01223 880751
(B W & E A Canning) www.thesycamorehouse.co.uk Map 154/549572
BB **C** ✕ nearby SI D2 Closed Xmas ⊡ ⊗ 🛏🖒🚗 Ⓜ ◆◆◆◆

● Kirtling (Newmarket)

☆ **Hill Farm**
Newmarket Road, CB8 9HQ ☎ 01638 730253 (Ann Bailey)
Map 154/682583
BB **D** ✕ nearby SI DI TI Closed Xmas
Ⓑ ⊡ 🛏🖒🚗 🛁 ◆◆◆

Picturesque 400-year-old farmhouse with superb views of rural Studland. Tea/coffee facilities, CH, en-suites available. Log fires, TV lounge, games room. Excellent home-cooking with menu choice. Special diets by arrangement. Licensed. Fire certificate. Access at all times. £32 single room, £60 double.

● Spaldwick (Huntingdon)

⌂🛶 Chestnut View, 8-10 High Street, PE28 0TD
☎ 01480 890216 (Joyce Leach)
www.chestnutview-bedbreakfast.co.uk Map 153/130727
BB **D** ✕ book first £10, 6-7:30pm T4 Ⓥ Ⓑ ⊡ ⊗ 🛏🖒🚗

● West Perry (Huntingdon)

☆ ⌂🛶 **West Perry B&B**
38 West Perry, PE28 0BX ☎ 01480 810225 (Diana Hickling)
www.westperrybandb.co.uk Map 153/146669
BB **C** ✕ nearby SI T2 Closed Xmas
Ⓑ ⊡ ⊗ 🛏🖒🚗 !

Victorian cottage situated in Perry village. 5 minutes' walk to Grafham Water with 10 miles of walking and cycle-track around the waterline. 2-minute walk to village pub/restaurant and Post Office shop. 1 mile to Three Shires Way. 5 miles to Ouse Valley Way. Offering quality, comfort and value for money.

ESSEX

● Bradfield (Manningtree)

ESSEX WAY

☆ **Emsworth House**
Ship Hill, CO11 2UP ☎ 01255 870860 (Penny Linton)
www.emsworthhouse.co.uk Map 168,169/142310
BB **D** ✕ nearby S3 D2 TI FI Closed Xmas
Ⓑ ⊡ ⊗ 🛏🖒🚗 ! 🛁 ◆◆◆◆

Emsworth House has stunning views of the countryside and River Stour.

A lovely place to stay.

All tastes catered for and your comfort my priority!

● Colchester

ESSEX WAY

Scheregate Hotel, 36 Osborne Street, CO2 7DB
☎ 01206 573034 (J Powell) Map 168/996250
BB **D** ✕ nearby SI5 D6 T8 FI Closed Xmas ⋙(Colchester)
Ⓑ ⊡ 🖒 ◆◆

● Feering (Colchester)
ESSEX WAY

☆ ●🍴 **Prested Hall**
CO5 9EE ☎ 01376 573300 www.prested.co.uk Map 168/882196
BB **D** ✕ £15, 6:30-8:30pm S/T3 D7 F1 ₩(Kelvedon)
Ⓥ Ⓑ Ⓓ ⊛ 🐾🛏🚗❗Ⓜ ★★★★
Wheelchair access. Guide dogs welcome.

Relaxing, 15th-century part-moated country house hotel in 75 acres.
Ideal for the Colne and Stour valleys, Dedham Vale, the Blackwater Valley and
Estuary, Abberton Reservoir, Fingringhoe Wick, Mark's Hall Arboretum and
many areas of ancient woodland. Close to Suffolk border.
Helpful staff, delicious food and great health club, with 20-metre pool, gym,
lawn and real tennis (the Tudor game), massage and beauty suite.
Individual walkers, groups and whole house bookings all welcome.

● Great Chesterford (Saffron Walden)
ICKNIELD WAY

Mill House, CB10 1NS ☎ 01799 530493 (Christine King)
Map 154/504431
BB **A** ✕ nearby S1 D4 T1 ₩(Gt Chesterford) Ⓓ ⊛ 🐾🛏🚗 🎒

● Great Dunmow
●🍴 Puttocks Farm B&B, Philpot End, CM6 1JQ
☎ 01371 872377 (Roger & Jane Hockley)
www.puttocksfarm.com Map 167/623196
BB **D** ✕ nearby D2 T2 Ⓥ Ⓑ Ⓓ ⊛ 🐾🛏🚗 ◆◆◆◆

● Ramsey (Harwich)
ESSEX WAY

●🍴 Woodview Cottage, Wrabness Road, CO12 5ND
☎ 01255 886413 (Anne Cohen)
www.woodview-cottage.co.uk Map 168,169/191310
BB **D** ✕ book first £4 (light supper) S1 D1 F1 Closed Xmas ₩(Wrabness)
Ⓥ Ⓑ Ⓓ ⊛ 🐾🛏🚗 🎒 ◆◆◆◆Ⓢ

HERTFORDSHIRE

● Hemel Hempstead
Alexandra Guest House, 40-42 Alexandra Road, HP2 5BP ☎ 01442 242897
www.alexandraguesthouse.co.uk Map 166/057074
BB **C** ✕ nearby S6 D5 T4 F3 Closed Xmas ₩(Hemel Hempstead)
Ⓥ Ⓑ 🐾🛏🎒 ◆◆◆

● Tring
RIDGEWAY

Rangers Cottage, Tring Park, Wigginton, HP23 6EB
☎ 01442 890155 (Sally Dawson) www.rangerscottage.com Map 165/936102
BB **D** ✕ nearby D2 T1 Closed Xmas ₩(Tring)
Ⓑ Ⓓ ⊛ 🐾🛏 ◆◆◆◆

NORFOLK

● Acle
WHERRYMAN'S WAY

●🍴 Fern House B&B, The Street, NR13 3QJ ☎ 01493 754142 (Denise Kett)
terrygkett@tiscali.co.uk Map 134/401105
BB **C** ✕ nearby D1 T1 F1 ₩(Acle) Ⓥ Ⓑ Ⓓ ⊛ 🐾🛏🚗❗🎒Ⓜ

● Aldborough
Butterfly Cottage, The Green, NR11 7AA ☎ 01263 768198 (Janet Davison)
www.butterflycottage.com Map 133/184343
BB **C** ✕ book first £12-£15, 6:30-7:30pm S1 D1 T1 F1
Ⓥ Ⓑ Ⓓ ⊛ 🐾🛏🚗❗🎒 ◆◆◆◆

● Aylsham (Norwich)
☆ ●🍴 **The Old Pump House**
2 Holman Road, NR11 6BY ☎ 01263 733789
www.smoothhound.co.uk/hotels/oldpumphouse.html Map 133,134/190270
BB **D** ✕ book first £20, 6.30pm D2 T2 F1 Closed Xmas
Ⓥ Ⓑ Ⓓ ⊛ 🐾🛏🎒 ◆◆◆◆Ⓢ

18th C family home by thatched pump near
marketplace, convenient for Weavers Way.
Centrally located heated rooms (5 en-suite)
with TV and hot drinks. Hearty breakfasts in
pine-shuttered sitting room overlooking
peaceful garden. Evening meals Oct-April by
arrangement. Non-smoking.

● Dersingham (King's Lynn)
PEDDARS WAY & NORFOLK COAST PATH

●🍴 Holkham Cottage, 34 Hunstanton Road, PE31 6HQ
☎ 01485 544562 (Jane Curtis) www.holkhamcottage.co.uk Map 132/685305
BB **B/C** ✕ book first £10, 6:30pm S1 D2 T1
Ⓥ Ⓑ Ⓓ ⊛ 🐾🛏🚗❗🎒 ◆◆◆◆
Accommodation suitable for disabled guests.

●🍴 Ashdene House, 60 Hunstanton Road, PE31 6HQ
☎ 01485 540395 (Martin Bruce) www.ashdene-house.co.uk Map 132/686306
BB **D** ✕ book first £12, 7-8pm D2 T2 F1 Closed Dec
Ⓥ Ⓑ Ⓓ ⊛ 🐾🛏❗🎒 ◆◆◆

● Great Cressingham (Swaffham)
PEDDARS WAY & NORFOLK COAST PATH

The Vines, IP25 6NL ☎ 01760 756303 (Mike & Vanessa Woolnough)
www.thevines.fsbusiness.co.uk Map 144/850016
BB **B** ✕ nearby D2 T1 F1
Ⓑ Ⓓ ⊛ 🐾🛏🚗❗🎒 ◆◆◆◆

● Hickling (Norwich)
Black Horse Cottage, The Green, NR12 0YA ☎ 01692 598691 (Yvonne Pugh)
www.blackhorsecottage.com Map 134/410234
BB **C** ✕ nearby S1 D2 Closed Xmas Ⓓ ⊛ 🐾🛏🚗❗ ◆◆◆◆

●🍴 Dairy Barns, Lound Farm, NR12 0BE ☎ 01692 598243 (Hannah Deane)
www.dairybarns.co.uk Map 134/419255
BB **C** ✕ book first £7.95, 6-7pm D2 T4
Ⓥ Ⓑ Ⓓ ⊛ 🐾🛏❗ ★★★★Ⓢ Ⓦ Wheelchair access.

● Hunstanton
PEDDARS WAY & NORFOLK COAST PATH

🛏🍴 The Gables, 28 Austin Street, PE36 6AW ☎ 01485 532514
(Barbara Bamfield) www.thegableshunstanton.co.uk Map 132/674411
BB **C** ✕ book first £14.99, 6:30pm D2 T2 F3 Closed Xmas
Ⓥ Ⓑ Ⓓ 🐾♨🚗!Ⓜ ◆◆◆ Discounts for groups.

☆ 🛏🍴 **The Burleigh House Hotel**
7 Cliff Terrace, PE36 6DY ☎ 01485 533080 (Ram/Sharon Chauhan-Jennings)
www.theburleigh.com Map 132/673411
BB **C/D** ✕ book first £17, 6-7pm S1 D4 T2 F4
Ⓥ Ⓑ Ⓓ 🐾♨ ◆◆◆

Charming, Victorian, family-run guest house ideally situated close to Peddars Way and the coastal path at the quieter end of Hunstanton. We offer spacious, comfortable rooms, a licensed restaurant and cosy lounge. An ideal base for walkers and birdwatchers.

● Little Cressingham (Thetford)
PEDDARS WAY & NORFOLK COAST PATH

☆ **Sycamore House B&B**
IP25 6NE ☎ 01953 881887 (Mr J Wittridge)
Map 144/872001
BB **C** ✕ nearby S2 D2 T1
Ⓑ Ⓓ 🐾♨🚗! ◆◆◆◆

Sycamore House is a large country home in a tranquil village. Close to Thetford Forest, which is host to many activities to suit people of all ages. It is situated on The Peddars Way and near the historical market towns of Watton, Swaffham & Thetford.

● Little Walsingham
PEDDARS WAY & NORFOLK COAST PATH

🛏🍴 St David's House, Friday Market, NR22 6DB ☎ 01328 820633
(Mrs J Renshaw) www.stdavidshousewalsingham.co.uk Map 132/933366
BB **C** ✕ book first £14, 6-8:30pm D2 T2 F1
Ⓥ Ⓑ Ⓓ ⊛ 🐾♨🚗 ◆◆◆

● Morston (Holt)
PEDDARS WAY & NORFOLK COAST PATH

Scaldbeck Cottage, Stiffkey Rd, NR25 7BJ ☎ 01263 740188 (E Hamond)
ned@hamond.co.uk Map 133/004440
BB **C** ✕ nearby D1 T1 Closed Dec-Jan Ⓓ ⊛ ♨🚗!

● Neatishead (Norwich)
THE BROADS

🛏🍴 Regency Guest House, The Street, NR12 8AD ☎ 01692 630233
(Sue Wrigley) www.regencyguesthouse.com Map 133,134/340210
BB **C** ✕ book first D1 T1 F1 Ⓑ Ⓓ 🐾♨!🏊 ◆◆◆◆

● North Walsham
🛏🍴 Green Ridges, 104 Cromer Road, NR28 0HE
☎ 01692 402448 (Yvonne Mitchell) www.greenridges.com Map 133/272307
BB **B/C** ✕ book first £14.99, 5:30-8:30pm D1 T1 F1 🚍(North Walsham)
Ⓥ Ⓑ Ⓓ ⊛ 🐾♨🚗!🏊 ◆◆◆◆

● Norwich
The Old Rectory, Crostwick, NR12 7BG ☎ 01603 738513 (Mrs D Solomon)
info@oldrectorycrostwick.com Map 133,134/256159
BB **D** ✕ book first £13.50, 6:30-8:30pm S1 D9 T5 F2
Ⓥ Ⓑ Ⓓ 🐾♨🏊 ★★

🛏🍴 Foxhole Farm, Windy Lane, Foxhole, Saxlingham Thorpe, NR15 1UG
☎ 01508 499226 (John & Pauline Spear)
foxholefarm@hotmail.com Map 134/218971
BB **C** ✕ book first £15 D1 T1 Ⓥ Ⓑ Ⓓ ⊛ 🐾♨ ◆◆◆◆

☆ 🛏🍴 **Butterfly Guest House**
240 Thorpe Road, NR1 1TW ☎ 01603 437740 (Lynn Wardle)
Map 134/251084
BB **B** ✕ nearby S1 D3 T3 F1 Closed Xmas 🚍(Norwich)
Ⓥ Ⓑ Ⓓ ⊛ 🐾♨Ⓜ ◆◆◆ Wheelchair access.

Restored Edwardian house one mile from Norwich centre.
On main bus route. Close to the Broads, local pubs and restaurants.
Private car park with CCTV.
Colour TV in all rooms.
Business and leisure guests welcome.

● Old Hunstanton (Hunstanton)
PEDDARS WAY & NORFOLK COAST PATH

☆ 🛏🍴 **The Neptune Inn & Restaurant**
85 Old Hunstanton Road, PE36 6HZ ☎ 01485 532122
www.theneptune.co.uk Map 132/686422
BB **D** ✕ book first £30, 6-9pm S1 D5 T1
Ⓥ Ⓑ ⊛ 🐾♨🏊 ◆◆◆◆Ⓢ

Award-winning accommodation and restaurant, near to Peddars Way & Norfolk Coast Path and bird reserves. All bedrooms en-suite, TV, DVD, coffee and tea-making facilities. Only fresh local produce served in our AA rosette restaurant.

● Salthouse (Holt)
PEDDARS WAY & NORFOLK COAST PATH

Cumfus Bottom, Purdy Street, NR25 7XA
☎ 01263 741118 Map 133/073437
BB **C** ✕ nearby D2 T1 Ⓑ Ⓓ 🐾♨!🏊

● Sedgeford (Hunstanton)
PEDDARS WAY & NORFOLK COAST PATH

☆ 🛏🍴 **The King William IV Country Pub & Restaurant**
Heacham Road, PE36 5LU ☎ 01485 571765
www.thekingwilliamsedgeford.co.uk Map 132/709365
BB **D** ✕ £8-£15, 6:30-9pm S4 D4 T4 F2
Ⓥ Ⓑ Ⓓ 🐾♨🏊

Close to ancient Peddars Way, north Norfolk coastline and coastal path, tucked away in village amid rolling countryside. Comfortable en-suite bedrooms, king-size beds, TV, coffee/tea. Two restaurants, bar and garden. Delightful escape for every season.

Park View, PE36 5LU ☎ 01485 571352 (Mrs J Frost) Map 132/711366
BB **B** ✕ book first £10 S1 D1 T1 Closed Dec-Feb
Ⓥ Ⓑ Ⓓ ⊛ 🐾 🛏 🚗 ! 🌑

● Sheringham
PEDDARS WAY & NORFOLK COAST PATH

Oakleigh, 31 Morris Street, NR26 8JY ☎ 01263 824993 (Diana North)
dnorthoak@hotmail.com Map 133/157434
BB **B/C** ✕ nearby S1 D1 Closed Dec-Feb ⋘(Sheringham)
Ⓑ Ⓓ ⊛ 🛏 🌑

▪◁ Elmwood, 6 The Rise, NR26 8QA ☎ 01263 825454 Map 133/160426
BB **B** ✕ nearby D1 T1 Closed Xmas ⋘(Sheringham)
Ⓑ Ⓓ ⊛ 🛏 🚗 ! 🌑 Ⓜ

☆ **The Beaumaris Hotel**
15 South St, NR26 8LL ☎ 01263 822370 (Alan & Hilary Stevens)
www.thebeaumarishotel.co.uk Map 133/155431
BB **D** ✕ book first £18.50, 7-8:30pm S5 D/T16 Closed Xmas-Feb
⋘(Sheringham) Ⓥ Ⓑ Ⓓ 🐾 🛏 🚗 ! ★★

Owned by the same family since 1947 with a reputation for personal service and excellent English cuisine. 5 mins' walk from Norfolk Coast Path. National Trust properties and bird-watching at Cley close by.

● Stalham (Norwich)
THE BROADS

Landell, Brick Kiln Lane, Ingham, NR12 9SX ☎ 01692 582349 (Barbara Mixer)
www.landell.co.uk Map 133,134/385255
BB **C** ✕ book first £12 D1 T1 F1 Closed Xmas
Ⓑ Ⓓ ⊛ 🐾 🛏 🚗 ! 🌑 Ⓜ

● Taverham (Norwich)

▪◁ Foxwood Guest House, Fakenham Road, NR8 6HR ☎ 01603 868474
www.foxwoodhouse.co.uk Map 133/154152
BB **C** ✕ book first £10, 6:30pm D1 T2 Closed Xmas
Ⓥ Ⓑ Ⓓ ⊛ 🐾 🛏 🚗 !

● Thompson (Thetford)
PEDDARS WAY & NORFOLK COAST PATH

▪◁ College Farm, IP24 1QG ☎ 01953 483318 (Lavender Garnier)
collegefarm83@amserve.net Map 144/933966
BB **C** ✕ nearby D2 T1 Ⓑ Ⓓ 🐾 🛏 🚗

▪◁ Thatched House, Mill Rd, IP24 1PH
☎ 01953 483577 (Brenda Mills)
thatchedhouse@amserve.net Map 144/919967
BB **D** ✕ nearby D1 T2 Closed Xmas Ⓥ Ⓑ Ⓓ ⊛ 🐾 🛏 🚗 ! 🌑 Ⓜ

FOUND SOMEWHERE GOOD THAT'S NOT IN THE GUIDE?
Fill in the Recommendation/Feedback Form on p123 and send it to the editor at our central office or email:
yearbook@ramblers.org.uk

● Titchwell (King's Lynn)
PEDDARS WAY & NORFOLK COAST PATH

☆ **Briarfields**
Main Street, PE31 8BB ☎ 01485 210742
www.norfolkhotels.co.uk Map 132/757438
BB **D** ✕ £15, 6:30-9pm D11 T7 F4
Ⓥ Ⓑ Ⓓ ⊛ 🐾 🛏 🚗 🌑 ★★

Briarfields is a renovated barn complex with sea views situated next to the RSPB reserve and marshes at Titchwell. We are the perfect getaway to explore the north Norfolk coast with Sandringham, Norfolk Lavender, Peddars Way and Holkham Hall nearby.
Old beams and oak floors, log fire, excellent bar & restaurant dishes, afternoon teas, real ales, four-poster beds and exceptional views of the RSPB marshes. All bedrooms are en-suite including family rooms.
We offer bed & breakfast packages and discounted rates over the winter period.

● Watton (Thetford)
PEDDARS WAY & NORFOLK COAST PATH

▪◁ The Hare & Barrel Hotel, 80 Brandon Road, IP25 6LB ☎ 01953 882752
(M Raven) www.hare-and-barrel-hotel-norfolk.co.uk Map 144/906007
BB **D** ✕ book first £8, 6.30-9pm S6 D4 T7 F1 Ⓥ Ⓑ 🐾 🛏 🌑

● Wells-next-the-Sea
PEDDARS WAY & NORFOLK COAST PATH

Meadowside, Two Furlong Hill, NR23 1HQ
☎ 01328 710470 (C & L Shayes) Map 132/913433
BB **C** ✕ nearby D1 T1 Closed Xmas Ⓑ Ⓓ ⊛ 🛏 ! Ⓜ

The Cobblers, Standard Road, NR23 1JU ☎ 01328 710155 (Mike Rivington)
www.cobblers.co.uk Map 132/918435
BB **D** ✕ nearby S3 D3 T/D2 Closed Xmas
Ⓥ Ⓑ ⊛ 🐾 🛏 🌑 ◆◆◆◆

● Weybourne
PEDDARS WAY & NORFOLK COAST PATH

Sedgemoor, Sheringham Road, NR25 7EY ☎ 01263 588533 Map 133/113429
BB **B** ✕ nearby D2 Closed Xmas ⋘(Weybourne) Ⓓ 🛏 🚗 🌑

SUFFOLK

● Beccles
THE BROADS

Catherine House, 2 Ringsfield Road, NR34 9PQ
☎ 01502 716428 (Mr & Mrs W T Renilson) Map 156/418897
BB **C/D** ✕ nearby D3 Closed Xmas ⋘(Beccles)
Ⓑ Ⓓ 🐾 🛏 ◆◆◆◆

▪◁ Pinetrees, Park Drive, NR34 7DQ ☎ 01502 470796 (Sue Bergin)
www.pinetrees.net Map 156/435900
BB **D** ✕ nearby D3 ⋘(Beccles)
Ⓥ Ⓑ Ⓓ ⊛ 🐾 🚗 ! ◆◆◆ Wheelchair access.

EAST

● Blaxhall (Woodbridge)

SUFFOLK COAST & HEATHS PATH

▨ The Ship Inn, School Road, IP12 2DY ☎ 01728 688316
shipblaxhall@aol.com Map 156/367570
BB **C** ✕ £9, 6-9pm T4 Ⓥ Ⓑ Ⓓ ⊛ 🐾🛏🚗! 🐄 ◆◆

● Bungay

▨ Bigod Holidays B&B, 22 Quaves Lane, NR35 1DF ☎ 01986 892907
(Mrs M Sheppard) bigod.holidays@tiscali.co.uk Map 156/336895
BB **C** ✕ nearby S1 D1 T1 Closed Xmas Ⓑ Ⓓ ⊛ 🐾🛏🚗!

● Bury St Edmunds

Rose Cottage & Laurels Stables, Horringer-cum-Ickworth, IP29 5SN
☎ 01284 735281 Map 155/825613
BB **C** ✕ nearby S1 D1 T1 ⚊(Bury St Edmunds)
Ⓓ ⊛ 🐾🛏🚗 🐄 Access Category 1.

▨ Oak Cottage, 54 Guildhall Street, IP33 1QF
☎ 01284 762745 (Sheila Keeley) sheekee@talk21.com Map 155/852638
BB **B/C** ✕ book first £15, 6:30-7pm S1 D1 T1 F1 ⚊(Bury St Edmunds)
Ⓥ Ⓑ Ⓓ ⊛ 🐾🛏 🐄 Ⓜ

● East Bergholt (Colchester)

ESSEX WAY & SUFFOLK COAST & HEATHS PATH

Rosemary, Rectory Hill, CO7 6TH ☎ 01206 298241 (Natalie Finch)
Map 155,169/073344
BB **B** ✕ nearby S1 T3 ⚊(Manningtree) Ⓓ ⊛ 🐾🛏🚗 🐄 ◆◆◆

● East Bridge (Leiston)

SUFFOLK COAST & HEATHS PATH

▨ The Eels Foot Inn, IP16 4SN ☎ 01728 830154
www.theeelsfootinn.co.uk Map 156/452660
BB **D** ✕ £12, 7-9pm S6 D6 T2 F1 Ⓥ Ⓑ Ⓓ 🐾🛏🚗!

● Felixstowe

SUFFOLK COAST & HEATHS PATH

Ranevale, 96 Ranelagh Road, IP11 7HU ☎ 01394 270001 Map 169/305348
BB **B** ✕ nearby S2 D2 T1 F1 Closed Dec ⚊(Felixstowe)
Ⓥ Ⓑ ⊛ 🐾🛏!

● Framsden (Stowmarket)

Greggle Cottage, Ashfield Rd, IP14 6LP ☎ 01728 860226 (Jim & Phil Welland)
wellands@ukgateway.net Map 156/194609
BB **B/C** S1 D1 T/D1 Closed Dec-Jan Ⓑ ⊛ 🐾🛏🚗! 🐄

● Lavenham (Sudbury)

Brett Farm, The Common, CO10 9PG ☎ 01787 248533 (Mrs M Hussey)
www.brettfarm.com Map 155/923491
BB **C** D2 T1 Closed Xmas ⚊(Sudbury) Ⓑ Ⓓ ⊛ 🐾🛏🚗! ◆◆◆◆

● Reydon (Southwold)

SUFFOLK COAST & HEATHS PATH

49 Halesworth Road, IP18 6NR ☎ 01502 725075 (Miss E A Webb)
www.southwold.info Map 156/498770
BB **C** ✕ nearby D2 T1 Ⓑ Ⓓ ⊛ 🐾🛏🚗! 🐄

● Saxmundham

▨ Georgian Guest House, 6 North Entrance, IP17 1AY ☎ 01728 603337
www.thegeorgian-house.com Map 156/385634
BB **D** ✕ nearby D4 T1 F2 Closed Xmas ⚊(Saxmundham)
Ⓑ Ⓓ ⊛ 🐾🛏🚗! 🐄 ★★★★★Ⓢ

● Sudbourne (Woodbridge)

Long Meadows, Gorse Lane, IP12 2BD ☎ 01394 450269 (Mrs A Wood)
Map 156/412532
BB **B** ✕ book first £10, 7:30pm S1 D1 T1 Closed Xmas
Ⓥ Ⓑ Ⓓ ⊛ 🐾🛏🚗! 🐄 ◆◆◆

● Wenhaston (Halesworth)

▨ Rowan House, Hall Road, IP19 9HF ☎ 01502 478407 (Patricia Kemsley)
pat@rowanhouse1.pms.com Map 156/427749
BB **C** ✕ book first £12, 7:30pm D1 T1 Closed Xmas
Ⓥ Ⓑ Ⓓ ⊛ 🐾🛏🚗! 🐄 ★★★★

● Woodbridge

Deben Lodge, Melton Road, IP12 1NH ☎ 01394 382740 (Rosemary Schlee)
Map 169/278498
BB **B** ✕ nearby S2 D1 T1 ⚊(Woodbridge)
Ⓓ ⊛ 🛏 🐄 ◆◆Ⓦ Hard tennis court. Oxfam B&B Scheme.

● Yoxford (Saxmundham)

Chapel Cottage Bed & Breakfast, High Street, IP17 3HP
☎ 01728 667096 (Deborah Gentry)
www.chapelcottage-yoxford.co.uk Map 156/393694
BB **C** ✕ nearby S1 D1 ⚊(Darsham) Ⓥ Ⓑ Ⓓ ⊛ 🐾🛏

SELF-CATERING

ESSEX

● Benfleet

Alice's Place ☎ 01268 756283 (Mr S Millward)
www.alices-place.co.uk
£450 Sleeps 4. 1 bungalow.
Family-size hot tub. ⊛ ⚊(Benfleet) ★★★★

NORFOLK

● Bacton

Castaways Holiday Park ☎ 01692 650436 www.castawaysholidaypark.co.uk
£116-£495 Sleeps 2-8. 3 log cabins, 5 apartments, 26 caravans.
A small site with great amenities. 🐄

● Cley-next-the-Sea

☆ **Archway Cottage**
☎ 01992 511303 (Mrs V Jackson)
£230-£500 Sleeps 2-7. 1 cottage.
Character cottage, comfortable and well-equipped
⊛ 🐄 ★★★

Archway Cottage, Cley-next-the-Sea.

Comfortable and well-equipped
character cottage – sleeps 7.

Another cottage in Wells-next-the-Sea.

Also telephone: 01992 503196

● Great Yarmouth
THE BROADS

Clippesby Hall ☎ 01493 367800 (John Lindsay) www.clippesby.com
£209-£949 Sleeps 2-8. 17 cottages & lodges.
Beautiful parkland setting. 🦽 ★★★★

● Mautby
THE BROADS

Lower Wood Farm Country Cottages ☎ 01493 722523 (Jill Nicholls)
www.lowerwoodfarm.co.uk
£295-£1,295 Sleeps 4-9. 7 cottages.
Indoor heated swimming pool. 😊 ★★★★

● West Raynham

Pollywiggle Cottage ☎ 01603 471990 (Marilyn Farnham-Smith)
www.pollywigglecottage.co.uk £340-£800 Sleeps 1-8. 1 cottage.
Character cottage, well equipped, coast 15 miles. 😊 🦽 ★★★★

● West Runton

Mrs J Marquart ☎ 01603 454801 jackie.marquart@tiscali.co.uk
£180-£300 Sleeps 3. 1 flint cottage.
National Trust conservation area, coastal path. ᴧᴧᴧ(West Runton) 😊 🦽

● Aldeburgh

Seaside Cottage ☎ 01728 746475 (Fiona Kerr) www.eastonfarmpark.co.uk
£421-£824 Sleeps 7. 1 cottage.
Seaside location. Ample parking. 😊 ★★★★

● Bures

Coppins Farm ☎ 01787 269297 (John McGlashan) http://coppinsfarm.co.uk
£215-£350 Sleeps 4. 1 showman's living van.
150-acre farm. Countryside stewardship. Hills. ᴧᴧᴧ(Bures) 😊

GROUPS

ESSEX

Prested Hall (BB) Hall Chase, Feering, Colchester CO5 9EE ☎ 01376 573300
www.prested.co.uk
BB £65 Min 6, max 22. 1 hotel. ᴧᴧᴧ(Kelvedon)
✕ 🦽 B D 😊 ⚓ ! ★★★★ See B&B also.

NORFOLK
PEDDARS WAY & NORFOLK COAST PATH

Deepdale Granary Group Hostel (SC) Burnham Deepdale
☎ 01485 210256
www.deepdalefarm.co.uk Map 132/804441
Max 18. ✕ nearby 🦽 B D 😊 ★★★W See Hostels also.

HOSTELS, BUNKHOUSES & CAMPSITES

NORFOLK
PEDDARS WAY & NORFOLK COAST PATH

Deepdale Backpackers and Camping (C/IH) Burnham, Deepdale
☎ 01485 210256
www.deepdalefarm.co.uk Map 132/803443
Bednight £10.50 ✕ nearby 🦽
B D 😊 🦽 ★★★★W See Groups also.

EAST

EAST MIDLANDS

Long Distance Paths

Derwent Valley
Heritage Way ....DER

Macmillan Way ....MCM

Midshires Way ....MDS

Nene Way............................NEN

Pennine Bridleway ....PNB

Pennine Way ....PNN

Staffordshire Way ....SFS

Trans Pennine Trail................TPT

Viking Way ....VIK

See Paths & Access p25 for full details of LDPs and waymarks

National Parks

Peak District

See Useful Contacts p99 for full details of national parks

FOOTPATH ALONG MAM TOR TO LOSE HILL
RIDGE IN THE PEAK DISTRICT

WALK...   ...THE DANELAW WAY

Danelaw was the Viking-settled area of ninth-century England that included the old 'burghs' of Derby, Nottingham, Leicester, Lincoln and Stamford, and this recently established, 96km/60-mile trail links those last two borough towns via some of the region's most beautiful countryside.

Devised by the late Brett Collier – a stalwart local Ramblers volunteer and author – his accompanying guidebook features plenty of historic and poetic background, plus details of a 13km/8-mile circular route from the picturesque village of Ryhall. To order it, see Local Ramblers Publications, p89.

VISIT...
...THE DERVENTIO HERITAGE VILLAGE

If the grand stately homes and UNESCO-hailed heritage along the Derwent Valley Heritage Way aren't enough to slake your historical thirst (and you must be one thirsty walker!), then take a detour at Derby to visit the newly created Derventio Heritage Village. The 1.6-hectare site by Derbyshire County Cricket Club takes you on an even steeper journey through Derby's history, recreating village life from Roman times to World War II, including a Celtic roundhouse, Viking longhouse and a whole host of archaeological treasures.

A Viking re-enactment is promised for Easter Bank Holiday. Visit www.derventio.org or ☎ 01332 613576 for details.

SEE...   ...THE DEVIL'S ARSE

You might feel quite rightly insulted if someone invited you to take a hike up the Devil's Arse, but hold back on your knuckled response! Because it is in fact a spectacular cave near the Peak District village of Castleton, approached by an awesome 280ft-deep gorge with the ruins of Peveril Castle towering above. And the reason for its mirthsome name? It was a fond monicker given by craftsmen who for centuries lived and made rope in its massive (ahem!) entrance. After a storm, water and air are sucked into the cavern, which creates an incredible noise, the vibrations of which can be felt through the floor.

For more details of guided tours and admission, visit www.cavern.co.uk or ☎ 01433 620285.

EAST MIDLANDS

LOCAL RAMBLERS GROUPS... A series of seven leaflets by the Dearne Valley Group detailing some picturesque shorter walks around the region are available to download free from their website (see p77)... **Derbyshire Family Rambling Group organises weekend walks at a pace and length suitable for families with children that are free and open to all. Contact them for a full programme (p70)**... A survey of all new access land in the Peak District, together with access points and grid references, is available from South Yorkshire and NE Derbyshire Area's website (see p77)... **Find a walker-friendly pub in Leicestershire and Rutland with the help of Leicester Group's list on their website (see p73).**

The Cardigan area is truly a walker's paradise. Whether you're looking for a taste of beautiful Cardigan Bay, Pembrokeshire Coastal Path, the mysterious Teifi Valley or the magical Preseli Hills – Cardigan Festival of Walking has it all!

©Janet Baxter 200

CARDIGAN FESTIVAL OF WALKING
GŴYL CERDDED ABERTEIFI
5-7 OCTOBER / HYDREF 2007

For further details contact Menter Aberteifi Tel: 01239 615554
Email: info@menter-aberteifi.co.uk Website: www.visitcardigan.com

VISIT LINCOLNSHIRE

Lincolnshire Wolds
Walking
Festival

19th May - 3rd June 2007

- 2 weeks of great walking
- Come and explore this wonderful Area of Outstanding Natural Beauty
- A healthy and enjoyable way to explore some of Lincolnshire's hidden treasures

To find out more and to order a Festival programme
Tel 01507 609289 Email louthinfo@e-lindsey.gov.uk
visitlincolnshire.com

MAP 193

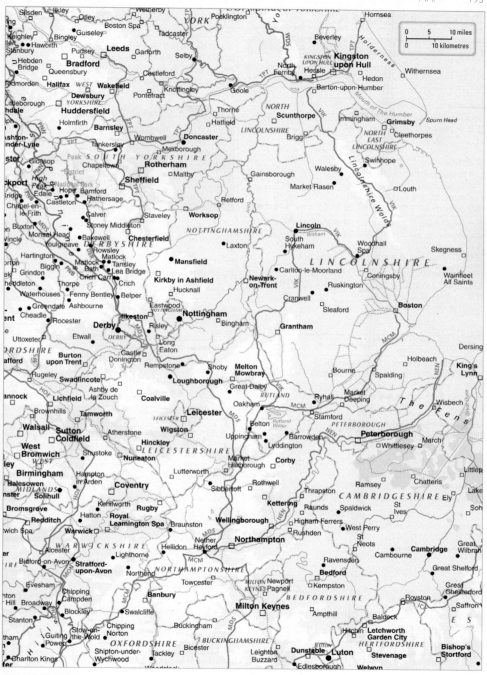

BED & BREAKFAST

DERBYSHIRE

● Alsop en le Dale (Ashbourne)
PEAK DISTRICT
PENNINE BRIDLEWAY

Dove Top Farm, Coldeaton, DE6 1QR ☎ 01335 310472 (Ann Wainwright)
www.dovetopfarm.co.uk Map 119/147566
BB **B** ✗ book first £10 D1 F1 Closed Dec-Jan
Ⓥ Ⓑ Ⓓ ⊛ ⬮⬮ ♨ ⬮ ⬮

● Ashbourne

☞☜ Mercaston Hall, Mercaston, DE6 3BL
☎ 01335 360263 (Angus & Vicki Haddon)
www.mercastonhall.com Map 119, 128/279419
BB **D** ✗ nearby D1 T2 Closed Xmas Ⓑ Ⓓ ⊛ ⬮⬮ ♨ ⬮ ⬮ ◆◆◆◆

☞☜ Compton House, 27-31 Compton, DE6 1BX ☎ 01335 343100 (Jane Maher)
www.comptonhouse.co.uk Map 128,119/180464
BB **C** ✗ nearby D3 T1 F1
Ⓑ ⊛ ⬮⬮ ♨ ⬮ ! ⬮ ◆◆◆ Tissington Trail on doorstep.

☞☜ Mona Villas B&B, Church Lane, Middle Mayfield, DE6 2JS
☎ 01335 343773 www.mona-villas.fsnet.co.uk Map 128,119/149448
BB **D** ✗ nearby D2 T1 Closed Xmas
Ⓑ Ⓓ ⊛ ⬮⬮ ♨ ⬮ ◆◆◆◆

● Bakewell
PEAK DISTRICT
DERWENT VALLEY HERITAGE WAY

Mandale House, Haddon Grove, nr Over Haddon, DE45 1JF
☎ 01629 812416 (Mrs J Finney) www.mandalehouse.co.uk Map 119/184664
BB **D** ✗ nearby D2 T1 Closed Dec-Jan
Ⓑ Ⓓ ⊛ ⬮⬮ ♨ ! ◆◆◆◆

☞☜ 1 Glebe Croft, Monyash Rd, DE45 1FG ☎ 01629 810013 (Mrs P Green)
www.glebecroft-bakewell.co.uk Map 119/214684
BB **D** ✗ nearby D2 T1 Closed Xmas
Ⓑ Ⓓ ⊛ ⬮⬮ ♨ ⬮ ! ◆◆◆◆Ⓢ

Holly Cottage, by Pilsley Post Office, Bun Alley, Pilsley, DE45 1UH
☎ 01246 582245 (Julie & Phil Rodgers)
www.hollycottagebandb.co.uk Map 119/241709
BB **D** ✗ nearby D2 T1 Closed Xmas Ⓑ Ⓓ ⊛ ⬮⬮ ♨ ⬮ ! ◆◆◆◆

☞☜ Ridgefield, Monyash Road, DE45 1FG ☎ 01629 815277 (Julie Horsfield)
www.ridgefieldbakewell.co.uk Map 119/212683
BB **C** ✗ nearby D1 Closed Xmas
Ⓑ Ⓓ ⊛ ⬮⬮ ♨ ◆◆◆◆

● Bamford (Hope Valley)
PEAK DISTRICT

The White House, S33 0BG ☎ 01433 651487 (Fiona Middleton)
Map 110/200818
BB **B** ✗ nearby S2 D2 T1 Closed Xmas ⋙(Bamford)
Ⓓ ⬮⬮ ♨ ⬮ ⬮ ◆◆◆

DON'T FORGET!
You can use your Discount Vouchers on p121
at any B&B listed with a ☞ symbol

● Biggin-by-Hartington (Buxton)
PEAK DISTRICT

☆ ☞☜ **Biggin Hall Hotel**
SK17 0DH ☎ 01298 84451
www.bigginhall.co.uk Map 119/153594
BB **D** ✗ book first £18, 7pm S1 D8 T8 F3
Ⓥ Ⓑ Ⓓ ⊛ ⬮⬮ ♨ ⬮ ★★

17th-century Old Hall, 1,000ft up in the Peak District National Park, close to Dovedale, in peaceful open countryside with beautiful uncrowded footpaths and bridleways.

20 en-suite rooms, log fires, warmth, comfort, quiet, and fresh home-cooked dinner. Licensed. Telephone 01298 84451 for a free brochure
or
Fax: 01298 84681
Email: enquiries@bigginhall.co.uk

● Buxton
PEAK DISTRICT
MIDSHIRES WAY

☆ **Devonshire Lodge Guest House**
2 Manchester Road, SK17 6SB ☎ 01298 71487 (Mrs S Pritchard)
www.devonshirelodgeguesthouse.co.uk Map 119/055738
BB **C** D2 T1 Closed Dec-Feb ⋙(Buxton)
Ⓑ Ⓓ ⊛ ⬮ ♨ ◆◆◆◆Ⓢ

Set in the elegant town of Buxton, in the heart of the English Peak District, Devonshire Lodge is a friendly, family-run guest house offering quality accommodation. This fine Victorian house is just three minutes' walk from the Opera House, Pavilion Gardens and the town centre.

The Old Manse, 6 Clifton Road, Silverlands, SK17 6QL ☎ 01298 25638
(T W & P A Cotton) www.oldmanse.co.uk Map 119/063734
BB **B** ✗ book first £12, 6:30pm S1 D4 T2 F2 Closed Xmas ⋙(Buxton)
Ⓥ Ⓑ Ⓓ ⊛ ⬮⬮ ♨ ◆◆◆

Linden Lodge, 31 Temple Rd, SK17 9BA ☎ 01298 27591 (Eileen Blane)
www.lindentreelodge.co.uk Map 119/052727
BB **C** ✗ nearby D1 T1 Closed Xmas ⋙(Buxton)
Ⓑ Ⓓ ⊛ ⬮⬮ ♨ ★★★★Ⓦ

☆ Kingscroft Guest House

10 Green Lane, SK17 9DP ☎ 01298 22757 (David Sedgwick)
Map 119/056727

BB **D** ✗ nearby S2 D5 T2 ⚌(Buxton)
Ⓥ Ⓑ Ⓓ 🛏☕🚗🛁❗🏷 ◆◆◆◆Ⓢ🅦

We welcome you to stay in our late Victorian luxury guest house, situated in a central yet quiet position in Buxton, in the heart of the Peak District. Here you will find everything you need for a relaxing break in comfortable surroundings with period decor and furnishings. Enjoy our hearty, delicious home-cooked and veggie breakfasts.

☆ ⚌ Portland Hotel

32 St Johns Road, SK17 6XQ ☎ 01298 22462
www.portlandhotelbuxton.net Map 119/054734

BB **C** ✗ £10, 7-9pm S5 D8 T9 ⚌(Buxton)
Ⓥ Ⓑ Ⓓ 🛏🛁🏷

Rambler-friendly, Peak District National Park hotel.

- 22 en-suite rooms with singles available (no single supplement)
- Real ale bar
- Traditional, fresh local food
- BB & DBB rates available
- Competitive rates for groups
- Packed lunches available if required
- Drying facilities
- Open socialising area available
- Modern but homely atmosphere with friendly and efficient service
- Car and coach parking and bike storage available
- Across the road from the famous Buxton Opera House

Please contact us to ascertain availability. portland.hotel@btinternet.com

● Calver (Hope Valley)
PEAK DISTRICT
DERWENT VALLEY HERITAGE WAY

⚌ Pear Tree Cottage, Main Street, S32 3XR ☎ 01433 631243 (Dianne Payne)
diannepayne1@aol.com Map 119/238745

BB **B** ✗ nearby S2 D1 Closed Xmas ⚌(Grindleford)
Ⓥ Ⓑ Ⓓ ⊗🛏🛁🚗❗

● Castleton (Hope Valley)
PEAK DISTRICT
PENNINE WAY & PENNINE BRIDLEWAY

⚌ Dunscar Farm, S33 8WA ☎ 01433 620483 (Janet Glennerster)
www.dunscarfarm.co.uk Map 110/143835

BB **C** ✗ nearby D3 T2 Closed Xmas ⚌(Hope)
Ⓑ Ⓓ ⊗🛁🚗❗ ★★★★

Cryer House, S33 8WG ☎ 01433 620244 (Mr & Mrs T Skelton)
fleeskel@aol.com Map 110/149829

BB **C** ✗ nearby D2 Closed Xmas ⚌(Hope) Ⓑ Ⓓ ⊗🛏🛁 ◆◆◆

☆ Rambler's Rest

Mill Bridge, S33 8WR ☎ 01433 620125 (Mary Gillott)
www.ramblersrest-castleton.co.uk Map 110/150831

BB **C** ✗ nearby S2 D5 T2 F1 Closed Xmas ⚌(Hope)
Ⓑ Ⓓ 🛏🛁🏷 ◆◆◆

A 17th-century guesthouse in the picturesque village of Castleton. The house is pleasant and olde worlde with 5 bedrooms, 3 en-suite. All have central heating, colour TV and tea-making facilities. Own car park.

⚌ Bargate Cottage, Market Place, S33 8WQ ☎ 01433 620201 (Fiona Saxon)
www.bargatecottage.co.uk Map 110/150827

BB **C** ✗ nearby D2 T1 Closed Xmas ⚌(Hope)
Ⓑ Ⓓ ⊗🛏🛁🚗❗ ◆◆◆◆ Guide dogs welcome.

☆ ⚌ Losehill Hall

Peak District National Park Centre, S33 8WB ☎ 01433 620373
www.losehillconferences.org.uk Map 110/153838

BB **C** ✗ book first £16.80, 7pm S22 D4 T14 F1 Closed Xmas ⚌(Hope)
Ⓥ Ⓑ Ⓓ ⊗🛏 ◆◆◆

Set in 27 acres of beautiful parkland in the heart of the Peak District, Losehill Hall offers stunning scenery, a relaxed environment and friendly staff. Close to the Pennine Way and Limestone Way. We also offer Walking and Navigation Skills holidays.

☆ ⚌ Ye Olde Cheshire Cheese Inn

How Lane, S33 8WJ ☎ 01433 620330 (Ken Slack)
www.cheshirecheeseinn.co.uk Map 110/152830

BB **B** ✗ £10, until 8:30pm S1 D11 T1 ⚌(Hope)
Ⓥ Ⓑ Ⓓ 🛏🛁🚗❗ ★★★★

This delightful 17th-century free house is situated in the heart of the Peak District and is an ideal base for walkers and climbers.
All bedrooms are en-suite.
A 'Village Fayre' menu is available all day, all dishes home-cooked in the tradtional manner. There is also a selection of daily specials.
All credit cards accepted. Special golf packages.
Email: kslack@btconnect.com

☆ ⚌ Ye Olde Nags Head

Cross Street, S33 8WH ☎ 01433 620248 (Nigel Birks)
nigel.birks@optimalfinance.net Map 110/151829

BB **D** ✗ £9, 5:30-9pm D7 T1 F2 ⚌(Hope)
Ⓥ Ⓑ 🛏🛁 ★★★

Traditional family-run 17th-century inn. En-suite rooms from £25pp. Four-posters and jacuzzis. Delicious home-cooked food, famous all-you-can-eat weekend carvery. Cosy bar with real fire, real ales. Leave your car and head for the hills — fantastic views guaranteed! Secure cycle storage.

● Chapel-en-le-Frith (High Peak)
PEAK DISTRICT

☆ **High Croft Guesthouse**
High Croft, Manchester Road, SK23 9UH ☎ 01298 814843 (Elaine Clarke)
www.highcroft-guesthouse.co.uk Map 119/041799
BB **C** ✕ nearby D4 F2 ᴀᴡ(Chapel-en-le-Frith)
Ⓑ Ⓓ ⊛ 🐾🛏🚗❗🐾 ◆◆◆◆◆Ⓦ

A luxurious Edwardian country house in 1.5 acres of peaceful, mature gardens adjoining Chapel-en-le-Frith golf course and Combs Reservoir with magnificent views and superb walks from the door. Four beautiful en-suite rooms, sitting room, elegant dining room and extensive breakfast menu.

● Crich
MIDSHIRES WAY & DERWENT VALLEY HERITAGE WAY

Clovelly Guest House, Roe's Lane, DE4 5DH ☎ 01773 852295 (Janice Lester)
Map 119/352545
BB **B** ✕ book first £6, 6pm S1 D2 Closed Xmas ᴀᴡ(Whatstandwell)
Ⓥ Ⓓ ⊛ 🐾🛏🚗❗ ◆◆

● Crich Carr (Whatstandwell)
PEAK DISTRICT
MIDSHIRES WAY & DERWENT VALLEY HERITAGE WAY

🐾🛏 Riverdale, Middle Lane, DE4 5EG ☎ 01773 853905 (Mrs V A Durbridge)
www.riverdaleguesthouse.co.uk Map 119/336542
BB **C** ✕ book first £12, 7pm D2 T1 Closed Xmas ᴀᴡ(Whatstandwell)
Ⓥ Ⓑ Ⓓ ⊛ 🐾🛏🚗🐾 Ⓜ ◆◆◆◆

● Edale (Hope Valley)
PEAK DISTRICT
PENNINE WAY & DERWENT VALLEY HERITAGE WAY

Brookfield, S33 7ZL ☎ 01433 670227 (J E Chapman) Map 110/113847
BB **B** ✕ nearby D1 T1 Closed Nov-Mar ᴀᴡ(Edale) Ⓓ ⊛ 🐾🛏🚗

🐾🛏 Mam Tor House, S33 7ZA ☎ 01433 670253 (Caroline Jackson)
www.mamtorhouse.co.uk Map 110/123858
BB **B** T2 F1 Closed Xmas ᴀᴡ(Edale) Ⓓ ⊛ 🐾🛏🐾 ◆◆◆

☆🐾🛏 **Rambler Country House Hotel**
Lane Head Green, S33 7ZA ☎ 01433 670268 (David Cairney)
www.theramblerinn.co.uk Map 110/123855
BB **D** ✕ £10, 12-9:30pm S1 D3 T1 F4 ᴀᴡ(Edale)
Ⓥ Ⓑ 🐾🛏 ◆◆◆

An attractive country house situated in Edale Valley, which lies in a beautiful setting below Kinder Scout and at the start of the Pennine Way — England's first and most famous long-distance footpath.

All our rooms are en-suite with colour TV, coffee & tea making facilities, hairdryer and phone.
You can see our hotel and rooms in the Virtual Tour on our website.

☆🐾🛏 **Ollerbrook Barn**
S33 7ZG ☎ 01433 670200 (Theresa Skillen)
www.ollerbrook-barn-cottage.co.uk Map 110/128859
BB **C** ✕ book first £10, 7:30pm D2 T1 ᴀᴡ(Edale)
Ⓥ Ⓑ Ⓓ ⊛ 🐾🛏🚗❗🐾 See SC also.

Friendly, family-run guest house situated a few minutes' walk from the Pennine Way and in the foothills of Kinder Scout.
It is an ideal base for walkers of any ability wishing to explore the wonders of the Peak District.

● Etwall (Derby)
🐾🛏 The Barn at Ashe Hall, Ash Lane, DE65 6HT ☎ 07875 250716
(Judy Chau) www.thebarnretreat.co.uk Map 128/257332
BB **D** ✕ book first £2, 6:30pm S5 T1
Ⓥ Ⓑ Ⓓ ⊛ 🐾🛏 ◆◆◆ On-site cafe.

● Fenny Bentley (Ashbourne)
PEAK DISTRICT

🐾🛏 Cairn Grove, Ashes Lane, DE6 1LD ☎ 01335 350538 (Thelma Wheeldon)
www.cairngrove.co.uk Map 119/173501
BB **C** ✕ nearby D2 T1 Closed Xmas
Ⓑ Ⓓ ⊛ 🐾🛏🚗❗🐾 ◆◆◆◆

● Foolow (Hope Valley)
PEAK DISTRICT
DERWENT VALLEY HERITAGE WAY & PENNINE BRIDLEWAY

🐾🛏 Housley Cottage, Housley, S32 5QB ☎ 01433 631505 (Kevin Tighe)
www.housleycottages.co.uk Map 119/194759
BB **C/D** ✕ nearby D3 T3 F1 Closed Dec-Jan
Ⓑ Ⓓ ⊛ 🐾🛏🚗❗ ◆◆◆◆

● Glossop
PEAK DISTRICT
PENNINE WAY, TRANS PENNINE TRAIL & PENNINE BRIDLEWAY

🐾🛏 Birds Nest Cottage, 40 Primrose Lane, SK13 8EW ☎ 01457 853478
(Brenda Howlett) birds@nest49.freeserve.co.uk Map 110/025939
BB **B** ✕ nearby S2 T2 F2 ᴀᴡ(Glossop)
Ⓑ Ⓓ ⊛ 🐾🛏🐾 Mini kitchen for guests.

● Grangemill (Matlock)
PEAK DISTRICT
MIDSHIRES WAY & PENNINE BRIDLEWAY

🐾🛏 Avondale Farm, DE4 4HT ☎ 01629 650820 (Louise Wragg)
www.avondalefarm.co.uk Map 119/244577
BB **B/C** ✕ nearby T1 Closed Xmas
Ⓑ Ⓓ ⊛ 🛏🚗❗🐾 ◆◆◆◆Ⓢ

● Hartington (Buxton)
PEAK DISTRICT
MIDSHIRES WAY & PENNINE BRIDLEWAY

Bank House, Market Place, SK17 0AL ☎ 01298 84465 (Mrs H Harrison)
Map 119/128604
BB **C** ✕ book first £11-£14.50, 6:30pm S1 D1 T1 F2 Closed Xmas
Ⓥ Ⓑ Ⓓ ⊛ 🐾🛏🚗❗ ◆◆◆

For an explanation of the symbols and abbreviations used in this guide, see the Key on the fold-out flap at the back.

● Hathersage (Hope Valley)
PEAK DISTRICT
DERWENT VALLEY HERITAGE WAY

☆ **Cannon Croft**
Cannonfields, S32 1AG ☎ 01433 650005 (Sandra Oates)
www.cannoncroft.fsbusiness.co.uk Map 110/226815
BB **D** ✕ nearby D3 T2 F2 ⋘(Hathersage)
🄱 🄳 ⊛ 🐾🛏 ◆◆◆◆Ⓖ

Stunning panoramic views.

Famous for our hospiatlity and breakfast: try Sundancer eggs or porridge with whiskey for example!

The standard of cleanliness is exceptional, as is the friendliness and caring attention provided throughout your stay, in keeping with our gold award status. Off road and private parking. All rooms en-suite.

Recommended by Holiday Which? Country Walking and Food and Travel Magazines. AA 4 RED dimanonds, VB Gold Award and Egg Cup Award also.

● Hope (Hope Valley)
PEAK DISTRICT
DERWENT VALLEY HERITAGE WAY

🏠 Round Meadow Barn, Parsons Lane, S33 6RB ☎ 01433 621347
(Gill & Geof Harris) http://mysite.freeserve.com/rmbarn Map 110/185831
BB **C** ✕ nearby D2 T1 F2 ⋘(Hope) 🄱 🄳 ⊛ 🐾🛏 🏺

● Lea Bridge (Matlock)
PEAK DISTRICT
DERWENT VALLEY HERITAGE WAY, PENNINE BRIDLEWAY & MIDSHIRES WAY

🏠 Pear Tree Farm Creative Holidays, Lea Road, DE4 5JN
☎ 01629 534215 (Sue Barber) www.derbyshirearts.co.uk Map 119/319572
BB **D** ✕ book first £15, 6:30-7:30pm D4 T4 F1 ⋘(Cromford)
Ⓥ 🄱 🄳 ⊛ 🐾🛏🚗! 🏺 ◆◆◆◆ Wheelchair access.

● Matlock
PEAK DISTRICT
DERWENT VALLEY HERITAGE WAY

☆ **Glendon**
Knowleston Place, DE4 3BU ☎ 01629 584732 (Mrs S Elliott)
Map 119/301598
BB **C** ✕ nearby D2 T2 F1 Closed Xmas ⋘(Matlock)
🄱 🄳 ⊛ 🐾🛏 ◆◆◆◆

This Grade II-listed building by the river and park is on the Heritage Way. It is conveniently situated near the town centre and bus/rail stations. Comfortable, well equipped accommodation in a relaxed atmosphere. Large private car park.

Riverbank House, Derwent Avenue, DE4 3LX ☎ 01629 582593
bookings@riverbankhouse.co.uk Map 119/299599
BB **D** ✕ nearby D3 T1 F2 Closed Xmas ⋘(Matlock)
🄱 🄳 ⊛ 🐾🛏Ⓜ ◆◆◆◆

Woodside, Stanton Lees, DE4 2LQ ☎ 01629 734320 (Mrs K M Potter)
www.stantonlees.freeserve.co.uk Map 119/254633
BB **C** ✕ nearby D2 T1 Closed Xmas 🄱 🄳 ⊛ 🐾🛏 ◆◆◆◆

🏠 Sheriff Lodge, Dimple Road, DE4 3JX ☎ 01629 760760
(Kate & Alan Richmond) www.sherifflodge.co.uk Map 119/295606
BB **D** ✕ nearby D2 T2 ⋘(Matlock) 🄱 🄳 ⊛ 🐾🛏 ◆◆◆◆Ⓖ

● Matlock Bath (Matlock)
PEAK DISTRICT
DERWENT VALLEY HERITAGE WAY

🏠 The Firs, 180 Dale Road, DE4 3PS ☎ 01629 582426 (Bernhard Trotman)
bernhard@thefirs180.demon.co.uk Map 119/295594
BB **C** ✕ nearby D1 T/D2 Closed Xmas ⋘(Matlock Bath)
🄱 🄳 ⊛ 🐾🛏🚗! 🏺 ◆◆◆

● Monsal Head (Bakewell)
PEAK DISTRICT

☆ 🏠 **Castle Cliffe**
DE45 1NL ☎ 01629 640258 (Mrs J Mantell)
www.castle-cliffe.com Map 119/185716
BB **C** ✕ nearby D3 T2 F2 Closed Xmas
🄱 🄳 ⊛ 🐾🛏🚗! 🏺 ◆◆◆◆

Stunning position overlooking the beautiful Monsal Dale.
Noted for its friendly atmosphere, hearty breakfasts and exceptional views.
Drinks in the garden or around an open log fire in winter.
Choice of dinner venues within an easy stroll.
Walks in all directions. Groups of all sizes welcome.
Guest lounge available and licensed to sell drinks.
Plenty of car parking space.

● Risley
MIDSHIRES WAY

🏠 Braeside Guest House, 113 Derby Rd, DE72 3SS ☎ 01159 395885
www.braesideguesthouse.co.uk Map 129/457357
BB **D** ✕ nearby D4 T2 🄱 🄳 ⊛ 🐾🛏 ◆◆◆◆

● Rowsley (Matlock)
PEAK DISTRICT
DERWENT VALLEY HERITAGE WAY

🏠 Eastfield, Chatsworth Road, DE4 2EH ☎ 01629 734427
www.east-field.co.uk Map 119/260662
BB **B** ✕ nearby D1 T2 Closed Xmas 🄳 ⊛ 🐾🛏🚗! Ⓜ

● Stoney Middleton (Hope Valley)
PEAK DISTRICT
DERWENT VALLEY HERITAGE WAY

🏠 Lovers Leap, The Dale, S32 4TF ☎ 01433 630300
www.loversleap.biz Map 119/227756
BB **B** ✕ £7-£18, 7pm-12am D3 Ⓥ 🄱 🄳 ⊛ 🐾🛏🚗! 🏺

● Tansley (Matlock)
DERWENT VALLEY HERITAGE WAY, PENNINE BRIDLEWAY & MIDSHIRES WAY

☆ ⬛ B&B Yew Tree Cottage
The Knoll, DE4 5FP ☎ 01629 583862 (Teanie Dornan)
www.yewtreecottagebb.co.uk Map 119/321601
BB D ✗ nearby D3 🚌(Matlock)
Ⓑ Ⓓ ⊗ 🍵 ♨ 🚗 ! ◆◆◆◆

Award-winning B&B. Memorable breakfasts.
Historic cottage, sympathetically restored,
providing outstanding comfort and cleanliness
whilst retaining originality and charm. Stunning
views, tranquil grounds. Good pub food nearby.
Ideally situated for Derwent Valley Heritage
Way, High Peak Trail, Peaks and Dales.

● Thorpe (Ashbourne)
PEAK DISTRICT
PENNINE BRIDLEWAY

☆ ⬛ Hillcrest House
Dovedale, DE6 2AW ☎ 01335 350436 (Margaret Sutton)
hillcresthouse@freenet.co.uk Map 119/152505
BB B ✗ book first £14.50 S1 D4 T1 F1 Closed Xmas
Ⓥ Ⓑ Ⓓ ⊗ 🍵 ♨ 🚗 ! ◆◆◆◆

Start your day with a full English
breakfast and finish off with a
nightcap in our lounge. Plenty of
off-road car parking. All king-size
beds and four-posters. En-suite,
TV, tea/coffee making facilities,
radio alarm and hairdryer.

⬛ Jasmine Cottage, DE6 2AW ☎ 01335 350465 (Liz Round)
Map 119/155502
BB B ✗ nearby D1 T1 Closed Xmas Ⓑ Ⓓ ⊗ 🍵 ♨ 🚗

● Whaley Bridge (High Peak)
MIDSHIRES WAY & PENNINE BRIDLEWAY

Springbank Guest House, 3 Reservoir Rd, SK23 7BL ☎ 01663 732819
(Margot Graham) www.whaleyspringbank.co.uk Map 110/009813
BB D ✗ book first £8, 7pm D2 T2 F1 🚌(Whaley Bridge)
Ⓥ Ⓑ Ⓓ ⊗ 🍵 ♨ 🚗 ! ◆◆◆◆

● Youlgreave (Bakewell)
PEAK DISTRICT
PENNINE BRIDLEWAY & MIDSHIRES WAY

The Old Bakery, Church Street, DE45 1UR ☎ 01629 636887 (Anne Croasdell)
www.cressbrook.co.uk/youlgve/oldbakery Map 119/210643
BB C ✗ nearby D2 T2 Closed Xmas Ⓑ Ⓓ ⊗ 🍵 ♨ ! ◆◆◆

LEICESTERSHIRE

● Great Dalby (Melton Mowbray)
MIDSHIRES WAY

Dairy Farm, 8 Burrough End, LE14 2EW ☎ 01664 562783 (Mrs L Parker)
www.dairy-farm.co.uk Map 129/744141
BB B ✗ nearby D2 T1 Ⓑ Ⓓ ⊗ 🍵 ♨ 🚗 ! 🐾 ◆◆◆

● Loughborough
Peachnook Guest House, 154 Ashby Road, LE11 3AG
☎ 01509 264390 (Valerie Wood)
www.smoothhound.co.uk/hotels/peachno-html Map 129/529196
BB B ✗ nearby S1 D1 T1 F2 🚌(Loughborough)
Ⓑ 🍵 ♨ ◆◆ Special diets. Guide dogs welcome.

● Rempstone (Loughborough)
MIDSHIRES WAY

⬛ Guesthouse At Rempstone, LE12 6RH ☎ 01509 881886 (Mark Cosgrove)
www.guesthouse-rempstone.co.uk Map 129/577243
BB B ✗ £6, 7pm S5 D3 T4 F2 Ⓥ Ⓑ Ⓓ 🍵 ♨ 🚗 ! 🐾

LINCOLNSHIRE

● Carlton-le-Moorland (Lincoln)
VIKING WAY

⬛ Grange Bed & Breakfast, 16 Broughton Road, LN5 9HN
☎ 01522 788286 (Diane Swales) www.thegrangebnb.co.uk Map 121/907581
BB B ✗ nearby S2 D1 T2 Ⓑ Ⓓ ⊗ 🍵 ♨ ! 🐾

● Cranwell (Sleaford)
VIKING WAY

⬛ Byards Leap Cottage, NG34 8EY
☎ 01400 261537 (Anne Wood) Map 130/011498
BB B ✗ book first £12, 6:30pm onwards D1 T1 Closed Xmas
Ⓥ Ⓓ ⊗ 🍵 ♨ 🚗 ! Ⓜ ◆◆◆ Special diets. Guide dogs welcome.

● Lincoln
VIKING WAY

Old Rectory Guest House, 19 Newport, LN1 3DQ
☎ 01522 514774 (Tony Downes) Map 121/975722
BB C ✗ nearby S1 D3 T1 F1 Closed Xmas 🚌(Lincoln)
Ⓑ Ⓓ ⊗ ♨ ◆◆◆

● Market Rasen
VIKING WAY

☆ ⬛ Waveney Cottage
Willingham Road, LN8 3DN ☎ 01673 843236 (Mrs J Bridger)
www.waveneycottage.co.uk Map 121,113/111890
BB C ✗ book first £12.50, 6pm D/F1 T2 Closed Xmas 🚌(Market Rasen)
Ⓥ Ⓑ Ⓓ ⊗ 🍵 ♨ 🚗 ◆◆◆◆

Comfortable, smoke-free en-suite
accommodation offering a choice of
delicious breakfasts. Hospitality tray,
hairdryer and TV in all rooms. Situated
close to all amenities, providing an
ideal base to explore the beauty and
peace of the Lincolnshire Wolds AONB.

● Ruskington (Sleaford)
Sunnyside Farm, Leasingham Lane, NG34 9AH ☎ 01526 833010 (Daphne Luke)
www.sunnysidefarm.co.uk Map 121/074502
BB B ✗ nearby D1 T1 🚌(Ruskington) Ⓑ Ⓓ 🍵 ♨ 🚗 ! 🐾 ◆◆◆

● South Hykeham (Lincoln)
VIKING WAY

⬛ Wellbeck Cottage B&B, 19 Meadow Lane, LN6 9PF ☎ 01522 692669
(Margaret Driffill) maggied@hotmail.co.uk Map 121/938645
BB C ✗ book first £10, 6-8:30pm D2 T1 🚌(North Hykeham)
Ⓥ Ⓑ Ⓓ ⊗ 🍵 ♨ 🚗 🐾 ★★★★Ⓦ

● Swinhope (Binbrook)

☆ ▪━◀ **Hoe Hill House Bed & Breakfast**
LN8 6HX ☎ 01472 399366 (Sally Ward)
www.hoehill.co.uk Map 113/217955
BB C ✕ book first £10, to suit D2 T1 Closed Xmas
Ⓥ Ⓑ Ⓓ ⊛ 🐾👜 ! 🛏 ★★★★

Characterful late 18th-century warren
bailiff's (rabbit catcher's) cottage.
Focus on excellent regional produce and
homemade wherever possible.
In rural spot, its pretty bedrooms enjoy
lovely views across the Wolds. Close to Viking
Way and unspoilt countryside.

● Wainfleet (Skegness)
▪━◀ Willow Farm, Thorpe Fendykes, PE24 4QH ☎ 01754 830316
www.willowfarmholidays.co.uk Map 122/452611
BB B ✕ £5, 6-9pm D1 T1 Closed Xmas ⇢(Thorpe Culvert)
Ⓥ Ⓑ Ⓓ 🐾👜 🚗 ! 🛏

● Walesby (Market Rasen)
VIKING WAY
▪━◀ Blaven, Walesby Hill, LN8 3UW ☎ 01673 838352 (Jacqy Braithwaite)
www.blavenhouse.co.uk Map 113/135924
BB D D2 T1 Closed Xmas Ⓑ Ⓓ ⊛ 🐾👜 🚗 ◆◆◆◆◆

● Woodhall Spa
VIKING WAY
Claremont Guest House, 9/11 Witham Road, LN10 6RW
☎ 01526 352000 (Claire Brennan)
www.woodhall-spa-guesthouse-bedandbreakfast.co.uk Map 122/191630
BB A/B ✕ nearby S3 D2 T1 F5 Closed Xmas Ⓑ Ⓓ 🐾👜 ! 🛏 ◆◆

NORTHAMPTONSHIRE

● Braunston (Daventry)
The Old Castle, London Road, NN11 7HB ☎ 01788 890887
Map 152/533660
BB B ✕ nearby D2 Closed Dec-Jan Ⓑ Ⓓ 👜 🛏

HAVE YOU TRIED
OUR GROUP
WALKS FINDER YET?

You can search our online database
and get details of thousands of Group walks the
length and breadth of Britain, all led by
Ramblers walk leaders and linked to the
accommodation guide.

Visit www.ramblers.org.uk/walksfinder

● Hellidon (Daventry)

☆ ▪━◀ **Hellidon Lakes**
NN11 6GG ☎ 01327 262550
www.marstonhotels.com Map 151/512578
BB D ✕ £29.95, 7-9:45pm S7 D75 T28
Ⓥ Ⓑ 🐾👜 ★★★★ Wheelchair access.

Hellidon Lakes offers splendid views overlooking lakes and rural countryside,
with many wonderful walks through conservation villages, delightful hamlets,
meadows and pastures nearby.

Our golf course and comfortable bedrooms allow Hellidon Lakes to offer you a
rejuvenating break.

The hotel is situated in 220 acres of walkable rolling countryside on the borders
of Warwickshire and Northamptonshire.

Please ask about our exclusive rates for walking parties.

● Nether Heyford (Northampton)
NENE WAY & MIDSHIRES WAY
▪━◀ Heyford B&B, 27 Church Street, NN7 3LH ☎ 01327 340872
(Pam Clements) http://heyfordguesthouse.co.uk Map 152/659586
BB C ✕ nearby S1 T3 Closed Xmas Ⓑ Ⓓ 🐾👜 🚗 ! ◆◆

● Sibbertoft (Market Harborough)
The Wrongs, LE16 9UJ ☎ 01858 880886 (Mrs M J Hart)
www.brookmeadow.co.uk Map 141/666829
BB B ✕ nearby S1 D1 Closed Xmas
Ⓓ ⊛ 🐾👜 🚗 ! 🛏 See Broadmeadow, Leics in SC also.

NOTTINGHAMSHIRE

● Laxton (Newark)
Manor Farm, Moorhouse Road, NG22 0NU ☎ 01777 870417 (Pat Haigh)
Map 120/724666
BB B ✕ nearby D1 F2 Closed Xmas Ⓓ 🐾👜 🛏 ★★★

● Mansfield
▪━◀ Bridleways Holiday Homes & Guest House, Newlands Rd, Forest Town,
NG19 0HU ☎ 01623 635725 (Gillian & Michael Rand)
www.stayatbridleways.co.uk Map 120/579624
BB D ✕ nearby S5 D4 T1 F1 Ⓑ ⊛ 👜 ◆◆◆

EAST MIDLANDS

● Nottingham (West Bridgford)

☆ ◼ The Nottingham Belfry
Mellor's Way, off Woodhouse Way, NG8 6PY ☎ 0115 9739393
www.marstonhotels.com Map 120/515420
BB **D** ✗ £25.50, 7-9:30pm D98 T22
Ⓥ Ⓑ ⊛ 🐾🍵🛏 ★★★★ Wheelchair access.

A contemporary hotel, on the edge of the city, offering every comfort with excellent leisure facilities. Predominantly a non-smoking hotel. Take time out to explore the wide variety of local attractions. Please ask about our exclusive rates for walking parties.

RUTLAND

● Barrowden (Oakham)
◼ The Spinneys, 31 Wakerley Road, LE15 8EP
☎ 01572 747455 (Valerie & John Hennessy) Map 141/950002
BB **B/C** ✗ book first £6, 6:30-7:30pm S1 T1 F1 Closed 12
Ⓥ Ⓑ Ⓓ ⊛ 🐾🛏 🚗 Facilities for disabled guests.

● Belton-in-Rutland (Oakham)
MACMILLAN WAY

☆ ◼ The Old Rectory
LE15 9LE ☎ 01572 717279
www.theoldrectorybelton.co.uk Map 141/814010
BB **B/C/D** ✗ nearby S1 D2 T3 F1 Closed Xmas
Ⓑ Ⓓ ⊛ 🐾🛏 🚗 ! 🍵 ★★★ See SC also.

Macmillan Way, Leicestershire Round, Rutland Water, Barnsdale gardens. Comfortable B&B accommodation in conservation village. Pub 200 yards, serving meals by arrangement. Packed lunch available with 24hrs notice.

● Lyddington (Oakham)
◼ Lydbrooke, 2 Colley Rise, LE15 9LL ☎ 01572 821471 (Pauline Brown)
lydbrookebb@hotmail.com Map 141/872973
BB **C** ✗ nearby S1 D1 T1 Closed Dec Ⓑ Ⓓ ⊛ 🐾🛏 🚗

● Oakham
MACMILLAN WAY & VIKING WAY
◼ The Old Wisteria Hotel, 4 Catmose Street, LE15 6HW
☎ 01572 722844 (Emad Saleeb) www.wisteriahotel.co.uk Map 141/862086
BB **D** ✗ book first £12.50+, 7-9pm S7 TD/18 ▲(Oakham)
Ⓥ Ⓑ Ⓓ 🐾🍵🛏 ★★★ See Groups also.

● Ryhall
MACMILLAN WAY
◼ Manorcroft, Essendine Road, PE9 4HE ☎ 01780 754876 (Julie Headland)
manorcroft@hotmail.com Map 130/036114
BB **D** ✗ nearby D1 T2 Closed Xmas Ⓑ Ⓓ ⊛ 🛏 🚗 ★★★★

● Uppingham
Meadow Sweet Lodge, South View, LE15 9TU ☎ 01572 822504
Map 141/867995
BB **B** ✗ nearby S1 T1 Closed Xmas Ⓑ Ⓓ ⊛ 🐾🛏 🚗 ! 🍵

SELF-CATERING

DERBYSHIRE

● Ashbourne
PEAK DISTRICT

☆ Sandybrook Country Park
☎ 01335 300000 (Pinelodge Holidays Ltd)
www.pinelodgeholidays.co.uk/sandybrook.ihtml
£260-£995 Sleeps 2-8. 41 pine lodges. Pinelodges sleep 2-8, indoor swimming pool. ⊛ 🛏 ★★★★ See Matlock also.

Luxurious pinelodges with glorious views, excellent base for Peak District.

Indoor pool, spa, sauna and play areas. Woodland walk.

The Coach House bar and restaurant serves an extensive menu and takeaways.

The luxurious pinelodges have satellite television and DVD players.
Fully fitted kitchens and a range of appliances. Each has a verandah with garden furniture. All linen is included. Weeks and short breaks available year round.
Email: enquiries@pinelodgeholidays.co.uk

☆ Offcote Grange Cottage Holidays
☎ 01335 344795 (Pat Walker)
www.offcotegrange.com
£970-£1,950 Sleeps 10-14 + 2 cots. 2 cottages. Oak beams, log fires, beautiful gardens. ⊛ ★★★★★ Car collection from station

Hillside Croft and Billy's Bothy

Two large, luxurious 5-star five-bedroom detached country cottages in peaceful rural locations, own landscaped gardens within beautiful scenery. Patio and BBQs. Private parking.

Each with separate lounge and dining rooms, exceptional farmhouse kitchens, quality bath/shower rooms. Billy's Bothy is all en-suite.

An excellent walking area, central Derbyshire, ideal base for all attractions.
Close to Chatsworth House and Carsington Water.
Soon — gymnasium, sauna and conference facility.

Ann Brown ☎ 01335 344799
ann@canalside00.freeserve.co.uk
£280 Sleeps 3. 1 cottage.
Available for short breaks. Good walking countryside. ⊛ 🛏 Ⓜ

☆ Granary Court
☎ 01283 820917 (Lynne Statham) www.granarycourt.demon.co.uk
£300-£1,800 Sleeps 1-26. 4 barn conversions, I cottage.
Spa, great celebration room, games room.
🚭 Ⓜ ★★★★ See Groups also.

Situated on the Staffordshire & Derbyshire borders, this venue offers plenty of scope for different grades of walking and outdoor activities. After a day's exertion, relax in our spa or book an on-site treatment with our therapists. Very relaxing.

● Ashford-in-the-Water
PEAK DISTRICT

I, Sunny Lea ☎ 01629 815285 (Mrs D Furness)
£230-£395 Sleeps 4 + cot. I cottage.
Beamed cottage, high standard, owner maintained.
🚭 ★★★★ Short breaks available.

● Bakewell
PEAK DISTRICT

Rock House ☎ 01298 872418 (Paul Steverson)
www.rockhouse-peakdistrict.co.uk
£245-£450 Sleeps 2-7. I cottage. 🚭 🐾

● Belper
PEAK DISTRICT

☆ Chevin View
☎ 01773 823061 (Mrs T Sowerby)
www.spacelocations.co.uk
£378-£429 Sleeps 7. I cottage.
Luxury listed cottage with contemporary design. ⋙(Belper) 🚭

Newly available, completely renovated and professionally designed, spacious 200-year-old mill worker's cottage.
Excellent location for historic walks in and around Belper, World Heritage Corridor and beautiful Peak District.

3 bedrooms and 2 bathrooms over 3 floors, newly fitted designer bathrooms and kitchen. Broadband wired/WiFi internet access.

Very convenient location, in a peaceful conservation area. Walking distance to train and bus stations.

● Castleton
PEAK DISTRICT

Riding House Cottages ☎ 01433 620257 (Denise Matthews)
www.riding-house-cottages.co.uk
£330-£500 Sleeps 2-4. 2 cottages.
Walker's paradise, spectacular views, working farm. ⋙(Hope)
🚭 ★★★★-★★★★★★

● Chatsworth
PEAK DISTRICT

☆ Chatsworth Estate
☎ 01246 565379 (Tissie Reason)
www.chatsworth.org
£345-£1,413 Sleeps 2-10. I farmhouse, I hunting tower, 12 cottages/barns.
Wonderful walks on your doorstep. 🚭 🐾 ★★★★-★★★★★★

Wonderful walks on your doorstep.

Come to stay on the Chatsworth Estate, home to the Duke and Duchess of Devonshire. Our range of holiday cottages, in four stunning locations throughout Derbyshire and the Peak District, comprise of fourteen properties: from the 16th-century Hunting Tower to our beautifully renovated barns, providing well equipped and very comfortable accommodation.

Free tickets to Chatsworth House and Gardens for weekly bookings.
Groups and 'good' dogs welcome.

● Chinley
PEAK DISTRICT

Pam Broadhurst ☎ 01663 750566 www.cotebank.co.uk
£230-£600 Sleeps 2-6. 2 cottages.
Footpaths from the door. ⋙(Chinley) 🐾 ★★★★

● Curbar
PEAK DISTRICT

Curbar Cottages ☎ 01433 631885 (Dr Morrisy)
http://curbarcottages.com
£175-£275 Sleeps 2-6. 2 cottages. Walks from the door. 🐾 ★★★

● Edale
PEAK DISTRICT

☆ Ollerbrook Barn Cottage
☎ 01433 670200 (Mark & Theresa Skillen)
www.ollerbrook-barn-cottage.co.uk
£350-£500 Sleeps 4. I cottage.
Four-poster bed. Log burning stove. ⋙(Edale) 🐾 ★★★ See B&B also.

A cosy, well equipped cottage situated a few minutes' walk from the Pennine Way and in the foothills of Kinder Scout.

It is an ideal base for walkers of any ability wishing to explore the wonders of the Peak District.

EAST MIDLANDS

● Eyam
PEAK DISTRICT

☆ Dalehead Court Country Cottages
☎ 01433 620214 (Dorothy Neary)
www.peakdistrictholidaycottages.com
£195-£500 Sleeps 2-6. 3 cottages. Unique village square setting, private parking. ⊗ ★★★★-★★★★★ See Hope also.

Historic Eyam. A fine house, a delightful 17th-century barn and cosy cottage overlooking Derbyshire's most historic village square.
Exceptional decor and furnishings, walled courtyard garden and private parking. Village inn, shops 2 mins.
Breaks from £115. Phone for a brochure or email laneside@lineone.net

● Hartington
PEAK DISTRICT

Patrick Skemp ☎ 01298 84447
www.cotterillfarm.co.uk
£220-£950 Sleeps 2-6. 6 cottages.
Superb location and views, near River Dove. ⊗ Ⓜ ★★★★

● Hope
PEAK DISTRICT

☆ Laneside Farm Holiday Cottages
☎ 01433 620214 (Dorothy Neary)
www.peakdistrictholidaycottages.com
£185-£395 Sleeps 2-4. 4 cottages. Delightful riverside setting bordering Hope village. ⋘(Hope) ⊗ 🛁 ★★★★-★★★★★ See Eyam also.

Hope – riverside setting. Award-winning conversion of 3 beamed farm barns into delightful self-catering cottages. River & hill walks abound. Train/buses nearby for walk and ride-back options. Conveniently located near village amenities.
Breaks from £110. Phone for a brochure or email laneside@lineone.net

Mrs Gill Elliott ☎ 01433 620640
www.farfield.gemsoft.co.uk
£250-£575 Sleeps 2-5. 3 cottages. Spacious, well-equipped accommodation in scenic location. ⋘(Hope) ⊗ ★★★★

● Matlock
PEAK DISTRICT

☆ Carpenters Cottage
☎ 0115 9233455 (Iris & Bob Wilmot)
www.carpenters-cottage.com
£220-£400 Sleeps 4-6. 1 cottage.
⋘(Matlock) ⊗ Ⓜ ★★★★

Warm, well equipped, fully modernised stone cottage. Located within sensitively converted 18th-century mill complex in Derbyshire Dales. 3 bedrooms (one en-suite).
Small sunny garden. Lovely views. Doorstep walks. Designated private parking for 2 cars.
Short stroll to Matlock, pubs/restaurants.

☆ Darwin Forest Country Park
☎ 01629 732428 (Pinelodge Holidays Ltd)
www.pinelodgeholidays.co.uk/darwin_forest.ihtml
£260-£995 Sleeps 2-8. 85 pine lodges. Pinelodges sleep 2-8, indoor swimming pool. ⊗ 🛁 ★★★★ See Ashbourne also.

Set in 44 acres of stunning woodland, excellent base for exploring Peak District.
Tennis courts, children's play areas, indoor pool, sauna, steam, gym and beauty therapy.

The Forester's Inn serves an extensive menu and takeaways.

The luxurious pinelodges have satellite television and DVD players.
Fully fitted kitchens and a range of appliances. Each has a verandah with garden furniture. All linen is included. Weeks and short breaks available year round.

Email: enquiries@pinelodgeholidays.co.uk

● Parwich
PEAK DISTRICT

☆ High Barn Cottage
http://highbarn.ctranter.co.uk
£250-£540 Sleeps 7-9. 1 cottage.
Suitable for individuals with mobility difficulties.
⊗ 🛁

Large converted barn in picturesque village of Parwich. Excellent base for walking, cycling and climbing. High Peak and Tissington trails close by. Alton Towers 30 minutes away. Parking for up to 4 vehicles. Groups welcome.
Email: highbarnparwich@tiscali.co.uk

● Sheen
PEAK DISTRICT

☆ Sheen Cottage
☎ 01270 874979 (Janice Mills)
www.sheencottage.co.uk
£200-£380 Sleeps 1-4. 1 cottage.
Open fire, beams, warm and cosy. ⊗

Lovely Grade-II listed cottage. Modernised to high standards while maintaining character and charm. Clean, warm and welcoming.
Excellent base for exploring White Peak.
Adjoins quiet pub serving good food. Includes heating, electricity, coal, logs and bed linen.
Email: janice@sheencottage.co.uk

● Sutton-on-the-Hill
Windlehill Farm ☎ 01283 732377 (Keith & Joan Lennard)
www.windlehill.btinternet.co.uk
£140-£450 Sleeps 2-6. 1 apt, 1 cottage.
Beamed barns on small organic farm. ⊗ 🛁 ★★★★

● Tideswell
PEAK DISTRICT

Rebethnal Cottage ☎ 07775 597787 (Amanda Greenland)
www.rebethnalcottage.com
£150-£475 Sleeps 6. 1 cottage. Closed Nov-Mar
200-year-old fully modernised cottage. 🚫 ★★★

LEICESTERSHIRE

● Market Harborough
Brookmeadow ☎ 01858 880886 (Mary & Jasper Hart)
www.brookmeadow.co.uk
£180-£490 Sleeps 3-6. 3 chalets.
Peaceful lakeside setting, camping. Jurassic Way.
🛏 ★★★-★★★★ See The Wrongs, Northants in B&B also.

LINCOLNSHIRE

● Louth
Louth Holiday Home ☎ 0117 9315033 (Julia Mullett)
www.louth-holidayhome.co.uk
£210-£280 Sleeps 3. 1 house.
Victorian townhouse with private parking. 🚫 Ⓜ ★★★

Goulceby Post ☎ 01507 343230 (Gordon and Louise Reid)
www.goulcebypost.co.uk
£210-£265 Sleeps 2. 1 cottage.
Situated on Viking Way. 🚫 ★★★★

RUTLAND

● Belton-in-Rutland
The Old Rectory ☎ 01572 717279 (Richard & Vanessa Peach)
bb@iepuk.com
£150-£295 Sleeps 2-5. 1 apartment.
On Macmillan Way and Leicestershire Round. 🚫 🛏 See B&B also.

GROUPS

DERBYSHIRE
PEAK DISTRICT

The Glenorchy Centre (SC) West Derbyshire United Reformed Church, Coldwell Street, Wirksworth, DE4 4FB ☎ 01629 824323 (Mrs E M Butlin)
www.glenorchycentre.org.uk Grid Ref: SK287541
SC £10pppn for groups of 10-20 Max 30. Closed Dec-Feb ✗ nearby
➳(Cromford) Ⓓ

Cliff College (BB) Calver, Hope Valley, Nr Sheffield S32 3XG
☎ 01246 584206 (Ian Phipps) bookings@cliffcollege.org
FB £33.25 Max 276. 2 buildings with twin/single rooms, 2 with dormitories.
✗ 🐄 Ⓑ Ⓓ 🚫

☆ **Granary Court** (BB/SC)
Draycourt-in-the-Clay, Ashbourne
☎ 01283 820917 (Lynne Statham)
SC £300+ Min 10, max 26. 1 barn conversion.
✗ 🐄 Ⓑ Ⓓ 🚫 Ⓜ ★★★★ See SC also.

Great for groups. Situated on the Staffordshire/Derbyshire borders this venue offers plenty of scope for different grades of walking or outdoor activities. Wonderful Garden Room to dine or relax in with catering available. Adult spa and treatments available.

RUTLAND

The Old Wisteria Hotel (BB) 4 Catmose St, Oakham, Rutland LE15 6HW
☎ 01572 722844
www.wisteriahotel.co.uk Map 141/862086
DBB £47.50 Min 15, max 45. ➳(Oakham)
✗ 🐄 Ⓑ Ⓓ 🚫 ★★★ See B&B also.

HOSTELS, BUNKHOUSES & CAMPSITES

DERBYSHIRE

Bushey Heath Farm (C/BHB) Tideswell Moor, Buxton SK17 8JE
☎ 01298 873007 (Rod Baraona)
www.busheyheathfarm.co.uk Grid ref: 146785
Camping £4pppn, sole use of bunkhouse £100-£140pw
Camping summer only. Ⓓ 🚫

LINCOLNSHIRE

Brook House Farm (BHB) Watery Lane, Scamblesby, Louth LN11 9XL
☎ 01507 343266 (The Strawsons)
www.brookhousefarm.com
Bednight from £12 ✗ nearby 🐄 Ⓑ Ⓓ 🚫

EAST MIDLANDS

WEST MIDLANDS

Long Distance Paths

Heart of England Way ....HOE

Herefordshire Trail ....HFT

Macmillan Way ....MCM

Monarch's Way ....MON

Offa's Dyke Path ....OFD

Sandstone Trail ....SAN

Severn Way ....SVN

Shropshire Way ....SHS

Staffordshire Way ....SFS

Wye Valley Walk ....WVL

See Paths & Access p25 for full details of LDPs and waymarks

THE IRON BRIDGE SPANNING
THE SEVERN GORGE, SHROPSHIRE

WALK...   ...SHAKESPEARE'S WAY

Linking the Globe at London's Bankside to Stratford-upon-Avon, this new 235km/146-mile waymarked path is a true Shakespearean epic. Retracing the playwright's likely journey between his birthplace and most celebrated theatrical venue (give or take a few more picturesque stretches along the Grand Union canal into London), it visits the Cotswolds, Blenheim Palace, Oxford and the Chilterns. Creator Peter Titchmarsh also devised the Macmillan Way.

A full-colour guide, route-planner and supplements are available from the website www.shakespearesway.org or ☎ 01789 740852 for more information.

NIK MILNE/SHAKESPEARE'S GLOBE THEATRE

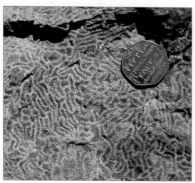

VISIT...   ...THE MONKEY FOREST

There are more than just squirrels playing in the trees at Trentham Estate, near Stoke-on-Trent. A 25-hectare woodland and meadow there is home to hundreds of free-roaming Barbary macaques – an endangered species from north Africa. A forest path allows visitors to observe the monkeys functioning in their fascinating society as they would in the wild, with no bars coming between you! Admission is charged, as is entrance to the estate's famous Italian garden, but 162 hectares of signed woodland and lakeside trails are free to explore.

Visit www.trenthamleisure.co.uk or ☎ 01782 657341 for details.

SEE...   ...THE BEACH AT WENLOCK EDGE

You might not expect to stumble across coral and seashells in the middle of the Shropshire Hills, but Wenlock Edge near Church Stretton is awash with them. A world-famous geological site, the area is made up mostly of limestone formed 425 million years ago when Shropshire was about level with the Seychelles. Ancient fossilised sea lilies and shellfish are abundant among the now wooded and flooded former quarries in the area. The Shropshire Way climbs the ridge going south from Ironbridge and offers fantastic views from its summit.

The Shropshire Geological Society is putting together a series of Geotrails for the area; details are on their website www.shropshiregeology.org.uk or ☎ 01746 716674.

KEITH HOTCHKISS

WEST MIDLANDS

LOCAL RAMBLERS GROUPS... Rail Rambles offers a programme of free led walks for all throughout the year covering the Marches and Mid Wales region. Routes start from various stations in Shropshire and Wales in association with Arriva trains. Call the Ramblers Wales office for a leaflet on ☎ 029 2064 4308 or email: cerddwyr@ramblers.org.uk... **Sandwell Group runs a series of free weekly 45-minute Stride Health Walks across the region that are open to anyone aiming to lose weight and get fit. For details, contact the Health Walks Coordinator ☎ 0121 612 1651 or see the Sandwell Group's website (p77).**

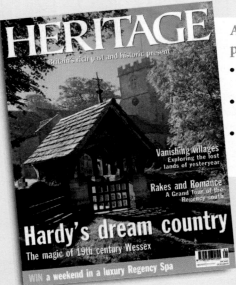

MAP 207

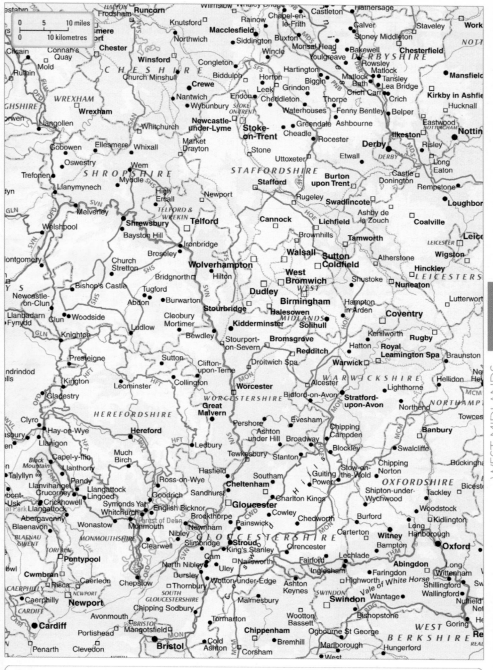

BED & BREAKFAST

BIRMINGHAM & THE BLACK COUNTRY

● Hampton-in-Arden (Solihull)
HEART OF ENGLAND WAY

▪️◄ The Cottage, Kenilworth Road, B92 0LW ☎ 01675 442323 (Roger)
www.smoothhound.co.uk/hotels/cottage.html Map 139/224792
BB **D** ✕ nearby S4 D4 T2 F2 Closed Xmas ⋙(Hampton-in-Arden)
Ⓑ Ⓓ♨🛏🚗 🏵 ◆◆◆◆

▪️◄ The White Lion, High Street, B92 0AA ☎ 01675 442833 (Liz Thorne)
www.thewhitelioninn.com Map 139/203808
BB **D** ✕ £15, 6:30pm D4 T4 ⋙(Hampton-in-Arden)
Ⓥ Ⓑ Ⓓ🐄♨🛏🚗!🏵

● Solihull
HEART OF ENGLAND WAY

▪️◄ Ivy House, Warwick Road, Heronfield Knowle, B93 0EB
☎ 01564 770247 (Mr & Mrs J Townsend)
www.ivyhouseguesthouse.co.uk Map 139/194750
BB **D** ✕ nearby S1 D2 T3 F1 ⋙(Dorridge) Ⓑ ⊛♨🏵 ◆◆◆

HEREFORDSHIRE

● Clyro (Hay-on-Wye)
HEREFORDSHIRE TRAIL

☆ ▪️◄ **Baskerville Arms Hotel**
HR3 5RZ ☎ 01497 820670 (Dave & June Slade)
www.baskervillearms.co.uk Map 161,148/214438
BB **D** ✕ £10, 6-9pm S1 D9 T2 F1
Ⓥ Ⓑ Ⓓ🐄♨🛏🚗!🏵

Central Welsh border area, 1 mile to Hay-on-Wye.
Family-run country hotel.
En-suite rooms. Restaurant and bar.
Close to the Offa's Dyke path.
Ideally placed for short breaks!
info@baskervillearms.co.uk

● Collington (Bromyard)
HEREFORDSHIRE TRAIL

The Granary, Church House Farm, HR7 4NA
☎ 01885 410345 (Margaret Maiden) Map 149,138/655600
BB **B** ✕ book first £13+, 6-9pm D1 T4 Closed Xmas
Ⓥ Ⓑ Ⓓ🐄♨🛏🚗 ◆◆◆

● Gladestry (Kington)
OFFA'S DYKE PATH

▪️◄ Gobe Farm, HR5 3PW ☎ 01544 370606 (June Lloyd)
lloyd@gobefarm.freeserve.co.uk Map 148/226545
BB **B** ✕ nearby D2 Ⓓ⊛🐄♨🛏!🏵

● Goodrich (Ross-on-Wye)
WYE VALLEY WALK & HEREFORDSHIRE TRAIL

▪️◄ Jolly's Of Goodrich, HR9 6HX ☎ 01600 890352
www.jollysofgoodrich.co.uk Map 162/574194
BB **D** ✕ nearby D1 T1 F1 Closed Xmas Ⓑ ⊛🐄♨

● Hereford
WYE VALLEY WALK

▪️◄ Hopbine Hotel, Roman Road, HR1 1LE ☎ 01432 268722 (Doreen Horne)
www.hopbine.com Map 149/512420
BB **D** ✕ nearby S4 D6 T6 F4 ⋙(Hereford) Ⓑ Ⓓ🐄♨🛏! ◆◆

● Kington
OFFA'S DYKE PATH & HEREFORDSHIRE TRAIL

☆ ▪️◄ **Burton Hotel**
Mill Street, HR5 3BQ ☎ 01544 230323
www.hotelherefordshire.co.uk Map 148/296565
BB **D** ✕ £8.50, 6:30pm onwards S2 D6 T5 F3
Ⓥ Ⓑ Ⓓ🐄♨🛏!🏵 ★★★

A family-run 3-star hotel with local reputation for good ales and food with relaxed ambience.

Even if you have a cold or wet walk you can be refreshed in our new inviting pool, spa and fitness club — free to hotel guests.

Church House, Church Road, HR5 3AG
☎ 01544 230534 (Mr & Mrs Darwin)
www.churchhousekington.co.uk Map 148/291567
BB **C** ✕ nearby D1 T1 Closed Xmas Ⓓ 🐄♨🛏!🏵

▪️◄ Southbourne, Newton Lane, HR5 3NF ☎ 01544 231706
(Geoff & Patsy Cooper) www.southbournebandb.co.uk Map 148/290570
BB **B** ✕ book first £11, 7pm S1 D2 T2
Ⓥ Ⓓ⊛🐄♨🛏!

● Ledbury
HEREFORDSHIRE TRAIL

▪️◄ Wall Hills House, Hereford Road, HR8 2PR ☎ 01531 632833
(David & Jennifer Slaughter) www.wallhills.com Map 149/701386
BB **D** ✕ £17.50, 7:30-9:30pm D2 T1 ⋙(Ledbury)
Ⓥ Ⓑ Ⓓ⊛🐄♨ ◆◆◆◆

● Leominster

▪️◄ Lavender House, 1 Richmond Villas, Barons Cross Road, HR6 8RS
☎ 01568 617559 (Caroline Richmond)
www.lavenderhouse.012webpages.com Map 148,149/483587
BB **C** ✕ nearby D3 T1 ⋙(Leominster)
Ⓑ Ⓓ⊛🐄♨🛏! ◆◆◆◆

● Much Birch (Hereford)
HEREFORDSHIRE TRAIL

☆ ▪️◄ **Pilgrim Hotel**
Ross Road, HR2 8HJ ☎ 01981 540742
www.pilgrimhotel.co.uk Map 149/498310
BB **D** ✕ £20, 7-9pm S4 D12 T4 F2
Ⓥ Ⓑ Ⓓ🐄♨🛏🚗!🏵 ★★★ Cater for special diets.

Beautiful country house hotel set in 4 acres of parkland, in sleepy village of Much Birch. A wonderful base for a walking holiday, convenient for the Wye Valley Walk. Cosy beamed bar and award winning restaurant.
Country breaks: DB&B from £38 pp.

● Ross-on-Wye
WYE VALLEY WALK & HEREFORDSHIRE TRAIL

Sunnymount Hotel, Ryefield Road, HR9 5LU ☎ 01989 563880
(Denise & Bob Robertson) sunnymount@tinyworld.co.uk Map 162/606242
BB **C** ✕ nearby S1 D4 T2 B D 🛏️🐾👓🚗!🛁 ◆◆◆◆

● Symonds Yat (Ross-on-Wye)
WYE VALLEY WALK

☆ **The Royal Hotel**
Symonds Yat East, HR9 6JL ☎ 01600 890238 (Jill Wilson)
www.royalhotel-symondsyat.co.uk Map 162/561160
BB **D** ✕ £12, 6:30-9pm S2 D10 T1 F6
V B D 🛏️🐾👓🚗!🛁 ★★

Symonds Yat East is situated in a beautiful woodland gorge in the heart of the Wye Valley, nestling below Symonds Yat Rock, and is in close proximity to the market towns of Ross-on-Wye and Monmouth.

The Royal Hotel is adjacent to the Forest of Dean with lovely walks and cycling paths. These continue along the line of the Ross-on-Wye-to-Monmouth railway line, with no roads to cross!

● Whitchurch (Ross-on-Wye)
HEREFORDSHIRE TRAIL, OFFA'S DYKE PATH & WYE VALLEY WALK

Biblins Lodge, The Doward, HR9 6DX
☎ 01600 890126 (Suzanne Marfell) Map 162/549145
BB **B** ✕ book first £5, 6:30-7pm S1 D1 V 👓🛏️🛁

SHROPSHIRE

● Abdon (Craven Arms)
SHROPSHIRE WAY

Earnstrey Hill House, SY7 9HU
☎ 01746 712579 (Jill Scurfield) Map 137/587873
BB **C/D** ✕ book first £18.50, to suit D1 T2 Closed Xmas
V B D 👓🛏️🐾👓🚗! ◆◆◆◆

● Bayston Hill (Shrewsbury)
SHROPSHIRE WAY

Lythwood Hall B&B, 2 Lythwood Hall, Lythwood, SY3 0AD
☎ 07074 874747 (Julia Bottomley)
lythwoodhall@msn.com Map 126/470085
BB **C** ✕ book first £14, 6-8pm S2 D1 T1 ᴡᴡ(Shrewsbury)
V D 👓🛏️🐾👓🚗!🛁 Ⓜ ◆◆◆◆

● Bishop's Castle
SHROPSHIRE WAY

The Old Brick Guesthouse, 7 Church Street, SY9 5AA ☎ 01588 638471
(Norm & Rosie Reid) www.oldbrick.co.uk Map 137/323885
BB **D** ✕ nearby D2 T1 F1 B D 👓🛏️🐾👓🚗!🛁

Old Time, 29 High Street , SY9 5BE ☎ 01588 638467 (Jane Carroll)
www.oldtime.co.uk Map 137/323888
BB **C** ✕ nearby D2 T1 B D 🛏️🐾👓🚗!🛁

Claremont, Bull Lane, SY9 5BW ☎ 01588 638170 (Audrey Price)
www.priceclaremont.co.uk Map 137/324889
BB **D** ✕ nearby D1 T2 Closed Xmas B D 👓🛏️🐾👓🚗!

The Porch House, 33/35 High Street, SY9 5BE
☎ 01588 638854 (Gill Lucas) www.theporchhouse.com Map 137/323888
BB **D** ✕ nearby D/T2 F1 Closed Xmas
B D 👓🛏️🐾👓🚗! See SC also.

● Broseley

Orchard House, 40 King Street, TF12 5NA ☎ 01952 882684
(Diane Kaiser) mbkbroseley@yahoo.co.uk Map 127/671022
BB **B** ✕ nearby S1 D1 T1 F1 Closed Xmas
B D 👓🛏️🐾👓🚗 ◆◆◆

● Church Stretton
SHROPSHIRE WAY

Belvedere Guest House, Burway Road, SY6 6DP ☎ 01694 722232
www.belvedereguesthouse.co.uk Map 137/451941
BB **C** ✕ nearby D4 T1 F2 Closed Xmas ᴡᴡ(Church Stretton)
B D 👓🛏️🐾👓🚗!🛁 ◆◆◆◆

☆ **Brookfields Guest House**
Watling Street North, SY6 7AR ☎ 01694 722314 (Angie & Paul Bradley)
www.churchstretton-guesthouse.co.uk Map 137,138/459937
BB **D** ✕ book first £20 (groups only), 6:30-7:30pm S1 D2 T1 F1
Closed Xmas ᴡᴡ(Church Stretton) V B D 👓🛏️🐾👓🚗 ★★★★★

Large comfortable Edwardian house & grounds, ample parking. Stroll to town & train station. Luxury en-suite bedrooms. Ideal base for walkers & tourers. Great views of Long Mynd. Licensed. Non-smoking. Drying room. Special rates for weekly or party bookings.

☆ **The Longmynd Hotel**
Cunnery Road, SY6 6AG ☎ 01694 722244
www.longmynd.co.uk Map 137/449935
BB **D** ✕ £27, 6:45-9pm S6 D23 T15 F6 ᴡᴡ(Church Stretton)
V B D 👓🛏️🐾👓🚗🛁 ★★★ See Groups also.

Breathtaking views, fine restaurant and bar facilities. Ideal location for walking the Shropshire hills and touring the area.

Special interest packages and many amenities (including sauna, outdoor heated pool, golf) available.

Sayang House, Hope Bowdler, SY6 7DD ☎ 01694 723981
(Patrick & Madeline Egan) www.sayanghouse.com Map 137,138/476924
BB **C** ✕ book first £15, 6:30pm onwards D3 T1 F/D2 ᴡᴡ(Church Stretton)
V B D 👓🛏️🐾👓🚗!🛁 ◆◆◆◆

Old Rectory House, Burway Road, SY6 6DW ☎ 01694 724462 (Mike Smith)
info@oldrectoryhouse.co.uk Map 137/452938
BB **B** ✕ nearby D2 T1 Closed Xmas ᴡᴡ(Church Stretton)
B D 👓🛏️🐾👓🚗 ◆◆◆◆

☆ **Malt House Farm**
Lower Wood, SY6 6LF ☎ 01694 751379 (Lyn Bloor)
Map 137,138/466974
BB C ✗ book first £15, 7pm D2 TI Closed Dec
Ⓥ Ⓑ Ⓓ ⊘ 🐾 ♿ ◆◆◆

The Malthouse is a centuries-old working farm situated on the lower slopes of the Long Mynd Hills AONB. Peace, quiet and stunning scenery. Excellent walking from our door. Many places of interest to visit. Half an hour drive from Ludlow, Shrewsbury and Ironbridge Gorge.
All rooms en-suite, colour television, hairdryers and beverage tray.
Comfortable guest lounge.
Home cooked dinners available in the beamed dining room.
Warm welcome.
Regret: no children or pets. No smoking.

🚶 Ragdon Manor, Ragdon, SY6 7EZ ☎ 01694 781389 (Wendy Clark)
www.ragdonmanorbandb.co.uk Map 137,138/455915
BB C DI TI Closed Xmas ⇢(Church Stretton)
Ⓑ Ⓓ ⊘ 🐾 ♿ �car 🛏 ◆◆◆◆

● Cleobury Mortimer (Kidderminster)
Cox's Barn, Bagginswood, DY14 8LS ☎ 01746 718415 (Dinah M Thompson)
www.visitbridgnorth.co.uk Map 138/682805
BB C ✗ book first £8–£12, 6:30-8:30pm D3
Ⓥ Ⓑ Ⓓ ⊘ 🐾 ♿ 🛏 ◆◆◆◆

● Clun
SHROPSHIRE WAY
🚶 The White Horse Inn, The Square, SY7 8JA ☎ 01588 640305
www.whi-clun.co.uk Map 137/300808
BB C ✗ £10, 6:30-8:30pm DI F3 Closed Xmas
Ⓥ Ⓑ Ⓓ 🐾 ♿ 🚗 ! 🛏 ★★★

☆ **Clun Farm House**
High Street, SY7 8JB ☎ 01588 640432 (Anthony & Sue Whitfield)
www.clunfarmhouse.co.uk Map 137/302808
BB D ✗ book first £20-£25 S2 D/FI T/DI FI Closed Xmas
Ⓥ Ⓑ Ⓓ ⊘ 🐾 ♿ 🚗 !

Book yourself a treat. Stumble into the friendly atmosphere at Clun Farm House and enjoy award-winning marmalade at breakfast and local produce for dinner. In the heart of the village with real ale pubs and amenities on the door step. Come and indulge!

☆ 🚶 **Crown House**
Church Street, SY7 8JW ☎ 01588 640780 (Reg Maund & Judy Bailey)
www.smoothhound.co.uk Map 137/300805
BB C ✗ nearby SI DI TI Closed Xmas
Ⓑ Ⓓ ⊘ 🐾 ♿ 🚗 ! 🛏 Ⓜ ◆◆◆◆

Walking the Shropshire Way or Offa's Dyke? If you visit Clun, visit us! We welcome muddy boots, wet anoraks & happy people. We have superb accommodation in a self-contained annexe. Lifts and luggage transfers by arrangement.

● Ellesmere
Hordley Hall, Hordley, SY12 9BB ☎ 01691 622772 (Hazel Rodenhurst)
Map 126/381308
BB C ✗ book first £12-£14, 6-7pm SI D2 TI
Ⓥ Ⓑ Ⓓ ⊘ 🐾 ♿ ◆◆◆◆

● Gobowen (Oswestry)
Clevelands, Station Road, SY11 3JS ☎ 01691 661359 (Miss O Powell)
Map 126/302334
BB B ✗ nearby S2 DI Closed Xmas ⇢(Gobowen) ⊘ 🛏

● High Ercall (Telford)
SHROPSHIRE WAY & SEVERN WAY
🚶 The Mill House, Shrewsbury Road, TF6 6BE ☎ 01952 770394 (Judy Yates)
www.ercallmill.co.uk Map 126/584163
BB D ✗ nearby DI TI FI Ⓑ Ⓓ ⊘ 🐾 ♿ 🚗 ! 🛏 ◆◆◆◆

● Hilton (Bridgnorth)
SEVERN WAY, STAFFORDSHIRE WAY & MONARCH'S WAY
🚶 The Old House, WV15 5PJ ☎ 01746 716560 (Fifi Sharplin)
www.oldhousehilton.co.uk Map 138/775952
BB C ✗ nearby DI T2 Ⓑ Ⓓ ⊘ 🐾 ♿ 🚗 🛏 ◆◆◆◆

● Ironbridge
SHROPSHIRE WAY & MONARCH'S WAY
🚶 Post Office House, 6 The Square, TF8 7AQ ☎ 01952 433201
(Janet Hunter) www.pohouse-ironbridge.fsnet.co.uk Map 127/673034
BB D ✗ nearby DI TI FI Ⓑ Ⓓ 🐾 ♿ 🚗 ! 🛏 ◆◆◆

☆ 🚶 **Woodville B&B**
4a The Woodlands, TF8 7PA ☎ 01952 433343 (Peter & Hilary Fox)
foxpeter3@aol.com Map 127/676038
BB B ✗ nearby DI TI
Ⓑ Ⓓ ⊘ 🐾 ♿ 🚗 ! 🛏

Delightful bungalow in a secluded spot on the Ironbridge Way — ideal base to explore Shropshire. All rooms ground floor, equipped with tea/coffee making facilities. Full English, vegetarian or continental breakfast. Ample secure parking. Brochure on request.

● Ludlow
SHROPSHIRE WAY
🚶 The Mount Guest House, 61 Gravel Hill, SY8 1QS ☎ 01584 874084
(Mandy Callender) www.themountludlow.co.uk Map 137,138/515751
BB C/D ✗ nearby SI D3 TI ⇢(Ludlow)
Ⓑ Ⓓ ⊘ 🐾 ♿ 🚗 ! 🛏 Ⓜ ★★★★

☆ Cecil Guest House

Sheet Road, SY8 1LR ☎ 01584 872442 (Ron Green)
Map 137,138/525742
BB **D** ✗ book first £18, 6:30pm S2 D2 T4 F1 Closed Xmas ⋙(Ludlow)
Ⓥ Ⓑ Ⓓ 🛏🐾🛁🚗!🐾 ◆◆◆

Comfortable guesthouse offering relaxed atmosphere, freshly cooked food & spotlessly clean surroundings. 9 bedrooms (7 ensuite), with CH & TV. Residents bar & lounge. Smoking only in bar. Off-street parking. Double/ twin ensuite £28-£31pp (dual occupancy) £38-£41 (single) Standard single £22.   Fax/Tel: 01584 872442

● Melverley (Oswestry)
SEVERN WAY

🛏🚪 Church House, SY10 8PJ ☎ 01691 682754 (Jane Sprackling)
www.members.aol.com/melverley Map 126/332166
BB **C** ✗ nearby D1 T1 Closed Xmas Ⓑ Ⓓ ⊛ 🐾🛁🚗🐾

● Myddle (Shrewsbury)

🛏🚪 Oakfields, Baschurch Road, SY4 3RX
☎ 01939 290823 (Gwen Frost) Map 126/465235
BB **B** ✗ nearby D1 T1 F1 ⋙(Yorton) Ⓓ ⊛ 🐾🛁🐾 ◆◆◆

● Newcastle-on-Clun (Craven Arms)
SHROPSHIRE WAY & OFFA'S DYKE PATH

🛏🚪 The Quarry House, Church Rd, SY7 8QJ
☎ 01588 640774 (Michelle Evans) www.quarry-house.com Map 137/255827
BB **B** ✗ £11.50, 6-9pm D1 T1 F1
Ⓥ Ⓑ Ⓓ ⊛ 🐾🛁🚗!🐾 Free afternoon tea on arrival.

● Oswestry
OFFA'S DYKE PATH

BJ's, 87 Llwyn Rd, SY11 1EW ☎ 01691 650205 (Barbara Williams)
barbara@williams87.fsnet.co.uk Map 126/294303
BB **B** ✗ nearby D1 T1 Closed Xmas Ⓓ 🐾🛁🚗🐾 ★★

● Shrewsbury
SHROPSHIRE WAY

☆🛏🚪 Sydney House Hotel

Coton Crescent, Coton Hill, SY1 2LJ ☎ 01743 354681
www.sydneyhousehotel.co.uk Map 126/490135
BB **C** ✗ nearby S2 D3 T1 F1 ⋙(Shrewsbury)
Ⓑ Ⓓ 🐾🛁🚗🐾 ◆◆◆

Within 10 minutes' walk of town centre & train/bus stations. All en-suite rooms. Private car park. Walkers' special needs happily catered for.
Residents bar. £25-30 per person. Major credit cards accepted.

🛏🚪 Abbey Court House, 134 Abbey Foregate, SY2 6AU ☎ 01743 364416
(Mrs VA Macleod) www.abbeycourt.biz Map 126/503122
BB **D** ✗ nearby S2 D3 T4 F1 ⋙(Shrewsbury) Ⓑ 🐾🛁 ◆◆◆◆

● Trefonen (Oswestry)

The Pentre, SY10 9EE ☎ 01691 653952 (Helen & Stephen Gilbert)
www.thepentre.com Map 126/238260
BB **D** ✗ book first £18, 7:30pm D1 T1 F1 Closed Xmas
Ⓥ Ⓑ Ⓓ ⊛ 🐾🛁🚗!🐾 ◆◆◆◆

● Tugford (Craven Arms)
SHROPSHIRE WAY

Tugford Farm Holiday Cottages, SY7 9HS ☎ 01584 841259 (Bronwen Williams)
www.tugford.com Map 137,138/558872
BB **D** ✗ book first £15, 7-10pm D2 T1 F1
Ⓥ Ⓑ Ⓓ ⊛ 🐾🛁🚗!🐾 ◆◆◆Ⓦ See SC also.

● Wem (Shrewsbury)
SHROPSHIRE WAY

Forncet, Soulton Road, SY4 5HR ☎ 01939 232996 (Anne James)
Map 126/521292
BB **C** ✗ nearby S1 D1 T1 Closed Xmas ⋙(Wem) Ⓓ ⊛ 🐾🛁🚗!

● Whixall (Whitchurch)
SHROPSHIRE WAY

Roden View, Dobson's Bridge, SY13 2QL ☎ 01948 710320 (Jean James)
www.roden-view.co.uk Map 126/493343
BB **C** ✗ book first £12, 6-8:30pm D1 T2 F1
Ⓥ Ⓑ Ⓓ ⊛ 🐾🛁🚗!🐾 ★★★★

● Woodside (Clun)
SHROPSHIRE WAY

The Old Farmhouse, SY7 0JB ☎ 01588 640695 (Conor Digby)
www.theoldfarmhousebandb.co.uk Map 201/310800
BB **C** ✗ book first £12.50, 6-8pm D2 T2 Closed Dec
Ⓥ Ⓑ Ⓓ ⊛ 🐾🛁🚗!🐾 ◆◆◆◆

STAFFORDSHIRE

● Cheddleton (Leek)
STAFFORDSHIRE WAY

🛏🚪 Prospect House Guest House, 334 Cheadle Road, ST13 7BW
☎ 01782 550639 (Rolf & Jackie Griffiths)
www.prospecthouseleek.co.uk Map 118/967506
BB **B** ✗ book first £14 S1 D1 T1 F2 Ⓥ Ⓑ ⊛ 🐾🛁🚗! ◆◆◆◆

● Endon (Stoke-on-Trent)
STAFFORDSHIRE WAY

Hollinhurst Farm, Park Lane, ST9 9JB ☎ 01782 502633 (Mrs J Ball)
www.smoothhound.co.uk/hotels/hollinhurst.html Map 118/942531
BB **B** ✗ nearby D2 T1 F1 Ⓑ ⊛ 🐾🛁🚗!🐾 ◆◆◆

● Greendale (Oakamoor)
STAFFORDSHIRE WAY

🛏🚪 The Old Furnace, ST10 3AP ☎ 01538 703331
www.oldfurnace.co.uk Map 128,119/041435
BB **B** ✗ book first £7.50 S2 D2 T1 Ⓥ Ⓓ ⊛ 🐾🚗! See SC also.

● Grindon (Leek)
PEAK DISTRICT

☆ Summerhill Farm

ST13 7TT ☎ 01538 304264 (Mrs P Simpson)
www.summerhillfarm.co.uk Map 119/083534
BB **B** ✗ book first £12, 6:30-7pm D2 T/D1 F1 Closed Xmas - NY
Ⓥ Ⓑ Ⓓ ⊛ 🐾🛁🚗🐾 ◆◆◆◆

Tastefully furnished, en-suite facilities, tea/coffee, colour TV. Amid rolling countryside overlooking the Dove and Manifold Valleys — wonderful for walkers. Ideally situated for Buxton, Chatsworth House, the Potteries and Alton Towers. Email: info@summerhillfarm.co.uk, or visit our website.

● Horton (Leek)
STAFFORDSHIRE WAY

Croft Meadows Farm, ST13 8QE ☎ 01782 513039 (Irene Harrison)
Map 118/921577
BB **B** ✕ book first £10 S3 D1 T1 Ⓥ Ⓑ Ⓓ ☺ 🐾👤🚗❗Ⓜ

● Rocester (Uttoxeter)
STAFFORDSHIRE WAY

🏠◀ The Riversholme, High Street, ST14 5JU ☎ 01889 590900
www.riversholme.co.uk Map 128/108393
BB **D** ✕ book first £17, 7-9pm D4 T1 F2 Ⓥ Ⓑ Ⓓ 🐾👤

● Waterhouses (Stoke-on-Trent)
PEAK DISTRICT

Leehouse Farm, Leek Road, ST10 3HW ☎ 01538 308439 (Josie Little)
Map 119/081503
BB **C** D2 T1 Closed Xmas Ⓑ Ⓓ ☺ 🐾👤🚗❗ ◆◆◆◆Ⓢ

WARWICKSHIRE

● Bidford-on-Avon
HEART OF ENGLAND WAY

🏠◀ Fosbroke House, 4 High Street, B50 4BU ☎ 01789 772327 (M Swift)
www.smoothhound.co.uk/hotels/fosbroke.html Map 150/101519
BB **D** ✕ nearby D1 T1 F1 Closed Xmas Ⓑ Ⓓ ☺👤❗ ◆◆◆◆

● Hatton
HEART OF ENGLAND WAY & MONARCH'S WAY

Northleigh House, Five Ways Road, CV35 7HZ ☎ 01926 484203
www.northleigh.co.uk Map 139,151/222689
BB **C** ✕ £8, 7pm S5 D5 T2 F2 ➖(Hatton)
Ⓥ Ⓑ Ⓓ ☺ 🐾👤🚗❗🏨 Wheelchair access.

● Kenilworth

Banner Hill Farmhouse Accom., Rouncil Lane, CV8 1NN
☎ 01926 852850 (Patricia Snelson) Map 140/268708
BB **B** ✕ book first £8.50 S2 D2 T4 F2 Ⓥ Ⓑ Ⓓ 🐾👤🚗❗🏨

● Lighthorne

Church Hill Farm, CV35 0AR ☎ 01926 651251 (Susan Sabin)
www.churchhillfarm.co.uk Map 151/336558
BB **D** ✕ nearby D2 T1 Ⓥ Ⓑ Ⓓ ☺ 🐾👤 ★★★★

● Northend
MACMILLAN WAY

☆🏠◀ **The Stables**
The Farmhouse, Top Street, CV47 2TW ☎ 01295 770765
www.thestablesnorthend.co.uk Map 151/393526
BB **D** ✕ nearby D/T1
Ⓑ Ⓓ ☺ 🐾👤 DIY continental breakfasts.

Enjoy a peaceful stay in a converted stable at the rear of The Farmhouse. Situated in the village of Northend at the foot of the Burton Dassett Hills Country Park. Excellent local pubs and country walks. Convenient for Stratford and Cotswolds.

● Shustoke (Coleshill, Birmingham)
HEART OF ENGLAND WAY

Priory Farmhouse, B46 2AZ ☎ 01675 481550 (Margaret Manley)
Map 139/220900
BB **C** ✕ nearby S2 D2 T1 F1 Closed Xmas Ⓑ Ⓓ 🐾👤🚗 🏨

● Stratford-upon-Avon
HEART OF ENGLAND WAY

☆🏠◀ **Parkfield Guest House**
3 Broad Walk, CV37 6HS ☎ 01789 293313 (Jo & Roger Pettitt)
www.parkfieldbandb.co.uk Map 151/197546
BB **C** ✕ nearby S1 D3 T2 F1 Closed Xmas ➖(Stratford-upon-Avon)
Ⓑ Ⓓ ☺ 🐾👤 ★★★

Attractive Victorian house in quiet location, 5 minutes' walk to town centre and Royal Shakespeare Theatre, 1 min from Greenway leading to Heart of England Way. Most rooms en-suite, with colour TV. Large breakfast menu. Brochure on request. Large private car park. Non-smoking. Email: parkfield@btinternet.com

☆🏠◀ **Stratford Victoria**
Arden Street, CV37 6QQ ☎ 01789 271000
www.marstonhotels.com Map 151/197551
BB **D** ✕ £29.50, 6-9:30pm S10 D52 T32 F8 ➖(Stratford-upon-Avon)
Ⓥ Ⓑ 🐾👤🏨 ★★★★ Wheelchair access.

Stratford Victoria is a convenient base for exploring historic Stratford-upon-Avon and its variety of walks, with many starting from the River Avon via field paths, bridleways and a disused railway.

Located in the town centre, near to the train station, guests can walk to many of the town's attractions, such as Shakespeare's theatre and house.

Enjoy great food and fine wines in our award-winning restaurant. A comfortable modern hotel incorporating the style and character of Victorian architecture.

Please ask about our exclusive rates for walking parties.

🏠◀ Arden Way, 22 Shipston Road, CV37 7LP
☎ 01789 205646 (Jeanne Hallworth)
info@ardenwayguesthouse.co.uk Map 151/207544
BB **C/D** ✕ nearby S1 D2 T2 F1 ➖(Stratford-upon-Avon) Ⓑ ☺ 🐾👤

☆ ▸◂ Stratford Manor
Warwick Road, CV37 0PY ☎ 01789 731173
www.marstonhotels.com Map 151/230587
BB **D** ✕ £32.50, 7-9.45pm D50 T51 F3
Ⓥ Ⓑ 🖐 ★★★★ Wheelchair access.

Perfectly located for the Welcombe Hills Nature Reserve, Stratford Manor is a modern hotel with excellent leisure facilities situated in the pleasant Warwickshire countryside, only 4 miles from historic Stratford-upon-Avon with its picturesque canal walks, including Wilmcote – home to the well-kept house of Shakespeare's mother.

The hotel offers a new bar and restaurant, and the Reflections Leisure Club offers a sauna, swimming pool, gym and tennis courts.

Ideal for exploring the area, especially Warwick Castle, Leamington Spa and Stratford-upon-Avon.

Please ask about our exclusive rates for walking parties.

WORCESTERSHIRE

● Ashton-under-Hill (Evesham)
▸◂ Holloway Farm House, WR11 7SN ☎ 01386 881910 (M Sanger-Davies)
www.hollowayfarmhouse.btinternet.co.uk Map 150/998382
BB **B** ✕ nearby T2 F1 Closed Xmas Ⓑ Ⓓ ⊛ 🐾 🚗 ! 🎿

● Bewdley
SEVERN WAY
▸◂ Tarn, Longbank, DY12 2QT ☎ 01299 402243 (Topsy Beves)
www.topsybandb.com Map 138/764749
BB **C** ✕ nearby S2 T2 Closed Dec-Jan Ⓓ ⊛ 🐾 🚗 ! 🎿

Severn Valley Guest House, 240 Westbourne St, DY12 1BS ☎ 01299 402192
(Mary Jane & Rob) www.severnvalleyguesthouse.co.uk Map 138/790754
BB **B** ✕ nearby S1 D2 T2 F2 Ⓑ 🐾 🖐 🎿

● Broadway
COTSWOLD WAY
Brook House, Station Road, WR12 7DE ☎ 01386 852313 (Marianne Thomas)
www.brookhousebandb.co.uk Map 150/090379
BB **C** ✕ nearby S1 D2 T1 F1 Closed Xmas Ⓑ Ⓓ 🖐 🎿

Old Station House, Station Drive, WR12 7DF ☎ 01386 852659
www.broadway-cotswolds.co.uk/oldstation.html Map 150/090380
BB **D** ✕ nearby S1 D2 T2 F1 Closed Xmas
Ⓑ Ⓓ ⊛ 🐾 🖐 ! ◆◆◆◆Ⓢ

☆ ▸◂ Small Talk Lodge
32 High Street, WR12 7DP ☎ 01386 858953 (Laurie Avery)
www.smalltalklodge.co.uk Map 150/097375
BB **C** ✕ book first £10, 7pm D4 T2
Ⓥ Ⓑ Ⓓ ⊛ 🐾 🖐 ◆◆◆◆ Wheelchair access.

Small Talk Lodge is situated in a pretty, secluded courtyard in the centre of Broadway, which lies on the Cotswold Way.
We are an ideal base to explore some of the Cotswolds' most picturesque villages and countryside.

▸◂ Dove Cottage, Colletts Fields, WR12 7AT ☎ 01386 859085
www.broadway-cotswolds.co.uk Map 150/101376
BB **C** ✕ book first D1 T1 Ⓥ Ⓑ Ⓓ ⊛ 🐾 ◆◆◆◆Ⓢ

● Clifton-upon-Teme
▸◂ Pitlands Farm, WR6 6DX ☎ 01886 812220 (Diane Mann)
www.pitlandsfarm.co.uk Map 149,138/728609
BB **C** ✕ nearby T2 F1 Closed Xmas
Ⓑ Ⓓ ⊛ 🐾 🚗 ! ★★★★ See SC also.

● Evesham
▸◂ Anglers View B&B, 88-90 Albert Rd, WR11 4LA
☎ 01386 442141 (Sarah Tomkotowicz) Map 150/033441
BB **C** ✕ book first £5+ S2 D1 T3 F2 〰(Evesham)
Ⓥ Ⓑ Ⓓ ⊛ 🐾 🚗 ! 🎿

● Great Malvern
SEVERN WAY
Sidney House, 40 Worcester Road, WR14 4AA ☎ 01684 574994
www.sidneyhouse.co.uk Map 150/775463
BB **B/C** ✕ nearby S1 D4 T2 F1 〰(Great Malvern)
Ⓑ Ⓓ 🐾 🖐 🎿 ◆◆◆

Croft Guest House, Bransford, WR6 5JD ☎ 01886 832227 (Ann Porter)
www.croftguesthouse.com Map 150/795524
BB **C/D** ✕ book first £10-£12.50, 7-7:30pm D4 T/F1
Ⓑ Ⓓ ⊛ 🐾 🖐 🎿 ★★★

☆ ▸◂ Abbey Hotel
Abbey Road, WR14 3ET ☎ 01684 892332
www.sarova.co.uk/sarova/hotelcollection/abbey/ Map 150/775458
BB **D** ✕ £23.50, 7-9:30pm S10 D47 T37 F9 〰(Great Malvern)
Ⓥ Ⓑ 🐾 🖐 🎿 Ⓜ ★★★

The Abbey is an historic hotel situated at the foot of the Malvern Hills.
The bedrooms are comfortable; many have breathtaking views.
The Priory View restaurant is open for evening meals and the bar serves refreshments throughout the day.

Local walking attractions include:
Malvern Hills
Wye Valley
Severn Valley
Family rooms and group accommodation are available. For further information please see our website or contact us quoting Ramblers' Association.

WEST MIDLANDS

● **Kidderminster**
🚩 Victoria House, 15 Comberton Road, DY10 1UA
☎ 01562 67240 (Terry & Clare Turner)
www.smoothhound.co.uk/hotels/victoriahousebb Map 138/840763
BB **C** ✗ nearby S3 D2 T1 F1 ▲(Kidderminster) Ⓑ Ⓓ ⊗ 🐾♨ ◆◆◆

● **Sutton (Tenbury Wells)**
Kyre Equestrian Centre & B&B, Lower House Farm, WR15 8RL ☎ 01885 410233
(Anne Durston-Smith) www.kyre-equestrian.co.uk Map 149,138/615649
BB **C** ✗ book first £10, 7:30-8:30pm S1 D1 T2 Ⓑ Ⓓ ⊗ 🐾♨! 🐎

SELF-CATERING

HEREFORDSHIRE

● **Hereford**

☆ **Hermit Holidays**
☎ 01432 760022 (Ron Zahl)
www.hermitholidays.co.uk
£265-£595 Sleeps 2-6. 2 cottages, 3 apartments.
250-acre woodland. Spring water. ⊗ ★★★★

Four-star converted coachhouse and stables and apartments with stunning views over Hertfordshire countryside. Secluded and surrounded by 250-acre natural woodland with footpaths and trails. Spring water, comfy beds, self-catering with optional international vegetarian meals available on request.

● **Kington**

Crossing Cottage ☎ 01625 582550 (N Passey) www.crossingcottage.info
£224-£416 Sleeps 6. 1 cottage. Rural riverside cottage.
Offa's Dyke Path. ⊗ 🐎

● **Ross-on-Wye**

Main Oaks ☎ 01531 650448 (Mrs P Unwin) www.mainoaks.co.uk
£230-£790 Sleeps 2-7. 6 farm cottages.
Beside River Wye, short breaks available. 🐎 ★★★-★★★★

Fiddlers Rest Cottage ☎ 01989 750853 (Lisa Lown)
www.fiddlersrestcottage.co.uk £120-£150 Sleeps 2. 1 cottage annexe.
Cosy, secluded rural accommodation. Country walks. ⊗ 🐎

● **Whitbourne**

Dial House ☎ 01886 821534 (Anne Evans) www.whitbourne-estate.co.uk
£390-£690 Sleeps 11 +cot. 19th century farmhouse.
Spacious, personally maintained, 5 bedrooms. Fishing. ⊗ 🐎 ★★★

SHROPSHIRE

● **Bishop's Castle**

Maureen Thuraisingham ☎ 01588 638560 www.thefirscolebatch.co.uk
£190-£285 Sleeps 2-4. 1 bungalow.
Open views, garden, log stove, spacious. 🐎 ★★★

Annette Bedford ☎ 01588 620770 www.bordercottages.co.uk
£250-£629 Sleeps 1-7. 1 cottage, 1 flat.
Relaxing and picturesque country house setting. ⊗ 🐎 ★★★★★

The Porch House ☎ 01588 638854 (Gill Lucas) www.theporchhouse.com
£177-£294 Sleeps 2-4. 2 apartments.
Historic Elizabethan town centre house. Short breaks. ⊗ See B&B also.

● **Craven Arms**

Hesterworth ☎ 01588 660487 (Roger & Sheila Davies) www.hesterworth.co.uk
£123-£426 Sleeps 2-8. 11 cottages & flats.
Beautiful area, caring owners, short breaks. ▲(Broome) 🐎 ★★-★★★

Tugford Farm Holiday Cottages ☎ 01584 841259 (Bronwen Williams)
www.tugford.com
£208-£2,008 Sleeps 4-10. 1 cottage, 2 barn conversions.
Designated AONB on Shropshire Way footpath.
⊗ 🐎 ★★-★★★★ See B&B also.

● **Knighton**

The Garden Lodge ☎ 01547 529542 (Sue & Roger Morris)
sue@graigcottage.fsnet.co.uk
£125-£210 Sleeps 2-3. 1 lodge. Closed Dec
Stunning views, ground floor accommodation. ⊗ 🐎

● **Ludlow**

☆ **Sutton Court Farm**
☎ 01584 861305 (Jane Cronin)
www.suttoncourtfarm.co.uk
£210-£500 Sleeps 2-6. 6 cottages.
Short breaks all year (minimum 2 nights) 🐎 ★★★★

Six special cottages set around a peaceful, rural, courtyard in the Corvedale. Walk from the door or explore further afield in the beautiful south Shropshire countryside. Enjoy a cream tea or evening meal on your return (by prior arrangement).

Goosefoot Barn ☎ 01584 861326 (Sally Loft) www.goosefootbarn.co.uk
£200-£460 Sleeps 2-6. 4 cottages.
Tranquil setting. Games room. Short breaks. ⊗ 🐎 ★★★★

☆ **Mocktree Barns**
☎ 01547 540441 (Clive & Cynthia Prior)
www.mocktreeholidays.co.uk
£195-£410 Sleeps 1-6 +cot. 5 cottages.
Walking from door. Good food nearby. ⊗ 🐎 ★★★Ⓦ Access Category 1.

Comfortable well-equipped, character cottages in lovely peaceful countryside. Gardens, wildlife, super views. Great walks from the door. Offa's Dyke, Mortimer Trail, Herefordshire Trail, Shropshire Hills all convenient. Maps and advice available. Groups welcome. Disabled-friendly. Short breaks (3 nights minimum).

Mrs Jean Mellings ☎ 01584 873315 www.shropshirecottage.co.uk
£370-£750 Sleeps 6 +cot. 1 cottage.
Cottage, village location, garden. Near Ludlow. ⊗ 🐎 ★★★★★

Elm Lodge ☎ 01584 872308 (Barbara Weaver)
www.elm-lodge.org.uk
£320-£400 Sleeps 2-5. 2 flats. ⊗ ♨(Ludlow) Ⓦ

● Much Wenlock

Bramley ☎ 01952 728153 (Miss M Revell & Mrs D Revell)
www.stmember.com/bramley
£150-£230 Sleeps 2. 1 separate annexe.
Short breaks, AONB, peaceful location. ⊗ ★★

STAFFORDSHIRE

● Calton
PEAK DISTRICT

☆ **Field Head Farmhouse Holidays**
☎ 01538 308352 (Janet Hudson)
www.field-head.co.uk
£602-£1,280 Sleeps 12-14. 1 farmhouse.
Groups welcome, Sky TV, spa bath. ⊗ ♨ ★★★★

Grade II-listed farmhouse, 5 bedrooms, 2 bathrooms, plus spa bath/shower room. Well equipped, secluded location set in beautiful surroundings close to Dovedale and the Manifold Valley. Open all year, short breaks, bargain mid-week breaks. Email: info@field-head.co.uk

● Leek

☆ **Blackshaw Grange**
☎ 01538 300165 (Carolyn Williams)
www.btinternet.com/~blackshawgrange
£170-£450 Sleeps 2-6. 3 cottages.
⊗ ♨ ★★★★

Welcome to Blackshaw Grange where each cottage is well appointed and cosy. An excellent base to walk the Peak District, visit the Potteries and check out the tourist sites such as Chatsworth House and Snugborough Hall. Phone or email Carolyn for details on kevwilliams@btinternet.com

● Oakamoor

☆ **The Old Furnace**
☎ 01538 703331 (Annette Baxter)
www.oldfurnace.co.uk
£30-£50 per day Sleeps 1-3. 1 annexe.
Transport available. Adjoins Staffordshire Way ⊗ ♨ ★★★ See B&B also.

Comprising one twin and one single room, The Annexe is situated beside a trickling stream in beautiful Dimmingsdale. Superb walking all around; Staffordshire Way and National Trust Nature Reserve both 400 yards. Adjoins Peak District National Park. Short breaks available all year.

● Waterfall (Ashbourne)
PEAK DISTRICT

Croft House Barn ☎ 01538 308125 (Stephanie Cadenhead)
www.crofthousebarn.co.uk
£298-£575 Sleeps 2-6. 1 cottage. Characterful, lovely setting. Doorstep walks/pub. ⊗ ★★★★ Guide dogs welcome.

● Winkhill

Broomyshaw Country Cottages ☎ 01538 308298 (Mr & Mrs Saul)
www.broomyshaw.co.uk
£120 Sleeps 4-8. 3 cottages.
Secluded, not isolated, with panoramic views. ♨ ★★★

WORCESTERSHIRE

● Clifton-upon-Teme

Pitlands Farm Holidays ☎ 01886 812220 (Diane Mann)
www.pitlandsfarm.co.uk
£160-£600 Sleeps 2-6. 3 lodges, 1 cottage, 1 bungalow.
Drop off & pick-up service. Near Worcestershire Way.
⊗ ♨ ★★★★ See B&B also.

● Great Malvern

Greenbank ☎ 01684 567328 (Mr D G Matthews)
matthews.greenbank@virgin.net
£150-£210 Sleeps 2-4. 1 flat.
Conservatory, drying room. Near Worcestershire Way. ♨(Colwall) ♨ ★★★

Rosehill Cottage ☎ 01684 561074 (Mrs Gwyn Sloan)
sloaniain@hotmail.com
£195-£225 Sleeps 2. 1 detached studio.
Situated in Malvern Hills, stunning views. ⊗ ♨ ★★★

GROUPS

HEREFORDSHIRE

Hollytree House (SC) Symonds Yat West HR9 6BL
☎ 01600 772929 (Sue Wadley) www.hollytreehouse.info Map 141/862086
SC £1,800pw, £1,400w/e Max 20. 1 house. ✗nearby Ⓑ Ⓓ ★★★

☆ **Best Western Talbot Hotel** (BB)
Leominster HR6 8EP ☎ 01568 616347
www.smoothhound.co.uk/hotels/talbot2.html
BB £32-£48pppn Min 10, max 42. ♨(Leominster)
✗ 🍷 Ⓑ Ⓓ ! ★★★

Originally a 15th-century coaching house sympathetically updated with ensuite bedrooms. Ideal location for ramblers visiting Herefordshire. Designated Black and White Trail through picturesque villages and beautiful countryside. Group rates offered for Ramblers Group block-bookings. Email: talbot@bestwestern.co.uk

SHROPSHIRE

☆ **Longmynd Hotel** (BB)
Cunnery Rd, Church Stretton ☎ 01694 722244 (Rowena Jones)
www.longmynd.co.uk Map 137/449935
DBB £44-£64 Min 20, max 100. ⚆(Church Stretton)
✕ 🐾 Ⓑ Ⓓ See B&B also.

Breathtaking views, fine restaurant and
bar facilities. Ideal location for walking
the Shropshire hills and touring the area.

Special interest packages and many
amenities (including sauna, outdoor
heated pool, golf) available.

**FOUND SOMEWHERE GOOD
THAT'S NOT IN THIS GUIDE?**
Or got a complaint about one that is?
Use the Recommendation/Feedback Form
on p123 and send it to the editor
at our central office or email:
yearbook@ramblers.org.uk

HOSTELS, BUNKHOUSES & CAMPSITES

HEREFORDSHIRE

Berrow House Camping/Bunkhouse (C/B/IH/OC) Hollybush, Ledbury HR8 1ET
☎ 01531 635845 www.berrowhouse.co.uk Map 150/763368
Bednight £8 ⊗   Near Worcestershire Way and Three Choirs Way.

SHROPSHIRE

Sallow View (C) Park Lane, Craven Arms ☎ 01588 673295 (Steve Rudge)
www.sallowview.co.uk Map 137/422825
£50 per night (max 4 people) ⚆(Craven Arms) ✕ nearby Ⓓ

☆ **Springhill Farm** (B/IH)
Selattyn, Oswestry SY10 7NZ ☎ 01691 718406 (Sue Sopwith)
www.atspringhill.co.uk Grid ref: 210346
Bednight £16
🐾 Ⓑ Ⓓ 🚭

Set at 1,475ft overlooking
the Ceiriog Valley and
Berwyns. Offa's Dyke 3
miles. A new quality
conversion with 6 bedrooms,
sleeping 1-6. Breakfast and
transfer available.

NORTH WEST

Long Distance Paths

See **Paths & Access p25** for full
details of LDPs and waymarks

National Parks

Lake District

Peak District

Yorkshire Dales

See **Useful Contacts p99** for full
details of national parks

A SNOW-CAPPED SKIDDAW VIEWED ACROSS
DERWENTWATER IN THE LAKE DISTRICT

WALK...   ...A LAKELAND LLAMA TREK

There's a distinctively Andean flavour about the Cumbrian Lakes these days. Llamas more used to the mountains of Peru, Bolivia or Chile can now be found on trail heads near Keswick thanks to Lakeland Llama Treks. The animals make excellent walking companions: not only do they carry your backpack, but their sharp hearing and eyesight mean they can also spot wildlife en route quicker than humans. A range of treks is available, from a couple of hours to day-long excursions; some include speed dating, a picnic or a curry in a pub. Visit www.lakelandllamatreks.co.uk or ☎ 0870 770 7175 for further information.

VISIT...   ...EAST LANCASHIRE'S PANOPTICONS

'Panopti-what?' you might ask. A panopticon is apparently 'a structure, space or device providing a comprehensive or panoramic view'. East Lancashire's REMADE project is planning to reclaim areas of neglected land across the region to site six of them by the end of the year, all linked by extensive and improved footpath networks. Already, a derelict cannon battery in Blackburn's Grade II-listed Corporation Park has been restored as an impressive hilltop viewing platform. And a former landfill site at Haslingden has been reclaimed to site the Halo (pictured) – an 18m-diameter circular steel dish with solar-powered panels that glow, so by night it appears to hover. For more information, visit www.panopticons.uk.net, www.lancashire.gov.uk/environment/remade or call Mid Pennine Arts ☎ 01282 421986.

NORTH WEST

SEE......THE SADDLEWORTH RUSHCART FESTIVAL

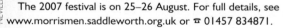

Revived in 1975, the annual Rushcart festival in Saddleworth – a Pennine valley near Oldham – is now the largest Morris Dancing event in Britain. Up to 150 Morris Men gang together to pull the three-tonne cart, stacked five metres high with rushes, through the streets of six moorland villages. Centuries ago, the rushes were mixed with fragrant herbs and spread across the bare floors of churches to insulate against the winter cold. Now symbolically performed at St Chad's Church, Uppermill, an afternoon of gurning, wrestling and entertainment follows.

The 2007 festival is on 25–26 August. For full details, see www.morrismen.saddleworth.org.uk or ☎ 01457 834871.

LOCAL RAMBLERS GROUPS... The Speke Garston Coastal Park opened last year after four years of hard work by Ramblers in Merseyside with local partners. The 2.4-hectare site overlooking the River Mersey contains the only natural shoreline in Liverpool city centre and has been extensively landscaped with many new pathways. Visit www.merseywaterfront.com for more details... **The Hodder Way is a new 43km/27-mile route devised by Clitheroe Group that follows the course of the river Hodder from its source in the Bowland Fells, over new access land in rural Lancashire, to its confluence with the Ribble. See p89 to order the guidebook.**

WALKING & CYCLING BREAKS

Discover a wealth of experiences at your own pace on self guided holidays, designed to offer you the very best in breathtaking countryside and interesting places to visit

The breathtaking scenery of Cumbria - The Lake District is a natural adventure playground.

www.lakedistrictoutdoors.co.uk

Where else could you find such a variety of world-class outdoor activities in so accessible and compact a region?

CUMBRIA TOURIST BOARD

ROAM
RECOGNISED OUTDOOR ACTIVITY MEMBER

PlayHard RestEasy

ROAM is an accreditation scheme for Cumbria's outdoor activity providers offering a professional assessment of both safety and quality.

Choose your adventure with a **Recognised Outdoor Activity Member** and you can rest assured that their service has been judged against national codes of good practice.

MAP 221

BED & BREAKFAST

CHESHIRE

● Altrincham
TRANS PENNINE TRAIL

🚶🍴 Oasis Hotel, 46-48 Barrington Road, WA14 1HN ☎ 0161 928 4523
www.oasishotel.co.uk Map 109/769885
BB **D** ✕ £10, 5:30-10:30pm S10 D11 T9 F3 ⋙ (Altrincham)
Ⓥ Ⓑ Ⓓ 🐾☕ ★★

● Church Minshull (Crewe)
Higher Elms Farm, Cross Lane, Minshull Vernon, CW1 4RG
☎ 01270 522252 (Mrs AM Charlesworth)
http://members.aol.com/tomsworld/higherelmsfarmhomepage.html
Map 118/669607
BB **C** ✕ nearby S1 D1 T1 F1 Ⓑ Ⓓ 🐾 🐾☕🚗 🐾 ★★★

● Congleton
STAFFORDSHIRE WAY

🚶🍴 Yew Tree Farm, North Rode, CW12 2PF ☎ 01260 223569 (Sheila Kidd)
www.yewtreebb.co.uk Map 118/890665
BB **C/D** ✕ book first £16, 6:30pm D1 T1 Closed Xmas
Ⓥ Ⓑ Ⓓ 🐾🐾☕🚗 ★★★★

● Crewe

☆ 🚶🍴 **Crewe Hall**
Weston Road, CW1 6UZ ☎ 01270 253333
www.marstonhotels.com Map 118/732540
BB **D** ✕ £37.50, 7-9:30pm D63 T2 ⋙ (Crewe)
Ⓥ Ⓑ 🐾☕ ★★★★ Wheelchair access.

An ideal base for a multitude of walks in the attractive Cheshire countryside, including the Shropshire Union and Trent & Mersey Canals, Crewe Hall is a beautiful four-star stately home with a sympathetic modern wing.

Enjoy a break in the comfortable and stylish West Wing and dine in the Brasserie with its unique revolving bar while soaking in the atmosphere of history.

Convenient for the Little Moreton Walk and Crewe station.

Please ask about our exclusive rates for walking parties.

● Macclesfield
PEAK DISTRICT

☆ 🚶🍴 **Ryles Arms**
Hollin Lane, Higher Sutton, SK11 0NN ☎ 01260 252244 (Ian Brown)
www.rylesarms.com Map 118/939695
BB **C** ✕ £9, 5:30-9pm D3 T1 F1 Closed Xmas
Ⓥ Ⓑ Ⓓ ⊗ 🐾☕ ♦♦♦♦

Highly celebrated and long established traditional country inn.

Offers homemade food, locally sourced. English cuisine from the traditional to the most contemporary alongside fine wine and real ale.
Experience spectacular views of rolling Cheshire countryside, only three miles from Macclesfield centre.
Luxury en-suite B&B popular with business travellers and walking groups, providing comfort at an affordable price.
Plenty of car parking available.
Visit for a true taste of Cheshire.

● Northwich
Ash House Farm, Chapel Lane, Acton Bridge, CW8 3QS ☎ 01606 852717
(Mrs SM Schofield) www.ashhousefarm.co.uk Map 117/587755
BB **C** ✕ S1 D1 T1 F1 ⋙ (Acton Bridge) Ⓑ Ⓓ 🐾☕🚗 🐾 ★★★★

● Rainow (Macclesfield)
PEAK DISTRICT
STAFFORDSHIRE WAY

☆ 🚶🍴 **Common Barn Farm B&B**
Smith Lane, SK10 5XJ ☎ 01625 574878 (Rona Cooper)
www.cottages-with-a-view.co.uk Map 118/968764
BB **D** ✕ nearby S2 D1 T2 F1
Ⓑ Ⓓ ⊗ 🐾☕🚗 ⚠️

A luxury barn conversion with en-suite facilities in all rooms, including power showers and under-floor central heating. Fully accessible room with en-suite wetroom and wheelchair-friendly bathroom. Situated in the Peak District National Park with unrivalled views across the Cheshire plain to the Welsh mountains.

● Siddington (Macclesfield)
🚶🍴 The Golden Cross Farm, SK11 9JP ☎ 01260 224358 (Hazel Rush)
Map 118/848707
BB **B** ✕ nearby S2 D2 Closed Xmas Ⓑ Ⓓ ⊗ 🐾☕🚗 ♦♦♦

● Willaston (South Wirral)
Pollards Inn, Village Sq, CH64 2TU ☎ 0151 3274615
www.liverpool-wirral.com Map 117/329776
BB **B** ✕ book first, 7-9pm D4 ⋙ (Hooton)
Ⓥ Ⓑ Ⓓ 🐾☕ ⚠️ Bar food available during day.

● Wincle (Macclesfield)
PEAK DISTRICT

Hill Top Farm, SK11 0QH ☎ 01260 227257 (Susan Brocklehurst)
c_brock_22@hotmail.com Map 118/965661
BB **C** ✗ book first £12, 6-6:30pm D1 T1 Closed Jan-Feb
Ⓥ Ⓑ Ⓓ ⊗ 🐾👜☕🚗 ! ★★★★

● Wybunbury (Nantwich)

☆ 🍴 **Lea Farm**
Wrinehill Road, CW5 7NS ☎ 01270 841429 (Jean E Callwood)
www.smoothhound.co.uk/hotels/leafarm.html Map 118/716489
BB **C** ✗ nearby D1 T1 F1
Ⓑ Ⓓ 🐾👜☕! 🛁 ◆◆◆

Charming farmhouse set in landscaped
gardens where peacocks roam. 150 acres of
peaceful family farm.
Delightful bedrooms. All amenities, some
en-suite rooms.
Snooker/pool table. Fishing available.
Email: contactus@leafarm.freeserve.co.uk

CUMBRIA

● Alston
PENNINE WAY

🍴 Greycroft, Middle Park, The Raise, CA9 3AR
☎ 01434 381383 (Mrs P M Dent) www.greycroft.co.uk Map 86/706463
BB **C** ✗ nearby D1 T/F1 Closed Xmas
Ⓑ Ⓓ ⊗ 🐾👜☕ ◆◆◆◆Ⓢ

High Field, Bruntley Meadows, CA9 3UX ☎ 01434 382182 (Celia Pattison)
cath@cybermoor.org.uk Map 87/720461
BB **A** ✗ £8, 7-9pm S1 D1 T1 F1 Closed Xmas Ⓥ Ⓑ Ⓓ 🐾👜☕🚗

🍴 Lowbyer Manor Country House, Hexham Road, CA9 3JX ☎ 01434 381230
www.lowbyer.com Map 86,87/717469
BB **D** ✗ nearby S1 D5 T2 F1 Ⓑ Ⓓ ⊗ 🐾👜☕🛁 ◆◆◆◆

● Ambleside
LAKE DISTRICT
COAST TO COAST WALK & CUMBRIA WAY

☆ 🍴 **Broadview Guest House**
Low Fold, Lake Road, LA22 0DN ☎ 015394 32431 (Alan & Sue Clarke)
www.broadview-guesthouse.co.uk Map 90/377036
BB **B/C/D** ✗ nearby D4 T2 F1 Closed Xmas
Ⓑ Ⓓ ⊗ 🐾👜☕ ★★★★

Comfortable AA 4* non-smoking B&B in
Ambleside, short stroll from village and Lake
Windermere at Waterhead. Always a warm
welcome and a hearty breakfast. Packed lunches,
morning weather reports and drying facilities.
Walks start from our front door.
Special breaks available all year.

🍴 Claremont House, Compston Road, LA22 9DJ ☎ 015394 33448
www.claremontambleside.co.uk Map 90/375043
BB **C** ✗ nearby D3 T1 F2
Ⓑ Ⓓ ⊗ 🐾👜☕🛁 ◆◆◆◆Ⓦ Wheelchair access.

☆ 🍴 **The Old Vicarage**
Vicarage Road, LA22 9DH ☎ 015394 33364
www.oldvicarageambleside.co.uk Map 90/373044
BB **D** ✗ nearby D8 T2 F2
Ⓑ Ⓓ 🐾👜☕🛁Ⓜ ◆◆◆◆

Quality Bed & Breakfast accommodation.
Quiet central location. Own car park. Pets
welcome. All bedrooms have TV, hairdryer,
alarm clock radio, video, mini fridge,
kettle, CH, private bath/shower and WC.
Indoor heated pool, sauna and hot-tub.
Email: the.old.vicarage@kencomp.net

☆ 🍴 **Croyden House**
Church Street, LA22 0BU ☎ 015394 32209 (Sylvia & John Drinkall)
www.croydenhouseambleside.co.uk Map 90/376043
BB **C** ✗ nearby S3 D6 T4 F2 Closed Xmas
Ⓑ Ⓓ ⊗ 👜☕ ◆◆◆

A guest house centrally situated on a quiet street,
2 minutes' walk from the main bus stop and centre of
Ambleside.

Offering a friendly welcome, generous homecooked
breakfasts, comfortable rooms with TV, tea/coffee making
facilities and private car park.

☆ **Nab Cottage**
Rydal, LA22 9SD ☎ 015394 35311 (Liz & Tim Melling)
www.rydalwater.com Map 90/355064
BB **C** ✗ book first £15, 7pm S1 D3 T2 F1
Ⓥ Ⓑ Ⓓ ⊗ 🐾👜☕! 🛁 ◆◆◆

A Grade II-listed 16th C. cottage
overlooking Rydal Water. Once
home of Thomas de Quincey and
Hartley Coleridge. Superb walks in
every direction. Delicious home
cooked food. Informal atmosphere.
Email: tim@nabcottage.com

☆ 🍴 **Smallwood House Hotel**
Compston Road, LA22 9DJ ☎ 015394 32330
www.smallwoodhotel.co.uk Map 90/375044
BB **D** ✗ £20, 6:30-7pm S2 D4 T3 F3 Closed Xmas
Ⓥ Ⓑ Ⓓ 🐾👜☕🛁 ◆◆◆◆ See Groups also.

We pride ourselves on a
quality, friendly service in
the traditional way.

Dinners and packed lunches.
Drying facilities. Newly
refurbished bedrooms with
luxurious bathrooms each
with underfloor heating.
Leave your cars in our car-
park and walk from here.

Please telephone Anthony or
Christine Harrison for a full
brochure and tariff.

enq@smallwoodhotel.co.uk

NORTH WEST

▧◄ Lyndale Guest House, Lake Road, LA22 0DN ☎ 015394 34244 (Alison Harwood) www.lyndale-guesthouse.co.uk Map 90/377036
BB **C** ✗ nearby S2 D2 T2 F2 Ⓑ Ⓓ ⊗ 🐾♨️🏔️ ◆◆◆

☆ **Stepping Stones**
Under Loughrigg, LA22 9LN ☎ 015394 33552 (Amanda Rowley)
www.steppingstonesambleside.co.uk Map 90/366055
BB **D** ✗ nearby D3 T1 Closed Xmas
Ⓑ Ⓓ ⊗ ♨️ ◆◆◆◆ See SC also.

Lakeland stone Victorian house, set in outstanding location with spectacular views over river, stepping stones and fells. Beautifully appointed, spacious bedrooms with period furnishings. Walks from door. Landscaped gardens with ample private parking.

▧◄ Brantfell House, Rothay Road, LA22 0EE
☎ 015394 32239 (Chris & Jane Amos) www.brantfell.co.uk Map 90/374041
BB **C/D** ✗ nearby S1 D6 T3 Ⓑ Ⓓ ⊗ 🐾♨️🏔️ ◆◆◆◆

● Appleby-in-Westmorland

☆▧◄ **Limnerslease**
Bongate, CA16 6UE ☎ 017683 51578 (Kathleen Coward)
http://mysite.freeserve.com/limnerslease Map 91/689200
BB **B** ✗ nearby D2 T1 Closed Xmas ⚡(Appleby)
Ⓓ ⊗ 🐾♨️🏔️

Limnerslease is a charming guest house situated in the historic picturesque market town of Appleby-in-Westmorland. You are assured a warm welcome and clean, comfortable accommodation. 5 mins walk from town centre and 10 mins walk from the famous Carlisle to Settle line.

▧◄ Bongate House, CA16 6UE ☎ 017683 51245 (Mary & John Geary)
www.bongatehouse.co.uk Map 91/689200
BB **C/D** ✗ book first £15, 6:30pm latest S1 D3 T2 F2 Closed Dec-Jan
⚡(Appleby) Ⓥ Ⓑ Ⓓ 🐾♨️🚗!🏔️ ◆◆◆◆

● Arnside
Willowfield Hotel, The Promenade, LA5 0AD
☎ 01524 761354 (Janet & Ian Kerr) www.willowfield.uk.com Map 97/456788
BB **C** ✗ book first £16, 7pm S2 D3 T4 F2 ⚡(Arnside)
Ⓥ Ⓑ Ⓓ ⊗ 🐾♨️🚗! ★★★★ Evening meal weekends only.

● Bampton (Penrith)
LAKE DISTRICT
COAST TO COAST WALK

☆ **Mardale Inn**
CA10 2RQ ☎ 01931 713244 (Neil & Katherine Stocks)
www.mardaleinn.co.uk Map 90/514181
BB **D** ✗ £8.95, 6-8pm D3 T3 Closed Jan
Ⓥ Ⓑ ⊗ 🐾♨️🏔️ ◆◆◆

Cosy, non-smoking, 18th-century inn with en-suite accommodation, near Haweswater. Wooden beams, log fire, real ales and over 45 malt whiskies. Home-made food featuring local produce. Tranquil location surrounded by beautiful countryside, by Coast to Coast Walk.

● Bampton Grange (Penrith)
LAKE DISTRICT
COAST TO COAST WALK

▧◄ Crown & Mitre Hotel, CA10 2QR ☎ 01931 713225
www.crownandmitrehotel.co.uk Map 90/520179
BB **C** ✗ £6-£9, 6-9pm S2 D2 T1 F2 Closed Xmas Ⓥ Ⓑ Ⓓ 🐾♨️🏔️

● Boot (Eskdale)
LAKE DISTRICT

The Post Office, Dale View, CA19 1TG ☎ 019467 23236 (John & Leigh Gray)
www.booteskdale.co.uk Map 89,90/176010
BB **B** ✗ nearby S1 D2 T1 Closed Xmas ⚡(Dalegarth) Ⓓ ⊗ 🐾♨️

▧◄ Wha House, CA19 1TH ☎ 019467 23322
mariehodgkiss@aol.com Map 89,90/190009
BB **B** ✗ nearby S1 D1 T2 ⚡(Ravenglass & Eskdale)
Ⓓ ⊗ 🐾♨️🏔️ Guest kitchen available. See SC also.

● Borrowdale (Keswick)
LAKE DISTRICT
COAST TO COAST WALK & CUMBRIA WAY

☆▧◄ **Royal Oak Hotel**
CA12 5XB ☎ 017687 77214
www.royaloakhotel.co.uk Map 90/259148
BB **D** ✗ £10, 7pm S2 D5 T2 F6 Closed Xmas
Ⓥ Ⓑ Ⓓ 🐾♨️🏔️🚗!🏔️ ★

Traditional, family-run Lakeland hotel situated beside Stonethwaite Beck in the heart of Borrowdale. Good home cooking, cosy bar, open fire and friendly service. Brochure, tariffs and special mid-week and long weekend breaks available.

● Boustead Hill (Burgh-by-Sands)
HADRIAN'S WALL

▧◄ Hillside Farm, CA5 6AA ☎ 01228 576398 (Sandra Rudd)
www.hadrianswalkbnb.co.uk Map 85/293591
BB **B** D1 T1 Closed Dec-Feb ⚡(Carlisle)
Ⓓ 🐾♨️🚗!🏔️ ◆◆◆ See Hostels also.

● Bowness-on-Solway
HADRIAN'S WALL

Kings Arms, CA7 5AF ☎ 016973 51426
www.kingsarmsbowness.co.uk Map 85/222627
BB **C** ✗ £5.50, 6-9pm T2 F2 Closed Xmas Ⓥ Ⓓ 🐾♨️!🏔️

☆ **The Old Chapel**
CA7 5BL ☎ 016973 51126 (Maureen Miller)
www.oldchapelbownessonsolway.com Map 85/224627
BB **B** ✗ nearby S1 T2 F1
Ⓑ Ⓓ ⊗ 🐾♨️🚗!🏔️ Wheelchair access.

Recently converted former chapel and cottage at the end of Hadrian's Wall. Ideally suited for walkers with all facilities provided — including foot spas! Price includes a substantial continental breakfast and a packed lunch for the following day. Full disabled access and facilities.

● Bowness-on-Windermere (Windermere)
LAKE DISTRICT & DALES WAY

☆ 🍴 Lingwood Lodge
Birkett Hill, LA23 3EZ ☎ 015394 44680 (Mrs J Fry)
www.lingwoodlodge.co.uk/ Map 96,97/402963
BB **D** ✗ nearby D4 T1 F1 ⏴(Windermere)
B D ⊗ 🛁 å ♿ ! ◆◆◆◆

A modern, family-run guest house in a quiet location but within 400 yards of Lake Windermere. A 10-minute walk from the end of the Dales Way and free off-road parking whilst you walk it!

🍴 Blenheim Lodge, Brantfell Road, LA23 3AE
☎ 015394 43440 (Janz Duncan) www.blenheim-lodge.com Map 96,97/404967
BB **D** ✗ nearby S3 D8 T2 F2 ⏴(Windermere) B D ⊗ å ◆◆◆◆

● Brampton
HADRIAN'S WALL

New Mills House, CA8 2QS ☎ 016977 3376 (Janet Boon)
www.newmillshouse.co.uk Map 86/549617
BB **B/C** ✗ book first £15+, 7:30-8pm D1 T1 Closed Xmas ⏴(Brampton)
V B D ⊗ 🛁 å ♿ ◆◆◆

● Broughton-in-Furness
LAKE DISTRICT

Middlesyke, Church Street, LA20 6ER ☎ 01229 716549 (David & Sarah Hartley)
www.middlesyke.co.uk Map 96/208876
BB **D** ✗ nearby D2 Closed Xmas ⏴(Foxfield)
B D ⊗ 🛁 å ♿ Ⓜ ◆◆◆◆ⓢ

● Buttermere (Cockermouth)
COAST TO COAST WALK

☆ 🍴 Dalegarth Guest House
CA13 9XA ☎ 017687 70233 (Ramblers Holidays)
www.dalegarthguesthouse.co.uk Map 89,90/186160
BB **C** ✗ book first, 7pm D4 T5
V B D ⊗ 🛁 Ⓜ

Our guesthouse is situated in the grounds of the Hassness Estate on the shore of Buttermere 1¼ miles south of Buttermere village. Bed and breakfast: standard £24pp, ensuite £30pp, evening meal from £5. Ask about midweek specials.

● Caldbeck (Wigton)
LAKE DISTRICT & CUMBRIA WAY

☆ 🍴 The Briars
Friar Row, CA7 8DS ☎ 016974 78633 (Dorothy H Coulthard)
Map 90/325399
BB **B** ✗ nearby S1 D1 T1 Closed Xmas
B D ⊗ å !

Situated in Caldbeck village, overlooking Caldbeck Fells. Ideal for touring Lake District, Scottish Borders and Roman Wall. We are right on the Cumbria Way. Near Reivers cycle route. Tea-making facilities. Rooms en-suite with TV. 2 mins walk to village inn.

☆ Swaledale Watch
Whelpo, CA7 8HQ ☎ 016974 78409 (Mr & Mrs Savage)
www.swaledale-watch.co.uk Map 90/309396
BB **B/C** ✗ nearby D2 T1 Closed Xmas
B D ⊗ 🛁 å ♿ ! ◆◆◆◆ⓢ

Enjoy comfort, beautiful surroundings and peaceful countryside on our farm. Central for touring or walking the northern fells. Lifts to and from Caldbeck village available. A warm welcome awaits you. Ideal for the Cumbria Way. All rooms have private facilities.

● Carlisle
HADRIAN'S WALL, CUMBRIA WAY & PENNINE WAY

Angus Hotel & Almonds Bistro, 14 Scotland Road, Stanwix, CA3 9DG
☎ 01228 523546 www.angus-hotel.co.uk Map 85/400571
BB **D** ✗ £15, 6-9pm S3 D3 T4 F4 ⏴(Carlisle)
V B D 🛁 å ! 🏠 ◆◆◆◆
Free packed lunch for walk BRITAIN readers!

Craighead, 6 Hartington Place, CA1 1HL
☎ 01228 596767 (Pam Smith) Map 85/406559
BB **B** ✗ nearby S1 D2 T1 F1 Closed Xmas ⏴(Carlisle)
B D ⊗ 🛁 å ! 🏠 ◆◆◆

🍴 Knockupworth Hall, Burgh Road, CA2 7RF
☎ 01228 523531 (Patricia Dixon) www.knockupworthdi.co.uk Map 85/370566
BB **D** ✗ book first £10+, 7pm D2 T2 F1 Closed Dec-Feb ⏴(Carlisle)
V B D ⊗ 🛁 å ♿ !

Abberley House, 33 Victoria Place, CA1 1HP ☎ 01228 521645
www.abberleyhouse.co.uk Map 85/406561
BB **C** ✗ nearby S3 D2 T2 F1 Closed Xmas ⏴(Carlisle)
B D ⊗ å ! ◆◆◆◆

☆ No 1 Guest House
1 Etterby St, Stanwix, CA3 9JB ☎ 01228 547285 (Sheila Nixon)
sheila@carlislebandb.co.uk Map 85/399571
BB **C** ✗ book first £10, 6:30pm S2 D1 T1 Closed Xmas ⏴(Carlisle)
V B D ⊗ 🛁 å ♿ !

A warm welcome awaits at No 1 Guest House situated on the line of the Roman Wall. 10min walk from Sand Centre, close to Solway coastal walk. 2 miles from Rockliffe. Four diamond, all rooms ensuite with power showers, central heating. Special diets catered for. Packed lunches ordered in advance. Laundry service available.

🍴 Cambro House, 173 Warwick Rd, CA1 1LP
☎ 01228 543094 (David & Alice) davidcambro@aol.com Map 85/412559
BB **B** ✗ nearby D2 T1 Closed Xmas ⏴(Carlisle)
B D ⊗ 🛁 å ! ◆◆◆◆

🍴 Kenilworth Guest House, 34 Lazonby Terrace, London Road, CA1 2PZ
☎ 01228 526179 (Robert & Anne Glendinning)
www.kenilworth-guesthouse.co.uk Map 85/414545
BB **C** ✗ nearby S1 D3 T1 F1 ⏴(Carlisle) V B ⊗ 🛁 å ◆◆◆

🍴 Howard Lodge Guest House, 90 Warwick Road, CA1 1JU
☎ 01228 529842 (Charlotte Davies) www.howard-lodge.co.uk Map 85/407558
BB **C** ✗ nearby S2 D3 T3 F2 ⏴(Carlisle) B D 🛁 å 🏠 ◆◆◆

NORTH WEST

●◄ Cornerways Guest House, 107 Warwick Road, CAI IEA ☎ 01228 521733
(Steve & Be Coggan) www.cornerwaysbandb.co.uk Map 85/406559
BB **C** ✕ nearby S4 D2 T2 F2 Closed Xmas ⋙(Carlisle)
Ⓑ Ⓓ ⊗ 🐾🛏🚿 ! ★★★★Ⓦ

● Cartmel (Grange-over-Sands)

Bank Court Cottage, The Square, LAII 6QB ☎ 015395 36593 (Mrs PC Lawson)
Map 96,97/378787
BB **C** ✕ book first £15, 7pm DI Closed Xmas ⋙(Grange)
Ⓥ Ⓑ Ⓓ ⊗ 🐾🛏🌡 ★★★

● Coniston
LAKE DISTRICT
CUMBRIA WAY

☆ **Beech Tree House**
Yewdale Road, LA2I 8DX ☎ 015394 41717
Map 96/302976
BB **C** ✕ nearby D6 T2 Closed Xmas
Ⓑ Ⓓ ⊗ 🐾🛏🚲 ⋙ ◆◆◆◆

Charming 18th-century house with
attractive gardens situated 150m from
the village centre and all amenities.
Ideally situated for a walking holiday
or overnight stay on the Cumbria Way.
Good drying facilities, ample parking.
En-suites available.

Lakeland House Guest House, Coffee & Eating Hse,Tilberthwaite Ave, LA2I 8ED
☎ 015394 41303 www.lakelandhouse.com Map 96,97/304976
BB **C/D** SI D3 TI F5 Closed Xmas Ⓑ Ⓓ ⊗ 🐾🛏🌡! 🌡 ◆◆◆

☆●◄ **Thwaite Cottage**
Waterhead, LA2I 8AJ ☎ 015394 41367 (Marguerite & Graham Aldridge)
www.thwaitcot.freeserve.co.uk Map 96/311977
BB **C** ✕ nearby D2 TI Closed Xmas
Ⓑ Ⓓ ⊗ 🐾🛏 ★★★★

A beautiful 17th C. cottage in
a peaceful wooded garden,
close to village and lake.
Central heating, log fires,
beamed ceilings. Bathrooms,
private or en-suite. Off-road
parking. Non-smoking.

Waverley, Lake Road, LA2I 8EW ☎ 015394 41127 (Jenny Graham)
Map 96,97/302974
BB **B/C** ✕ nearby SI DI TI FI Closed Xmas Ⓑ Ⓓ ⊗ 🐾🛏🌡

●◄ Crown Inn, LA2I 8ED ☎ 015394 41243
www.crown-hotel-coniston.com Map 96, 97/304976
BB **D** ✕ £10, until 9pm D6 T4 F2 Closed Xmas
Ⓥ Ⓑ Ⓓ ⊗ 🐾🛏🌡 ◆◆◆◆

Orchard Cottage, 18 Yewdale Road, LA2I 8DU ☎ 015394 41319 (Jean Johnson)
www.conistonholidays.co.uk Map 96,97/302976
BB **D** ✕ nearby D2 TI Closed Xmas
Ⓑ Ⓓ ⊗ 🐾🛏⋙! Ⓜ ◆◆◆◆

Oaklands, Yewdale Rd, LA2I 8DX ☎ 015394 41245 (Mr & Mrs J Myers)
www.oaklandsconiston.co.uk Map 96,97/302977
BB **C** ✕ nearby SI D2 TI Ⓑ Ⓓ ⊗ 🐾🛏⋙! ◆◆◆◆

☆●◄ **Wheelgate Country Guest House**
Little Arrow, LA2I 8AU ☎ 015394 41418 (Steve & Linda Abbott)
www.wheelgate.co.uk Map 96,97/290950
BB **D** ✕ nearby S2 D3 TI Closed Xmas
Ⓑ Ⓓ ⊗ 🛏 ⋙ ◆◆◆◆◆ See Coniston Country Cottages in SC also.

17th-century farmhouse with
beamed ceilings, spacious en-suite
bedrooms and cosy bar. Excellent
breakfasts cater for all tastes.
Ideally situated for access to central
lakes, with superb local walks to
suit all ages and abilities.

Coniston Lodge, Station Road, LA2I 8HH ☎ 015394 41201 (Mr & Mrs Robinson)
www.coniston-lodge.com Map 96/301975
BB **D** ✕ book first £26, 7pm D3 T3
Ⓥ Ⓑ Ⓓ ⊗ 🐾🛏🌡! ◆◆◆◆◆Ⓖ

● Dent (Sedbergh)
YORKSHIRE DALES
DALES WAY

●◄ Garda View Guest House, Main Street, LA10 5QL
☎ 015396 25209 (Rita Smith) rita@gardaview.co.uk Map 98/705870
BB **B** ✕ nearby SI D2 TI Closed Xmas Ⓑ Ⓓ ⊗ 🐾🛏

Stone Close Tea Room, Main Street, LA10 5QL
☎ 015396 25231 (Janet Browning) www.dentdale.com Map 98/705869
BB **C** DI T2 Ⓑ Ⓓ ⊗ 🐾🛏🌡 ◆◆◆
Special diets catered for. Wheelchair access.

● Dubwath (Cockermouth)
LAKE DISTRICT
CUMBRIA WAY

●◄ Ouse Bridge Hotel, Bassenthwaite Lake, CAI3 9YD ☎ 017687 76322
www.ousebridge.com Map 89,90/197312
BB **D** ✕ book first £14, 7:15-8pm S2 D5 T2 F2 Ⓥ Ⓑ Ⓓ ⊗ 🐾🛏 ★★

● Dufton (Appleby)
PENNINE WAY & TEESDALE WAY

Coney Garth, CAI6 6DA ☎ 017683 52582 (Mrs J T Foster)
www.coneygarth.co.uk Map 91/685257
BB **C** ✕ book first £12.50, 7-7:30pm DI TI FI
Ⓥ Ⓑ Ⓓ ⊗ 🐾🛏🌡! 🌡

● Eamont Bridge (Penrith)
River View, 6 Lowther Glen, CAI0 2BP ☎ 01768 864405 (Mrs C O'Neil)
http://river-view.co.uk Map 90/524285
BB **C** ✕ nearby S2 D2 T2 ⋙(Penrith) Ⓑ Ⓓ 🐾🛏🌡

● Eskdale Green
LAKE DISTRICT

☆ **Forest How Guest House**
CAI9 ITR ☎ 019467 23201
www.foresthow.co.uk Map 96/136999
BB **D** ✕ nearby SI D4 T3 FI Closed Xmas ⋙(Ravenglass & Eskdale)
Ⓑ Ⓓ ⊗ 🐾🛏🌡

Secluded, warm, comfortable guest
house. Excellent home cooking.
Delightful gardens with spectacular
views. TVs, H&C, beverage trays. Some
en-suite. Parking. Friendly and
informal atmosphere.
Brochure available.

● Gilsland (Brampton)

HADRIAN'S WALL & PENNINE WAY

🚶🚲 The Hill on the Wall, CA8 7DA ☎ 016977 47214 (Elaine Packer)
www.hadrians-wallbedandbreakfast.com Map 86/624668
BB **D** ✗ book first £15, 7-7:30pm D1 T2
Ⓥ Ⓑ Ⓓ ⊗ 🐾 ☕ 👜 ◆◆◆◆◆Ⓢ

● Grange-over-Sands

🚶🚲 Corner Beech Guest House, 1 Methven Terr, Kents Bank Rd, LA11 7DP
☎ 015395 33088 (Ian Wright) www.cornerbeech.co.uk Map 96,97/402772
BB **D** ✗ book first £17.50, 6:30pm D3 T1 F1 Closed Dec-Jan
🚌(Grange-over-Sands) Ⓥ Ⓑ Ⓓ ⊗ 🐾 ☕ 👜 🚗 ! ◆◆◆◆

● Grasmere (Ambleside)

LAKE DISTRICT

COAST TO COAST WALK & CUMBRIA WAY

☆ **Dunmail House**
Keswick Road, LA22 9RE ☎ 015394 35256 (Tony & Shirley Evans)
www.dunmailhouse.com Map 90/339084
BB **D** ✗ nearby S1 D3 T1 Closed Xmas
Ⓑ Ⓓ ⊗ 🐾 ☕ ★★★★★

A traditional stone house with a friendly
family atmosphere. Beautiful views from
all rooms and the spacious gardens.
Convenient for lake and village.
Non-smoking. Car park.
info@dunmailhouse.com

☆ **Forest Side Hotel**
Forest Side, LA22 9RN ☎ 015394 35250
www.forestsidehotel.com Map 90/342080
BB **B** ✗ £10.50, 6-9pm S10 D9 T9 F5
Ⓥ Ⓑ Ⓓ ⊗ 🐾 ☕ 👜 🚗 Ⓜ

Family-run hotel just ten minutes' walk from the centre of Grasmere, set in 43
acres of wooded and landscaped gardens.

Forest Side is an ideal base for exploring the Lake District or a stopover for the
Coast to Coast Walk.

Homecooked meals: traditional English breakfast. Packed lunches are available
daily.

Licensed bar and log fires. Non-smoking throughout. Tea/coffee making
facilities and TV available in all rooms. Most rooms en-suite. Boot drying room.

Self-catering apartments and large private car park also available.

Oak Lodge, Easedale Rd, LA22 9QJ ☎ 015394 35527 (Alison Dixon)
www.oaklodge-grasmere.co.uk Map 90/331081
BB **C/D** ✗ nearby D2 T1 Closed Xmas Ⓑ Ⓓ ⊗ 🐾 ☕

● Helton (Penrith)

LAKE DISTRICT

🚶🚲 Beckfoot Country House, Guest Accommodation, CA10 2QB
☎ 01931 713241 (Lesley White) www.beckfoot.co.uk Map 90/500210
BB **D** ✗ nearby S1 D3 T2 F1 Closed Dec-Feb
Ⓑ Ⓓ 🐾 ☕ 👜 🚗 ◆◆◆◆

● Hesket Newmarket (Caldbeck)

LAKE DISTRICT

CUMBRIA WAY

Newlands Grange, CA7 8HP ☎ 016974 78676 (Dorothy Studholme)
studholme_newlands@hotmail.com Map 90/350394
BB **B** ✗ book first £12, 6:30pm S1 D1 T1 F2 Closed Xmas
Ⓑ Ⓓ ⊗ 🐾 ☕ 👜 🚗 ! 🐄 See SC also.

● Kendal

LAKE DISTRICT

DALES WAY

🚶🚲 Hillside Bed & Breakfast, 4 Beast Banks, LA9 4JW ☎ 01539 722836
(Joanne Buchanan) www.hillside-kendal.co.uk Map 97/513925
BB **B/C** ✗ nearby S3 D2 T1 Closed Xmas 🚌(Oxenholme)
Ⓑ Ⓓ ⊗ 🐾 ☕ 🚗 ◆◆◆

Sundial House, 51 Milnthorpe Road, LA9 5QG ☎ 01539 724468
(Sue & Andrew McLeod) info@sundialguesthousekendal.co.uk Map 97/516916
BB **B** ✗ nearby S2 D2 T2 F/D/T1 Closed Xmas 🚌(Oxenholme)
Ⓑ Ⓓ ⊗ 🐾 ☕ 👜

☆ 🚶🚲 **The Glen**
Oxenholme, LA9 7RF ☎ 01539 726386 (Chris Green)
www.glen-kendal.co.uk Map 97/534900
BB **C** ✗ nearby S1 D3 T1 F2 Closed Xmas 🚌(Oxenholme)
Ⓑ Ⓓ ⊗ 🐾 ☕ 👜 🚗 ! 🐄 ◆◆◆◆

We are situated in a quiet location on
the outskirts of Kendal under 'The
Helm', where there is a local walk &
viewpoint of the Lakeland Mountains,
but within short walk of country pub
and restauarnt. Ideal for touring the
Lakes & Yorkshire Dales.

🚶🚲 Bridge House, 65 Castle Street, LA9 7AD ☎ 01539 722041
(Sheila Brindley) www.bridgehouse-kendal.co.uk Map 97/521930
BB **C** ✗ nearby S1 D1 T1 🚌(Kendal) Ⓑ Ⓓ ⊗ 🐾 ☕ 🚗

● Kentmere (Kendal)

LAKE DISTRICT

Maggs Howe, LA8 9JP ☎ 01539 821689 (Christine Hevey)
www.smoothhound.co.uk/hotels/maggs Map 90/462041
BB **B/C** ✗ book first £12.50, 7pm S1 D1 T1 F1 Closed Xmas
Ⓥ Ⓑ Ⓓ 🐾 ☕ 🚗 ! 🐄

● Keswick

LAKE DISTRICT

CUMBRIA WAY

🚶🚲 Lincoln Guest House, 23 Stanger Street, CA12 5JX ☎ 017687 72597
www.lincolnguesthouse.com Map 89,90/265236
BB **C** ✗ nearby S2 D3 T1 F1 Ⓑ Ⓓ ⊗ 🐾 ☕

☆ Seven Oaks Guest House

7 Acorn Street, CA12 4EA ☎ 017687 72088 (L Furniss & C Firth)
www.sevenoaks-keswick.co.uk Map 89,90/269232
BB **C** ✕ nearby D4 T2 F1 Closed Xmas
🅱 🅳 ⊗ 🐾 🚗 ! ◆◆◆

There's a warm welcome at our non-smoking en-suite guest accommodation, peacefully located only a few minutes from the town centre and Lake Derwentwater.
The bedrooms are furnished with your comfort in mind, and the rear rooms have mountain views.

☆ Tarn Hows

3-5 Eskin Street, CA12 4DH ☎ 017687 73217 (Mr & Mrs T Bulch)
www.tarnhows.co.uk Map 89, 90/268233
BB **C/D** ✕ book first £20 (groups only), 5-8pm S2 D6 Closed Xmas
🆅 🅱 🅳 ⊗ 🐾 ◆◆◆◆

Traditional Victorian residence pleasantly situated in a quiet location, Tarn Hows is only a few minutes' walk from the town centre, with easy access to the lake and the surrounding fells. Private car park. Non-smoking. Drying facilities.

☆ Hedgehog Hill

18 Blencathra Street, CA12 4HP ☎ 017687 74386 (Nel & Keith Nicholls)
www.hedgehoghill.co.uk Map 89,90/269233
BB **B/C** ✕ nearby S2 D3 T1 Closed Xmas
🅱 🅳 ⊗ 🐾 ★★★★

A warm welcome awaits at our Victorian guesthouse near the town centre, fells and lake.

Freshly prepared breakfast with choice. Vegetarian and special diets catered for. Flask filled for free.

All rooms are centrally heated with colour TV and tea/coffee making facilities. Most are en-suite with fell views.

Non-smoking.
Credit cards accepted.

rambler@hedgehoghill.co.uk

☆ Glencoe Guest House

21 Helvellyn, CA12 4EN ☎ 017687 71016 (Teresa Segasby)
www.glencoeguesthouse.co.uk Map 89,90/269233
BB **C** ✕ nearby S1 D3 T2
🅱 🅳 ⊗ 🐾 ◆◆◆◆

Teresa & Karl await you with a warm friendly welcome, ensuring an enjoyable stay in comfortable, quiet and relaxing accommodation.
Excellent breakfasts. Keswick centre 5 mins, drying room, free flask filling, weather reports, local knowledge and more.

☆ 🚩 Cumbria House

1 Derwentwater Place, Ambleside Road, CA12 4DR ☎ 017687 73171
(Barry & Cathy Colam) www.cumbriahouse.co.uk Map 89,90/268232
BB **B/C/D** ✕ book first £15 (groups only), 6:45pm S3 D2 T3 F1 Closed
Dec-Jan 🆅 🅱 🅳 🐾 🛏 Ⓜ ◆◆◆◆ Discounts for car-free guests.

We can't guarantee the weather – but at least we have an efficient drying room and provide a local weather forecast twice a day.

Award-winning breakfast using local produce with plenty of choice, home-made rolls, marmalade and jams, plus Fairtrade teas, coffees and fruit juices.

Advice on walks freely given or "Pace the Peaks" with Cathy & Kim. See Walking Holidays section and www.pacethepeaks.co.uk

☆ Badgers Wood

30 Stanger Street, CA12 5JU ☎ 017687 72621 (Anne Paylor)
www.badgers-wood.co.uk Map 89,90/265235
BB **C** ✕ nearby S2 D4 T1 Closed Jan
🅱 🅳 ⊗ 🛏 ◆◆◆◆

Quality accommodation and a friendly welcome await at this no-smoking, traditional Lakeland guest house, carefully restored and retaining much charm and character. Situated in a quiet cul-de-sac just two minutes' walk from the market square and bus station.

All rooms are en-suite, attractively furnished and smartly decorated with views towards the fells. High standards of housekeeping are our trademark.

Maps and guide books available. Owners' extensive fells knowledge gladly shared.

☆ 🚩 Hawcliffe House

30 Eskin Street, CA12 4DG ☎ 017687 73250 (Diane & Ian McConnell)
www.hawcliffehouse.co.uk Map 89,90/270232
BB **B** ✕ nearby D3 T2 Closed Xmas
🅱 ⊗ 🐾 🛏 ◆◆◆

Small, family-run guest house.
Warm welcome assured.
Non-smoking.
Packed lunches available on request.
Short walk from town centre.

Call Diane for more information.

☆ Hazeldene Hotel

The Heads, CA12 5ER ☎ 01768 772106
www.hazeldene-hotel.co.uk Map 89,90/264232
BB **D** ✕ nearby D7 T1 F2 Closed Jan
🅱 🅳 ⊘ 🐾 ♿ 🐧 ★★★★

Hazeldene is a welcoming family-run hotel in a magnificent location, ideally placed for both town and country.

Well-appointed en-suite bedrooms, beautiful views & an excellent breakfast make Hazeldene Hotel the perfect haven for your visit to the Lake District National Park.

Games room with table tennis and pool table. Private parking is available for 8 cars.

☆ High Hill Farm

High Hill, CA12 5NY ☎ 017687 74793 (Lillian & Keith Davies)
lillankei@btinternet.com Map 89/262238
BB **B** ✕ nearby D2 T1 Closed Xmas
🅱 🅳 ⊘ 🐾 ♿ Ⓜ

Former farmhouse, 5 mins level walk to town centre. B&B for non-smokers in 3 en-suite rooms with tea/coffee and beautiful views. Parking. Special breaks of 3 days plus — except bank holidays. Excellent centre for walking.

☆ ▪◀ Littlefield

32 Eskin Street, CA12 4DG ☎ 017687 72949 (Maureen Hardy)
www.keswick98.fsnet.co.uk Map 89,90/270233
BB **B/C** ✕ nearby S1 D3 T1 Closed Xmas
🅱 🅳 ⊘ 🐾 ♿

Small, friendly bed and breakfast.

Convenient for shops, lake and many lovely walks.

We pride ourselves on our warm, relaxed hospitality and attention to detail.

☆ ▪◀ Rivendell Guest House

23 Helvellyn St, CA12 4EN ☎ 01768 773822 (Pat & Linda Dent & June Muse)
www.rivendellguesthouse.com Map 89,90/269233
BB **B** ✕ nearby S2 D6 T4 F2
🅱 🅳 ⊘ 🐾 ♿ ! Ⓜ

A warm friendly welcome awaits you at our lovely Victorian home run by RA members. Set in quiet location close to town centre & Fitz Park with lots of parking. Most rooms en-suite. Drying facilities. Pets welcome (by arragement). Groups up to 15 welcome. Lots of local knowledge — map and walks to suit all levels. Email: info@rivendellguesthouse.com

Cragside Guest House, 39 Blencathra St, CA12 4HX
☎ 01768 773344 (Wayne & Alison Binks)
www.smoothhound.co.uk/hotels/cragside Map 89,90/271234
BB **B** ✕ nearby D2 T1 F1 Closed Xmas 🅱 🅳 ⊘ 🐾 ♿ ◆◆◆◆

☆ ▪◀ Craglands Guest House

Penrith Road, CA12 4LJ ☎ 017687 74406 (Ella Ferguson)
www.craglands-keswick.co.uk Map 89,90/279238
BB **C** ✕ nearby S2 D3 T2
🅱 🅳 ⊘ 🐾 ♿ ! ◆◆◆◆

Elevated position on the peaceful edge of town with stunning mountain views. Single, twin and double rooms. Walking route advice, guide books, drying facilities. Breakfasts from home-made and quality local produce with Fairtrade beverages. Packed lunches with Ella's famous flapjack! En-suite, non-smoking, private parking.

▪◀ Portland House, 19 Leonard Street, CA12 4EL
☎ 017687 74230 (Linda Ball) www.portlandhouse.net Map 89,90/269233
BB **C** ✕ nearby S1 D3 T1 F1
🅱 🅳 ⊘ 🐾 ♿ ! Wheelchair access.

☆ Easedale House

1 Southey Street, CA12 4HL ☎ 017687 72710
www.easedalehouse.com Map 89,90/268234
BB **C/D** ✕ nearby D6 T2 F1
🅱 🅳 ⊘ 🐾 ♿ ◆◆◆◆

Easedale House is a family-run guest house offering high quality B&B accommodation, situated close to the town centre and a short stroll from Derwentwater and the fells. Walker-friendly, with early breakfasts, packed lunches and drying room available.

● Kirkby Stephen
COAST TO COAST WALK

☆ Redmayne House

Silver Street, CA17 4RB ☎ 017683 71441 (Mrs C J Prime)
Map 91/774088
BB **B** ✕ nearby S1 D1 T1 F1 Closed Xmas 〰(Kirkby Stephen)
🅳 ⊘ 🐾 ♿

A spacious and attractive Georgian home set in a large garden. Glorious walking country. Home-made bread and preserves, walkers' breakfasts, private sitting room, parking.

£23.00 — one price for all.

Lockholme, 48 South Road, CA17 4SN ☎ 017683 71321 (Mrs M E Graham)
www.lockholme.co.uk Map 91/772079
BB **B** ✕ nearby S1 D1 T1 F1 〰(Kirkby Stephen) 🅱 🅳 ⊘ 🐾 ♿ ! Ⓜ

● Long Marton (Appleby-in-Westmorland)
PENNINE WAY & TEESDALE WAY

Broom House, CA16 6JP ☎ 017683 61318 (Sandra Bland)
http://broomhouseappleby.co.uk Map 91/666238
BB **C** ✕ book first S1 D1 T1 Closed Dec-Jan
🅱 🅳 ⊘ 🐾 ♿ ◆◆◆◆

NORTH WEST

● Low Crosby (Carlisle)

HADRIAN'S WALL & CUMBRIA WAY

Madgwick, Green Lane, CA6 4QN ☎ 01228 573283 (MJ Plane)
www.madgwickonwall.co.uk Map 85/445593
BB **B** ✕ nearby S1 T1 Closed Dec-Jan Ⓓ ⊗ 🐾 🔥 !

● Motherby (Penrith)

☆ 🍴◀ **Motherby House**
CA11 0RJ ☎ 017684 83368 (Jacquie Freeborn)
www.motherbyhouse.co.uk Map 90/429285
BB **B** ✕ book first £14.50, 7pm F2 Closed Xmas
Ⓥ Ⓓ ⊗ 🐾 🔥 See Greystone in SC also.

18th C. warm and friendly guest house with beamed lounge and log fires. Drying facilities. Packed lunches and flask filling. Excellent 3-course meal for healthy outdoor appetites. Near Ullswater Helve, Ilyn and Blencathra. Small groups & muddy boots welcome.

● Patterdale (Ullswater)

LAKE DISTRICT
COAST TO COAST WALK

☆ **Wordsworth Cottage**
CA11 0NP ☎ 017684 82084 (Joan B Martin)
www.wordsworthcottage-ullswater.co.uk Map 90/400160
BB **C** ✕ nearby D2 T1 Closed Xmas
Ⓑ Ⓓ ⊗ 🐾 🔥 !

A warm welcome awaits you at this charming and historic cottage. Built in 1670 it was once owned by Wordsworth himself. Ideally located for the Coast to Coast Walk, Helvellyn and High Street ranges.
View website for more details.

☆ **Old Water View**
CA11 0NW ☎ 017684 82175
www.oldwaterview.co.uk Map 90/398158
BB **C** ✕ nearby D3 Closed Xmas
Ⓑ Ⓓ ⊗ 🐾 🔥

Elegant and welcoming, this bed & breakfast is beautifully situated on the banks of Goldrill Beck. Guests are welcome to enjoy the guest lounge and garden at any time during their stay. Telephone for a brochure or view the website. Credit cards accepted.

🍴◀ Brotherswater Inn & Sykeside Camping Park, Brotherswater, CA11 0NZ
☎ 017684 82239 www.sykeside.co.uk Map 90/407130
BB **C** ✕ £10, 5:30-9:30pm D6 T8 Closed Xmas
Ⓥ Ⓑ Ⓓ 🐾 🔥 🅜

Barco House, CA11 0NW ☎ 017684 82474
www.barcohouse.com Map 90/397157
BB **D** ✕ nearby S3 D2 T2 F2 Ⓑ Ⓓ ⊗ 🐾 🔥 🚗 🅜

● Portinscale (Keswick)

LAKE DISTRICT
CUMBRIA WAY

🍴◀ The Mount Guest House, CA12 5RD ☎ 017687 73970
(Lindsay & Ann Ferguson) www.mountferguson.co.uk Map 89/252236
BB **C** ✕ nearby S1 D1 T1 F1 Closed Xmas Ⓑ Ⓓ ⊗ 🐾 🔥 🏔

● Rydal (Ambleside)

LAKE DISTRICT
COAST TO COAST WALK & CUMBRIA WAY

Rydal Hall, LA22 9LX ☎ 015394 32050 www.rydalhall.org Map 90/366063
BB **D** ✕ book first £12.50, 6:30pm S8 D4 T16 F2
Ⓥ Ⓑ Ⓓ ⊗ 🐾 🔥 Wheelchair access. See SC also.

● Sedbergh

YORKSHIRE DALES
DALES WAY

Holmecroft, Station Road, LA10 5DW ☎ 015396 20754 (Mrs S Sharrocks)
www.holmecroftbandb.co.uk Map 97/650919
BB **B** ✕ nearby S1 D1 T1 Closed Nov-Feb Ⓓ ⊗ 🐾 🚗 !

🍴◀ Wheelwright Cottage, 15 Back Lane, LA10 5AQ ☎ 015396 20251
(Miss M Thurlby) antique.thurlby@amserve.net Map 97/659921
BB **B** ✕ nearby D1 T1 Ⓓ ⊗ 🐾 🔥 🚗 ! 🏔 ◆◆

☆ 🍴◀ **St Mark's**
Cautley, LA10 5LZ ☎ 015396 20287 (Barbara Manwaring)
www.saintmarks.uk.com Map 98/690944
BB **C** ✕ book first £10.50, 7-7:30pm S1 T3 F1 Closed Xmas
Ⓥ Ⓑ Ⓓ ⊗ 🐾 🔥 🚗 ! 🏔 ◆◆◆◆

Treat yourself to the tranquil Howgill Fells (Cautley Spout 2 miles). Outstanding setting, Yorkshire Dales National Park. Victorian vicarage, comfortable en-suite rooms (3 bath, 2 shower), open fires, delicious aga-cooked breakfasts. Full board accommodation and excellent studio available for groups of 6 +.

🍴◀ Yew Tree Cottage, 35 Loftus Hill, LA10 5SQ ☎ 015396 21600 (Anne Jones)
www.sedbergh.org.uk Map 97/658917
BB **B** ✕ nearby D1 T1 Closed Xmas Ⓓ ⊗ 🐾 🔥 ! 🏔 ◆◆◆

🍴◀ Brantrigg, Winfield Rd, LA10 5AZ ☎ 015396 21455 (Linda Hopkins)
www.brantrigg.co.uk Map 97/658923
BB **D** ✕ nearby T1 Closed Xmas Ⓑ Ⓓ ⊗ 🐾 🔥 🚗

☆ 🍴◀ **The Bull Hotel**
44 Main Street, LA10 5BL ☎ 015396 20264
www.bullhotelsedbergh.co.uk Map 97/657921
BB **C** ✕ £8, 6-9pm S2 D6 T5 F2
Ⓥ Ⓑ Ⓓ 🐾 🔥 🏔 ◆◆◆◆

17th-century former coaching inn with fifteen en-suite bedrooms, two bars, restaurant and beer garden.
Warm welcome.
Award-winning ales. Great food.
Dogs and families welcome.
Beautiful views and walks.

● St Bees

COAST TO COAST WALK

Fairladies Barn Guest House, Main Street, CA27 0AD ☎ 01946 822718
(Susan & John Carr) www.fairladiesbarn.co.uk Map 89/970114
BB **B** ✕ nearby D5 T4 F2 🚉(St Bees) Ⓑ Ⓓ ⊗ 🐾 🔥 ! ◆◆◆◆

Stonehouse Farm, Main Street, CA27 0DE ☎ 01946 822224 (Carole Smith)
www.stonehousefarm.net Map 89/971119
BB **C** ✕ nearby S1 D3 T2 F3 Closed Xmas ⋙(St Bees)
Ⓑ Ⓓ 🍳🚌🚗 ! 🛏 ◆◆◆

1 Tomlin House, Beach Road, CA27 0EN ☎ 01946 822284
(Mr & Mrs Whitehead) id.whitehead@which.net Map 89/963118
BB **B** ✕ nearby D1 T2 F1 Closed Xmas ⋙(St Bees) Ⓑ Ⓓ ⊗🍳🚌🚗 🛏

● Staveley (Kendal)
    LAKE DISTRICT
    DALES WAY

🚶⊲◀ Ramblers Cottage, 1 School Lane, LA8 9NU
☎ 01539 822120 (Mrs Craven) www.ramblers-cottage.co.uk Map 97/469984
BB **C** ✕ nearby D1 T1 Closed Xmas ⋙(Staveley) Ⓑ Ⓓ 🍳🚌🚗 ! 🛏

● Threlkeld (Keswick)
    LAKE DISTRICT
    CUMBRIA WAY

☆ **Scales Farm Country Guest House**
CA12 4SY ☎ 01768 779660 (Alan & Angela Jameison)
www.scalesfarm.com Map 90/341268
BB **C** ✕ nearby D3 T2 F1 Closed Xmas
Ⓑ Ⓓ ⊗🍳🚌🚗 🛏 ★★★★

Stunning views & a warm welcome await you at this 17th C. fells farmhouse sensitively modernised to provide accommodation of the highest standard. The farm is on the lower slopes of Blencathra, with a Lakeland inn next door.

● Troutbeck (Windermere)
    LAKE DISTRICT
    DALES WAY

🚶⊲◀ High Fold Guest House, LA23 1PG ☎ 015394 32200
(Les & Susan Bradley) www.highfoldbedandbreakfast.co.uk Map 90/408027
BB **D** ✕ nearby D4 T1 F1 Ⓑ Ⓓ ⊗🍳🚌🛏 ! ★★★★

● Ulverston
    CUMBRIA WAY

The Walkers Hostel, Oubas Hill, LA12 7LB ☎ 01229 585588 (Jan Nicholson)
www.walkershostel.co.uk Map 96,97/296787
BB **A** ✕ book first £10, 7pm S1 D3 T3 F4 ⋙(Ulverston)
Ⓥ Ⓑ Ⓓ ⊗🍳 ! 🛏 Ⓜ

🚶⊲◀ St Mary's Mount, Belmont, LA12 7HD ☎ 01229 583372 (Marlon Bobbett)
www.stmarysmount.co.uk Map 96,97/290788
BB **D** ✕ book first £17.50, 2:30-9pm S1 D2 T1 ⋙(Ulverston)
Ⓥ Ⓑ Ⓓ ⊗🍳🚌🛏 See SC also.

🚶⊲◀ Sefton House, 34 Queen Street, LA12 7AF ☎ 01229 582190
www.seftonhouse.co.uk Map 96,97/285782
BB **C** ✕ nearby S1 D3 T1 F1 ⋙(Ulverston) Ⓑ ⊗🍳🚌🛏 Ⓜ

● Watermillock (Ullswater)
    LAKE DISTRICT

☆ **Land Ends Country Lodge**
CA11 0NB ☎ 017684 86438 (Barbara Murphy)
www.landends.co.uk Map 90/433245
BB **D** ✕ nearby S2 D5 T1 F1 Closed Xmas-Jan
Ⓑ Ⓓ 🍳🚌🛏 Ⓜ ◆◆◆ See SC also.

Peaceful setting in 25 acres with 2 lakes and lovely courtyard with flowers, pots and fishpond. Red squirrels, ducks, owls and other fabulous birdlife live in the grounds. Ullswater 1.3 miles. Rooms are light, clean and airy. Great breakfasts.

● Windermere
    LAKE DISTRICT
    DALES WAY

🚶⊲◀ Holly Lodge, 6 College Road, LA23 1BX ☎ 015394 43873
(Anne & Barry Mott) http://hollylodge20.co.uk Map 96,97/411985
BB **C** ✕ nearby S1 D4 F4 Closed Xmas ⋙(Windermere)
Ⓑ Ⓓ ⊗🍳🛏 ◆◆◆

☆ **Lynwood**
Broad Street, LA23 2AB ☎ 015394 42550 (Mrs F Holcroft)
www.lynwood-guest-house.co.uk Map 96,97/413982
BB **B/C** ✕ nearby S1 D4 T1 F3 ⋙(Windermere)
Ⓑ Ⓓ ⊗🍳🚌🛏 ◆◆◆◆

Relax in our elegant Victorian house in the heart of Windermere. Each bedroom is individually furnished and smoke-free with en-suite shower and wc, colour TV, hairdryer & beverages. Convenient for bus and train stations and close to parking. We look forward to your stay with us.

Brendan Chase, 1-3 College Road, LA23 1BU ☎ 015394 45638 (David Maloney)
www.placetostaywindermere.co.uk Map 96,97/411985
BB **B** ✕ nearby S2 D2 T3 F5 ⋙(Windermere) Ⓑ Ⓓ ⊗🛏

LANCASHIRE

● Burnley
    PENNINE BRIDLEWAY

Rosehill House Hotel, Rosehill Ave, BB11 2PW ☎ 01282 453931
www.rosehillhousehotel.co.uk Map 103/834315
BB **D** ✕ £8+, 7-9:30pm S9 D21 T4 F4 ⋙(Burnley)
Ⓥ Ⓑ Ⓓ🍳🚌🛏 ! 🛏 ★★★

● Chatburn (Clitheroe)
    RIBBLE WAY

Greenside Bed & Breakfast, 13 Downham Road, BB7 4AU ☎ 01200 440370
(Marguerite Mortimer) marguerite.mortimer@tesco.net Map 103/771441
BB **C** ✕ nearby D1 T2 ⋙(Clitheroe) Ⓥ Ⓑ Ⓓ ⊗🍳🚌

NORTH WEST

● Chipping (Clitheroe)

☆ ☜ **Rakefoot Farm**
Thornley Rd, Chaigley, BB7 3LY ☎ 01995 61332 (Pat Gifford)
www.rakefootfarm.co.uk Map 103/663416
BB **B/C/D** ✗ book first £15-£18, 5-7pm S2 D2 T2 F2
Ⓥ Ⓑ Ⓓ 🍴🫖🚶🚗❗️🛁 ★★★★ See SC also.

17th C. farmhouse and traditional stone barn on family farm. Original features, woodburners, home cooked meals/ convenient restaurants, laundry, en-suite and ground floor available. Longridge Fell/ Forest of Bowland/ AONB/ panoramic views. Transport available. See self-catering also.

● Clitheroe
RIBBLE WAY

☆ ☜ **Foxhill Barn**
Howgill Lane, Gisburn, BB7 4JL ☎ 01200 415906 (Janet & Peter Moorhouse)
www.foxhillbarn.co.uk Map 103/843467
BB **C** D1 T2 F1 Closed Dec
Ⓓ ⊗ 🍴🫖🚗🛁 ◆◆◆◆

A newly converted barn with beautiful panoramic views close to the Lancashire/Yorkshire border. Many scenic walks traversing the farm. Ribble Way and Pendle nearby. Unwind afterwards with a jacuzzi, or in our homely guest lounge with wood burner and oak beams.

● Colne

☆ ☜ **Wickets**
148 Keighley Road, BB8 0PJ ☎ 01282 862002 (Mrs Etherington)
wickets@colne148.fsnet.co.uk Map 103/897402
BB **B/C** ✗ nearby D1 T1 Closed Xmas-Feb 🚶(Colne)
Ⓑ Ⓓ ⊗ 🍴🫖 ◆◆◆◆

Spacious Edwardian family home providing quality accommodation in attractive & comfortable en-suite rooms. All the local amenities of the town yet close to open countryside, lovely walks & breathtaking views. Pick up a bargain in the Mill shops.

● Delph (Oldham)
PENNINE WAY & PENNINE BRIDLEWAY

☜ Wellcroft House, Bleak Hey Nook, OL3 5LY
☎ 01457 875017 (Mr & Mrs E Landon) Map 110/004094
BB **B** ✗ book first £10, 7:30pm D2 T1
Ⓥ Ⓑ Ⓓ ⊗ 🍴🫖🚶🚗❗️🛁

● Eccleston (Chorley)

☆ **Parr Hall Farm**
Parr Lane, PR7 5SL ☎ 01257 451917 (Mike & Kate Motley)
parrhall@talk21.com Map 108/519174
BB **C** ✗ nearby S1 D9 T3 F2
Ⓑ Ⓓ ⊗ 🍴🫖🚶❗️ ◆◆◆◆

Charming property with mature gardens peacefully located in the countryside, a few miles from the M6. Built in 1721, it has been renovated, providing comfortable guest rooms with en-suite facilities, TV & hospitality trays. With many attractions nearby, it is a good stopover from Scotland & the Lake District.

● Grains Bar (Oldham)

☜ Grains Bar Hotel, Ripponden Road, Grains Bar, OL1 4SX
☎ 0161 624 0303 www.grainsbarhotel.co.uk Map 109/963085
BB **D** ✗ book first £5, 7pm S4 D6 T4 F10 🚶(Shaw & Crompton)
Ⓥ Ⓑ Ⓓ 🍴🫖 ◆◆◆ Facilities suitable for disabled guests.

● Silverdale (Carnforth)

Spring Bank House, 19 Stankelt Rd, LA5 0TA ☎ 01524 702693 (Nancy Bond)
www.springbankhousesilverdale.co.uk Map 97/463749
BB **C** ✗ nearby S1 D1 T2 F1 🚶(Silverdale) Ⓑ Ⓓ ⊗ 🍴🫖🚗 Ⓜ

● Wycoller (Colne)

☜ Parson Lee Farm, BB8 8SU ☎ 01282 864747 (Pat Hodgson)
www.parsonleefarm.co.uk Map 103/937385
BB **B** ✗ book first £9, 6:30-8pm D1 T1 F1 Closed Xmas
Ⓥ Ⓑ Ⓓ 🍴🫖🚗❗️🛁 ◆◆◆

SELF-CATERING

CHESHIRE

● Audlem
Berry Cottage ☎ 01270 811573 (Jane Hardwick)
http://homepages.tesco.net/hardwork/index.html
£180-£350 Sleeps 4 + cot. 1 bungalow.
Canalside village. Rural, private. Donkeys, chickens. ⊗ 🛁 ★★★

● Macclesfield
Acorn Cottages ☎ 01260 223388 (Susan Bullock)
www.acorncottages-england.co.uk
£220-£320 Sleeps 2-9. 2 cottages.
Oak beams, stone floors, undulating scenery. ⊗ ★★★★

● Rainow
PEAK DISTRICT
Common Barn Farm ☎ 01625 574878 (Rona Cooper)
www.cottages-with-a-view.co.uk
£250-£500 Sleeps 4-10. 2 cottages.
Fabulous views. Underfloor heating. Footpath from door. ⊗ ★★★★

CUMBRIA

☆ Cumbrian Cottages
☎ 01228 599960
www.cumbrian-cottages.co.uk
£250-£3,200 Sleeps 2-15. 700 cottages, apartments, houses & cabins.
All our properties are VisitBritain annually inspected. ♿ 🐾

Choose from over 700 self-catering cottages, houses, apartments and log cabins situated in superb locations throughout the Lake District.
Ideal for great outdoor holidays at anytime of the year.
All properties are VisitBritain graded to at least 3-star quality.
Visit our website to browse cottages, check availability and book online.
Or call 01228 599960, lines open 7 days-a-week until 9pm (5:30pm Saturday).

● Ambleside
LAKE DISTRICT

Ramsteads ☎ 015394 36583 (Gareth Evans) www.ramsteads.co.uk
£165-£395 Sleeps 4-6. 7 lodges. Closed Dec-Feb
Secluded woodland setting in central Lakeland. ★-★★

P F Quarmby ☎ 015394 32326 paulfquarmby@aol.com
£140-£240 Sleeps 4. 1 flat. Closed Nov-Feb
Opens on to garden. Private parking. ♿ 🐾

☆ Grove Cottages
☎ 015394 33074 (Peter & Zorika Thompson)
www.grovecottages.com
£250-£650 Sleeps 2-6. 4 cottages.
Superior cottages, centre of the Lakes. ♿ ★★★★-★★★★★

4 beautiful, traditional cottages set in our 200 acres of Stockghyll Valley. Magnificent views to Coniston Old Man and The Langdales but only 1.5 miles from Ambleside shops and restaurants. Wonderful walks from your doorstep and a warm personal welcome.

☆ Rydal Holiday Lettings
☎ 015394 31043 (Neil Rowley)
www.steppingstonesambleside.co.uk
£240-£430 Sleeps 2-4. 4 flats.
Lovely apartments in idyllic riverside setting. ♿ 🐾 ★★★★ See B&B also.

Superbly situated apartments, furnished and equipped to high, clean standard with video and CD player. Large landscaped gardens with BBQ area and spectacular views. Ample private parking. Private water supply.

Rydal Hall ☎ 015394 32050 (Alison Butland/Alasdair Galbraith)
www.rydalhall.org
£275-£600 Sleeps 4-10. 2 cottages.
Situated in heart of Fairfield Horseshoe. ♿ 🐾 See Groups also.

● Appleby
Scalebeck Holiday Cottages ☎ 01768 351006 (Keith & Diane Budding)
www.scalebeckholidaycottages.co.uk
£235-£460 Sleeps 4-5. 3 cottages. Games room. ♿ 🐾 ★★★★

● Bassenthwaite
LAKE DISTRICT

Brook House Cottages ☎ 017687 76393 (Alison Trafford)
www.holidaycottageslakedistrict.co.uk
£120-£850 Sleeps 2-20. 3 cottages, 1 studio.
Village cottages & B&B by stream/farm. 🐾

Irton House Farm ☎ 017687 76380 (Mrs J Almond) www.irtonhousefarm.com
£315-£730 Sleeps 2-6. 5 apartments, 1 caravan.
Superb views. Table tennis, snooker/pool. ♿ 🐾 ★★★★

Skiddaw View Holiday Park ☎ 016973 20919 (Philip Carr)
www.skiddawview.co.uk £121-£633 Sleeps 1-18. 15 caravans, 4 lodges.
Pet-friendly accommodation. ♿ 🐾 ★★★★
See Big White House in Groups also.

● Boot
LAKE DISTRICT

☆ The Chalets
☎ 019467 23128 (Lisa & Philip)
www.thechalets.co.uk
£250-£500 Sleeps 2-6. 4 timber cottages. Peaceful riverside location, perfect for lakes. ♿ ➰(Ravenglass & Eskdale) 🐾 ★★★★

Surrounded by stunning scenery, The Chalet has four immaculately presented cottages. Each cottage has two bedrooms, a modern kitchen and pristine bathroom, large living/dining area, mature south-facing riverside gardens. BBQ, charming pubs and spectacular walks from the door.

● Borrowdale
LAKE DISTRICT

Kilnhow ☎ 017687 77356 (Peter & Nicola Davis-Merry) www.kilnhow.com
£160-£515 Sleeps 2-6. 4 apartments, 1 cottage.
Converted farmhouse, unrivalled location, parking, garden. ♿ ★★★

● Bowness-on-Windermere
LAKE DISTRICT

☆ Mrs J Kay ☎ 01925 755612
£205-£390 Sleeps 4. 1 flat.
Closed Nov-March
Modern, central, lake view, private parking.
♿ ➰(Windermere)

2-bedroom flat. Very attractively furnished. Central situation near shops, restaurants and places of interest. Lake view. Private parking. No dogs or children under 10. No smoking.

● Brampton

Long Byres Cottages ☎ 016977 3435 (Harriet Sykes) www.longbyres.co.uk
£190-£405 Sleeps 2-6. 7 cottages.
Homecooked meal service. Working farm. ⚂(Brampton Junction) 🏠 ★★★

● Caldbeck
LAKE DISTRICT

Monkhouse Hill ☎ 016974 76254 (Jennifer or Andy Collard)
www.monkhousehill.co.uk
£340-£2,280 Sleeps 2-46. 9 cottages.
Award-winning. Rural setting. Evening meals. ⊗ 🏠 ★★★★-★★★★★

Newlands Grange ☎ 016974 78676 (Dorothy Studholme)
studholme_newlands@hotmail.com £100-£140 Sleeps 6. 1 caravan.
On working farm, lovely views. ⊗ See B&B also.

● Cockermouth
LAKE DISTRICT

Wood Farm Cottages ☎ 01900 829533 (Mrs A Cooley)
www.woodfarmcottages.com £270-£415 Sleeps 6. 2 cottages.
Great access Cockermouth, Buttermere, Keswick, Loweswater. ⊗ 🏠

● Coniston
LAKE DISTRICT

☆ **Coniston Country Cottages**
☎ 015394 41114 (Steve, Linda or Sharon)
www.conistoncottages.co.uk
£220-£750 Sleeps 2-7. 17 cottages. Quality cottages in superb surroundings.
⊗ 🏠 ★★★-★★★★ See Wheelgate in B&B also.

Cosy Lakeland cottages in superb surroundings.

Tastefully furnished and well-equipped.

Easy access to central Lakes, with local walking to suit all ages and abilities.

● Elterwater
LAKE DISTRICT

☆ **Langdale Cottages**
☎ 0161 980 0634 (Pat Locke)
www.langdale-cottages.co.uk
£240-£2,200 Sleeps 2-10. 1 house, 1 cottage. Leisure club. Unspoilt village.
Luxury accommodation. Ⓜ ★★★-★★★★

Two luxury Lake District self-catering holiday cottages at the entrance to the Langdale valley, in the unspoilt village of Elterwater, Cumbria. These beautifully refurbished houses are set in well-landscaped gardens with fine views to the beck and fells.

● Eskdale
LAKE DISTRICT

Mrs J Holland ☎ 01732 459168
£350-£650 Sleeps 8. 1 farmhouse.
17th century farmhouse, elevated position, stunning views. ⊗ 🏠 Ⓜ

Wha House ☎ 019467 23322 (Marie Crowe) mariehodgkiss@aol.com
£180-£350 Sleeps 2. 1 cottage. Ideal starting point for Scar/Harter Fell.
⚂(Ravenglass & Eskdale) ⊗ 🏠 See B&B also.

Irton Hall Country Cottages ☎ 0161 976 5440 (Steve Cottrell)
www.irtonhall.co.uk
£210-£440 Sleeps 5. 2 cottages.
Peacefully set in 19 acres of grounds. ⚂(Ravenglass) 🏠

● Grange-over-Sands

Lynn Branson ☎ 01253 813682
£200-£250 Sleeps 2. 1 cottage. Close to all amenities.
⚂(Grange-over-Sands) ⊗

● Grasmere
LAKE DISTRICT

☆ **Broadrayne Farm**
☎ 015394 35055 (Jo Dennison Drake)
www.grasmere-accommodation.co.uk
£254-£580 Sleeps 2-5. 3 cottages. Dramatic views, quiet location, colour brochure. ⊗ 🏠 ★★★★ See Hostels & Groups also.

Broadrayne Farm is at the heart of the Lake District. Superb traditional cottages. Quiet location.Open fires, C/H & parking. Dogs welcome. Dramatic views. Classic Lakeland walks from front door. Brochure. Sauna and drying room on site. Resident owners.
Email: jo@grasmere-accommodation.co.uk

● Greystoke

Motherby House ☎ 017684 83368 (Jacquie Freeborn)
www.motherbyhouse.co.uk
£176-£306 Sleeps 4-6. 1 cottage. Closed Xmas
Converted coach house. Use of walled garden. ⊗ 🏠 See B&B also.

● Hawkshead
LAKE DISTRICT

☆ **High Dale Park Barn**
Grizedale Forest ☎ 01229 860226 (Mr P Brown)
www.lakesweddingmusic.com/accomm/
£195-£650 Sleeps 2-6. 17th century barn.
Quiet valley, superb position, many walks. ⊗ 🏠 ★★★

Idyllic setting in Grizedale Forest. Charming 17th-century barn conversion. Two centrally heated units, sleeping six and two, or eight altogether. Totally non-smoking. Off road parking.

Fully fitted, well equipped kitchens. Popular catering service available.
Owner managed. Trout fishing nearby.
Secure undercover cycle storage. High Dale Park Barn is a recently converted 17th-century barn that nestles in a small, peaceful valley within Grizedale Forest — Lakeland's largest forest area.
Woodland walks literally seconds away.
Email: peter@lakesweddingmusic.com

☆ Esthwaite Farm
☎ 0845 0992398 (Ruth or Lesley)
www.lakeland-hideaways.co.uk
£235-£510 Sleeps 2-7. 11 cottages & flats.
Converted farm, stunning views, free fishing. ⊗ 🐾 ★★★

This converted Lakeland farm is beautifully situated between Near Sawrey (the home of Beatrix Potter) and Esthwaite Water.

The farm offers 11 very comfortable, warm cottages with wood-burning stoves.

Lake access and shoreline for the sole use of guests a short stroll away with free fishing. A lovely, quiet location — tucked away from the main road, close to village pub — a good base from which to explore the Lakes or simply walk in the gentle surrounding countryside.

We also have a wonderful selection of cottages in and around Hawkshead and we produce our own guide book for local walks.

● Keswick
LAKE DISTRICT

☆ Birkrigg
☎ 017687 78278 (Mrs Beaty)
£200-£340 Sleeps 1-4. 1 cottage. Closed Jan
Pleasantly situated, exceptional view, walker's paradise!
⊗ ★★★

Enjoy the peace and quiet of a Lakeland valley, five miles from Keswick. Cosy oakbeamed cottage converted from a stable nestled between the farm guesthouse and barn. Wonderful view of the Newlands range of mountains, Blencathra in the distance.

☆ Derwent House Holidays
☎ 01889 505678 (Mary & Oliver Bull)
www.dhholidays-lakes.com
£115-£385 Sleeps 2-6. 4 flats.
Central heating & parking. ⊗ 🐾 ★★★

Traditional stone Lakeland building now four comfortable well-equipped self-catering holiday suites at Portinscale village on Derwentwater, 1 mile from Keswick. Central heating and linen included. Parking. Open all year. Short breaks. Prices £115 to £385. Some reductions for two people only.

Mrs Smith ☎ 01992 463183
£100-£350 Sleeps 2-8. 2 flats. Near bus station and Lake Derwentwater.

☆ Brigham Farm
☎ 017687 79666 (N Green)
www.keswickholidays.co.uk
£140-£365 Sleeps 2-4. 6 apartments. Lovely garden. Ample parking.
Owner maintained. ⊗ 🐾 ★★★★ See The Studio (below) also.

Quietly situated 5 minutes' walk from town centre, former farmhouse converted to six spacious self-contained apartments. Handsomely furnished and well equipped, gas-fired CH, with garden and plenty of parking space. Carefully owner maintained.

Email: selfcatering@keswickholidays.co.uk

☆ The Studio
☎ 017687 79666 (N Green)
www.keswickholidays.co.uk
£140-£320 Sleeps 2-4. Apartments. Tasteful barn conversion with stunning views. ⊗ ★★★★ See Brigham Farm (above) also.

Tasteful barn convesion in the lovely Vale of St Johns. Well equipped, handsomely furnished with beautiful views. Five miles from Keswick. Personally maintained.

Email: selfcatering@keswickholidays.co.uk

Hope Cottages ☎ 01900 85226 (Christine M England)
www.hope-farm-holiday-cottages.co.uk £240-£440 Sleeps 3-4. 2 cottages.
Closed Nov-Feb Quiet and comfortable, lovely views/walks. 🐾 ★★★

☆ Croft House Holidays
☎ 017687 73693 (Jan Boniface)
www.crofthouselakes.co.uk
£270-£940 Sleeps 2-8. 5 cottages.
Stunning, panoramic views. Peaceful rural settings. ⊗ Ⓜ ★★★★

Cottage and ground floor apartment in a Victorian country house and three other cottages — including a spacious barn conversion with snooker room. All in Applethwaite village — just one mile from Keswick. Open all year, short breaks available.

☆ Aura
☎ 0161 4450630 (Bill Murray)
www.aura-keswick.co.uk
£250-£450 Sleeps 4. 1 flat. Spacious, warm and superbly furnished.
⊗ Ⓜ ★★★★

Spacious, two double-bedroomed accommodation close to centre of Keswick, yet in quiet location. Warm, well furnished and comfortable with all mod cons. Large lounge/diner and separate kitchen. Convenient outer entrance hall for boots and wet weather gear.

NORTH WEST

☆ Keswick Cottages
☎ 017687 78555 (Anthony Fearns)
www.keswickcottages.co.uk
£180-£1,015 Sleeps 2-8. 40 cottages & apartments.
⊗ 🛁 Ⓜ ★★★★

Keswick Cottages offer fabulous cottages and apartments in and around Keswick. All properties offer warm, very clean, well-equipped accommodation with all the comforts of home. Short breaks & reduced occupancy prices offered. Walks from every doorstep. Email: info@keswickcottages.co.uk

● Kirkby-in-Furness
LAKE DISTRICT

The Annexe ☎ 01543 676552 (R C Clague-Smith) theannexeuk@aol.com
£175 Sleeps 2. 1 bungalow.
Duddon estuary, Furness fells, Cumbrian Coastal Way. ᗯᗯ(Kirkby-In-Furness) ⊗

● Loweswater
LAKE DISTRICT

D Bell ☎ 01900 85227£250-£300 Sleeps 2-6. 1 cottage.
Quiet country location, ideal for walking. 🛁

● Patterdale
LAKE DISTRICT

☆ Patterdale Hall Estate
☎ 017684 82308 (Jon Holdsworth)
www.patterdalehallestate.com
£159-£490 Sleeps 2-6. 17 varying types..
Private 300 acre estate below Helvellyn. ⊗ 🛁 ★★-★★★

Between Helvellyn and the picturesque shores of Ullswater, the private 300-acre Estate offers a range of 17 self-catering properties in an idyllic and relaxing setting with stunning views.

With its own foreshore, woodland and gardens, it is perfect for peaceful leisurely holidays and is an ideal starting point for many great Lakeland walks. The Estate's central location makes it a perfect base from which to explore the entire Lake District.

Lesley Hennedy ☎ 01539 622069
www.hartsop-fold.co.uk
£131-£459 Sleeps 5-6. 12 lodges.
Scandinavian lodges on small secluded site. ⊗ 🛁 ★★★

● Penrith

Howscales ☎ 01768 898666 (Mrs E Webster)
www.howscales.co.uk
£220-£500 Sleeps 2-4. 5 cottages.
Set in open, tranquil countryside. ᗯᗯ(Lazonby) ⊗ 🛁 ★★★★

☆ Dukes Meadow
☎ 0121 705 4381 (Jane Hounsome)
www.dukesmeadow.co.uk
£150-£450 Sleeps 6. 1 pine lodge.
Quiet, peaceful location. ⊗ ★★★

Three-bedroomed holiday lodge, recently refurbished to a high standard (including D/W). Good base for the north Lakes and Eden Valley, and within easy reach of the excellent facilities in Penrith (15 mins). Mon-Fri and weekend lets available. Email: janeandben@hotmail.co.uk

● Silverdale

Dot McGahan ☎ 0114 2338619 dotmcgahan@aol.com
£190-£320 Sleeps 2-5. 1 cottage. Closed Feb
AONB/nature reserve location, lake views. ᗯᗯ(Silverdale) ⊗ Ⓜ

● Ulverston
LAKE DISTRICT

St Mary's Mount ☎ 01229 583372 (Marion Bobbett) www.stmarysmount.co.uk
£400-£500 Sleeps 4 + 2. 1 converted stable. Lovely views. Peaceful location.
Large garden. ᗯᗯ(Ulverston) ⊗ 🛁 See B&B also.

● Watermillock
LAKE DISTRICT

☆ Land Ends
☎ 017684 86438 (Barbara Murphy)
www.landends.co.uk
£290-£550 Sleeps 2-5. 4 log cabins.
Peaceful 25 acre grounds, 2 ponds. 🛁 ★★★ See B&B also.

For real countrylovers! Peaceful fellside setting in 25 acres with 2 lakes. Red squirrels, ducks, moorhens, owls and fabulous birdlife on your doorstep. Lake Ullswater only 1.3 miles. Dramatic scenery and superb walks close by! Warm and cosy interiors.

LANCASHIRE

● Chipping

Fell View ☎ 01995 61160 (Mrs J Porter) www.fellviewchipping.co.uk
£170-£220 Sleeps 2. 1 coach house.
Superb fell views, excellent walking. Woodburner. ⊗ 🛁 ★★★★

☆ Rakefoot Farm
☎ 01995 61332 (Pat Gifford)
www.rakefootfarm.co.uk
£100-£595 Sleeps 2-22. 4 cottages in barn conversion.   Woodburners, meals, laundry, CH, panoramic views. 🛁 ★★★-★★★★ See B&B also.

Past winner of North West Tourist Board Silver Award. Traditional stone barn conversion. Family farm in the Forest of Bowland. Most bedrooms en-suite, some groundfloor. Original features with comforts of modern living. Gardens, games room, meals service.

● Clitheroe

Weavers Cottage ☎ 01200 423086 (Pam Bowell) www.clitheroe-selfcatering.co.uk
£125-£185 Sleeps 1-2. 1 cottage.
Bowland Forest, Yorkshire Dales, Ribble Valley. ᗯᗯ(Clitheroe) ⊗ 🛁 Ⓜ

● Cowpe

☆ **Tippett Farm**
☎ 01706 224741 (Wendy Davison)
www.tippettfarm.co.uk
£195-£495 Sleeps 2-8. 1 cottage.
20 + good walks, spectacular views, peaceful setting. 🏠 ★★★★Ⓦ

Spacious, 4-bedroom stone cottage with original features and exceptional views. Variable tariff depending on number of bedrooms used. Attractive gardens to front, patio and outdoor dining area to rear.

Set in a quiet, hidden valley 285m (920ft) above sea-level, motorway 10 mins. 20 + walks outlined in 'Rossendale Rambles' by Ian Goldthorpe (copies available for guests to use), plus Rossendale Way and Pennine Bridleway National Trail (Mary Towneley Loop) right on the doorstep.

Typical landscape: upland and moorland punctuated by dry stone walls with some wooded areas. Great for birdwatching too!

● Holcombe
Top o'th' Moor Cottage   ☎ 07976 034196 (Michele Richardson)
www.topofthemoorcottage.com £350 Sleeps 2. 1 cottage.
Snooker room, tennis court, panoramic views. 🚫 ★★★★

GROUPS

CUMBRIA

Big White House (SC) Nr Cockermouth
☎ 016973 20919 (Philip Carr) www.bigwhitehouse.co.uk
SC £930-£1,848 Min 10, max 18. 1 house.
✗ nearby Ⓑ Ⓓ 🚫   See Skiddaw View, Bassenthwaite in SC also.

Shackleton Lodge (SC) Brathay Exploration Group, Brathay Hall, Ambleside LA22 0HP ☎ 015394 33942 www.brathayexploration.org.uk Map 90/366028
SC £955 Max 32. 1 lodge. Ⓓ Ⓧ

☆ **Ambleside Backpackers** (IH/SC)
Old Lake Road, Ambleside LA22 0DJ
☎ 015394 32340 www.englishlakesbackpackers.co.uk
SC £15.50pppn Min 10, max 72. Hostel.
✗ nearby 🌿 Ⓓ 🚫 🚗 ❗

The best backpacker facilities in the area. Reasonable charges with longer stay reduction. Ideally situated, 5 mins from bus. 72 beds in a large traditional Lakeland cottage. Newly refurbished, clean, comfortable and warm. Manager on site, no lock out/curfew. Mountain & valley walks from door. Internet access

☆ **Smallwood House Hotel** (BB)
Compston Road, Ambleside LA22 9DJ
☎ 015394 32330 (Christine & Anthony Harrison)
www.smallwoodhotel.co.uk
BB £33 Min 10, max 24. ✗ Ⓑ Ⓓ 🌿 ◆◆◆◆ See B&B also.

We pride ourselves on a quality, friendly service in the traditional way.

Special prices for groups of 11 or more - pay for 10 and one stays free Sun-Thurs. Do you want to organise a group but need help? Contact us for assistance. All your walking needs catered for.

Please telephone Anthony or Christine for a full brochure & tariff.

enq@smallwoodhotel.co.uk

Rydal Hall (B/C/SC) Rydal, Ambleside LA22 9LX ☎ 015394 32050
www.rydalhall.org SC £175 + FB £57pppn Min 1, max 90.
1 hotel, 1 bunkhouse, campsite. ✗ 🌿 Ⓑ Ⓓ 🚫   See SC also.

Grasmere Independent Hostel (SC), Broadrayne Farm, Grasmere LA22 9RU
☎ 015394 35055 (Bev Dennison) www.grasmerehostel.co.uk Grid ref: 336094
Bednight £14.50, SC £275-£350 Min 1, max 24.
✗ nearby 🌿 Ⓑ Ⓓ 🚫 ❗ ★★★★ See Hostels & SC also.

HOSTELS, BUNKHOUSES & CAMPSITES

CUMBRIA

Stables Lodge (IH) The Racecourse, Cartmel LA11 6QF
☎ 015395 36340 (Shaun Hodgson/Jessica Taylor)
www.cartmel-racecourse.co.uk Bednight £10 ✗ nearby Ⓓ 🚫

Catbells Camping Barn (CB) Newlands ☎ 01946 758198 (Ann Grave)
Map 90/243208 Bednight £6 Min 1, max 12 Ⓓ 🚫 ❗ 🚗

Tarn Flatt Barn (CB) Sandwith, Whitehaven CA28 9UX
☎ 01946 692162 (Janice Telfer) www.lakelandcampingbarns.co.uk
Bednight £6 🌿 On Coast to Coast Path.

Hillside Farm (BHB) Boustead Hill, Burgh-by-Sands, Carlisle
☎ 01228 576398 (Sandra Rudd) www.hadrianswalkbnb.co.uk
Grid ref: 293591 Bednight £5 Closed Dec-Feb 🌿 Ⓓ 🚫 See B&B also.

☆ **Grasmere Independent Hostel** (IH)
Broadrayne Farm, Grasmere LA22 9RU ☎015394 35055 (Bev Dennison)
www.grasmerehostel.co.uk Grid ref: 336094
Bednight £14.50
✗ nearby 🌿 Ⓑ Ⓓ 🚫 ★★★★ Hostel See Groups & SC also.

Quiet, clean and friendly. Ensuite bedrooms. Sleeps 24. Beds made up. Superb SC kitchens, dining, drying rooms, laundry, sauna, full C/H, parking. Fantastic walks from door. Individuals to whole hostel group hire welcome. Colour brochure. Hostel is behind farmhouse
bev@grasmere-accommodation.co.uk

NORTH WEST

YORKSHIRE

Long Distance Paths

Cleveland Way.....................CVL

Coast to Coast Walk C2C

Dales Way ....DLS

Nidderdale Way....................NID

Pennine Bridleway ....PNB

Pennine Way ....PNN

Ribble Way...........................RIB

Teesdale Way ....TSD

Trans Pennine Trail................TPT

Yorkshire Wolds Way...........WDS

See Paths & Access p25 for full details of LDPs and waymarks

National Parks

North York Moors

Yorkshire Dales

See Useful Contacts p99 for full details of national parks

HIKING UP THE GREEN SLOPES OF THE DALES, NORTH YORKSHIRE

JOE CORNISH/AE11

WALK...

...THE DARLINGTON DOORSTEP WALKS

Darlington is proving that anyone can enjoy the pleasures of walking with these eight superbly-planned short walks in and around the town, for walkers of all ages and abilities. Each no more than 5km/3 miles long, the routes take in three local nature reserves (Brinkburn, Drinkfield Marsh and Rockwell Pastures), the Skerne and Tees riversides, suburban woodland and popular parks. Well-designed route cards provide distances in steps, public transport links and details of walking surfaces, including gradients, steps and stiles – ideal for users of wheelchairs, walking aids or pushchairs.

Download the free pack from www.darlingtonpct.nhs.uk or contact Darlington TIC ☎ 01325 388666.

VISIT...

...THE YORKSHIRE WHEEL

After the success of the London Eye, it's not surprising that other British cities wanted some Ferris-wheel fun of their own. So following the successes of wheels in Birmingham and Manchester, York completed construction of its 54m-high Yorkshire Wheel last year. The 13-minute ride offers some spectacular panoramic views of the historic city, the River Ouse and surrounding countryside. Back on the ground, you could visit the National Rail Museum next door, or attempt the two-hour walk of the City Walls.

Visit www.nrm.org.uk or ☎ 01904 621261 for details of the Wheel's opening times and admission.

SEE...

...PEREGRINE FALCONS AT MALHAM COVE

Britain's largest falcon, the peregrine, is also the fastest animal on earth, reaching speeds of over 120mph when plunging from the sky after prey. Visitors to the Yorkshire Dales can see this magnificent bird in action at Malham Cove, which becomes a hunting and training ground for young peregrines in early summer. The RSPB offers a free public viewpoint during April to July, staffed by experts with binoculars, to spot the aerial acrobatics close up.

See www.rspb.org.uk/birds/brilliant for opening times, and visit www.malhamdale.com for details of walks around Malham's dramatic limestone scenery.

LOCAL RAMBLERS GROUPS... Sheffield Group has put together six free local walks leaflets, titled *Walking with the Ramblers*, offering a great variety of routes in and around the city, from short urban walks to longer treks over open moorland. They're available from local TICs or downloadable at the Group's website (see p93)... **Local Ramblers will be leading walks through beautiful 18th-century parkland at the Yorkshire Sculpture Park during the summer months. Check the events diary at www.ysp.co.uk for details...** Celebrating the 25th birthday of the Yorkshire Wolds Way, East Yorkshire & Derwent Area will be walking the entire 126km/79-mile national trail in sections from June to September. Contact them for full details (see p71).

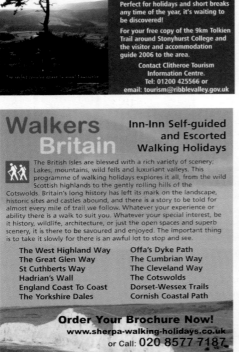

MAP   241

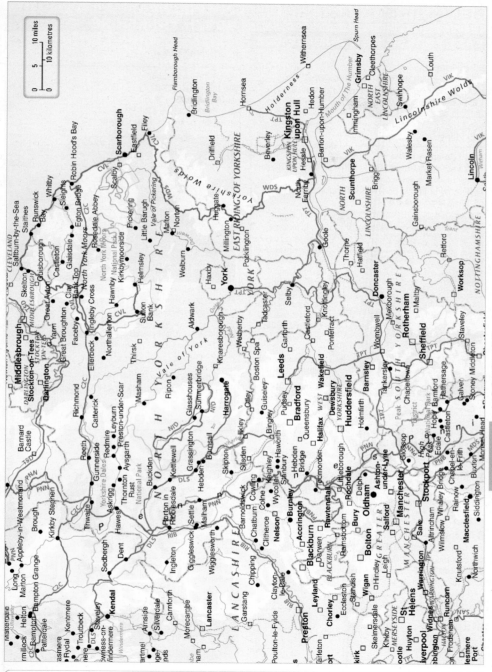

YORKSHIRE

BED & BREAKFAST

EAST YORKSHIRE & HUMBERSIDE

● Beverley

▪◗◄ I Woodlands, HUI7 8BT ☎ 01482 862752 (Sarah King)
www.number-one-bedandbreakfast-beverley.co.uk Map 106,107/029395
BB **C** ✕ book first £15, 7pm SI DI T2 Closed Xmas ᴧᴧ(Beverley)
Ⓥ Ⓑ Ⓓ ⊗ 🐾🛏🚗! ◆◆◆

● Bridlington

☆ ▪◗◄ **Rosebery House**
I Belle View, Tennyson Avenue, YOI5 2ET ☎ 01262 670336 (Helen Gallagher)
helengallagher99@btinternet.com Map 101/186671
BB **D** ✕ nearby D3 TI F3 Closed Xmas ᴧᴧ(Bridlington)
Ⓑ Ⓓ ⊗ 🐾🛏 ◆◆◆◆

A Grade II-listed Georgian house with a long garden and sea view. Amenities close by. Ideal for walking and touring. Near Flamborough Head and Bempton Bird Reserve. High standard of comfort and friendliness. All rooms en-suite, CH, TV, tea/coffee facilities. Some parking. Vegetarians/vegans welcome, packed lunches available.

● Goole

TRANS PENNINE TRAIL

The Briarcroft Hotel, 49-51 Clifton Gardens, DNI4 6AR ☎ 01405 763024
www.briarcrofthotel.co.uk Map 105,106,112/739241
BB **C** ✕ nearby S5 D5 T6 FI ᴧᴧ(Goole Town) Ⓑ Ⓓ ⊗ 🐾🛏 ◆◆◆

● Huggate

The Wolds Inn, Driffield Road, YO42 IYH ☎ 01377 288217 (John & Jane Leaver)
huggate@woldsinn.freeserve.co.uk Map 106/882550
BB **C** ✕ £9, 6:30-9pm S3 D2 TI Closed Xmas Ⓥ Ⓑ ⊗ 🐾🛏 ◆◆◆

● Millington (York)

▪◗◄ Laburnum Cottage, YO42 ITX ☎ 01759 303055 (Maureen Dykes)
roger&maureen@labcott.fslife.co.uk Map 106/830517
BB **B** ✕ book first £9+, 7pm TI FI Closed Dec-Feb
Ⓥ Ⓑ Ⓓ ⊗ 🐾🛏🚗! 🛁 ◆◆◆

● North Ferriby

TRANS PENNINE TRAIL

B&B at 103, 103 Ferriby High Road, HUI4 3LA
☎ 01482 633637 (Margaret Simpson)
www.bnb103.co.uk Map 106/999260
BB **B** ✕ nearby SI DI TI FI Closed Xmas ᴧᴧ(Ferriby)
Ⓑ Ⓓ ⊗ 🐾🛏🛁 ★★★

NORTH YORKSHIRE

● Aldwark (York)

☆ ▪◗◄ **Aldwark Manor**
YO6I IUF ☎ 01347 838146
www.marstonhotels.com Map 100/469631
BB **D** ✕ £35, 7-9:30pm D37 TI2 F6
Ⓥ Ⓑ 🐾🛏 ★★★★ Wheelchair access.

Incorporating an invigorating mix of old and new styles, Aldwark Manor is a great place to stay, convenient for York walks, the Nidderdale Way and the Castle Howard circular route.

Set in 100 acres of walkable parkland on the picturesque River Ure, the golf course and Reflections Leisure Club facilities are excellent, with indoor pool, spa and body treatments.

Aldwark Manor is a hotel with wonderful contrasts offering maximum comfort, and an award-winning restaurant offering fine dining, complemented by wonderful wines.

Please ask about our exclusive rates for walking parties.

● Askrigg (Leyburn)

YORKSHIRE DALES

▪◗◄ Milton House, DL8 3HJ ☎ 01969 650217 (Mrs B Percival)
stay_miltonhouse@btinternet.com Map 98/948910
BB **B/C** ✕ nearby DI TI Closed Xmas
Ⓑ Ⓓ ⊗ 🐾🛏 ★★★★

▪◗◄ Whitfield, Helm, DL8 3JF ☎ 01969 650565 (Kate Empsall)
www.askrigg-cottages.co.uk Map 98/934916
BB **C** DI TI Closed Xmas Ⓑ Ⓓ ⊗ 🐾🛏🚗!🛁 ◆◆◆◆

▪◗◄ Thornsgill House, Moor Rd, DL8 3HH ☎ 01969 650617 (Wendy Turner)
www.thornsgill.co.uk Map 98/949512
BB **C** ✕ nearby SI DI TI Closed Xmas
Ⓑ Ⓓ ⊗ 🐾🛏🚗! ★★★★

● Aysgarth (Leyburn)
YORKSHIRE DALES

☆ ⌖◀ **Stow House Hotel**
Aysgarth Falls, DL8 3SR ☎ 01969 663635
www.stowhouse.co.uk Map 98/014883
BB **D** ✕ book first £20, 7:30pm D5 T4 Closed Xmas
Ⅴ Ⓑ Ⓓ 🐾🛁! 🏛 ◆◆◆◆

Family-run former Victorian Vicarage with magnificent views near Aysgarth Falls. Superb walks from the door. En-suite rooms, comfortable lounge and cosy bar. The house overlooks Wensleydale and Bishopdale and stands in 2 acres of garden with tennis and croquet lawns. Excellent food and hospitality.
Email: info@stowhouse.co.uk

● Buckden (Skipton)
YORKSHIRE DALES
DALES WAY & PENNINE WAY

Romany Cottage, BD23 5JA ☎ 01756 760365 (Tim & Gwen Berry)
www.thedalesway.co.uk/romanycottage Map 98/942772
BB **C** ✕ nearby S1 D1 T2 Closed Xmas Ⓓ 🐾🛁 🚗! 🏛

⌖◀ West Winds Yorkshire Tearooms, BD23 5JA
☎ 01756 760883 (Lynn Thornborrow)
www.westwindsinyorkshire.co.uk Map 98/942772
BB **B** ✕ £8, Before 6pm S1 D1 T1 Closed Xmas Ⅴ Ⓓ ⊗ 🐾🛁!

● Burnsall (Skipton)
YORKSHIRE DALES
DALES WAY

Wharfe View B&B, Wharfe View Farm, BD23 6BP ☎ 01756 720643
www.burnsall.net Map 98/032614
BB **B** ✕ nearby S1 D1 T2 Ⓑ Ⓓ ⊗ 🐾🛁🚗! 🏛

● Castleton (Whitby)
NORTH YORK MOORS

⌖◀ Greystones, 30 High Street, YO21 2DA
☎ 01287 660744 (Della Wedgwood)
thewedgwoods@aol.com Map 94/684079
BB **B** ✕ nearby D3 Closed Xmas ⋘(Castleton Moor)
Ⓑ Ⓓ ⊗ 🐾🛁🚗! ◆◆◆ Sauna available.

● Catterick Village (Richmond)
COAST TO COAST WALK

⌖◀ Rose Cottage Guest House, 26 High Street, DL10 7LJ
☎ 01748 811164 (Carol Archer) Map 99/249979
BB **B** ✕ book first £14, 6:30pm S1 D1 T2 Closed Xmas
Ⅴ Ⓑ 🐾🛁 🏛 Ⓜ ◆◆◆

● Clay Bank Top (Bilsdale)
NORTH YORK MOORS
COAST TO COAST WALK

Maltkiln House, Urra, Chopgate, TS9 7HZ
☎ 01642 778216 (Wendy & Gerry Broad) www.maltkiln.co.uk Map 93/571019
BB **B** ✕ £11.50, 7pm D1 T2 Ⅴ Ⓑ Ⓓ ⊗ 🐾🛁!

● Cowling (Skipton)
PENNINE WAY

⌖◀ Woodland House, 2 Woodland Street, BD22 0BS
☎ 01535 637886 (Susan Black) www.woodland-house.co.uk Map 103/973432
BB **B** ✕ nearby D1 T1 Ⓑ Ⓓ ⊗ 🐾🛁 🚗! Ⓜ ◆◆◆◆

● Egton Bridge
NORTH YORK MOORS
COAST TO COAST WALK

☆ ⌖◀ **Broom House**
Broom House Lane, YO21 1XD ☎ 01947 895279 (Mr & Mrs D White)
www.egton-bridge.co.uk Map 94/796054
BB **D** ✕ book first (groups only), 7pm S1 D/T4 T1 F1 ⋘(Egton Bridge)
Ⅴ Ⓑ Ⓓ ⊗ 🐾🛁 🚗! ◆◆◆◆Ⓢ See SC also.

An excellent place to stay. Comfortable en-suite rooms and an idyllic setting with views of the Esk valley. En-route Coast to Coast & Esk Valley Walks. Local pubs serving good meals within easy walking distance. In house evening meals for large parties.
Email: mw@broom-house.co.uk

● Ellerbeck (Northallerton)
CLEVELAND WAY

The Old Mill, The Old Mill House, Nr Osmotherley, DL6 2RY ☎ 01609 883466
(Gillian Shepherd) www.shepherd-online.com/b&b Map 99/433967
BB **C** ✕ nearby D2 T1 Closed Dec Ⓓ ⊗ 🐾🛁 🚗

● Faceby (Middlesbrough)
NORTH YORK MOORS
CLEVELAND WAY & COAST TO COAST WALK

Four Wynds B&B, Whorl Hill, TS9 7BZ ☎ 01642 701315 (Sue Barnfather)
Map 93/487033
BB **B/C** ✕ book first £9, 5-7pm D1 T1 F1 Closed Xmas
Ⅴ Ⓑ Ⓓ 🐾🛁 🚗! ◆◆◆

● Giggleswick (Settle)
YORKSHIRE DALES
RIBBLE WAY

☆ ⌖◀ **Harts Head Hotel**
Belle Hill, BD24 0BA ☎ 01729 822086
www.hartsheadhotel.co.uk Map 98/812640
BB **C** ✕ book first £8.95, 5:30-9pm S2 D5 T2 F1 ⋘(Settle)
Ⅴ Ⓑ Ⓓ 🐾🛁! ◆◆◆◆

Significantly refurbished country inn offering 10 en-suite bedrooms, superb food (30 main courses), listed in CAMRA Good Beer Guide for the last 5 years. Emphasis on quality & service. Great base for exploring the Dales. Special rate for 3-night stay – ring or see website for details.

● Glaisdale (Whitby)
NORTH YORK MOORS
COAST TO COAST WALK

☆ Red House Farm
YO21 2PZ ☎ 01947 897242 (Tom or Sandra Spashett)
www.redhousefarm.com Map 94/771049
BB **C/D** ✕ nearby S1 D2 T1 F1 Closed Xmas ᴧᴧᴧ(Glaisdale)
🅱 🅳 ⊗ 🐾🛁 See SC also.

Listed Georgian Farmhouse featured in Houses of the North Yorkshire Moors. Completely refurbished to the highest standards & retaining all original features. All bedrooms en-suite, with CH, TV & tea making facilities. Wonderful walking country. Coast to Coast Walk 400 yds from house.

● Glasshouses (Harrogate)
NIDDERDALE WAY

Arran House, 3 Glencoe Terrace, HG3 5DU
☎ 01423 712785 (Lynda Coates)
suite4two@hotmail.com Map 99/175647
BB **C** ✕ nearby D1 T1 F1 Closed Xmas-Jan 🅱 🅳 ⊗ 🐾🛁🚗! 🍵

● Grassington (Skipton)
YORKSHIRE DALES
DALES WAY

Springroyd House, 8a Station Road, BD23 5NQ ☎ 01756 752473
(Mrs P Robertshaw) www.springroydhouse.co.uk Map 98/001639
BB **C** ✕ nearby T/D2 F1 Closed Xmas 🅱 🅳 ⊗ 🐾🛁 ◆◆◆

Lythe End, Wood Lane, BD23 5DF
☎ 01756 753196 (Andrew & Cynthia Colley) Map 98/000647
BB **C** ✕ nearby D1 F1 Closed Xmas 🅱 🅳 ⊗ 🐾🛁🚗!

● Great Ayton
NORTH YORK MOORS

Crossways, 116 Newton Road, TS9 6DL ☎ 01642 724351 (Sue Drennan)
susieds@crossways26.fsnet.co.uk Map 93/563115
BB **B** ✕ nearby S2 D1 T1 ᴧᴧᴧ(Great Ayton)
🅱 🅳 ⊗ 🐾🛁🚗! ◆◆◆◆

● Great Broughton
CLEVELAND WAY & COAST TO COAST WALK

Holme Farm, 12 The Holme, TS9 7HF ☎ 01642 712345 (Don Robinson)
www.donathome.demon.co.uk Map 93/546062
BB **B** ✕ nearby D1 T2 🅳 ⊗ 🚗

● Gunnerside (Richmond)
YORKSHIRE DALES
COAST TO COAST WALK & PENNINE WAY

Oxnop Hall, DL11 6JJ ☎ 01748 886253 (Mrs Al Porter) Map 98/931973
BB **D** ✕ nearby S1 D2 T2 Closed Nov-Feb 🅱 🅳 ⊗ 🐾🛁! ◆◆◆◆

● Harrogate
YORKSHIRE DALES

Barker's Guest House, 204 Kings Road, HG1 5JG
☎ 01423 568494 (Mrs E Barker)
eebarkeruk@yahoo.co.uk Map 104/304563
BB **B** ✕ nearby S1 D1 F/T/D1 ᴧᴧᴧ(Harrogate) 🅱 🅳 ⊗ 🐾🛁 ◆◆◆

● Hawes (Wensleydale)
YORKSHIRE DALES
PENNINE WAY

☆ Dalesview
East Marry, Gayle, DL8 3RZ ☎ 01969 667397 (Mrs S McGregor)
Map 98/871893
BB **B** ✕ nearby D1 T1 Closed Nov-Mar
🅱 🅳 ⊗ 🐾🛁

A modern comfortable bungalow situated in the picturesque village of Gayle, ½ mile from the small market town of Hawes. 100m from Pennine Way. Lovely views, quiet location, an ideal centre for touring, cycling and walking in the Yorkshire Dales.

Ebor House, Burtersett Road, DL8 3NT ☎ 01969 667337
(Mr & Mrs McLoughlin) www.eborhouse.co.uk Map 98/876897
BB **C** ✕ nearby S1 D4 T1 F1 🅱 🅳 ⊗ 🐾🛁!

White Hart Inn, Main Street, DL8 3QL ☎ 01969 667259 (Diane Horner)
www.whiteharthawes.co.uk Map 98/875897
BB **C** ✕ £8.50, 6:45-8:30pm S1 D4 T2 Closed Xmas
🆅 🅱 🅳 🐾🛁🚗! 🍵 ◆◆◆

☆ Thorney Mire House
Appersett, DL8 3LU ☎ 01969 667159 (Mrs S Turner)
www.thorneymire.yorks.net Map 98/852899
BB **C** ✕ nearby S1 D2 Closed Nov-Feb
🅱 🅳 ⊗ 🐾🛁🚗 Ⓜ ◆◆◆◆

Recommended in the Which? Good Bed & Breakfast Guide. A warm welcome awaits you at our traditional Dales house, surrounded by woods, fells & meadows, a place to unwind. Excellent walking, ideal for birdwatchers. Off-road parking.

● Hawnby (Helmsley)
NORTH YORK MOORS

☆ The Hawnby Hotel
Hilltop, YO62 5QS ☎ 01439 798202 (Dave & Kathryn Young)
www.hawnbyhotel.co.uk Map 100/542898
BB **D** ✕ book first £12, 7-9pm D6 T3 Closed Xmas
🆅 🅱 🅳 🐾🛁🚗! ◆◆◆◆

Situated in an unspoilt village in the heart of the North Yorkshire Moors National Park. An ideal spot for a walking holiday. Group bookings available.

● Hebden (Skipton)
YORKSHIRE DALES
DALES WAY

Court Croft, Church Lane, BD23 5DX
☎ 01756 753406 (Philippa Kitching)
Map 98/026630
BB **C/D** ✕ nearby T3 🅱 🅳 🐾🛁🚗 🍵 ◆◆◆

● Helmsley
NORTH YORK MOORS
CLEVELAND WAY

● Carlton Grange, YO62 5HH ☎ 01439 770259 (Ann Kirby)
Map 100,94/615879
BB **B** ✗ book first £4 (light supper) S1 D1 Closed Nov-Feb
Ⓥ Ⓓ 🍵 🏃 🚗

● Ingleby Cross (Northallerton)
NORTH YORK MOORS
COAST TO COAST WALK & CLEVELAND WAY

● Park House, DL6 3PE ☎ 01609 882899 (Mr & Mrs Cameron)
www.parkhouse.co.uk Map 93/453995
BB **C** ✗ £10-£12, 6-9pm S1 D1 T4 Ⓥ Ⓑ Ⓓ 🍵 🏃 🚗 ! 🎿

● Ingleton (Carnforth)
YORKSHIRE DALES

☆ ● **The Dales Guest House**
Main Street, LA6 3HH ☎ 015242 41401 (Penny & Paul Weaire)
www.dalesgh.co.uk Map 98/692727
BB **B** ✗ book first £13, 6:30pm S1 D3 T1 Closed Xmas
Ⓥ Ⓑ Ⓓ 🕮 🍵 🏃 🏧 Ⓜ ◆◆◆

A friendly welcome, comfortable en-suite rooms and high quality food will make your stay one to remember.

The perfect base for exploring the Dales, Forest of Bowland, southern Lakes and Lancs/Cumbrian coast. Nearby are the Waterfalls Walk, White Scar and Ingleborough show caves and the scenic Settle-Carlisle railway.

We offer excellent value and considerable savings for longer stays.
Visit our website, phone or e-mail dalesgh@hotmail.com for a full tariff.

● Newbutts Farm, High Bentham, LA2 7AN
☎ 015242 41238 (Jean Newhouse) Map 98/696695
BB **B** ✗ book first £13.50, 6-7pm S2 D2 T2 F2
Ⓥ Ⓑ Ⓓ 🍵 🏃 ◆◆◆

The Station Inn, Ribblehead, LA6 3AS ☎ 015242 41274
www.thestationinn.net Map 98/779799
BB **D** ✗ £5, 6:30-8:30pm S1 D3 T1 F1 Closed Xmas 🚂(Ribblehead)
Ⓥ Ⓑ Ⓓ 🍵 🏃 🚗 ! 🎿 Ⓜ ◆◆◆ See Hostels also.

☆ ● **Riverside Lodge**
24 Main Street, LA6 3HJ ☎ 015242 41359 (Andrew Foley)
www.riversideingleton.co.uk Map 98/691727
BB **C** ✗ book first £15 D/T7 Closed Xmas
Ⓥ Ⓑ Ⓓ 🕮 🍵 🏃 🚗 ★★★★

Beautiful riverside location, rooms with views of Ingleborough or wooded riverbank. Nearby waterfalls walk, 2 ground floor rooms, all rooms en-suite, large lounge, open fire, T.V. Snooker table, sauna, licensed, conservatory dining room, private car park.

● Inglenook Guest House, 20 Main Street, LA6 3HJ
☎ 015242 41270 (Phil & Carolyn Smith)
www.inglenookguesthouse.com Map 98/691727
BB **B/C** ✗ book first £15, 6:30pm D2 T2 F1
Ⓥ Ⓑ Ⓓ 🍵 🏃 ◆◆◆◆

● Kettlewell (Skipton)
YORKSHIRE DALES
DALES WAY

Lynburn, BD23 5RF ☎ 01756 760803 (Lorna Thornborrow)
lorna@lthornborrow.fsnet.co.uk Map 98/970720
BB **C** ✗ nearby D1 T1 Closed Xmas Ⓓ 🕮 🍵 🏃 ◆◆◆

● Kilburn (York)
NORTH YORK MOORS
CLEVELAND WAY

● Church Farm, YO61 4AH ☎ 01347 868318 (Mrs C Thompson)
churchfarmkilburn@yahoo.co.uk Map 100/516796
BB **B** ✗ book first £10, 6-8pm D1 F1 Closed Xmas
Ⓥ Ⓑ Ⓓ 🕮 🍵 🏃 🏧 ◆◆

● Kirkbymoorside (York)
NORTH YORK MOORS

Mount Pleasant, Rudland, Fadmoor, YO62 7JJ ☎ 01751 431579 (Mary Clarke)
www.mountpleasantbedandbreakfast.co.uk Map 100/657917
BB **B** ✗ book first £6.50, 6:30-8pm T1 F1 Closed Xmas
Ⓥ Ⓓ 🍵 🏃 🚗 ★★★

● Leyburn
The Haven, Market Place, DL8 5BJ ☎ 01969 623814 (Paula & David Burke)
www.havenguesthouse.co.uk Map 99/111904
BB **D** ✗ nearby D4 F2 Closed Xmas Ⓑ 🕮 🍵 🏃 🚗 ! ◆◆◆◆

● Malham (Skipton)
YORKSHIRE DALES
PENNINE WAY

☆ ● **River House Hotel**
BD23 4DA ☎ 01729 830315
www.riverhousehotel.co.uk Map 98/901628
BB **C** ✗ book first £15, 7-8pm D6 T2
Ⓥ Ⓑ Ⓓ 🕮 🍵 🏃 ! 🎿 ◆◆◆◆

A Victorian country house hotel, originally built in 1664, offering superb breakfasts & evening meals. Centrally located in this beautiful Dales village amidst stunning scenery, with the Pennine Way running just past the front door. A warm welcome awaits you on your arrival. Walking parties welcome. Midweek breaks available.

☆ ● **Beck Hall Guest House**
BD23 4DJ ☎ 01729 830332 (Simon Maufe)
www.beckhallmalham.com Map 98/898631
BB **C** ✗ £7.50, 6pm S1 D6 T3 F1 Closed Xmas
Ⓥ Ⓑ Ⓓ 🕮 🍵 🏃 ! 🎿 ◆◆◆

A friendly family welcome to all at 18th C. Beck Hall. 3 nights price of 2 Nov-Feb midweek. Located on Pennine Way. Riverside location. Special diets catered for. Meals until 6pm or 2 pubs 100 yards away. Internet PC. Group discounts.

YORKSHIRE

● Masham (Ripon)

▪▪◢ Bank Villa Guest House, HG4 4DB ☎ 01765 689605
www.bankvilla.com Map 99/224810
BB **C** ✕ book first £15, 7:30pm D3 T2 Fl
Ⓥ Ⓑ Ⓓ ⊛ 🐾 🛁 🚗 ! ◆◆◆◆

● Northallerton

COAST TO COAST WALK

▪▪◢ Alverton Guest House, 26 South Parade, DL7 8SG ☎ 01609 776207
(Mrs M Longley) www.alvertonguesthouse.com Map 99/367934
BB **B** ✕ nearby S3 D2 Tl Fl Closed Xmas ⋘(Northallerton)
Ⓑ Ⓓ ⊛ 🐾 🛁 🚗 ◆◆◆

● Pickering

NORTH YORK MOORS

▪▪◢ Swan Cottage, Newton-upon-Rawcliffe, YO18 8QA ☎ 01751 472502
(Marjorie Heaton) swancottagenewton@yahoo.co.uk Map 100,94/812907
BB **C** ✕ book first £12 Dl Fl
Ⓥ Ⓑ Ⓓ ⊛ 🐾 🛁 🚗 ! 🛁 Ⓜ ◆◆◆◆

Vivers Mill, Mill Lane, YO18 8DJ ☎ 01751 473640
www.viversmill.com Map 100/796835
BB **C** ✕ nearby D5 T2 Fl Closed Xmas Ⓑ ⊛ 🛁 🛁 ◆◆◆◆

☆ ▪▪◢ **Bramwood Guest House**
19 Hallgarth, YO18 7AW ☎ 01751 474066 (Marilyn Bamforth)
www.bramwoodguesthouse.co.uk Map 100/800840
BB **C/D** ✕ book first £17.50, 6:30pm S2 D4 Tl Fl ⋘(Pickering)
Ⓥ Ⓑ Ⓓ ⊛ 🐾 🛁 🚗 ! Ⓜ ◆◆◆◆Ⓢ See SC also.

Elegant Georgian Grade II-listed building in quiet location close to town centre. All rooms are en-suite with TV & generous hospitality trays. Hearty breakfasts. Lounge with log fire & TV. Private parking. Charming walled garden. Steam railway nearby.

● Preston-under-Scar (Leyburn)

▪▪◢ Hawthorn Cottage, DL8 4AQ ☎ 01969 624492 (Helen Francis)
www.hawthorn-wensleydale.com Map 99/071910
BB **C** ✕ book first £15-£20, 7-7:30pm Dl Tl
Ⓥ Ⓑ Ⓓ ⊛ 🐾 🛁 🚗 🛁 ★★★★

● Redmire (Leyburn)

YORKSHIRE DALES
COAST TO COAST WALK

▪▪◢ The Old Town Hall Guest House & Tea Room, DL8 4ED ☎ 01969 625641
(Julie & Simon Greenslade) www.theoldtownhall.co.uk Map 98/045911
BB **D** ✕ nearby D2 Tl Ⓑ Ⓓ ⊛ 🐾 🛁 🚗 ! ◆◆◆◆

● Reeth (Richmond)

YORKSHIRE DALES
COAST TO COAST WALK

▪▪◢ Springfield House, Quaker Close , DL11 6UY
☎ 01748 884634 (Denise Guy) denise.guy@tiscali.co.uk Map 98/039993
BB **B** ✕ nearby Dl Tl Closed Xmas
Ⓑ Ⓓ ⊛ 🐾 🛁 🚗 ◆◆◆◆ Free refreshments on arrival.

▪▪◢ The Buck Hotel, DL11 6SW ☎ 01748 884210
www.buckhotel.co.uk Map 98/038993
BB **D** ✕ £10, 6-9pm Sl D6 T2 Fl
Ⓥ Ⓑ Ⓓ 🐾 🛁 ! 🛁 ◆◆◆◆

● Richmond

COAST TO COAST WALK

The Old Brewery Guest House, 29 The Green, DL10 4RG ☎ 01748 822460
www.oldbreweryguesthouse.com Map 92/168006
BB **D** ✕ nearby Sl D3 T2 Ⓑ Ⓓ ⊛ 🐾 🛁 ! 🛁 ◆◆◆◆

▪▪◢ Beechfield, 16 Beechfield Road, DL10 4PN ☎ 01748 824060
(Thelma Jackson) www.beechfieldrichmond.co.uk Map 92/176015
BB **C** ✕ nearby Sl Dl Tl Ⓑ Ⓓ ⊛ 🐾 🛁

● Ripon

Bishopton Grove House, HG4 2QL ☎ 01765 600888 (Susi Wimpress)
wimpress@bronco.co.uk Map 99/301711
BB **D** ✕ nearby Dl Tl Fl Ⓑ Ⓓ 🐾 🛁 🚗 🛁 ◆◆◆

● Robin Hood's Bay (Whitby)

NORTH YORK MOORS
CLEVELAND WAY & COAST TO COAST WALK

South View, Sledgates, Fylingthorpe, YO22 4TZ
☎ 01947 880025 (Mrs Reynolds) Map 94/940048
BB **B** ✕ nearby D2 Closed Xmas Ⓓ 🐾 🛁

● Rosedale Abbey (Pickering)

NORTH YORK MOORS

☆ ▪▪◢ **Sevenford House**
Thorgill, YO18 8SE ☎ 01751 417283 (Linda Sugars)
www.sevenford.com Map 100,94/724949
BB **C** ✕ nearby Dl Tl Fl Closed Xmas
Ⓑ Ⓓ ⊛ 🐾 🛁 🚗 ! ◆◆◆◆Ⓢ

Originally a vicarage, built from the stones of Rosedale Abbey, Sevenford House stands in 4 acres of lovely gardens in the heart of the beautiful Yorkshire Moors National Park.

The tastefully furnished bedrooms offer wonderful views of valley and moorland & overlook Rosedale. There is a relaxing guests' lounge where a roaring log fire can be enjoyed on colder evenings. An excellent base for exploring the region with over 500 square miles of open moorland, with ruined abbeys, Roman roads and a steam railway. Non-smoking. ETC & AA 4 Diamonds, Silver Award.
Email: sevenford@aol.com

● Runswick Bay (Saltburn-by-the-Sea)

NORTH YORK MOORS
CLEVELAND WAY

☆ **The Firs**
26 Hinderwell Lane, TS13 5HR ☎ 01947 840433
www.the-firs.co.uk Map 94/791168
BB **D** ✕ book first £19.50, 6-9pm Sl D4 T2 F4 Closed Nov-Feb
Ⓥ Ⓑ Ⓓ 🐾 🛁 🛁 ◆◆◆ See Groups also.

Situated at the top of the bank in the beautiful scenic coastal village of Runswick Bay. An ideal base for moors and coast, on the edge of the North Yorkshire Moors NP, Cleveland Way and Coast to Coast paths, 5 minutes from the beach.

● **Saltburn-by-the-Sea (Middlesborough)**
CLEVELAND WAY

⌗◣◢ The Rose Garden, 20 Hilda Place, TS12 1BP
☎ 01287 622947 (Anna Jastrzabek)
www.therosegarden.co.uk Map 94/661212
BB **D** ✗ nearby D/T2 T1 Closed Xmas-Jan ⋙(Saltburn)
🅱 🅳 ⊛ 🐾🏃 ★★★★

● **Scarborough**
CLEVELAND WAY

⌗◣◢ Russell Hotel, 22 Ryndleside, YO12 6AD ☎ 01723 365453
www.russellhotel.net Map 101/033893
BB **C** ✗ book first £10, 5:45pm S2 D3 T2 F3 ⋙(Scarborough)
🆅 🅱 🅳 ⊛🐾🏃🚗! 🛁🧼 ◆◆◆◆

Rayvil Hotel, 133 Queen's Parade, YO12 7HY ☎ 01723 364901
(Mrs B Rigg/Mrs C Mills) www.rayvilhotel.co.uk Map 101/040892
BB **B** ✗ nearby S3 D3 F1 Closed Dec-Feb ⋙(Scarborough)
🅱 🅳 ⊛ 🏃 ◆◆◆

⌗◣◢ The Ainsley Hotel, 4 Rutland Terrace, Queens Parade, YO12 7JB
☎ 01723 364832 (Mrs Mitchell)
www.ainsleyhotel.scarborough.co.uk Map 101/044890
BB **B** ✗ nearby S3 D5 T1 ⋙(Scarborough) 🅱 ⊛ 🐾🏃🛁🧼

● **Settle**
YORKSHIRE DALES
RIBBLE WAY & PENNINE WAY

☆ **Whitefriars Country Guest House**
Church Street, BD24 9JD ☎ 01729 823753
www.whitefriars-settle.co.uk Map 98/819637
BB **B/C** ✗ nearby S1 D3 T3 F2 Closed Xmas ⋙(Settle)
🅱 🅳 ⊛ 🐾🏃! ◆◆◆◆

Delightful 17th C. family home, standing in secluded gardens in the heart of the market town of Settle. Ideal for walking, cycling and touring: Yorkshire Dales National Park, The Three Peaks and Settle-Carlisle Railway.

Golden Lion Hotel, Duke Street, BD24 9DU ☎ 01729 822203
www.yorkshirenet.co.uk/stayat/goldenlion Map 98/819635
BB **D** ✗ book first £18, 6-9:30pm D10 T2 F2 ⋙(Settle)
🆅 🅱 🅳 🐾🏃🛁🧼 ◆◆◆◆

● **Skelton (Saltburn-by-the-Sea)**
CLEVELAND WAY

⌗◣◢ Westerland's Guest House, 27 East Parade, TS12 2BJ
☎ 01287 650690 (B Bull) Map 94/655185
BB **B** ✗ book first £6, 6:30-7pm S2 D3 F1 Closed Xmas ⋙(Saltburn)
🆅 🅱 🅳 ⊛ 🐾🏃🚗! 🛁 ◆◆◆◆

Wharton Arms, 133 High Street, TS12 2DY
☎ 01287 650618 (Pat Cummings)
p.cummings4@ntlworld.com Map 94/658189
BB **B** ✗ nearby S1 D1 T1 F2 Closed Xmas ⋙(Saltburn)
🅱 🅳 🐾🏃🚗! 🛁 ◆◆

For an explanation of the symbols used in this guide, see the fold-out flap at the back of the book.

● **Skipton**
YORKSHIRE DALES

☆ **Low Skibeden House**
Harrogate Rd, BD23 6AB ☎ 01756 793849 (Mrs Simpson)
www.yorkshirenet.co.uk/accgde/lowskibeden Map 104/012524
BB **C** D2 T1 F2 Closed Xmas ⋙(Skipton)
🅱 🅳 ⊛ 🏃 ◆◆◆◆

16th-century farmhouse. Quiet country location set in private grounds. Beautiful views, garden & parking. Offering home-from-home comforts and little luxuries in guests' lounge. Close to many areas of AONB. 2 mins by car to the market town of Skipton.

● **Sleights (Whitby)**
NORTH YORK MOORS
COAST TO COAST WALK

☆ **Ryedale House**
156 Coach Road, YO22 5EQ ☎ 01947 810534 (Pat Beale)
www.ryedalehouse.co.uk Map 94/866070
BB **B/C** ✗ nearby S2 D2 Closed Dec-Mar ⋙(Sleights)
🅱 ⊛ 🐾🏃 ◆◆◆◆

Welcoming home at foot of the moors in National Park 4 miles from Whitby. Magnificent scenery, superb walking, picturesque harbours, cliffs, beaches, scenic railways— it's all here!

Beautifully appointed rooms, private facilities, many extras. Guest lounge, extensive breakfast menu served with panoramic views, facing large landscaped gardens. Local inn and fish restaurant just a short walk.
Minimum booking 2 nights. Regret no pets/children. B&B £ 25-30.
Exclusive to non-smokers.

● **Staithes (Saltburn-by-the-Sea)**
NORTH YORK MOORS
CLEVELAND WAY

Brooklyn, Brown's Terrace, TS13 5BG ☎ 01947 841396 (Margaret Heald)
m.heald@tesco.net Map 94/782187
BB **B/C** ✗ nearby D2 T1 Closed Xmas 🅳 🐾🏃🚗! 🛁 ◆◆◆

● **Summerbridge (Harrogate)**
NIDDERDALE WAY

⌗◣◢ Dalriada, Cabin Lane, Dacre Banks, HG3 4EE
☎ 01423 780512 (Mrs J E Smith) Map 99/196621
BB **B/C** ✗ nearby S1 D1 T1 Closed Xmas 🅱 🅳 ⊛ 🐾🏃🚗! 🛁 ◆◆◆

● **Sutton Bank (Thirsk)**
NORTH YORK MOORS
CLEVELAND WAY

High House Farm, YO7 2HJ ☎ 01845 597557 (Mrs K M Hope) Map 100/521839
BB **B** ✗ book first £12, 6pm S1 D1 T1 F1 Closed Xmas
🆅 🅳 🐾🏃 ! 🛁

Cote Faw, YO7 2EZ ☎ 01845 597363 (Mrs J Jeffray) Map 100/522829
BB **B** ✗ nearby S1 D1 T1 Closed Xmas 🅳 🐾 ◆◆

YORKSHIRE

● Thornton Rust (Leyburn)

☆ ▦◂ **Thornton Lodge**
DL8 3AP ☎ 01969 663375 (Vanessa Kilvington)
www.thorntonlodgenorthyorkshire.co.uk Map 98/967890
BB **D** ✖ £10, 7pm S1 D4 T1 F3
Ⓥ Ⓑ Ⓓ ⊛ 🐾🛏 ⛟ ! Wheelchair access.

Thornton Lodge is a beautifully restored Edwardian mansion set in stunning grounds on a spur road off the A684 near Aysgarth.

Bespoke carpeting and sumptuous curtains are accentuated by Edwardian antiques and exquisite decor, whilst our modern en-suite bathrooms are luxuriously appointed to the highest possible standards.

Fantastic breakfasts. Wheelchair accessible. Large car park.

● Thwaite (Richmond)

Kearton Country Hotel, DL11 6DR ☎ 01748 886277 (I & J Danton)
www.keartoncountryhotel.co.uk Map 98/892982
BB **C** ✖ book first £12, 6:30-7pm S1 D3 T6 F2 Closed Jan
Ⓥ Ⓑ ⊛ 🐾🛏 ◆◆◆

● Welburn (York)
▦◂ Welburn Lodge, Castle Howard Station Road, YO60 7EW
☎ 01653 618885 (Stella & Steve Serowka)
www.welburnlodge.com Map 100/733669 BB **D** D3 Ⓑ ⊛ 🐾🛏

● Whitby

▦◂ Prospect Villa, 13 Prospect Hill, YO21 1QE ☎ 01947 603118 (J Gledhill)
janceeprospectvilla@hotmail.co.uk Map 94/894105
BB **C** ✖ nearby S2 D1 T1 F2 Closed Xmas ▦(Whitby)
Ⓑ Ⓓ ⊛ 🐾🛏 ★★★

Rosewood, 3 Ocean Rd, YO21 3HY ☎ 01947 820534 Map 94/890113
BB **B** ✖ nearby D2 ▦(Whitby) Ⓑ Ⓓ ⊛ 🐾🛏 ◆◆◆◆Ⓢ

▦◂ Saxonville Hotel, Ladysmith Ave , YO21 3HX
☎ 01947 602631 (Richard Newton) www.saxonville.co.uk Map 94/891113
BB **D** ✖ £11, 7-8:30pm S4 D8 T9 F2 Closed Nov-Jan ▦(Whitby)
Ⓥ Ⓑ Ⓓ ⊛ 🐾🛏 ★★★ See Groups also.

● Wigglesworth (Skipton)

▦◂ Cowper Cottage, BD23 4RP ☎ 01729 840598 (Marion Howard)
www.yorkshirenet.co.uk/stayat/cowper Map 103/810569
BB **C** ✖ nearby D1 T1 Closed Xmas Ⓑ Ⓓ ⊛ 🐾🛏 ⛟ ! ◆◆◆◆

● York

▦◂ Ambleside Guest House, 62 Bootham Crescent, Bootham, YO30 7AH
☎ 01904 637165 (Keith Hugill)
www.ambleside-gh.co.uk Map 105/598527
BB **D** ✖ nearby D4 T1 F1 Closed Jan ▦(York) Ⓑ ⊛ 🛏 ★★★

▦◂ Coxwold Tearooms, School House, YO61 4AD
☎ 01347 868077 (Mervyn Poulter)
www.coxwoldschoolhouse.co.uk Map 100/534771
BB **B** ✖ nearby D2 T1 Closed Jan Ⓓ ⊛ 🐾🛏 ⛟ !

☆ ▦◂ **Ascot House**
80 East Parade, YO31 7YH ☎ 01904 426826
www.ascothouseyork.com Map 105/616525
BB **C/D** ✖ nearby S1 D8 T3 F3 Closed Xmas ▦(York)
Ⓑ 🐾🛏 ⊛ 🏃 ◆◆◆◆Ⓢ

A family-run Victorian villa with four-poster and canopy beds. Situated midway between the Dales and Moors and fifteen minutes' walk from the historic York city centre. Delicious English, Continental and vegetarian breakfasts. Residential licence, sauna and private enclosed car park.

SOUTH YORKSHIRE

● Tankersley (Barnsley)

☆ ▦◂ **Tankersley Manor**
S75 3DQ ☎ 01226 744700
www.marstonhotels.com Map 110,111/341993
BB **D** ✖ £29.50, 7-9:30pm S2 T22 F75
Ⓥ Ⓑ 🐾🛏 ⊛ ★★★★ Wheelchair access.

Backing onto the accessible Trans Pennine Trail, Tankersley Manor sensitively incorporates a 17th-century building with a modern hotel with many original features retained.

Relax and enjoy a meal in the Manor Restaurant or the The Onward Arms, Tankersley Manor's own traditional pub, complete with beams and roaring fires.

The Reflections Leisure Club offers a heated indoor swimming pool, gym, steam, sauna and spa offering body treatments.

Take the time to explore the delights of South Yorkshire and its picturesque moorland scenery.

Please ask about our exclusive rates for walking parties.

WEST YORKSHIRE

● Guiseley (Leeds)
DALES WAY

Lyndhurst, Oxford Road, LS20 9AB
☎ 01943 879985 (Alison Button)
www.guiseley.co.uk/lyndhurst Map 104/190421
BB **C** ✗ nearby DI TI ⋙(Guiseley) Ⓑ Ⓓ ⊗ 🐾🛁 Ⓜ ◆◆◆

● Haworth
PENNINE WAY

Apothecary Guest House, 86 Main Street, BD22 8DP
☎ 01535 643642 (Mr N J Sisley)
http://theapothecaryguesthouse.co.uk Map 104/030372
BB **C** ✗ nearby SI D3 T2 FI ⋙(Haworth)
Ⓑ Ⓓ ⊗ 🐾🛁 ◆◆◆

Rosebud Cottage Guest House, I Belle Isle Rd, BD22 8QQ
☎ 01535 640321 (Caroline Starkey)
www.rosebudcottage.co.uk Map 104/034370
BB **D** ✗ book first £15, 7pm SI D2 TI FI ⋙(Haworth)
Ⓥ Ⓑ Ⓓ ⊗ 🐾🛁 ★★★★

☆ ⋙ **Aitches Guest House**
II West Lane, BD22 8DU ☎ 01535 642501 (Philomena Evans)
www.aitches.co.uk Map 104/030372
BB **B** ✗ nearby S2 D2 TI FI ⋙(Haworth)
Ⓑ Ⓓ ⊗ 🐾🛁🚗❗🔥 ◆◆◆◆

Elegant Victorian house in quiet location
overlooking Bronte parsonage two minutes'
stroll from village centre, pubs, eateries and
shops. We offer comfortable, well-equipped
rooms, cosy guest lounge, sumptious
five-course breakfasts and a warm welcome,
especially to walkers.

● Hebden Bridge
PENNINE WAY & PENNINE BRIDLEWAY

Mytholm House, Mytholm Bank, HX7 6DL
☎ 01422 847493 (Brenda & Jim Botten)
www.mytholmhouse.co.uk Map 103/983274
BB **B/C/D** ✗ book first £15, To suit. SI D/T2 Closed Xmas
⋙(Hebden Bridge) Ⓥ Ⓑ Ⓓ ⊗ 🐾🛁🚗 Ⓜ ◆◆◆◆Ⓢ

● Holmfirth (Huddersfield)
Uppergate Farm, Hepworth, HD9 ITG
☎ 01484 681369 (Alison Booth)
www.uppergatefarm.co.uk Map 110/162068
BB **D** ✗ nearby T2 FI Closed Xmas
Ⓑ Ⓓ ⊗ 🐾🛁🚗❗ ★★★★

DON'T FORGET!
You can use your Discount Vouchers on p121
at any B&B listed with ⋙ next to their entry.

● Stanbury (Keighley)
PENNINE WAY

☆ ⋙ **Ponden House**
BD22 0HR ☎ 01535 644154 (Mrs Taylor)
www.pondenhouse.co.uk Map 103/992371
BB **C** ✗ book first £16, 7pm DI TI FI
Ⓥ Ⓑ Ⓓ ⊗ 🐾🛁 Ⓜ ◆◆◆◆

'Brontë Country'
Relax in a tranquil historic setting.
Enjoy panoramic views over reservoir and
moors, log fires, imaginative home cooking and
warm hospitality.
Call Brenda Taylor for a brochure .

● Todmorden
PENNINE WAY

Cherry Tree Cottage, Woodhouse Road, OLI4 5RJ ☎ 01706 817492
(Jean Butterworth) Map 103/951245
BB **C** ✗ nearby DI T2 Closed Jan ⋙(Todmorden)
Ⓥ Ⓑ Ⓓ ⊗ 🐾🛁 ◆◆◆◆

Highstones Guest House, Rochdale Road, Walsden, OLI4 6TY
☎ 01706 816534 (Heather Pegg) Map 103/939208
BB **B** ✗ book first £10, 7-7:30pm SI D2 Closed Xmas ⋙(Walsden)
Ⓥ Ⓑ Ⓓ ⊗ 🐾🛁 ★★★

SELF-CATERING

☆ **Yorkshire Cottages**
☎ 01228 406701
www.yorkshire-cottages.info
£220-£950 Sleeps 2-15. Over 100 cottages, apartments, houses & cabins.
Many properties are VisitBritain inspected annually. ⊗ 🛁

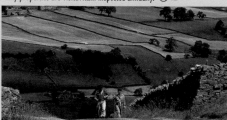

We have quality self-catering cottages, houses, apartments and log cabins in
superb locations throughout the Yorkshire Dales, North York Moors and on the
Yorkshire coast.
Lovely properties, ideal for great outdoor holidays, starting from as little as
£10pppn, pets go free and short breaks all year round. Visit our website to
browse cottages, check availability and book online, or call 01228 406701.

NORTH YORKSHIRE

● Askrigg
YORKSHIRE DALES

Elm Hill Cottages ☎ 01969 624252 (Peter & Liz Haythornthwaite)
www.elmhillholidaycottages.co.uk
£250-£515 Sleeps 4-6. 2 cottages.
High quality, central heating, private parking. ⊗ ★★★

YORKSHIRE

☆ Country Hideaways
☎ 01969 663559 (Nadine Bell)
www.countryhideaways.co.uk
£166-£1,115 Sleeps 2-10. 40 cottages & apartments. Unique watermill apartments, houses and cottages. ⊗ 🛏 ★★-★★★★

Choose from 40 beautiful properties in stunning locations in Wensleydale, Swaledale, Coverdale and Bishopdale, all carefully chosen for their quality and individual style. Enjoy the timeless, unspoilt beauty of these wonderful dales whilst walking the many footpaths and open areas here.

Visit our website to check availability and book online if you wish, or call us on 01969 663559 for friendly help and advice and to book your chosen cottage.

● Austwick
YORKSHIRE DALES

Spoutscroft Cottage ☎ 01524 251052 (Christine Hartland)
www.cottageguide.co.uk/spoutscroft
£250-£495 Sleeps 1-4. 1 cottage.
Traditional Dales cottage for the discerning. ⊗ 🛏 ★★★★★

● Aysgarth Falls
YORKSHIRE DALES

☆ Meadowcroft
☎ 01792 280068 (M C Mason)
www.meadowcroftcottage.co.uk
£192-£356 Sleeps 5. 1 cottage.
Wensleydale, unspoiled village in National Park. ⊗ 🛏 ★★★★

Wensleydale. Unspoilt village with pub and shop. Modern comfortable conversion of large traditional Dales barn in heart of National Park. Network of footpaths directly from cottage – a walker's pardise. Lovely views. Secure off-street parking and private paddock.

● Ebberston (Pickering)
NORTH YORK MOORS

Cliff House Cottage Holidays ☎ 01723 859440 (Simon Morris)
www.cliffhouse-cottageholidays.co.uk
£225-£975 Sleeps 2-6.
6 cottages, 2 apts. Indoor heated swimming pool. ★★★★

● Egton Bridge
NORTH YORK MOORS

☆ Broom House Cottages
☎ 01947 895279 (M White)
www.egton-bridge.co.uk
£220-£595 Sleeps 2-4. 3 cottages. Riverside location, private garden.
Local inns. 🚶(Egton Bridge) ⊗ ★★★★ See B&B also.

Broom Cottage and Riverside Cottage, Egton Bridge. North Yorkshire Moors National Park. 4-star cosy cottages well equipped to a high standard. Quiet village setting with superb views. For a virtual tour visit our website. For further details and a brochure please phone or Email: mw@broom-house.co.uk

● Glaisdale
NORTH YORK MOORS

Red House Farm ☎ 01947 897242 (TJ Spashett) www.redhousefarm.com
£200-£620 Sleeps 2-4. 2 cottages, 1 studio flat.
Award winning, listed barn conversions. 🚶(Glaisdale) 🛏 See B&B also.

● Grosmont
NORTH YORK MOORS

5 Hardstruggle Cottages ☎ 01636 815572 (Miriam Duffy) www.esk.org.uk
£275-£500 Sleeps 8. 1 cottage.
Stunning location, fantastic walks, luxury. 🚶(Grosmont) ⊗ 🛏

● Hawes
YORKSHIRE DALES

Mile House Farm ☎ 01969 667481 (Anne Fawcett)
www.wensleydale.uk.com
£250-£675 Sleeps 2-7. 4 cottages.
Lovely character old dales stone cottages. ⊗ 🛏 ★★★★

Mrs Metcalfe ☎ 01609 881302 info@adventuretoys.co.uk
£125-£325 Sleeps 4. 1 cottage. Cosy, open fire, fishing, short breaks. 🛏

● Kirkbymoorside
NORTH YORK MOORS

Rose Cottage ☎ 01751 417588 (Mrs AM Wilson)
£150-£210 Sleeps 3. 1 cottage. Closed Dec-Jan
Good walking country, in National Park. 🛏

● Lealholm
NORTH YORK MOORS

Rachel Woolley ☎ 07889 199445 rachelsjewels@aol.com
£250 Sleeps 6. 1 cottage.
Fully modernised, patio area. Stunning views. 🚶(Lealholm) 🛏

● Leyburn

☆ Throstlenest Cottages
☎ 01969 623694 (Tricia Smith)
www.throstlenestcottages.co.uk
£210-£450 Sleeps 1-6. 6 cottages. Closed Jan
Glorious view, rural, town half mile. 🚶(Leyburn) ⊗ Ⓜ ★★★

Six cosy, comfortable, well-equipped cottages converted from stone barns. All have a glorious panoramic view over Wensleydale and the high fells of Coverdale. Rural, yet town centre only half a mile. Sorry – no pets.

Dales View Hoiday Homes ☎ 01969 623707/622808 (Mr Chilton)
www.daleshols.co.uk
£140-£305 Sleeps 3-4. 3 cottages, 3 apts.
Secluded courtyard off marketplace. ᴍᴍ(Leyburn) 🛏 ★★★-★★★★

● Pateley Bridge

☆ Edge Farm
☎ 01422 240829 (Michael O'Byrne)
www.edgefarm.co.uk
£950-£1,450 Sleeps 12. 1 farmhouse.
Quality accommodation with peace & tranquility. ⊗ ★★★★

Edge Farm is a 4-star, spacious, 5-bedroom detached property on the privately-owned Summerstone Estate, set in the remote and picturesque Upper Nidderdale Valley. This fully modernised, well equipped accommodation is ideal for walkers, groups of friends or a family get-together.

● Pickering
NORTH YORK MOORS

☆ Keld Head Farm Cottages
☎ 01751 473974 (Penny & Julian Fearn)
www.keldheadcottages.com
£189-£1,050 Sleeps 2-8 +cot. 9 cottages.
Off-peak discounts, couples, senior citizens. ⊗ ★★★★ Access category I.

In open countryside on the edge of the market town, a picturesque group of stone cottages with beamed ceilings and stone fireplaces. Furnished with emphasis on comfort, some with four-poster bedrooms. Large gardens with garden house, play and barbecue area. Some single storey and one-bedroom cottages. Excellent base for the York Moors, Heritage Coast, Cleveland Way, Wolds Way and Lyke Wake Walk. See virtual tour on website.

Let's Holiday ☎ 01751 475396 (John & Penny Wicks)
www.letsholiday.com
£282-£790 Sleeps 2-6. 1 cottage, 2 apts.
Indoor heated pool, jacuzzi and sauna. ⊗ 🛏 ★★★★

Bramwood Cottages ☎ 01751 473446 (Marilyn Bamforth)
www.bramwoodguesthouse.co.uk
£195-£480 Sleeps 2-4. 2 cottages. Tastefully converted stables, Grade II-listed.
ᴍᴍ(Pickering) ⊗ Ⓜ ★★★★ See B&B also.

● Redmire

Ashes House ☎ 01969 622201 (Mrs S L Robinson)
sue.asheshouse@virgin.net
£195-£325 Sleeps 6. 1 house.
Excellent walks, superb views, homely accommodation. 🛏

● Reeth
YORKSHIRE DALES

Chetwynd Holiday Cottage ☎ 0131 449 7435 (Richard & Maureen Porter)
http://reeth-holiday-cottages.pwp.blueyonder.co.uk
£240-£395 Sleeps 5. 1 cottage.
Three bedrooms (one en-suite), spacious, well-equipped. ⊗ 🛏

● Robin Hood's Bay
NORTH YORK MOORS

Lingers Hill Farm ☎ 01947 880608 (Mrs F Harland)
£190-£355 Sleeps 2-4. 1 cottage. Grid ref: NZ 94634 05241
Cosy character cottage. 🛏 ★★★

● Scarborough
NORTH YORK MOORS

☆ Wrea Head Country Cottages
☎ 01723 375844 (Steve Marshall)
www.wreahead.co.uk
£255-£1,450 Sleeps 2-8. 9 cottages.
Indoor swimming pool, panoramic sea views. ⊗ ★★★★

National winners of the ETC England for Excellence award. Superb residents-only, indoor heated swimming pool, sauna and jacuzzi. Ideal base for North York Moors, coastal path and forest walks. Excellent off-season breaks. A rural haven with inspiring charm, character and tranquility.

Bedwyn's Holidays ☎ 01723 516700 (Diane Crampton)
www.bedwyns.co.uk
£145-£845 Sleeps 2-12. 20 houses, flats, bungalows and cottages.
🛏 ★★★-★★★★★

☆ Wayside Farm
☎ 01723 870519 (Peter & Jane Halder)
www.waysidefarm.co.uk
£120-£489 Sleeps 2-6. 4 cottages.
Private woodland walk and nature trail. ⊗ 🛏 ★★-★★★

Set in 34 acres, Wayside Farm is in the heart of the North Yorkshire Moors. Ideal for walking or visiting the nearby towns of Scarborough (9 miles) and Whitby (10 miles). Four original sandstone farm building conversions creating excellent family accommodation, fully central heated. Open all year.

● Settle
YORKSHIRE DALES

Selside Farm ☎ 01729 860367 (Mrs S E Lambert)
www.selsidefarmholidaycottage.co.uk
£260-£445 Sleeps 2-6. 1 barn conversion.
Centre Three Peaks. Selside, Horton-in-Ribblesdale. 🛏 ★★★★

● Skipton

Bankfoot Farm ☎ 07753 747912 (Peter Smith)
www.bankfootsutton.co.uk
£391-£624 Sleeps 2-6. 1 cottage.
Well equipped farmhouse with amazing views. ⊗ 🛏 ★★★★

YORKSHIRE

● Staithes

NORTH YORK MOORS

David Purdy ☎ 01751 431452
£230-£360 Sleeps 4. 1 cottage.
Coast, moors. On Cleveland Way. Harbourside ⊗ 🛏 ★★

● Whitby

NORTH YORK MOORS

Grange Farm ☎ 01947 881080 (Denise Hooning)
www.grangefarm.net
£435-£1,595 Sleeps 2-14. 1 farmhouse, 1 cottage.
Excellent base to explore coast & moors. ⊗ ★★★★

☆ **Aislaby Lodge Cottages**
☎ 01947 811822 (Mrs S Riddolls)
www.aislabylodgecottages.co.uk
£200-£650 Sleeps 2-25 + 3 cots. 5 farmhouse cottages.
Stunning views, quiet location. Sleeps 25. ⋙(Ruswarp) 🛏 ★★★-★★★★

Traditional stone cottages with stunning views over Esk Valley. 4 miles from Whitby and coastal villages. Ideal base for North Yorkshire Moors and coast. Excellent facilities, including laundry and drying room. Quiet location, ample parking.

The Crows Nest ☎ 01642 492144 (Mr E Tayler)
www.crowsnestwhitby.co.uk
£190-£665 Sleeps 2-11. 1 house, 2 apartments.
Spacious five-bedroom house. Apartments. Panoramic views. ⋙(Whitby)
⊗ 🛏 ★★★

WEST YORKSHIRE

● Hebden Bridge
Robin Hood Cottage ☎ 07977 459913 (Liz Woznicki)
www.robinhoodcottage.co.uk
£150-£240 Sleeps 3. 1 cottage.
Cosy beams, real fire, weekends available. ⋙(Mytholmroyd) ⊗ 🛏 ★★★

GROUPS

NORTH YORKSHIRE

Saxonville Hotel (BB) Ladysmith Ave, Whitby YO21 3HX ☎ 01947 602631
www.saxonville.co.uk
DBB from £39 Min 20, max 42. Closed Dec-Jan, July-Aug ⋙(Whitby)
✕ 🐾 B D ⊗ ★★★Ⓢ See B&B also.

NORTH YORK MOORS
CLEVELAND WAY & COAST TO COAST WALK

Whitby Backpackers At Harbour Grange (SC/IH/B)
Spital Bridge, Whitby YO22 4EF ☎ 01947 600817 (Birgitta)
www.whitbybackpackers.co.uk Map 94/901104
SC £240pn Max 24. ⋙(Whitby) ✕ nearby 🐾 D ⊗ See Hostels also.

NORTH YORK MOORS

The Firs (BB) 26 Hinderwell Lane, Runswick Bay, Nr Whitby TS13 5HR
☎ 01947 840433 (Mandy Shackleton)
www.the-firs.co.uk Map 94/791168
BB £30 Min 2, max 24. Closed Nov-Feb
✕ 🐾 B D ◆◆◆◆ See B&B also.

York Youth Hotel (BB/SC) 11/13 Bishophill Senior, York YO1 6EF
☎ 01904 625904 (Maureen Sellers) www.yorkyouthhotel.com
BB £30 Min 4, max 100. 1 hostel. ⋙(York)
✕ 🐾 D ⊗ ! ★★ Hostel See Hostels also.

HOSTELS, BUNKHOUSES & CAMPSITES

NORTH YORKSHIRE

York Youth Hotel (IH) 11/13 Bishophill Senior, York YO1 6EF
☎ 01904 625904 (Charles Stuart)
www.yorkyouthhotel.com Map 105/600515
Bednight £14 ⋙(York) ✕ nearby D ⊗ ★★ Hostel See Groups also.

YORKSHIRE DALES
DALES WAY

Skirfare Bridge Dales Barn (IH/BHB) Kilnsey
☎ 01756 761028 (Mrs J L Foster)
www.skirfaredalesbarn.co.uk Map 98/971689
Bednight £12 ✕ nearby D ⊗

YORKSHIRE DALES
DALES WAY & PENNINE WAY

The Station Inn (B) Ribblehead, Ingleton
☎ 015242 41274
www.thestationinn.net Map 98/764792
Bednight £8.50 ⋙(Ribblehead) ✕ 🐾 D ◆◆◆ See B&B also.

NORTH YORK MOORS
CLEVELAND WAY & COAST TO COAST WALK

Whitby Backpackers At Harbour Grange (IH) Spital Bridge, Whitby YO22 4EF
☎ 01947 600817
www.whitbybackpackers.co.uk Map 94/901104
Bednight £12 ✕ nearby ⋙(Whitby)
🐾 ⊗ D See Groups also.

FOUND SOMEWHERE GOOD THAT'S NOT IN THIS GUIDE?
Or got a complaint about one that is?
Fill in the Recommendation/Feedback Form on p123 and send it to the editor at our central office address, or email: yearbook@ramblers.org.uk

Free Hotel Accommodation all year round

Treat yourself to a break

Do you enjoy getting away from it all? With a Privilege Hotel Pass from Travel Offers Ltd, you and a partner can stay for free at over 320 hotels and sample their culinary delights without paying for your room.

How it works

For only £29.95, your Privilege Hotel Pass gives you the freedom to enjoy as many hotel breaks as you wish over 12 months. All you have to do is pay for your meals – dinner and breakfast – your accommodation is absolutely free! Twin or double rooms are available and meal prices range from £19 to £30 and over per person for award-winning dining.

With your pass you will also receive the Travel Offers Hotel Directory which provides details on each of our featured hotels. With so many to choose from, you'll be spoilt for choice!

£29.95
for as many hotel breaks as you wish over 12 months*

TRAVEL OFFERS ★ LTD

Stay for just 1 night or more – however long you stay, just pay for your meals and any additional items you choose to purchase, e.g drinks and spa treatments.

Where you can stay

We have an extensive range of hotels in a wide variety of impressive locations across the UK and Ireland.

Choose from over 320 hotels:	
England	213
Channel Islands	6
Wales	26
Scotland	62
N. Ireland & Ireland	21

Whether you're looking for a relaxing break by the coast, a weekend away in the country or fancy exploring a new town, we have the perfect break for you. Many of our featured hotels have won awards for their cuisine, boast top leisure facilities and have a stunning selection of attractions and amenities close by – all you have to do is decide where you want to go!

Telephone:
0871 282 2882

Lines are open
Mon-Fri 8.30am-9pm, Sat 10am-4pm, Sun 2pm-6pm

www.travel-offers.co.uk

NORTH EAST

Long Distance Paths

Cleveland Way CVL

Hadrian's Wall Path ....HNW

Pennine Way.......................PNN

South Tyne Trail ....STY

St Cuthbert's Way ....STC

Teesdale Way......................TSD

See Paths & Access p25 for full details of LDPs and waymarks

National Parks

Northumberland

See Useful Contacts p99 for full details of national parks

SUMMERHILL FORCE CASCADING OVER GIBSON'S CAVE IN UPPER TEESDALE, CO DURHAM

WALK...

...THE NORTHUMBERLAND COAST PATH

This new 103km/64-mile route between Berwick and Cresswell forms part of the vast North Sea Trail – a European long-distance path totalling 4,900km of coast along Holland, Denmark and Scandinavia. Divided into six day-long stages, the Coast Path takes in many of the AONB's highlights, including Druridge Bay's golden sands and the dramatic ruins of Dunstanburgh Castle (pictured), and at one stage briefly picks up St Cuthbert's Way to Holy Island.

Visit www.northseatrail.org for more information. Guidebooks are available from local TICs or the Northumberland Coast AONB ☎ 01670 534078.

VISIT...

...THE PARKLAND AT DALTON PARK

It's not often a trip to an out-of-town shopping centre can double as a family nature trail. But the developers of Dalton Park, near Murton in Durham, have incorporated an excellent child-friendly nature park, with wetlands, meadows and hundreds of trees planted across the 27-hectare site of what was formerly a colliery spoil tip. There are three easy, colourful trails rich with wildlife (hares and kites are frequently sighted), a children's centre with a nursery, and regular organised bug hunts. Various lookouts offer great views of the sea and surrounding countryside, including a Bronze Age burial mound at nearby Batter Law.

For details of upcoming events and a downloadable map of the trails, visit www.dalton-park.co.uk or ☎ 0191 526 6157.

SEE...   ...THE RED SQUIRREL AT WALLINGTON

When it comes to squirrels, seeing red is getting rarer and rarer with so much of Britain going grey. Only 160,000 of our native red squirrels survive, compared to 2.5 million greys. But Wallington, in Northumberland, is one of their few strongholds. The National Trust-owned estate – partly landscaped by 'Capability' Brown – encompasses high moorland and wooded valleys where specially erected hides attract the creatures close up with food. A 3km/2-mile Red Squirrel Walk (downloadable from www.nationaltrust.org.uk) tours their locations and offers spectacular views of Wansbeck river and Shafto Crag escarpment to the south. ☎ 01670 773600 or visit the website (above) for opening times and admissions.

NORTH EAST

LOCAL RAMBLERS GROUPS... Berwick Group have devised an epic 192km/120-mile walk around the borough that encompasses majestic countryside, five castles, a palace and a mountain, and is beautifully detailed in Arthur Wood's hand-drawn booklet (see p90 to order)... **Northumbria Short Circuits Group guarantees walks of no more than six miles, with many far shorter, and welcomes newcomers to join what is the Area's fastest growing Group. See p76 for contact details**... Northumbria Area has successfully pressured the county council to replace a vital footbridge for walkers near Otterburn that was demolished in 2000 for being unsafe.

Walk the biggest leisure centre in the British Isles

If your boots are made for walking then here are some dates for your diary: The Isle of Man June Walking Festival takes place on the 24th-29th of June and our October Walking Festival from the 11th-14th October.

Itineraries are devised for walkers to experience the beauty of the island plus a chance to spend evenings taking part in all manner of varied and exciting social events.

Festival packages available: visit www.isleofmanwalking.com or call 01624 66 11 77

Isle OF man
VisitIsleofMan.com

MAP 257

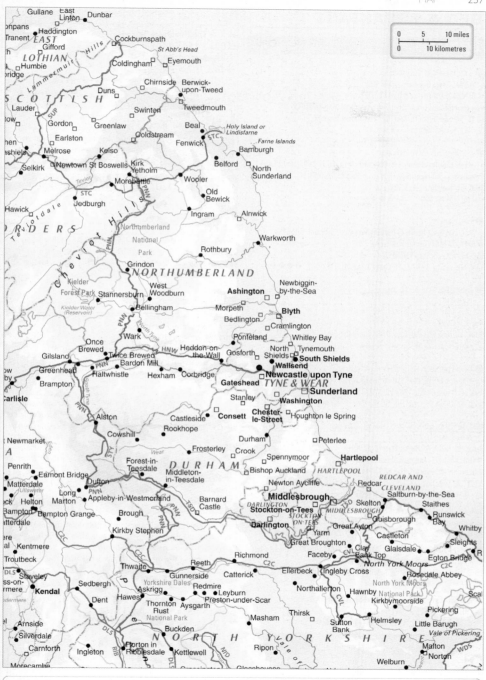

BED & BREAKFAST

DURHAM

● Castleside (Consett)
Bee Cottage Guesthouse, DH8 9HW
☎ 01207 508224 (Melita & David Turner)
www.smoothhound.co.uk/hotels/beecottage.html Map 87/070453
BB **D** ✗ book first £18, 7pm D2 T2 F4 Closed Xmas
Ⓥ Ⓑ Ⓓ ⊗ ⛯⛯ ⛱⛲ ★★★★

● Cowshill (Wearhead)
Low Cornriggs Farmhouse, DL13 1AQ ☎ 01388 537600 (Janet Elliott)
www.alstonandkillhoperidingcentre.co.uk Map 86,87/845413
BB **C** ✗ book first £16, 6.30pm D2 TI
Ⓥ Ⓑ Ⓓ ⊗ ⛯⛯ ⛱⛲ ◆◆◆◆

● Durham
Hillrise Guest House, 13 Durham Road West, Bowburn, DH6 5AU
☎ 0191 377 0302 (George Webster)
www.hill-rise.com Map 93/306376
BB **C** ✗ nearby SI D2 T2 FI Closed Xmas Ⓑ Ⓓ ⊗ ⛱ ◆◆◆◆

● Forest-in-Teesdale
PENNINE WAY & TEESDALE WAY
The Dale, DL12 0EL ☎ 01833 622303 (Jean Bonnett)
Map 91/869298
BB **A** ✗ book first £10, 7pm DI FI Closed Dec-Feb
Ⓥ ⊗ ⛯⛯ ⛱⛲ Ⓜ

● Frosterley (Bishop Auckland)
Newlands Hall, DL13 2SH ☎ 01388 529233 (Carol Oulton)
www.newlandshall.co.uk Map 92/043372
BB **C** F2 Closed Dec-Mar Ⓑ Ⓓ ⊗ ⛯⛯ ⛱⛲ ◆◆◆◆

● Middleton-in-Teesdale (Barnard Castle)
PENNINE WAY & TEESDALE WAY
Brunswick House, 55 Market Place, DL12 0QH
☎ 01833 640393 (Andrew & Sheila Milnes)
www.brunswickhouse.net Map 91,92/946255
BB **D** ✗ book first £18, 7:30pm D3 T2 Closed Xmas
Ⓥ Ⓑ Ⓓ ⊗ ⛯⛯ ⛱⛲ ★★★★⑤

Belvedere House, 54 Market Place, DL12 0QA ☎ 01833 640884 (Mrs J A Finn)
www.thecoachhouse.net Map 91,92/947254
BB **B** ✗ nearby D2 TI Closed Xmas Ⓑ ⊗ ⛯⛯ ⛱⛲ ◆◆◆◆

Wemmergill Hall Farm, Lunedale, DL12 0PA ☎ 01833 640379 (Irene Stoddart)
www.wemmergill-farm.co.uk Map 91,92/901218
BB **B** ✗ book first £15, 6:30pm S/DI T/FI Closed Oct-Mar
Ⓥ Ⓑ Ⓓ ⊗ ⛯⛯ ⛱⛲ ★★★★

Lonton South Farm, DL12 0PL ☎ 01833 640 409 (Irene Watson)
Map 91,92/954245
BB **C** ✗ nearby SI DI TI Ⓓ ⊗ ⛯⛯ ⛱⛲ ◆◆◆

● Rookhope (Bishop Auckland)

☆ The Rookhope Inn
DL13 2BG ☎ 01388 517215 (Chris Jones)
www.rookhope.com Map 87/938428
BB **C** ✗ £7, 7pm T4 FI
Ⓥ Ⓑ Ⓓ ⊗ ⛯⛯ ⛱⛲ Ⓜ ★★ See Groups also.

This is upper Weardale in the North
Pennines, secluded 300-year-old
village inn offering en-suite
accommodation, good food and cask
ales. Groups of up to 12 welcome.
Drying facilities, maps and excellent
walking venues. B&B: £30 / DBB: £36

NORTHUMBERLAND

● Bardon Mill (Hexham)
NORTHUMBERLAND NATIONAL PARK
PENNINE WAY & HADRIAN'S WALL
Twice Brewed Inn, Military Rd, NE47 7AN ☎ 01434 344534 (Brian Keen)
www.twicebrewedinn.co.uk Map 86,87/753669
BB **C** ✗ £6.50, 6-8:30pm S2 D4 T7 FI Closed Xmas (Bardon Mill)
Ⓥ Ⓑ ⊗ ⛯⛯ ⛱⛲! ◆◆◆

● Beal (Berwick-upon-Tweed)
ST CUTHBERT'S WAY

☆ Brockmill Farmhouse
TD15 2PB ☎ 01289 381283
www.lindisfarne.org.uk/brock-mill-farmhouse Map 75/060436
BB **C** ✗ nearby SI DI TI FI Closed Xmas
Ⓓ ⊗ ⛯⛯ ⛱⛲ ◆◆◆◆

Brock Mill
Farmhouse is
peacefully situated
1½ miles from the
AI on the road to
Holy Island.
The St Cuthbert's
Way is just
1½ miles away.

Four Diamonds.

Ideally situated for touring and exploring north Northumberland and Borders.
A warm welcome awaits in superbly furnished quality rooms with TV,
tea-making facilities, vanity units and 2-seater settees. Pick-ups available for
ramblers. Evening meals nearby. Full English or vegetarian breakfasts.

● Belford
The Old Vicarage, I North Bank, NE70 7LY ☎ 01668 213025 (Annette Monnelly)
www.belfordoldvicarage.co.uk Map 75/108340
BB **C** ✗ nearby DI TI Ⓑ Ⓓ ⊗ ⛯⛯!

● Berwick-upon-Tweed
Orkney Guest House, 37 Woolmarket, TD15 1DH
☎ 01289 331710 (Helen Rutherford)
orkneyguesthouse@yahoo.co.uk Map 75/000528
BB **B** ✗ nearby D2 T2 FI (Berwick-upon-Tweed) Ⓑ Ⓓ ⊗ ⛯⛯ ⛱⛲

● Corbridge
HADRIAN'S WALL

🔹◢ The Hayes, Newcastle Rd, NE45 5LP
☎ 01434 632010 (Mrs MJ Matthews)
www.hayes-corbridge.co.uk Map 87/996643
BB **D** ✕ nearby S1 T1 F2 Closed Xmas ₩(Corbridge)
Ⓑ Ⓓ ⊗ 🐾🚻🛏🚗 ! ◆◆◆

☆ 🔹◢ **Dyvels Hotel**
Station Rd, NE45 5AY ☎ 01434 633633
dyvels.corbridge@virgin.net Map 87/989636
BB **C** ✕ £7, until 8:30pm D1 T1 Closed Xmas ₩(Corbridge)
Ⓥ Ⓑ Ⓓ ⊗ 🐾🚻🛏 !

Cosy, friendly atmosphere. Fully stocked bar, offering a good selection of cask ales, lagers and fine wines. Separate restaurant, serving a full English Breakfast and excellent home-cooked food. Beer Garden. All rooms tastefully decorated and furnished and equipped with TV and beverage tray.

● East Wallhouses (Corbridge)
HADRIAN'S WALL

The Barn B&B, Military Rd, NE18 0LL
☎ 01434 672649 (Brenda Walton)
www.smoothhound.co.uk/hotels/thebarn1.html Map 87/047683
BB **D** ✕ nearby D1 T2 Closed Dec ⊗ 🐾🛏 ! 🦽

● Fenwick (Berwick-upon-Tweed)
ST CUTHBERT'S WAY

🔹◢ The Manor House, TD15 2PQ ☎ 01289 381016 (Kate Moore)
www.manorhousefenwick.co.uk Map 75/066401
BB **C** ✕ nearby D2 T1 F1 Ⓑ Ⓓ ⊗ 🐾🛏🚗 !

☆ 🔹◢ **Cherry Trees**
TD15 2PJ ☎ 01289 381437
Map 75/066401
BB **B/C** ✕ book first £12, 6-7:30pm D1 T1 F1 Closed Sep-Apr
Ⓥ Ⓑ Ⓓ 🐾🛏

Large detached house in large private grounds with ample parking. Ideally situated for St Cuthbert's Way, walking and touring. 6 miles to Holy Island. Spacious rooms, hospitality tray and countryside views.

● Greenhead (Brampton)
NORTHUMBERLAND NATIONAL PARK
HADRIAN'S WALL, PENNINE WAY & SOUTH TYNE TRAIL

10 Blenkinsopp Terrace, Bankfoot, CA8 7JN
☎ 016977 47429 (Robin & Jean Fuller)
robingfuller@yahoo.co.uk Map 86/663645
BB **B** ✕ book first £8-£12, 7pm S1 D1 T/F1 Ⓥ Ⓑ Ⓓ ⊗ 🐾🛏🚗 ! Ⓜ

🔹◢ Holmhead Guest House, CA8 7HY
☎ 016977 47402 (Brian & Pauline Staff) www.holmhead.com Map 86/661659
BB **D** ✕ book first £24, 7:30pm D2 T2 Closed Xmas
Ⓥ Ⓑ Ⓓ ⊗ 🐾🛏 ! ◆◆◆◆

● Grindon (Hexham)
NORTHUMBERLAND NATIONAL PARK
PENNINE WAY & HADRIAN'S WALL

☆ **Old Repeater Station**
Military Road, NE47 6NQ ☎ 01434 688668 (Les Gibson)
www.hadrians-wall-bedandbreakfast.co.uk Map 86,87/816701
BB **C** ✕ £8, 7pm D1 T3 F1
Ⓥ Ⓑ Ⓓ ⊗ 🐾🛏🚗 ! 🦽 ★★★ Wheelchair access.

Whether planning a short walking or cycling holiday, a long weekend exploring the surrounding areas such as the Lake District and Kielder, or just enjoying the unspoilt county of Northumberland itself – the Old Repeater Station is well placed to serve your needs.

● Haltwhistle
PENNINE WAY, HADRIAN'S WALL & SOUTH TYNE TRAIL

🔹◢ Hall Meadows, Main Street, NE49 0AZ
☎ 01434 321021 (Heather Humes)
Map 86,87/708641
BB **B/C** ✕ nearby S1 D1 T1 Closed Xmas ₩(Haltwhistle)
Ⓑ Ⓓ 🐾🛏🚗 ◆◆◆◆

☆ 🔹◢ **Kellah Farm B&B**
NE49 0JL ☎ 01434 320816 (Lesley Teasdale)
www.kellah.co.uk Map 86/659612
BB **C** ✕ book first D2 T1 F2
Ⓥ Ⓑ Ⓓ ⊗ 🐾🛏🚗 ! 🦽

New for 2007. Farmhouse breakfasts using all local produce, including our own free-range eggs, comfortable accommodation with a warm welcome, and stunning views of the Northumberland countryside will be our recipe for a relaxing stay at Kellah Bed & Breakfast accommodation.

● Heddon-on-the-Wall
HADRIAN'S WALL

Ramblers' Repose, 8 Killiebrigs, NE15 0DD
☎ 01661 852419 (Mrs P A Millward)
Map 88/130665
BB **D** ✕ nearby D1 T1 Closed Xmas ⊗ 🛏 ◆◆◆

Tyne Valley Views, 9 Killiebrigs, NE15 0DD
☎ 01661 853509 (Jillian Riddell)
www.holiday-rentals.co.uk Map 88/130665
BB **C** ✕ nearby S1 D1 T1 Closed Dec ₩(Wylam)
Ⓓ ⊗ 🐾🛏🚗 !

● Ingram (Powburn)
NORTHUMBERLAND NATIONAL PARK

🔹◢ Reaveley Farmhouse B&B, NE66 4LS
☎ 01665 578268 (Mary Shaw)
reaveleyfarm@aol.com Map 81/021170
BB **C** ✕ book first £10 S1 D2 T1 Closed Xmas
Ⓥ Ⓑ Ⓓ ⊗ 🐾🛏🚗 ◆◆◆ On the Inn Way.

NORTH EAST

● Old Bewick (Alnwick)

☆ ☛⌂ **Old Bewick Farmhouse**
NE66 4DZ ☎ 01668 217372 (Catherine Lister)
www.oldbewick.co.uk Map 75/069213
BB **C** ✗ book first £10, to suit DI FI
Ⓥ Ⓑ Ⓓ ⊗ 🐾🍴🅗 🚗 ❗

A Georgian farmhouse situated in the unspoilt beautiful countryside of North Northumberland with panoramic views of the Cheviot Hills. An ideal location for walkers and cyclists of all abilities. We provide guided walks, packed lunches and evening meals on request.

● Rothbury

☛⌂ Well Strand, NE65 7UD
☎ 01669 620794 (Helen & David Edes)
Map 81/056016
BB **B** ✗ nearby SI DI TI Closed Xmas Ⓓ ⊗ 🚗 ❗ 🅗

☛⌂ Beechy Hedge, 18 Cragside View, NE65 7YU
☎ 07896 061949 (Freda Bettany)
www.beechyhedge.co.uk Map 81/054018
BB **A** ✗ book first £10, 6-8pm SI DI TI Closed Jan-Mar
Ⓥ Ⓑ Ⓓ ⊗ 🐾🍴 🅗 Ⓜ

● Stannersburn

☆ ☛⌂ **The Pheasant Inn**
NE48 IDD ☎ 01434 240382
www.thepheasantinn.com Map 80/721866
BB **D** ✗ £7.95-£15, 7-9pm D4 T/S3 FI Closed Xmas
Ⓥ Ⓑ 🐾🍴🅗 ◆◆◆◆Ⓢ

380-year-old traditional family-run country inn bursting with character and charm, beamed ceiling, open fires.
Bar lunches and evening meals available daily.
Excellent area for walking and cycling in and around Kielder Water and Forest.

● Twice Brewed (Haltwhistle)

☛⌂ Saughy Rigg Farm, NE49 9PT ☎ 01434 344120 (Kath Dowle)
www.saughyrigg.co.uk Map 86,87/755675
BB **C** ✗ book first £15, 7-9pm SI DI D4 T4 F2 Closed Xmas
Ⓥ Ⓑ Ⓓ 🐾🍴 🅗 ◆◆◆◆

● Wark (Hexham)

☆ ☛⌂ **Battlesteads Hotel & Restaurant**
NE48 3LS ☎ 01434 230209 (Richard & Dee Slade)
www.battlesteads.com Map 87/860770
BB **C** ✗ £3.50-£15, 6:30-9:30pm SI D4 T7 F2
Ⓥ Ⓑ Ⓓ 🐾🍴🅗 ★★ Wheelchair access.

Originally built as a farmstead in 1747, this stone-built inn and restaurant features a cosy open fire, sunny walled beer-garden, excellent bar meals and a la carte menus (including vegetarian) using fresh, local produce, good choice of wines, 3 cask ales and a wide range of bottle conditioned beers from local micro-breweries. Situated in quiet village of Wark, 15 miles north of Hexham. 14 bedrooms carefully modernised to provide comfortable accommodation, all en-suite with freeview colour television, ironing boards and hairdryer. Four ground floor rooms specifically for visitors with disabilities and close to parking.

● Warkworth (Morpeth)
Bide a While, 4 Beal Croft, NE65 0XL ☎ 01665 711753 (Mrs D Graham)
Map 81/249053 BB **B** ✗ nearby DI TI FI Ⓑ Ⓓ ⊗ 🚗 🅗

● West Woodburn (Hexham)

☛⌂ Yellow House Farm, NE48 2SB ☎ 01434 270070 (Avril A Walton)
www.yellowhousebandb.co.uk Map 80/898870
BB **C** ✗ nearby DI TI FI Ⓑ Ⓓ ⊗ 🐾🍴 🚗 ❗ 🅗 ◆◆◆◆

● Wooler

☆ ☛⌂ **Winton House**
39 Glendale Road, NE71 6DL ☎ 01668 281362 (Terry & Veronica Gilbert)
www.wintonhousebandb.co.uk Map 75/991283
BB **C/D** ✗ nearby D2 TI Closed Dec-Feb
Ⓑ Ⓓ ⊗ 🐾🍴 🚗 ◆◆◆

Charming Edwardian house with spacious, comfortable rooms. Situated on a quiet road close to village centre just 250m from St Cuthbert's Way. Much praised breakfasts, using local produce. Walkers very welcome.

☆ ☛⌂ **Tilldale House**
34/40 High Street, NE71 6BG ☎ 01668 281450 (Julia Devenport)
tilldalehouse@freezone.co.uk Map 75/990281
BB **B/C** ✗ nearby D3 T3
Ⓑ Ⓓ ⊗ 🐾🍴 🚗 ❗ 🅗 ◆◆◆◆ Special diets catered for.

Our stone built 17th C. home offers spacious comfortable en-suite bedrooms. An ideal base for walking, cycling, fishing, golf or riding. Located off the main road, 150 yards from St Cuthbert's Way. Further details on request.

TYNE & WEAR

● Newcastle-upon-Tyne
HADRIAN'S WALL

🏠🍴 Clifton House Hotel, 46 Clifton Rd, NE4 6XH
☎ 0191 2730407 (Caterina Love) Map 88/226639
BB **B/C** ✕ book first £16, 8-9pm S3 D2 T2 F3 ⚡(Newcastle)
Ⓥ Ⓑ Ⓓ🐾🚭🚿🚗❗🛏 ◆◆◆

● Ponteland (Newcastle-upon-Tyne)
HADRIAN'S WALL

Stonehaven Lodge B&B, Prestwick Road Ends, NE20 9BX
☎ 01661 872363 (Brendan Anderson)
Map 88/180717
BB **C** ✕ nearby S1 D1 T2 Ⓑ ⊗ 🐾🚭🚿🚗❗ ★★★★

● South Shields
HADRIAN'S WALL

Seaways Guest House, 91 Ocean Road, NE33 2JL
☎ 0191 4271226 (Karon Dickinson)
seawayshouse@aol.com Map 88/368674
BB **B** ✕ book first £8, 6:30-7pm S2 D3 T2 F2
Ⓥ Ⓑ Ⓓ🐾🚿🚗❗🛏

🏠🍴 Royale Guest House, 13 Urfa Terrace, NE33 2ES
☎ 0191 4559085 (Joe Redhead) Map 88/367676
BB **B** ✕ book first £6, 5-6pm S2 D1 T2 F2
Ⓥ Ⓑ Ⓓ⊗🐾🚭🚿🚗

● Wallsend
HADRIAN'S WALL

🏠🍴 Dorset Arms Hotel, Dorset Avenue, NE28 8DX ☎ 0191 2099754
Map 88/292670
BB **C** ✕ £5.99, 6-9pm S2 D2 T2 F2 ⚡(Wallsend)
Ⓥ Ⓓ🚭🚿🚗❗🛏 ★★

SELF-CATERING

DURHAM

● Barnard Castle

☆ East Briscoe Farm Cottages
☎ 01833 650087 (Emma Wilson)
www.eastbriscoe.co.uk
£130-£470 Sleeps 2-6. 6 cottages.
Beautiful countryside, superb area for walking. 🛏 ★★★★

East Briscoe is a beautiful riverside estate which makes a superb base for walkers in scenic Teesdale. Offering well-equipped, comfortable cottages. Walkers welcome accreditation. Close to many new right to roam areas. Pets welcome in three cottages. Linen, towels and heating included.

☆ Dove Cottage
☎ 0191 5102720 (Stephen Collins)
stephen@collins1899.freeserve.co.uk
£215-£330 Sleeps 2 adults + 2 children. 1 cottage.
Peaceful cottage. Superb walks on doorstep. 🛏

Nestled in a quiet part of the historical market town of Barnard Castle, only a short stroll from the town.

Newly refurbished compact cottage, which is in a perfect location for exploring the walks and reservoirs of the northern Dales.

● Bowes
Mellwaters Barn ☎ 01833 628181 (Mrs S Tavener)
www.mellwatersbarn.co.uk
£110-£330 Sleeps 2-4. 5 cottages.
Spacious cottages, Pennine Way, walking country.
⊗ ★★★★ Guide dogs accepted.

● Cowshill
Lynn Taylor ☎ 01388 537683
ltaylor_blakeleyfield@yahoo.com
£295-£435 Sleeps 4-6. 1 cottage.
Short breaks available. Near Weardale Way. ⊗ 🛏

● Wolsingham

☆ Pasture Cottage
☎ 01388 527864 (Carolyn Ramsbotham)
www.pasturecottage.co.uk
£295-£495 Sleeps 4-6. 1 cottage.
Warm welcome. Relaxing haven for walkers. ⊗ 🛏 ★★★★

Extremely comfortable, well equipped cottage. Sleeps 4-6. Situated in idyllic rural Durham Dales and an AONB.
Lovely walks from cottage. Wolsingham 1 mile. Guests welcome throughout year. Games room. Garden. Parking. Ideal for exploring County Durham/Northumberland.

Mrs M Gardiner ☎ 01388 527538
£150-£233 Sleeps 4. 2 terraced cottages.
Cosy cottages, excellent scenic walking area. ⊗ 🛏 ★★★

NORTHUMBERLAND

Northumbria Byways
☎ 016977 46777 (Vicky Reed)
www.northumbria-byways.com
£170-£1,400 Sleeps 1-10. 145 cottages, apartments, bungalows and castle.
Locations by coast, Cheviots and Hadrian's Wall. Brochure available.

NORTH EAST

● Alnwick

Northumberland Cottage ☎ 0191 2528765 (Anna Scantlebury)
www.northumberland-cottage.com
£380-£480 Sleeps 6. 1 cottage.
Baby/child friendly. Log-burning stove.

● Berwick-upon-Tweed

The Courtyard ☎ 01289 308737 (Mrs J Morton)
www.berwickselfcatering.co.uk
£200-£750 Sleeps 9-12. 1 maisonette..
Special overnight rates for budget walkers. (Berwick-upon-Tweed)
★★★

● Craster

Jill Carden ☎ 020 7272 1720
jill.carden@btinternet.com
£277-£585 Sleeps 6. 1 cottage.
Coastal route, castle views, kingsize bed.

● Embleton

Doxford Farm ☎ 01665 579348 (Sarah Shell)
www.doxfordfarmcottages.com
£175-£550 Sleeps 2-7. 7 cottages.
Quiet, working farm, farm walk and wildlife. ★★★-★★★★

● Newton-by-the-Sea

☆ **Link House Farm Holiday Cottages**
☎ 01665 576820 (Mrs Hellmann)
www.linkhousefarm.com
£280-£880 Sleeps 2-10. 3 cottages, 2 houses, 1 lodge. Closed Dec
Located in an AONB. ★★★★

Secluded, quality cottages on a working farm, 2 minutes' walk from our beautiful, picturesque beach. 2 to 4-bedroom accommodation. Ideal for families and couples. Good central base for touring, sightseeing and walking, or just 'getting away'. Playground. Sorry, no pets.

● Rothbury

NORTHUMBERLAND NATIONAL PARK

The Lodge & Gatehouse
☎ 01669 630210 (Jenny Sordy)
http://alnhamfarm.co.uk
£180-£480 Sleeps 4-6. 2 properties.
Tennis court, fishing. Excellent walking. ★★★★

Bracken Lea Cottage
☎ 01670 519629 (Mr J Dalrymple)
www.brackenleacottage.co.uk
£215-£365 Sleeps 3. 1 cottage.
Walks from door, drying facilities, nearby pub. ★★★

GROUPS

DURHAM

The Rookhope Inn (BB) Rookhope, Weardale DL13 2BG
☎ 01388 517215 (Dale Alderson)
www.rookhope.com Map 87/939428
BB £27, DBB £36 Min 1, max 14. Village inn.
☒ ☒ B D See B&B also.

HOSTELS, BUNKHOUSES & CAMPSITES

DURHAM

Hole House Bunkhouse (B) Eastgate, Weardale
☎ 01388 517184 (Nick & Lorraine Thwaites)
nick@holehousefarm.wanadoo.co.uk Map 92/951398
BB £17.50 ☒ nearby ☒ B D ☒

NORTHUMBERLAND

Shitlington Crag Bunkhouse (B) Wark, Hexham NE48 3QB
☎ 01434 230330 (Jo Marsh)
www.penninewayaccommodation.co.uk
Bednight £10 ☒ ☒ D ☒

WALKING FESTIVAL WALES VALLEYS

14th - 17th September 2007

A fantastic opportunity to explore the Valleys of Rhondda Cynon Taf and Merthyr Tydfil in South Wales. 4 days of guided walks to suit all abilities and interests.

For further details please contact:
www.walkingwalesvalleys.com
E-mail:walkingwalesvalleys@uk2.net

WALES

Long Distance Paths

Cambrian Way ....CAM

Clwydian Way ....CLW

Glyndŵr's Way...................GLN

Isle of Anglesey
Coastal Path ....ANC

Offa's Dyke Path ....OFD

Pembrokeshire
Coast Path ....PSC

Severn Way..........................SVN

Valeways Millennium
Heritage Trail......................VMH

See **Paths & Access p25** for full
details of **LDPs** and waymarks

National Parks

Brecon Beacons
Pembrokeshire Coast
Snowdonia

See **Useful Contacts p99** for full
details of national parks

VIEW OVER MYNYDD ILLTYD COMMON TO PEN-Y-FAN
AND CORN DU NEAR BRECON, POWYS

WALK...   ...THE ALWEN TRAIL

Opened in July, this fully waymarked 11km/7.5-mile trail circles the
Alwen Reservoir near Cerrigydrudion, on the border of Conwy and
Denbighshire. The going is easy on forest tracks and paths along
the water's edge, with fantastic views across the reservoir to the
Snowdonian mountains. From there, it takes walkers up on to moorland
at Mynydd Hiraethog (Denbigh Moors). Illustrated panels around the
route describe the wildlife, culture and even folk tales associated with
the area. But sharp-eyed walkers could also pick out rare black grouse,
lapwing, large heath butterfly and red squirrel along the way.

Part of a scheme to encourage more visitors to this little-known
area of North Wales. Contact Conwy Countryside Service for more
details on ☎ 01492 575123 or visit www.conwy.gov.uk

VISIT...

...THE CENTRE FOR ALTERNATIVE TECHNOLOGY (CAT)

Set in three hectares of the Dyfi Valley, and surrounded by rugged mountains and
unspoilt forests, CAT is located in a remote and breathtaking part of the country near
Machynlleth, Powys – and it's the Centre's intention to keep it that way. Using
interactive displays and educational programmes, it encourages greener transport and
energy production, demonstrating practical, everyday solutions in its own day-to-day
running. The Centre's Straw Bale Theatre offers drama and science workshops for
children, and adults can peruse the state-of-the-art AtEIC (Environmental Information
Centre) showcasing the latest technology for energy and water conservation.

A fascinating stopover for 'eco-hikers' on the Glyndŵr's Way or Dyfi Valley Way.
Visitors arriving by foot, bike, train or even in-line skates receive discounts on
admission. ☎ 0845 330 8373 or visit www.cat.org.uk for full details.

SEE.......THE GREEN LADY OF CAERPHILLY CASTLE

Built in the 13th-century by Gilbert de Clare, lord of Glamorgan,
Caerphilly Castle is one of Western Europe's great medieval
castles and the largest castle in Britain after Windsor. The spirit of
de Clare's wife, Alice de Lusignan, is said to haunt the site. She fell
in love with a prince from the nearby village of Brithdir, but died
of a broken heart when he was hanged by her husband. Now on
frosty mornings a green lady appears on the ruins of the north-
west tower gazing towards Brithdir in search of her lost love.

Close to the Taff Trail and Cambrian Way. For opening times
and admission, call Caerphilly Visitor Centre on ☎ 029 2088 0011
or visit www.caerphillycastle.org.uk

WALES

LOCAL RAMBLERS GROUPS... Bunny Walks are six new short walks around the Llantrisant area
in Rhondda Cynon Taf devised by Taff Ely (Llantrisant) Group. All are 4–6km/2.5–4 miles long and
well detailed in a series of free leaflets. To order, see p94... **Eryri 20.30 organise family-friendly
walks in north Wales all year round, with many also suitable for buggies. Contact them for
a full programme (p82)...** Cardiff and South Gwent Groups have both set up monthly walks for
the visually impaired in south-east Wales. Contact either Group for further information (p81).

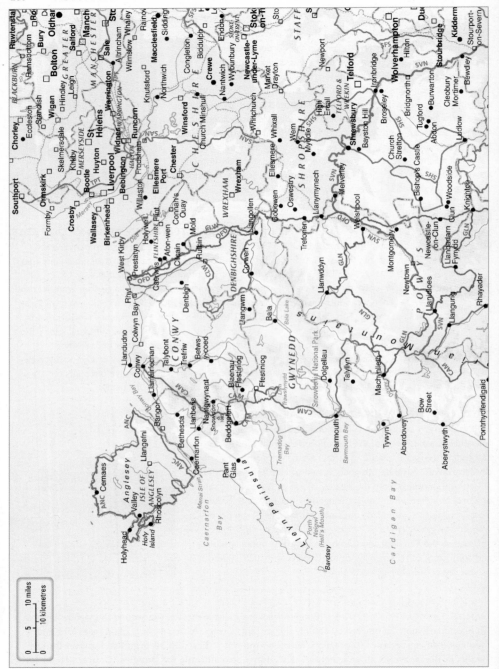

MAP 267

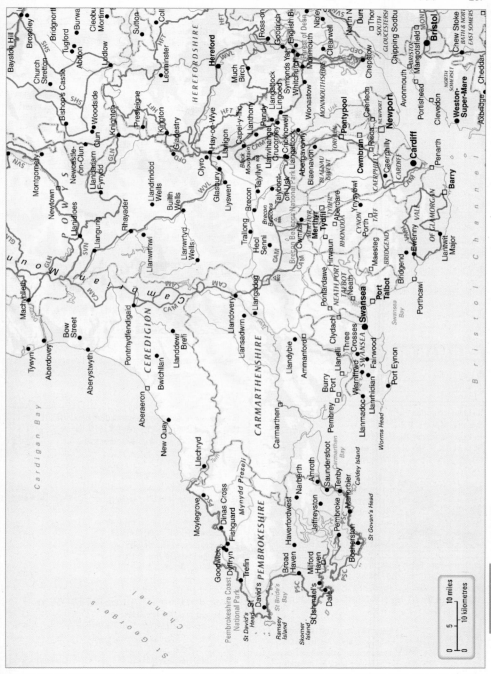

BED & BREAKFAST

ANGLESEY

● Cemaes
ISLE OF ANGLESEY COASTAL PATH

Tredolphin Guest House, Cemaes Bay, LL67 0ET
☎ 01407 710388 (Frances & Bill O'Donnell)   Map 114/370935
BB **C** ✗ nearby S2 D2 T1 F2 Closed Xmas
Ⓑ Ⓓ ⊗ 🐾🦮👜 ★★★ Guide dogs welcome.

● Holyhead
ISLE OF ANGLESEY COASTAL PATH

Quayside Guest House, 3 Stanley Crescent, LL65 1DD
☎ 01407 769202 (Ken Collett) quayside3@tiscali.co.uk Map 114/248827
BB **B** ✗ nearby D1 T4 ∿∿(Holyhead) Ⓥ   Ⓓ🐾👜🚗∿

● Rhoscolyn (Holyhead)
ISLE OF ANGLESEY COASTAL PATH

Glan Towyn, LL65 2NJ ☎ 01407 860380 (Carol Gough)
www.glantowyn-rhoscolyn.co.uk Map 114/272752
BB **B/C** ✗ nearby S1 D2 T1 Closed Nov-Jan Ⓑ ⊗ 🐾👜🚗! ★★★

● Valley (Holyhead)
ISLE OF ANGLESEY COASTAL PATH

Ty Mawr, LL65 3HH ☎ 01407 740235 (Anne Lloyd)
www.angleseybedandbreakfast.co.uk Map 114/296784
BB **C** ✗ nearby D1 T1 Closed Xmas-Jan ∿∿(Valley) Ⓓ ⊗ 👜🚗∿ ★★★

CARMARTHENSHIRE

● Llandovery
BRECON BEACONS
CAMBRIAN WAY

☆ LLanerchindda Farm
Cynghordy, SA20 0NB ☎ 01550 750274 (Lynn & Martin Hadley)
www.cambrianway.com Map 160/808429
BB **D** ✗ £14.50, 7pm S1 D3 T3 F2 ∿∿(Cynghordy)
Ⓥ Ⓑ Ⓓ🐾👜🚗!∿Ⓜ ★★

Family-run guesthouse with experienced new management and spectacular views. En-suite bedrooms, comfortable lounge bar, excellent homecooked food, log fires, drying room, map room, ideal base for exploring mid/south Wales. Self-catering cottages also available. Special mid-week offers.

☆ Dan-y-Parc Farm Guest House
Cynghordy, SA20 0LD ☎ 01550 720401 (Diane Brown)
www.danyparcholidays.co.uk Map 146,160/795378
BB **B** ✗ book first £15, 7pm S1 D1 T1 F1 Closed Xmas ∿∿(Llandovery)
Ⓥ Ⓑ Ⓓ🐾👜🚗!∿ ★★★

Beautifully situated 17th C. farmhouse bordering the Brecon Beacons and Cambrian mountains. Comfortable en-suite rooms with tea/coffee facilities, hearty cooked breakfasts & homemade evening meals. Woodland walk and many waymarked routes nearby. Pets very welcome.

● Llandybie

☆ The Glynhir Estate
Glynhir Mansion, Glynhir Road, SA18 2TD ☎ 01269 850438 (Justine Jenkins)
www.theglynhirestate.com Map 159/639152
BB **D** ✗ book first £17 for groups of 6+ only, 7pm S1 D3 T1 F2
Closed Xmas ∿∿(Llandybie) Ⓥ Ⓑ Ⓓ 🐾🚗 !

200-acre estate nestling in the foothills of the Black Mountains. Explore its secret valleys and rivers – wonderful walking country with spectacular scenery and plenty of wildlife. Perfect for groups, excellent homecooked food and a large private car park.

● Llansadwrn (Llanwrda)

☆ Myrtle Hill
SA19 8HL ☎ 01550 777530 (Lizzie Johnson)
www.myrtlehillhouse.com Map 146,160/696316
BB **C** ✗ nearby D2 T1 ∿∿(Llanwrda)
Ⓥ Ⓑ Ⓓ ⊗ 🐾👜🚗!∿

Comfortable, cosy Georgian farmhouse in stunning and secluded location. Ideal base for walking locally in Carmarthen Fans or exploring Brecon Beacons and Pembrokeshire. All rooms en-suite. Pub 100 yards. Also available: self-contained cottage, sleeps 4-6. Brochure on request.

CEREDIGION

● Aberystwyth

Marine Hotel, Promenade, Marine Terrace, SY23 2BX ☎ 0800 0190020 (Freephone) www.marinehotelaberystwyth.co.uk Map 135/583821
BB **D** ✗ £8-£18.95, 6:30-8:30pm S6 D24 T6 F12 ∿∿(Aberystwyth)
Ⓥ Ⓑ Ⓓ🐾👜🚗!∿Ⓜ Wheelchair access.

● Bow Street (Aberystwyth)

Garreg Lwyd, Penygarn, SY24 5BE
☎ 01970 828830 (Mrs A Edwards) Map 135/625852
BB **B/C** ✗ nearby S1 D1 T1 F1 ∿∿(Aberystwyth) Ⓓ 🐾👜∿ ★★

● Llanddewi Brefi (Tregaron)
Ffynnonddewi, SY25 6NZ ☎ 01570 493269
www.ffynnonddewi.net Map 146/645545
BB **C** ✗ book first £20, 7pm D2 T1
Ⓥ Ⓑ Ⓓ ⊗ 🐾👜🚗!∿

● Llechryd (Cardigan)
Glanhelyg, SA43 2NJ ☎ 01239 682482 (Kath Sapey & Ann Williamson)
www.glanhelyg.co.uk Map 145/211444
BB **B** ✗ book first £12.50, 7pm S2 D1 T2 Closed Dec-Feb Ⓥ ⊗ 🐾∿

● New Quay
Ty Hen Farm, Llwyndafydd, SA44 6BZ ☎ 01545 560346 (Roni Kelly)
www.tyhencottages.co.uk Map 145/365553
BB **C** ✗ nearby D1 T1 Closed Nov-Mar
Ⓑ Ⓓ ⊗ 👜∿ Indoor pool. See SC also.

● Pontrhydfendigaid (Ystrad Meurig)
CAMBRIAN WAY

☆ 🖛🝙 **Black Lion Hotel**
Mill St, SY25 6BE ☎ 01974 831624 (Giles Polglase)
www.blacklionhotel.co.uk Map 135,147/731666
BB **D** ✕ £7.50, 5-9pm D2 T2 F1
Ⓥ Ⓑ Ⓓ 🚗🛏🥛! 🐾 Ⓜ ★★★

The Black Lion Inn is set in a fold of the Cambrian Mountains close to Strata Florida Abbey and Cors Caron Nature Reserve. Log fire, beamed ceilings and traditional music. Homemade food & real ale. Guided/self-guided walks arranged.

CONWY

● Betws-y-Coed
SNOWDONIA/ERYRI

☆ 🖛🝙 **Fairy Glen Hotel**
Beaver Bridge, LL24 0SH ☎ 01690 710269 (Mr & Mrs B Youe)
www.fairyglenhotel.co.uk Map 115/799547
BB **C** ✕ book first £16, 7pm S1 D5 T1 F1 Closed Dec-Feb
🚶(Betws-y-Coed) Ⓥ Ⓑ Ⓓ 🚗🛏 ★★

Built in the 17th C., commended for its food and hospitality in the 21st C. The hotel where you can enjoy your walking, relaxation and food. Residents licensed bar. Private car park.
fairyglen@youe.fsworld.co.uk

🖛🝙 Glan Llugwy, LL24 0BN ☎ 01690 710592 (Graham & Jean Brayne)
jean@glanllugwy.fsnet.co.uk Map 115/784565
BB **B** ✕ nearby S1 D2 T1 F1 Closed Xmas 🚶(Betws-y-Coed)
Ⓓ 🚗🛏🥛🚗! ★★★

☆ 🖛🝙 **The Ferns Guest House**
LL24 0AN ☎ 01690 710587 (Lynn & David Taylor)
www.ferns-guesthouse.co.uk Map 115/795562
BB **C** ✕ nearby D6 T1 F2 🚶(Betws-y-Coed)
Ⓑ Ⓓ 🚗🛏🥛 ★★★★

The Ferns Guest House is conveniently situated in the village of Betws-y-Coed. 9 en-suite rooms comfortably furnished and including TV, beverage trays, clocks and hairdryers. Your hosts Lynn and David offer the warmest hospitality with an emphasis on service and comfort.

🖛🝙 The Old Courthouse, Henllys, Old Church Rd, LL24 0AL ☎ 01690 710534 (Mark & Gillian Bidwell) www.guesthouse-snowdonia.co.uk Map 115/795568
BB **D** ✕ nearby D7 T1 F1 Closed Jan 🚶(Betws-y-Coed)
Ⓑ Ⓓ 🚗🛏🥛! Ⓜ ★★★

The Park Hill, Lanrwst Rd, LL24 0HD ☎ 01690 710540 (Jaap & Ghislaine Buis)
www.park-hill.co.uk Map 116/801565
BB **C/D** ✕ book first £19, 7pm D6 T3 🚶(Betws-y-Coed)
Ⓥ Ⓑ Ⓓ 🚗🛏🥛! ★★★

☆ 🖛🝙 **Afon View Non Smokers Guest House**
Holyhead Road, LL24 0AN ☎ 01690 710726 (Keith Roobottom)
www.afon-view.co.uk Map 115/795562
BB **D** ✕ nearby S1 D4 T1 F1 🚶(Betws-y-Coed)
Ⓑ Ⓓ 🚗🛏🥛! ◆◆◆◆

A warm welcome awaits you from your host Keith. Mountain bike hire is available nearby — secure overnight storage. You can choose from four-poster, twin, doubles and single room, all with en-suite shower. Guests who appreciate a relaxed, comfortable environment are well cared for here.

Bryn Bella Guest House, Lon Muriau, Llanwrst Rd, LL24 0HD
☎ 01690 710627 (Mark Edwards)
www.bryn-bella.co.uk Map 116/800565
BB **D** ✕ nearby D5 Closed Xmas 🚶(Betws-y-Coed)
Ⓑ Ⓓ 🚗🛏🥛🚗 Ⓜ ★★★★

● Conwy
CAMBRIAN WAY

☆ **Glan Heulog Guest House**
Llanwrst Road, LL32 8LT ☎ 01492 593845 (Stan & Vivien Watson-Jones)
www.walesbandb.co.uk Map 115/779772
BB **C** ✕ nearby D4 T2 F1 Closed Xmas 🚶(Conwy)
Ⓥ Ⓑ Ⓓ 🚗🛏🥛! 🐾 ★★★

Beautiful Victorian house coveniently situated in the World Heritage town of Conwy. Non-Smoking en- suite rooms, centrally heated with TV, beverage trays, clock radio and hairdryers. Lounge and conservatory to relax in. Car parking.

● Llandudno
CAMBRIAN WAY

🖛🝙 Vine House, 23 Church Walks, LL30 2HG
☎ 01492 876493 (Amanda Jacob)
www.vinehouse.org.uk Map 115/778827
BB **B** ✕ nearby D2 F2 🚶(Llandudno)
Ⓑ Ⓓ 🚗🛏🥛! 🐾 ◆◆◆

● Llanfairfechan
SNOWDONIA/ERYRI
CAMBRIAN WAY

☆ 🖛🝙 **Rhiwiau Isaf**
LL33 0EH ☎ 01248 681143 (Ruth Carrington)
www.rhiwiau.co.uk Map 115/678732
BB **C** ✕ book first £12.50, 6:15-8pm S2 D2 T2 F2 🚶(Llanfairfechan)
Ⓥ Ⓑ Ⓓ 🚗🛏🥛! 🐾 ★★

Set in secluded valley only 5 minutes from A55. Views across the Menai Straits to Anglesey. Walk through our 16 acres of woods onto the Snowdonia National Park, Carneddau and North Wales Path. Extremely comfortable en-suite rooms (all non-smoking). Own car park.

WALES

● Trefriw
SNOWDONIA/ERYRI

☆ ◄ Crafnant Guest House
LL27 0JH ☎ 01492 640809 (Mike & Jan Bertenshaw)
www.trefriw.co.uk Map 115/780631
BB **C** ✕ nearby D3 T1 F1 Closed Dec-Jan ₩(Llanrwst)
Ⓥ Ⓑ Ⓓ ⊛ 🍵☕🚗❗ ★★★

Whether you've discovered the mountain lakes which nestle above our village, conquered Snowdon or just strolled in the stunning Conwy Valley then rest assured of the comfort and warm welcome of Crafnant House. All bedrooms have cast-iron beds with fresh white linen.

GWYNEDD

● Aberdovey
SNOWDONIA/ERYRI

Awel Y Mor, 4 Bodfor Terrace, LL35 0EA ☎ 01654 767058 (Jennifer Johnson)
www.awelymor-aberdovey.co.uk Map 135/612959
BB **C/D** ✕ nearby S1 D3 T2 F1 ₩(Aberdovey)
Ⓑ Ⓓ ⊛ 🍵☕🚗🛶 ★★★

● Bala
SNOWDONIA/ERYRI

☆ Frondderw Country House
Stryd y Fron , LL23 7YD ☎ 01678 520301 (Paul Short)
www.frondderwhouse.co.uk Map 125/915361
BB **D** ✕ £26 S1 D4 T1 F1 Closed Xmas
Ⓥ Ⓑ Ⓓ ⊛ 🍵☕ ★★★★

Enjoying spectacular lake & mountain views, our early 17th C. Dower House is an ideal base for touring and walking holidays. Fully refurbished. Off street parking. Imaginative cuisine and outstanding wine list. Close to many local walks & attractions.

● Barmouth
SNOWDONIA/ERYRI
CAMBRIAN WAY

◄ The Gables, Mynach Rd, LL42 1RL ☎ 01341 280553 (Mrs D Lewis)
Map 124/609166
BB **C** ✕ nearby S1 D2 F1 Closed Dec-Feb ₩(Barmouth)
Ⓑ Ⓓ ⊛ 🍵☕🚗🛶

☆ Lawrenny Lodge
Aberamffra Road, LL42 1SU ☎ 01341 280466 (Toby & Chantal Simpson)
www.lawrennylodge.co.uk Map 124/617156
BB **D** ✕ £10, 6:30-8pm S1 D4 T2 F1 ₩(Barmouth)
Ⓥ Ⓑ Ⓓ ⊛ 🍵☕🛶 ★★Ⓦ

Lawrenny Lodge is situated in a quiet area of Barmouth overlooking Cardigan Bay and the Mawddach estuary.
Five minutes' walk from beach, town and harbour area.
We offer 7 en-suite rooms with TV and tea/coffee making facilities.

● Beddgelert (Caernarfon)
SNOWDONIA/ERYRI
CAMBRIAN WAY

☆ Plas Tan Y Graig
Smith Street, LL55 4LT ☎ 01766 890310 (Tony Love)
www.plas-tanygraig.co.uk Map 115/591482
BB **C** ✕ nearby D1 T/D3 F3
Ⓑ Ⓓ ⊛ 🍵☕Ⓜ

Comfortable Victorian house, village-centre location, surrounded by beautiful scenery, ideal base for activities in Snowdonia.

Our dining room and guest lounge provide a peaceful setting to enjoy a hearty homecooked breakfast, or end the day with a glass of wine.

● Blaenau Ffestiniog
SNOWDONIA/ERYRI
CAMBRIAN WAY

☆ ◄ Bryn Elltyd Guest House
Tanygrisiau, LL41 3TW ☎ 01766 831356 (Ann & Bob Cole)
www.accommodation-snowdonia.com Map 124/681448
BB **C** ✕ book first £12, 7.30pm S1 D2 T2 F1 ₩(Blaenau Ffestiniog)
Ⓥ Ⓑ Ⓓ ⊛ 🍵☕❗🛶Ⓜ ★★★ Guided walks.

One of the leading environmentally-friendly guest houses in Wales, located in a secluded mountain setting in the centre of Snowdonia National Park, ideal for all outdoor activities. Sauna, drying room, evening meals & packed lunches. Discount for ramblers and groups.

☆ ◄ Cae Du
Manod, LL41 4BB ☎ 01766 830847 (Chris Carswell & Sue Ashe)
www.caedu.co.uk Map 124/709438
BB **B** ✕ book first £14, 7pm D2 T1 Closed Xmas ₩(Blaenau Ffestiniog)
Ⓥ Ⓑ Ⓓ ⊛ 🍵☕❗ ★★★

Picturesque 16th C. former farmhouse in magnificent mountain setting. Stunning panoramic views, comfortable en-suite rooms, log fires, 2 lounges, satellite TV, private parking. Beautiful mature gardens & ponds. Centrally located for exploring Snowdonia with varied walks direct from Cae Du, guide if required. Great views, great walks, great homecooking, all make for ramblers to unwind with Chris & Sue. "It's our home — make it yours."

● Caernarfon

◄ Tegfan B&B, 4 Church Street, LL55 1SW ☎ 01286 673703
tegfanbb@yahoo.co.uk Map 114/476628
BB **B** ✕ nearby S2 D2 T2 F2
Ⓥ Ⓑ ⊛ 🍵☕🚗 ★

● Dolgellau
SNOWDONIA/ERYRI
CAMBRIAN WAY

☆ **Dwy Olwyn**
Coed-y-Fronallt, LL40 2YG ☎ 01341 422822 (Mrs N Jones)
www.dwyolwyn.co.uk Map 124/734183
BB **B/C** ✗ book first £13, 7pm D1 T1 F2 Closed Dec
Ⓥ Ⓓ ⊛ 🐾🛏♿ ★★★

"View of Cader Idris from Dwy Olwyn." A warm welcome awaits you in this comfortable guesthouse, set in an acre of landscaped gardens. Peaceful position only 10 mins walk into town. Ideal for touring Snowdonia NP, sandy beaches, gauge railways, RSPB sanctuary, picturesque walks including famous Precipice Walk above Mawddach estuary. Spacious bedrooms with colour TV, clock radio, hairdryer. Good home-cooking. Lounge with selection of maps, guide books and leaflets. Cleanliness and personal attention assured. Car parking.

☆ **Ivy House**
Finsbury Square, LL40 1RF ☎ 01341 422535 (J S & M Bamford)
www.ukworld.net/ivyhouse Map 124/727177
BB **B** ✗ book first £16, 6:30-7:30pm D3 T2 F1 Closed Xmas
Ⓥ Ⓑ Ⓓ ⊛ 🐾🛏♿ ! 🐕 ◆◆◆

At the centre of an idyllic walking area, a country town guesthouse, offering home made food: big breakfasts, evening meals & packed lunches. Fully centrally heated, all bedrooms have TV, hairdryers and tea/coffee making facilities, most en-suite. Email: marg.bamford@btconnect.com

Tanyfron, Arran Road, LL40 2AA ☎ 01341 422638 (Elfed & Sue Rowlands)
www.tanyfron.co.uk Map 124/735176
BB **C** ✗ nearby D1 T1 F1 Closed Jan Ⓑ Ⓓ ⊛ ♿ ★★★★

🐾 Fronallt, LL40 2YL ☎ 01341 422296 (Ewyn Price)
ewynprice@aol.com Map 124/730182
BB **C** ✗ nearby D1 T/F1 Closed Dec Ⓥ Ⓑ Ⓓ ♿ 🚗 ! 🐕 ★★★

● Llanberis (Caernarfon)
SNOWDONIA/ERYRI

Mount Pleasant Hotel, High Street, LL55 4HA ☎ 01286 870395
www.waterton.org.uk/mph Map 114,115/577602
BB **B/C** ✗ £15, 6-9pm S2 D2 T1 F2 Ⓥ Ⓑ Ⓓ 🐾🛏🚗 ! 🐕

🐾 Snowdon Cottage, 7 Pentre Castell, LL55 4UB
☎ 01286 872015 (Carol Anne Gerrard) Map 115/585596
BB **B** ✗ book first S1 D1 T1 Ⓥ Ⓓ ⊛ 🐾🛏🚗 🐕 Ⓜ

● Nantgwynant (Caernarfon)
SNOWDONIA/ERYRI

Pen-y-Gwryd Hotel, Pen-y-Gwryd, LL55 4NT ☎ 01286 870211 & 870768
www.pyg.co.uk Map 115/660558
BB **D** ✗ book first £25, 7:30pm S1 D8 T6 F1 Closed Xmas
Ⓥ Ⓑ Ⓓ 🐾 🐕 ★★ Closed weekdays Jan-Feb.

● Pant Glas (Garndolbenmaen)
SNOWDONIA/ERYRI

☆ 🐾 **Hen Ysgol (Old School)**
Bwlch Derwin, LL51 9EQ ☎ 01286 660701 (Terry & Sue Gibbins)
www.oldschool-henyysgol.co.uk Map 123,115/456474
BB **C/D** ✗ book first £15-£18, 7pm D1 T1 F1 Closed Xmas
Ⓥ Ⓑ Ⓓ ⊛ 🐾🛏🚗 ! 🐕 ★★★

A beautiful, historical 'Welsh Not' Country School provides a unique base for walking the re-opened network of paths linking Snowdonia with Lleyn Peninsular & Bardsey Island. Delicious homecooked evening meals & choice of breakfast menu. Terry & Sue offer a warm welcome.

● Talyllyn (Tywyn)
SNOWDONIA/ERYRI
CAMBRIAN WAY

Dolffanog Fawr Country House, LL36 9AJ ☎ 01654 761247 (Lorraine Hinkins)
www.dolffanogfawr.co.uk Map 124/729104
BB **D** ✗ book first £19, 7pm D2 T2 Closed Dec-Feb
Ⓥ Ⓑ Ⓓ ⊛ 🐾🛏♿ 🚗 🐕 ★★★★

● Tywyn
SNOWDONIA/ERYRI
CAMBRIAN WAY

Hendy Farm, LL36 9RU ☎ 01654 710457 (Anne Lloyd-Jones)
www.hendyfarmholidays.co.uk Map 135/594013
BB **C** ✗ nearby D2 T1 Closed Nov-Mar 🚍(Tywyn)
Ⓑ Ⓓ ⊛ ♿ ! 🐕 ★★★

MONMOUTHSHIRE

● Abergavenny
BRECON BEACONS
CAMBRIAN WAY

🐾 The Guest House, 2 Oxford Street, NP7 5RP ☎ 01873 854823
(Jenny Taylor) theguesthouseabergavenny@hotmail.com Map 161/303147
BB **B** S1 D2 T3 F1 🚍(Abergavenny) Ⓓ 🐾🛏🚗 ! 🐕 ★

🐾 Park Guest House, 36 Hereford Road, NP7 5RA ☎ 01873 853715
(Neil & Julia Herring) www.parkguesthouse.co.uk Map 161/303146
BB **B/C/D** ✗ nearby S1 D4 T1 F1 Closed Xmas 🚍(Abergavenny)
Ⓑ Ⓓ ⊛ 🐾🛏♿ ★★

● Chepstow
OFFA'S DYKE

🐾 Upper Sedbury House, Sedbury Lane, Sedbury, NP16 7HN
☎ 01291 627173 (Christine Potts)
www.smoothound.co.uk/hotels/uppersed.html Map 172/547943
BB **D** ✗ nearby D3 T2 F1 Closed Xmas 🚍(Chepstow)
Ⓑ Ⓓ ⊛ 🐾🛏! 🐕 ★★

🐾 Southam, Welsh Street, Chepstow, NP16 5LU
☎ 01291 621162 (Maureen & Richard Langston)
maureenlangston@hotmail.com Map 172,162/527943
BB **C/D** ✗ nearby D2 T1 F1 Closed Xmas Ⓑ Ⓓ ⊛ 🐾🛏!

● Llanfihangel Crucorney (Abergavenny)
BRECON BEACONS
OFFA'S DYKE

Penyclawdd Farm, NP7 7LB ☎ 01873 890591 (Ann Davies)
www.penyclawdd.co.uk Map 161/312200
BB **C** ✗ nearby S/D/F1 D2 T2 F1 Closed Xmas 🚍(Abergavenny)
Ⓑ Ⓓ ⊛ 🐾🛏🚗 ! 🐕 ★★★

WALES

● Llangattock-Lingoed (Abergavenny)

BRECON BEACONS
OFFA'S DYKE

The Old Rectory, NP7 8RR ☎ 01873 821326 (Karen Ball)
www.rectoryonoffasdyke.co.uk Map 161/362201
BB **B/C** ✕ book first £12.50, 6:30-7pm S1 D2 T1
Ⓥ Ⓑ Ⓓ ⊗ 🍴🫖🛁🚗! ★★★

● Llanthony (Abergavenny)

BRECON BEACONS
OFFA'S DYKE & CAMBRIAN WAY

🚶◀ The Half Moon Hotel, NP7 7NN ☎ 01873 890611 (George Lawrence)
halfmoon@llanthony.wanadoo.co.uk Map 161/287276
BB **B** ✕ £5+, 7-9pm S1 D4 T4 F1 Ⓥ Ⓑ Ⓓ 🍴🫖🛁🚗!🚲

● Monmouth

OFFA'S DYKE & WYE VALLEY WALK

☆ 🚶◀ **Church Farm Guest House**
Mitchel Troy, NP25 4HZ ☎ 01600 712176 (Rosey & Derek Ringer)
www.churchfarmmitcheltroy.co.uk Map 162/492103
BB **C** ✕ book first £15, 7-7:30pm S2 D3 T2 F3 Closed Xmas
Ⓥ Ⓑ Ⓓ ⊗ 🍴🫖🛁🚗!🚲 Ⓜ ◆◆◆

Set in large garden with stream, a 16th C.
former farmhouse with oak beams and
inglenook fireplaces. Excellent base for Wye
Valley, Forest of Dean, Black Mountains.
Central heating. Mainly en-suite bedrooms.
Groups welcome (discounts available).
Also self-catering unit.

🚶◀ Penylan Farm, The Hendre, NP25 5NL ☎ 01600 716435
(Cathy & Dave Bowen) www.penylanfarm.co.uk Map 161/445162
BB **C** ✕ book first £12, 7:30pm D1 T1 F1 Closed Xmas
Ⓥ Ⓑ Ⓓ ⊗ 🍴🫖🛁🚗! ◆◆◆◆ See Hendre in SC also.

Ramblers Rest, 7 Levitsfield Close, NP25 5BZ ☎ 01600 715611 (Mrs MC Atkins)
secretswd@hotmail.com Map 162/496133
BB **C** ✕ book first £7.50 S1 D1 T1 Ⓥ Ⓑ Ⓓ ⊗ 🍴🫖🛁🚗 Ⓜ

● Pandy (Abergavenny)

BRECON BEACONS
OFFA'S DYKE

Brynhonddu Country House B&B, Bwlch Trewyn Estate, NP7 7PD
☎ 01873 890535 (Carol White) www.brynhonddu.co.uk Map 161/326224
BB **C** ✕ nearby S1 D2 T1 Closed Xmas
Ⓑ Ⓓ 🍴🫖🛁🚗 🚲 ★★★

● Wonastow (Monmouth)

OFFA'S DYKE & WYE VALLEY WALK

☆ 🚶◀ **Old Hendre Farm B&B**
NP25 4DJ ☎ 01600 740447 (Val Barrell)
valerie@ohfs.fsnet.co.uk Map 161/460123
BB **C** ✕ book first £10-£12, 7-9pm S1 D2 T1 Closed Nov-Feb
Ⓥ Ⓑ Ⓓ ⊗ 🍴🫖🛁🚗!🚲 Horses welcome.

Modern farmhouse in quiet location on
Offa's Dyke. Ideal base for exploring
local walks and places of interest in
north Monmouthshire.
All rooms ensuite with colour TV and
courtesy tray. Full English or vegetarian
breakfast. Dogs and horses welcome.

NORTH EAST WALES

● Bodfari (Mold)

OFFA'S DYKE & CLWYDIAN WAY

🚶◀ Moel-y-Park, Mountain View, The Bungalow, Afon-Wen, CH7 5UB
☎ 01352 720338 (Mrs HL Priestley)
www.afonwen-guesthouse.co.uk Map 116/127716
BB **B** ✕ nearby D2 T1 Closed Xmas ⊗ 🍴🫖🛁🚗

● Caerwys (Mold)

OFFA'S DYKE

🚶◀ Plas Penucha, CH7 5BH ☎ 01352 720210 (Mrs N Price)
www.plaspenucha.co.uk Map 116/108733
BB **C** ✕ book first £16, 7pm S4 D2 T2 Closed Xmas
Ⓥ Ⓑ Ⓓ ⊗ 🍴🫖🛁🚗!🚲 ★★★

● Cilcain

CLWYDIAN WAY & OFFA'S DYKE

🚶◀ Ashview House, 1 Lon Cilan, CH7 5PL ☎ 01352 740979
(Fiona & Ray Wright) fiona-ray@ashview.wanadoo.co.uk Map 116/177655
BB **A** ✕ nearby S1 D2 Ⓑ Ⓓ ⊗ 🍴🫖🛁🚗!

● Corwen

CLWYDIAN WAY

Corwen Court Private Hotel, London Road, LL21 0DP ☎ 01490 412854
Map 125/080434
BB **A** S6 D4 Closed Dec-Feb Ⓑ Ⓓ 🍴🫖 🚲

☆ 🚶◀ **Bron-y-Graig**
LL21 0DR ☎ 01490 413007
www.north-wales-hotel.co.uk Map 125/082433
BB **D** ✕ book first £18, 6:30-9pm S/D/T8 F2
Ⓥ Ⓑ Ⓓ 🍴🫖🛁🚗!🚲 ◆◆◆◆◆Ⓦ

Bron-y-Graig is a
superbly located AA
5-Diamond guest
house set in the
Upper Dee Valley
between Llangollen
and Bala — ideal for
Offa's Dyke, Clwydian
Way, the Berwyns
and the Dee Valley —
on the edge of
Snowdonia National
Park.

Its 10 en-suite luxury
bedrooms can be
configured as single, double, twin or triple rooms. Prices are £29.50pppn for bed
and breakfast, single rooms are £39.50pppn.

Chose from our excellent a la carte menu and take dinner, bed and breakfast at
£39.50pppn (see www.northwales-wales-hotel.co.uk for full details and
conditions).

Member of Walkers' Welcome Scheme with minibus available.

● Denbigh
CLWYDIAN WAY

Cayo Guest House, 74 Vale Street, LL16 3BW ☎ 01745 812686
stay@cayo.co.uk Map 116/055663
BB **B** ✗ nearby S1 D2 T2 Closed Xmas Ⓑ ⊗ 🍴👤🔥🚗🛁 ★★★

● Holywell
Gerddi Bueno Guest House, Whitford Street, CH8 7NJ
☎ 01352 712392 (Pamela Hunt) Map 116/182760
BB **B** ✗ book first £5, 5:30-8:30pm S2 D1 T1 F1 Ⓥ Ⓓ🍴👤🔥🚗🛁

● Llangollen
CLWYDIAN WAY & OFFA'S DYKE

☆ ✉= **New Ross**
Dinbren Rd, LL20 8TF ☎ 01978 861334 (Mrs EA Roberts)
www.newrossllan.co.uk Map 117/217418
BB **C** ✗ nearby D2 T1 Closed Xmas
Ⓑ Ⓓ⊗🍴👤🔥🚗! ★★★★

Set in a spectacular location by Offa's Dyke Path and overlooking Llangollen marina. The warm welcome and excellent breakfast inspired one visitor to comment "wonderful, friendly, relaxing B&B. Immaculate and with views to die for".

Squirrels, Abbey Rd, LL20 8SP ☎ 01978 869041 (Lilian Speake)
www.squirrels-b-and-b.co.uk Map 117/211423
BB **C** ✗ nearby D3 T2 Ⓑ Ⓓ⊗🍴👤🔥🚗🛁 ★★★

☆ **Oakmere**
Regent Street, LL20 8HS ☎ 01978 861126 (Lyndsey Knibbs)
www.oakmere.llangollen.co.uk Map 117/218418
BB **C** ✗ nearby D4 T2
Ⓑ Ⓓ⊗🍴👤🔥🚗! ◆◆◆◆

Large country house set in its own grounds, five minutes' walk from Llangollen's town centre. Easy access to Offa's Dyke and the Dee Valley Way. Rooms either en-suite or with private facilities providing a relaxing atmosphere of spacious comfort. Private parking and non-smoking.

● Llangwm (Corwen)
Bryn Awel B&B, LL21 0RB ☎ 01490 420610 (Jenni Miller)
www.brynawelbnb.co.uk Map 125/963439
BB **B** S1 D1 T1 Closed Xmas
Ⓓ⊗🍴👤🔥🚗! ★★ Walking routes, notes & maps available.

PEMBROKESHIRE

● Amroth (Narberth)
PEMBROKESHIRE COAST PATH & NATIONAL PARK

Ashdale Guest House, SA67 8NA ☎ 01834 813853 (Roy & Edith Williamson)
Map 158/160071
BB **B** ✗ book first £9.95, 6pm S1 D4 T3 F0 Closed Nov-Feb ⋙(Kilgetty)
Ⓓ🛁🚗!

● Bosherston (Pembroke)
PEMBROKESHIRE COAST PATH & NATIONAL PARK

St Govan's Country Inn, SA71 5DN ☎ 01646 661643 (Marcia Giardelli)
trefalen@trefalen.force9.co.uk Map 158/966947
BB **D** ✗ £8, 6:30-9pm S4 D2 T2 F1 Ⓥ Ⓑ🍴👤🔥🚗! ★★★

● Broad Haven (Haverfordwest)
PEMBROKESHIRE COAST PATH & NATIONAL PARK

✉= Albany Guesthouse, 27 Millmoor Way, SA62 3JJ
☎ 01437 781051 (Mrs Morgan) www.albanyguesthouse.co.uk Map 157/861138
BB **C/D** ✗ nearby S1 D1 T1 Closed Oct-Feb Ⓑ Ⓓ⊗🍴👤🔥!

● Dale (Haverfordwest)
PEMBROKESHIRE COAST PATH & NATIONAL PARK

Allenbrook, SA62 3RN ☎ 01646 636254 (Elizabeth Webber)
www.ukworld.net/allenbrook Map 157/811059
BB **D** ✗ nearby S1 D1 T1 F1 Closed Xmas Ⓑ Ⓓ⊗🍴👤🔥🚗! ★★★★

✉= Point Farm, SA62 3RD ☎ 01646 636541 www.pointfarm.info
Map 157/815053
BB **C** ✗ nearby S1 D1 F1 Closed Dec-Mar Ⓓ⊗🍴👤🔥🚗! Ⓜ ★★★

● Dinas Cross (Newport)
PEMBROKESHIRE COAST NATIONAL PARK

Dolwern, Feidr Fawr, SA42 0UY ☎ 01348 811266 (Annette Keylock)
dolwernb@tiscali.co.uk Map 157,145/011390
BB **B** ✗ nearby S1 D2 T1 Ⓑ Ⓓ⊗🍴👤🔥🚗!🛁 ★★

● Dyffryn (Goodwick)
PEMBROKESHIRE COAST PATH & NATIONAL PARK

✉= Ivybridge, Drim Mill, SA64 0JT ☎ 01348 875366
www.ivybridge.cwc.net Map 157/943371
BB **D** ✗ book first £20, 6:30-7:30pm S1 D3 T3 F4 Closed Xmas
⋙(Fishguard) Ⓥ Ⓑ Ⓓ🍴👤🔥🚗!🛁 ★★★

● Fishguard
PEMBROKESHIRE COAST PATH & NATIONAL PARK

✉= Cartref Hotel, 15-19 High Street, SA65 9AW ☎ 01348 872430
(Kristina Bjorkqvist) www.cartrefhotel.co.uk Map 157/956369
BB **D** ✗ £16, 6:30-8:30pm S4 D2 T2 F2 ⋙(Fishguard Harbour)
Ⓥ Ⓑ Ⓓ🍴👤🔥🚗🛁 ★★

● Goodwick (Fishguard)
PEMBROKESHIRE COAST PATH & NATIONAL PARK

✉= Seaside Steps, 6 New Hill Villas, SA64 0DS ☎ 01348 874076
(Anne Strawbridge) seasidesteps@seasidesteps.plus.com Map 157/947385
BB **C** ✗ nearby D1 F1 Closed Xmas ⋙(Fishguard)
Ⓑ Ⓓ⊗🍴👤🔥🚗!🛁

● Haverfordwest
☆ **Cuckoo Mill Farm**
Pelcomb Bridge, SA62 6EA ☎ 01437 762139 (Margaret Davies)
cmflimited@aol.com Map 157,158/933172
BB **B** ✗ book first £13-£15, 6-8:30pm S1 D2 T1 F1 ⋙(Haverfordwest)
Ⓥ Ⓑ Ⓓ🍴👤🔥🛁 ★★★

Mixed farm in central Pembrokeshire. Country walking. Six miles to coastal path. Meal times to suit guests. Excellent home cooking. Cosy farmhouse. Warm, well-appointed rooms. En-suite facilities. Gold Welcome Host.

WALES

College Guest House, 93 Hill St, St Thomas Green, SA61 1QL ☎ 01437 763710
(Colin Larby) www.collegeguesthouse.com Map 157,158/951152
BB **D** ✕ nearby S1 D2 T2 F3 ⋙(Haverfordwest)
Ⓑ Ⓓ ⊛ 🛏👤♨🚗❗🛏 ★★★★

● Jeffreyston (Kilgetty)
PEMBROKESHIRE COAST PATH

⋘ Jeffreyston Grange, SA68 0RE ☎ 01646 650159 (Tony Hesslegrave)
www.jeffreystongrange.co.uk Map 158/089065
BB **B** ✕ book first £10, 6:30pm S1 D2 T2 F1 Closed Jan-Feb
Ⓥ Ⓑ Ⓓ ⊛ 🛏👤♨🚗❗ Wheelchair access.

● Moylegrove (Cardigan)
PEMBROKESHIRE COAST PATH & NATIONAL PARK

⋘ Swn-y-Nant B&B, SA43 3BW ☎ 01239 881244
www.moylegrove.co.uk Map 145/117446
BB **C** ✕ book first £15 D2 T1 Closed Jan
Ⓥ Ⓑ Ⓓ ⊛ 🛏👤♨🚗❗ ★★★

● Pembroke
PEMBROKESHIRE COAST PATH & NATIONAL PARK

⋘ High Noon Guest House, Lower Lamphey Road, SA71 4AB
☎ 01646 683736 (The Barnikel Family)
www.highnoon.co.uk Map 157,158/990011
BB **B/C** ✕ nearby S3 D3 T1 F2 Closed Xmas ⋙(Pembroke)
Ⓑ Ⓓ ⊛ 🛏👤♨🚗❗🛏 ★★

● Saundersfoot
PEMBROKESHIRE COAST PATH & NATIONAL PARK

Jubilee Guest House, Stammers Road, SA69 9HH
☎ 01834 813442 (Diane Cotton) Map 158/135046
BB **B** ✕ nearby, 6:30pm D3 T1 F1 ⋙(Saundersfoot)
Ⓑ Ⓓ ⊛ 🛏👤♨🚗 ★★ Facilities available for disabled guests.

⋘ Vine Cottage Guesthouse, The Ridgeway, SA69 9LA ☎ 01834 814422
(Helen & David Trimmings) www.vinecottageguesthouse.co.uk Map 158/127052
BB **D** T/D3 F/D2 ⋙(Saundersfoot) Ⓥ Ⓑ Ⓓ ⊛ 🛏👤♨🚗 ★★★

● St Davids
PEMBROKESHIRE COAST PATH & NATIONAL PARK

☆ **Ramsey House**
Lower Moor, SA62 6RP ☎ 01437 720321 (Ceri & Elaine Morgan)
www.ramseyhouse.co.uk Map 157/747250
BB **D** ✕ nearby D3 T2 Closed Nov-Feb
Ⓑ Ⓓ ⊛ 🛏👤♨🚗❗ ◆◆◆◆

Quality 4 Diamond accommodation catering exclusively for adults. Quiet location situated just half mile from centre of St Davids, coast path and cathedral. Ideal for walking, bird watching, watersports and beaches. Congenial relaxed hospitality and licensed bar complete your enjoyment.

Alandale Guest House, 43 Nun Street, SA62 6NU
☎ 01437 720404 (Rob & Gloria Pugh)
www.stdavids.co.uk/guesthouse/alandale.htm Map 157/754256
BB **D** ✕ nearby S1 D3 T1 Ⓑ Ⓓ ⊛ 🛏🚗❗ ◆◆◆◆

Glendower, Ynun Street, SA62 6NS ☎ 01437 721650 (JJ Darby)
Map 157/753253
BB **C** ✕ nearby D4 Ⓥ Ⓑ Ⓓ ⊛ 🛏👤

☆ **Lochmeyler Farm Guest House**
Llandeloy, Pen-y-Cwm, Solva, SA62 6LL ☎ 01348 837724 (Mrs MM Jones)
www.lochmeyler.co.uk Map 157/855275
BB **D** ✕ book first £15, 7pm S1 D4 T3 F3 Closed Xmas
Ⓥ Ⓑ Ⓓ ⊛ 🛏👤♨🛏 ★★★★★

11 en-suite non-smoking luxury bedrooms, TV & refreshment facilities. Centre St Davids peninsula. Ideal for exploring Pembrokeshire Coast Path and countryside. B&B £25-50pppn. Optional evening dinner £15pp. Closed Christmas and New Year. 10% discount on advance bookings for inclusive evening dinner, B&B for 7 nights or more. Email: stay@lochmeyler.co.uk

● St Ishmael's (Haverfordwest)
PEMBROKESHIRE COAST PATH & NATIONAL PARK

⋘ Skerryback Farmhouse, Sandy Haven, SA62 3DN ☎ 01646 636598
(Mrs M Williams) www.pfh.co.uk/skerryback Map 157/852074
BB **B/C** ✕ nearby D1 T1 F1 Closed Xmas Ⓑ Ⓓ ⊛ 🛏👤♨🚗❗ ★★★

● Tenby
PEMBROKESHIRE COAST PATH & NATIONAL PARK

Sea Breezes B&B, 18 The Norton, SA70 8AA ☎ 01834 842753
www.seabreezesonline.co.uk Map 158/132007
BB **B/C** ✕ nearby S/D1 D/T2 ⋙(Tenby) Ⓥ Ⓑ 🛏🛏 ★★

⋘ Glenholme, Picton Terrace, SA70 7DR ☎ 01834 843909 (Sandra Milward)
www.glenholmetenby.co.uk Map 158/134002
BB **C** ✕ nearby S1 D4 T1 F2 ⋙(Tenby) Ⓑ Ⓓ ⊛ 🛏👤♨ ★★★

⋘ Dove's Nest, St Florence, SA70 8LU ☎ 01834 871136 (Meurig Jones)
www.doves-nest.co.uk Map 158/083010
BB **C** ✕ nearby D2 T1 ⋙(Manorbier) Ⓥ Ⓑ Ⓓ 🛏👤♨🚗❗🛏 Ⓜ

● Trefin (St Davids)
PEMBROKESHIRE COAST PATH & NATIONAL PARK

Bryngarw, Abercastle Rd, SA62 5AR ☎ 01348 831211
(Anthony & Judith Johnson) www.bryngarwguesthouse.co.uk Map 157/842325
BB **D** ✕ book first £20, 7pm D4 T2 Closed Nov-Dec
Ⓥ Ⓑ Ⓓ ⊛ 🛏👤♨🛏 ★★★

⋘ Hampton House, 2 Ffordd-y-Felin, SA62 5AX ☎ 01348 837701
(Vivienne & Chris Prior) viv.kay@virgin.net Map 157/840324
BB **B** ✕ nearby S1 D1 T1 Closed Dec-Jan
Ⓑ Ⓓ ⊛ 🛏👤♨🚗❗🛏 ★★★

POWYS

● Brecon
BRECON BEACONS

The Grange , The Watton, LD3 7ED ☎ 01874 624038 (Meryl, Ian & John)
www.thegrange-brecon.co.uk Map 160/048283
BB **C/D** ✕ nearby D4 F4 Closed Xmas
Ⓑ Ⓓ ⊛ 🛏👤♨ ★★★ Guide dogs welcome.

☆ **Lodge Farm**
Talgarth, LD3 0DP ☎ 01874 711244 (Mrs M Meredith)
marionlodgefarm@fwi.co.uk Map 161/173344
BB C/D ✗ book first £17, 7pm D1 T1 F1 Closed Xmas
Ⓥ Ⓑ Ⓓ ⊛ ☕ ♨ ★★★

Welcome to our 17th century farm house situated in the Brecon Beacons National Park, well placed for walking the Black Mountains and Brecon Beacons. En-suite bedrooms, tea-making facilities. Good, freshly prepared food including vegetarian. Sheep's cheese made on farm. FHB members.

☆ ⌂ **The Old Mill**
Felinfach, LD3 0UB ☎ 01874 625385
Map 161/091332
BB C ✗ nearby D1 T2 Closed Oct-Feb
Ⓑ Ⓓ ♨ ★★★Ⓦ

A 16th C. converted corn mill, peacefully situated in its own grounds. Inglenook fireplace, exposed beams, TV lounge, beverage trays. Ideally situated for walks & touring the Brecon Beacons NP & Black Mountains or just relaxing. Local inn within walking distance. A friendly welcome awaits you.

⌂ Canal Bank, Ty Gardd, LD3 7HG
☎ 01874 623464 (Peter & Barbara Jackson)
www.accommodation-breconbeacons.co.uk Map 160/047281
BB D ✗ nearby D2 T1 Closed Xmas
Ⓑ Ⓓ ☕ ♨ ♨ ★★★★★

⌂ The Beacon, 4 The Watton, LD3 7ED ☎ 01874 625862
(Joanna & Dafydd Jones) www.beaconguesthouse.co.uk Map 160/048283
BB B ✗ £7, 6:30pm T1 Ⓥ Ⓑ Ⓓ ⊛ ☕ ♨ ♨ !

● **Builth Wells**
WYE VALLEY WALK
⌂ Little Smithfield, Cwmbach, LD2 3RS ☎ 01982 552973 (Philippa Wright)
andrew.wright91@virgin.net Map 147/024548
BB C ✗ book first £15, 7:30pm S2 D1 F1 Closed Xmas ⚞(Builth Road)
Ⓥ Ⓑ Ⓓ ⊛ ☕ ♨ ♨ ! ★★★

● **Capel-y-Ffin (Abergavenny)**
BRECON BEACONS
CAMBRIAN WAY & OFFA'S DYKE
The Grange, NP7 7NP ☎ 01873 890215/157 (Griffiths Family)
www.grangeguesthouse.co.uk Map 161/251315
BB B ✗ book first £14, 7-7:45pm S1 D1 T1 F2 Closed Nov-Feb
Ⓥ Ⓑ Ⓓ ☕ ♨ ♨ ! ♨ ★

● **Crickhowell**
BRECON BEACONS
CAMBRIAN WAY
⌂ Dragon Hotel, High Street, NP8 1BE ☎ 01873 810362
(Andrew & Sian Powell) www.dragonhotel.co.uk Map 161/217183
BB D ✗ £6-£15, 6:30-9pm S2 D6 T6 F1 Closed Xmas
Ⓥ Ⓑ Ⓓ ☕ ♨ ★★

⌂ Ty Croeso Hotel, The Dardy, NP8 1PU ☎ 01873 810573 (Linda Jarrett)
www.ty-croeso.co.uk Map 161/206183
BB D ✗ £18, 7-9pm S2 D4 T2 Closed Jan Ⓥ Ⓑ Ⓓ ⊛ ☕ ♨ ♨ ! Ⓜ

Ty Gwyn, Brecon Road, NP8 1DG
☎ 01873 811625 (Sue & Pete)
Map 161/216188
BB C ✗ nearby D1 T2 Ⓑ Ⓓ ⊛ ☕ ♨ ♨ ! Ⓜ ★★★★

● **Glasbury (Hay-on-Wye)**
WYE VALLEY WALK
Aberllynfi B&B, HR3 5NT
☎ 01497 847107 (Catherine Sturgeon)
www.hay-on-wye.co.uk/aberllynfi Map 161/179390
BB B ✗ nearby S1 T2 Closed Xmas Ⓓ ⊛ ☕ ♨ !

● **Hay-on-Wye**
BRECON BEACONS
OFFA'S DYKE & HEREFORDSHIRE TRAIL
Fernleigh, Hardwick Road, Cusop, HR3 5QX
☎ 01497 820459 (Winnifred Hughes)
Map 161,148/235422
BB B ✗ nearby D2 T1 Closed Nov-Feb Ⓥ Ⓑ Ⓓ ⊛ ☕ ♨ Ⓜ

La Fosse Guest House, Oxford Road, HR3 5AJ
☎ 01497 820613 (Bob & Annabel Crook)
www.hay-on-wye.co.uk/lafosse Map 161/232423
BB B ✗ nearby D3 T1 Closed Xmas Ⓑ Ⓓ ⊛ ☕ ♨ ! ♨ ★★

⌂ Oxford Cottage, Oxford Road, HR3 5AJ
☎ 01497 820008 (Ed Moore)
www.oxfordcottage.co.uk Map 161,148/232423
BB C/D D2 T1 Ⓓ ⊛ ♨ Kitchen for guests.

⌂ Baskerville Hall Hotel, Clyro Court, Clyro, HR3 5LE ☎ 01497 820033
www.baskervillehall.co.uk Map 161/208428
BB D ✗ £6, 7-9pm S7 D10 T12 F5 Closed Xmas
Ⓥ Ⓑ Ⓓ ☕ ♨ ♨ ! ♨ See Groups also.

● **Heol Senni (Brecon)**
BRECON BEACONS
⌂ Maeswalter Farm, LD3 8SU ☎ 01874 636629 (Mrs MJ Mayo)
www.maeswalter.co.uk Map 160/931236
BB C/D ✗ book first £12-£15, 6:30-7pm D3 T1 F1
Ⓥ Ⓑ Ⓓ ⊛ ☕ ♨ ! ♨ ◆◆◆

● **Knighton**
GLYNDWR'S WAY & OFFA'S DYKE
The Fleece House, Market Street, LD7 1BB ☎ 01547 520168 (Dana Simmons)
www.fleecehouse.co.uk Map 148,137/284723
BB D ✗ nearby T3 ⚞(Knighton)
Ⓑ Ⓓ ⊛ ♨ ! ★★★ Local information available.

⌂ The Plough, 40 Market Street, LD7 1EY ☎ 01547 528041
sarahscotford@aol.com Map 148,137/284723
BB B/C ✗ £3 (bar snacks), 7-9pm S4 D1 T3 ⚞(Knighton)
Ⓥ Ⓑ ☕ ♨ ! ♨

● **Llanbadarn Fynydd (Llandrindod Wells)**
GLYNDWR'S WAY
Hillside Lodge Guest House, LD1 6TU
☎ 01597 840364 (Mr WT & Mrs B Ainsworth)
Map 136/085764
BB B ✗ nearby T1 F2 Closed Xmas Ⓑ Ⓓ ☕ ♨ ♨ ! ♨ ★★★

WALES

Please mention walk BRITAIN
when booking your accommodation

● Llandrindod Wells

☆ **Holly Farm**
Howey, LD1 5PP ☎ 01597 822402 (Ruth Jones)
www.ukworld.net/hollyfarm Map 147/049589
BB **C** ✕ book first £12-£14, 7pm D2 T2 F1 Closed Xmas
⋘(Llandrindod Wells) Ⓥ Ⓑ Ⓓ ⊛ 🐾🛏️🖐️ ◆◆◆◆

Tastefully restored Tudor farmhouse on working farm in peaceful location.
En-suite bedrooms with breathtaking views over fields and woods. CTV and
beverage trays. Two lounges, log fires, delicious cuisine using farm produce.
Excellent area for walking, birdwatching or relaxing. Near red kite feeding
station. Weekly reductions. Packed lunches. Safe parking.
Call Mrs Ruth Jones for a brochure.

● Llangattock (Crickhowell)
BRECON BEACONS
CAMBRIAN WAY

🏠 Park Place Guesthouse, The Legar, NP8 1HH ☎ 01873 810878
(Maxine Wheaton) www.parkplaceguesthouse.co.uk Map 161/215179
BB **B** ✕ book first £6.95, 7-8pm S2 D1 T1 F2
Ⓥ Ⓑ Ⓓ ⊛ 🐾🛏️🚗🖐️🛁 ★★

● Llangurig (Llanidloes)
WYE VALLEY WALK

🏠 The Old Vicarage, SY18 6RN ☎ 01686 440280 (Margaret Hartey)
www.theoldvicaragellangurig.co.uk Map 147/912799
BB **B/C** ✕ book first £15, 7pm D3 T2 F1 Closed Xmas
Ⓥ Ⓑ Ⓓ 🐾🛏️🛁 Ⓜ ◆◆◆◆

● Llanidloes
GLYNDWR'S WAY

🏠 Lloyds Hotel & Restaurant, Cambrian Place, SY18 6BX ☎ 01686 412284
(Tom Lines & Roy Hayter) www.lloydshotel.co.uk Map 136/955844
BB **D** ✕ book first £30, 8pm S2 D3 T2 Closed Feb
Ⓥ Ⓑ Ⓓ ⊛🛏️ ★★★

● Llanigon (Hay-on-Wye)
BRECON BEACONS
OFFA'S DYKE & WYE VALLEY WALK

🏠 The Old Post Office, HR3 5QA ☎ 01497 820008 (Linda Webb)
www.oldpost-office.co.uk Map 161/213401
BB **C/D** D1 T1 F1 Closed Jan Ⓑ Ⓓ ⊛ 🐾🛏️🛁

● Llanwddyn (Oswestry)
GLYNDWR'S WAY

🏠 Gorffwysfa, 4 Glyn Du, Lake Vyrnwy, SY10 0NB ☎ 01691 870217
www.vyrnwy-accommodation.co.uk Map 125/019190
BB **D** ✕ book first £17.50, 7pm D2 T1 F1
Ⓥ Ⓑ Ⓓ ⊛ 🐾🛏️🚗🖐️🛁 Jacuzzi for walkers.

☆🏠 **The Oaks**
Lake Vyrnwy, SY10 0LZ ☎ 01691 870250 (Michael & Daphne Duggleby)
www.vyrnwyaccommodation.co.uk Map 125/017190
BB **C** ✕ nearby D1 T2 Closed Xmas
Ⓥ Ⓑ Ⓓ ⊛ 🐾🛏️🖐️🛁 ★★★

Located by Lake Vyrnwy on
Glyndwr's Way. A warm and
friendly welcome into a
comfortable family home.
Brilliant breakfasts. Excellent
for walkers.
Email: mdugg99@aol.com

● Llanwrthwl (LLandrindod Wells)
WYE VALLEY WALK

🏠 Dolifor, LD1 6NU ☎ 01597 811051 (Mrs J Austin)
www.stayatdolifor.co.uk Map 147/958658
BB **B** D2 Ⓥ Ⓑ Ⓓ 🐾🛏️🖐️ Ⓜ ★★★

● Llanwrtyd Wells

🏠 Neuadd Arms Hotel, The Square, LD5 4RB
☎ 01591 610236 (Lindsay Ketteringham)
www.neuaddarmshotel.co.uk Map 147/879467
BB **C** ✕ £5-£10, 6-8:30pm S5 D7 T8 ⋘(Llanwrtyd Wells)
Ⓥ Ⓑ Ⓓ 🐾🛏️🖐️🛁 ★ See Groups & Walking Holidays also.

☆🏠 **Belle Vue Hotel**
LD5 4RE ☎ 01591 610237 (Eileen & Bernie Dodd)
www.bellevuewales.co.uk Map 147/879467
BB **B** ✕ £4-£14, 6:30-9:30pm S4 D3 T8 F2 Closed Xmas
⋘(Llanwrtyd Wells) Ⓥ Ⓑ Ⓓ 🐾🛏️🚗🛁 See Groups also.

Situated midway between Builth Wells and Llandovery on the A483 trunk road.
Built in 1843 the Belle View Hotel is the oldest hotel in Llanwrtyd Wells.
Combining village pub and local meeting place, which gives this small,
comfortable, family-run hotel the charm and character of the friendly
inhabitants of this town.

● Llanymynech
OFFA'S DYKE

🏠 Orchard Holidays, Unity House, Llandrinio, SY22 6SG
☎ 01691 831976 (Maxine Roberts)
www.orchard-holidays.com Map 126/290160
BB **C** ✕ nearby S3 D2 T1 Closed Nov-Feb Ⓑ Ⓓ ⊛ 🐾🛏️🚗🖐️ ★★★

● Llyswen (Brecon)
BRECON BEACONS
WYE VALLEY WALK

☆ 🚶🚲 **Wye Knot Stop**
LD3 0UR ☎ 01874 754247 (Susan Beck)
www.wyeknotstop.co.uk Map 161/133378
BB **D** ✗ £8–£10, to suit D1 T1 F1
Ⓥ Ⓑ Ⓓ 🚫 🐾 ♿ 🚗 🛏 Wheelchair access.

Situated in the pretty village of Llyswen, half-a-mile from the Wye Valley Walk and 8-miles from Offa's Dyke. Ideal for exploring Black Mountains and Brecon Beacons. Ensuite family room sleeps 4, ensuite twin with disabled facilities and double. Large car park.

● Machynlleth
GLYNDWR'S WAY

🚶🚲 Maenllwyd, Newtown Road, SY20 8EY ☎ 01654 702928 (Mrs M Vince)
www.cyber-space.co.uk/maenllwyd.htm Map 135/752008
BB **C/D** ✗ nearby D4 T3 F1 Closed Dec-Feb 🚌(Machynlleth)
Ⓑ Ⓓ 🚫 🐾 🚗 ! 🛏 ◆◆◆◆

☆ 🚶🚲 **Talbontdrain Guest House**
Uwchygarreg, SY20 8RR ☎ 01654 702192
www.talbontdrain.co.uk Map 135/777959
BB **C** ✗ book first £15, 7:30pm S1 D1 T2
Ⓥ Ⓑ Ⓓ 🚫 🐾 🚗 ! 🛏

Remote and comfortable farm guesthouse – Glyndwr's Way runs through the yard. Homemade food with generous helpings. Newly renovated in 2006. Much more information on the website.

● Montgomery
OFFA'S DYKE

Dragon Hotel, SY15 6PA ☎ 01686 668359 (Mark & Sue Michaels)
www.dragonhotel.com Map 137/222964
BB **D** ✗ £7–£20, 7-9pm S2 D9 T5 F4 Ⓥ Ⓑ Ⓓ 🐾 ♿ 🚗 ! 🛏 ★★★

☆ 🚶🚲 **Hendomen Farmhouse**
Hendomen, SY15 6HB ☎ 01686 668004 (Jo & Bruce Lawson)
www.offasdykepath.com Map 137/218981
BB **C** ✗ nearby S1 D1 T1
Ⓑ Ⓓ 🚫 🐾 🚗 ! 🛏 Ⓜ ★★

Stay in Montgomery and walk the Dyke. Transport of walkers between Knighton and Llangollen and Glyndwr's Way. Discounts for 3 nights. Owners are walkers. Flexible breakfast times. 5 pubs (1 with pool) nearby. Fabulous views. Email: bruce.lawson@btinternet.com

● Presteigne
OFFA'S DYKE

Carmel Court, King's Turning Road, LD8 2LD ☎ 01544 267986
(Marenee & Terry Monaghan) www.carmelcourt.co.uk Map 148,137/320639
BB **C** ✗ nearby S1 D5 T3 F2 Closed Xmas Ⓑ Ⓓ 🐾 ♿ 🚗 ! 🛏 ★★

🚶🚲 Lower Dolley Farm, Dolley Green, LD8 2EE ☎ 01547 560430
(Claire & Neil Reid-Warrilow) reidwarrilow@aol.com Map 148,137/284654
BB **B** ✗ book first £8, 7:30pm S1 D1 Ⓥ Ⓓ 🐾 🚗 ! 🛏

● Rhayader
WYE VALLEY WALK

Brynteg, East Street, LD6 5EA ☎ 01597 810052 (Mrs B Lawrence)
brynteg@hotmail.com Map 147,136/972681
BB **B** ✗ nearby S1 D2 T1 Closed Xmas
Ⓑ Ⓓ 🐾 ♿ 🚗 ! Ⓜ ★★★ Local footpath information.

● Talybont-on-Usk (Brecon)
BRECON BEACONS

🚶🚲 Gethinog, LD3 7YN ☎ 01874 676258 (Christina & Roy Gale)
www.gethinog.co.uk Map 161/108233
BB **C** ✗ book first £16, 7pm D1 T1 Closed Xmas Ⓥ Ⓑ 🚫 🐾 ♿ !

● Talyllyn (Brecon)
BRECON BEACONS

🚶🚲 Dolycoed, LD3 7SY ☎ 01874 658666 (Mary Cole) Map 161/107271
BB **B** S1 D1 T1 Ⓑ Ⓓ 🚫 🐾 ♿ 🚗 🛏

● Trallong (Brecon)
BRECON BEACONS

☆ **Beech Copse**
2 Pentrebach Cottage, LD3 8HS ☎ 01874 636125 (Joy & Alan Bloss)
www.beechcopsebb.co.uk Map 160/971297
BB **C** ✗ book first £7, 7pm D1 Closed Dec-Feb
Ⓥ Ⓑ Ⓓ 🚫 🐾 ♿ ! Ⓜ ★★★ Special diets by arrangement.

Comfort and tranquillity in delightful cottage. Northern edge of Brecon Beacons National Park. Gorgeous countryside and wildlife. Gentle/moderate walking in immediate vicinity. Lifts available. One double en-suite room. Comfortable adult put-you-up also available.

● Welshpool
GLYNDWR'S WAY & OFFA'S DYKE

Tynllwyn Farm, SY21 9BW ☎ 01938 553175 (Jane & Caroline Emberton)
www.tynllwynfarm.co.uk Map 126/215086
BB **D** ✗ book first £14, 6:30pm D1 F4 Closed Xmas 🚌(Welshpool)
Ⓥ Ⓑ Ⓓ 🚫 🐾 ♿ 🚗 ! 🛏 ★★★

Severn Farm, SY21 7BB ☎ 01938 555999 (T & J Jones)
www.severnfarm.co.uk Map 126/231070
BB **B** ✗ nearby S2 D1 T1 F2 Closed Xmas 🚌(Welshpool)
Ⓓ 🚫 🐾 🚗 ! 🛏

🚶🚲 Ty-Isaf, Llanerfyl, SY21 0JB ☎ 01938 820143 (Sheenagh Carter)
sheen.carter@virgin.net Map 125/024082
BB **C** ✗ book first £10, 6:30-9pm D1 F1
Ⓥ Ⓑ Ⓓ 🚫 🐾 ♿ ! 🛏 ★★★

SOUTH WALES

● Caerphilly

Lugano Guest House, Hillside, Mountain Road, CF83 1HN ☎ 029 2085 2672
(Marian Dowson) nick@dowson.4145.freeserve.co.uk Map 171/156863
BB **D** ✗ nearby D1 T2 🚌(Caerphilly) Ⓥ Ⓑ Ⓓ 🚫 🐾 ♿ Ⓖ

WALES

● Cardiff

CAMBRIAN WAY

Avala Hotel, 156 Newport Road, CF24 IDJ ☎ 029 2048 1412
www.avalahotel.co.uk Map 171/198774
BB **D** ✗ nearby S4 D1 T6 F1 ⚬⚬⚬(Cardiff Central)
Ⓓ ⊛ 🐾👤☕🚗 See Groups & Hostels also.

● Cwmtaf (Merthyr Tydfil)

BRECON BEACONS

Llwyn Onn Guest House, CF48 2HT
☎ 01685 384384 (Mrs M Evans)
www.llwynonn.co.uk Map 160/012115
BB **D** D6 T4 F1 Closed Xmas Ⓑ Ⓓ🐾👤🚗 ★★★★

● Ewenny (Bridgend)

VALEWAYS MILLENNIUM HERITAGE TRAIL

Ewenny Farm Guest House, Ewenny Cross, CF35 5AB
☎ 01656 658438 (Howard R Jennings)
www.ewennyfarm-guesthouse.co.uk Map 170/901771
BB **D** ✗ nearby S8 D8 T4 ⚬⚬⚬(Bridgend)
Ⓥ Ⓑ Ⓓ ⊛ 🐾👤🚗! ★★★ Wheelchair access.

● Fairwood (Swansea)

☆ ⚬⚬ **Seren Retreat**
Bryncoch Farm, SA2 7LB ☎ 01792 371421 (Rex & Alaea Beynon)
www.serenretreat.com Map 159/556921
BB **C/D** D2 F4
Ⓥ Ⓑ Ⓓ ⊛ 🐾👤🚗! ★★★

Idyllic 23-acre farm with ancient oak forest, river and wildflower meadows. Ideal base to explore the natural beauty of the Gower peninsula. Walkers can follow the river from our farm down the Ilston valley to Three Cliffs Bay. All rooms are en-suite.

● Llanmadoc (Gower)

Tallizmand, SA3 1HA ☎ 01792 386373 (Mrs A Main)
http://tallizmand.co.uk Map 159/444933
BB **C** D1 T2 Ⓑ Ⓓ ⊛ 🐾👤🚗 ★★★Ⓦ

Forge Cottage, SA3 1DB ☎ 01792 386302 (Mike Downie)
www.forgecottagegower.co.uk Map 159/446932
BB **D** ✗ nearby D1 T1 F1 Closed Xmas-Jan Ⓑ ⊛ 🐾👤🚗 ★★★

● Llanrhidian (Gower)

☆ ⚬⚬ **North Gower Hotel**
SA3 1EE ☎ 01792 390042
www.northgowerhotel.co.uk Map 159/501919
BB **C/D** ✗ £7, 6-9pm D/S10 T1 F7
Ⓥ Ⓑ Ⓓ🐾👤☕🚗!🚲 ★★

Privately owned, professionally run 2-star AA hotel.

Our central Gower location overlooking the Loughar Estuary is an ideal base for exploring the beautiful Gower peninsular.

All our rooms are en-suite with modern facilities. We can provide our guests a full laundry service and a clothes drying service. Our hotel prides itself on its catering standards, from light snacks up to a four course dinner, and also provides a packed lunch on request.

We also have discounts for group bookings and mid-week breaks.

For more information visit our website.

● Llantwit Major

VALEWAYS MILLENNIUM HERITAGE TRAIL

The Curriers Guest House, Wine Street, CF61 1RZ
☎ 01446 793506 (Sally Bagstaff) www.thecurriers.co.uk Map 170/966688
BB **C** ✗ nearby S1 D2 T2 F1 ⚬⚬⚬(Llantwit Major)
Ⓥ Ⓓ🐾👤☕🚗! ★★ⒼⓌ

● Port Eynon (Gower)

☆ ⚬⚬ **Culver House Hotel**
SA3 1NN ☎ 01792 390755 (Mark & Susan Cottell)
www.culverhousehotel.co.uk Map 159/468853
BB **D** ✗ nearby S2 D7 T3 F1 Closed Nov-Jan
Ⓑ Ⓓ ⊛ 👤🚲 ★★

A family-run hotel with a warm friendly atmosphere, superb food and quality service. Most rooms have beautiful seaviews with en-suite facilities. Ideally situated for rambling the Gower peninsula. Groups welcome. Discounts available.

● Swansea

The Coast House, 708 Mumbles Road, SA3 4EH ☎ 01792 368702
(Jan & Len Clarke) www.thecoasthouse.co.uk Map 159/622877
BB **C** ✗ nearby S1 D3 F2 Closed Nov-Dec Ⓑ ⊛ 👤🚲 ★★★

● Three Crosses (Swansea)
◄● Gower Golf Club, Cefn Goleu, SA4 3HS
☎ 01792 872480 (Michelle Beswick) www.gowergolf.co.uk Map 159/573952
BB **D** ✗ £12, Until 9pm T11 ⋙(Gowerton)
Ⓥ Ⓑ Ⓓ 🍵☕! ★★★★ Wheelchair access.

● Wernffrwd (Llanmorlais)
◄● Ael-y-Bryn, SA4 3TY ☎ 01792 850187 (Heather Bergfeld)
ael-y-bryn@tesco.net Map 159/514937
BB **B** ✗ nearby D1 F1 Closed Dec-Jan Ⓥ Ⓑ Ⓓ 🚫🍵☕🚗🐴

● Ynysybwl
BRECON BEACONS

☆ **Tyn-y-Wern**
CF37 3LY ☎ 01443 790551 (Hermione Bruton)
www.tyn-y-wern.co.uk Map 170/065945
BB **C** D2 T1 Closed Xmas
Ⓑ Ⓓ 🚫🍵☕🚗!🐴 ★★★ See Pontypridd in SC also.

A Victorian mine manager's residence lovingly restored to its former glory. Offers a tranquil country retreat just 30 minutes from Cardiff.
Spectacular walking.
Phone for brochure.

SELF-CATERING

ANGLESEY

● Brynsiencyn
Cerrig Y Barcud Holidays ☎ 01248 430056 (Julia Harfitt)
www.cerrigybarcud.co.uk
£170-£535 Sleeps 2-4. 4 cottages.
Tranquil location superb views. Adults only. 🚫 ★★★★★

CEREDIGION

● Aberporth
Frances & Peter Miller ☎ 01239 810595
milldrove@aol.com
£180-£350 Sleeps 4. 2 cottages.
Rural setting. Walks & beach minutes away. 🚫🐴

● Cardigan
Glanafon Bach Cottage ☎ 01239 682931 (Sally Sparkes)
glanafon.bach@virgin.net
£150-£320 Sleeps 2. 1 cottage.
Village location, linen, CH, log fire. 🚫🐴 ★★★★

● Llanilar
Nantclyd ☎ 01974 241543 (Liz Findlay) www.nantclydorganics.co.uk
£150-£180 Sleeps 6. 1 caravan.
An organic farm producing eggs & vegetables. 🚫

● New Quay
Tyhen Farm Cottages ☎ 01545 560346 (Roni Kelly) www.tyhencottages.co.uk
£250-£800 Sleeps 2-6. 7 cottages. Closed Nov-Jan
Private indoor heated pool & facilities. 🚫🐴 See B&B also.

Romantic Garden Cottage ☎ 01545 560846 (Mr N Makepeace)
www.romantic-garden-cottage.co.uk
£250-£415 Sleeps 2. 1 property. Peaceful location. Good walking.
Gardens. Dolphins. 🚫 Ⓜ ★★★★★

☆ **Park Hall**
☎ 01545 560996 (Carol Burgess)
www.park-hall.co.uk
£1,585-£2,575 Sleeps 20. 1 house.
Beautiful tranquil location, licensed for weddings. 🚫🐴 ★★★

Nestling within a beautiful valley, 300m from Cwmtydu Beach on the Ceredigion Heritage Coast. Set in 2.5 acres of lovely, lawned gardens.
Outstanding views of the sea.
Spacious, comfortable and perfect venue for walking holidays, reunions, family holidays, weddings or special anniversaries.
Eight bedrooms (7 en-suite), two lounges both with open fires and one with a piano. Large, sunny conservatory/dining room and games room.
Walking from the door, horse-riding, sea and fresh water fishing, clay pigeon shooting, canoeing, golf, bowls, tennis, quad-biking all within easy reach.
Snowdon, Tenby and the Gower peninsula within driving distance.

● Ystrad Meurig

☆ **Mr Ian Poyser**
☎ 01974 831471
£300 Sleeps 1-2. 1 bungalow.
Closed Nov & Jan
🚫 ★★★★

Beautifully presented spacious bungalow with magnificent views in quiet location. Superbly situated in the heart of Kite country, adjacent to Cors Canon nature reserve. Ideally placed for walking the Cambrian Mountains or Cardigan Bay coast. Brochure on request.

GWYNEDD

● Bangor
SNOWDONIA/ERYRI
Ogwen Valley Holidays ☎ 01248 600122 (Jill Jones)
www.ogwensnowdonia.co.uk
£160-£565 Sleeps 2-6. 1 flat, 1 cottage.
Cosy Welsh cottage, great views and walking. 🐴 ★★★★

WALES

● Barmouth
SNOWDONIA/ERYRI

Rose & Terry Holland ☎ 01341 247033
bethellvt@btopenworld.com
£190-£250 Sleeps 2. 1 cottage. Closed Jan
Delightfully rural. Sea/mountain views. Peaceful ⚓(Dyffryn Ardudwy) ☺ 🐾

● Beddgelert
SNOWDONIA/ERYRI

Glaslyn Leisure Ltd ☎ 01766 890880 (Joan Firth)
www.snowdonia-cottages.net
£275-£750 Sleeps 1-6. 5 cottages.
Excellent accommodation, village location. Families/groups. ☺ ★★★★★

Red Dragon Holiday Cottages ☎ 01766 890646
www.reddragonholidays.co.uk
£175-£540 Sleeps 2-8+. 3 cottages, 1 log cabin.
Set in private woodland. ☺ 🐾

● Caernarfon

☆ **Hafoty Farm Cottages**
☎ 01286 830144 (Elaine Moss)
www.hafoty.co.uk
£170-£630 Sleeps 2-6. 6 cottages. Closed Jan-Feb
Stunning views over the Menai Straits. ☺ ★★★★

Set on the edge of Snowdonia, Hafoty Farm Cottages provide the perfect base for exploring Anglesey, the Llyn Peninsula, Caernarfon and the surrounding countryside of Snowdonia. The cottages have been converted from old farm barns to provide the highest standard in self-catering facilities.

☆ **Ty'n yr Onnen Holiday Caravan & Camping Park**
☎ 01286 650281 (Tom Griffith)
£120-£450 Sleeps 6-10.
4 caravans.
☺ 🐾 ★★★★

Set on a traditional Welsh hill-farm owned by the same family for over 300 years. Ty'n yr Onnen's extensive area 'off the beaten track' offers seclusion, peace and tranquility unequalled in Wales, coupled with all the modern facilities the modern day camper demands.

● Criccieth

☆ **Arwel Williams**
☎ 01766 515015
getaway2northwales@hotmail.com
£200-£350 Sleeps 4. 2 apartments. ⚓(Criccieth)
☺ 🐾

Two comfortable apartments in a Victorian house near seafront, coastal path and 14 miles from Snowdon.

Ideal base to visit Llyn Peninsula and Snowdonia – close to all local amenities with train station nearby.

● Dolgellau
SNOWDONIA/ERYRI

☆ **Brynygwin Isaf**
☎ 01341 423481 (Gilbert Gauntlett)
www.holidaysinwales.fsnet.co.uk
£140-£729 Sleeps 2-24. 2 cottages, 2 parts country house.
Walk guidesheets provided. Large bird-rich garden. 🐾

Two self-contained sections of family country house built 1806 with large, comfortably furnished rooms, superb views, extensive garden and character cottages. 1 mile from Dolgellau. Over 30 walk guidesheets provided. Log fires. Open all year. Children and pets welcome. Email: holidays_wales@onetel.com

Mrs O Williams ☎ 01341 430277
£150-£180 Sleeps 6. 1 caravan. Closed Nov-Feb
Working farm. Estuary views, countryside walks. ☺ 🐾

● Harlech
SNOWDONIA/ERYRI

☆ **Ystumgwern**
☎ 01341 247249 (John & Jane Williams)
www.ystumgwern.co.uk
£200-£1250 Sleeps 2-12. 10 cottages. Working farm, games room, play area.
⚓(Harlech/Dyffryn Ardudwy) ☺ 🐾 ★★★★★

A truly Welsh welcome awaits you at Ystumgwern where the mountains of Snowdonia slope down to the sea.

Please view our website or ask for a copy of our colour brochure.

● Llanbedr
SNOWDONIA/ERYRI

Gwynfryn Farm ☎ 01341 241381
www.gwynfrynfarm-cottages.co.uk
£200-£1,500 Sleeps 2-10. 5 cottages.
Log-burning stoves, digital TV. ⚓(Llanbedr Halt/Pensarn)
☺ 🐾 ★★★★-★★★★★★

● Porthmadog
SNOWDONIA/ERYRI

Rhos Country Cottages ☎ 01758 720047 (Anwen Jones)
www.rhos-cottages.co.uk
£200-£1,000 Sleeps 2-8. 4 varying types.
Good walks from your door. 🐾 ★★★★★

MONMOUTHSHIRE

● Hendre

Ciderhouse Cottage ☎ 01600 716435 (Cathy Bowen)
www.penylanfarm.co.uk
£275-£520 Sleeps 6-7. 1 cottage.
Converted barn, slate floors, underfloor heating. ☺ See Monmouth in B&B also.

● Trellech
Mrs S D M Poulter ☎ 01600 860681
alanpoulter@beeb.net
£150-£550 Sleeps 1-6. 1 cottage.
Characterful 17th-century stone property. Historic village. 🏠 ★★★★★ⓖ

NORTH EAST WALES

● Bodfari
Ty'r Aer Bach Holidays ☎ 01745 710553 (Sue Hudson)
www.tabholidays.co.uk
£150-£200 Sleeps 4-6. 1 mobile home. Closed Nov-Mar
Offa's Dyke and Clwydian Hills. ⓧ 🏠

● Llangollen

☆ **Tan Y Ddol**
☎ 01206 855244 (Judith Watts)
www.visitwales.com
£240-£450 Sleeps 2-5. 1 house.
Maps and guides available. ⓧ ★★★★

Tan Y Ddol is a modern house ideally placed for walking the beautiful Dee valley and surrounding hills.
A wide variety of easy and challenging walks are available straight from the door, including the Llangollen Canal and Offa's Dyke Path.

● Prestatyn

☆ **Plasse Holiday Cottages**
☎ 01745 571036 (Jenny Christian)
www.plasseholidaycottages.co.uk
£225-£490 Sleeps 5-8. 3 cottages.
Offa's Dyke, Clwydian Hills, Snowdonia nearby. ⓧ

Three delightful cottages situated amidst the beautiful Vale of Clwyd, alongside Offa's Dyke Path. An ideal base to explore the North Wales coast and Snowdonia. A Ramblers package is available on request, to include an evening meal and breakfast provisions.

PEMBROKESHIRE

● Boncath

☆ **Clydey Country Cottages**
☎ 01239 698619 (Jacqui Davies)
www.clydeycottages.co.uk
£250-£950 Sleeps 2-6. 9 cottages.
Indoor heated pool, gym, sauna, hot-tub. ★★★★★

In an elevated position with glorious views over the Pembrokeshire countryside, these beautifully furnished and decorated cottages have been converted from 18th-century farm buildings.

Four-poster beds, wood-burning stoves and pretty furnishings all add to their charm. Enjoy the luxurious indoor heated pool with sun terrace, together with the gym, sauna, games room and outdoor hottub – the ultimate relaxing experience after a day exploring.

The cottages are surrounded by 20 acres of attractive grounds, including a woodland trail. For children there is a sandpit, rope swings and slide, eggs to collect from the resident chickens, and ponies and sheep to feed.

● Broad Haven
PEMBROKESHIRE COAST NATIONAL PARK
Morawelon ☎ 01494 714612 (Sandra Rollins) www.morawelon.co.uk
£215-£625 Sleeps 4. 1 apartment.
Seafront apartment next to coast path. ⓧ ★★★★★

● Dale
PEMBROKESHIRE COAST NATIONAL PARK
The Anchorage Holiday Cottage ☎ 01672 871684 (David Snell)
www.holidaycottagepembs.co.uk £240-£775 Sleeps 6. 1 cottage.
Cosy cottage, coast path, pub nearby. ⓧ 🏠 ★★★★

● Freshwater East
PEMBROKESHIRE COAST NATIONAL PARK

☆ **Nantucket**
☎ 01437 765777 (Coastal Cottages of Pembrokeshire)
www.coastalcottages.co.uk
£446-£1,155 Sleeps 10. 1 cottage. ⓧ 🏠
10% discount off a week (restrictions apply). See Lydstep & St Davids also.

Situated above the bay, this unique property enjoys the most stunning uninterrupted sea views.

With the sandy beach, Pembrokeshire Coast National Park and Path on your doorstep, and local pub just a short walk away you have everything you need for a wonderful walking break.

WALES

● **Haverfordwest**

☆ **Newton East**
☎ 01348 840375 (Richard & Elizabeth James)
newtoneast@tiscali.co.uk
£200-£400 Sleeps 1-6. 1 log cabin. Closed Jan-Feb
Central location, wildlife haven, peaceful, views. ⊗ 🐾

Beautiful log cabin. Three bedrooms, one ensuite. Furnished to a high standard. Private grounds and parking. Ideal base for walking and exploring Pembrokeshire. Coast Path and Preseli Hills within 15 minutes. Local walks, fabulous views, variety of habitats and wildlife.

● **Lydstep**
PEMBROKESHIRE COAST NATIONAL PARK

☆ **Westhills**
☎ 01437 765777 (Coastal Cottages of Pembrokeshire)
www.coastalcottages.co.uk
£333-£837 Sleeps 7. 1 cottage. ⊗ 🐾
10% discount off a week (restrictions apply). See Freshwater East & St Davids also.

Charming property on private lane to Lydstep's pretty bay and stunning National Trust headland. Relax in front of the open fire or garden BBQ after a day exploring the Coast Path. Pub 5 mins' walk away serving food. Recommended for any season. Near to Tenby & Saundersfoot's sandy beaches.

● **Moylegrove**
PEMBROKESHIRE COAST NATIONAL PARK

Ty Newydd Cottage ☎ 01239 881280 (Dawn Cotton)
£270-£398 Sleeps 2-5. 3 cottages. Coast Path within 10 mins walk. 🐾

● **St Davids**
PEMBROKESHIRE COAST NATIONAL PARK

☆ **Quality Cottages**
☎ 01348 837871
www.qualitycottages.co.uk
£250-£2290 Sleeps 2-17. 225 cottages & houses.
🐾 ★★★-★★★★★

Outstanding self-catering cottages in superb locations ideal for exploring near, safe and sandy beaches. Walk around the spectacular coastline or in the magnificent countryside of Lleyn, Pembrokeshire, Snowdonia and Anglesey. Enjoy birdwatching kites, puffins etc. Pets welcome free.

☆ **Poppy Cottage**
☎ 01437 765777 (Coastal Cottages of Pembrokeshire)
www.coastalcottages.co.uk
£282-£612 Sleeps 5. 1 cottage. ⊗ 🐾
10% discount off a week (restrictions apply). See Freshwater East & Lydstep also.

Poppy Cottage is a beautifully renovated, mid terrace house located in this tiny city. Many period features, exposed stonework and original doors. Tastefully furnished providing quality and comfort. Views of cathedral and Bishops Palace from bedrooms to rear of house. Perfectly situated to explore the city & coastline.

St Nons Bay Cottages ☎ 01437 720616 (Thelma M Hardman)
www.stnbc.co.uk
£195-£995 Sleeps 2-16. 4 cottages.
Beautiful location, near Coast Path.
⊗ 🐾 ★★★★★ See High View in Groups also.

● **St Dogmaels**

Trenewydd Farm Cottages ☎ 01239 612370 (Cheryl Hyde)
www.cottages-wales.com
£200-£875 Sleeps 4-9. 5 cottages.
Coastal Path, river valleys, Bluestone country. 🐾 ★★★★★

● **Tenby**
PEMBROKESHIRE COAST NATIONAL PARK

☆ **Celtic Haven**
☎ 01834 870000
www.celtichaven.com
£272-£2,445 Sleeps 2-12. 26 cottages. Private beach access. Coast path, golf, pool. ∿∿(Manorbier) ★★★★★ See The Hunting Lodge below also.

An award-winning village set in the Pembrokeshire Coast National Park. 26 5-star luxury cottages nestling above a private beach and set in acres of parkland.

An amazing spa with over 80 therapies and treatments awaits to pamper you, while the headland golf course and the coast path walks are ideal for the more energetic!

Celtic Haven really is a unique escape with its own superb terrace restaurant, heated pool and fitness suite.

☆ **The Hunting Lodge**
☎ 01834 870000
www.escapedirectory.com
£596-£1,411 Sleeps 8. 1 lodge. Lovely lodge, secluded, own private beach. ∿∿(Tenby) 🐾 ★★★★★ See Celtic Haven above also.

In Pembrokeshire's beautiful coastal national park, this lovely lodge is in the secluded setting of Waterwynch Estate.
The Hunting Lodge has access on to the estate's own private beach, 30 acres of forest and miles of inspiring walks.
The property sleeps 8 people in 4 bedrooms, has 3 bathrooms, a beamed ceiling lounge and a wonderful kitchen and dining room.
A unique experience for people looking for something different and very special.

☆ The Old Vicarage
☎ 01834 842773 (Phil & Denise Walters)
www.happy-holidays.co.uk
£190-£580 Sleeps 2-4. 7 apartments.
Close to coastal path. ⊗ ⋙(Penally/Tenby) ★★★★★

A perfect spot to enjoy a quieter base while investigating the coastal walks of Pembrokeshire, the Preseli Mountains or the ancient castles of Carew, Manorbier, Pembroke and Tenby.

Seven luxury apartments with individual private access. Ample carparking. The railway station at Penally is only five minutes' walk away. Just over a mile from Tenby, ten minutes' walk from the South Beach and the renowned coastal path.

Spectacular views over golf course and sea. Penally has pubs, restaurants and a post office/general store.

POWYS

● Brecon
BRECON BEACONS

☆ Penpont
☎ 01874 636202 (Davina & Gavin Hogg)
www.penpont.com
£1,200-£1,700 Sleeps 14-17. West wing of large house.
Tennis court, flyfishing, extensive gardens, peace. 🐾 ★★★★

Penpont, a Grade I-listed building, lies beside the River Usk within the heart of the Brecon Beacons National Park. It was first built in 1665 and whose descendants still live there today.

The wing has six bedrooms, a large kitchen/dining area and a comfy sitting room. There are 40 acres of gardens, woodlands and maze to explore including a productive organic kitchen walled garden. Laundry facilities on-site.

Wern-y-Marchog ☎ 01874 665329 (Ann Phillips)
www.wernymarchog.co.uk
£150-£600 Sleeps 1-6. 1 bungalow, 2 apartments, 1 farmhouse.
Excellent walking country. Lovely, homely cottages. 🐾 ★★★★

● Lake Vyrnwy
SNOWDONIA/ERYRI

☆ Eunant
☎ 01691 870321 (Bronwen Davies)
eunant@terrafirmatravel.com
£237-£385 Sleeps 1-7. Gites.
Gorgeous lakeside scenery, edge of Snowdonia. 🐾

Lovely self-catering accommodation; large farmhouse, woodburning stove, spacious conservatory. Fabulous walking, cycling and fishing in this area of outstanding natural beauty, on the edge of the beautiful Berwyn hills, not far from Snowdonia. Castles, beaches and more...

● Machynlleth
SNOWDONIA/ERYRI

Lynn & John Williams ☎ 01654 702952
www.lynn.john.williams.care4free.net
£170-£220 Sleeps 4-5. 2 cottages.
Local walks, wildlife, rivers, varied landscape. ⋙(Machynlleth) ⊗ 🐾 ★★★

SOUTH WALES

● Cardiff
Victoria Hall ☎ 029 2035 9500 (Sez)
www.victoriahall.com
£75-£81 Sleeps 3-5. 86 flats. Closed Sep-Jun ⋙(Cardiff Central) ★★★★

● Gower
Mrs M Jeffreys ☎ 01792 391175 www.pittoncrossfarmhouse.co.uk
£300-£750 Sleeps 2-6. 1 farmhouse.
Varied scenery. Central heating. Weekends available.
⊗ 🐾 Ⓜ ★★★★

● Pontypridd
BRECON BEACONS

☆ Tyn-y-Wern Country House
☎ 01443 790551 (Hermione Bruton)
www.tyn-y-wern.co.uk
£225-£335 Sleeps 2-4. 2 lodges. Beautiful location, Welsh valleys, spectacular walking. ⊗ 🐾 ★★★★ See Ynysybwl in B&B also.

Stylish conversion of old building offering modern facilities in tranquil country retreat just 30 minutes from Cardiff. Spectacular walking. Phone for further inormation. OS Map 170 - 065945
Email: tynywern2002@yahoo.co.uk

WALES

● Port Eynon (Gower)
Bay View Farm ☎ 01792 390234 (Pat Jeffreys) www.bayviewfarmgower.co.uk
£230-£630 Sleeps 2-6 + cott. 1 cottage, 1 wing of farmhouse.
Inclusive price: sheets and towels suppplied. ⊗ ★★★★

GROUPS

CARMARTHENSHIRE

Gwilimill (SC) Llanpumsaint, Camarthen SA33 6BY
☎ 01267 253486 (Carolyn Smethurst) www.gwilimill.co.uk
SC £850-£2,000 Max 18 + children. 1 house.
✗ B D ⊗ ★★★★★

CEREDIGION

Maesnant (SC) Ponterwyd, Aberystwyth SY23 3AG
☎ 07747 017371 (Julie Bellchambers)
www.maesnant.org.uk Map 135/774881
SC £140-£560 Min 4, max 16. 1 bunkhouse. Closed Nov-Feb ⊗

GWYNEDD

☆ **The Old School Lodge** (SC)
Deiniolen, Caernarfon LL55 3HH ☎ 0151 677 5703 (The Booking Secretary)
www.oldschoollodge.org.uk Map 115/584628
SC £50pppw Min 4, max 38.
✗ nearby B D ⊗

High standard, excellent value
accommodation for groups of up to
38 persons. All en-suite rooms plus
good disabled facilities.
Attractive rural location – 4 miles from
Llanberis – with many local attractions
and activities. All welcome!

MONMOUTHSHIRE

PEMBROKESHIRE COAST NATIONAL PARK

Millenium Youth Hostel (SC) Lawrenny, SA68 0PN ☎ 01646 651270
www.lawrenny-village.co.uk
SC £180pn (sole use) Min 10, max 23.
✗ nearby 🐾 D ⊗ ★★★★ Hostel

PEMBROKESHIRE

PEMBROKESHIRE COAST PATH & NATIONAL PARK

Upper Neeston Lodges (SC) Herbrandston, Milford Haven ☎ 01646 690750
(Mandy Tilling) www.upperneeston.co.uk Grid ref: 878077
SC £12.50-£15pppn Min 6, max 17. 2 bunkhouses.
✗ nearby 🐾 B D ⊗ 🚗 ! ★★★★

High View (SC) St Davids ☎ 01437 720616 (Thelma Hardman)
www.stnbc.co.uk Map 175/740731
SC £395-£2,195 Min 2, max 16. 4 cottages.
✗ nearby B D ⊗ ! 🚗 See St Nons Bay Cottages, St Davids in SC also.

Pen Rhiw Group & Retreat Centre for Groups (BB)
St Davids, Haverfordwest SA62 6PG
☎ 01437 721821 www.penrhiw.co.uk
DBB £38 ✗ 🐾 B D ⊗ ! 🚗 ★★

POWYS

BRECON BEACONS

Baskerville Hall Hotel (BB) Clyro Court, Clyro, Hay-on-Wye HR3 5LE
☎ 01497 820033
www.baskervillehall.co.uk Map 161/208428
BB £16 Min 1, max 60. 1 hotel, 1 bunkhouse.
✗ 🐾 B D See B&B also.

☆ **Belle Vue Hotel** (BB)
Llanwrtyd Wells ☎ 01591 610237 (Eileen & Bernie Dodd)
www.bellevuewales.co.uk Map 147/879467
BB £19.50 Min 10, max 24. 🚂(Llanwrtyd Wells)
✗ 🐾 B D ! 🚗 See B&B also.

Situated midway between Builth Wells and Llandovery on the A483 trunk road.
Built in 1843 the Belle Vue Hotel is the oldest Hotel in Llanwrtyd Wells.
Combining village pub and local meeting place and so giving this small,
comfortable, family run hotel the charm and character representative of the
friendly inhabitants of this town.

☆ **Neuadd Arms Hotel** (BB)
The Square, Llanwrtyd Wells LD5 4RB ☎ 01591 610236 (Lindsay & Catherine
Ketteringham) www.neuaddarmshotel.co.uk Map 147/879467
BB £22+ Min 10, max 37. 1 hotel. 🚂(Llanwrtyd Wells)
✗ 🐾 B D ⊗ ! ★ See B&B also.

Family run Grade II listed Victorian
hotel with 21 en-suite rooms, situated
at the heart of Britain's smallest town.
Accommodation, food and facilities
are ideally tailored to suit rambling
groups. Comfortable, clean and
friendly and always a warm welcome.

SOUTH WALES

Avala Hotel & Backpackers (BB/SC) 156 Newport Road, Cardiff CF24 1DJ
☎ 029 2048 1412
www.avalahotel.co.uk Map 151/198774
BB £15pppn SC £630-£2,730 Min 6, max 50. 1 hotel, 1 self-catering, 1 hostel.
✗ nearby 🚂(Cardiff Central/Queen St) 🐾 D ⊗ 🚗
See B&B also Hostels also.

HOSTELS, BUNKHOUSES & CAMPSITES

GWYNEDD

SNOWDONIA/ERYRI

Llwyn Celyn Bach (C) Llanberis ☎ 07796 420179 (Fiona Davies)
daviesllanberis@aol.com Grid Ref: SH573595
Camping £3 🐾nearby D ★

Silver Birches Camping (C) Betws Garmon, Caernarfon LL54 7YR
☎ 01286 650707 (Ian & Marion MacLeod)
www.silver-birches.org.uk Map 115/545567
Camping £5 Closed Nov-Feb 🗙 🐾

PEMBROKESHIRE

PEMBROKESHIRE COAST PATH & NATIONAL PARK

Tycanol Farm (C/CB/B/IH/BB/OC) Newport ☎ 01239 820264
www.caravancampingsites.co.uk/pembrokeshire/tycanolfarm.htm
Map 157, 145/043396
Bednight £10 🗙nearby B D

POWYS

BRECON BEACONS

Canal Barn Bunkhouse (B) Ty Camlas, Canal Bank, Brecon LD3 7HH
☎ 01874 625361 (Ralph Day)
www.canal-barn.co.uk Map 160/052280
Bednight £15 🗙nearby D ⊛ ★★★★

The Held Bunkhouse (B) Cantref, Brecon
☎ 01874 624646 (Christina)
www.theheldbunkhouse.co.uk
Bednight £12.50 🗙 🐾 D ⊛

☆ **Woodhouse** (B)
St Harmon, Rhayader ☎ 01597 870081 (Mr J Adams) www.woodhouse-farm.org.uk Map 147/998750
Bednight £12
🗙 🐾 D ⊛

Camping and caravan site with electric hook up. Tipi hire, perfect for small groups. Bunkhouse under construction, opening 2007. Nature reserve. Glyndwr's Way and Wye Valley Walk within easy reach. Located within the heart of red kite country.

SOUTH WALES

Avala Backpackers (IH) 156 Newport Road, Cardiff CF24 1DJ
☎ 029 2048 1412
www.avalahotel.co.uk Map 151/198774
Bednight £17 🗙nearby ⇄(Cardiff Central/Queen St)
🐾 D ⊛ See B&B and Groups also.

For an explanation of the symbols and abbreviations used in this guide, see the Key on the fold-out flap at the back of the book.

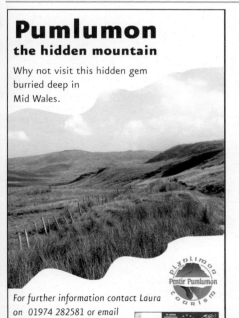

WALES

SCOTLAND

Long Distance Paths

Cateran Trail ....CAT

Cowal Way ....COW

Fife Coastal Path ....FFC

Great Glen Way ....GGN

Pennine Way ....PNN

Rob Roy Way........................RRY

Southern Upland Way..........SUP

Speyside Way ....SPS

St Cuthbert's Way................STC

West Highland Way............WHL

See Paths & Access p25 for full details of LDPs and waymarks

National Parks

Cairngorms

Loch Lomond & The Trossachs

See Useful Contacts p99 for full details of national parks

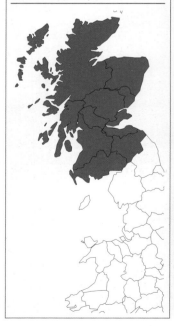

SUNSET OVER COASTLINE AT
ARISAIG, INVERNESS-SHIRE

WALK...   ...THE RIVER AYR WAY

This 66km/44-mile route, launched in June last year, is Scotland's first source-to-sea path, following the river from Glenbuck to the sea at Ayr. En route, it takes in some of Ayrshire's most stunning scenery and numerous sites of interest, including the 14th-century Sorn Castle, a beautiful woodland reserve at Ayr Gorge, and Ballochmyle Viaduct – the world's largest masonry span arch when built in 1848.

Part of East Ayrshire's Paths to Health scheme. A detailed information pack is available from local TICs priced £3.99, or by calling ☎ 01563 554753. For further details of the route, visit www.theriverayrway.org

VISIT...   ...THE NESS ISLANDS

This well-known Inverness beauty spot has undergone a radical make-over thanks to a grant from Scottish Natural Heritage. Situated at the northern end of the Great Glen Way, a mile from Inverness, the Islands are all linked to the shore by footbridges and two Victorian suspension bridges. A delightful network of wheelchair-accessible paths winds through woodland and along the River Ness – home to a variety of wildlife, such as mergansers, dippers, salmon and otters.

A new arena on the largest island is planned for outdoor performances and educational exhibitions, while nearby Bught Park will host the world's largest Highland Games on 21–22 July. For details of forthcoming events, contact the Highlands of Scotland Tourist Board ☎ 01997 421160 or visit www.highland.gov.uk

SEE...   ...MELROSE ABBEY

Melrose – on the Southern Upland Way and start of St Cuthbert's Way – sits among the beautiful Eildon Hills on the Scottish borders, and the town's decorative but war-weary abbey reflects the area's rich, turbulent history. Founded in AD660, it was home to the famed St Cuthbert, apostle of the Borders, before being razed by the first king of Scotland in AD839. Over the next millennium, the abbey would be rebuilt and destroyed three times before Sir Walter Scott restored the ruins to their current state. The lintel over the bell-stair carries the apt inscription 'Be halde to ye hende' – meaning 'Keep in mind the end, your salvation' – now the motto of Melrose itself.

For details of admission, ☎ 01896 822562 or visit www.historic-scotland.gov.uk/properties

LOCAL RAMBLERS GROUPS... St Andrews & North East Fife Group has teamed up with the Bums Off Seats healthy walking scheme to provide short, easy walks of 5–8km/3–5 miles. Walks are spread right across north-east Fife, providing lots of opportunities for a local ramble... **For a full list of Ramblers Groups offering shorter walks in Scotland, see p82 or visit www.ramblers.org.uk/scotland/walking/your-area.html...** North Berwick Group successfully prevented developers fencing out walkers from right to roam woodland in East Lothian. In the so-called Archerfield court case, volunteers regularly visited the site, reported on developments and attended court hearings.

SCOTLAND

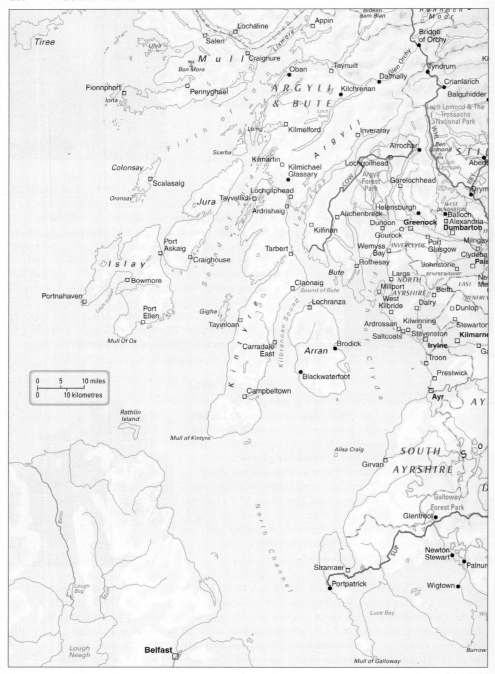

MAP   289

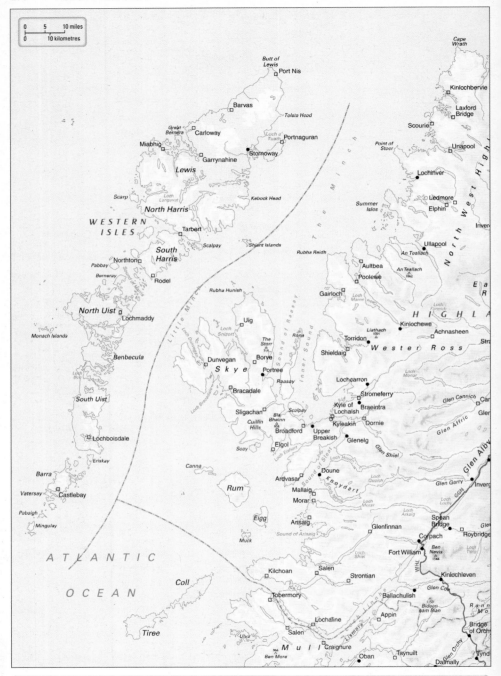

MAP 291

BED & BREAKFAST

ARGYLL & BUTE

● Bridge of Orchy (Argyll)
WEST HIGHLAND WAY

Inveroran Hotel, PA36 4AQ ☎ 01838 400220
www.inveroran.com Map 50/274414
BB **D** ✕ £9-£16, 6:30-8pm S1 D3 T3 F1 Closed Xmas
Ⓥ Ⓑ Ⓓ ⊛ 🐾🛁🚗🎒 ★★

● Dalmally
Craigroyston, Monument Rd, PA33 1AA ☎ 01838 200234 (Sandra Boardman)
www.craigroyston.com Map 50/158271
BB **B** ✕ nearby S1 D1 T1 Closed Xmas �(Dalmally)
Ⓑ Ⓓ ⊛ 🐾🛁🚗🎒 ★★★Ⓦ

● Helensburgh
LOCH LOMOND & THE TROSSACHS

Balmillig, 64B Colquhoun Street, G84 9JP
☎ 01436 674922 (Anne & John Urquhart) www.balmillig.co.uk
Map 56/297830 BB **D** ✕ nearby D1 T1 F1 ᴗᴗ(Helensburgh Central)
Ⓑ Ⓓ ⊛ 🛁🎒 ★★★★

● Kilchrenan (Taynuilt)
Roineabhal, PA35 1HD ☎ 01866 833207 (Maria Soep)
www.roineabhal.com Map 50/033239
BB **D** ✕ book first £30-£35, 7pm D2 T1
Ⓥ Ⓑ Ⓓ ⊛ 🐾🛁🚗🎒! 🎒 ★★★★

● Kilmichael Glassary (Lochgilphead)
The Horseshoe Inn, PA31 8QA ☎ 01546 606369
www.horseshoeinn.biz Map 55/852930
BB **C** ✕ £9, 6-9pm D2 T2 F1 Closed Xmas Ⓥ Ⓑ ⊛ 🐾🛁🚗

● Oban
Kathmore, Soroba Road, PA34 4JF ☎ 01631 562104 (Mrs M Wardhaugh)
www.kathmore.co.uk Map 49/860292
BB **B/C/D** ✕ nearby D4 T3 F2 Closed Xmas ᴗᴗ(Oban)
Ⓑ Ⓓ ⊛ 🐾🛁 ★★★

Beechgrove Guest House, Croft Road, PA34 5JL ☎ 01631 566111 (Joyce Millar)
beechgroveguesthouse@btinternet.com Map 49/860308
BB **C** ✕ nearby D2 T1 F1 Closed Nov-Jan ᴗᴗ(Oban)
Ⓥ Ⓑ Ⓓ ⊛ 🐾🛁 ★★★★

CENTRAL BELT

● Aberdour (Fife)
FIFE COASTAL PATH

Aberdour Hotel, 38 High Street, KY3 0SW ☎ 01383 860325
www.aberdourhotel.co.uk Map 65,66/189852
BB **D** ✕ £15, 6-9pm D6 T6 F4 ᴗᴗ(Aberdour)
Ⓥ Ⓑ Ⓓ ⊛ 🐾🛁🚗! Ⓜ ★★★

● Broughton (Biggar)
The Glenholm Guesthouse, ML12 6JF ☎ 01899 830408
(Neil Robinson/Fiona Burnett) www.glenholm.co.uk Map 72/101329
BB **D** ✕ £16, 7:30pm D1 T2 F1 Closed Jan
Ⓥ Ⓑ Ⓓ ⊛ 🐾🛁🚗🎒 ★★★ Wheelchair access.

● Dunbar
Springfield Guest House, Belhaven Road, EH42 1NH
☎ 01368 862502 (Joy Smeed) smeed@tesco.net Map 67/669787
BB **C** ✕ nearby S1 D2 T1 F1 Closed Dec ᴗᴗ(Dunbar) Ⓥ Ⓓ ⊛ 🛁 ★★

● Edinburgh
Barrosa Guest House, 21 Pilrig Street, EH6 5AN
☎ 0131 554 3700 (Miss Y Pretty) Map 66/264753
BB **C/D** ✕ nearby D3 T3 F2 Closed Xmas ᴗᴗ(Waverley)
Ⓑ ⊛ 🛁 ★★

Elderfields Guest House, 23 Spring Gardens, Holyrood, EH8 8HU
☎ 0131 620 2222 (M Elderfield)
www.guest-houses-edinburgh.com Map 66/274741
BB **B** ✕ nearby S1 D2 T2 ᴗᴗ(Wavereley) Ⓥ Ⓑ Ⓓ ⊛ 🐾🛁

● Glasgow
WEST HIGHLAND WAY

Adelaide's, 209 Bath Street, G2 4HZ ☎ 0141 248 4970
www.adelaides.co.uk Map 64/584657
BB **C** ✕ nearby S2 D2 T2 F2 Closed Xmas ᴗᴗ(Glasgow Central)
Ⓑ Ⓓ ⊛ 🐾🛁

Barrisdale Guest House, 115 Randolph Road, G11 7DS
☎ 0141 339 7589 (Ron Phillips) www.barrisdale-bnb.co.uk Map 64/546678
BB **B** ✕ nearby S3 D3 T3 F1 ᴗᴗ(Hyndland) Ⓥ Ⓑ Ⓓ ⊛ 🐾🛁

● Haddington
Eaglescairnie Mains, Gifford, EH41 4HN
☎ 01620 810491 (Barbara Williams) www.eaglescairnie.com Map 66/516689
BB **C/D** S2 D1 T1 Closed Xmas Ⓑ Ⓓ ⊛ 🐾🛁🎒 ★★★★

● Leven
FIFE COASTAL PATH

Fluthers Wood B&B, Cupar Road, KY8 5NN ☎ 01333 351167
(Rosemary Lawson) www.flutherswood.freeuk.com Map 59/380043
BB **D** ✕ book first £12, 6-8pm D2 Closed Nov-Feb
Ⓥ Ⓑ Ⓓ ⊛ 🐾🛁🚗 ★★★Ⓦ

DUMFRIES & GALLOWAY

● Gatehouse of Fleet (Castle Douglas)

☆ **The Bobbin Guest House**
36 High Street, DG7 2HP ☎ 01557 814229 (Mr & Mrs Green)
bobbinguesthouse@btconnect.com Map 83/601564
BB **C** ✕ nearby D3 T1 F1
Ⓥ Ⓑ Ⓓ ⊛ 🐾🛁🚗! ★★★

Family guesthouse, central location, pubs and restaurants 3 minutes' walk. Ideally situated as an admirable base from which to explore the surrounding countryside walks with the birds, wildflowers, historical remains, forests, hills and seaside.

● Glentrool (Bargrennan)
SOUTHERN UPLAND WAY

Lorien, 61 Glentrool Village, DG8 6SY ☎ 01671 840315
(Morag McIlwraith) morag.lorien61@btinternet.com Map 77/358783
BB **B** ✕ nearby T2 Ⓥ Ⓑ Ⓓ ⊛ 🐾🚗! 🎒

● Kirkcudbright
Number 3 B&B, 3 High Street, DG6 4JZ ☎ 01557 330881 (Miriam Baker)
www.number3-bandb.co.uk Map 83,84/681509
BB **D** ✕ nearby D1 T2 Ⓑ Ⓓ ⊛ 🍵🛏🕯🎀 ★★★★

● Langholm
◾◼ Carnlea, 16 Hillside Crescent, DG13 0EE
☎ 013873 80284 (Meg Braithwaite) www.carnlea.co.uk Map 79/370839
BB **B/C** ✕ nearby D1 T1 Closed Xmas Ⓑ Ⓓ ⊛ 🍵🛏🚗🎀 ★★★

● Lochmaben (Lockerbie)

☆◾◼ **Ardbeg Cottage**
19 Castle Street, DG11 1NY ☎ 01387 811855 (Bill Neilson)
bill@neilson.net Map 78/081826
BB **B** ✕ book first £12, 6:30pm D/T1 T1 Closed Xmas
Ⓥ Ⓑ Ⓓ ⊛ 🍵🛏Ⓜ ★★★

Munro-bound? Break your journey here,
A74(M) Junction 18, 4 miles.
At leisure? Don't miss seeing beautiful
southwest Scotland. 'See and Do' guides
and walks info. Ground floor en-suite
bedrooms, one twin, one double/twin.
Comfortable beds. Substantial breakfasts.

● Moffat
  SOUTHERN UPLAND WAY
◾◼ Seamore House, Academy Road, DG10 9HW ☎ 01683 220404
(Heather & Allan Parkinson) www.seamorehouse.co.uk Map 78/083055
BB **C** ✕ nearby, Xmas D3 F2 Ⓑ Ⓓ ⊛ 🍵🛏🕯🎀 ★★★

◾◼ Morag, 19 Old Carlisle Road, DG10 9QJ ☎ 01683 220690 (Mrs L Taylor)
morag_moffat44@btopenworld.com Map 78/093046
BB **B/C** ✕ nearby S1 D2 T1 Closed Dec-Feb Ⓑ Ⓓ ⊛ 🍵🛏 ★★★

North Nethermiln, Old Carlisle Road, DG10 9QJ
☎ 01683 220325 (Heather Quigley) Map 78/093046
BB **B** ✕ £10, 6-9pm S/T1 D2 F1 Closed Xmas Ⓥ Ⓓ ⊛ 🍵🛏🚗🕯

☆◾◼ **Bridge House**
Well Road, DG10 9JT ☎ 01683 220558 (Danyella & Russell Pearce)
www.bridgehousemoffat.co.uk Map 78/091057
BB **B** ✕ book first £20, 7-8pm D4 T2 F1
Ⓥ Ⓑ Ⓓ ⊛ 🍵🛏🚗🕯🎀 ★★★★

A fine Victorian property, Bridge House lies in
attractive gardens in a quiet residential area
on the fringe of the town.
Family-run, the atmosphere is friendly
and relaxed.
The chef/proprietor provides excellent
dinners for both residents and non-residents.

● New Abbey
◾◼ Abbey Arms Hotel, 1 The Square, DG2 8BX ☎ 01387 850489
http://abbeyarms.co.uk Map 83/963662
BB **C** ✕ £7.50, until 8pm S1 D2 T5 F2 Closed Xmas
Ⓥ Ⓑ Ⓓ 🍵🛏🎀 ★★

● Newton Stewart
Kilwarlin, 4 Corvisel Road, DG8 6LN ☎ 01671 403047 (Hazel Dickson)
hazel@kilwarlin.plus.com Map 83/409650
BB **B** ✕ nearby S1 D1 F1 Closed Nov-Feb Ⓓ ⊛ 🍵🛏🚗 ★★★Ⓦ

☆◾◼ **Sherwood**
4 Stronord, Palnure, DG8 7BD ☎ 01671 401174 (Mrs G Pullen)
Map 83/450643
BB **B** ✕ book first £6, 7pm D1 T1 Closed Xmas
Ⓥ Ⓑ Ⓓ ⊛ 🍵🛏🚗🕯!

Galloway Forest trails direct
from the door. Cairnsmore of
Fleet opposite. Red squirrels
are daily visitors along with
numerous bird life. Come and
enjoy Scotland's secret corner.
Non-smoking, en-suite rooms.

Benera, Corsbie Rd, DG8 6JD ☎ 01671 403443 (Mrs EM Prise)
ethel_prise@hotmail.com Map 83/405655
BB **B** ✕ nearby D1 T1 Closed Nov-Mar
Ⓑ Ⓓ ⊛ 🍵🛏🚗🕯! ★★★

◾◼ Bargaly Estate, Bargaly House, Palnure, DG8 7BH ☎ 01671 401048
(Gene & Peter Jones) www.bargaly.net Map 83/464664
BB **B/C** ✕ book first £10-£15, 6:30-9pm D2 T1
Ⓥ Ⓑ Ⓓ ⊛ 🍵🛏🚗🕯! 🎀 See SC also.

☆◾◼ **Eskdale**
Princes Avenue, DG8 6ES ☎ 01671 404195 (Marie Sergeant)
peter-sergeant@ntlworld.com Map 83/409652
BB **B** ✕ nearby S1 D1 T1
Ⓥ Ⓑ Ⓓ ⊛ 🍵🛏

Comfortable house offering spacious
bedrooms and a friendly welcoming
atmosphere.
Within 5 minutes' walk of Newton Stewart's
varied amenities and easy access to all that
Galloway has to offer the outdoor enthusiast.
Forest, hill and coastal walks all nearby.

● Portpatrick (Stranraer)
  SOUTHERN UPLAND WAY

☆◾◼ **Dunskey Guest House**
Heugh Road, DG9 8TD ☎ 01776 810241 (Gareth Cole)
www.dunskeyguesthouse.co.uk Map 82/994544
BB **C** ✕ nearby D4 T3 F2
Ⓑ Ⓓ ⊛ 🍵🛏🚗!

Dunskey Guest House sits in private grounds overlooking the picturesque village of Portpatrick (the
start of Southern Upland Way) — the ideal base for
your walking break. 9 ensuite rooms with TV/DVD,
hospitality tray. Packed lunches & early breakfasts
available. Locked storage/drying room. Car park.
Transport arranged. 2 mins from local amenities.

● Sanquhar
  SOUTHERN UPLAND WAY
Newark Farm, DG4 6HN ☎ 01659 50263 (Frances Barbour)
www.newarkfarm.com Map 71,78/789091
BB **A** ✕ book first, to suit D1 F2 ⚡(Sanquhar)
Ⓥ Ⓑ Ⓓ 🍵🛏🚗🎀 ★★★Ⓦ Access Category 2.

HIGHLAND

● Aviemore
CAIRNGORMS
SPEYSIDE WAY

◄ Ravenscraig Guest House, Grampian Road, PH22 1RP
☎ 01479 810278 (Jonathan Gatenby)
www.aviemoreonline.com Map 35,36/895131
BB C/D ✕ nearby S2 D3 T3 F4 Closed Xmas ⋘(Aviemore)
Ⓑ Ⓓ ⊛ 🐾 🖐 ★★★

◄ Cairngorm Guest House, Grampian Road, PH22 1RP
☎ 01479 810630 (Gail & Peter Conn)
www.cairngormguesthouse.com Map 35,36/895131
BB D ✕ nearby D5 T3 F2 Closed Xmas ⋘(Aviemore)
Ⓑ Ⓓ ⊛ 🐾 🖐 ★★★

● Ballachulish (Argyll)
Park View, 18 Park Road, PH49 4JS
☎ 01855 811560 (Diana Macaskill)
www.glencoe-parkview.co.uk Map 41/080582
BB B ✕ nearby S1 D2 T1 Closed Xmas Ⓓ ⊛ 🐾 🖐 ★★★Ⓦ

● Balloch
LOCH LOMOND & THE TROSSACHS
GREAT GLEN WAY

Anchorage Guest House, 31 Balloch Road, G83 8SS ☎ 01389 753336
www.anchorage-guesthouse-balloch.com Map 63/389819
BB C ✕ nearby D3 T2 F1 ⋘(Balloch)
Ⓥ Ⓑ Ⓓ ⊛ 🖐 🎋 ★★ Wheelchair access.

● Braeintra (Plockton)

☆ **Soluis Mu Thuath**
IV53 8UP ☎ 01599 577219 (Margaret Arscott)
www.highlandsaccommodation.co.uk Map 24/864324
BB C ✕ book first £13, 7:30pm D1 T3 ⋘(Strome Ferry)
Ⓥ Ⓑ Ⓓ ⊛ 🐾 🖐 ➡ ! 🎋 ★★ Facilities available for disabled guests.

Ideally situated for Torridon, Kintail, Skye or Glen Carron for the energetic, and the picture postcard village of Plockton for the less energetic, Soluis Mu Thuath is a family-run guest house where a warm welcome awaits all walkers.

● Corpach (Fort William)
WEST HIGHLAND WAY & GREAT GLEN WAY

◄ Mansfield Guest House, Corpach, PH33 7LT
☎ 01397 772262 (Toby & Bev Richardson)
www.fortwilliamaccommodation.com Map 41/101768
BB B/C ✕ book first £15, 7pm S1 D2 T2 F2 ⋘(Corpach)
Ⓥ Ⓑ Ⓓ ⊛ 🐾 🖐 ★★★

**REMEMBER TO USE
YOUR DISCOUNT VOUCHERS!**
Turn to p121 and save money on any establishment
where you see 🐾 next to their entry.

● Doune (Knoydart)

☆ **Doune Stone Lodges**
PH41 4PL ☎ 01687 462667 (Martin Davies)
www.doune-knoydart.co.uk Map 33/705035
BB D ✕ £25, 7:30pm F3 Closed Oct-Mar
Ⓥ Ⓑ Ⓓ ⊛ 🐾 🖐 ! Full board only. See Groups also.

Remote and unique holiday setting on the western tip of Knoydart with views to the magnificent Skye Cuillin.

Spectacular low and high level walking.

There is no road access — we collect you from Mallaig in our own boat.

Enjoy every comfort: delicious home cooking, a warm welcome and total relaxation. Mountains, sea, boat trips, wildlife — a truly great escape.

● Fort Augustus
GREAT GLEN WAY

☆ ◄ **St Joseph's Bed & Breakfast**
Fort William Road, PH32 4DW ☎ 01320 366771 (Ann Taylor)
stjosephsftaug@tiscali.co.uk Map 34/375088
BB C ✕ nearby D2
Ⓥ Ⓑ Ⓓ ⊛ 🐾 🖐 ! 🎋

St Joseph's is a former hospital run by the Benedictine nuns from around 1871. Fort Augustus has a lot to offer. Enjoy peace & tranquility or be energetic. Walk along the Great Glen Way with stunning views over Loch Ness.

◄ Bank House, PH32 4AY
☎ 01320 366755 (Mike Buchanan)
www.visitlochness.co.uk Map 34/377091
BB B/C ✕ nearby S1 D1 T1 F1 Ⓥ Ⓑ Ⓓ ⊛ 🐾 🖐 🎋

● Fort William
WEST HIGHLAND WAY & GREAT GLEN WAY

Craig Nevis Guest House, Belford Road, PH33 6BU ☎ 01397 702023
www.craignevis.co.uk Map 41/108741
BB B ✕ nearby S2 D3 T3 F1 Closed Xmas ⋘(Fort William)
Ⓑ Ⓓ ⊛ 🐾 🖐 ! ★★

◄ Glenlochy Guest House, Nevis Bridge, PH33 6LP
☎ 01397 702909 (Hugh MacPherson) www.glenlochy.co.uk Map 41/114742
BB B/C/D ✕ nearby S1 D7 T3 F2 Closed Xmas ⋘(Fort William)
Ⓑ Ⓓ ⊛ 🖐 ★★★

◄ Alltonside Guest House, Achintore Road, PH33 6RW
☎ 01397 703542 (Elizabeth Ann Allton) www.alltonside.co.uk Map 41/085718
BB B ✕ book first D3 T2 F1 ⋘(Fort William)
Ⓥ Ⓑ Ⓓ ⊛ 🖐 🎋 ★★★

☆ ◼▬◼ **Distillery House**
Nevis Bridge, PH33 6LR ☎ 01397 700103 (Stuart & Mandy McLean)
www.stayinfortwilliam.co.uk Map 41/113744
BB **D** ✗ nearby S2 D3 T2 FI Closed Xmas ▬(Fort William)
Ⓑ Ⓓ ⊛ 🍴☕! 🛏 ★★★★ See SC also.

Set in the grounds of the old Glenlochy
Distillery against the backdrop of Ben
Nevis. Lovely homecooked breakfast
and well equipped en-suite bedrooms.
Recommended in the *Daily Mail*
article 'Great Glen Way'.
Enjoy a complimentary whiskey upon arrival. Email: disthouse@aol.com

◼▬◼ II Castle Drive, Lochyside, PH33 7NR ☎ 01397 702659 (Mrs M Grant)
www.moygrant.co.uk Map 41/118758
BB **B** ✗ book first £12 DI TI Closed Xmas ▬(Fort William)
Ⓥ Ⓓ ⊛ 🍴☕🚗! 🛏 ★★★

◼▬◼ Ashburn House, Achintore Rd, PH33 6RQ ☎ 01397 706000
(Christine MacDonald) www.highland5star.co.uk Map 41/095732
BB **D** ✗ nearby S3 D4 Closed Xmas ▬(Fort William)
Ⓑ Ⓓ ⊛ ◆◆◆◆◆

☆ ◼▬◼ **Kismet Villa**
4 Hillside Estates, PH33 6RS ☎ 01397 703654
www.kismetvilla.com Map 41/099703
BB **C** ✗ nearby D2 TI ▬(Fort William)
Ⓥ Ⓑ Ⓓ ⊛ 🍴☕🛏

An ideal location overlooking Loch
Linnhe and the Ardnamurchan
Peninsular. Ben Nevis and Glen Nevis are
a short walk away, with Glen Coe and
Glenfinnian a 15 minute drive. Combined
with the host's local knowledge, this
ensures a wonderful holiday.

◼▬◼ Constantia House, Fassifern Road, PH33 6BD ☎ 01397 702893
(Derek Walker) derek.walker61@tiscali.co.uk Map 41/104739
BB **B** ✗ nearby S3 D2 TI ▬(Fort William) Ⓥ Ⓑ Ⓓ ⊛ 🍴☕🚗! 🛏

● Garve
◼▬◼ Birch Cottage, 6/7 Station Road, IV23 2PS ☎ 01997 414237
www.birchcottagebandb.com Map 20/395611
BB **C** ✗ £8.50-£15, 7-8pm D2 TI ▬(Garve)
Ⓥ Ⓑ Ⓓ ⊛ 🍴☕🚗 🛏 ★★★

● Glenelg (Kyle)
Marabhaig, 7 Coullindune, IV40 8JU ☎ 01599 522327 (Margaret Cameron)
Map 33/808189
BB **B** ✗ book first £12, 6-8:30pm D3 TI Closed Xmas & Jan
Ⓥ Ⓑ Ⓓ ⊛ 🍴☕🚗! ★★★

● Invergarry
GREAT GLEN WAY
◼▬◼ Craigard Guest House, PH35 4HG ☎ 01809 501258
(Robert & Barbara Withers) www.craigard.saltire.org Map 34/292010
BB **B/C** ✗ nearby SI D4 T2 Ⓑ Ⓓ ⊛ 🍴☕🚗!

● Kincraig (Kingussie)
CAIRNGORMS
Insh House, PH21 INU ☎ 01540 651377 (Nick & Patsy Thompson)
www.kincraig.com/inshhouse Map 35/836038
BB **B** ✗ nearby S2 DI TI FI Closed Nov-Dec
Ⓑ Ⓓ ⊛ 🍴☕! 🛏 ★★★

● Kingussie
CAIRNGORMS

☆ **Ardselma**
The Crescent, PH21 IJZ ☎ 07786 696384 (Valerie Johnston)
valerieardselma@aol.com Map 35/757009
BB **B** ✗ nearby SI DI T3 F2 Closed Xmas ▬(Kingussie)
Ⓑ Ⓓ ⊛ 🍴☕! 🛏

Situated within the Cairngorms
National Park, Ardselma is quiet and
peaceful, set in its private grounds of
three acres with ample parking and
safe bicycle storage. Large bedrooms,
log fire sitting room, 5 mins from
train station and less from bus stop.

● Kinlochewe (Achnasheen)
Hill Haven, IV22 2PA ☎ 01445 760204 (David & Lilah Ford)
www.kinlochewe.info Map 19/029620
BB **D** ✗ nearby D2 TI
Ⓥ Ⓑ Ⓓ ⊛ 🍴☕! ★★★

● Kinlochleven
WEST HIGHLAND WAY
◼▬◼ Hermon, 5 Rob Roy Rd, PH50 4RA ☎ 01855 831383 (Miss MacAngus)
hughenamacangus@tiscali.co.uk Map 41/189622
BB **B** ✗ nearby DI T2 Closed Dec-Jan
Ⓑ Ⓓ ⊛ 🍴☕🚗! 🛏 Ⓜ ★★★

Edencoille Guest House, Garbhien Rd, PH50 4SE
☎ 01855 831358 (Elsie Robertson)
www.kinlochlevenbed&breakfast.co.uk Map 41/181617
BB **C/D** ✗ £15, 6:30-9pm D2 T2 F2
Ⓥ Ⓑ Ⓓ ⊛ 🍴☕🚗! ★★★

☆ **Tigh na Cheo Guest House**
Garbhein Road, PH50 4SE ☎ 01855 831434 (Nicola Lyden)
www.tigh-na-cheo.co.uk Map 41/182617
BB **C** ✗ nearby S2 D6 T6 FI
Ⓥ Ⓑ Ⓓ ⊛ 🍴☕🚗! Facilities available for disabled guests.

The ideal accommodation on the
penultimate stop of the famous West
Highland Way.
With views of Am Bodach Mountain and
River Leven, we offer walkers practical yet
luxurious accommodation including en-suite
baths, open fires and drying room facilities.

● Lochinver (Sutherland)
◼▬◼ Ardglas Guest House, IV27 4LJ
☎ 01571 844257 (Arthur & Meryl Quigley)
www.ardglas.co.uk Map 15/093231
BB **B** SI D4 TI F2 Closed Xmas Ⓓ ⊛ 🍴☕🚗 Ⓜ ★★★

● Nethy Bridge (Inverness)
CAIRNGORMS
SPEYSIDE WAY
◼▬◼ Mondhuie, PH25 3DF ☎ 01479 821062 (David Mordaunt)
www.mondhuie.com Map 36/991207
BB **A** ✗ book first £10, 7:30pm DI TI Closed Nov-Dec ▬(Broomhill)
Ⓥ Ⓓ ⊛ 🍴☕🚗! 🛏 See SC also.

● Newtonmore (Kingussie)
CAIRNGORMS

☆ ●━ **Craigerne House Hotel**
Golf Course Rd, PH20 1AT ☎ 01540 673281 (David & Jane Adamson)
www.craigernehotel.com Map 35/716991
BB **C** ✕ £21, 7-9pm S1 D3 T6 F1 Closed Xmas ⚍(Newtonmore)
Ⓥ Ⓑ Ⓓ ⊛ 🐾🍵🚗 🛁

A detached Victorian villa with mature gardens commanding magnificent views of the Monadhliath & Cairngorm Mountains & the Spey Valley. Only 100 yards from the centre of Newtonmore, "The walking centre of Scotland". Most rooms en-suite with tea/coffee making facilities.

● Spean Bridge
GREAT GLEN WAY

●━ Inverour Guest House, PH34 4EU ☎ 01397 712218 (Lesley Brown)
www.inverourguesthouse.co.uk Map 41,34/223816
BB **B/C** ✕ book first £12.50, 7pm S2 D3 T3 F1 ⚍(Spean Bridge)
Ⓥ Ⓑ Ⓓ ⊛ 🐾🍵🚗 Ⓜ ★★★

●━ Marlaw Bed & Breakfast, 3 Lodge Gardens, PH34 4EN
☎ 01397 712603 (Cynthia & Martin)
www.marlawbandb.co.uk Map 41,34/220816
BB **B/C** ✕ nearby D2 T1 ⚍(Spean Bridge)
Ⓑ Ⓓ ⊛ 🐾🍵🚗 !🛁 Ⓜ ★★★

●━ Achnabobane Farmhouse, PH34 4EX
☎ 01397 712919 (Neil & Elizabeth Ockenden)
www.achnabobanefarmhouse.dial.pipex.com Map 41,34/195810
BB **D** ✕ book first £15, 7pm S1 D1 T1 F1 ⚍(Spean Bridge)
Ⓥ Ⓑ Ⓓ ⊛ 🐾🍵🚗 !🛁 ★★★

● Tomatin (Inverness-shire)
Glenan Lodge Guest House, IV13 7YT ☎ 0845 6445793 (Lesley Smithers)
www.glenanlodge.co.uk Map 35/791296
BB **C** ✕ £12-£15, 6:30-8pm S1 D3 T1 F2
Ⓥ Ⓑ Ⓓ ⊛ 🐾🍵🚗 !🛁

● Tongue (Sutherland)
●━ Rhian Guest House, Rhian Cottage, IV27 4XJ
☎ 01847 611257 (Mrs JM Anderson)
www.rhiancottage.co.uk Map 10/588555
BB **C** ✕ nearby D2 T2 F1 Ⓥ Ⓑ Ⓓ ⊛ 🐾🍵🚗 !🛁 ★★★

● Torridon
Ben Bhraggie, Diabaig, IV22 2HE ☎ 01445 790268 (Mrs I Ross)
Map 24,19/802605
BB **A** ✕ book first £10.50, 7:30pm S1 D1 T1 Closed Nov-Feb
Ⓥ Ⓑ ⊛ 🐾!

Riverside, Inveralligin, IV22 2HB ☎ 01445 791333 (Mary Mackay)
Map 24/845577
BB **B** D2 T1 Closed Dec Ⓓ ⊛

● Ullapool
●━ The Ceilidh Place Clubhouse, West Argyle Street, IV26 2TY
☎ 01854 612103
www.theceilidhplace.com Map 19/126939
BB **B** ✕ £20, 6:30-9pm S4 T3 F4 Closed Jan Ⓥ Ⓓ ⊛ 🐾🍵 Ⓜ

● Blackwaterfoot (Brodick)
Lochside , KA27 8EY ☎ 01770 860276 (Marjorie Bannatyne)
george.bannatyne@virgin.net Map 68,69/903268
BB **C** ✕ book first £9, 6:30pm S1 D2 T1 F1 Closed Xmas
Ⓥ Ⓑ Ⓓ ⊛ 🐾🍵🛁 See SC also.

● Brodick
☆ **Rosaburn Lodge**
KA27 8DP ☎ 01770 302383
www.smoothhound.co.uk/hotels/rosaburn.html Map 69/009367
BB **D** ✕ nearby D3 T2
Ⓑ Ⓓ ⊛ 🐾🍵🛁! ★★★

Beautifully located on the banks of River Rosa. Nearest guest house to the Arran Hills.

Comfortable bedrooms and bathrooms.

Excellent breakfasts. Private parking.

● Stornoway
Hebridean Guest House, 61 Bayhead Street, HS1 2DZ ☎ 01851 702268
(Linda & Kevin Johnson) www.hebrideanguesthouse.co.uk Map 8/425334
BB **D** ✕ nearby S6 D3 T3 Ⓥ Ⓑ Ⓓ ⊛ 🐾🍵🚗! ★★★

● Upper Breakish
Tir Alainn, 8 Upper Breakish, IV42 8PY ☎ 01471 822366 (Pam & Ron Davison)
www.visitskye.com Map 32/680231
BB **B** ✕ book first £15, 7-7:30pm S1 D1 F1 Closed Nov-Dec
Ⓥ Ⓑ Ⓓ ⊛ 🐾🍵🚗!🛁 ★★★★ Guided walking available.

● Inverurie
●━ Glenburnie Guest House, Blackhall Road, AB51 4JE
☎ 01467 623044 (Iain Ogilvie) Map 38/770216
BB **B** ✕ nearby D1 T5 Closed Xmas ⚍(Inverurie) Ⓥ Ⓑ ⊛ 🍵🛁🚗

● Letham (Angus)
●━ Whinney-Knowe, 8 Dundee Street, DD8 2PQ
☎ 01307 818288 (Ellen Mann) www.whinneyknowe.co.uk Map 54/525485
BB **B** ✕ book first £10, 6-8pm S1 D2 T1 Ⓥ Ⓑ Ⓓ ⊛ 🐾🍵🛁 ★★★

● Rothes (Elgin)
SPEYSIDE WAY

●━ Eastbank Hotel, 15-17 High Street, AB38 7AU ☎ 01340 831564
(Maureen Humphreys) www.eastbankhotel.activehotels.com Map 28/277491
BB **C** ✕ £7-£15, until 8:30pm S3 D3 T4 F2
Ⓥ Ⓑ Ⓓ ⊛ 🐾🍵🚗 !🛁 ◆◆◆ Group discounts also available on request.

● Tomintoul (Ballindalloch)
CAIRNGORMS
SPEYSIDE WAY
⌂ Morinsh, 26 Cults Drive, AB37 9HW ☎ 01807 580452 (Jean Birchall)
www.tomintoul-glenlivet.org Map 36/166189
BB A ✗ nearby S1 D1 T1 Closed Xmas D ⊗ 🛁🚲🚗!🛏

PERTH & KINROSS

● Acharn (Aberfeldy)
ROB ROY WAY
Travellers Haven, 12 Ballinlaggan, PH15 2HT ☎ 01887 830409 (June Spiers)
www.bandbacharn.co.uk Map 51,52/753437
BB B ✗ book first £7.50 S1 T1 V D ⊗ 🛁🚗!

● Blairgowrie
CATERAN TRAIL
⌂ Shocarjen House, Balmoral Rd , PH10 7AF ☎ 01250 870525
(Shonaidh Beattie) shocarjen@btinternet.com Map 53/180456
BB B ✗ book first £8, 7pm D1 T1 Closed Xmas
V B D ⊗ 🛁🛏🚗!🛏 ★★★★

● Kirkmichael (Blairgowrie)
CATERAN TRAIL

☆ ⌂ Strathardle Inn
PH10 7NS ☎ 01250 881224 (Tim Hancher)
www.strathardleinn.co.uk Map 52,53/082599
BB D ✗ £15, 6-9pm D3 T1 F3
V B D ⊗ 🛁🛏🛏

The Cateran Trail runs in front of this cosy,
family-run hotel set in the glorious Perthshire
Highlands.

For the weary walker we offer plentiful
refreshment, real ales, malts, open fires, lots of hot water, comfortable beds
and drying facilities.

● Perth
Beeches, 2 Comelybank, PH2 7HU ☎ 01738 624486 (Pat & Brian Smith)
www.beeches-guest-house.co.uk Map 53, 58/124245
BB B ✗ nearby S2 D1 T1 🚌(Perth) B D ⊗ 🛁🛏 ★★★

● Pitlochry
Dalshian House, Old Perth Road, PH16 5TD ☎ 01796 472173 (Joan Graham)
www.dalshian.com Map 52,53/956565
BB C ✗ nearby D4 T1 F2 🚌(Pitlochry) V B D ⊗ 🛁🛏🛏 Ⓦ

● Stanley (Perth)
Glensanda House, Six Acres, Station Road, PH1 4NS ☎ 01738 827016
www.altouristguide.com/glensandahouse/ Map 53/108334
BB B ✗ nearby S1 D1 T1 Closed Xmas B ⊗ 🛁🛏 ★★★

SCOTTISH BORDERS

● Galashiels (Selkirk)
SOUTHERN UPLAND WAY & ST CUTHBERT'S WAY
Ettrickvale, 33 Abbotsford Road, TD1 3HW ☎ 01896 755224 (Mrs S Field)
www.ettrickvalebandb.co.uk Map 73/499352
BB B ✗ book first £10, 6-8pm D1 T2 Closed Xmas
V B D ⊗ 🛁🛏🛏 ★★★

● Jedburgh
ST CUTHBERT'S WAY

☆ Ferniehirst Mill Lodge
TD8 6PQ ☎ 01835 863279 (Alan & Christine Swanston)
www.ferniehirstmill.co.uk Map 80/654171
BB B ✗ book first £15, 7:30pm S2 D2 T4
V B D ⊗ 🛁🛏🛏 ★

Just 2½ miles south of Jedburgh,
this chalet-style guesthouse is set in
its own grounds of 25 acres beside
Jed Water. Homecooking including
vegetarian. Dogs welcome.
A country-lover's paradise.
Email: ferniehirstmill@aol.com

● Kelso
Mo Dhachaigh, 11 Kings Croft, TD5 7NU ☎ 01573 225480 (Moira Ferguson)
Map 74/723348
BB C ✗ nearby D1 T1 V D ⊗ 🛁 ★★★

● Kirk Yetholm (Kelso)
PENNINE WAY & ST CUTHBERT'S WAY
⌂ Blunty's Mill, TD5 8PG ☎ 01573 420288 (Gail Brooker)
Ggailrowan@aol.com Map 74/825283
BB B ✗ nearby T2 D ⊗ 🛁🛏🚗!🛏Ⓜ ★★

● Melrose
ST CUTHBERT'S WAY & SOUTHERN UPLAND WAY
⌂ The George & Abbotsford Hotel, High St, TD6 9PD
☎ 01896 822308 (Philip & Janette Titley)
www.georgeandabbotsford.co.uk Map 73/546340
BB D ✗ £7, 12-9pm S6 D8 T15 F1 V B D 🛁🛏!🛏 ★★

● Morebattle (Kelso)
ST CUTHBERT'S WAY
⌂ Linton Farm, TD5 8AE ☎ 01573 440362 (Mary Ralston)
ralston@ecosse.net Map 74/773264
BB B ✗ book first £10 S1 D1 T1 Closed Nov-Feb
V B D ⊗ 🛁🛏🚗!

● Peebles
Whitestone House, Innerleithen Road, EH45 8BD
☎ 01721 720337 (Mrs M Muir)
www.aboutscotland.com/peebles/whitestone.html Map 73/251408
BB B ✗ nearby S1 D1 T2 F1 Closed Xmas D 🛁Ⓜ ★★★

● Selkirk
⌂ Ivy Bank, Hillside Terrace, TD7 4LT ☎ 01750 21270 (Janet MacKenzie)
Iannet@aol.com Map 73/473286 BB B ✗ nearby S1 D1 T1
Closed Xmas-Jan B D ⊗ 🛁🛏🚗!🛏 ★★

● Traquair (Innerleithen)
SOUTHERN UPLAND WAY
The School House, EH44 6PL ☎ 01896 830425 (Mrs J A Caird)
www.old-schoolhouse.ndo.co.uk Map 73/331344
BB B D1 T1 F1 Closed Xmas D 🛁🛏🚗!🛏 ★★

● Walston (Carnwath)
⌂ Walston Mansion Farmhouse, ML11 8NF ☎ 01899 810334
(Margaret Kirby) www.walstonmansion.co.uk Map 72/057454
BB B ✗ £10, 7pm D1 T1 F2 V B D ⊗ 🛁🛏 ★★★

SCOTLAND

STIRLING

● Balquhidder
LOCH LOMOND & THE TROSSACHS
ROB ROY WAY

▰◀ Kings House Hotel, FKI9 8NY ☎ 01877 384646
www.kingshouse-scotland.co.uk Map 51,57/543209
BB **D** ✕ £13-£15, until 8:30pm D5 T2 Closed Xmas
Ⓥ Ⓑ Ⓓ ⊛ 🐾 ♨ 🚗 ❗ ★★

● Crianlarich
LOCH LOMOND & THE TROSSACHS
WEST HIGHLAND WAY

▰◀ Suie Lodge Hotel, Glen Dochart, FK20 8QT ☎ 01567 820417
www.suielodge.co.uk Map 51/488278
BB **C/D** ✕ £9, until 8:30pm S2 D4 T3 FI Closed Xmas
Ⓥ Ⓑ Ⓓ ⊛ 🐾 ♨ ★★

▰◀ Inverardran House, FK20 8QS ☎ 01838 300240 (John & Janice Christie)
www.inverardran.demon.co.uk Map 364/393249
BB **C** ✕ £12, until 9:30pm D3 T2 ⋙(Crianlarich)
Ⓥ Ⓑ Ⓓ ⊛ 🐾 ♨ 🚗 ❗ 🐾 Ⓜ ★★★

● Drymen (Glasgow)
LOCH LOMOND & THE TROSSACHS
WEST HIGHLAND WAY & ROB ROY WAY

Ceardach, Gartness Road, G63 0BH ☎ 01360 660596 (Betty Robb)
Map 57/477884
BB **B** ✕ nearby DI TI FI Closed Xmas Ⓓ ⊛ 🐾 ♨ 🚗 ❗ 🐾 ★★

Hillview B&B, The Square, G63 0BL ☎ 01360 661000 (Margaret Welsh)
hillview@drymensquare.co.uk Map 57/473885
BB **B** ✕ nearby SI DI TI FI Closed Xmas Ⓓ ⊛ 🐾 ♨ 🚗 ❗ 🐾

Green Shadows, Buchanan Castle Estate, G63 0HX
☎ 01360 660289 (Gail Lisa Goodwin)
www.visitdrymen.co.uk Map 57/460887
BB **C** ✕ nearby SI DI TI FI Closed Dec-Jan Ⓑ Ⓓ ⊛ 🐾 ♨ 🚗 ❗ ★★★

● Falkirk
▰◀ Ashbank Guest House, 105 Main St, Redding, FK2 9UQ
☎ 01324 716649 (Betty Ward) www.bandbfalkirk.com Map 65/922787
BB **C** ✕ nearby DI TI FI Closed Xmas ⋙(Polmont)
Ⓑ Ⓓ 🐾 ♨ 🚗 ❗ ★★★

● Lochearnhead
LOCH LOMOND & THE TROSSACHS & ROB ROY WAY

☆ ▰◀ **Lochearnhead Hotel**
Lochside, FKI9 8PU ☎ 01567 830229
www.lochearnhead-hotel.com Map 51/596238
BB **D** ✕ £10, 6-9pm D4 T5 FI
Ⓥ Ⓑ Ⓓ ⊛ 🐾 ♨ 🐾

Enjoying wonderful views over Loch Earn. A family-run hotel with 10 ensuite bedrooms, lounge bar, restaurant and residents' lounge. Lots of wonderful walking in the vicinity of the hotel. There is ample parking with secure garage parking for motorbikes/bicycles.

● Strathyre (Stirling)
LOCH LOMOND & THE TROSSACHS
ROB ROY WAY

Rosebank House, Main Street, FKI8 8NA ☎ 01877 384208 (Mal Dingle)
www.rosebankhouse.co.uk Map 57/561171
BB **C** ✕ nearby D4 T2 FI Ⓥ Ⓑ Ⓓ ⊛ 🐾 ♨ 🚗 🐾

SELF-CATERING

ARGYLL & BUTE

● Dunoon
LOCH LOMOND & THE TROSSACHS

Lyall Cliff ☎ 01369 702041 (Mr P Norris)
www.lyallcliff.co.uk
£200-£625 Sleeps 2-8. 2 houses.
Beautifully situated spacious accommodation on promenade. ⊛ ★★★

● Inveraray
The Anchorage ☎ 07751 105345 (Margaret Muir)
www.scottishholidays.co.uk
£180-£350 Sleeps 6 +cot. I bungalow.
Loch facing bungalow, cosy open fire. ⊛ 🐾 ★★★

● Kilmelford
Mrs G H Dalton ☎ 01866 844212
www.assc.co.uk/maolachy
£240-£350 Sleeps 1-2 +cot. I cottage. Closed Feb
Great walking among hills & forests. ★★★Ⓦ

● Oban

☆ **The Melfort Club**
☎ 01852 200257 (Christine Roberts)
www.melfortvillage.co.uk
£330-£1,050 Sleeps 4-10. 32 cottages.
Fantastic walking area, local walks booklet. 🐾 ★★★★

A small holiday village nestled in the hills and oak woods at the head of Loch Melfort, amidst some of the most beautiful scenery on the west coast of Scotland. A really relaxing holiday is guaranteed by the combination of beautifully furnished cottages, excellent leisure facilities and a friendly rural atmosphere.

Argyll Mansions ☎ 01289 306103 (Elaine Paterson)
www.oban-self-catering.co.uk
£350-£450 Sleeps 7. I apartment.
Historic seafront building. Views to Mull. ⋙(Oban) ⊛

● Taynuilt

☆ Airdeny Chalets
☎ 01866 822648 (Jenifer Moffat)
www.airdenychalets.co.uk
£265-£695 Sleeps 4-6. 7 chalets. Peaceful, natural habitat. Stunning views.
⋀⋀(Taynuilt) ⊗ 🐾 ★★★-★★★★

Set in a peaceful natural habitat with stunning mountain views, one mile from Taynuilt and 12 miles from Oban, Airdeny Chalets provides an ideal base for walking, cycling, fishing, bird-watching, touring the Western Highlands and Islands or just relaxing.

The 7 two and three bedroomed chalets are furnished to a very high standard and immaculately maintained by the resident owner. Each chalet enjoys its own privacy with parking and plenty of space for children to play safely.

An added bonus is that it is a 'midge free zone'!

CENTRAL BELT

● Auchtermuchty
Pitcairlie ☎ 01337 827418 (Rosemary Jones)
www.pitcairlie-leisure.co.uk
£306-£871 Sleeps 2-6. 4 apartments, 1 gatekeeper's lodge.
Indoor heated swimming pools. Rooms all ensuite. ⊗ 🐾 ★★★★

● Biggar

☆ Carmichael Cottages
☎ 01899 308336 (Richard Carmichael)
www.carmichael.co.uk/cottages
£205-£595 Sleeps 2-6. 14 cottages & houses. Great walking country.
Lovely cosy cottages. ⊗ 🐾 ★★-★★★★ See Kincraig also.

Lovely stone cottages, many with log fires, in beautiful countryside. Great walking includes Tinto Hills and Falls of Clyde from cottage door. Outdoor spa for your aches. Indoor driers and Sky TV. Dogs. Fishing lochan. Tennis court. Tearoom. Walking maps.

Please mention walk BRITAIN when booking your accommodation

DUMFRIES & GALLOWAY

● Dumfries
Nunland Country Holidays ☎ 01387 730214 (Mrs E Chambers)
www.nunland.co.uk
£195-£495 Sleeps 2-5. 4 cottages, 6 lodges. Ideal location to walk and relax.
🐾 ★★★-★★★★★Ⓦ Access Category 1 for one lodge.

● Moffat
Fran Considine ☎ 01784 740892 www.holidayelegance.co.uk
£250-£425 Sleeps 1-6. 1 apartment.
Luxury refurbished Victorian villa. Splendid views. ⊗ ★★★★

● Newton Stewart
Bargaly Estate ☎ 01671 401048 (Gene & Peter Jones) www.bargaly.net
£250-£650 Sleeps 2-6. 3 cottages.
Cottages in grounds of historic estate. ⊗ 🐾 See B&B also.

● Thornhill

☆ Templand Cottages
☎ 01848 330775 (Andrew & Ruth Snee)
www.templandcottages.co.uk
£280-£590 Sleeps 2-6. 6 cottages.
Beautiful unspoilt location, ideal for walking. ⊗ 🐾

Six luxury well-equipped cottages with heated pool/sauna, games room and cycle hire. Located in valley near the river Nith (famous for salmon) and Southern Upland Way. Attractive village of Thornhill with shops, restaurants and pubs only half a mile away.

HIGHLAND

● Aviemore
CAIRNGORMS

☆ Pine Bank Chalets
☎ 01479 810000 (Alex Burns-Smith)
www.pinebankchalets.co.uk
£350-£699 Sleeps 2-6. 11 cabins & 2 apartments. ⋀⋀(Aviemore)
🐾 ★★★-★★★★

Cosy log cabins, chalets and apartments in the heart of the Cairngorm National Park. Great location to bag a Munro or climb a Corbitt. For the less energetic we have some wonderful forest, river and lochside walks.

We are a 5 minute walk from Aviemore village centre where you'll find plenty of places to eat and drink. We can also offer you temporary membership to the MacDonald's Leisure Club.

SCOTLAND

☆ **High Range Chalets**
☎ 01479 810636 (Mrs J Hyatt)
www.highrange.co.uk
£200-£595 Sleeps 2-6. 8 chalets. Peaceful complex with stunning
mountain views. ₩(Aviemore) See Hostels also.

1-3 bedroom chalets sleeping 2-6,
providing all that is necessary for your
comfort. Situated in its own birch
woodland park with magnificent views of
the Spey valley and Cairngorm mountains.
Five hundred yards from Aviemore centre.
Ristorante, pizzeria and bar on site.

☆ **Speyside Leisure Park**
☎ 01479 810236
www.speysideleisure.com
£210-£875 Sleeps 2-8. 14 chalets, 3 cabins, 9 caravans.
Heated indoor pool. Sauna. ₩(Aviemore) ★★-★★★

Self-catering chalets and caravans in
a quiet riverside setting with views to
the Cairngorm Mountains. An ideal
location at the centre of the
Cairngorms National Park for couples,
families or groups wishing to explore
this magnificent walking area.

● **Fort William**
Distillery Cottages ☎ 01397 700103 (Stuart McLean)
www.distillerycottages.co.uk
£240-£490 Sleeps 2-4. 3 apartments. West Highland Way and Ben Nevis.
₩(Fort William) ⊗ ★★★ See B&B also.

● **Invergarry**
Ardochy House Cottages ☎ 01809 511292 (Mr C Sangster)
www.ardochy.ukgateway.net
£225-£455 Sleeps 4-6. 3 cottages.
Variety of walks and Munros nearby. ⊗

☆ **Highland Lodges**
☎ 01809 501225 (Janet Loney)
www.highlandlodges.org.uk
£200-£455 Sleeps 5. 2 pine lodges..
⊗ Ⓜ ★★★

Two solid pine lodges located on the Great
Glen Way and situated beneath the majestic
Ben Tee.
Ideal location for guests who enjoy the
outdoor life, but equally caters for those
who just want to relax in their
refurbished lodge.

● Kincraig
CAIRNGORMS

☆ **Feshiebridge**
☎ 01899 308336 (Richard Carmichael)
www.carmichael.co.uk/cottages.feshie.htm
£300-£400 Sleeps 1-2. 1 chalet.
⊗

Cedar chalet in birch woodlands beside
the bridge at Feshiebridge. Fantastic
access walking in Glen Feshie and on
Cairngorm massif. Very comfortable, well
equipped chalet. 7 day minimum letting
period. Shops, restaurant 2 miles. Sky TV.
Washer/dryer. Walking maps.

● Kingussie
CAIRNGORMS

☆ **Landseer and Carrick Houses**
☎ 01926 640560 (Mary E Wheildon)
www.holidaysinthehighlands.co.uk
£195-£600 Sleeps 5-6 + cot. 2 houses.
For Scotlands mountain peaks & rushing rivers. ₩(Kingussie) ★★★

Landseer House and
Carrick House.

Two traditional granite
houses at the foot of
both the Cairngorms
and Monadhliath
Mountains.

Each offer three most comfortable bedrooms and well-equipped homely public
rooms. These popular accommodations offer a splendid base from which to walk
the Cairngorm National Park – explore the many outdoor activities, spot the
wildlife and encompass the district.
Quiet village location, easy parking with local amenities.

Email: m_e_wheildon@hotmail.com

● Nethy Bridge
CAIRNGORMS
Mondhuie ☎ 01479 821062 (David Mordaunt) www.mondhuie.com
£135-£285 Sleeps 3-6. 2 chalets. Closed Nov-Dec
Speyside Way. Owner is a mountaineer. ₩(Broomhill) See B&B also.

● Newtonmore
CAIRNGORMS

☆ **Inveralder Holiday Homes**
☎ 01540 673575 (Alex Gillies)
£175-£400 Sleeps 4-6. 5 cottages.
Cottages are "home from home". ₩(Newtonmore)

Our quality holiday cottages offer the
perfect blend of comfort and value for
money, each well equipped and can
sleep either four or six. Many of our
guests return year after year. You are
advised to book early to avoid
disappointment.

● Poolewe
Innes-Maree Bungalows ☎ 01445 781454 (Ken MacLean)
www.poolewebungalows.com
£205-£495 Sleeps 6. 6 bungalows. ♿ ★★★

● Thurso
Dunnet Head Outdoor Activities ☎ 01847 851774 (Brian Sparks)
www.dunnethead.co.uk
£150-£450 Sleeps 2-4. Three various types of lodging. Closed Nov-Mar
En-suite rooms, superb views, renovated croft. ☺ ♿ ★★★

● Ullapool
Custom House ☎ 01854 612107 (Mrs P Campbell)
www.ullapool.co.uk/customhouse
£180-£300 Sleeps 2-4. 1 cottage. Closed Nov-March
Quiet conservation area, near shops/harbour. ♿

Corran Self-catering ☎ 01854 612501 (Barbara D Peffers)
www.corranullapool.co.uk £350-£600 Sleeps 6. 1 house.
Traditional village house, mountains, sea views. ☺

ISLE OF ARRAN

● Blackwaterfoot
Lochside ☎ 01770 860276 (Mrs M Bannatyne) george.bannatyne@virgin.net
£220-£380 Sleeps 2-6. 2 cottages.
Centrally heated, near beach/village. Aga. ♿ See B&B also.

ISLE OF BUTE

● Rothesay

☆ **Kames Castle Cottages**
☎ 01700 504500 (Julie Robertson)
www.kamescastlecottages.co.uk
£385-£885 Sleeps 4-8. 4 cottages. Closed Nov-Mar
All cottages listed of historical & architectural interest. ☺

Kames Castle is a truly lovely private estate by Kames Bay to the north of the Isle of Bute. Within the grounds are four listed period cottages, each refurbished to an exceptional standard of comfort and amenity.

Within the estate is a magnificent, two-acre 18th-century walled garden which has been progressively restored so that guests may enjoy its peace, colour and produce.

The cottages provide the perfect venue from which to explore the varied beauty of this green and lovely island as well as the wonderful coastline of Argyll and Kintyre. Ferry crossings are frequent from two mainland points.

NORTH EAST SCOTLAND

● Forfar
Hunters Cabins ☎ 01575 573480 (Yvonne or Robert Campbell)
www.hunterscabins.co.uk
£190-£490 Sleeps 2-6. 5 cabins. ☺ ♿

● Forres

☆ **Tulloch Holiday Lodges**
☎ 01309 673311 (Ian Dawson)
www.tullochlodges.com
£300-£750 Sleeps 4-6. 8 lodges.
Beautiful lodges in woodland/lochside setting. ☺ ★★★-★★★★

Situated in gloriously peaceful woodland by an enchanting loch, the eight lodges stand in a sheltered valley four miles from the lovely country town of Forres.

Walking, birdwatching, fishing, riding and lots of beaches and coastal walks.

PERTH & KINROSS

● Blairgowrie
Pondfauld Holidays ☎ 01250 873284 (Mel Thomson)
www.pondfauldholidays.co.uk
£190-£466 Sleeps 1-6. 2 cottages, 2 lodges, 2 caravans.
Family-run, quiet site, beautiful views. ♿ ★★-★★★

● Crieff

☆ **Gamekeepers Cottages & Norwegian Lodges**
☎ 01764 652586 (Stephen Brown)
www.monzievaird.com
£350-£1000 Sleeps 2-8. 23 lodges, 1 cottage.
Fishing, designated designed landscape ☺ ♿ ★★★★Ⓦ

Gamekeeper's Cottage & Norwegian Lodges in a designated designed landscape.

Beautiful, mature and extensive grounds. Private and well spread out.

Elevated positions with magnificent views.
"Holidays like they used to be" — space — wildlife — bring your dog — build dens & dams — net tadpoles — paddle — walk — tennis —fishing. Large local path network on our doorstep. Many other local activities.

For an explanation of the symbols used in this guide, see the Key on the fold-out flap at the back

SCOTLAND

● **Glenshee**

CAIRNGORMS

☆ **Finegand Cottages**
☎ 01250 885234 (Shona Haddow)
www.finegandestate.com
£173-£399 Sleeps 2-7. 4 cottages.
Individually sited, well equipped, magnificent views. 🏃 ★★

4 individual traditional highland cottages in this beautiful glen with its winding river. South edge of Cairgorm National Park: 17 Munros nearby; historic walks such as the Cateran Trail and Lairig Guru. Small trout loch and wonderful bird life. Email: finegand@tesco.net

● **Kenmore**

Bracken Lodges ☎ 01567 820169 (Mr & Mrs Palmer) www.bracken-lodges.com
£265-£630 Sleeps 2-6. 7 lodges.
Perfect location on Loch Tay. 🐾 🏃 ★★★★

SCOTTISH BORDERS

● **Peebles**

☆ **Ashlar Court**
☎ 07952 960626 (Phil Burnside)
www.peeblesholidaylets.co.uk
£275-£480 Sleeps 6. 1 apartment.
🏃 ★★★

24 Ashlar Court is a newly built 2 bed apartment in Mains Farm Steading, Cardrona. This picturesque rural location is in between Peebles and Innerleithen. Walking begins on your doorstep with Cardrona Forest 400m away. Email: philburnside@gmail.com

● **St Abbs**

Rock House ☎ 01890 771288 (Alison Aitchison)
www.rockhousediving.com £15pppn Sleeps 5-10.
1 cottage, 1 bunkhouse, 2 B&B rooms. 🐾 🏃 See Groups also.

GROUPS

HIGHLAND

☆ **Doune Bay Lodge** (BB/SC)
Doune, Knoydart ☎ 01687 462656 (Liz Tibbetts)
www.doune-knoydart.co.uk Map 33/705035
FB £50, SC £750 Min 6, max 14. 1 lodge.
✕ 🐾 🆔 ! 🚗 See B&B also.

Views across Sound of Sleat to Skye Cuillins. 20 metres from own beach. Accommodation for up to 14 guests in 2 single, 4 twin and 2 double rooms. All have excellent sea/hillside views. Fully or self-catered. Our fast charter boat provides access to Skye, Rum, Eigg, Canna and the remoter parts of the Knoydart coastline.

Fort William Backpackers (SC) Alma Road, Fort William PH33 6BH
☎ 01397 700711 (Andrea Krudde) www.scotlandstophostels.com
SC £12-13pppp Min 2, max 30. 1 hostel. ◢◣◢(Fort William)
✕ nearby 🆔 🐾 ★★ Hostel See Hostels also.

ISLE OF ARRAN

Kilmory Lodge (SC) Kilmory, KA27 8PQ ☎ 01770 870345 (Ann Rhead)
www.kilmoryhall.com Grid ref: NS 960215
SC £230pn Min 15, max 23. 1 bunkhouse.
✕ nearby 🅱 🅳 🐾 ! 🚗 ★★★

SCOTTISH BORDERS

☆ **Whithaugh Park** (BB/SC)
Newcastleton, Roxburghshire TD9 0TY ☎ 01387 375394
www.barnabas.org.uk Grid ref: NY 492882
SC £79+ Min 5, max 200. 28 log cabins.
✕ book first 🆔 🐾

Attractive 100-acre venue offering comfortable, warm Scandinavian log cabins with hot showers, pine furnishings & excellent self-catering facilities with option of catering. Situated in heart of Liddesdale. Stunning views to Priesthill and Newcastleton Forest.

Rock House (BB/SC) St Abbs, Berwickshire
☎ 01890 771288 (Alison Aitchison) www.rockhousediving.com
SC £15pppn, BB £19pppn Min 2, max 15. 1 cottage, 1 bunkhouse, 2 B&B rooms.
🐾 🅱 🅳 🐾 See SC also.

HOSTELS, BUNKHOUSES & CAMPSITES

HIGHLAND

CAIRNGORMS

High Range Caravan and Camping Park (C) Grampian Rd, Aviemore PH22 1PT
☎ 01479 810636 (Mrs J Hyatt) www.highrange.co.uk
£14-£15 per pitch ✕ ◢◣◢(Aviemore) 🐾 🅳 See SC also.

Sail Mhor Croft Hostel (IH) Dundonnell IV23 2QT ☎ 01854 633224
www.sailmhor.co.uk Map 19/064983
Bednight £11.50 🅳 🐾 On Teallach Ridge route.

Sheenas Backpackers Lodge (IH) Mallaig, Inverness
☎ 01687 462764
Bednight £13 ✕ nearby ◢◣◢(Mallaig) 🅳 🐾

Bunroy Park Caravan & Camping Site (C) Roy Bridge, Inverness
☎ 01397 712332 www.bunroycamping.co.uk Map 41/274806
Camping up to £5pppn Closed Nov-Feb ◢◣◢(Roy Bridge)
🐾 nearby ★★★★

☆ **Fort William Backpackers** (IH)
Alma Road, Fort William PH33 6BH
☎ 01397 700711 www.scotlandstophostels.com
Bednight £12-£13 ◢◣◢(Fort William)
✕ nearby 🅳 🐾 ★★ See Groups also.

Tranquil location just minutes from the town, with beautiful views of the Great Glen. Our comfy hostel provides everything you'll need after a day in the hills!

Perfect for outdoor enthusiasts, groups and foot sore travellers. Dorms and twin rooms.

☆ **Chase The Wild Goose Hostel** (IH)
Lochiel Crescent, Banavie, Fort William ☎ 01397 772531
www.great-glen-hostel.com
Bednight £13.50 ✗ nearby ⋙(Banavie)
D ⊗ ★★★★ Hostel

Located on the Great Glen Way and Cycle route within the village of Banavie,
just three miles from Fort William, is Scotland's newest backpackers' hostel,
serving the accommodation needs of walkers, cyclists, individuals on activity
holidays, families and groups.

Enjoy a relaxing break to the Scottish Highlands. Be inspired with fantastic
views of Ben Nevis. Take an evening walk along the banks of the Caledonian
Canal and Neptune's Staircase. Or enjoy a glass of wine or beer on the patio.

Above all, share your experiences with like-minded travellers.

Quality hostel accommodation sleeping 40. We are open all year.

Give us a call or visit our website for more information.

ISLE OF SKYE

☆ **Skye Backpackers** (IH)
Kyleakin ☎ 01599 534510
www.scotlandstophostels.com
Bednight £9.50-£15 ⋙(Kyle)
✗ nearby D ⊗ ★

A sanctuary with great facilities for the
weary traveller!
Real fire, garden, cosy lounge, kitchen, bike
hire, mini-bus tours.
Handy for all the attractions of Skye, Kintail
and the Cuillin mountains, with easy bus/train
connections. Dorms, doubles, twins.

PERTH & KINROSS

☆ **Pitlochry Backpackers Hotel** (IH)
134 Atholl Road PH16 5AB ☎ 01796 470044
www.scotlandstophostels.com
Bednight £12-£13.50 Closed Nov-Mar ⋙(Pitlochry)
✗ nearby B D ⊗ ★★

Ideal location set in the heart of beautiful,
rural Perthshire the hostel provides some of
the most luxurious backpacker's
accommodation in Scotland.
All the comforts of a hotel, the ambience and
facilities of a hostel, plus a wonderful sunny
lounge. Dorms, twins, doubles.

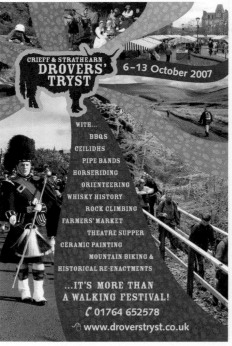

WALKING HOLIDAYS

BRITAIN

The companies listed here have chosen to advertise with us and their inclusion should not imply any recommendation by the Ramblers' Association

ENGLAND

ENGLAND

Curlew Guided Walking, 26 De Vitre Cottages, Ashton Road, Lancaster LA1 5AN Tel: 01524 35601
Email: info@curlewguidedwalking.co.uk
Web: **www.curlewguidedwalking.co.uk** Walking holidays and short breaks, comfortable accommodation and transport included. Covers: Lake District, Yorkshire Dales, Hadrian's Wall and other areas of Northern England

Footprints of Sussex, Pear Tree Cottage, Jarvis Lane, Steyning, West Sussex BN44 3GL Tel: 01903 813381
Email: footprintwalks@tinyworld.com
Web: **www.footprintsofsussex.co.uk** Self-guided holidays along the South Downs Way with baggage transfers and lots of local knowledge. Covers: South Downs

Skylark Holidays
Guided walks – classical Peak District and the new, ever-changing National Forest. Walking activities – getting started with Map reading. Responsible tourism with shared transport into the Peak District National Park and supporting the National Forest, the boldest environmental project in the UK.
Tel: 01283 701739
Web: **www.skylarkholidays.co.uk**

Step by step walking holidays at Hambledon Hotel
Guided and unescorted walks, tailor-made to suit you.
11 Queen's Road, Shanklin, Isle of Wight PO37 6AW
Tel: 01983 862403 (Bill Grindley)
Web: **www.step-by-step.co.uk**
See advert on page 179

ENGLAND

Orchard Trails, 5 Orchard Way, Horsmonden, Tonbridge, Kent TN12 8JX Tel: 01892 722680 Fax: 01892 722680 Email Grabham@btinternet.com Web: **www.kent-esites.co.uk/orchardtrails** Unescorted walking/cycling holidays. Kent and East Sussex. Luggage transported. Covers: Kent, East Sussex

Byways Breaks, 25 Mayville Road, Liverpool L18 0HG Tel: 0151 722 8050 Web: **www.byways-breaks.co.uk** Self-led walking and cycling holidays. Flexible routes, comfortable accommodation, luggage transported. Covers: Shropshire, Welsh borders, Offa's Dyke, Cheshire

Pace the Peaks – Guided Lake District Fell Walking. Local knowledge is the key to wonderful walking. Join Cathy for guided walks or practical navigation. Individuals and groups welcome. Cathy Colam, Keswick, Cumbria Tel: 017687 73171 Web: **www.pacethepeaks.co.uk**

Lodge in the Forest - Delightful Peak District alpine lodge (sleeps 5). Well equipped self-catering with luxury pool in forest setting. Guides or self-guided routes or just relax with the family. Tel: 020 8741 8277 Web: **www.lodgeintheforest.co.uk**

WALES, SCOTLAND AND IRELAND

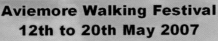

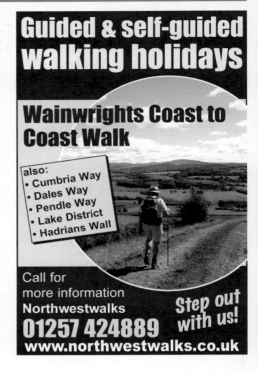
About Argyll Walking Holidays, Letters Lodge South, Strathlachlan, Argyll PA27 8BZ Tel/Fax: +44 (0)1369 860272 Email: info@aboutargyll.co.uk Web: **www.aboutargyll.co.uk** Guided walking holidays designed for people who like to explore the beautiful countryside and discover the secrets of its history and wildlife.Covers: West Highlands & Islands of Scotland

North-West Frontiers, Tigh na Creig, Garve Road, Ullapool IV26 SX Tel/Fax: 01854 612 628 Email: info@nwfrontiers.com Web: **www.nwfrontiers.com** Widest range of guided small group quality walking holidays in NW Scotland, Skye & Western Isles, Orkney, Shetland and Faroes. Walking, Munros, Ridges.

ACCOMMODATION INDEX

ACCOMMODATION INDEX

ACCOMMODATION INDEX

ACCOMMODATION INDEX

ADVERTISING INDEX

Bet your dog loves the great outdoors.

Now there's a company making specialist gear for your dog too.

Ruff Wear For Dogs On The Go™.

Ruff Wear is available from specialist outdoor retailers nationwide.

Visit **www.rosker.co.uk** for the very latest in dog gear from Ruff Wear.

RUFFWEAR

For Dogs On The Go

Siemens recommends Nikwax TX.DIRECT

WIN stuff at www.nikwax.

An EASY formula to STAY DRY ✓

Nikwax® + washing machine = clean, waterproofed, breathable cloth

EASIER

Wash and proof in a washing machine. It's **EASY**.

SAFER

No propellant gases or fluorocarbons, non-toxic and environmentally safe. It's **WATERBASED**.

DRIER

Maintains and enhances the waterproofing of your gear so you stay warm and **DRY** in wet weather

NIKWA WATERPROOF

For more information call **01892 786400** and ask for Emma.
To **WIN** a Nikwax® product visit **www.nikwax.net**